Latin American Economic Outlook 2023

INVESTING IN SUSTAINABLE DEVELOPMENT

Please cite this publication as:
OECD et al. (2023), *Latin American Economic Outlook 2023: Investing in Sustainable Development*, OECD Publishing, Paris, https://doi.org/10.1787/8c93ff6e-en.

ISBN 978-92-64-56136-6 (print)
ISBN 978-92-64-54693-6 (pdf)
ISBN 978-92-64-46677-7 (HTML)
ISBN 978-92-64-66750-1 (epub)

Latin American Economic Outlook
ISSN 2072-5159 (print)
ISSN 2072-5140 (online)

CAF Reference Number: CAF-513i-2023

ECLAC Reference Number: LC/PUB.2023/21

European Union
ISBN 978-92-68-09679-6 (PDF)
Catalogue number: MN-09-23-582-EN-N (PDF)
ISBN 978-92-68-09678-9 (print)
Catalogue number: MN-09-23-582-EN-C (print)

Revised version, January 2024
Details of revisions available at: https://www.oecd.org/about/publishing/Corrigendum_notice_Latin_American_Economic_Outlook_2023.pdf

Photo credits: Cover design by Aida Buendía and Mélodie Ly Descours (OECD Development Centre).

Corrigenda to OECD publications may be found on line at: www.oecd.org/about/publishing/corrigenda.htm.

Foreword

The *Latin American Economic Outlook* (LEO) analyses critical aspects related to sustainable and inclusive development in Latin America and the Caribbean (LAC). Since the first LEO launch in November 2007, the annual report has compared LAC's performance with that of other regions, analysed main development challenges and put forward policy recommendations, experiences and good practices.

The LEO benefits from the expertise and inputs of co-authors. Since 2011, the LEO has been published in partnership with the United Nations Economic Commission for Latin America and the Caribbean. In 2013, the Development Bank of Latin America and the Caribbean joined the team of authors and in 2018, the European Commission joined as a main partner of the LEO.

This 16th LEO, *Investing in Sustainable Development*, underscores the urgent need for more and better investment strategies to promote a more sustainable and inclusive future in the region. The report provides policy recommendations to mobilise and attract investments that help advance a better production model, create quality jobs and improve citizens' well-being. LEO 2023 analyses investment and socioeconomic trends, presents concrete innovative financing mechanisms and highlights the key role of governance and institutions in promoting further investment while responding to Latin Americans' demands. Finally, the report underscores the necessity for strengthened international partnerships to propel better investment and enhance regional integration.

Acknowledgements

Partners of this report are the United Nations Economic Commission for Latin America and the Caribbean (ECLAC), the Development Bank of Latin America and the Caribbean (CAF), the European Union (EU) and the Development Centre of the Organisation for Economic Co-operation and Development (OECD). This report is supported by the Directorate-General for International Partnerships of the European Commission (INTPA).

The contribution of the OECD Development Centre to this report was led and managed by Sebastián Nieto-Parra, Head of the Latin America and the Caribbean - LAC Unit at the OECD Development Centre. Co-ordination was led by Luis Cecchi, Policy Analyst at the LAC Unit of the OECD Development Centre, under the guidance of Ragnheiður Elín Árnadóttir, Director of the OECD Development Centre, and Federico Bonaglia, Deputy Director of the OECD Development Centre. Juan Vázquez Zamora, Deputy Head of the LAC Unit at the OECD Development Centre, René Orozco and Olivia Cuq, economist and policy analyst respectively at the same Unit contributed extensively to the production and co-ordination of the report. ECLAC's contribution was led by Marco Llinás, Director of the Production, Productivity and Management Division, and Sebastián Rovira, Economic Affairs Officer in Charge of the Innovation and New Technologies Unit, under the guidance of José Manuel Salazar-Xirinachs, Executive Secretary of ECLAC. The contribution from CAF was led by Adriana Arreaza, Director of Macroeconomic Studies, under the guidance of Veronica Frisancho Robles, Chief Economist, and Sergio Díaz-Granados, Executive President of CAF. The European Commission contribution was led by Diana Montero Melis, Deputy Head of Unit at the Directorate-General for International Partnerships of the European Commission (INTPA), with the assistance of Rodolfo Lazarich Gener, International Aid / Cooperation Officer, and Claudia Pablos Lorenzo, Cooperation consultant, under the guidance of Olivier Luyckx, Head of Unit South America and regional operations, and Felix Fernández-Shaw, Director of INTPA Latin America and the Caribbean relations with overseas countries and territories.

The report benefited from the research, drafting and fruitful collaboration among various authors across these organisations, including Adriana Arreaza (CAF), María Carolina Arcila (OECD), Laura Buchet (OECD), Adriana Caicedo (OECD), Luis Cecchi (OECD), Olivia Cuq (OECD), Rita Da Costa (OECD), Samuel Elrington (OECD), Andrés Espejo (ECLAC), Sofia Faurie (OECD), Sonia García Lorenzana (OECD), Nicolo Gligo Saez (ECLAC), Laura Gutiérrez Cadena (OECD), Michael Hanni (ECLAC), Sebastián Herreros (ECLAC), Ingrid Jenezova (EC), Andrea Laplane (ECLAC), Juan Ramón Larraín Aylwin (OECD), Martina Lejtreger (OECD), Carlos Maldonado (ECLAC), Thomas Manfredi (OECD), Nathalia Montoya González (OECD), Sebastián Nieto Parra (OECD), Georgina Nuñez (ECLAC), René Orozco (OECD), Ramón Pineda (ECLAC), Marti Pera Planas (ECLAC), Esteban Pérez (ECLAC), Noel Pérez Benitez (ECLAC), Juan Vázquez Zamora (OECD), Helvia Velloso (ECLAC), and Cecilia Vera (ECLAC). Rosario Hernando Cruz (OECD), Daniela Sánchez Galvis (OECD), Agustina Vierheller (OECD) and Paul Wonder (ECLAC) provided invaluable administrative support throughout the elaboration of the report.

A group of experts and colleagues have been particularly active and supportive during the production process, providing views, inputs and comments. We would like to highlight the support of Jose Antonio Ardavín (OECD), Jens Arnold (OECD), Julia Benn (OECD), Eric Bensel (OECD), Francesca Borgonovi (OECD), Monica Brezzi (OECD), Aida Caldera Sanchez (OECD), Maya Camacho (OECD), Jorge Carbonell (OECD), Olivier Cattaneo (OECD), Claire Charbit (OECD), Helena Cravinho (OECD), Pietrangelo De Biase (OECD), Rachida Dkhissi (OECD), Falilou Fall (OECD), Priscilla Fialho (OECD), Jacobo Garcia Villareal (OECD), Paula Garda (OECD), Daniela Ibarra (OAS), Stratos Kamenis (OECD), Fatos Koc (OECD), Michael

Koelle (OECD), Sarah Kups (OECD), Alessandro Maravalle (OECD), Ida Mcdonnell (OECD), Jeroen Meyer (OECD), Veerle Miranda (OECD), Letizia Montinari (OECD), Ana Novik (OECD), Alberto Gonzalez (OECD), Lorenzo Pavone (OECD), Bertrand Pluyaud (OECD), Annalisa Primi (OECD), Kim Osbone (OAS), Adolfo Rodríguez-Vargas (OECD), Ana Maria Ruiz Rivadeneira (OECD), Carlos Santiso (OECD), Daniela Sena Rojas (OECD), Luz Serrano (OAS), Rebeca Vidal (CAF), Martin Wermelinger (OECD), Bettina Wistrom (OECD) and Yumika Yamada (OECD).

The content of the report was enriched by constructive feedback received during an informal consultation with the LAC countries and members of the OECD Development Centre Governing Board on 22 February 2023; virtual Experts' Meeting on 30 and 31 May 2023; and a private-sector consultation meeting that took place on 27 June 2023. In addition to the LAC delegates to the Governing Board of the OECD Development Centre, we are particularly grateful to the experts, academics, private-sector representatives and other public servants who joined us during the Experts' Meeting, the private-sector consultation meeting and informal meetings: Graciela Altruda (MEF, Uruguay), Daniela Araujo (EU-LAC Foundation), Maria Paula Arenas (MINCIT, Colombia), Patricia Benavente (WB), Juan Benavides (Fedesarrollo), Antoine Berthou (OECD), Janos Bertok (OECD), San Bilal (European Centre for Development Policy Management), Marie-Pierre Bourzai (AFD), Ana Capilla (OEI), Lucio Castro (IFC), Mario Coronado (Telefónica Hispam), Andrea Costafreda (OXFAM), Humberto Cote (DNP), Manuel Escudero (Permanent Delegation of Spain to the OECD), Ministra Elisa Facio (MIEM, Uruguay), Almudena Fernández (UNDP), Juan Miguel Gallego (DNP Colombia), Andrés García Suaza (Universidad del Rosario), Pilar Garrido (OECD), Cecilia Giffuni (RREE, Uruguay), Elaine Godoy (AUCI), Carla Fernández-Durán Gortazar (IDB), Martín Francos (Ministry of Economy, Dominican Republic), Fernando Jaramillo Mejía (Universidad del Rosario), Fidel Jaramillo (FLAR), Juan Labraga (MEF, Uruguay), Antón Leis (AECID), Guilherme Magacho (AFD), Analia Maguna (MEF, Uruguay), Ana Fernanda Maiguashca (Private Council for Competitiveness, Colombia), Juan Carlos Moreno-Brid (UNAM), Natalia Moreno Rigollot (Telefónica), José Antonio Ocampo (Columbia University), Laura Oroz (AECID), Eric Parrado (IDB), Javier Pérez (Banco de España), Meghann Puloch (AFD), Fazia Pusterla (IDB), Olga Lucía R. Ramirez (DLA Piper), Juan Ruiz (BBVA Research), José Antonio Sanahuja (Fundación Carolina), Verónica Santini (MEF, Uruguay), Verónica Suarez (AUCI), Daniel Titelman, (ECLAC), Manuel Toledo (CAF), Ana Valero (Telefónica Hispam), Marco Varea (AFD), and Felipe Zaccheo (International Partnerships of the European Commission).

The country notes benefited from constructive inputs, scrutiny and verification by delegations to the OECD from Chile, Colombia, Costa Rica and Mexico, as well as the embassies in France of Argentina, Brazil, Dominican Republic, Ecuador, El Salvador, Guatemala, Panama, Paraguay, Peru and Uruguay. OECD delegations and embassies have also co-ordinated the relevant inputs from different national ministries and governmental areas.

The OECD Development Centre would also like to express its sincere gratitude to the *Agence française de développement* (AFD), the *Departamento Nacional de Planeación* (DNP) of Colombia, the European Union, the Spanish Ministry of Foreign Affairs, the Swiss Agency for Development and Co-operation, Telefónica, and Universidad del Rosario (Colombia) for their support of the Latin American Economic Outlook.

Finally, many thanks go to the Publications and Communications Division of the OECD Development Centre, in particular Aida Buendia, Mélodie Descours, Delphine Grandrieux, Elizabeth Nash, Irit Perry, Henri-Bernard Solignac-Lecomte and Felix Zimmermann, for their steadfast patience and expedient work on the production of this report and associated materials. The authors also sincerely appreciate the editing and proofreading activities undertaken by Mary Bortin and Marilyn Smith; the co-ordination of the Spanish translation by Alejandro Barranco, Julia Gregory, Alexander Summerfield; and the Spanish editing services by Liliana Tafur.

Table of contents

Figures

Tables

Boxes

Acronyms and abbreviations

5G	Fifth-generation mobile network
AAAA	Addis Ababa Action Agenda
ABS	Access and benefit sharing
AECID	Spanish Agency for International Development Cooperation
AEO	Authorised Economic Operator
AFD	Agence française de développement
ALIDE	Latin American Association of Development Financing Institutions
APEP	Americas Partnership for Economic Prosperity
AUCI	Uruguayan Agency for International Cooperation (*Agencia Uruguaya de Cooperación Internacional*)
BAU	Business as usual
BIICC	Bond indexed to indicators of climate change
BIT	Bi-lateral investment treaty
BNDES	Brazilian Development Bank
BRI	Belt and Road Initiative (China's)
C2F	Canadian Climate Fund for the Private Sector in the Americas
CAF	Development Bank of Latin America and the Caribbean (*Banco de Desarrollo de América Latina y el Caribe*)
CALAS	Centro Maria Sibylla Merian de Estudios Latinoamericanos Avanzados en Humanidades y Ciencias Sociales
CAPEX	Capital expenditures
CACM	Central American Common Market
CAN	Andean Community of Nations
CASEIF IV	Central America Small Enterprise Investment Fund IV
Caricom	Caribbean Community
CECCA	Clean Energy Corridor of Central America
CEPLAN	Centro Nacional de Planeamiento Estratégico del Perú
CET	Common external tariff
CIF	Caribbean Investment Facility
CIT	Corporate income tax
CIV	Collective investment vehicles
CO2	Carbon dioxide
CoGs	Centres of government
CONAGEBIO	National commission for biodiversity management of Costa Rica (*Comisión nacional para la gestión de la biodiversidad de Costa Rica*)
COVID 19	Coronavirus
CPI	Consumer price index
CSO	Civil society organisation
D4D	Digital Development Hub (Europe)
DAC	Development assistance committee
DFC	International Development Finance Corporation (United States)
DFIs	Development finance institutions
DIC	Direct investment in companies
DNP	National Planning Department of Colombia (*Departamento Nacional de Planeación de Colombia*)
DPR	Diversified Payment Rights

EATR	Effective Average Tax Rate
ECA	Export Credit Agencies
ECLAC	United Nations Economic Commission for Latin America and the Caribbean
ECSC	European Coal and Steel Community
EFAD	European Financial Architecture for Development
EFSD	European Fund for Sustainable Development
EMBL-EBI	European Bioinformatics Institute
EIB	European Investment Bank
EMBI	Emerging Market Bond Index (J.P. Morgan)
ESG	Environmental, social and governance
ETR	Effective tax rate
EU	European Union
FDI	Foreign direct investment
fintech	Financial technology
G20	Group of Twenty
GBP	Green Bond Principles
GCF	Gross capital formation
GDP	Gross domestic product
GFCF	Gross fixed capital formation
GGIA	Global Gateway Investment Agenda (European Union)
GHG	Greenhouse gases
GNI	Gross national income
GSSS	Green, social, sustainability and sustainability-linked
HEI	Higher education institutions
ICMA	International Capital Market Association
ICT	Information and communication technologies
ICTCR	Costa Rican Tourism Board (*Instituto Costarricense de Turismo de Costa Rica*)
IDB	Inter-American Development Bank
IFAD	International Fund for Agricultural Development
IFC	International Finance Corporation
IFI	International finance institutions
IIF	Institute of International Finance
IIT	International investment treaties
ILO	International Labour Organization
IMF	International Monetary Fund
INEGI	National Institute of Statistics and Geography of Mexico (*Instituto Nacional de Estadística y Geografía de México*)
IPA	Investment promotion agencies
IPO	Initial public offering
IRENA	International Renewable Energy Agency
ISCED	International Standard Classification of Education
ISCO	International Standard Classification of Occupations
ISDS	Investor-State dispute settlement
ISIC	International Standard Industrial Classification
KPI	Key performance indicators
LAC	Latin America and the Caribbean
LACIF	Latin America and Caribbean Investment Facility

LAIF	Latin America Investment Facility
LCRs	Local content requirements
LDC	Least-developed countries
Mbps	Megabytes per second
MCIT	Ministry of Commerce, Industry and Tourism of Colombia (*Ministerio de Comercio, Industria y Turismo de Colombia*)
MDBs	Multilateral development banks
MECON	Ministry of Economy of Argentina (*Ministerio de Economía de Argentina*)
ME	Ministry of Energy of Chile (*Ministerio de Energía de Chile*)
MEB	Ministry of Economy of Brazil (*Ministério da Economia do Brasil*)
MEF	Ministry of Economy and Finance of Uruguay
MEPyD	Ministry of Economy, Planning and Development of the Dominican Republic (*Ministerio de Economía, Planificación y Desarrollo de la República Dominicana*)
Mercosur	Common Market of the South (*Mercado Común del Sur*)
mHRDD	Mandatory human rights due diligence
MIDEPLAN	Ministry of National Planning and Economic Policy of Costa Rica (*Ministerio de Planificación Nacional y Política Económica de Costa Rica*)
MIEM	Ministry of Industry, Energy and Mining of Uruguay
MINAE	Ministry of Environment and Energy of Costa Rica (*Ministerio de Ambiente y Energía de Costa Rica*)
MLG	Multi-level governance
MPDB	Ministry of Development Planning of Bolivia (*Ministerio de Planificación del Desarrollo de Bolivia*)
MRREE	Ministry of Foreign Affairs of Uruguay
MSMEs	Micro-, small- and medium-sized enterprises
Mt	Metric tonnes
MtCO2	Metric tonnes of carbon dioxide
NAFTA	North America Free Trade Agreement
NCPs	National contact points
NCREs	Non-conventional renewable energies
NDBs	National development banks
NDCs	Nationally Determined Contributions
NDICI	Neighbourhood, Development, and International Co-operation Instrument
NDP	National development plan
NGO	Non-governmental organisation
NPIS	National public investment systems
NTBs	Non-tariff barriers
OAS	Organization of American States
ODA	Official development assistance
OECD	Organisation for Economic Co-operation and Development
PFI	OECD Policy Framework for Investment
PIT	Personal income tax
PNP	Private non-profit organisations
PPI	Private Participation in Infrastructure (World Bank)
PPP	Public-private partnerships

PREUM	Presidency of the Republic of the United Mexican States (*Presidencia de la República de los Estados Unidos Mexicanos*)
QII	Quality infrastructure investment
R&D	Research and development
RBC	Responsible business conduct
REIF	Renewable Energy Innovation Fund (Uruguay)
RELAC	Renewable Energy for Latin America and the Caribbean
SBG	Sustainability Bond Guidelines
SBP	Social Bond Principles
SDBs	Subnational development banks
SDGs	Sustainable Development Goals (United Nations)
SICA	Central American Integration System
SLBs	Sustainability-Linked Bonds
SLBP	Sustainability-Linked Bond Principles
SMEs	Small- and medium-sized enterprises
SNA	System of national accounts
SNPE	National Planning Secretariat of Ecuador (*Secretaría Nacional de Planificación del Ecuador*)
SOP	Second-party option
SPPPG	Planning and Programming Secretariat of the Presidency of Guatemala (*Secretaría de Planificación y Programación de la Presidencia de Guatemala*)
SPTs	Sustainability performance targets
SPV	Special purpose vehicles
STI	Science, technology and innovation
STPP	Technical Secretariat for Economic and Social Development Planning of Paraguay (*Secretaría Técnica de Planificación del Desarrollo Económico y Social del Paraguay*)
STR	Statutory tax rate
STT	Standard tax treatment
TFA	Trade Facilitation Agreement (World Trade Organization)
TFP	Total factor productivity
TIP	Treaty with investment provisions
UN	United Nations
UNAM	National Autonomous University of Mexico (*Universidad Nacional Autónoma de México*)
UNASUR	Union of South American Nations
UPME	Mining Energy Planning Unit of Colombia (*Unidad de Planeación Minero Energética de Colombia*)
USA	United States of America
USD	United States dollar
USMCA	United States, Mexico and Canada Agreement
VAT	Value-added tax
VET	Vocational education and training
VIX	Volatility Index
WTO	World Trade Organization

Editorial

Latin America and the Caribbean (LAC) has enormous potential to secure a stronger and more sustainable development trajectory. To seize this potential, the region needs a more ambitious and comprehensive investment agenda. The 16th edition of the *Latin American Economic Outlook: Investing in Sustainable Development* proposes strategies to boost investment in the LAC region, to help support policy makers, the private sector and international partners.

The region has unique assets. LAC boasts a wealth of natural resources, biodiversity and green energy. It has a young and culturally diverse population, and its economy offers opportunities in sectors as varied as agribusiness, sustainable tourism, renewable energies and health-related manufacturing. It has a large untapped internal market and is well-placed to further integrate into global value chains.

Despite these assets, socio-economic progress in the region has stalled in recent years. Poverty, at 29%, and extreme poverty, at 11.2%, remain on average at pre-pandemic levels, and inequalities are high. Persistent structural challenges constrain the LAC region. LAC countries need to invest in education and skills building and create more and better formal jobs, as in around 43% of households in the region all members work informally. They need to implement ambitious production development policies to increase local value added, harness the growth potential of new sectors, maximise the benefits of the digital transformation, and help tackle global challenges, in particular the green transition.

To achieve these goals, LAC countries must massively scale up domestic and foreign investment, from both public and private sources. At just 20% of gross domestic product, total investment in LAC represents one of the lowest shares among all regions globally.

This Outlook highlights how LAC countries can address their investment gaps. Fiscal reforms can increase revenues while rendering tax and expenditure systems more efficient and equitable. Development finance institutions and innovative financing tools can play a key role to help boost investment.

The report emphasises the importance of effective public institutions and a strong dialogue across socio-economic actors to ensure that investment aligns with national development strategies and addresses social priorities.

International partnerships can help promote a new investment agenda, by bringing together governments, international organisations, development finance institutions and the private sector. We welcome the EU-LAC Global Gateway Investment Agenda as a key step forward.

We stand ready to work together to support the LAC region's efforts and trust that this Outlook provides a solid basis for defining an investment agenda that sets the region on a path towards greater well-being for all.

Mathias Cormann Secretary-General OECD	Sergio Díaz-Granados Executive President CAF – Development Bank of Latin America and the Caribbean	José Manuel Salazar-Xirinachs Executive Secretary ECLAC	Jutta Urpilainen European Commissioner for International Partnerships

Executive summary

Countries in the Latin America and the Caribbean (LAC) region have enormous potential to embark on a stronger and more sustainable development trajectory. Yet, to seize that potential, the region needs a more ambitious and comprehensive investment agenda.

LAC needs to improve potential growth and social conditions in a challenging context

After the post-pandemic rebound in growth experienced in 2021 in LAC, external conditions became less favourable, public transfers were reduced, monetary policy tightened and the effects of the reopening of economies dissipated in 2022. The deceleration of economic activity in LAC in 2023 suggests that the region is returning to the low levels of growth seen in the years before the pandemic. Socio-economic conditions remain challenging in LAC, with poverty (29%) and extreme poverty (11.2%) still above pre-pandemic levels in more than half of LAC countries in 2022. One of the main challenges to addressing this situation is labour informality, entailing lower wages and lack of access to social protection networks. On average, 42.8% of the region's population lived in a household that depended only on informal employment. Moreover, purchasing power in LAC has been progressively eroded by increased inflation, with a more severe impact on the most vulnerable populations. In the first six months of 2023, households in extreme poverty confronted an average price increase that was around 4.0 percentage points higher than for average households.

More and better investment to drive sustainable development in LAC

At only 20% of GDP the LAC region exhibits one of the lowest levels of total investment across all regions globally. This can be partly explained by the region's low levels of national savings. Since the year 2000 gross domestic savings averaged 20% of GDP compared to 35% of GDP in East Asia and Pacific economies. The private sector is the largest source of investment in almost every LAC country (78% of total investment in 2019 on average), although private investment remains concentrated in large enterprises. The public sector has a crucial role to play notably by investing in strategic public infrastructure and mobilising private investment. The public sector can also mobilise private investment for example by updating regulatory investment frameworks and implementing well-regulated public-private partnerships (PPPs) under sound institutional frameworks.

FDI represents an opportunity to boost productivity, innovation and create quality jobs

Despite low domestic investment in LAC, the region has attracted relatively high levels of foreign direct investment (FDI). In 2022, it was the region that received relatively the largest FDI flows globally (equivalent to 4% of the region's GDP). To put these FDI inflows into perspective, while the Marshall Plan to promote Europe's recovery after World War II amounted to around 2% of the combined national incomes of the recipient countries between 1948 and 1951 (USD 13 billion in 1948, equivalent to USD 160 billion in 2022), FDI in LAC surpassed 3% of GDP in the periods 2017-19 (USD 464 billion) and 2020-22 (USD 445 billion), reaching 4% of GDP in 2022. Foreign firms tend to be more productive and invest more in product innovation and research and development (R&D) than domestic firms. This suggests a potential for knowledge and technology spillovers from foreign to domestic firms. Moreover, foreign firms in LAC tend to offer higher average wages and employ a higher proportion of unskilled workers, offering them training opportunities that can upgrade their skills and increase their employability. The impact of FDI in terms of job creation varies significantly depending on the country of origin and the sector receiving the investment. FDI from the EU and the United States had a particularly positive impact on the creation of jobs in the manufacturing sector in LAC. Additionally, FDI in renewables creates more jobs than it does in fossil fuels in LAC.

Investment in R&D and emerging sectors can transform the production structure

The production structure in LAC is characterised by low productivity levels. Investments in physical capital, knowledge and innovation, both from domestic and foreign sources, will be a fundamental driver of production transformation. R&D investment has remained low in the past two decades at around 0.65% of GDP on average, well below the OECD average of around 2.7% of GDP in 2022, and nearly 60% is driven by governments. Moreover, investment in strategic sectors will allow the region to harness untapped opportunities, notably those associated with the green transition and digital transformation. These sectors can be grouped into four broad areas, which are interlinked among them and where there are new opportunities for investment and job creation: i) the green transition; ii) the digital transformation; iii) health and the care economy; and iv) sustainable agriculture and food systems. In terms of green job creation, several activities show high potential, including sustainable food manufacturing, public administration (e.g. related to the planning and implementation of sustainable policies); sustainable construction; sustainable transport; and sustainable commerce (e.g. linked to more sustainable and circular business models). As new green occupations are mostly related to advanced scientific knowledge and skills, they are more likely to be assigned to highly educated men and tend to be formal jobs. This means that green jobs have an important potential contribution to increasing formalisation in LAC, particularly if paired with active labour market policies and with policies to improve female employability.

A new investment agenda demands mobilising resources through innovative instruments

An ambitious and comprehensive investment agenda will require substantially greater involvement both from the public and private sectors. Advancing towards more effective and progressive tax systems, more efficient public spending and debt management, and stronger and more sustainable fiscal frameworks is essential to expand public investment in a context of limited fiscal space. Two promising areas have the potential to improve the flow of both private and public financial resources towards development objectives. First, the role played by development finance institutions (DFIs), which can support access to finance – particularly for MSMEs, given that 75% of their financing needs remain unfunded – and can drive investments in key sectors. The second area is the development of innovative financing instruments, including Green, Social, Sustainability and Sustainability-linked (GSSS) bonds. These bonds represent 32% of total international LAC bond issuance.

Stronger institutions are key to linking investments with countries' and citizens' needs

Favouring dialogue around the investment agenda is key to enabling the implementation of investment and production transformation efforts in LAC by helping increase their legitimacy and thus strengthening the social contract. Building trust is an important goal as more than half of Latin Americans had low trust in national and international companies in 2020, and positive views on FDI have gone down, reaching 53%. Governments must establish mechanisms to promote effective citizen participation, impact assessments, and more equitable distribution of the benefits of investment projects. National development plans (NDPs) can provide the well co-ordinated, long-term and comprehensive policy frameworks needed to advance coherent investment and production transformation strategies. NDPs can also act as a catalyst to attract private investment by enhancing policy predictability and transparency and can include policy guidelines associated with strategic sectors with high development potential in the region.

International partnerships for better investments

International partnerships can create synergies between international organisations, governments, experts, development agencies and private-sector institutions to attract investments that are conducive to LAC's production transformation. These partnerships can attract private investments through innovative mechanisms, such as blended finance, to mobilise additional resources towards sustainable development projects. During the last decade, private finance mobilised by official development finance interventions in LAC, increased from USD 3 billion in 2016 to USD 9 billion in 2021. International partnerships can also help yield greater socio-economic impact of investments by creating an enabling environment for investment; fostering collaboration among institutions, such as multilateral development banks and DFIs, export credit agencies, investment promotion agencies and the private sector; or boosting local development by implementing local content requirements. Regional integration and efforts towards production integration can be an additional source of mobilisation of greater and better investments. Finally, the EU-LAC Global Gateway investment agenda identifies investment opportunities in strategic sectors. This agenda, accompanied by renewed mechanisms of dialogue and co-ordination among the investment, trade and development communities, can further support LAC's reindustrialisation efforts. To achieve this, the agenda should be aligned with national priorities, and ensure investment flows follow a shared criteria on quality, sustainability and inclusiveness.

Overview

Investing in sustainable development

Latin America and the Caribbean (LAC) needs an ambitious and comprehensive investment agenda to embark on a stronger and more sustainable development trajectory. To close existing investment gaps and overcome the region's structural challenges, it is essential to scale up domestic and foreign investment. These investments should be a catalyst for better quality jobs and an upgraded production structure, harnessing the potential of LAC's endowments and of the green and digital transitions. Strong public institutions are fundamental to promoting effective and efficient public and private investments and aligning them with national development strategies and social priorities. Moreover, innovative financing mechanisms, a renewed role for development finance institutions and reinvigorated international partnerships are key aspects to make this new investment agenda an instrument that sets the region on a path towards greater well-being for Latin Americans.

LAC needs to improve potential growth and social conditions in a challenging context

Economic activity in Latin America and the Caribbean (LAC) has slowed in 2023. Following the contraction caused by the COVID-19 pandemic, gross domestic product (GDP) growth in the region had rebounded to above 6% in 2021. This expansion was mainly due to fiscal and monetary stimuli, improved external conditions and base effects. In 2022, external conditions became less favourable, public transfers were reduced, monetary policy tightened and the effects of reopening economies dissipated. GDP grew by almost 4% on average in LAC in 2022, with most countries in the region regaining pre-pandemic GDP levels. Nevertheless, the deceleration of economic activity in 2023 suggests that the region is returning to the low levels of growth seen in the years before the pandemic.

This decline reflects enduring structural weaknesses that limit the region's growth potential, compounded by the impact of an unfavourable global context. Potential GDP per capita growth has been below 1% since 1980, although it increased slightly following the commodity boom between 2003 and 2013. Since then, potential per capita output growth has stagnated at around 0.7%. It has remained consistently below the average rate in advanced economies, which is close to 1 percentage point higher, thus hindering convergence (Figure 1). Global conditions are also denting growth in LAC countries. The global economic outlook remains weak, with tight monetary and fiscal conditions across major economies, including a weaker recovery in the People's Republic of China (hereafter "China") than expected (ECLAC, 2023[1]; OECD, 2023[2]).

Figure 1. **Potential GDP per capita growth in LAC and advanced economies**

Estimated under different methods since 1980

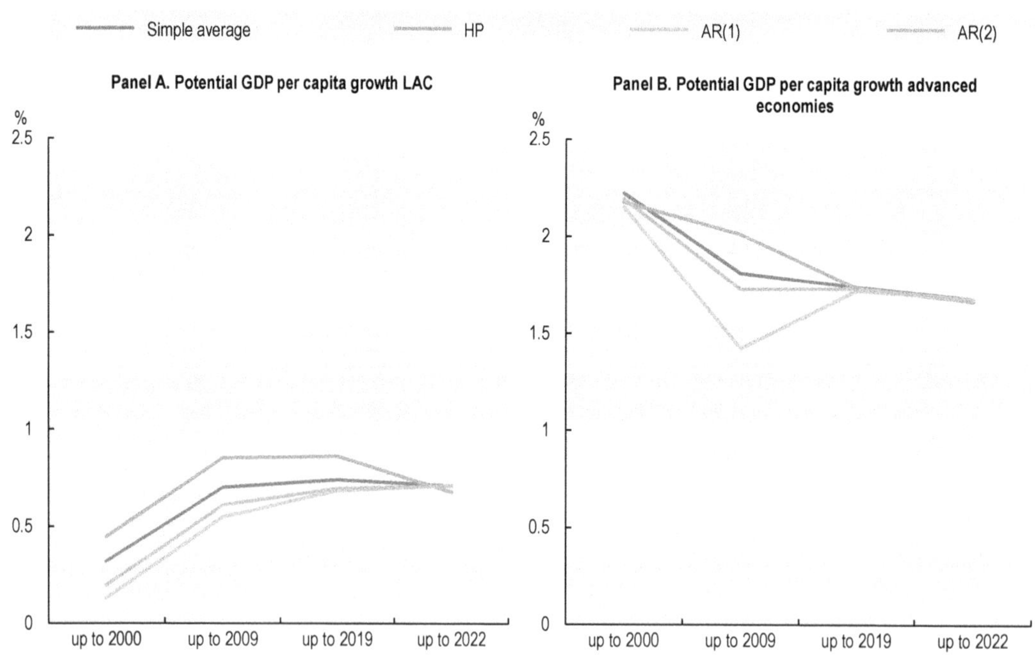

Note: Average growth is a simple average over the period analysed. HP = the Hodrick-Prescott filter, which was used as an alternative model due to its resilience to short-term shocks to create a smoothed curve (lambda 100). AR = autoregressive model, which uses GDP per capita growth data. The number of lags (1 and 2) was determined by analysing the autocorrelation function and choosing the model that maximised the log-likelihood. The LAC and advanced economies series refers to countries covered by the IMF's World Economic Outlook database, April 2023.
Source: Authors' calculations based on (IMF, 2023[3]).

StatLink https://stat.link/wi3cjx

Socio-economic conditions remain challenging in LAC, with poverty and extreme poverty above pre-pandemic levels in more than half of LAC countries. In 2022, 29% of the LAC population was in poverty and 11.2% in extreme poverty. One of the main challenges for addressing this situation is the persistence of high levels of labour informality, entailing lower wages and lack of access to social protection. On average, the informal employment rate in LAC was 48.7% in 2022 (ECLAC/ILO, 2023[4]). Before the pandemic, 42.8% of the region's population lived in a household that depended entirely on informal employment, and 21.8% lived in mixed households, i.e. households with both formal and informal workers. This implies that two-thirds of the region's population depended totally or partially on informal employment, though with important variations between countries (Figure 2).

Figure 2. **Distribution of informal workers at the household level, selected LAC economies**

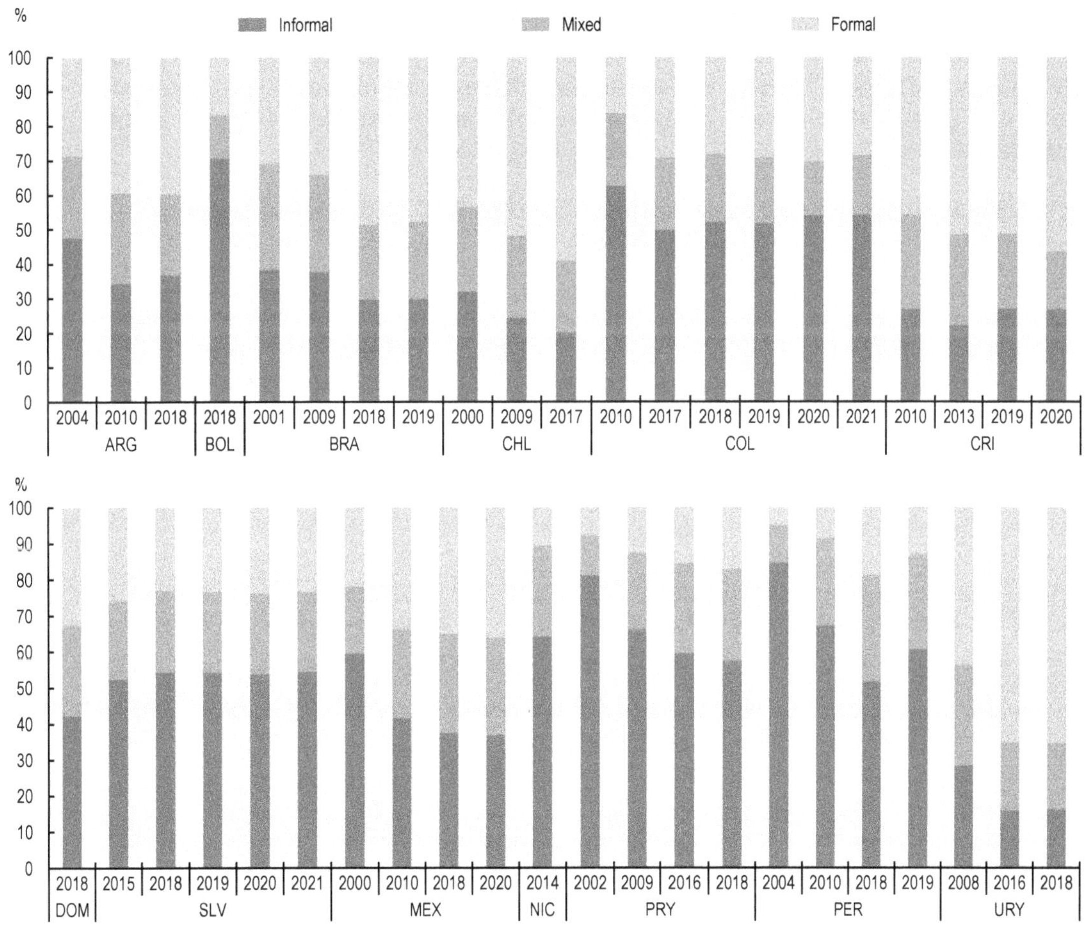

Note: The selected economies are Argentina, Bolivia, Brazil, Chile, Colombia, Costa Rica, Dominican Republic, El Salvador, Mexico, Nicaragua, Paraguay, Peru and Uruguay.
Source: Authors' elaboration based on (OECD, 2021[5]).

StatLink https://stat.link/1b3xf5

Increased inflation eroded purchasing power in LAC, with a more severe impact on the most vulnerable populations. In the first half of 2023, the detrimental effect of inflation was considerably higher for households in extreme poverty. Compared to average households, households in extreme poverty faced an average price increase that was 4.1 percentage points higher. From a sample of LAC economies, the highest difference between the impact of inflation on the average population and on extremely poor households was observed in Argentina (11.6 percentage points) and Peru (7.0 percentage points).

Investment can drive sustainable development in the region

More and better investments are needed to expand potential growth and create more formal jobs; to drive production transformation and leverage the opportunities of LAC's unique advantages; and to harness the potential of profound global transformations, notably the green and digital transitions.

The public and private sectors should mobilise further and better investments

The LAC region exhibits one of the lowest levels of total investment across all regions globally – only 20% of GDP – although with important divergencies across countries in the region (Figure 3). After reaching 23.3% in 2008, investment levels as a share of GDP have been relatively low, particularly between 2016 and 2020, when they were below 20% of GDP, only to recover slightly in 2021 and 2022. Within the region, investment as a percentage of GDP varies significantly. The only countries that achieved a steady increase in investment levels from 2014 to 2022 were Antigua and Barbuda, the Dominican Republic, Grenada, St. Vincent and the Grenadines, El Salvador and Paraguay.

Figure 3. **Total investment as a percentage of GDP in LAC and selected regions, 1990-2022**

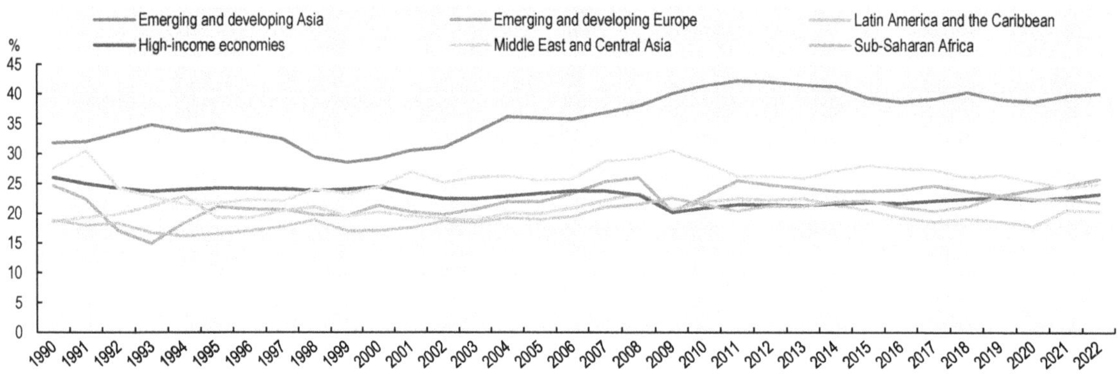

Note: As in the IMF database, data for each region corresponds to weighted averages. Investment, defined as gross capital formation, is measured by the total value of gross fixed capital formation and changes in inventories and acquisitions less disposals of valuables for a unit or sector [SNA 1993]. Investment is expressed as a ratio of total investment in current local currency and GDP in local currency.

Source: (IMF, 2023[6]).

StatLink https://stat.link/ibu4z2

Investment levels vary considerably across economic sectors. Almost half of the total investment in LAC from 1990 to 2018 was received by manufacturing (22.7%) and general services (21.1%). Commerce received 13.7%, mining 12.4%, agriculture 9.4% and transportation 10.9%. Essential services including electricity, gas and water accounted for 7.2% of total investment in the same period (ECLAC, 2022[7]).

Low levels of investment in LAC can be partly explained by the region's low levels of national savings. On average, for every percentage point of GDP increase in national savings, domestic investment increases by 0.39 percentage point, although with strong heterogeneity in the region (Cavallo and Pedemonte, 2015[8]). Despite those wide variations across countries, the region has consistently presented low levels of gross domestic savings, accounting on average for around 20% of GDP since 2000. This is considerably lower than the 35% of GDP saved by East Asia and Pacific economies.

The private sector is the largest source of investment in almost every LAC country, but this investment remains concentrated in large enterprises. The private sector accounted for 78% of total investment in 2019, below the OECD average of 84%. Private investment in LAC is highly concentrated, with 1%, 5% and 10% of the region's top companies being responsible, on average, for 25%, 55% and 69% of long-term investment.

The public sector has a crucial role to play in fostering sustainable development, notably by investing in strategic public infrastructure. However, public investment in infrastructure has remained low in the last decades, particularly since 2008, and stood at a level of 1.6% of GDP in 2021 (Infralatam, 2022[9]). Key sectors where investments in public infrastructure are needed are clean energy, sustainable transport, telecommunications and water. Investment in telecommunications and transport infrastructure can act as a catalyst for further growth and connectivity, at national and subnational levels, by allowing national and international firms to connect with other regions and integrate with national, regional and global markets. Similarly, quality infrastructure in energy, telecommunications and water can provide better equipment to ensure that both the digital and green transitions benefit all citizens in the LAC region.

In 2021, the largest public investments in LAC were in the transport sector (0.8% of GDP), followed by energy (0.3%), telecommunications (0.25%) and water (0.2%). Most public investment in infrastructure in LAC is directed towards the roads subsector; further efforts are needed in other modalities to make transportation sustainable. The strategic nature of infrastructure in energy, telecommunications and water underscores the importance of increasing public investment efforts in these areas.

Public sector investment can attract more and better private investment through various frameworks and tools. LAC governments can promote the development of innovative environments to attract higher levels of investment, for example by updating regulatory investment frameworks to set clear and transparent conditions for investors. Moreover, public-private partnerships (PPPs) can accelerate the development of strategic sectors and advance a more sustainable production matrix. PPPs require effective regulatory and institutional frameworks to avoid unexpected fiscal costs due to renegotiation of concession contracts. Even if as a share of GDP PPPs for public infrastructure in the region remains modest (0.46%), in 2021 LAC was above other developing regions like Sub-Saharan Africa (0.31%), South Asia (0.26%), East Asia and the Pacific (0.16%), the Middle East and North Africa (0.05%), and below Europe and Central Asia (0.47%) (World Bank, 2023[10]).

Overall, to achieve the Sustainable Development Goals (SDGs) by 2030, LAC countries need a substantial increase in both the levels and quality of investment. To close the gap between current investment levels and those necessary to achieve the SDGs, the LAC region will need an estimated investment of nearly USD 2.22 trillion in public infrastructure – the equivalent of USD 282 per capita per year by 2030 (IDB, 2021[11]). Low levels of domestic savings mean that LAC countries must borrow abroad to finance their investments, although this can sometimes be more costly and increases exposure to fluctuating external conditions.

While domestic investment has been low, the region has been successful in attracting FDI

While investment levels are low in the region, LAC has attracted relatively high levels of foreign direct investment (FDI) compared to other emerging economies. In 2022, it was the region that received the largest FDI flows globally relative to GDP, a position it has also held between 2018 and 2020 on average. FDI inflows were equivalent to 4% of the region's GDP in 2022 (Figure 4). Although global FDI decreased by 24% in 2022, FDI inflows increased by 55% in LAC, reaching almost USD 225 billion. To put these FDI inflows into perspective, for the periods 2017-19 and 2020-22 FDI represented the equivalent to

290% (USD 464 billion) and 278% (USD 445 billion), respectively, of the financial resources provided by the Marshall Plan to promote Europe's recovery after World War II (USD 13 billion in 1948 equivalent to USD 160 billion in 2022). Similarly, while the Marshall Plan amounted to around 2% of the combined national incomes of the recipient countries between 1948 and 1951 (Eichengreen, 2010[12]), FDI in LAC surpassed 3% of GDP in the periods 2017-19 and 2020-22, reaching 4% of GDP in 2022.

Figure 4. **FDI inflows as a share of GDP, by region, 2010-22**

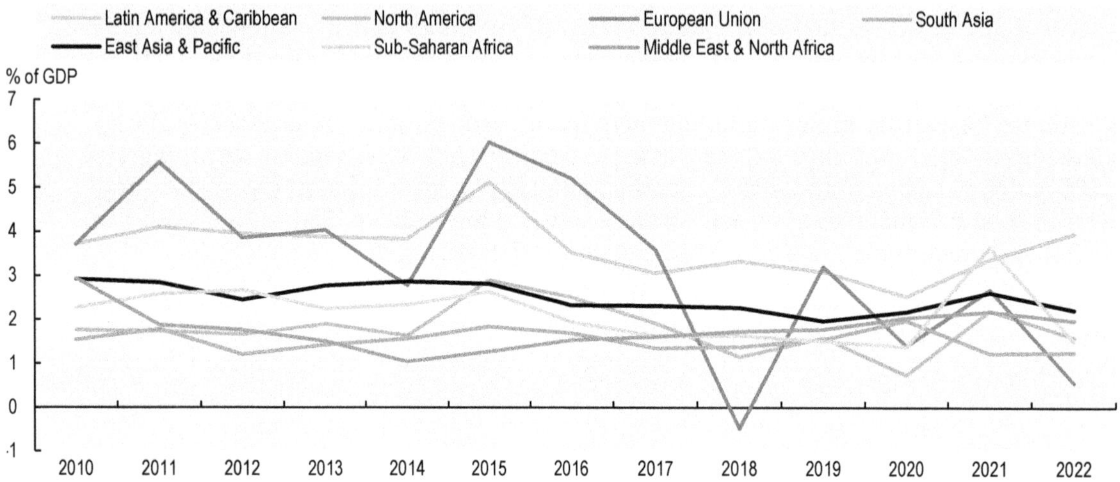

Note: As in (World Bank, 2023[13]), data for each region corresponds to weighted averages. For the LAC region, 37 countries were taken into account with available data for 2022: Antigua and Barbuda, Argentina, Aruba, Bahamas, Barbados, Belize, Bolivia, Brazil, Cayman Islands, Chile, Colombia, Costa Rica, Curacao, Dominica, Dominican Republic, Ecuador, El Salvador, Grenada, Guatemala, Guyana, Haiti, Honduras, Jamaica, Mexico, Nicaragua, Panama, Paraguay, Peru, Saint Kitts and Nevis, Saint Lucia, Saint Vincent and the Grenadines, Saint Maarten, Suriname, Trinidad and Tobago, Turks and Caicos, Uruguay and Venezuela. The latest data available for Aruba, Curacao and the Cayman Islands corresponds to 2021, while for Venezuela it corresponds to 2014.

Source: Authors' elaboration based on (World Bank, 2023[13]).

StatLink https://stat.link/6giqkh

Wide heterogeneity in FDI inflows is evident across LAC countries, both in terms of their origin and destination. More than half of FDI inflows to the LAC region in 2022 were directed to Brazil and Mexico, while Central America saw a decline of 11.9% that year. In terms of origin, and based on project announcements, the European Union (EU) and the United States have consistently accounted for more than half of the region's FDI inflows. About 8% of FDI in the region originated from LAC countries, followed by China (4%), the United Kingdom (4%) and Canada (2%) (fDi Markets, 2023[18]).

FDI represents an opportunity to boost productivity, innovation and the development of strategic sectors such as renewable energy. The OECD FDI Qualities Indicators, which seek to measure the impact of international investment on sustainable development, show that foreign investors are more productive than domestic firms across most LAC countries (Figure 5, Panel A), or more likely to introduce product innovation or invest in research and development (R&D). This productivity and innovation gap suggests that there is potential for knowledge and technology spillovers from foreign to domestic firms. In addition, regarding the development of strategic sectors, greenfield FDI in renewable energy has surpassed greenfield FDI in fossil fuels almost steadily since 2011 (Figure 5, Panel B), particularly in countries like Paraguay, Brazil, Uruguay, Dominican Republic, Honduras and Chile, where renewable energy FDI has dominated the energy sector and attracted a sizable share of total greenfield FDI over the 2003-22 period.

Figure 5. **FDI Qualities Indicator for productivity and evolution of greenfield FDI by energy type**

Selected LAC countries

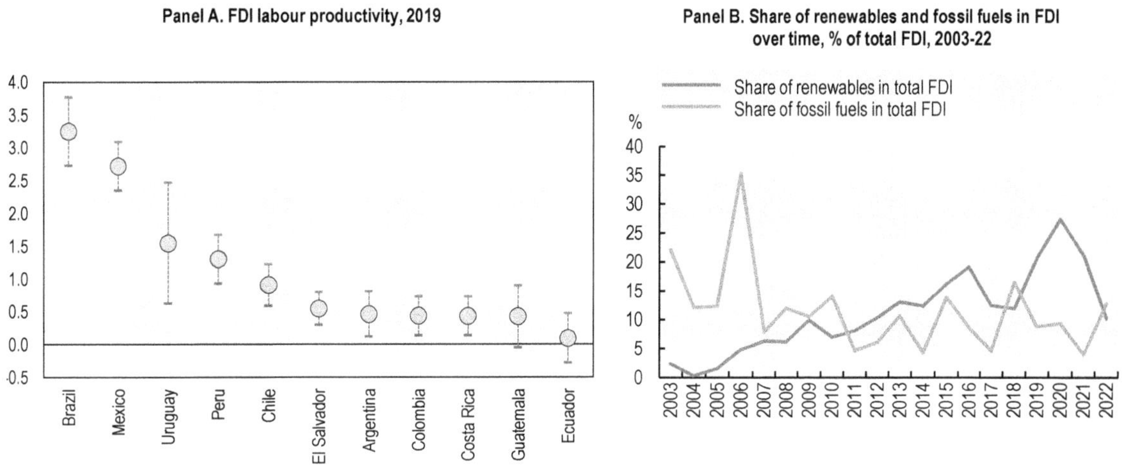

Note: In Panel A, the orange dots depict the estimation of the indicator while the dashed lines represent the corresponding confidence interval. If the value is >0, foreign firms perform better than domestic firms. Based on 2019 data or the latest data available. For methodological details, see www.oecd.org/fr/investissement/fdi-qualities-indicators.htm. Panel B shows the share of all opened and announced greenfield FDI projects in renewables and fossil fuels as a share of total greenfield FDI in LAC over time. In Panel B, LAC comprises Argentina, Brazil, Chile, Colombia, Costa Rica, the Dominican Republic, Ecuador, El Salvador, Guatemala, Honduras, Mexico, Paraguay, Peru and Uruguay.

Source: Based on (OECD et al., 2021[14]), (OECD, forthcoming[15]) and (OECD, 2019[16]).

StatLink https://stat.link/fjz0d8

Investment can be a catalyst for job creation and improved labour market conditions

Investments can create new formal jobs in the LAC region. However, the potential for investments to yield favourable effects on labour market outcomes will very much depend on the type of investments, the sectors where they take place and the policies surrounding those investments, including social protection, education and skills policies.

FDI has a particularly relevant impact on labour market conditions. Foreign firms in LAC tend to offer higher average wages and employ a higher proportion of unskilled workers than domestic firms do, and are also more likely to offer training opportunities (OECD, 2022[17]). Thus, foreign investors are an important source of employment for low-skilled workers in LAC and can make a significant contribution to upgrading their skills and increasing their employability.

The impact of FDI in terms of job creation varies significantly depending on the country of origin and the sector receiving the investment. FDI from the EU and the United States has had a particularly positive impact on the creation of jobs. However, results vary largely across economic activities, as seen in the manufacturing and the energy and extraction sectors, the main receivers of total FDI. In particular, 56% of jobs created in the region by FDI from the EU were in the manufacturing sector, which received 41% of the invested capital coming from the EU. Similarly, 61% of all jobs created in the region by FDI from the United States were in the manufacturing sector, which received 46% of total FDI from the United States. Conversely, 31% of the capital from the EU is invested in energy and extraction, but this created only 6% of new jobs. In the same vein, 24% of the region's FDI from the United States targeted the energy and extraction sector, but this only created 3% of jobs (Figure 6). Finally, FDI in renewables creates more jobs than it does in fossil fuels in LAC. For example, USD 1 billion invested in fossil fuels creates on average about 500 new jobs, while 800 jobs are being created with USD 1 billion worth of investment in renewables.

Figure 6. **Capital expenditure and formal jobs created by FDI in LAC, January 2003-May 2023**

By sector and countries of origin

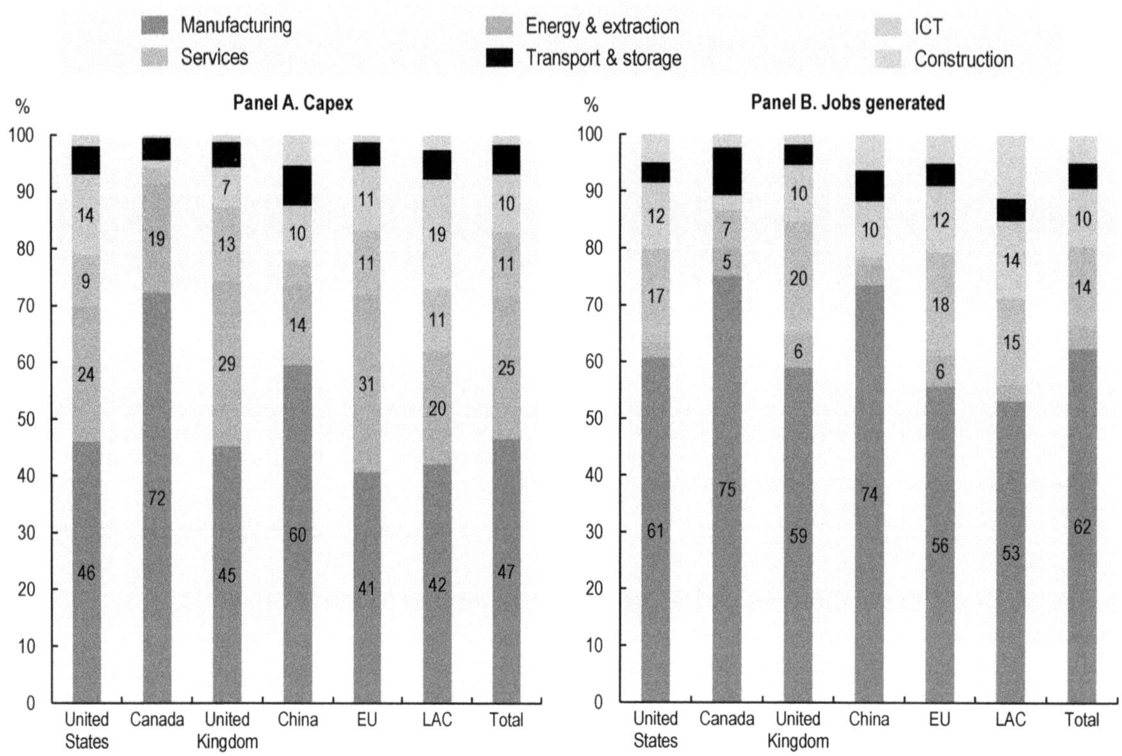

Note: ICT = information and telecommunication technologies. Capex = capital expenditures. Data covers January 2003 to May 2023. Energy and extraction includes: coal, oil and gas; minerals; and renewable energy. Services include: business services, financial services, health care, hotels and tourism, and leisure and entertainment. Construction includes: real estate. ICT includes: communications and software, and IT services. The LAC country group includes 27 countries: Antigua and Barbuda, Argentina, Bahamas, Barbados, Belize, Bolivia, Brazil, Chile, Colombia, Costa Rica, Cuba, Dominican Republic, Ecuador, El Salvador, Guatemala, Guyana, Honduras, Jamaica, Mexico, Nicaragua, Panama, Paraguay, Peru, Saint Lucia, Trinidad and Tobago, Uruguay and Venezuela.

Source: Authors' elaboration based on (fDi Markets, 2023[18]).

StatLink https://stat.link/i26hkt

Emerging sectors offer important opportunities for job creation. In a scenario where investments in green sectors increase by 3 percentage points annually, additional net job creation could reach 10.5% by 2030 (OECD et al., 2022[19]). In particular in terms of green job creation, several activities show high potential: sustainable food manufacturing (+18.8% green jobs by 2030) is related to more sustainable production models in agriculture, food and beverages, and sustainable intermediate products; public administration (+14.6%) includes activities related to the planning and implementation of sustainable policies (from general administration to sustainable local development or energy market policies). It also comprises supervision and administration of social and economic life such as public activities related to the care economy. Sustainable construction (+14.3%) is mainly linked to new sustainable building construction, installations and completions that should improve buildings' energy efficiency thanks to the use of new technologies. This also includes repair, additions and alterations to improve existing constructions from an environmental perspective; sustainable transport (+14.1%) reflects the need for more sustainable passenger and freight transportation systems, and to support sustainable transport activities, including the ones linked to digital transformation through telecommunications; finally, sustainable commerce (14.1%) represents the growing new business models of selling goods and services, and to repair goods that should contribute to developing the circular economy.

The development of green sectors requires well-targeted investments in human capital in order to leave no one behind. As new green occupations are mostly related to advanced scientific knowledge and skills, they are more likely to be assigned to highly educated men and tend to be formal jobs (Figure 7). This means that there is an important potential contribution of green jobs to increasing formalisation in LAC, particularly if paired with active labour policies to eradicate gender bias.

Figure 7. **Workers in green jobs are likely to be male, highly educated and formal**

Odds ratios

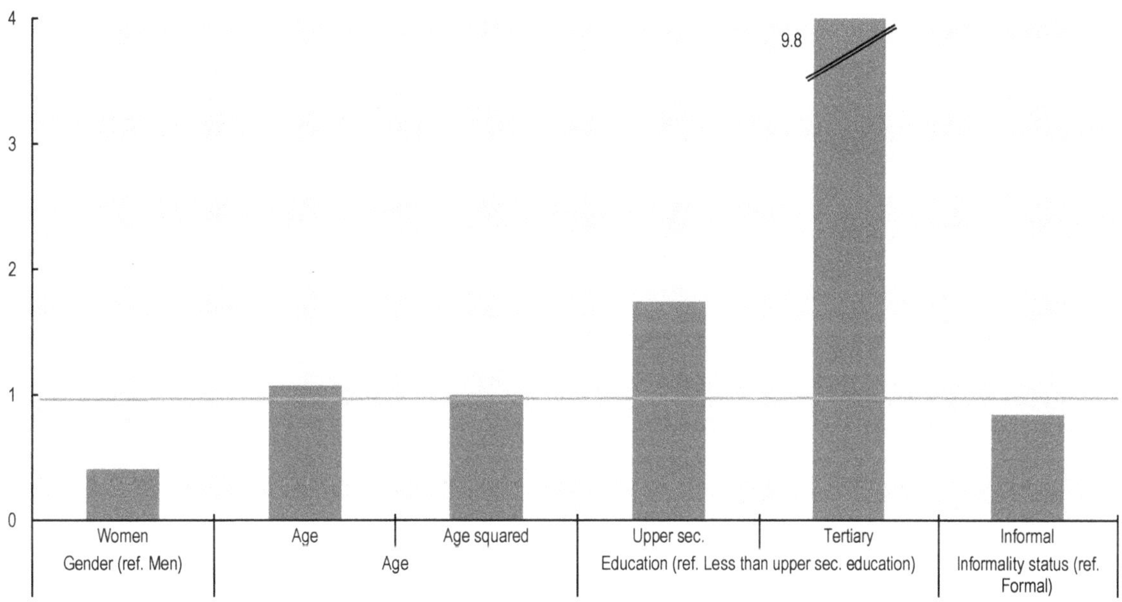

Note: An odds ratio greater than 1 indicates that the condition or event is more likely to occur in the first group. An odds ratio less than 1 indicates that the condition or event is less likely to occur in the first group. In the chart the odds of holding a green job for women is 0.4 times the odds for men, meaning that women are less likely than men to be employed in a green occupation. The data refer to a pooled sample of workers in Argentina, Bolivia, Brazil, Colombia, Ecuador, Guatemala, Mexico, Paraguay and Uruguay, in 2021. Green tasks are identified using the methodology of (Vona et al., 2018[20]).

Source: Authors' calculations based on national labour-force surveys.

StatLink https://stat.link/b80nez

Investment is key to transforming production and tapping into emerging sectors

The production structure in LAC is characterised by low productivity levels. Productivity in LAC economies has been low for decades, and the gap relative to advanced economies has been widening. In 2023, labour productivity in LAC relative to the United States was around 27%, down from around 40% in the early 1980s.

Significant productivity differentials exist both between and within sectors: very dynamic and high-productivity sectors that are generally export-oriented coexist with less dynamic sectors and with high rates of informality. This heterogeneity is also observed at the level of production units. The region's many informal, low-productivity micro, small and medium-sized enterprises (MSMEs) coexist with technology-based and fast-growing start-ups.

By transforming the production structure, LAC countries will be able to raise productivity, increase potential growth and create better job opportunities. Investments in physical capital, knowledge and innovation, both from domestic and foreign sources, will be a fundamental driver of this production transformation. Similarly, investment in strategic sectors will allow the region to harness untapped opportunities, notably those associated with the green transition and digital transformation. It will also help the region to increase dynamism through technological upgrading, diversification towards more knowledge-intensive activities across all economic sectors and higher-quality jobs.

Investment in R&D is needed for the transformation of LAC's production structure

Innovation is crucial for sustainable development and the transformation of the production structure in LAC as it is capable of spurring and prolonging long-term growth. Nevertheless, total investment in research and development in LAC has remained low for the past two decades, at around 0.65% of GDP between 2017 and 2020, or only 2.3% of total world investment, and well below the OECD average of around 2.7% of GDP in 2022 (RICYT, 2022[21]).

Significant heterogeneity in R&D expenditures is evident across LAC countries. In absolute terms, Argentina, Brazil and Mexico accounted for 86% of the region's R&D expenditures in 2020. Brazil, which alone accounted for 65%, invests the highest proportion of its GDP (nearly 1.2% in 2020), followed by Argentina and Cuba (0.52%). In contrast, R&D investment levels in Guatemala and Trinidad and Tobago are close to 0.05% (RICYT, 2022[21]). As capacities vary a lot across LAC countries, some of them face specific policy challenges in terms of improving their technological sophistication and the innovative potential of their structures of production.

Governments in LAC remain the main funding source of R&D investment, contributing nearly 60%[1] (Figure 8). This highlights the need to increase private investment in R&D. Private investment in R&D has been constantly growing in developed economies and currently exceeds 60% in the United States, the European Union and OECD member countries, and stands at nearly 80% in China.

Figure 8. **Share of R&D investments by funding source in LAC and other territories, 2011-20**

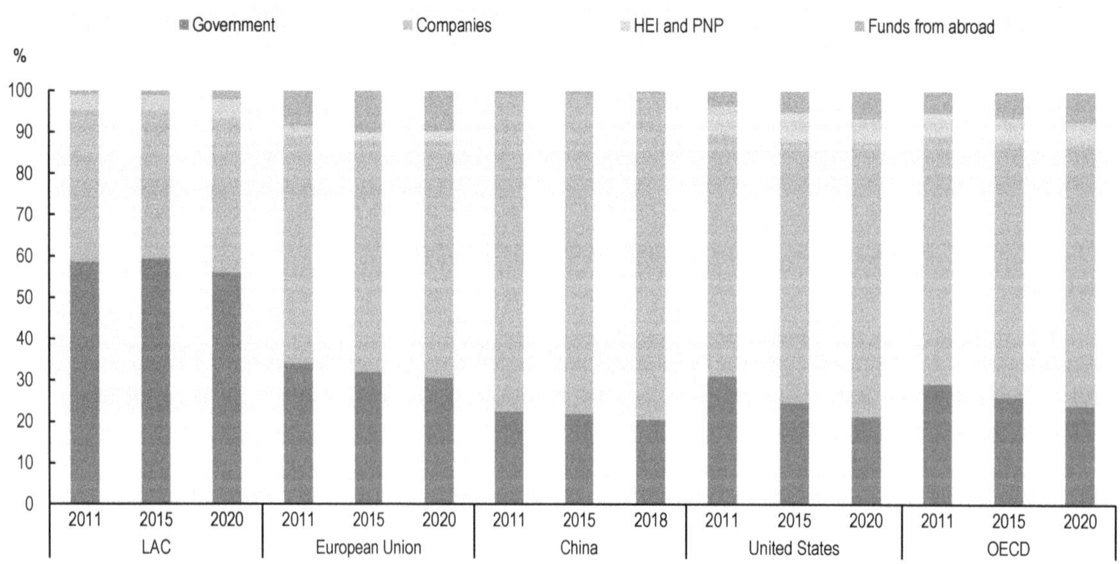

Note: HEI refers to higher education institutions. PNP refers to private non-profit organisations.

Source: Authors' elaboration based on (RICYT, 2020[22]) for LAC and OECD's STI Scoreboard for the other territories.

StatLink https://stat.link/4uge8z

Most sectors in LAC invest a medium to medium-low percentage of value added in R&D, while patent applications have been dominated by non-resident applicants in recent years (87%) (WIPO, 2023[23]). This contrasts with what is seen in more developed countries, where firms invest a higher percentage of value added in R&D and most patent applications are submitted by residents.

Investment should target strategic sectors such as the green and digital transitions

The sectors with the greatest potential for increasing productivity, creating better jobs and developing sustainable and inclusive value chains may be grouped into four broad areas, which are interlinked among them and where significant transformations are taking place, opening up new opportunities for investment and job creation: i) the green transition; ii) the digital transformation; iii) health and the care economy; and iv) sustainable agriculture and food systems (Figure 9).

Figure 9. **Sectors with high potential to drive sustainable development**

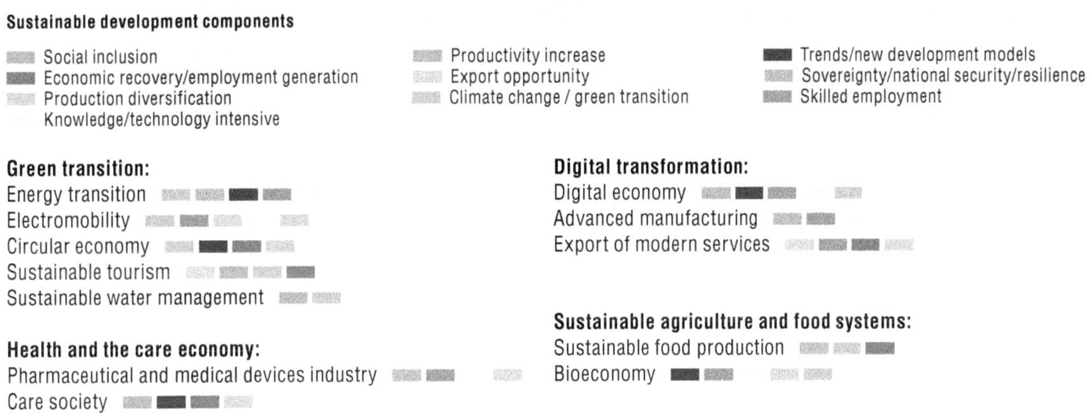

Source: Authors' elaboration based on (ECLAC, 2023[24]; OECD et al., 2022[19]).

The green transition requires substantial investment in new technologies and human talent, and it will involve a large reallocation of workers from brown to green sectors. In recent decades, green sectors in LAC have shown more dynamic growth (3.3% per year) than the total economy (2.8%). The development of the green hydrogen industry and the addition of local value to critical raw materials are two areas of particular potential in the region.

Digital transformation can help improve productivity and competitiveness and be a way to take advantage of technological progress. Health and the care economy can help to increase resilience and preparedness for future health crises by developing stronger and self-sufficient local industries, strengthening the region's scientific, technological and production capacities. This can contribute to building more inclusive societies by promoting affordable and quality care services. Advancing towards more sustainable agriculture and food systems is key to ensuring food security both in the region and in the rest of the world, as LAC has the world's largest reserve of land with agricultural potential.

Boosting investment requires mobilising innovative sources of finance

The LAC region needs to mobilise private and public sources on a large scale to finance the investments it needs. Tight fiscal space in many LAC countries limits the scope for public investment, which is already constrained by low levels of tax revenues. While the public sector can play an important role, particularly by investing in quality infrastructure, an ambitious and comprehensive investment agenda also requires much higher levels of private investment, which has been traditionally constrained by low levels of savings and high interest rates. To stimulate it, development finance institutions (DFIs) can support access to finance and drive investments in key sectors while leveraging the potential of private finance; and innovative financing instruments may be developed, including Green, Social, Sustainability and Sustainability-linked (GSSS) bonds.

Greater efficiency in taxation and spending can expand the scope for public investment

Expanding public investment will require mobilising resources from various sources of funding, yet most countries in the LAC region are constrained by limited fiscal space. This highlights the importance of advancing towards more effective and progressive tax systems, more efficient and effective public spending and debt management, and stronger and more sustainable fiscal frameworks (ECLAC, 2022[7]; OECD et al., 2022[19]; OECD et al., 2023[25]).

Regarding tax revenues, the average tax-to-GDP ratio in the LAC region in 2021 was 21.7%, considerably lower than the average of 34.1% in OECD economies. These revenues varied widely across LAC countries, from 12.7% of GDP in Panama to 33.5% in Brazil. LAC tax structures rely on indirect taxes more than direct taxes (Figure 10). In 2020, taxes on income and profits accounted for 25.2% of tax revenues in LAC on average, relative to 33.1% on average in the OECD.

Relatively high corporate income taxes (CIT) may hinder investment and entrepreneurship. Within income taxes, CIT accounted for 15.5% of total tax revenues in LAC, while personal income taxes (PIT) represented only 9.7%. In OECD economies, PIT account for a larger share of tax revenues (24.1%) than CIT (9.0%) (OECD et al., 2023[25]). Furthermore, effective corporate tax rates – i.e. the actual tax liabilities faced by companies after taking into account existing tax provisions – tend to be high due to relatively high statutory rates and tax provisions that are less generous than those observed in other jurisdictions.

Figure 10. **Average tax structure in the LAC region and the OECD, 2020**

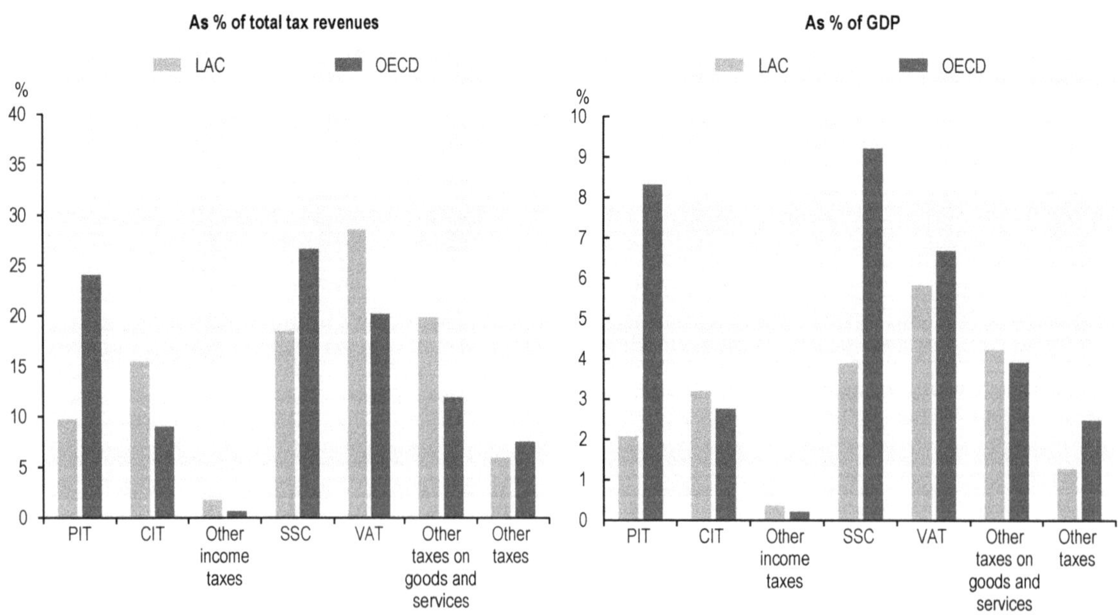

Note: PIT is personal income tax, CIT is corporate income tax, SSC is social security contributions and VAT is value-added tax.
Source: Authors' calculations based on (OECD et al., 2023[25]).

StatLink https://stat.link/9oys7g

On the expenditure side, more effective and efficient spending could be achieved through effective focalisation of public expenditures (including social spending and subsidies). Regarding public debt, it is above pre-pandemic levels and interest payments represent a larger fraction of spending, reducing the scope for countercyclical policies and investment.

Better debt management and economic growth are required for debt to stabilise or decrease, and investments are crucial for this. Capital investments are essential for the production transformation and can help to offset the contractionary effects of fiscal adjustment in the short term. Fiscal policy must therefore protect public investment with adequate fiscal frameworks, including fiscal rules that are flexible enough to accommodate exogenous shocks. This can be accomplished by including cyclically adjusted fiscal targets, setting well-defined escape clauses and practising differential treatment of investment expenditures.

DFIs can bolster access to finance for MSMEs and investments in strategic sectors

The potential of national and subnational public development finance institutions (DFIs) is often underutilised in LAC countries. With their diverse and innovative financial instruments, DFIs can play a crucial role in addressing the lack of depth in LAC's financial markets by redistributing risks and making markets more inclusive. In turn, DFIs also have the potential to bridge financing gaps faced by enterprises and to help expand the market.

As much as 75% of the financing needs of MSMEs in LAC remain unfunded, and DFIs can play a pivotal role in contributing to filling this gap. Public DFIs in LAC are already focused on MSMEs, as shown by an analysis in 2023 of 38 national and subnational public DFIs across 13 LAC countries. Of all instruments used by these DFIs, 42% target both MSMEs and large companies, 39% target only MSMEs, 7% target public institutions and 4% are directed only to large companies. Financing offered to MSMEs mainly targets investment (45%) and day-to-day operations (34%). This shows the commitment of DFIs to guaranteeing the working capital, liquidity and long-term investment needs of these firms.

DFIs offer MSMEs in LAC a variety of tailored financial instruments that cater to their financial needs at every stage of their development. Credits are the most common instrument offered to finance investment projects (87.6%) and to finance day-to-day expenses (69.6%), but other instruments are also used, including factoring, leasing, guarantees and mechanisms to access capital markets (Figure 11, Panel A).

DFIs can also promote innovation and long-term investments in strategic sectors, aligned with national development priorities. This will contribute to public-sector efforts for production transformation at the national, subnational and local levels. DFIs also support private-sector investments in key sectors. Of the total financial instruments offered to MSMEs with a sectoral perspective, 30% target agriculture, hunting and forestry; 14% target electricity, gas and water supply; 13% target manufacturing; and 7% target transport, storage and communications (Figure 11, Panel B).

Figure 11. **Financial instruments offered to MSMEs by DFIs in LAC, by type of financing and sector, 2023**

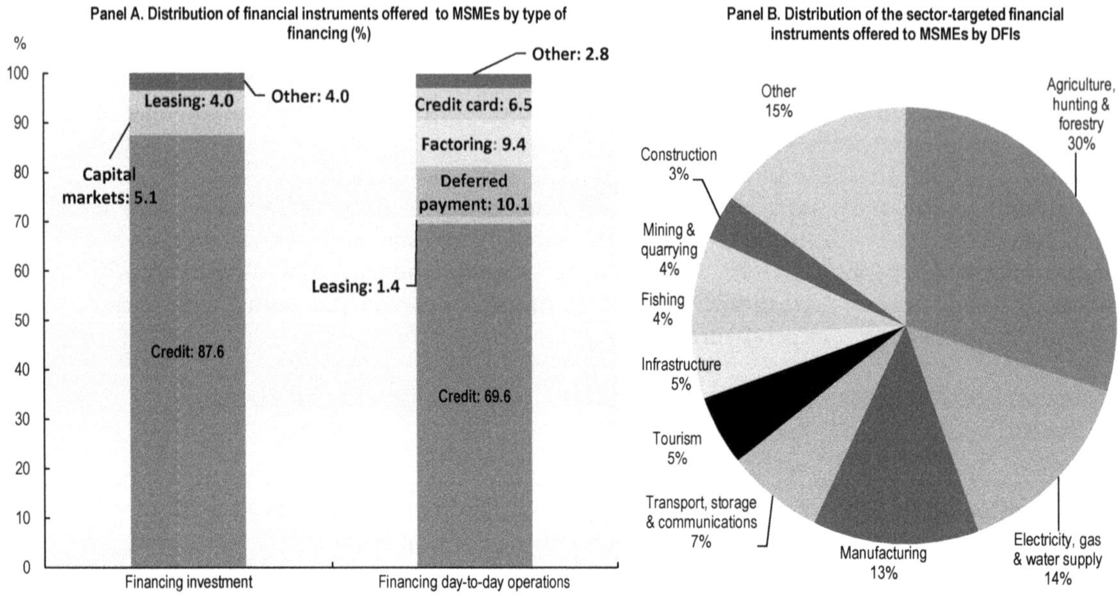

Note: The database covers 38 national and subnational public DFIs in 13 LAC countries: Argentina, Brazil, Chile, Colombia, Costa Rica, Dominican Republic, El Salvador, Guatemala, Mexico, Paraguay, Panama, Peru and Uruguay. Panel A: The category "Other" includes the following financial instruments: non-reimbursable financial support; credit fund; guarantee; trusts; and cancellation of liabilities. Panel B: The category "Other" includes the following sectors: wholesale and retail trade; financial intermediation; real estate, renting and business activities; public administration and defence; education; health and social work; other community, social and personal service activities; ICT; and creative industries.

Source: Authors' elaboration based on public data (annual and sustainability reports) accessed in 2023 from 38 public DFIs in 13 LAC countries.

StatLink *https://stat.link/gcflyh*

Scaling up innovative debt instruments can boost private and public investment in LAC

Developing sustainable debt market instruments can help mobilise resources where needs are greatest. While the GSSS bond market represents only 1% of total assets outstanding and around 2% of new issuances globally, it constitutes a promising avenue forward (OECD, 2022[26]). In the LAC region, even with tight financial markets, GSSS bonds are an attractive financing mechanism, representing 32% of total international LAC bond issuance. Between 2014 and 2022, the GSSS bond market reached a cumulative value of close to USD 100 billion, of which green bond issuance alone accounted for USD 33.4 billion, followed by bonds linked to sustainability criteria (USD 24.4 billion) (Figure 12, Panel A).

Sovereign GSSS issuance has been gaining prominence in recent years as a share of total GSSS bond issuance in LAC. In 2022, sovereign GSSS bond issuance in international markets in the region accounted for 35.7% of the total sovereign issuance of all types of bonds in international markets. During the first six months of 2023, this figure increased to 43.5%. Until June 2019, all GSSS bond issuances in LAC originated in the corporate sector. In 2022, sovereigns led, with a 57% share of total GSSS bond issuance in LAC, followed by corporates (23%) and supranational and quasi-sovereign issuers (20%).

GSSS bonds have also emerged as attractive instruments for specific sectors to raise capital and address the region's pressing sectoral challenges. Between 2014 and April 2022, the main sectors that issued GSSS bonds, after sovereign (39%), were finance (14%), the chemical industry (10%) and energy (9%) (Figure 12, Panel B).

Figure 12. **International GSSS bond issuance in LAC by type, as percentage of total and by sector, 2014-22**

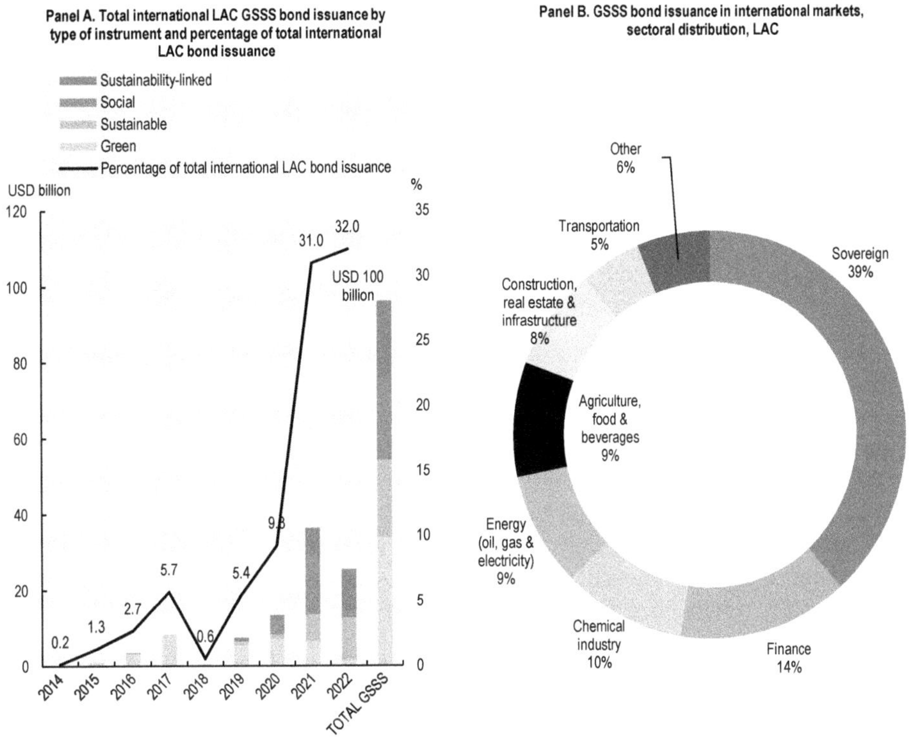

Note: GSSS refers to Green, Social, Sustainability and Sustainability-linked bonds. Total sustainable bonds for 2022 include two blue bonds issued by the Bahamas. Panel B: The category "Other" includes the following sectors: telecommunications; forestry & paper; and retail & consumer products.

Source: (Núñez, Velloso and Da Silva, 2022[27]; OECD et al., 2022[19])

StatLink https://stat.link/jv3682

Countries in LAC are focusing on expanding, improving and harmonising sustainable finance frameworks, which are essential to regulating, monitoring and verifying the issuance of GSSS bonds and other instruments. More consolidated frameworks have the potential to reduce transaction costs for investors, making capital markets in the region more attractive. Green and sustainable taxonomies have been developed in the region. They have been implemented in Mexico and Colombia, while they are under development in countries such as Brazil, Chile, Dominican Republic, Peru and subregions such as Central America. In June 2023, the United Nations system in LAC launched the first Common Framework of Sustainable Finance Taxonomies. This regional framework is intended as a voluntary guidance document for actors in the region who are in the process of developing or intend to develop taxonomies. The framework also provides guidance for the interoperability of taxonomies within LAC and globally (UNEP, 2023[28]). To maintain market transparency and avoid greenwashing/SDG-washing, it is also crucial to consolidate reliable monitoring and verification systems. LAC's GSSS bond market has made progress from self-labelling to becoming an externally reviewed market, yet there is still a long way to go. External reviews, i.e. pre-issuance and/or post-issuance reviews, must be installed and enhanced.

Strong public institutions should link investments with national and citizens' priorities

Better public institutions are fundamental to ensuring that investment and production transformation efforts address the priorities of citizens and are well connected with the broader development strategies in LAC countries. Similarly, by enhancing the rule of law, transparency and integrity, public institutions can create a conducive environment for investment, help build trust and reduce risk aversion.

Favouring dialogue around the investment agenda to strengthen the social contract

An ambitious investment agenda can have a significant impact on living standards across socio-economic groups in LAC. Engaging stakeholders to agree on the strategies for production transformation and investment will be crucial to making these efforts possible and to avoiding potential conflict. This involves understanding and incorporating stakeholders' priorities throughout the policy-making process, which increases the legitimacy of investment strategies, thus strengthening the social contract.

As enterprises are central to production transformation and a main source of investment, citizens' perceptions of their role are crucial. However, LAC citizens currently have low trust in national and international companies. In 2020, LAC citizens had either no trust at all (20.3% and 24.4%) or little confidence (35% and 34.2%) in national and international companies, respectively (Latinobarómetro, 2020[29]). In other words, lack of trust was expressed by more than half of those polled. In contrast, perceptions that FDI has positive impacts on economic development remain relatively high in LAC, though there has been slippage recently. FDI was seen as beneficial by 53.6% of the population surveyed in 2020, down from 70.7% in 2016 and the lowest level to date.

Inclusive dialogue throughout the investment cycle is particularly relevant to avoid conflict derived from the potential economic, social and environmental impacts of some investments on specific groups. Many social conflicts around environmental issues have erupted in the LAC region. Of 742 social conflicts that occurred in LAC from 2000 to 2022, 661 were still unresolved by the end of 2022. About one-third of the conflicts still open in 2022 concentrated on mining (33.7%), followed by water management (16.2%), biomass and land conflicts (14.8%), and fossil fuels and climate/energy justice (14.1%) (Figure 13).

Figure 13. **Number of open social conflicts in LAC linked to environment, by category, 2022**

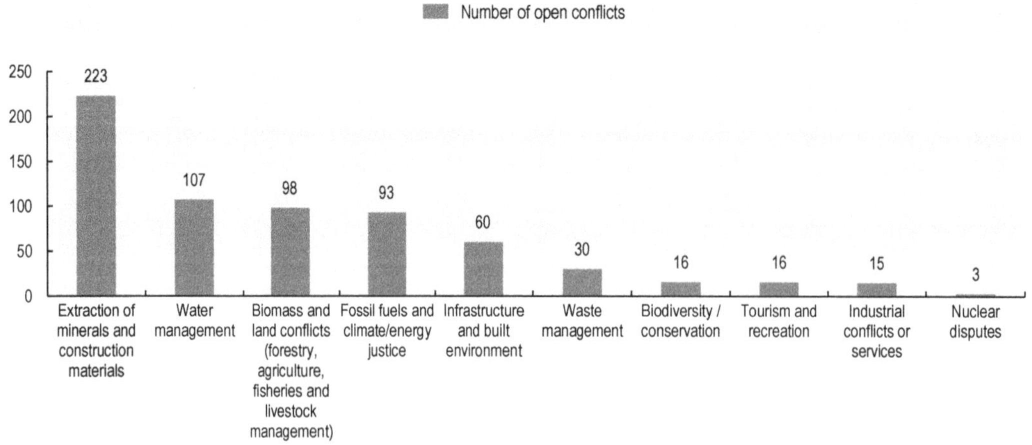

Note: These conflicts are defined as mobilisations by local communities and social movements, which might also include support of national or international networks against particular economic activities, such as infrastructure construction or waste disposal/pollution, whereby environmental impacts are a key element of the grievances. The figure shows unresolved conflicts that started in the period 2020-22.

Source: (Environmental Justice Atlas, 2023[30]).

StatLink https://stat.link/b4sk7r

To build support for the investment and production transformation agenda, while preventing and/or handling potential social conflicts and corruption, governments must establish mechanisms to ensure effective citizen participation, rigorous and standard environmental and social impact assessments, and more equitable distribution of the benefits of investment projects. Public consultations, access to information and data, participatory budgeting and representative deliberative processes are useful practices for engaging citizens in the process. Local governments have a vital role in promoting citizen participation, as investment projects often have direct impacts on specific communities and territories.

Aligning the investment agenda with national development strategies

National development plans (NDPs) can provide the well co-ordinated, long-term and comprehensive policy frameworks needed to advance coherent investment and production transformation strategies. The LAC region has frequently grappled with fragmented policies and political uncertainty, which discourage the domestic and foreign investments that are essential for production transformation. However, in most LAC countries, NDPs have emerged as a powerful instrument to provide strategic direction, enhance investor confidence and reinforce social contracts. The process of elaborating an NDP often includes mechanisms to incorporate civic participation and foster the inclusion of a diversity of views. NDPs can also contribute to adopting a whole-of-government strategy, which aligns public policies both horizontally (across sectors) and vertically (between government levels), facilitating efficient resource utilisation and investment planning.

NDPs can also act as a catalyst to attract private investment by enhancing policy predictability and transparency, and can include policy guidelines associated with strategic sectors with high development potential in the region. An analysis of the NDPs of 14 LAC countries indicates that agendas like digital transformation appear rather prominently, with greater relative relevance in countries such as Costa Rica, Ecuador and Peru. The pharmaceutical and health care industry receives significant attention in most countries, with Guatemala, Honduras and Panama addressing this agenda in particular. The energy transition is also addressed in most (but not all) NDPs, and is particularly emphasised in Argentina and Brazil. Interest surrounding the care economy also varies among countries, with nations like Chile, Colombia and the Dominican Republic leading in addressing this agenda. The approach to sustainable tourism is balanced across all countries, with Guatemala giving greater relative importance to this area. Sustainable agribusiness is addressed in all countries, although it receives slightly less relative attention than other topics, with countries such as Bolivia and Guatemala giving it greater relative importance. The circular economy is addressed in a balanced way in most NDPs, although in most countries it is not among the sectors receiving the most attention. Lastly, across countries, NDPs give low emphasis to sustainable mobility (Figure 14). It is worth mentioning that some countries may have specific sectoral strategies for certain sectors that are not particularly prominent in the NDPs. Sectoral development plans, often formulated in consultation with diverse stakeholders, provide additional, specialised frameworks for stimulating growth and development in key economic sectors. These planning tools are particularly important for aligning investments with broader socio-economic goals and for specifying implementation measures.

Figure 14. Prioritisation of strategic economic sectors in LAC national development plans, 2023

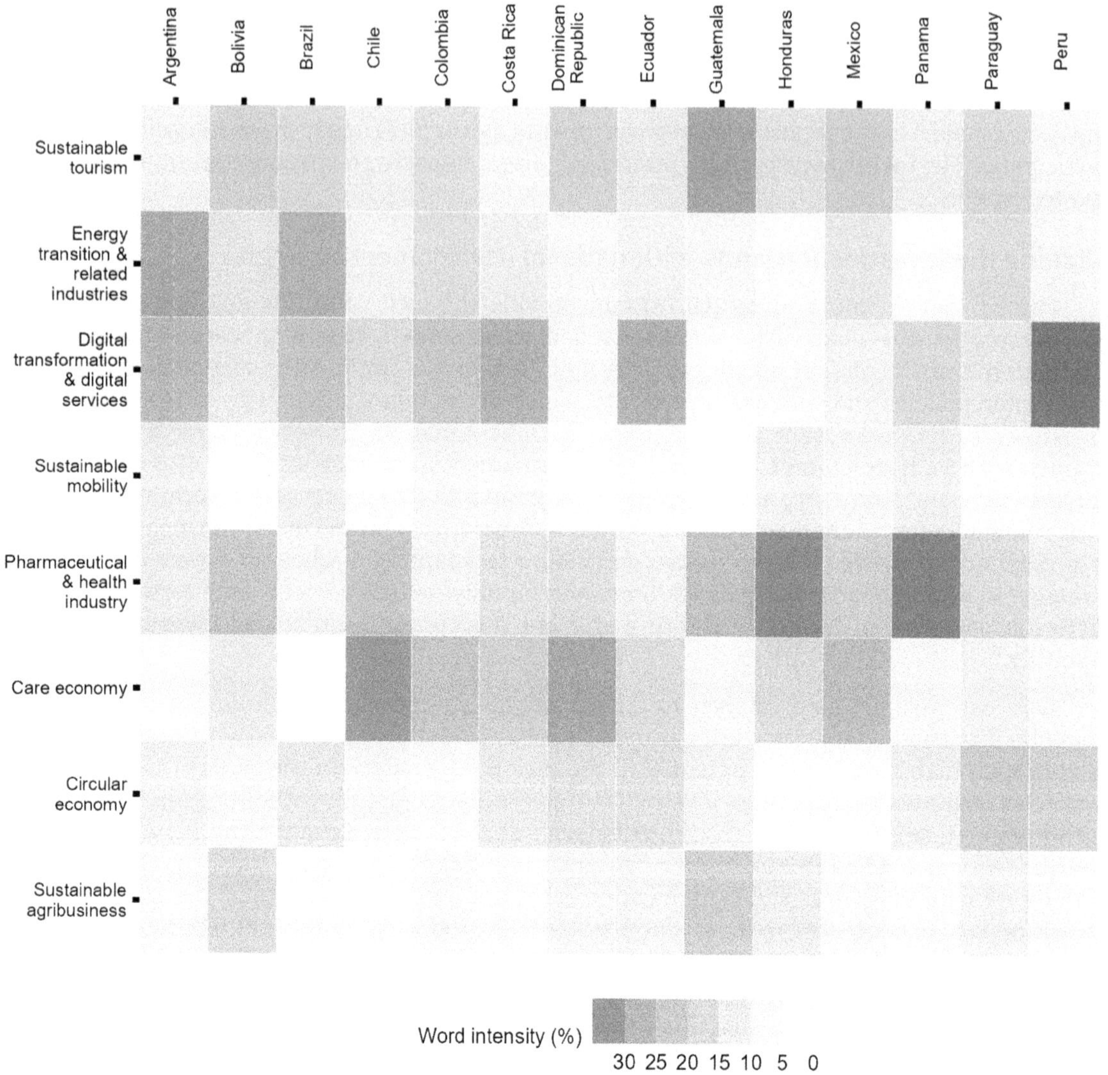

Note: Word intensity refers to the frequency with which a specific set of words associated with a strategic sector appears in each NDP. The idea is that the more frequently a set of words appears, the more "intense" or important they might be in the context of the text being analysed. This intensity, measured by frequency, can be indicative of the prominence or significance of a particular topic within the text. As a colour darkens, the frequency of references to a given strategic sector within the plan increases. The sum of the relative frequencies across all economic sectors in a country's national development plan is 100. Each country's text data comes from the latest development plan (or its equivalent), published by October 2023.
Source: Authors' elaboration using the national development plans of 14 LAC countries.

StatLink https://stat.link/i79mst

Other institutional arrangements offer additional co-ordination mechanisms. National public investment systems are pivotal in guiding public investment processes, offering an institutional framework that assures fiscal sustainability and enhances the economic and social impact of public spending. Effective multi-level governance (MLG) is crucial for aligning national policy objectives with local needs in investment and production transformation. Tools for MLG can operate both vertically and horizontally, involving various governmental tiers and stakeholders. Contracts specifying roles and co-financing clauses can enhance compliance and efficiency. Local governments play a pivotal role in attracting FDI and providing essential services, further supported by spatial planning policies.

International partnerships can help attract investments and enhance their development impact

To attract investments that are conducive to LAC's production transformation, international partnerships can create synergies between international organisations, governments, experts, development agencies and private-sector institutions. The nature of these partnerships is being reshaped by evolving global dynamics and trends, with a noticeable shift in development finance towards recognising the potential of the private sector to bridge the global investment gap.

International co-operation should contribute to attracting private investments that finance LAC's development and economic transformation. The region's heterogeneous economies and rich environmental resources can attract more FDI, impact investments and other international financial flows. Moreover, even if the region shows little and decreasing reliance on concessional sources of financing, such as official development assistance (when measured as a share of gross national income), development co-operation is still essential for LAC to further mobilise international financial flows through innovative mechanisms. For instance, blended finance can mobilise additional finance towards sustainable development projects. During the last decade, LAC has experienced an increase in the share of mobilised private finance by official development intervention as a percentage of GDP, from 0.06% (USD 3 billion) in 2016 to 0.18% (USD 9 billion) in 2021 (Figure 15). Most of the financing for banking and financial services came from guarantees, credit lines and syndicated loans, instruments that are generally used for supporting the development of MSMEs and financial inclusion (OECD, 2023[31]).

Figure 15. **Amounts mobilised from the private sector by official development finance interventions, 2012-21**

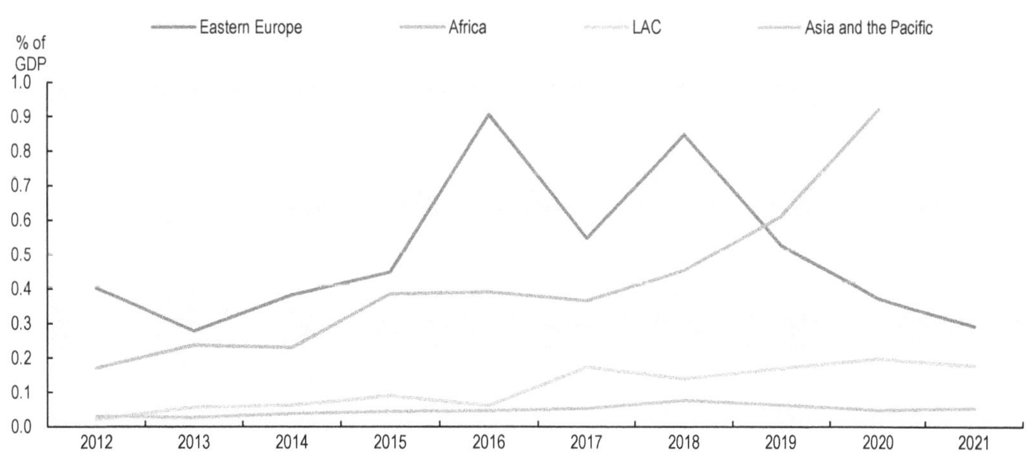

Note: Countries included in Eastern Europe: Albania, Belarus, Bosnia and Herzegovina, Kosovo*, Moldova, Montenegro, North Macedonia, Serbia, Türkiye and Ukraine. Countries included in Asia and the Pacific: Afghanistan, Armenia, Azerbaijan, Bangladesh, Bhutan, Cambodia, China, Fiji, Georgia, India, Indonesia, Iran, Iraq, Jordan, Kazakhstan, Kiribati, Kyrgyzstan, Lao PDR, Lebanon, Malaysia, Maldives, Micronesia, Mongolia, Myanmar, Nepal, Niue, Palau, Pakistan, Papua New Guinea, Philippines, Samoa, Solomon Islands, Sri Lanka, Syrian Arab Republic, Tajikistan, Thailand, Timor-Leste, Tonga, Turkmenistan, Tuvalu, Uzbekistan, Vanuatu, Viet Nam, West Bank and Gaza Strip, and Yemen. Countries included in LAC: Antigua and Barbuda, Argentina, Belize, Bolivia, Brazil, Chile, Colombia, Costa Rica, Cuba, Dominica, Dominican Republic, Ecuador, El Salvador, Grenada, Guatemala, Guyana, Haiti, Honduras, Jamaica, Mexico, Nicaragua, Panama, Paraguay, Peru, Saint Lucia, Saint Vincent and the Grenadines, Suriname, Uruguay, Venezuela. Africa includes all African countries. Data for 2021 are being reviewed.
* This designation is without prejudice to positions on status, and is in line with United Nations Security Council Resolution 1244/99 and the Advisory Opinion of the International Court of Justice on Kosovo's declaration of independence.

Source: Authors' calculations based on (OECD.Stat, 2023[32] and IMF, 2023[6]).

StatLink https://stat.link/xco6es

Beyond the opportunities presented by international financial flows, international partnerships play a crucial role not only in mobilising greater resources but also in ensuring that investments yield a greater socio-economic impact. Three main objectives can help international partnerships to ensure that they mobilise more and better investments. First, these partnerships can strive to create an enabling environment that attracts and facilitates investments that are conducive to the region's production transformation. This includes tools like international standards, frameworks and investment treaties, or capacity building and technology transfers, which improve the level playing field of countries in the region. Second, they can foster alignment and collaboration among investment-related actors, such as multilateral development banks (MDBs) and DFIs, export credit agencies (ECAs), investment promotion agencies (IPAs) and the private sector, to enhance co-ordination and effectiveness through specific platforms. Third, they can boost local development by implementing measures like local content requirements that strengthen local economies and value chains, and by aligning support with national development strategies (Table 1).

Table 1. **International mechanisms to promote better investments**

Objective	Existing or potential instrument
Create an enabling environment	International standards and frameworks
	International investment treaties
	Capacity building and technology transfer
Foster alignment between institutions	Co-ordination platforms among investment related actors with development and commercial purposes
Boost local development	Platforms for aligning investments with national priorities
	Local content requirements

Source: Authors' elaboration.

It is important to acknowledge that policies designed to attract FDI must be accompanied by measures to bolster the local capacity to absorb investments. This synergy is essential for FDI to serve effectively as a mechanism for knowledge and technology transfer. The measures include investing in education, strengthening institutional frameworks and developing physical, scientific and technological infrastructure. It is crucial to establish a comprehensive framework that combines efforts to attract FDI with production development policies. Development partners can support efforts to upgrade productive development policies via international partnerships and co-operation.

Deepening regional integration in LAC can be a source of mobilisation of better and stronger investments. For LAC countries to take advantage of regional and subregional integration opportunities, public policies geared to regional production integration, productive development and trade, international dialogue and co-operation among integration mechanisms are essential. LAC has made progress in regional integration – for instance, the region has significantly reduced tariff barriers, making entry to the regional market more attractive for FDI. As of 2019, the average tariff imposed on trade within the region was merely 2% (ECLAC, 2021[33]). Subregional trade blocs have contributed to this achievement and have also worked towards harmonising regulations and standards across member countries. Aligning regulations related to customs, taxation, investment procedures and business practices helps to reduce barriers for investors. Such alignment can also enhance transparency and predictability, making it easier for businesses to operate and invest across borders. To attract additional investment, further regional productive and commercial integration, economically viable regional production chains and a stable market that combines efficient scale with minimising transaction costs must be prioritised.

A new EU-LAC investment agenda

Strengthening partnerships and co-operation with the European Union can improve the development impact of investments in LAC countries. The European Union is not only the region's third-largest trading partner and the leading contributor to development co-operation, it is also one of the top investors in LAC. With a new impetus in EU-LAC relations, LAC is placed at the top of EU priorities for investment, especially with the launch of the EU-LAC Global Gateway Investment Agenda (European Commission, 2023[34]). The agenda identifies investment opportunities in LAC that will benefit the region's production transformation in sectors such as climate and energy, critical raw materials, infrastructure, SME development, electromobility and sustainable tourism, among others (Figure 16). This tool, accompanied by political and policy dialogue, can be supportive of LAC's production transformation by leveraging on a balanced mix of trade, investment and co-operation. Renewed mechanisms of dialogue and co-ordination among the investment, trade, and development communities, might be useful to accompany further LAC's reindustrialisation efforts aligning with national priorities, and ensure investment flows follow a shared criteria on quality, sustainability, and inclusiveness.

Figure 16. **Global Gateway Investment Agenda, number of projects by country and sector, 2023**

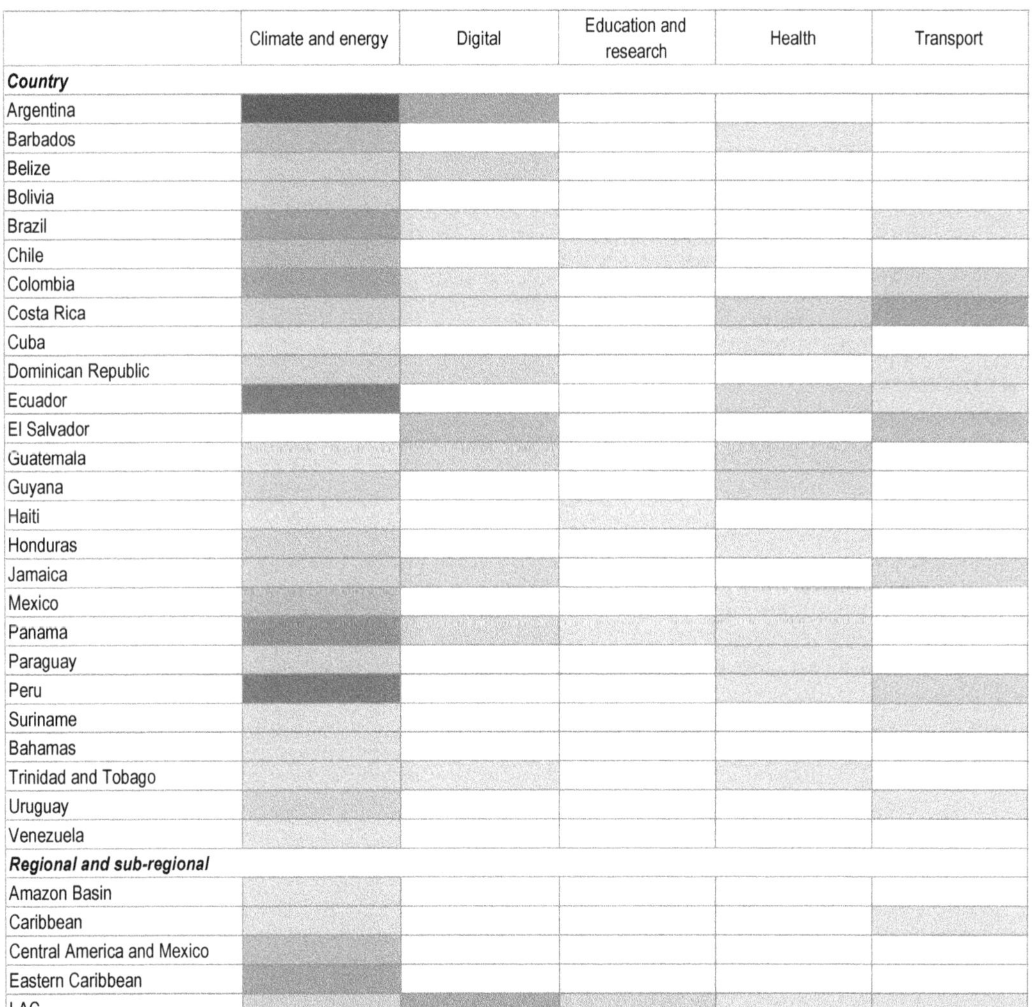

Note: The figure shows the total number of projects by country published by the European Commission. Darker blue shows a higher number of projects (lightest blue = 1 project; darkest blue =7 projects). In addition to the number of projects shown at country level, the number of projects at the regional and subregional level is also included in the Amazon Basin, Caribbean, Central America and Mexico, Eastern Caribbean and LAC regions.

Source: (European Commission, 2023[34]).

StatLink https://stat.link/5op6t9

Notes

1. This figure should be higher given that data on business investment includes investments made by state-owned enterprises.

References

Cavallo, E. and M. Pedemonte (2015), "What is the Relationship between National Saving and Investment in Latin America and the Caribbean?", *IDB Working Paper Series*, No. IDB-WP-617, https://publications.iadb.org/en/what-relationship-between-national-saving-and-investment-latin-america-and-caribbean. [8]

ECLAC (2023), *Estudio Económico de América Latina y el Caribe 2023*, United Nations Economic Commission for Latin America and the Caribbean, https://www.cepal.org/es/publicaciones/67989-estudio-economico-america-latina-caribe-2023-financiamiento-transicion. [1]

ECLAC (2023), *Iberoamérica: Espacio de oportunidades para el crecimiento, la colaboración y el desarrollo sostenible*, United Nations Economic Commission for Latin America and the Caribbean, https://www.cepal.org/es/publicaciones/48769-iberoamerica-espacio-oportunidades-crecimiento-la-colaboracion-desarrollo. [24]

ECLAC (2022), *Economic Survey of Latin America and the Caribbean 2022: Trends and Challenges of Investing for a Sustainable and Inclusive Recovery*, United Nations Commission for Latin America and the Caribbean, Santiago, https://repositorio.cepal.org/bitstream/handle/11362/48078/7/S2201057_en.pdf. [7]

ECLAC (2021), *International Trade Outlook for Latin America and the Caribbean: Regional Integration Is Key to Recovery After the Crisis*, United Nations Economic Commission for Latin America and the Caribbean, Santiago, https://www.cepal.org/en/publications/46614-international-trade-outlook-latin-america-and-caribbean-2020-regional-integration. [33]

ECLAC/ILO (2023), *Employment Situation in Latin America and the Caribbean: Towards the Creation of Better Jobs in the Post-pandemic Era*, UN-ECLAC and International Labour Organization, https://repositorio.cepal.org/handle/11362/48988. [4]

Eichengreen, B. (2010), "Lessons from the Marshall Plan", *World Development Report 2011 Background Case Note*, World Bank, https://documents1.worldbank.org/curated/en/907961468155715855/pdf/620420WP0Lesso0BOX0361475B00PUBLIC0.pdf. [12]

Environmental Justice Atlas (2023), *Global Atlas of Environmental Justice*, https://ejatlas.org/. [30]

European Commission (2023), *EU-LAC Global Gateway Investments Agenda - Infographics*, https://international-partnerships.ec.europa.eu/publications/eu-lac-global-gateway-investment-agenda-infographics_en. [34]

fDi Markets (2023), *fDi Markets: The Crossborder Investment Monitor*, https://www.fdimarkets.com/. [18]

IDB (2021), *The Infrastructure Gap in Latin America and the Caribbean: Investment Needed Through 2030 to Meet the Sustainable Development Goals*, Inter-American Development Bank, Washington, DC, https://publications.iadb.org/en/infrastructure-gap-latin-america-and-caribbean-investment-needed-through-2030-meet-sustainable. [11]

IMF (2023), *World Economic Outlook Database*, International Monetary Fund, Washington, DC, https://www.imf.org/en/Publications/WEO/weo-database/2023/April/weo-report (accessed on 8 November 2023). [6]

IMF (2023), *World Economic Outlook: A Rocky Recovery*, International Monetary Fund, Washington, DC, https://www.imf.org/en/Publications/WEO/Issues/2023/04/11/world-economic-outlook-april-2023. [3]

Infralatam (2022), *Data on Public Investment in Economic Infrastructure in Latin America and the Caribbean (database)*, http://infralatam.info/en/home/ (accessed on 5 September 2023). [9]

Latinobarómetro (2020), *Latinobarómetro (database)*, https://www.latinobarometro.org/latOnline.jsp (accessed on 18 September 2023). [29]

Núñez, G., H. Velloso and F. Da Silva (2022), "Corporate governance in Latin America and the Caribbean: Using ESG debt instruments to finance sustainable investment projects", *Project Documents*, United Nations Economic Commission for Latin America and the Caribbean, Santiago, https://repositorio.cepal.org/handle/11362/47778. [27]

OECD (2023), *OECD Economic Outlook, Volume 2023 Issue 2: Preliminary version*, OECD Publishing, Paris, https://doi.org/10.1787/7a5f73ce-en. [2]

OECD (2023), "Private finance mobilised by Official Development Finance Interventions", Development Co-operation Directorate, OECD, Paris, https://www.oecd.org/dac/2023-private-finance-odfi.pdf. [31]

OECD (2022), *FDI Qualities Policy Toolkit*, OECD Publishing, Paris, https://doi.org/10.1787/7ba74100-en. [17]

OECD (2022), "Green, social, sustainability and sustainability-linked bonds in developing countries: How can donors support public sector issuances?", OECD Publishing, Paris, https://www.oecd.org/dac/green-social-sustainability-and-sustainability-linked-bonds.pdf. [26]

OECD (2021), *Key Indicators of Informality Based on Individuals and Their Household (KIIbIH), (database)*, OECD Publishing, Paris, https://www.oecd.org/dev/key-indicators-informality-individuals-household-kiibih.htm. [5]

OECD (2019), *FDI Qualities Indicators: Measuring the Sustainable Development Impacts of Investment*, OECD Publishing, Paris, https://www.oecd.org/investment/FDI-Qualities-Indicators-Measuring-Sustainable-Development-Impacts.pdf. [16]

OECD (forthcoming), *Promoting investment for green growth in Latin America and the Caribbean*, OECD Publishing, Paris. [15]

OECD et al. (2023), *Revenue Statistics in Latin America and the Caribbean 2023*, OECD Publishing, Paris, https://doi.org/10.1787/a7640683-en. [25]

OECD et al. (2022), *Latin American Economic Outlook 2022: Towards a Green and Just Transition*, OECD Publishing, Paris, https://doi.org/10.1787/3d5554fc-en. [19]

OECD et al. (2021), *Latin American Economic Outlook 2021: Working Together for a Better Recovery*, OECD Publishing, Paris, https://doi.org/10.1787/5fedabe5-en. [14]

OECD.Stat (2023), *Mobilisation*, database, https://stats.oecd.org/Index.aspx?DataSetCode=DV_DCD_MOBILISATION# (accessed on 23 May 2023). [32]

RICYT (2022), *El estado de la ciencia: Principales indicadores de ciencia y tecnología Iberoamericanos / Interamericanos 2022, Red Iberoamericana de Indicadores de Ciencia y Tecnología*, Altuna Impresores S.R.L., Buenos Aires, https://oei.int/oficinas/argentina/publicaciones/el-estado-de-la-ciencia-principales-indicadores-de-ciencia-y-iberoamericanos-interamericanos-2022. [21]

RICYT (2020), *Network for Science and Technology Indicators – Ibero-American and Inter-American (RICYT)*, http://www.ricyt.org/en/. [22]

UNEP (2023), *Common Framework of Sustainable FInance Taxonomies for Latin America and the Caribbean*, United Nations Environment Programme, Geneva, http://www.unepfi.org/wordpress/wp-content/uploads/2023/07/Common-Framework-of-Sustainable-Finance-Taxonomies-LAC.pdf.[28]

Vona, F. et al. (2018), "Environmental Regulation and Green Skills: An empirical exploration", *Journal of the Association of Environmental and Resource Economists*, Vol. 5/4, https://www.journals.uchicago.edu/doi/suppl/10.1086/698859/suppl_file/2015197Appendix.pdf. [20]

WIPO (2023), *WIPO IP Statistics Data Center: Patent (database), World Intellectual Property Organization*, https://www3.wipo.int/ipstats/ips-search/patent. [23]

World Bank (2023), "Capitalización en el mercado de empresas nacionales que cotizan en bolsa (del PIB) (database)", *World Development Indicators*, World Bank Group, Washington DC, https://datos.bancomundial.org/indicator/CM.MKT.LCAP.GD.ZS?end=2020&start=1975&view=chart. [13]

World Bank (2023), *Private participation in infrastructure (database)*, https://ppi.worldbank.org/en/customquery (accessed on 5 September 2023). [10]

Chapter 1

Macro-structural perspective

This chapter describes the challenging economic context and critical factors driving a slowdown in economic activity in Latin America and the Caribbean (LAC) in 2023 following a rebound in growth after the COVID-19 pandemic. It also presents the socioeconomic challenges facing the region, where poverty and extreme poverty remain above pre-pandemic levels in more than half of LAC countries. The chapter first analyses macroeconomic policy in LAC, with a special focus on debt and taxes. It then reviews social conditions, presenting recent developments concerning poverty, inequality, and informality. Key policy messages point to the need to promote further and better investment to achieve more dynamic and sustainable growth and generate quality employment. It also highlights the need to protect the most vulnerable and, at the same time, ensure price stability.

Macro-structural perspective

Growth in LAC economies has slowed down in 2023 due to a complex global context and persistently low potential growth

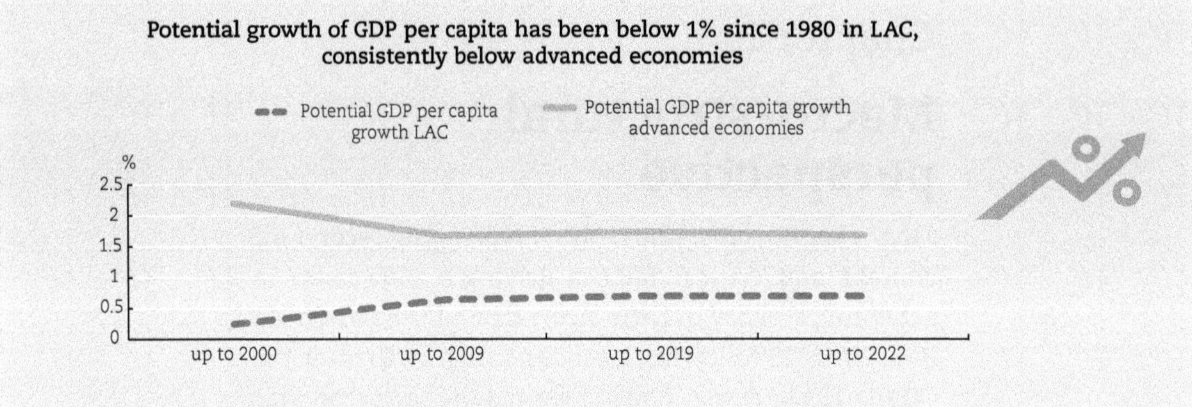

Social conditions remain challenging in the LAC region

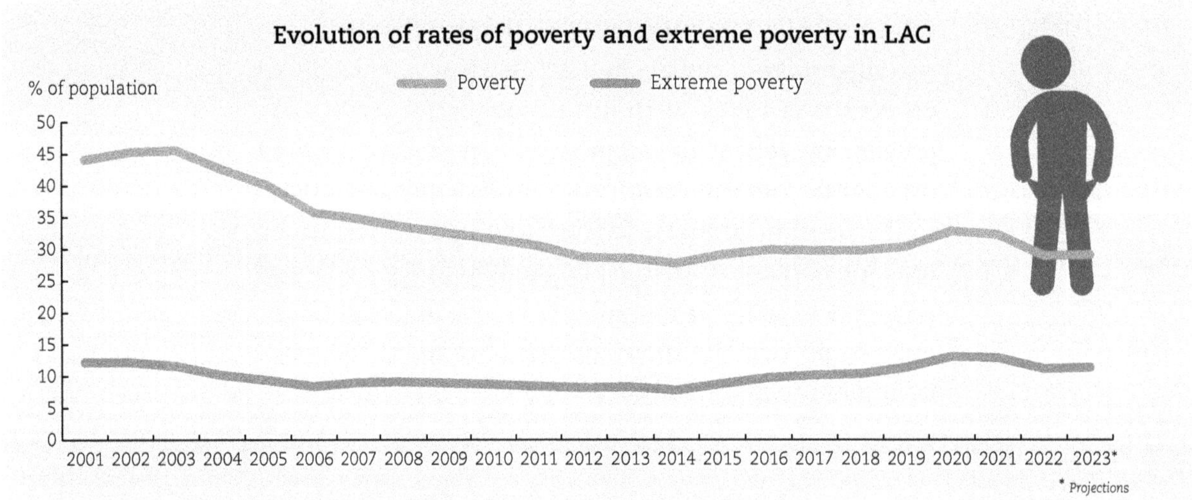

Informality: A major challenge to addressing poverty

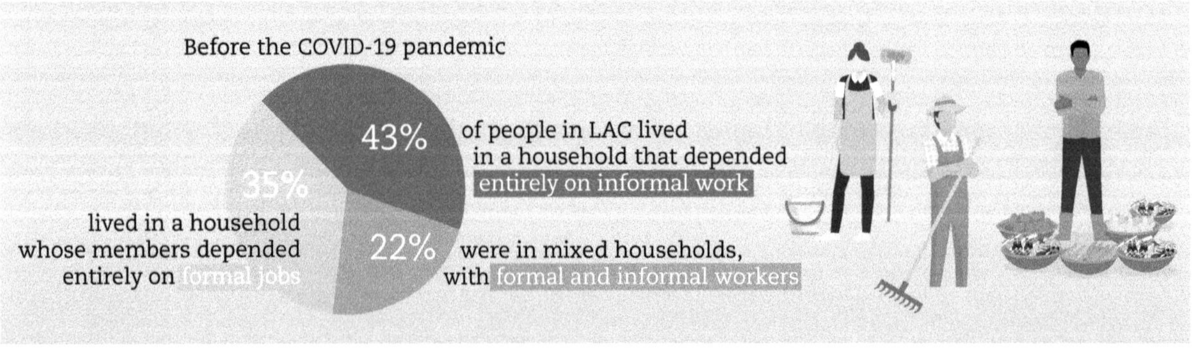

Introduction

Economic activity in Latin America and the Caribbean (LAC) will slow sharply in 2023 due to cyclical dynamics, subdued potential growth and low investment levels. The slowdown follows a post-pandemic rebound in growth as fiscal and monetary stimuli, more favourable external conditions, and the reopening of economies drove the recovery after 2020. The current slump in growth has been driven by a deterioration of external conditions, the roll-back of public transfers enacted to mitigate the effects of the pandemic and monetary policy tightening to curb inflation.

Although the relatively strong economic recovery in LAC came with an increase in employment and household income, challenging social conditions remain. Increased inflation eroded purchasing power, especially for the poorest, and poverty and extreme poverty in the region remain above pre-pandemic levels in more than half of LAC countries. In 2022, 29% of the population was in poverty and 11.2% in extreme poverty. One of the main challenges to address this situation is labour informality, entailing lower wages and lack of access to social protection systems. Before the pandemic, 42.8% of the LAC population lived in a household that depended entirely on informal employment and 21.8% lived in mixed households, i.e. households with both formal and informal workers. This implies that 64.6% of the regional population depended totally or partially on informal employment. Similarly, inequality in income distribution in Latin America, measured through the Gini index, remained relatively high and stagnant between 2017 and 2021; it did show a slight improvement from 0.46 in 2020 to 0.45 in 2022.

This chapter first examines the global context, which remains fragile. It then presents the macroeconomic performance in LAC, highlighting the region's heterogeneity, external accounts, inflationary conditions and tight fiscal space. It explores possible actions to improve taxation systems in order to promote investment, recover fiscal space and improve progressiveness, with a specific focus on corporate income tax. The chapter next examines social conditions in LAC, with a focus on poverty, extreme poverty, inequality and the evolution of informality at the household level. It concludes by presenting the main policy messages.

The global outlook remains fragile

The global economic outlook began to improve after the impacts of the pandemic, but the growth prospects remain weak. Although, for 2023, GDP growth has been stronger than expected, it remains subdued, and will moderate further in 2024. Core inflation is proving persistent and the impact of higher interest rates around the world is increasingly being felt, particularly in property and financial markets. Global growth is projected to moderate from 3.3% in 2022 to 2.9% in 2023 and 2.7% in 2024, with inflation projected to decrease in 2023 and in 2024 (OECD, 2023[1]; OECD, 2023[2]).

The global economy is expected to remain sub-par in 2024, due to macroeconomic policy tightening needed to rein in inflation. Risks to this outlook are tilted to the downside. Tight monetary policy for a more extended period could induce new episodes of financial fragility that further deteriorate credit conditions and depress demand more than anticipated. Lower-than-expected recovery in the People's Republic of China (hereafter "China"), geopolitical tensions, climate risks, debt distress, stickier inflation and geoeconomic fragmentation could also cloud the outlook (OECD, 2023[1]; OECD, 2023[2]).

Most commodity prices are normalising, easing inflation pressures (Figure 1.1). Russia's war of aggression against Ukraine pushed prices up against a backdrop of supply-demand imbalances from the COVID-19 pandemic. As a result of uncertainty stemming from the war, the prices of oil, gas, coal and industrial metals spiked in 2022 and fluctuated at higher levels in the following months. Food and energy prices have receded since the second half of 2022, but remain above levels recorded before the pandemic and the war in Ukraine. Even though Russia's invasion of Ukraine continues, a mild winter in 2022/23, the slowdown of global economic activity and the lifting of COVID-19 restrictions in China have helped decrease commodity prices.

Figure 1.1. **International commodity prices, January 2019 to August 2023**

Index, January 2019 = 100

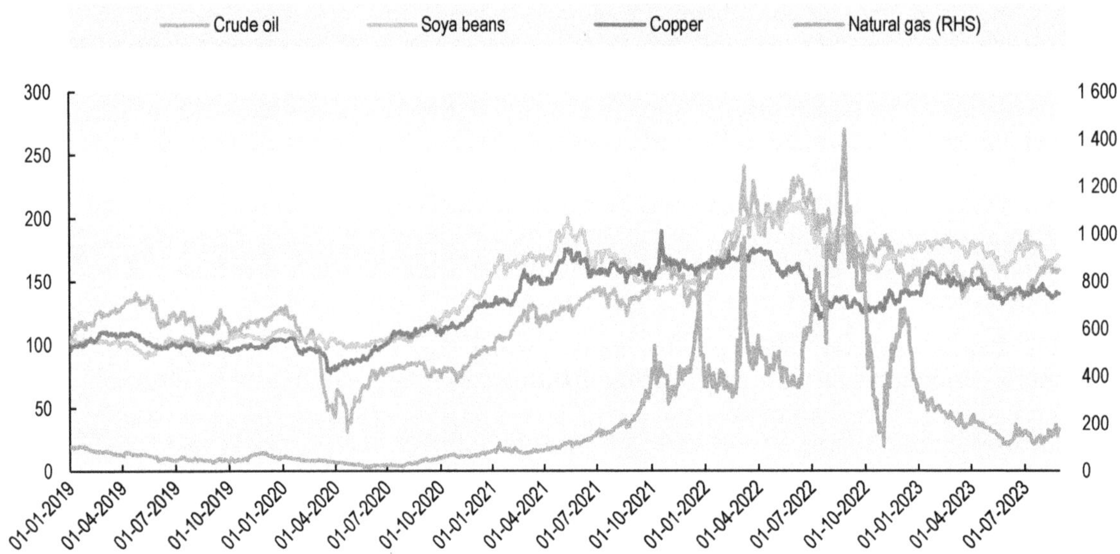

Source: (Refinitiv Eikon, 2023[3]).

StatLink https://stat.link/zjxvnh

Monetary policy dynamics in advanced economies affect the behaviour of capital markets. Following financial turmoil in March 2023 in the United States and Switzerland, stock market volatility measured by the Volatility Index (VIX index) has subsided and is back to pre-pandemic levels (Figure 1.2, Panel A). Credit conditions in the United States, measured by the Chicago Fed National Financial Conditions Credit Subindex, eased after turmoil caused by three failed US regional banks was resolved (Figure 1.2, Panel B). Similarly, risk premia in emerging sovereign bond markets, measured by the J.P. Morgan Emerging Market Bond Index (EMBI), have narrowed since the episode of financial fragility and remain well below the early months of the COVID-19 pandemic, signalling a recovery in appetite for emerging markets' assets. In LAC, sovereign bond spreads have remained higher than the global average but with high heterogeneity across countries. The average is affected by specific countries (Argentina, Ecuador, Venezuela and, more recently, Bolivia). Spreads in other LAC countries included in the EMBI are below the global average, suggesting that governments and firms can tap into international capital markets (Figure 1.2, Panel C), albeit at higher costs considering the increase in interest rates.

Figure 1.2. **Volatility and risk premia in financial markets**

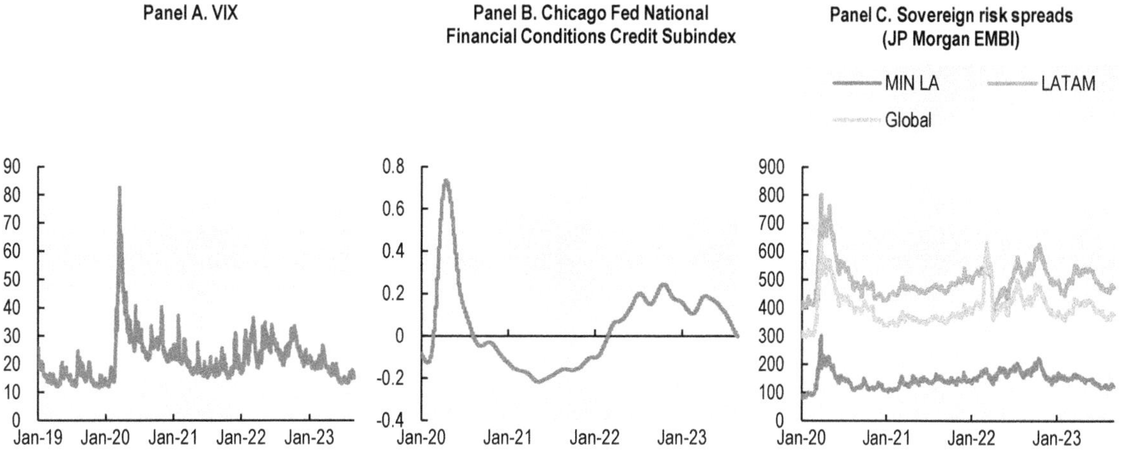

Note: Data from January 2020 until August 2023. In Panel A, a higher VIX index suggests that market participants anticipate more significant price swings and potential fluctuations. In Panel B, positive values on the Chicago Fed National Financial Conditions Credit Subindex indicate tighter financial conditions than average. In contrast, negative values indicate financial conditions that are looser than average. In Panel C, a larger index indicates that investor sentiment and risk appetite towards emerging market debt is decreasing. For Panel C, MIN LA refers to the country with the lowest sovereign risk spread.

Source: (Refinitiv Eikon, 2023[3]).

StatLink *https://stat.link/e6rn3j*

Growth in LAC reflects a complex juncture and pending structural challenges

Gross domestic product (GDP) growth in LAC rebounded to above 6% in 2021 and was close to 4% in 2022. The recovery was mainly driven by fiscal and monetary stimuli, better external conditions, and base effects. In 2022, however, external conditions were less favourable, public transfers were rolled back, monetary policy tightened and the effects of the reopening of economies dissipated. Nevertheless, activity in 2022 was more resilient than initially anticipated due to good performance of the labour market. But recovery has been uneven across the LAC region. By 2022, most LAC countries – including the largest economies – had regained pre-pandemic GDP levels; the exceptions were Ecuador and several Caribbean countries, which experienced deep economic recessions in 2020 and have suffered the impact of declining tourism flows and limited fiscal space (ECLAC, 2022[4]; Galindo and Nuguer, 2023[5]; Adler and Chalk, 2023[6]; Banco de España, 2023[7]).

There is little space for demand policies at this juncture. Headline inflation rates have receded in most countries, thanks to lower energy and food prices. However, inflation rates remain high in several countries, mainly due to the protracted dynamics of service prices. Consequently, most central banks are maintaining a contractionary monetary policy stance, with interest rates above neutral levels. The LAC region has little fiscal space. Much of the fiscal stimulus of 2020 has been withdrawn, while debt levels remain high and gradual fiscal consolidations continue (CAF, 2023[8]; ECLAC, 2023[9]). Risks to the outlook stem from a sharper and faster-than-expected slowdown across the region's key partners, as well as tightening financial conditions and political uncertainty within the region, and an escalation of Russia's war in Ukraine (Galindo and Nuguer, 2023[5]; Adler and Chalk, 2023[6]; IMF, 2023[10]; CAF, 2023[11]).

Low investment levels have been associated with low potential growth in the region. In the past decades investment has been one of the most important determinants of economic growth in Latin America (De Gregorio, 1992[12]). At only 20% over GDP, the LAC region exhibits one of the lowest levels of investment across all regions (Chapter 2) and therefore more and better investment is needed to boost potential growth. GDP per-capita growth was a pre-pandemic structural development challenge in LAC and remains a key determinant of slow progress in economic development. Potential GDP per-capita growth has been below 1% since 1980, although it increased slightly following the commodity boom (between 2003 and 2013). Since then, per-capita potential output growth has stagnated, remaining consistently below rates in advanced economies, thus hindering convergence (Figure 1.3).

Furthermore, higher productivity growth – based on more and better investments – should be central to closing the gap with developed economies (Chapters 2 and 3). Labour productivity in the LAC region, compared to the United States, explains almost the entire gap in per-capita GDP (Chapter 3). Countries that have managed to close the gap and increase productivity have diversified towards more technology and knowledge-intensive activities across all economic sectors. This has been achieved thanks to adequate investment in physical and human capital, as well as the implementation of deep production development policies that have helped the upgrading, diversification and structural change of these economies (OECD et al., 2022[13]; Álvarez et al., 2019[14]; ECLAC, 2022[15]).

Figure 1.3. **Potential GDP per-capita growth in LAC and advanced economies**

Estimated under different methods since 1980

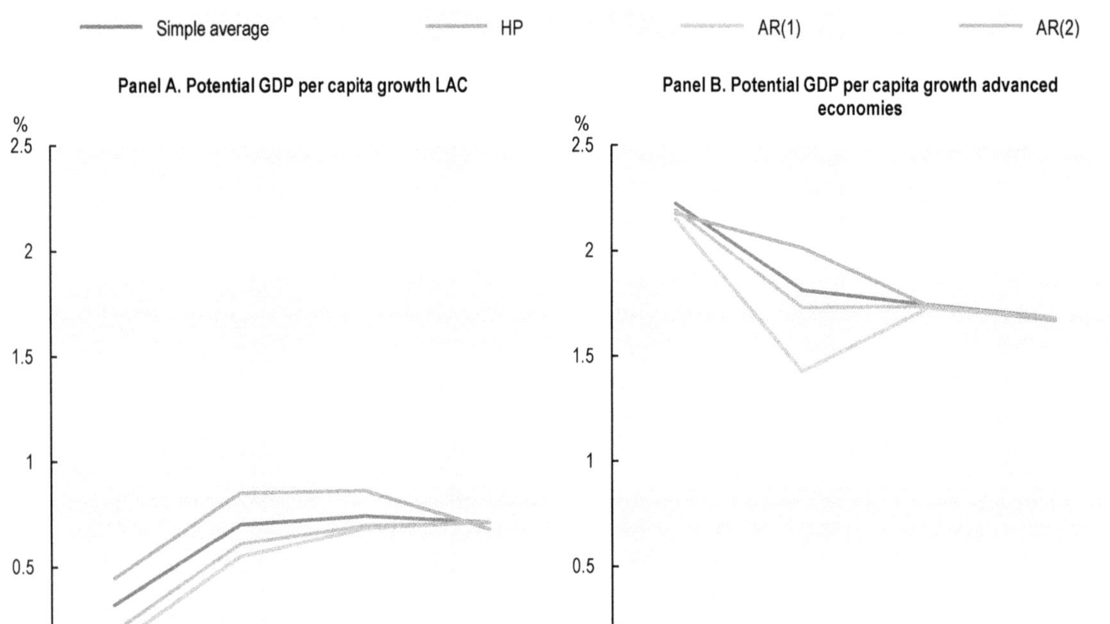

Note: Average growth is a simple average over the period analysed. HP = the Hodrick-Prescott filter, which was used as an alternative model due to its resilience to short-term shocks to create a smoothed curve (lambda equal to 100). AR = autoregressive model, which uses GDP per-capita growth data. The number of lags (1 and 2) was determined by analysing the autocorrelation function and choosing the model that maximised the log-likelihood. The LAC and advanced economies series refer to countries covered by the IMF's World Economic Outlook database, April 2023.

Source: Authors' calculations based on (IMF, 2023[10]).

StatLink https://stat.link/wi3cjx

The insufficient level of investment in LAC can be partly explained by the region's low levels of national savings. Individuals, business, and governments save money to smoothen their consumption (protect themselves against shocks) and invest respectively to improve their well-being, become more productive, and provide more public services. These savings in their turn, can be used to finance investments, thus there is a positive relationship between investment levels and domestic savings. On average in LAC for every 1 percentage point of GDP increase in national saving, domestic investment increases by 0.39 percentage points, although with strong heterogeneity in the region (Cavallo and Pedemonte, 2015[16]). Nevertheless, the region has consistently presented low levels of gross domestic savings accounting on average for around 20% of GDP since 2000. This is considerably lower than the 35% of GDP that East Asia and Pacific economies save. Economies with low levels of savings must look to borrow abroad to finance their investments but this can be more costly and increase the risk of crisis as international financial flows are volatile (Cavallo and Serebrisky, 2016[17]; World Bank, 2023[18]).

A complex global context and longstanding structural issues in the LAC region signal the importance of attracting and mobilising investment as a critical driver of regional production transformation (Chapter 3). This stands out even more prominently in a context where major world economies are taking decisive steps forward in promoting national industries: e.g. the United States with the Inflation Reduction Act and the Chips Act, or the European Union (EU) with its European Green Deal. This trend may significantly transform the global trade and investment landscape, opening new opportunities but also presenting challenges. Against this backdrop, LAC countries must create the conditions to benefit from the ongoing transformations and foster investments in sectors with emerging opportunities (Chapter 3).

External accounts are expected to improve

Current account deficits persisted in most LAC countries in 2022, particularly in net energy importers (Figure 1.4, Panel A). Current account dynamics have been marked by changes in terms of trade – particularly swings in energy and food prices – and domestic demand dynamics. External accounts should improve in 2023 as intermediate inputs and commodity prices normalise, and as domestic demand slows. Despite such normalisation, as commodity prices remain above historical means, the strain on net commodity exporters should not be significant.

Figure 1.4. LAC current account balance and capital flows to LAC countries

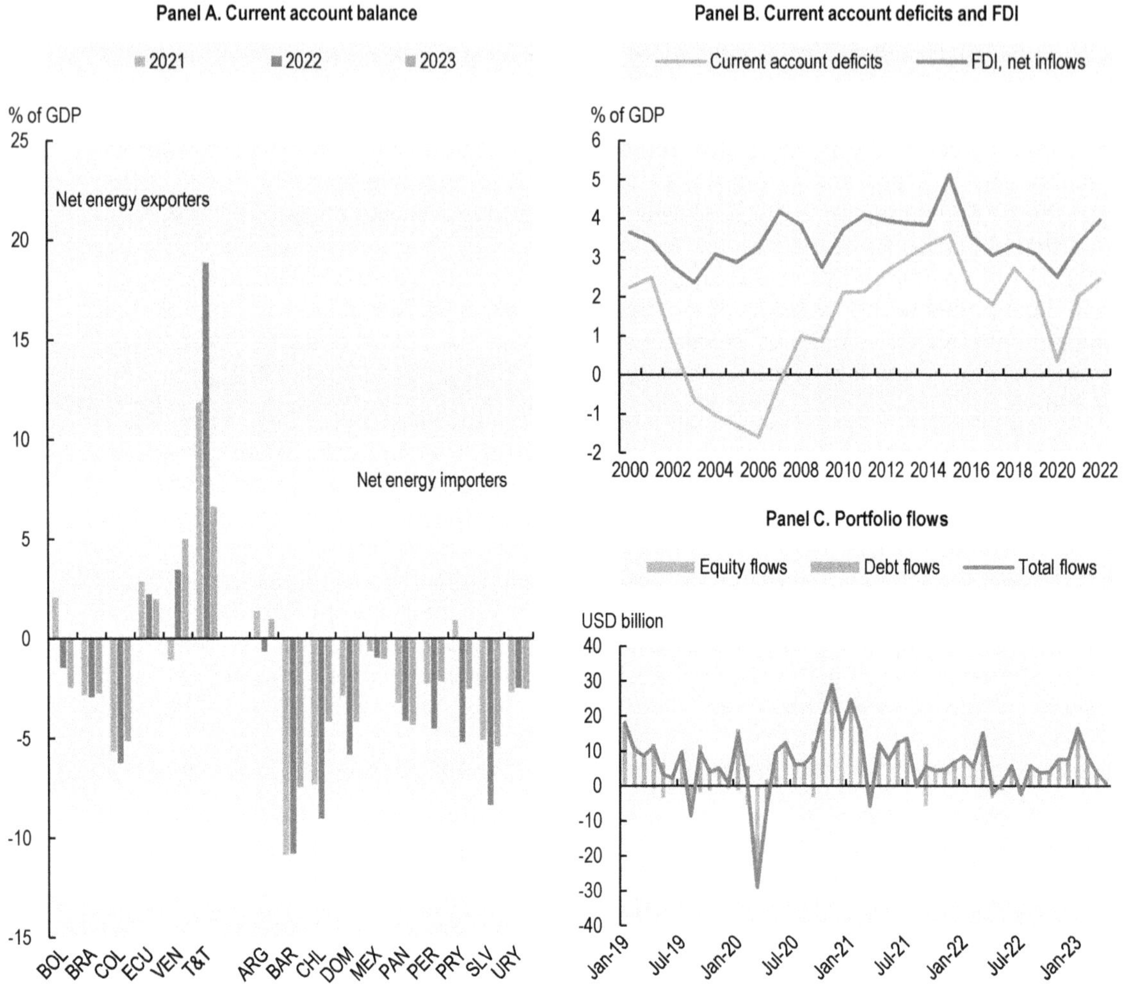

Note: FDI = foreign direct investment.

Source: (IMF, 2023[10]), (IIF, 2023[19]) and (World Bank, 2023[18]).

StatLink https://stat.link/i0al2n

The capital account continues to play a crucial role in financing the deficits of the current account. Portfolio flows to emerging markets have weakened in 2023, but most LAC countries have been able to tap into international capital markets (Figure 1.4, Panel C; see also Chapter 4). Current account deficits remain manageable in most LAC countries, mainly financed by foreign direct investment (FDI) (Figure 1.4, Panel B). FDI inflows have consistently helped to finance current account deficits since the mid-1980s. In 2022, FDI inflows experienced a 55.2% increase (reaching 4% of GDP), the highest level of the last three decades. This substantial increase was mainly driven by investments in services, hydrocarbons and manufactures. Regarding the main components of FDI, equity accounted for 36% in 2022, reaching levels similar to 2019 but still below 2013 levels. At 43%, reinvested earnings remained the main source of FDI in 2022 (ECLAC, 2023[20]). Not just the quantity but also the quality of FDI matters. Quality FDI can contribute to increasing productivity, increasing investment in research and development (R&D), delivering more quality jobs, and driving the development of key sectors (Chapter 2 and 3) (OECD, 2019[21]; OECD et al., 2021[22]).

The export basket needs greater value added and diversification

The LAC share in global exports has not changed in recent decades, remaining at values of 4% to 5%. Furthermore, if Mexico is excluded from LAC data, the overall export share falls by 1 percentage point. This contrasts with significant increases in the share of other developing regions. For example, East Asia and Pacific, driven by China, has seen its share in global exports increase from 19% in 1990 to 32% in 2022. Low participation of Latin American firms in international trade is partly due to the limited use of regional trade as part of a strategy to expand global export. In turn, one reason for this is that trade liberalisation has not generated high and sustained increases in intraregional trade. To foster regional integration and drive trade in LAC, it will be important to simplify border requirements and formalities, and lower tariffs and non-tariff barriers. Better connectivity is also needed to promote the exchange of merchandise, services and regional goods, including energy (Sanguinetti et al., 2021[23]).

LAC export performance over the last two decades shows scope to diversify and add greater value to the export basket. LAC weight in world shipments of manufactures (including those based on natural resources) has not exceeded 5%. Regarding services, the region's share in world exports has fallen since 2000, to 2.6% in 2021; it is just 1.7% in so-called modern digitally deliverable services (ECLAC, 2023[24]). Over this period, the main change in the structure of regional exports of goods has been the growing weight of primary goods. Within total merchandise exports, their share increased from an average of 27% between 1999 and 2001 to an average of 36% between 2019 and 2021. This increase correlates with a fall in the weight of low- and high-tech manufactures. Contrasting dynamics can be observed at the subregional level, however. In South America between the two periods, the share of primary goods increased by more than 16 percentage points to 58% of total exports. Central America shows the opposite trend: the weight of primary products in its export basket fell by more than 9 percentage points while the weight of natural resource-based manufactures and low- and medium-technology manufactures increased. Finally, in Mexico, the share of raw materials in total exports remained stable at around 11%, one of the lowest levels in the region. Mexico's main export segment is medium-technology manufactures, which account for almost half of the total value of its goods exports, and whose weight has increased by close to 10 percentage points in the last 20 years (Table 1.1).

Table 1.1. **Distribution of LAC goods exports by technology intensity, 1999-2001 and 2019-21**

LAC, selected subregions and Mexico (percentages)

	Primary goods		Manufactures based on natural resources		Low-tech manufactures		Medium-tech manufactures		High-tech manufactures	
	1999-2001	2019-21	1999-2001	2019-21	1999-2001	2019-21	1999-2001	2019-21	1999-2001	2019-21
Latin America and the Caribbean	26.7	36.2	18.2	18.3	13.5	7.8	25.3	26.4	16.4	11.3
Latin America and the Caribbean (excluding Mexico)	40.1	53.8	28.8	25.3	11.4	6.8	13.9	11.1	5.8	3
South America	41.9	58.4	29.4	25.1	9.4	4.2	14.2	10	5.1	2.3
Mexico	11.3	11.2	6.1	8.4	15.8	9.4	38.4	48.1	28.4	23
Central America	34.9	25.6	16	20.3	21.9	26.8	10.1	17.6	17.2	9.8
The Caribbean	20.4	11.4	30.2	38.7	37.2	21.5	9.1	19.2	3	9.1

Source: Based on United Nations Comtrade Database on International Trade Statistics (COMTRADE).

The heterogeneity of export patterns across LAC countries can also be seen in the share of medium- and high-technology in total manufactures exports. This proportion, which peaks at 80% in Mexico, equals or exceeds 40% in only six countries and is less than or equal to 10% in nine countries, all in South America and the Caribbean (Figure 1.5) (ECLAC, 2023[24]).

Figure 1.5. **Share of high- and medium-tech manufactures in total manufactures exports, latest year**

(Percentages)

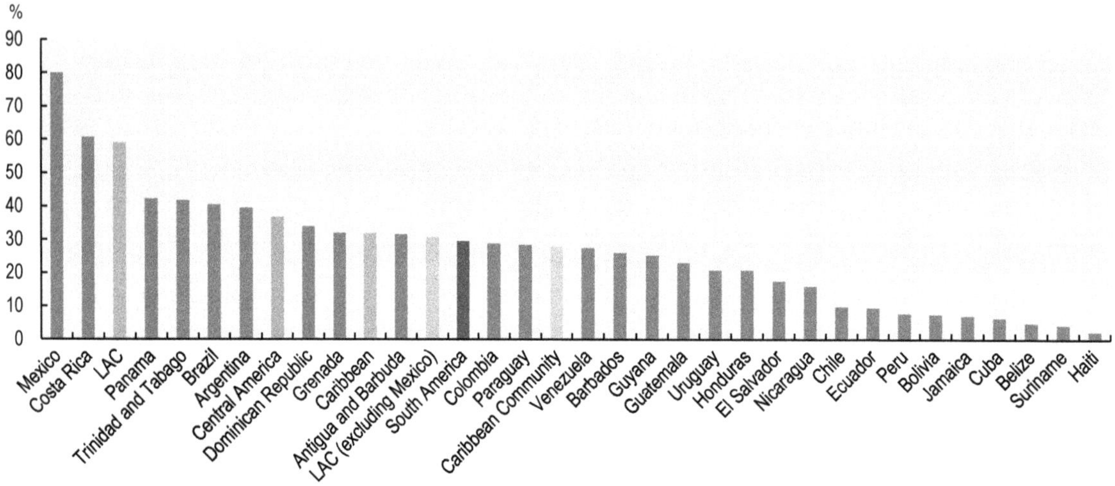

Note: Panama's exports include re-exports.

Source: (ECLAC, 2023[24]) based on United Nations, United Nations International Trade Statistics Database (COMTRADE).

StatLink https://stat.link/uzfo90

While growth of services exports in LAC has been low compared to the world trend, it has been above regional goods export growth. Between 2005 and 2019, regional services exports had an average annual growth rate of 5.6%. Although lower than the average expansion of world exports of services in the same period (6.3%), this exceeds the average annual growth rate expansion of regional exports of goods (4.2%). The value of LAC services exports reached an all-time high in 2019, exceeding USD 190 billion. In 2020, the COVID-19 pandemic led to an 18% plunge in global services trade due to the collapse in tourism and lower demand for transport services associated with the contraction in goods trade. At 37%, the drop in the LAC region services exports in 2020 was much larger than the global average, reflecting that tourism's share (47%) in pre-pandemic exports was twice as large as its share in world exports (23%).

The relative importance of trade in services varies widely across LAC countries. In general, its weight in GDP and total exports is inversely proportional to the size of the economies. Thus, for example, services account for more than 70% of total exports in Cuba and several economies of the English-speaking Caribbean but fall to more than 40% in Uruguay, Dominican Republic, Costa Rica, Panama and Belize (Figure 1.6).

Figure 1.6. **Share of services exports in GDP and total exports, 2019**

(Percentages)

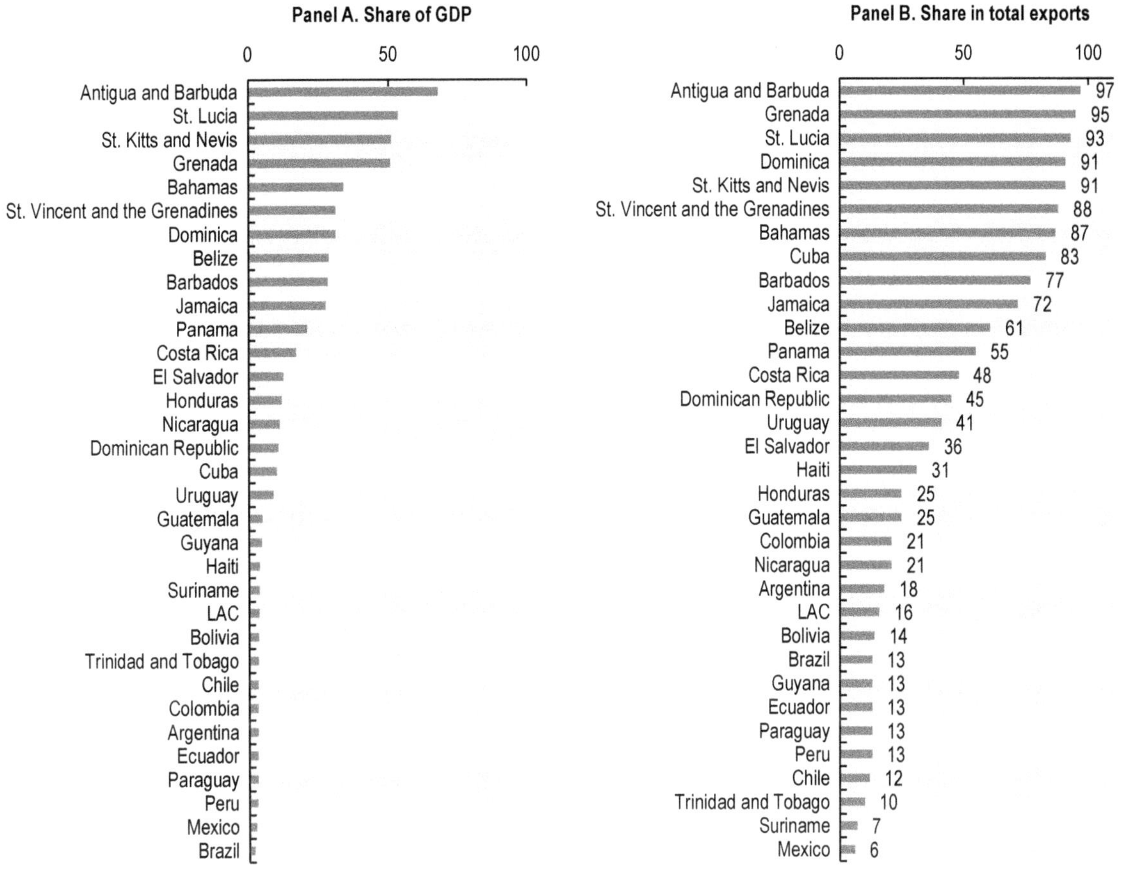

Source: (ECLAC, 2023[24]) based on UNCTADSTAT (exports) and CEPALSTAT (GDP).

StatLink https://stat.link/5hxi0z

Inflation eases but several central banks are expected to maintain a restrictive stance

Inflation in LAC has been declining in recent months, as food prices trend down and the effects of tighter monetary policies materialise. It peaked in mid-2022, rising to the highest level since the 2008 financial crisis. Several factors drove this inflation, including external factors in some countries, such as trade disruptions and supply bottlenecks caused by the pandemic and compounded by Russia's war in Ukraine, which further affected commodity prices. Domestic factors, such as the size of fiscal stimulus to address the pandemic and the consequent recovery, also played a role in some countries. Although these dynamics exerted particular pressure on energy and food prices, inflation has spread to other price categories in almost all countries. Inflation increased in all LAC countries, irrespective of their monetary regimes, although less so for the dollarised countries and more so in countries with no inflation-targeting regime. While inflation has been easing since mid-2022, for some LAC economies, it remains above central bank targets. Since the second half of 2021, countries with inflation-targeting regimes have rapidly increased interest rates to anchor inflation expectations. For some LAC economies, inflation rates remain above their targets in the first half of 2023 (Figure 1.7), particularly for those countries in which demand pressures were higher, such as Colombia and Chile. The normalisation of commodity prices is contributing to the decline in headline inflation, which is already below the upper band of the target range in several countries. However, stickier service prices have made the decline in core inflation more protracted (Adler and Chalk, 2023[6]; Galindo and Nuguer, 2023[5]; ECLAC, 2022[4]; Banco de España, 2023[7]; CAF, 2023[11]).

Figure 1.7. **Difference between headline inflation and the upper inflation target, 2023 (%)**

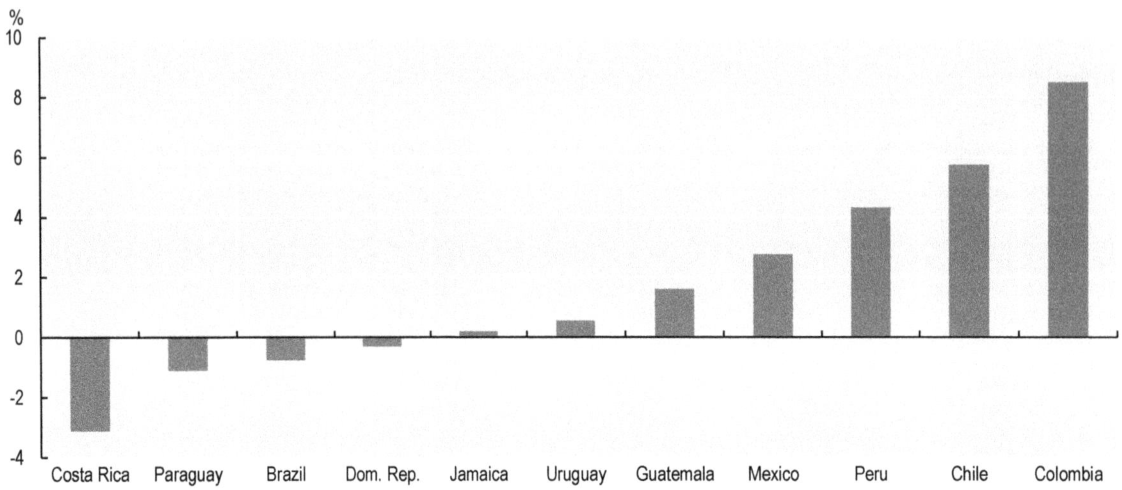

Note: Data include only economies that use inflation-targeting regimes. Data from January 2023 until August 2023.
Source: Authors' calculations based on (Refinitiv Eikon, 2023[3]).

StatLink https://stat.link/fixzuh

The decline in headline inflation is partly explained by the decrease in prices of energy and core components. Energy has made negative contributions to headline inflation over the last nine months. Similarly, the prices of core goods have started to decline, thanks to a reduction of supply bottlenecks and currency appreciation. However, inflationary pressures in food continue to be high and services continue to contribute significantly to inflation, without any noticeable easing of pressures (Banco de España, 2023[7]; CAF, 2023[11]).

Most central banks in the LAC region maintained a tight monetary policy stance during the first half of 2023, aiming to anchor inflation expectations while awaiting consolidation of its decline. Only a few countries, such as Costa Rica, started to reduce their policy rates in the first half of 2023. Other elements – such as the speed of the slowdown in economic activity, volatility in international financial markets and the resulting exchange rate fluctuations, or the impact of climate shocks such as *El Niño* – may condition monetary policy and the use of macroprudential instruments to preserve macrofinancial stability (ECLAC, 2022[4]; Banco de España, 2023[7]; CAF, 2023[11]).

Fiscal space remains limited despite the roll-back of fiscal stimuli

Fiscal accounts have been improving in LAC since 2021, as public revenues increased, and spending support introduced during the pandemic was rolled back. Consequently, a positive shift is seen (on average) in the fiscal accounts of central governments since the 2020 deficits (-6.9% of GDP) that resulted from the response to the COVID-19 crisis. Fiscal deficits narrowed to an average of -2.4% of GDP in 2022, compared to -4.2% in 2021. Caribbean economies continue to exhibit fiscal and primary balance deficits but have also been gradually improving (ECLAC, 2023[9]; CAF, 2023[8]).

In turn, narrowing fiscal deficits and the swift recovery of nominal GDP growth have contributed to decreases in public debt. In 2020, central government gross public debt (as a percentage of GDP) in the LAC region reached 56.3% (spiking to 87.4% in the Caribbean, its highest level in the last 30 years). In 2022, average debt levels declined to 51.5% of GDP (77.3% in the Caribbean). However, substantial heterogeneity is evident across countries in terms of debt levels, ranging from more than 100% of GDP in some Caribbean states (e.g. Barbados, Suriname) to less than 40% in Chile, Guatemala, Paraguay and Peru (ECLAC, 2023[9]; CAF, 2023[8]).

Despite recent consolidation efforts, fiscal space remains limited in LAC; as such, fiscal stability should not be compromised. On average, debt is above pre-pandemic levels and interest payments represent a larger fraction of spending, reducing the scope for countercyclical policies and investment. For debt to stabilise or decrease, it remains fundamental to promote economic growth at higher levels than real interest rates. Further public and private investments should be a key driver in the growth agenda for LAC countries (Chapters 2 and 3). Otherwise, the primary surplus should be high enough to compensate for the growth shortfall over interest rates.

Debt levels are likely to stabilise at manageable levels in most LAC economies. However, debt dynamics vary significantly across countries, depending on economic growth, primary balances, headline inflation, interest rates, exchange rates and the currency composition of the debt. Regarding the latter, a shock in international interest rates could derail debt dynamics, depending on exposure to foreign currency debt and the interplay with economic growth. For instance, in Argentina, Chile, Panama and Peru, a two-standard deviation shock in international interest rates could increase debt levels by approximately 5% of GDP by 2030 (Figure 1.8) (CAF, 2023[8]).

Figure 1.8. **Debt dynamics for selected LAC economies**

Public debt as % of GDP

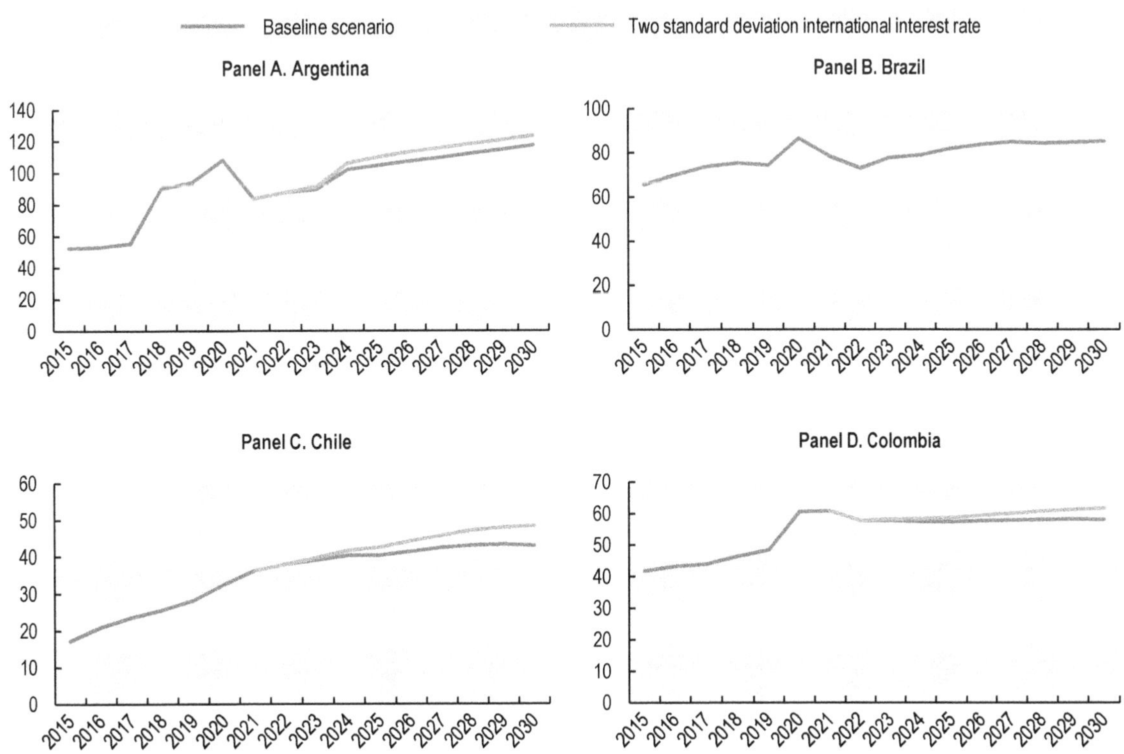

Figure 1.8. **Debt dynamics for selected LAC economies** *(cont.)*

Public debt as % of GDP

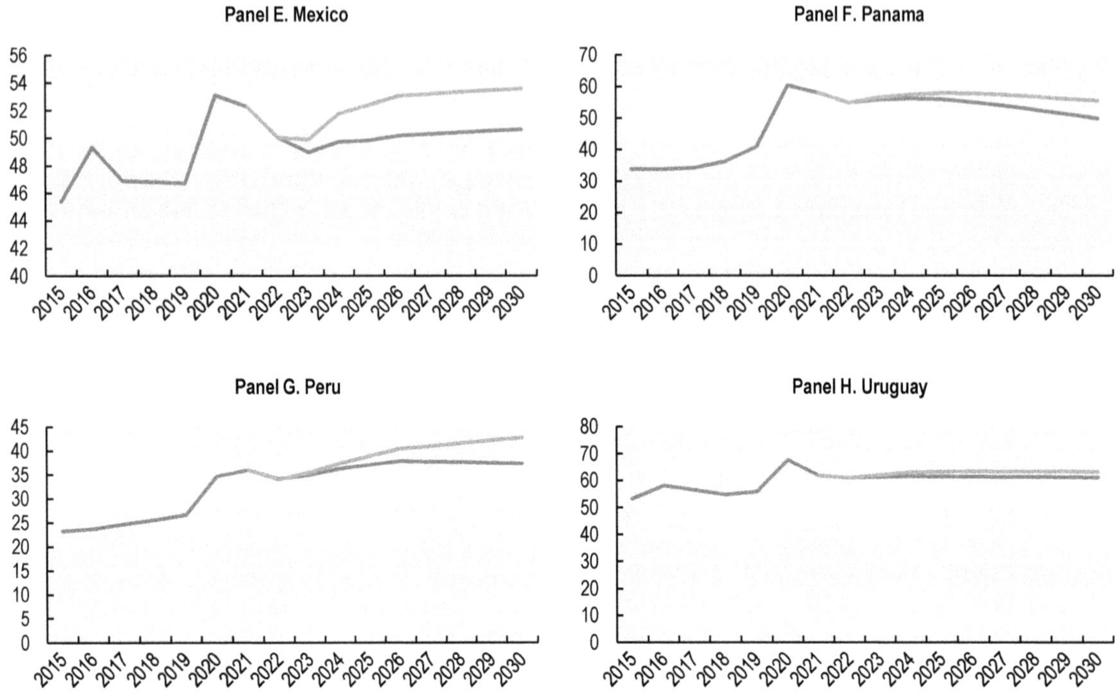

Note: Debt dynamics are modelled by a behavioural equation defined in Bohn (1998) and IMF (2018).

$$b_{t+1} = b_t \left\{ \frac{(1-\alpha)(1+i_t^d)+(\alpha)[1+d_t][1+i_t^*]}{1+g_t} \right\} - SP_t$$

It considers four variables that affect debt to GDP ratios (bt): real GDP growth (gt); real domestic and external interest rates (Id, I*); variation of the exchange rate (dt); and primary fiscal balance in terms of GDP (SPt). Random external interest rate shocks reflect an exercise of 1 000 stochastic simulations based on a "joint normal" distribution of the four fundamentals of the debt/GDP behaviour equation to compute the covariance matrix. For Uruguay only one standard deviation is calculated, and for Brazil only the base scenario is shown.

Source: (CAF, 2023[8]).

Both the composition of fiscal consolidation and its timing will be important to shape inclusive economic development (Powell and Valencia, 2023[25]). In the short term, the region must continue its fiscal consolidation efforts while, as a priority, protecting the most vulnerable from inflation. This can be done by strengthening the targeting of social protection systems and maintaining or implementing targeted support policies to counterbalance the negative effects of high inflation (OECD et al., 2021[22]).

For the long term, fiscal policy must protect public investment with adequate fiscal frameworks. Capital investments are essential for the production transformation and can (in the short term) help to offset the contractionary effects of fiscal adjustment. Nevertheless, in episodes of fiscal consolidation, governments find it easier to reduce capital expenditure than current expenditure, as the former tends to have lower political costs than cutting government consumption (Ardanaz and Izquierdo, 2022[26]). This not only has impacts on long-term growth but can also affect economic recovery. Protecting investment during the fiscal consolidation period can mitigate economic contraction and, in some cases, lead to an expansion (Ardanaz et al., 2021[27]). To protect public investment, the LAC region must develop or strengthen fiscal frameworks where fiscal rules can be an important tool. In addition, to protect investment, fiscal rules must be flexible enough to accommodate exogenous shocks. This can be accomplished by including cyclically adjusted fiscal targets, setting well-defined escape clauses and practising differential treatment of investment expenditures (OECD et al., 2022[13]; Arreaza et al., 2022[28]; Cavallo et al., 2020[29]).

Increasing fiscal space and public investment should be driven by better fiscal institutions, more efficient and effective public spending, more progressive tax revenues (OECD et al., 2022[13]; OECD et al., 2023[30]; ECLAC, 2022[31]), and better debt management. Stronger fiscal institutions increase confidence, which reduces risk premia and widens fiscal space by easing the required adjustment to stabilise debt (Arreaza et al., 2022[28]). Moreover, high debt levels in many LAC countries can hinder growth by reducing public investment, increasing financing costs and dampening private investment.

Aligning fiscal and monetary policy is fundamental for promoting sustainable growth. As demand is subdued by fiscal consolidation, this can help to reduce inflationary pressures. In addition, fiscal consolidation can create fiscal space by decreasing risk premia and minimising financing expenses, thus reducing the neutral monetary policy interest rate (Galindo and Nuguer, 2023[5]; Adler and Chalk, 2023[6]).

Tax systems need improvement to finance public services and investments

The LAC region must recover fiscal space to finance the investments needed for the production transformation, increase quality public services and ensure fiscal sustainability. This can be achieved via diverse instruments, including spending and taxes. More effective and efficient spending could be achieved through effective focalisation of public expenditures (including social spending and subsidies), as well as striving for a better balance between capital investment and current expenditure (OECD et al., 2021[22]; Izquierdo, Pessino and Vuletin, 2018[32]). Regarding taxes, the average tax-to-GDP ratio in the LAC region in 2021 was 21.7%, considerably lower than the average of 34.1% in OECD economies. In 2021, the level of tax revenues varied widely across LAC countries, from 12.7% of GDP in Panama to 33.5% in Brazil (Figure 1.9) (OECD et al., 2023[30]).

Figure 1.9. **Tax-to-GDP ratios in LAC countries and in other regions, 2021**

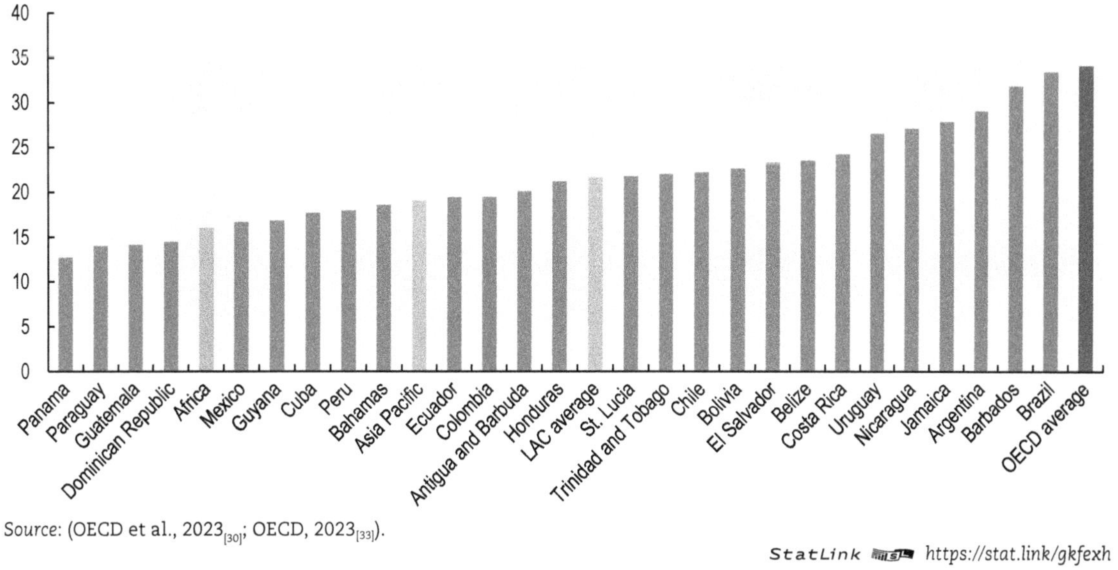

Source: (OECD et al., 2023[30]; OECD, 2023[33]).

StatLink https://stat.link/gkfexh

Most LAC economies need to increase tax revenues and reform their tax systems to pursue diverse social, economic and investment objectives. In a highly unequal region, improving the redistributive power of the tax system should be a priority (OECD et al., 2022[13]). Tax systems have a direct impact on key policy priorities, including job formalisation, entrepreneurship, investment and overall economic growth. Similarly, the tax system has a role in driving the green transition and reducing gender inequalities. To achieve these goals, relevant policy options include: reducing tax evasion and avoidance; increasing tax compliance; strengthening tax administration; increasing the progressivity of personal income tax; and eliminating tax expenditures that provide little benefit in terms of equity or job creation (Nieto-Parra, Orozco and Mora, 2021[34]). Achieving such goals will also require a gradual and well-co-ordinated approach to financing the green transition and reducing the dependence of some countries on hydrocarbon revenues.

By rebalancing the tax mix, LAC economies can achieve more progressive tax systems and reduce income inequalities. At present, LAC tax structures rely on indirect taxes more than direct taxes. Indirect or consumption taxes tend to be regressive as they place the greatest burden on low-income households. In 2020, general consumption taxes (mainly value-added tax [VAT] and sales taxes) accounted for almost half of tax revenues in LAC countries, compared to 32.1% in OECD countries (Figure 1.10). In contrast, income taxes are more progressive, as high-income households contribute a more significant proportion of their earnings in taxes than lower-income households. In 2020, taxes on income and profits accounted for 25.2% of tax revenues in LAC on average, relative to 33.1% on average in the OECD. Within income taxes, taxes on corporate income accounted for 15.5% of total tax revenues in LAC, while personal income tax represented only 9.7%. High corporate tax rates may hinder investment and entrepreneurship. In OECD economies, personal income taxes account for a larger share of tax revenues (24.1%) than corporate income taxes (9.0%) (OECD et al., 2023[30]).

Figure 1.10. **Average tax structure in the LAC region and OECD, 2020**

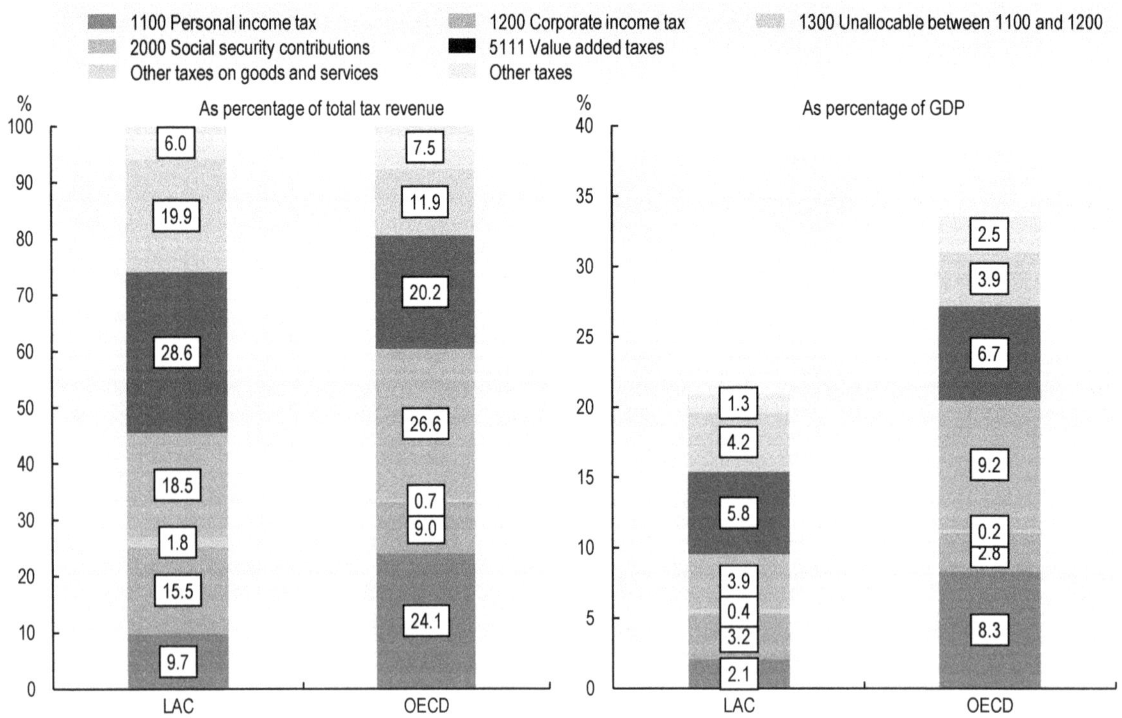

Source: (OECD et al., 2023[30]).

StatLink https://stat.link/kl6wds

In addition to raising revenue, tax systems can also help pursue environmental objectives. Increased environmental taxes can advance the green transition and digital transformation by reducing pollution, shifting consumption patterns in a more sustainable direction and stimulating technological innovation. The LAC region still has great potential to use environment-related taxes more effectively. On average in 2021, environmentally related tax revenues amounted to 1.0% of GDP in LAC countries – just half of the OECD average of 2.0% (OECD et al., 2023[30]).

However, environmental taxes may have negative repercussions on the most vulnerable populations and cause distorting effects that may affect economic activity. These taxes can, for example, further expose the most vulnerable by increasing the price of fossil-fuel-intensive products and services. Hence, it is essential to develop and enhance compensation schemes. These can include well-targeted cash and in-kind transfers, complemented by active labour market policies and self-employment and entrepreneurship programmes (OECD et al., 2022[13]). Environmental taxes may also distort tax bases or accentuate pre-existing distortions, with potential adverse effects on economic activity and entrepreneurship. It is thus necessary to use some of the revenue from environmental taxes to offset these effects (OECD, 2010[35]). If well designed, environmental taxes will produce the desired changes among consumers and businesses and should automatically phase out gradually.

Tax systems in LAC can also serve to promote gender equality. While men and women are generally subject to the same tax regulations, gender inequalities within the tax system can inadvertently be perpetuated by social and economic differences, such as income disparities or varying levels of labour participation. Within the region, the burden of both direct and indirect taxation affects women more than men. For instance, tax systems generally do not account for how women take on a larger share of unpaid work, making the tax burden disproportionate at the household level. Another example of gender bias in tax policy is tax relief for male-dominated economic sectors. It is therefore important to advance tax systems that remove all gender biases, whether explicit (i.e. when tax laws identify and treat women and men differently) or implicit (i.e. when tax laws or regulations treat women and men similarly but have an unequal outcome when applied). Removing both explicit and implicit biases in a country's tax system can increase gender equality – e.g. by changing the nature of asset ownership – while also increasing female labour force participation and entrepreneurship. This allows women to contribute to economic growth. Awareness of these issues is growing in the LAC region. Economies such as Argentina, Mexico and Uruguay have already implemented tax policies or reforms to improve gender equity; more needs to be done, however, and by a larger share of LAC economies (Astudillo et al., 2022[36]; OECD, 2022[37]; OECD et al., 2021[22]).

Fiscal measures should be co-ordinated under a well-defined sequence of policies. There needs to be a national dialogue and consensus, based on empirical evidence, regarding the timing and dimensions of required public spending and taxes. Such consensus can help to renew the social contract (OECD et al., 2021[22]).

Corporate tax incentives need to be improved to increase investments

Different types of tax instruments can influence private investment decisions. These can be taxes generally applied to companies, including income taxes, payroll taxes, taxes on goods and services (e.g. VAT) and other more specific taxes, such as corrective taxes and wealth taxes. In addition, certain provisions seek to reduce the cost of capital, such as investment credits or accelerated depreciation mechanisms. Each instrument has comparative advantages that are important to consider when designing an investment incentive programme (ECLAC, 2022[31]; ECLAC, 2013[38]).

In LAC, the vast majority of tax incentives focus on corporate income taxes (CIT), although some are also linked to import tariffs, VAT and other indirect taxes. Tax incentives are defined as targeted tax provisions that provide favourable deviations from standard tax treatment in a country, resulting in reduced or postponed tax liability (Celani, Dressler and Wermelinger, 2022[39]; OECD, 2022[40]). Incentives focused on CITs are a widely used tool to boost private investment, but they have a cost in public revenues. Such incentives can promote investment and positively affect output, employment, productivity and other objectives related to sustainable development. Nevertheless, if mismanaged or abused, incentives can lead to lower tax revenues, economic distortions, erosion of the principle of equity, and increased administrative and compliance costs, while potentially triggering harmful tax competition (Celani, Dressler and Wermelinger, 2022[39]).

Variations in the corporate tax base can significantly impact tax liabilities and can play a role in international competition and in promoting/discouraging investment. Fiscal depreciation rules or other related provisions (e.g. allowances for corporate equity, half-year conventions, inventory valuation methods) can help to explain variations in the tax bases across jurisdictions. To measure these provisions and compare them across economies, effective tax rates (ETRs) are a better measure than statutory tax rates (STR), as the former provide a more accurate picture of the actual tax liabilities faced by companies (OECD, 2022[41]).

In LAC, the effective average and marginal tax rates on corporate income are relatively high (Figure 1.11). This is due to relatively high STRs and to capital allowances that treat certain assets less generously compared to estimates of economic depreciation and with respect to other countries. These relatively higher ETRs could discourage potential investments (Hanappi et al., 2023[42]).

Figure 1.11. **Corporate effective tax rates in LAC, 2021**

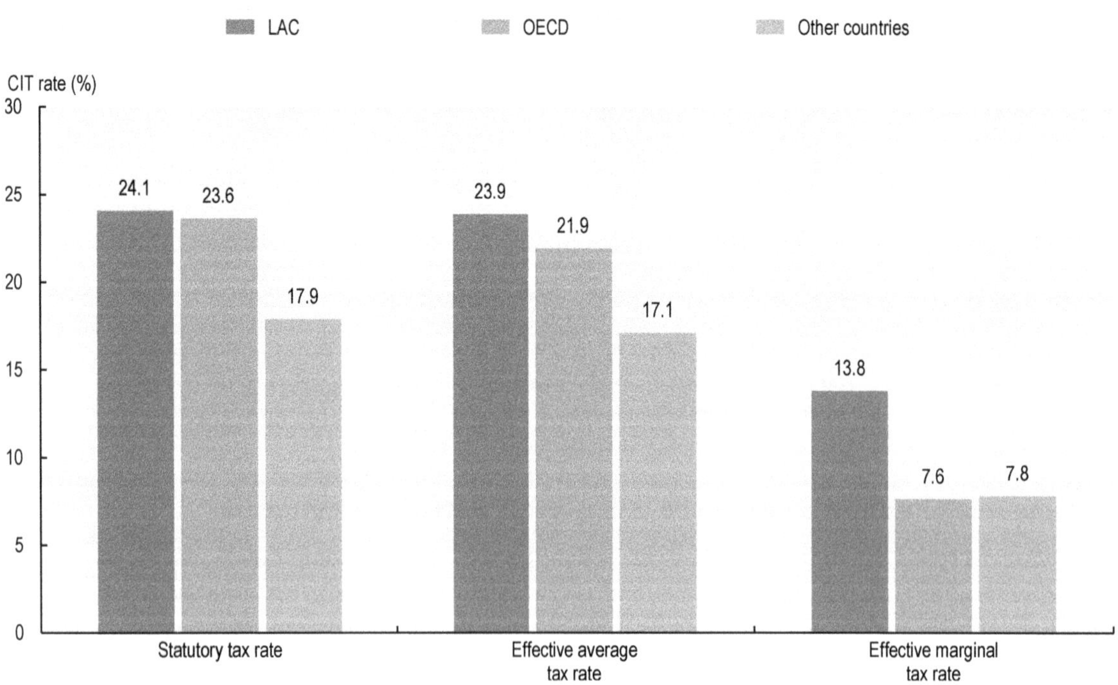

Note: Forward-looking effective tax rates. "Other countries" includes data from emerging Europe (9 countries), Middle East and Central Asia, emerging Asia, and Sub-Saharan Africa (16).

Source: (Hanappi et al., 2023[42]).

StatLink https://stat.link/d26fye

Several LAC countries grant targeted tax incentives or preferential tax treatments that reduce ETRs in specific activities, sectors and locations. Analysis currently exists for three countries (Dominican Republic, Ecuador and Paraguay) and three different industries (textile, metals and tourism) (Figure 1.12). While the Dominican Republic and Ecuador have a 25% standard ETR, they offer sector-specific tax incentives that substantially lower effective taxation in some of the industries. For example, ETRs can be as low as 0% in textiles in Dominican Republic and are up to 45% lower than standard taxation in the Ecuadorian metals industry (13.7% compared to 24.8%). While Paraguay does not use CIT incentives, it applies a relatively low standard CIT rate, resulting in the lowest ETR in the metals and tourism industries across the three countries (OECD, 2022[40]; Hanappi et al., 2023[42]; Celani, Dressler and Wermelinger, 2022[39]).

Figure 1.12. **Impact of sector-specific investment tax incentives on ETRs, selected LAC countries**

EATRs under standard tax treatment (STT) and investment tax incentives in the corresponding sector

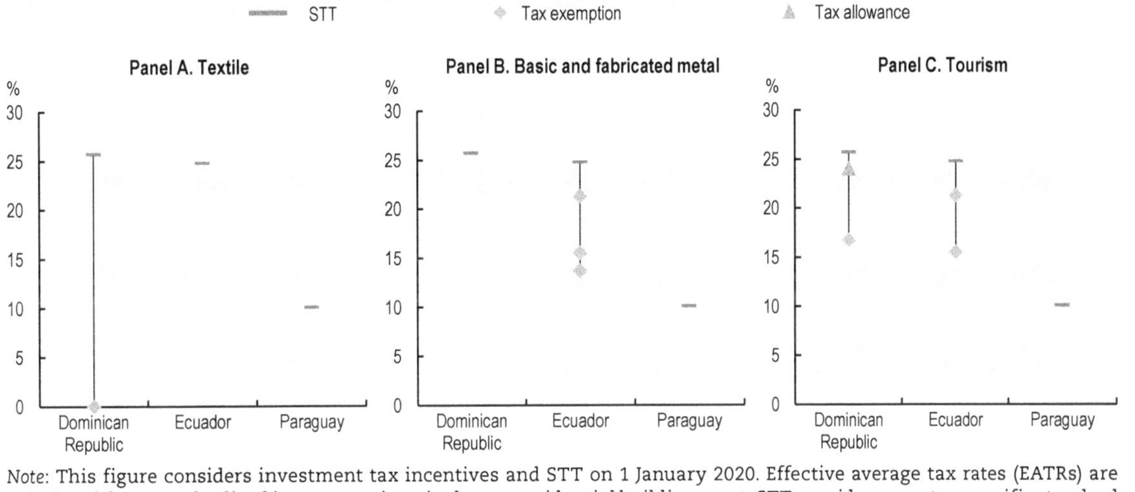

Note: This figure considers investment tax incentives and STT on 1 January 2020. Effective average tax rates (EATRs) are calculated for a standardised investment in a single non-residential building asset. STT considers country-specific standard CIT rates, asset-specific capital allowance rates and cost recovery method. Temporarily or permanently tax-exempt income does not give rise to standard capital allowances.

Source: (OECD, 2022[40]; Celani, Dressler and Wermelinger, 2022[39]).

StatLink https://stat.link/4eqp21

Revenues foregone due to tax incentives, deductions and reduced rates (among other factors) are significant in LAC. In 2021, foregone revenues averaged 3.7% of GDP, equivalent to 19% of general government tax revenues. If tax incentives are poorly designed, their effectiveness may be limited; they could also lead to windfall gains for projects that would have been carried out regardless of the incentives.

Tax incentives should be rationalised and properly designed to ensure that they achieve their development objectives. To accomplish this, LAC economies need to enhance their institutional frameworks to ensure good governance and reduce wasteful effects. This entails creating transparent and clear tax incentives with binding legal requirements for their quantification, including cost-benefit analyses and robust evaluation processes. Tax incentives with explicit terms of duration, clear eligibility criteria and corresponding review mechanisms have a higher success rate. Bringing together all aspects related to incentive design in a unified body of law, including information on the policy objectives of the incentives, could contribute positively (OECD, 2019[21]; ECLAC-OXFAM, 2019[43]; OECD, 2015[44]; Celani, Dressler and Wermelinger, 2022[39]; ECLAC, 2022[31]).

Evaluation of tax incentives is underdeveloped in the LAC region, with few comprehensive studies undertaken so far. Periodic reviews are a relevant exercise to determine whether tax incentives are justified. These involve weighing the costs associated with applying the incentive against the benefits to society, depending on the associated objective (industrial development, job creation or environmental protection, among others). The adoption of tax incentive programmes should also include an evaluation of their opportunity cost in comparison with other policy instruments that can also have a positive influence on investment dynamics, such as public investments, public procurement, targeted subsidies and government-guaranteed liquidity instruments. These comprehensive reviews must be complemented by an institutional framework that ensures good governance and creates binding legal requirements for the quantification of tax incentives, as well as for ongoing cost-benefit analysis and robust evaluation processes (OECD et al., 2023[30]).

Socioeconomic conditions remain challenging in the LAC region

Poverty and extreme poverty remain above pre-pandemic levels in LAC in more than half of LAC countries

In 2022, 29% of the LAC population was in poverty and 11.2% in extreme poverty (Figure 1.13). Estimates for 2023 show that both poverty and extreme poverty should remain at similar levels to 2022. Furthermore, poverty and extreme poverty remain above pre-pandemic levels in more than half of LAC countries. The poverty rate improved slightly between 2020 and 2022. After a sharp increase in 2020 due to the COVID-19 crisis, poverty decreased marginally in 2021 and 2022 owing to the strong economic rebound. However, extreme poverty has increased steadily every year since 2014, with the exception of it falling moderately in 2021 then returning in 2022 to the 2020 level. Poverty and extreme poverty combined were driven by two opposing factors in 2022. On the one hand, economic growth (while considerably lower than in 2021) generated an increase in employment and household income. On the other hand, 2022 was characterised by accelerated inflation, which eroded income purchasing power (ECLAC, 2023[45]; Cherkasky, 2022[46]).

Figure 1.13. **Evolution of rates of poverty and extreme poverty in LAC**

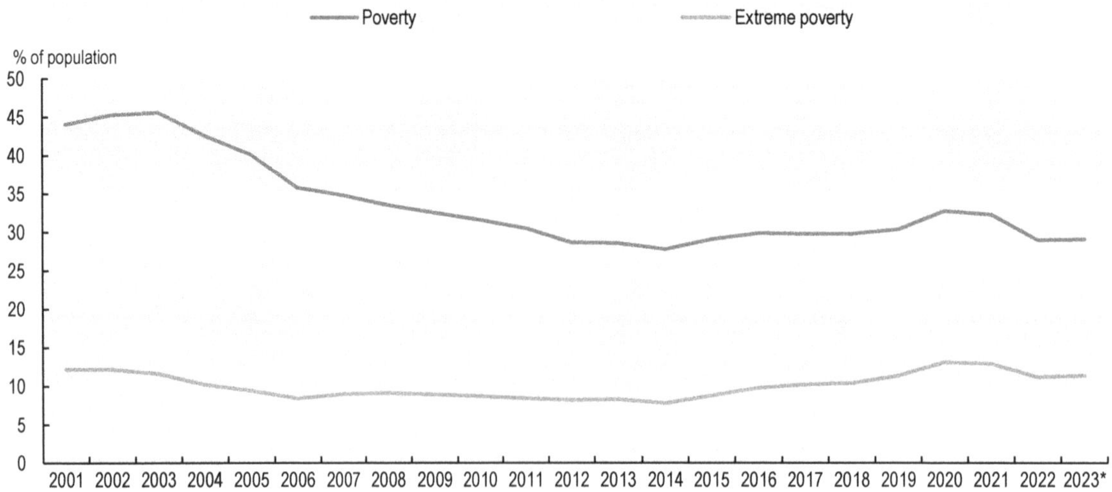

Note: Weighted average for the following countries: Argentina, Venezuela, Brazil, Chile, Colombia, Costa Rica, Dominican Republic, Ecuador, El Salvador, Guatemala, Honduras, Mexico, Nicaragua, Panama, Paraguay, Peru, Bolivia and Uruguay. *Estimates for 2023 are projections.

Source: (OECD et al., 2022[13]; ECLAC, 2023[45]).

StatLink https://stat.link/in5bvc

The detrimental effect of inflation on household incomes in LAC during the first halve of 2023 was considerably higher for households in extreme poverty, as they confronted an average price increase that was 4.1 percentage points higher than that of an average household at the national level (Figure 1.14). From a sample of LAC economies, Argentina and Peru showed the highest difference between the impact of inflation on the average population and on extremely poor households. For Argentina, this difference reached 11.6 percentage points and for Peru, this difference reached 7.0 percentage points.

Figure 1.14. **Impact of inflation on the general population and on the extremely poor in 2023**

Selected Latin American countries (%)

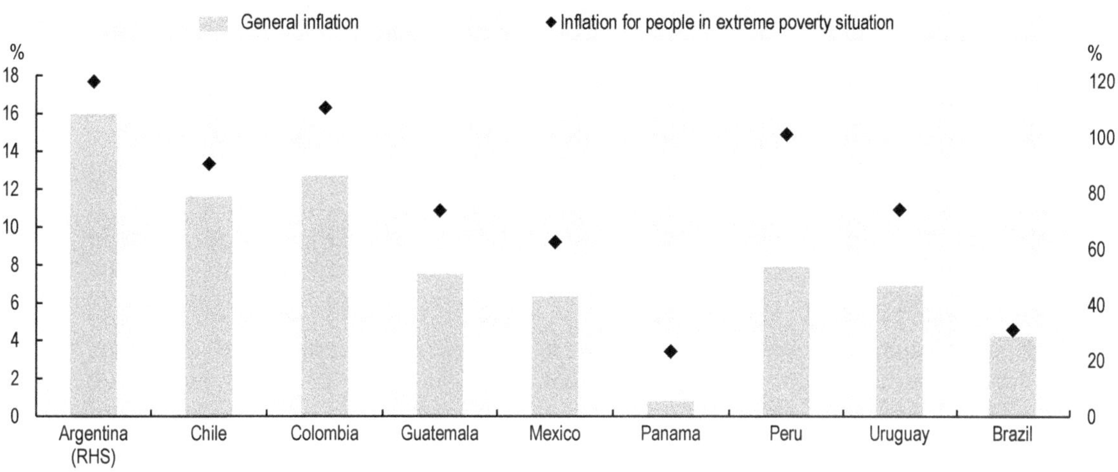

Note: Data from January to July 2023. Year-on-year average growth in national consumer price indices (CPI) versus average growth in extreme poverty thresholds. In the case of Panama data are up to June 2023 and for Chile the data are from 2022. Extreme poverty thresholds are based on the cost of a basic food basket that covers basic needs and provides the minimum caloric requirement of the members of a reference household. For Colombia and Peru, the food and non-alcoholic beverages item of their CPI was taken into consideration. In the case of Panama, the data include the districts of Panama and San Miguelito. For Uruguay, inflation in Montevideo is considered. To calculate inflation for people in extreme poverty in Brazil, the averages of the baskets of the 17 capitals considered by Dieese in the basic basket were used. Argentina is represented on the right axis.

Source: Authors' elaboration based on data from national statistical offices on CPI and poverty thresholds.

Economies in the LAC region have begun implementing policies to alleviate the effects of high inflation on the most vulnerable. These include policy tools such as: cash transfers; the sale or distribution of food at low prices or free of charge to isolated and socially marginalised populations; fuel and transport price subsidies; VAT reductions for some core products in the consumption basket of the poorest and most vulnerable; support for the food supply sector (with emphasis on family farming); the abolition or reduction of tariffs on some food goods; and reductions of certain charges. Several LAC economies have applied social measures – e.g. VAT or import exceptions, price freezes, or general measures to boost the supply of food – alongside price or competitiveness measures. Argentina provided income support to protect low-paid workers. Brazil expanded the coverage and amount of transfers in Auxílio Brasil and Auxílio Gás. Chile implemented the *Apoya* winter voucher to help the most vulnerable sectors cope with rising food price. Colombia expanded coverage of its Solidarity Income programme. Mexico established the Package Against Inflation and Scarcity, which strengthens traditional food security programmes. Peru implemented a one-off payment to beneficiaries of the non-contributory *Juntos* programmes (Pensión 65 and Contigo). Uruguay earmarked additional transfers to strengthen existing social programmes (ECLAC, 2023[45]). Looking forward, it is important that these support measures become targeted to low-income households and preserve incentives to reduce energy consumption (OECD, 2023[2]).

Inequality and low social mobility persist in the LAC region despite some progress

Inequality in income distribution in Latin America, measured through the Gini index, remained relatively stagnant from 2017 to 2022 after a significant decline in the 2000s and a smaller reduction in the 2010s. In 2022, the Gini index for the Latin American average showed a slight reduction, moving to 0.45 from 0.46 in 2020. Countries that showed the highest Gini coefficients (indicating higher inequality) in 2022 were Brazil and Colombia, with averages above 0.50. The lowest Gini coefficients were recorded in Argentina, Dominican Republic and Uruguay, with indices between 0.38 and 0.40 (ECLAC, 2023[45]).

To explain the evolution of inequality among LAC countries, it is useful to refer to the evolution of average household income. In countries where inequality increased, the higher-income quintiles gained more than the poorest (e.g. Uruguay). In contrast, three distinct patterns are observed in countries where inequality decreased. The first corresponds to countries (Dominican Republic, Argentina and Costa Rica) where the income of the poorest quintiles remained unchanged, while those of the highest-income quintile declined. The second pattern shows countries (Brazil, Panama and Peru) where the income of the poorest quintile increased significantly, while incomes in the rest of the quintiles fell, with higher-income households most affected. The third corresponds to countries (Chile, Ecuador and Mexico) where the incomes of the poorest quintile increased with those of almost all the other quintiles, but at a faster rate than in the highest-income quintile (ECLAC, 2023[45]).

Low levels of intergenerational mobility are a major contributor to the fact that inequality across LAC countries has not changed substantially or sustainably (CAF, 2022[47]). An analysis by the Development Bank of Latin America (CAF) takes a long-term perspective on how intergenerational mobility in the region evolved throughout the 20th century and the early 21st century. Persistence of low social mobility, the analysis shows, is closely related to the inequality of opportunity prevailing in the region. In turn, inequalities faced by people from different socioeconomic backgrounds define their opportunities for human capital formation, access to quality jobs and asset accumulation throughout their lives (CAF, 2022[47]).

Educational mobility is one dimension of intergenerational inequality. In LAC, the educational expansion in the last decades that benefited children and youth from disadvantaged families occurred at lower educational levels (mainly primary and, to a lesser extent, secondary). At higher educational levels, especially at university, the expansion of access was more concentrated among young people from middle and high socioeconomic families. Less progress at higher levels of education limits upward mobility, resulting in little progress in terms of relative mobility (CAF, 2022[47]).

Improving social mobility in LAC countries can strengthen incentives to put more effort and investment into education and training, thereby raising productivity. Moreover, if the region addresses the high intergenerational persistence resulting from inequality of opportunity, it can help increase people's trust in each other and in institutions. In that context, policy makers should consider policy actions in terms of relative mobility (ranking an individual against their peers) rather than only in terms of absolute mobility (comparing only to their parents) (CAF, 2022[47]).

Stronger social protection systems and more investments are needed to drive formalisation

Informality of work continues to be a main challenge to addressing poverty and extreme poverty in LAC, where the average informal employment rate was 48.7% in 2022 (ECLAC/ILO, 2023[48]). Informality at the household level also remains high. Before the pandemic (2018/19 depending on data availability), 42.8% of people in the region lived in a household that depended entirely on informal employment and 21.8% were in mixed households (with formal and informal workers). Taken together, a total of 64.6% of the region's people depended totally or partially on informal employment. Only the remaining one-third (35.4%) lived in households that depended entirely on formal employment. Among the countries with available data at the household level, people in Bolivia and Peru are especially vulnerable, with more than 60% of households depending exclusively on informal employment. By contrast, in Uruguay, Chile and Costa Rica more than half of people live in completely formal households (Figure 1.15) (OECD et al., 2022[13]; OECD, forthcoming[49]).

Figure 1.15. **Evolution of household informality in selected LAC economies**

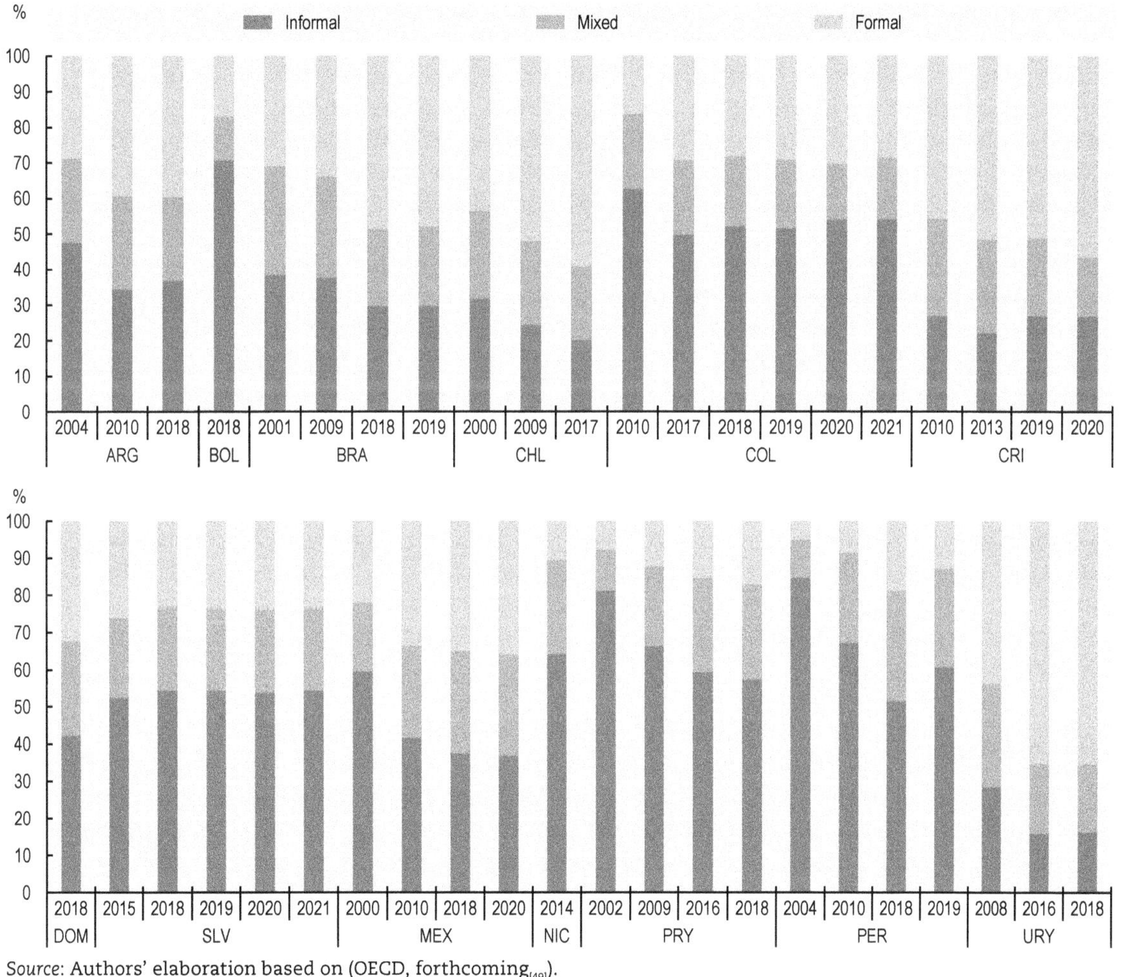

Source: Authors' elaboration based on (OECD, forthcoming[49]).

StatLink https://stat.link/1b3xf5

Informality has remained persistently high across most LAC countries over the last two decades. While negative economic shocks tend to increase informality levels, the specific features of the COVID-19 pandemic led to mixed results in the evolution of informality rates. One key factor was the prevalence of widespread informality in sectors that were heavily affected by lockdown and containment measures, compounded by the limited availability of telework opportunities. Similarly, a substantial number of workers within the informal sector became inactive, signifying their exclusion from the labour force (Acevedo et al., 2021[50]). As a result, informality showed different patterns across LAC economies when comparing indicators immediately post-COVID-19 with those of 2019. In Uruguay and Chile, labour formality grew, though for different reasons. In Uruguay, formalisation occurred due to a decline of total employment, with a larger fall in informality than formality. In Chile, total employment grew, and the process of formalisation occurred because informal job losses were offset by growth in formal jobs. Conversely, in the Dominican Republic, Ecuador and Peru, the labour market informalised, mainly because informal employment growth exceeded that for formal employment. Finally, in Argentina, Brazil, Costa Rica, Mexico and Paraguay, the share of informal employment in total employment remained similar to the level of 2019 (OECD, 2023[51]; OECD, forthcoming[49]).

Gaining a perspective on informality within households is essential for policy design. Informality has traditionally been measured at the individual level, which is useful for understanding its heterogeneity and making international comparisons. Nevertheless, this ignores the household context. The informal or formal status of working members within a household may have important implications for its dependent members. The formal employment of at least one household member may increase the household's access to social insurance schemes, which often cover the contributor's spouse and/or children. For this reason, households with only informal workers face vulnerabilities that are different – and often of a different magnitude – than mixed households. Adding the household dimension thus presents an opportunity to design targeted public policies that better address specific needs to mitigate the vulnerabilities and negative consequences of informality on individuals and households (OECD, forthcoming[52]). This is of particular importance in the post-pandemic context, in which, due to fiscal restrictions, countries need to improve the targeting and conditionality of social protection measures.

The investment agenda in LAC economies is an opportunity to drive job formalisation. Physical investments in economic sectors can create job opportunities that, if matched with the effective development of human capital, could reduce informality. Investments in human capital should aim to improve workers' skills to align with labour market demands, especially for those economic activities that are prioritised under the production development policies of LAC countries. In other words, specific support should be provided to informal workers to guarantee that the LAC investment agenda will leave no one behind (Chapter 3).

Key policy messages

The LAC region needs to address both short- and long-term challenges to minimise negative effects on the most vulnerable populations and achieve higher levels of well-being. Advancing production transformation, largely through increased investment and the implementation of well-designed production development policies, will be key to tackle LAC's structural challenges of low potential growth and low productivity. The region's investment agenda should prioritise the creation of quality formal jobs and investment in human capital creation.

To successfully implement this agenda, it will be necessary to regain monetary and fiscal policy space. On the monetary front, central banks should focus on guaranteeing price stability, thus anchoring long-term inflation expectations. Co-ordinating fiscal and monetary policies is essential, as policy makers must protect the most vulnerable individuals from the impact of significant price increases and prevent fiscally induced demand pressures on prices.

Regarding fiscal policy, public revenues need to be enhanced progressively. These additional resources can then be allocated towards financing improved public services that enhance long-term growth and overall well-being, and implementing production transformation policies. These revenues can also help to mitigate the adverse effects of economic shocks and contribute to establishing stronger social protection systems that are universal, comprehensive, resilient and sustainable (Box 1.1).

Overall, context-specific socioeconomic characteristics, challenges and possible solutions call for tailored approaches across LAC countries. However, some overarching considerations can help countries establish effective "policy menus" and achieve a good policy mix.

Box 1.1. **Key policy messages**

Strengthen investment and fiscal frameworks to address low growth in LAC

- More and better investment is needed in both physical and human capital to increase productivity and thus potential growth.
- Deeper and well-designed production development policies are needed to address the stagnant productivity challenge.
- The region must strengthen its fiscal frameworks, with fiscal rules at the core, to safeguard investments.

Support measures to protect the vulnerable from high inflation moderates

- Ensure that long-term inflation expectations are anchored while protecting the most vulnerable from high inflation.
- Support credible monetary frameworks via independent central banks and by implementing inflation-targeting regimes.

Expand fiscal space to finance investments under a sustainable fiscal framework

- The nature of fiscal consolidation and its timing will be important for shaping inclusive economic growth and development.
- Taxation systems may be improved by balancing policies that can be implemented in the short term with long-term policies. Policy makers may take action to achieve the following goals:
  - Reduce tax evasion and avoidance.
  - Increase tax compliance and strengthen tax administration.
  - Improve the weight of personal income taxes within total taxes in countries highly dependent on indirect taxes and high corporate income taxes.
  - Increase environmentally related taxes and revise general energy subsidies while protecting the most vulnerable populations from potential negative impacts of the green transition agenda.
  - Better promote gender equality throughout the tax system.
  - Rationalise tax incentives and align them with development goals and production transformation strategies. Improve their design by creating binding legal requirements with explicit terms of duration and clear eligibility criteria under a unified body of law.

Box 1.1. **Key policy messages** *(cont.)*

- o Align the treatment of capital allowances with investment development goals, as certain assets are treated less generously.
- o Undertake periodic reviews of investment tax incentives.

Continue improving the well-being of the most vulnerable populations

- Strengthen measures to protect the most vulnerable individuals and households while continuing to advance towards stronger universal social protection systems.
- Ensure that the investment agenda in LAC economies helps to create quality formal jobs and includes the necessary investment in human capital.

References

Acevedo, I. et al. (2021), *Informalidad en los tiempos del COVID-19 en América Latina: Implicaciones y opciones de amortiguamiento*, Inter-American Development Bank, https://doi.org/10.18235/0003220. [50]

Adler, G. and N. Chalk (2023), "In Latin America, Fiscal Policy Can Lighten the Burden of Central Banks", *IMF Blog*, International Monetary Fund, https://www.imf.org/en/Blogs/Articles/2023/04/13/in-latin-america-fiscal-policy-can-lighten-the-burden-of-central-banks. [6]

Álvarez, F. et al. (2019), *RED 2018: Institutions for productivity: towards a better business environment*, Development Bank of Latin America (CAF), Caracas, http://scioteca.caf.com/handle/123456789/1410. [14]

Ardanaz, M. et al. (2021), "The Output Effects of Fiscal Consolidations: Does Spending Composition Matter?", *IDB Working Paper*, No. IDB-WP-1302, http://publications.iadb.org/en/output-effects-fiscal-consolidations-does-spending-composition-matter. [27]

Ardanaz, M. and A. Izquierdo (2022), "Current expenditure upswings in good times and public investment downswings in bad times? New evidence from developing countries", *Journal of Comparative Economics*, Vol. 50(1), pp. 118-134. [26]

Arreaza, A. et al. (2022), *Reglas fiscales para la recuperación en América Latina: experiencias y principales lecciones*, Development Bank of Latin America and the Caribbean (CAF), Caracas, https://scioteca.caf.com/handle/123456789/1905. [28]

Astudillo, K. et al. (2022), "Making the Invisible Visible: Applying a Gender Perspective to Strengthen Tax Policy in Latin America and the Caribbean", *Technical Note*, No. IDB-TN-2504, Inter-American Development Bank, https://doi.org/10.18235/0004350. [36]

Banco de España (2023), *Informe de Economía: Moderación de la inflación, pausa en el endurecimiento monetario y vulnerabilidades fiscales, primer semestre 2023*, Banco de España, Departamento de Economía Internacional y Área del Euro, https://www.bde.es/f/webbe/SES/Secciones/Publicaciones/InformeEconomiaLatinoamericana/2023/S1/Fich/EconomiaLatinoamericana_012023.pdf. [7]

CAF (2023), *Latin American and Caribbean Outlook, April 2023*, Development Bank of Latin America and the Caribbean Internal Document, available upon request. [11]

CAF (2023), *Panorama Fiscal en América Latina y el Caribe*, Development Bank of Latin America and the Caribbean Internal document, available upon request. [8]

CAF (2022), *Inherited Inequalities: The Roles of Skills, Employment and Wealth in the Opportunities of New Generations, Executive Summary*, Development Bank of Latin America and the Caribbean (CAF), Bogota, https://scioteca.caf.com/bitstream/handle/123456789/1981/RED2022-Executive%20Summary.pdf?sequence=5&isAllowed=y. [47]

Cavallo, E. et al. (2020), "Growth-friendly fiscal rules? Safeguarding public investment from budget cuts through fiscal rule design", *IDB Working Paper*, No. IDB-WP-1083, Inter-American Development Bank, https://publications.iadb.org/en/growth-friendly-fiscal-rules-safeguarding-public-investment-budget-cuts-through-fiscal-rule-0. [29]

Cavallo, E. and M. Pedemonte (2015), "What is the Relationship between National Saving and Investment in Latin America and the Caribbean?", *IDB Working Paper Series*, No. IDB-WP-617, http://publications.iadb.org/en/what-relationship-between-national-saving-and-investment-latin-america-and-caribbean. [16]

Cavallo, E. and T. Serebrisky (2016), *Saving for Development: How Latin America and the Caribbean Can Save More and Better*, Inter-American Development Bank, https://publications.iadb.org/en/saving-development-how-latin-america-and-caribbean-can-save-more-and-better. [17]

Celani, A., L. Dressler and M. Wermelinger (2022), "Building an Investment Tax Incentives database: Methodology and initial findings for 36 developing countries", *OECD Working Papers on International Investment*, No. 2022/01, OECD Publishing, Paris, https://doi.org/10.1787/62e075a9-en. [39]

Cherkasky, M. (2022), *Inflación global en el bienio 2021-2022 y su impacto en América Latina*, Estudios y Perspectivas, United Nations Economic Commission for Latin America and the Caribbean, Santiago, https://www.cepal.org/es/publicaciones/48504-inflacion-global-bienio-2021-2022-su-impacto-america-latina. [46]

De Gregorio, J. (1992), "Economic growth in Latin America", *Journal of Development Economics*, Vol. 39/1, pp. 59-84, https://www.sciencedirect.com/science/article/pii/030438789290057G?ref=pdf_download&fr=RR-2&rr=80a169e11c62d712. [12]

ECLAC (2023), *Fiscal Panorama of Latin America and the Caribbean 2023: Fiscal Policy for Growth, Redistribution and Productive Transformation*, United Nations Economic Commission for Latin America and the Caribbean, Santiago, https://www.cepal.org/en/publications/48900-fiscal-panorama-latin-america-and-caribbean-2023-fiscal-policy-growth. [9]

ECLAC (2023), *Foreign Direct Investment in Latin America and the Caribbean 2023*, United Nations Economic Commission for Latin America and the Caribbean, Santiago, https://www.cepal.org/en/publications/48979-foreign-direct-investment-latin-america-and-caribbean-2023. [20]

ECLAC (2023), *International Trade Outlook for Latin America and the Caribbean 2022: The Challenge of Boosting Manufacturing Exports*, United Nations Economic Commission for Latin America and the Caribbean, Santiago, https://www.cepal.org/en/publications/48651-international-trade-outlook-latin-america-and-caribbean-2022-challenge-boosting. [24]

ECLAC (2023), *Social Panorama of Latin America and the Caribbean 2023: Labour inclusion as a key axis of inclusive social development*, United Nations Economic Commission for Latin America and the Caribbean, Santiago, https://repositorio.cepal.org/server/api/core/bitstreams/a4d96610-6048-4044-bf89-2eb3c31fc369/content. [45]

ECLAC (2022), *Economic Survey of Latin America and the Caribbean 2022: Trends and Challenges of Investing for a Sustainable and Inclusive Recovery*, United Nations Economic Commission for Latin America and the Caribbean, Santiago, https://www.cepal.org/en/publications/48078-economic-survey-latin-america-and-caribbean-2022-trends-and-challenges-investing. [31]

ECLAC (2022), *Preliminary Overview of the Economies of Latin America and the Caribbean 2022*, United Nations Economic Commission for Latin America and the Caribbean, Santiago, https://www.cepal.org/en/publications/48575-preliminary-overview-economies-latin-america-and-caribbean-2022. [4]

ECLAC (2022), *Towards Transformation of the Development Model in Latin America and the Caribbean: Production, Inclusion and Sustainability*, United Nations Economic Commission for Latin America and the Caribbean, Santiago, https://www.cepal.org/en/publications/48309-towards-transformation-development-model-latin-america-and-caribbean-production. [15]

ECLAC (2013), *Política tributaria para mejorar la inversión y el crecimiento en América Latina*, United Nations Economic Commission for Latin America and the Caribbean, Santiago, http://www.cepal.org/es/publicaciones/5361-politica-tributaria-mejorar-la-inversion-crecimiento-america-latina. [38]

ECLAC/ILO (2023), *Employment Situation in Latin America and the Caribbean: Towards the Creation of Better Jobs in the Post-pandemic Era*, ECLAC and International Labour Organization, https://repositorio.cepal.org/handle/11362/48988. [48]

ECLAC-OXFAM (2019), *Los incentivos fiscales a las empresas en América Latina y el Caribe*, https://www.cepal.org/es/publicaciones/44787-incentivos-fiscales-empresas-america-latina-caribe. [43]

Galindo, A. and V. Nuguer (2023), *Preparing the Macroeconomic Terrain for Renewed Growth*, Inter-American Development Bank, https://doi.org/10.18235/0004780. [5]

Hanappi, T. et al. (2023), "Corporate Effective Tax Rates in Latin America and the Caribbean", *Technical note No IDB-TN- 2782*, http://dx.doi.org/10.18235/0005168. [42]

IIF (2023), *The Institute of International Finance database*, https://www.iif.com/Research/Download-Data. [19]

IMF (2023), *World Economic Outlook: A Rocky Recovery*, International Monetary Fund, https://www.imf.org/en/Publications/WEO/Issues/2023/04/11/world-economic-outlook-april-2023. [10]

Izquierdo, A., C. Pessino and G. Vuletin (eds.) (2018), *Better Spending for Better Lives: How Latin America and the Caribbean Can Do More with Less*, Inter-American Development Bank, https://doi.org/10.18235/0001217-en. [32]

Nieto-Parra, S., R. Orozco and S. Mora (2021), "Fiscal policy to drive the recovery in Latin America: the "when" and "how" are key", *VOXLACEA*, https://vox.lacea.org/?q=blog/fiscal_policy_latam. [34]

OECD (2023), *Global Revenue Statistics Database*, https://www.oecd.org/tax/tax-policy/global-revenue-statistics-database.htm. [33]

OECD (2023), *Informality and Globalisation: In Search of a New Social Contract*, OECD Publishing, Paris, https://doi.org/10.1787/c945c24f-en. [51]

OECD (2023), *OECD Economic Outlook, Volume 2023 Issue 2: Preliminary version*, OECD Publishing, Paris, https://doi.org/10.1787/7a5f73ce-en. [2]

OECD (2023), *OECD Economic Outlook, Volume 2023 Issue 1*, OECD Publishing, Paris, https://doi.org/10.1787/ce188438-en. [1]

OECD (2022), *Corporate Tax Statistics: Fourth Edition*, https://www.oecd.org/tax/beps/corporate-tax-statistics-database.htm. [41]

OECD (2022), *Multi-dimensional Review of the Dominican Republic: Towards Greater Well-being for All*, OECD Development Pathways, OECD Publishing, Paris, https://doi.org/10.1787/560c12bf-en. [40]

OECD (2022), *Tax Policy and Gender Equality: A Stocktake of Country Approaches*, OECD Publishing, Paris, https://doi.org/10.1787/b8177aea-en. [37]

OECD (2019), *FDI Qualities Indicators: Measuring the sustainable development*, OECD Publishing, https://www.oecd.org/investment/fdi-qualities-indicators.htm. [21]

OECD (2015), *Policy Framework for Investment, 2015 Edition*, OECD Publishing, Paris, https://doi.org/10.1787/9789264208667-en. [44]

OECD (2010), *Taxation, Innovation and the Environment*, OECD Publishing, Paris, https://doi.org/10.1787/9789264087637-en. [35]

OECD (forthcoming), *Key Indicators of Informality based on Individuals and their Household (KIIbIH)*, OECD Publishing, Paris, https://www.oecd.org/dev/key-indicators-informality-individuals-household-kiibih.htm. [49]

OECD (forthcoming), *Portraying Informality and Households' Vulnerabilities in Latin America*, OECD Publishing, Paris. [52]

OECD et al. (2023), *Revenue Statistics in Latin America and the Caribbean 2023*, OECD Publishing, Paris, https://doi.org/10.1787/a7640683-en. [30]

OECD et al. (2021), *Latin American Economic Outlook 2021: Working Together for a Better Recovery*, OECD Publishing, Paris, https://doi.org/10.1787/5fedabe5-en. [22]

OECD et al. (2022), *Latin American Economic Outlook 2022: Towards a Green and Just Transition*, OECD Publishing, Paris, https://doi.org/10.1787/3d5554fc-en. [13]

Powell, A. and O. Valencia (eds.) (2023), *Dealing with Debt: Less Risk for More Growth in Latin America and the Caribbean*, Inter-American Development Bank, https://doi.org/10.18235/0004707. [25]

Refinitiv Eikon (2023), *Refinitiv Eikon Datastream*, https://www.refinitiv.com/en/products/datastream-macroeconomic-analysis. [3]

Sanguinetti, P. et al. (2021), *Pathways to integration: trade facilitation, infrastructure, and global value chains*, Development Bank of Latin America and the Caribbean (CAF), Caracas, https://scioteca.caf.com/handle/123456789/1907. [23]

World Bank (2023), *World Development Indicators*, https://datos.bancomundial.org/indicator/CM.MKT.LCAP.GD.ZS?end=2020&start=1975&view=chart. [18]

Chapter 2

Investment panorama in Latin America and the Caribbean: Challenges and opportunities

This chapter presents recent investment trends in Latin America and the Caribbean (LAC), with a focus on strategic and sustainable investment in public infrastructure. First, the chapter highlights the general low levels of investment in the region, examining the roles of both the public and private sectors. Second, it analyses how quality public infrastructure in energy, transport, telecommunications and water can contribute to creating a more sustainable and inclusive future. Third, the chapter stresses that good governance and transparency can enhance the investment climate. Fourth, it presents the main trends of public-private partnerships (PPPs) and how they can accelerate the development of strategic sectors. Fifth, the chapter considers the benefits of foreign direct investment (FDI) in terms of job creation, productivity and innovation. The chapter concludes with key policy messages to guide these efforts.

LAC needs more and better investments for more inclusive and sustainable development

Total investment as a percentage of GDP in LAC and selected regions, 1990-2022

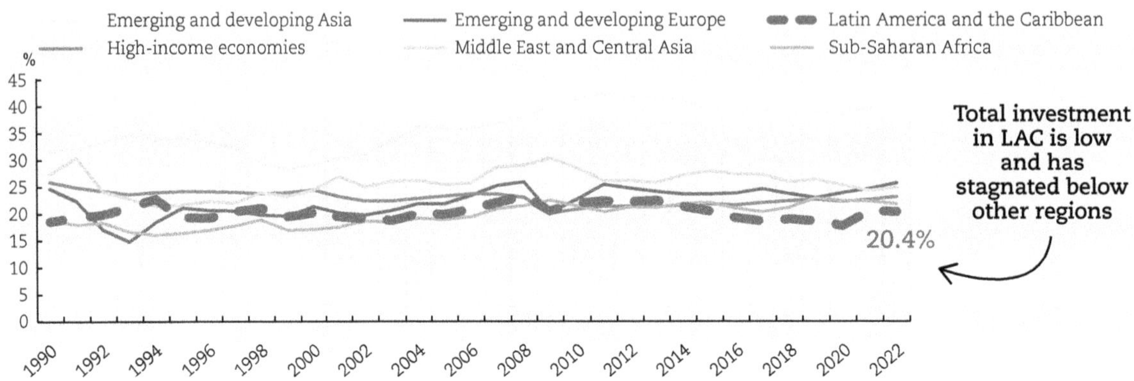

The public sector has a crucial role to play, notably by investing in strategic infrastructure

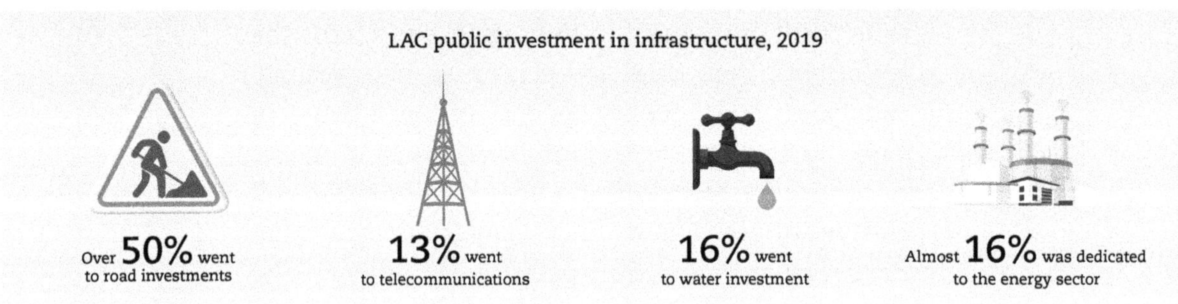

While domestic investment has been low, the region has been successful in attracting foreign investment

Foreign direct investment (FDI) inflows as a share of GDP, by region, 2010-22

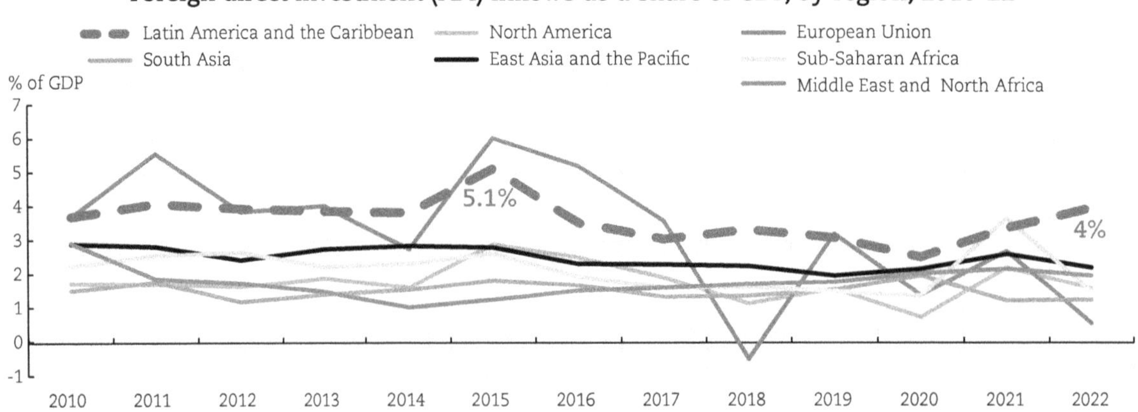

Introduction

Investment, if properly targeted, is a fundamental driver of sustainable development. It can be crucial in improving citizens' well-being while also achieving broader socio-economic and environmental objectives. Nonetheless, total investment in LAC has remained low over the last 30 years; and in the past decade its level has been consistently lower than in other developing regions. More and better investment in strategic sectors is needed to boost production transformation and to craft a more inclusive and sustainable development model.

This chapter devotes special attention to the importance of strategic investment in quality public infrastructure for stronger development in LAC, particularly in key sectors such as sustainable transportation, telecommunications and water. It explores public-private partnerships (PPPs) and foreign direct investment (FDI) as enablers of better investment to deliver social and environmental impact. Other key investment areas are covered in Chapter 3, such as human capital, which is directly connected to production transformation.

The public and private sectors have strategic roles to play in securing more and better domestic and international investment. The public sector is responsible for providing essential services and goods, and for mobilising strategic investment in public infrastructure (infrastructure owned or available for use by the public). Moreover, the amount and quality of investment that is attracted will be determined by good governance and institutional frameworks (e.g. regulations and laws); transparency; the quality of institutions (e.g. rule of law, institutional co-ordination); and well-designed policies and programmes (e.g. fiscal and financial incentives) across transversal sectors (e.g. labour-market policies, entrepreneurship) (OECD, 2022[1]). Similarly, governments in the LAC region will need to promote and generate reliable sources of information and data that provide a clear visualisation of public and private current investments. In turn, the private sector, both national and foreign, can engage in developing quality infrastructure that brings well-being to surrounding communities.

This chapter begins by analysing the main investment trends in LAC, detailing investment levels per sector and their respective sources. Second, it assesses the main sectors of public infrastructure and how they can promote wider well-being and help LAC countries to move towards achieving the UN Sustainable Development Goals (SDGs). Third, the chapter highlights the crucial role of good governance in boosting the impact of investment in infrastructure. Fourth, the chapter stresses the importance of carefully implementing PPPs to boost the potential of public infrastructure. Fifth, the impact of FDI is analysed, looking into the sectors funded, the main investors, job creation and the effects of foreign investment on productivity, innovation and environmental sustainability. The chapter concludes by providing main policy messages for further consideration and implementation. A methodological annex at the end of the chapter provides details about the information presented in selected figures. Box 2.1 presents a brief compilation of definitions and considerations related to investment and infrastructure.

Box 2.1. **Definitions, considerations and indicators for investment and infrastructure**

Gross fixed capital formation (GFCF): This measures the total value of investment made by businesses (both non-financial and financial corporations), governments and households within a given economy (OECD, 2023[2]). GFCF is defined as "the acquisition of produced assets (including purchases of second-hand assets), including the production of such assets by producers for their own use, minus disposals. The relevant assets relate to assets that are intended for use in the production of other goods and services for more than one year. The term "produced assets" includes only those assets that come into existence as a result of a production process and, therefore, does not include, for example, the purchase of land and natural resources" (OECD, 2023[2]). GFCF is measured by "the total value of acquisitions less disposals, of fixed assets during the accounting period plus certain specified expenditure on services that adds to the value of non-produced assets", such as the improvement of land (European Commission et al., 2008[3]). Since 2008, with the adoption of the new standards of the System of National Accounts (SNA), the expenses in research and development (R&D) and weapons systems are included in the GFCF (OECD, 2019[4]).

Gross capital formation (GCF): GCF is measured by "the total value of the GFCF, changes in inventories and acquisitions minus disposals of valuables" (European Commission et al., 2008[3]).

Investment: In this report, the term investment is used to refer to GFCF or GCF. According to the OECD Policy Framework for Investment, "investment can take many forms, from physical assets to human or intellectual capital. It can add capacity or simply improve the efficiency of existing assets such as through a change of ownership. Under the right conditions, it raises overall output both through factor accumulation and by introducing new techniques and processes which boost productivity and ultimately the country's standard of living" (OECD, 2015[5]).

Public investment: "Public investment includes public gross fixed capital formation and acquisitions, less the disposal of non-produced, non-financial assets. Public gross fixed capital formation is the main component of public investment, which consists mainly of transport infrastructure, but also includes other investments such as office buildings, housing, schools and hospitals. Public administration consists of central, state and local government and social security funds" (OECD, 2019[4]).

Private investment: The private sector's contribution to total investment refers to investment that has not been made by the government but is instead funded by households, companies or non-public organisations.

Quality public infrastructure: This concerns investment decisions in public infrastructure that "take into account the full externality effects of projects over the long term, including employment creation, social and environmental impacts, alignment with broader development strategies and the mobilisation of adequate resources" (OECD, 2021[6]). Public infrastructure is infrastructure owned or available for use by the public that encompasses essential services such as the energy, telecommunications, transport and water sectors.

Public-private partnerships: PPPs bring together the public and private sectors to finance and develop all phases of a public project, including construction, financing and operation (ECLAC, 2012[7]). PPPs tend to cover strategic public projects, such as hospitals, prisons, roads, schools, and water and sanitation (ECLAC, 2004[8]).

Foreign direct investment: FDI "is a category of cross-border investment in which an investor resident in one economy establishes a lasting interest in and a significant degree of influence over an enterprise resident in another economy. Ownership of 10% or more of the voting power in an enterprise in one economy by an investor in another economy is evidence of such a relationship" (OECD, 2023[9]).

Source: Based on (OECD, 2021[6]); (OECD, 2023[2]); (OECD, 2019[4]); (OECD, 2015[5]); (ECLAC, 2012[7]); (European Commission et al., 2008[3]); (ECLAC, 2004[8]); (OECD, 2023[9]).

Where does LAC stand in terms of investment?

The pattern of investment for the LAC region shows a general slowdown over the last three decades, which has stagnated below other developing regions. Total investment as a percentage of gross domestic product (GDP) dropped considerably even before the COVID-19 pandemic, declining by almost 2 percentage points from 2015 to 2019. By 2022, it averaged 20.4% of GDP, or around 2.8 percentage points less than total investment in high-income economies (23.2%). LAC also lags behind other developing regions in terms of total investment as a share of GDP. With 40% of GDP on average, emerging and developing economies in Asia show the highest levels of investment. Overall, the gap between LAC and other countries and regions has grown steadily since 2000. Since 2014, on average, every region has exhibited higher levels of total investment than LAC (Figure 2.1).

Figure 2.1. **Total investment as a percentage of GDP in LAC and selected regions, 1990-2022**

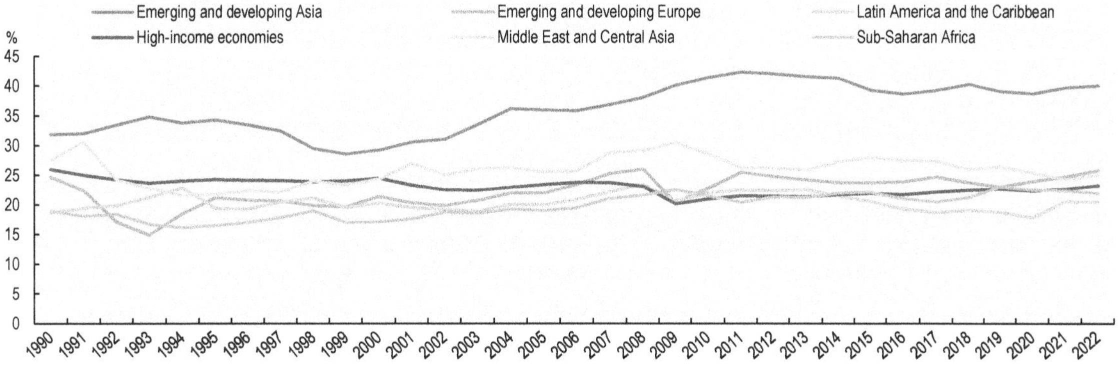

Note: As in (IMF, 2023[10]), data for each region corresponds to weighted averages. Investment, defined as gross capital formation, is measured by the total value of gross fixed capital formation and changes in inventories and acquisitions less disposals of valuables for a unit or sector [SNA 1993]. Investment is expressed as a ratio of total investment in current local currency and GDP in local currency. Middle East and Central Asia include 32 countries: Afghanistan, Algeria, Armenia, Azerbaijan, Bahrain, Djibouti, Egypt, Georgia, Iraq, Iran, Jordan, Kazakhstan, Kuwait, Kyrgyz Republic, Lebanon, Libya, Mauritania, Morocco, Oman, Pakistan, Qatar, Saudi Arabia, Somalia, Sudan, Syria, Tajikistan, Tunisia, Turkmenistan, United Arab Emirates, Uzbekistan and Yemen.

Source: (IMF, 2023[10]).

StatLink https://stat.link/ibu4z2

There is strong heterogeneity in LAC countries in terms of investment levels. In the Caribbean region, investment represented more than 32% of GDP in 2022 for countries such as Antigua and Barbuda, Dominican Republic, and St. Vincent and the Grenadines, while it was below 20% in Barbados, Puerto Rico and Haiti. In Central America and Mexico, average investment was 22.7% of GDP, while for South America the average was around 21% of GDP (Figure 2.2). From 2014 to 2020, countries that have shown a steady increase in investment levels are Antigua and Barbuda, Dominican Republic, Grenada, St. Vincent and the Grenadines, El Salvador and Paraguay (IMF, 2023[10]).

Figure 2.2. **Total investment as a percentage of GDP in selected LAC countries, 2022**

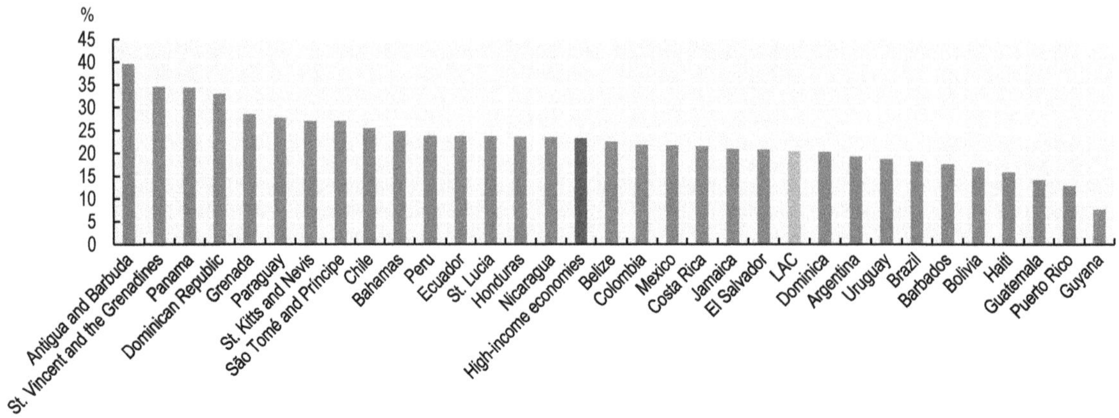

Note: As in (IMF, 2023[10]), data for LAC and high-income economies corresponds to weighted averages. Investment, defined as gross capital formation, is measured by the total value of the gross fixed capital formation and changes in inventories and acquisitions less disposals of valuables for a unit or sector [SNA 1993]. Investment is expressed as a ratio of total investment in current local currency and GDP in local currency.

Source: (IMF, 2023[10]).

StatLink https://stat.link/ty6g2f

Investment in LAC differs considerably across economic sectors. The share of investment per sector can be divided into three main groups. From 1990 to 2018, the largest proportions of total investment went to manufacturing (22.7%) and general services (21.1%). The second group – commerce (13.7%), mining industries (12.4%) and transportation (10.9%) – received almost 9 percentage points less investment. Finally, investments in agriculture (9.4%), electricity, gas and water (7.2%), and construction (2.6%) were below 10% of total investment (Figure 2.3). Notably, investment in construction goods as well as machinery and equipment has increased considerably over the last three decades in LAC. Over the period 1990 to 2020, the average annual growth rate of investment in machinery and equipment, at 4.4%, surpassed that of construction goods, at 3% (ECLAC, 2022[11]).

Figure 2.3. **Share of total investment per economic sector in LAC, 1990-2018**

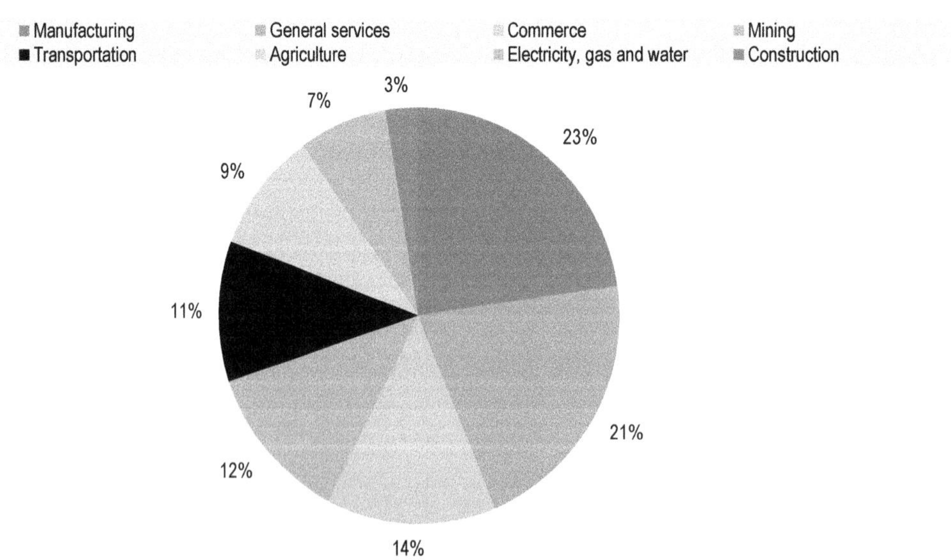

Source: (ECLAC, 2022[11]).

StatLink https://stat.link/h6lktb

As in other market-based economies, investments in most LAC countries are driven by the private and public sectors. The private sector includes what businesses, corporations, households and individuals invest in productive assets, such as investments in machinery, equipment, buildings, R&D, and other forms of fixed capital. Private investment is usually financed by private savings or by raising funds from financial markets and includes funding of infrastructure projects such as transport infrastructure, schools, hospitals, public transportation systems and other public assets as well as R&D. Public investment is typically financed by government expenditure or borrowing (Chapter 4). PPPs combine both sources of investment in collaborative projects (section below on PPPs).

The private sector is the main driver of investment in LAC; in 2019, it accounted for 78% of total investment. In Antigua and Bermuda, Bahamas, Chile, Dominican Republic and Guatemala, private investment represented more than 89% of total investment in 2019. The only LAC countries in which public sector investment exceeded private investment were Bolivia, Guyana and Venezuela. Overall, the share of private investment (78%) in total investment in LAC is below the OECD average of close to 84% (Figure 2.4). Historically (since 1990), private investment in LAC has represented 70% to 76% of total investment while public investment represented 24% to 30% (IMF, 2022[12]).

Figure 2.4. **Private vs. public investment as a share of total investment in LAC and OECD, 2019**

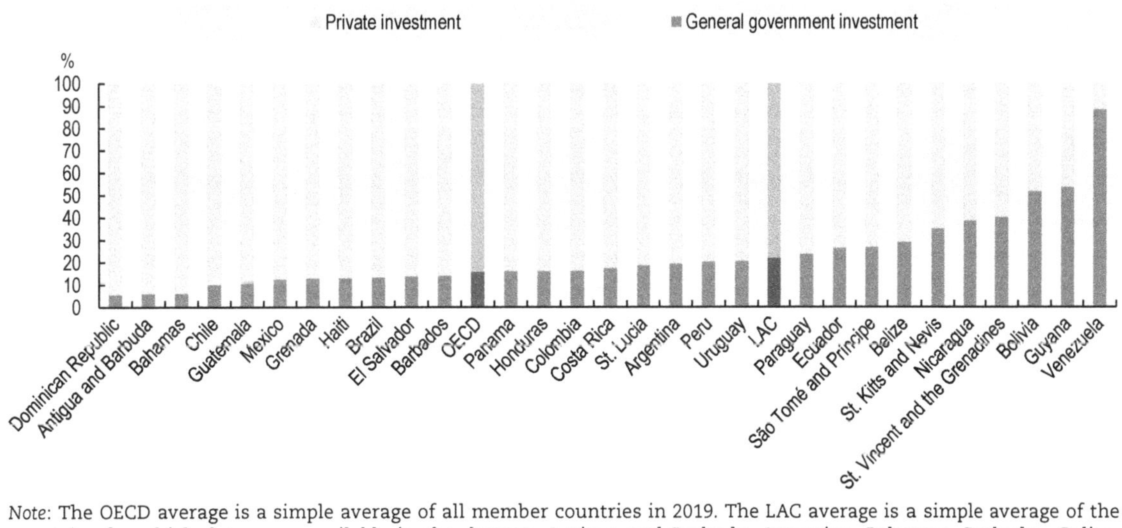

Note: The OECD average is a simple average of all member countries in 2019. The LAC average is a simple average of the countries for which data were available in the dataset: Antigua and Barbuda, Argentina, Bahamas, Barbados, Belize, Bolivia, Brazil, Chile, Colombia, Costa Rica, Dominican Republic, Ecuador, El Salvador, Grenada, Guatemala, Guyana, Haiti, Honduras, Mexico, Nicaragua, Panama, Paraguay, São Tomé and Príncipe, St. Kitts and Nevis, St. Lucia, St. Vincent and the Grenadines, Uruguay and Venezuela. See the Methodological Annex at the end of the chapter for general government and private investment calculations. The shares of total investment corresponding to private and general government investment were calculated taking into consideration the respective percentages of GDP represented by each category.

Source: (IMF, 2022[12]).

StatLink https://stat.link/tvn612

As the largest investor in LAC, the private sector should also be a key partner for the production transformation agenda, which requires more and better private investment. Until 2016, private investment showed high levels of concentration, with 1%, 5% and 10% of the region's top companies being responsible, on average, for 25%, 55% and 69% of long-term investment, respectively (ECLAC, 2018[13]). To promote more – yet less concentrated – private investment, LAC governments can pursue a wide variety of strategies and tools. Chapter 3 explores specific tools to promote small and medium-sized enterprises (SMEs). Chapter 5 highlights the potential impact of international partnerships to promote private investment in strategic sectors, following the example of the European Union's Global Gateway Investment Agenda (GGIA) in Latin America and the Caribbean. The next sections of this chapter cover strategic investment in quality infrastructure, effective PPPs and quality FDI.

Towards strategic investment in quality public infrastructure

This section focuses on the crucial role of the public sector and how quality public infrastructure can contribute to advancing a more sustainable and inclusive development model in LAC. It explores how better public infrastructure can promote private investment and act as a catalyst for further growth and connectivity. Particular attention will be given to the sustainable transportation, telecommunications and water sectors.

Public infrastructure encompasses essential services that have a direct impact on citizens' well-being, and tends to focus mainly on the energy, telecommunications, transport and water sectors. Public infrastructure in these four sectors will be of true quality only if designed and implemented to support a sustainable production model that brings direct benefits to citizens. Following the G20 principles, quality infrastructure should also be resilient over time and to the effects of climate change and should include gender and transparency considerations (OECD, 2020[14]).

Quality public infrastructure can help governments advance towards the SDGs. Investment in public infrastructure can catalyse the achievement of poverty reduction (SDG 1), good health and well-being (SDG 3), quality education (SDG 4), clean water and sanitation (SDG 6), affordable and clean energy (SDG 7), decent work and economic growth (SDG 8), industry, innovation, and infrastructure (SDG 9), and sustainable cities and communities (SDG 11).

In turn, quality public infrastructure can help to attract more and better private investment in strategic sectors, such as energy, telecommunications and transport infrastructure – all crucial for developing most economic activities. Investment in telecommunications and transport infrastructure can act as a catalyst for further growth and connectivity, at national and subnational levels, by allowing national and international firms to connect with other regions and integrate in national, regional and global markets. Similarly, quality infrastructure in energy, telecommunications and water can provide better equipment to achieve the digital transformation and the green transition needed in the LAC region.

Public investment in public infrastructure in LAC has remained relatively low (on average) since 2008, although fluctuations throughout the years show it has been particularly sensitive to external shocks. It reached its highest levels in 2009 (2.6% of GDP) and 2012 (2.5% of GDP) but has since been declining due to several factors, including lower commodity prices and limited fiscal space. In 2021, public investment in infrastructure represented 1.6% of LAC's GDP. The largest investments were in the transport sector (0.8% of GDP), followed by energy (0.3%), telecommunications (0.25%) and water (0.2%) (Figure 2.5, Panel A).

In general, transport infrastructure accounts for the largest public investment in the LAC region, with Bolivia (2.85%), Panama (2.2%) and Nicaragua (2.1%) showing the largest investments as a percentage of GDP in 2019. Energy received the second-largest share of investment, followed by telecommunications, leaving water receiving the lowest levels. With the single exception of Bolivia (1.12% of GDP), all LAC countries invested less than 1% of GDP in water infrastructure in 2019 (Figure 2.5, Panel B).

Figure 2.5. **Public investment in infrastructure in LAC as a percentage of GDP, 2008-21**

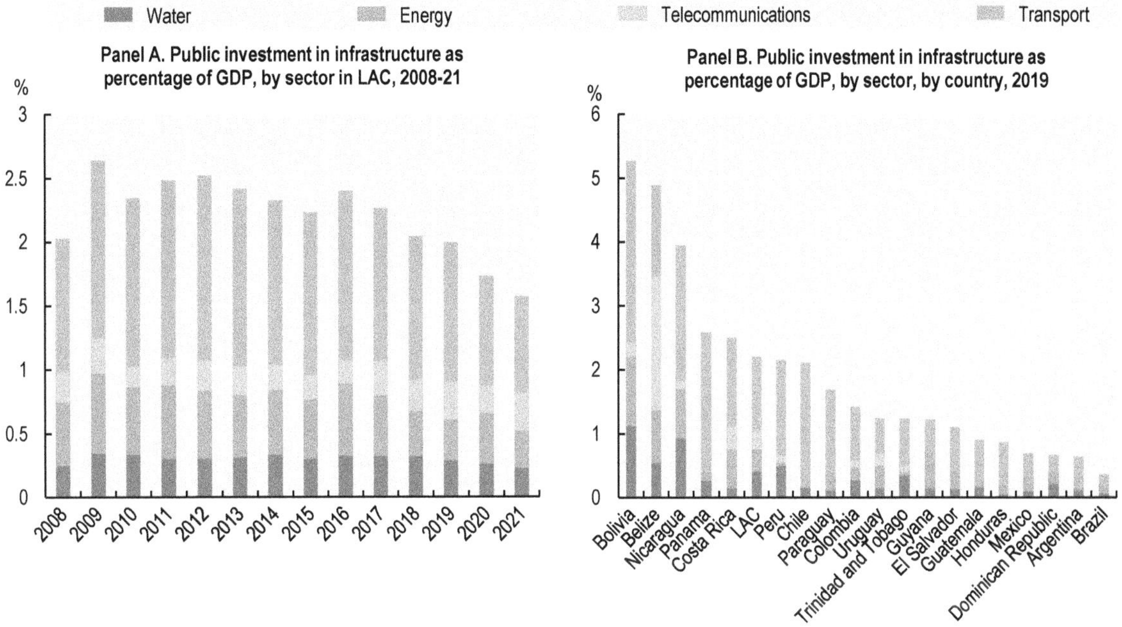

Note: See Methodological Annex for Panel B. Data from different countries were used depending on the sector and the year. Details provided in the source.
Source: (Infralatam, 2022[15]).

StatLink https://stat.link/nao149

Most of the public investment in infrastructure in LAC is directed towards the road subsector. In 11 of 20 LAC countries analysed, road investments represented more than half of public investment in infrastructure and exceeded 60% in Honduras (78%), Paraguay (77%), Guatemala (74%), Peru (66%) and Panama (64%) (Figure 2.6). For transportation to be sustainable, further public investment is necessary in sectors other than roads (section on sustainable transportation).

To ensure that the production transformation increases citizens' well-being and better aligns the region with the SDGs by 2030, governments in LAC need to increase substantially both the levels and the quality of investment in public infrastructure. To close the gap between current levels of investment and those necessary to achieve the 2030 SDGs, the LAC region will need an estimated investment of USD 2.22 trillion in public infrastructure – the equivalent of USD 282 per capita per year by 2030 (IDB, 2021[16]).

Figure 2.6. **Public investment in infrastructure in LAC as a percentage of total investment, 2019**

By subsector, by country

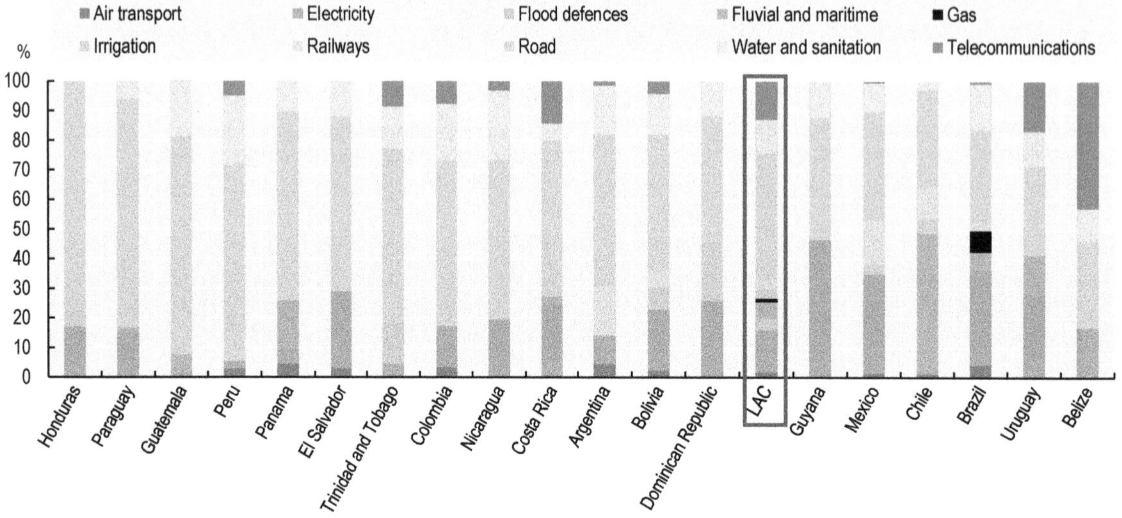

Note: Sectors under consideration (including water, transportation, energy and telecommunications) centre primarily around infrastructure services and essential utilities. As such, infrastructure investment related to oil and gas production, oil refinement and petrochemistry is excluded. Social infrastructure is also excluded (e.g. schools, hospitals, dwellings and security infrastructure). Telecommunications represents fixed-line telephone services, mobile and satellite telephony, and data and internet connection services. The other sectors are subdivided into subsectors. Water includes water and sanitation (drinking water supply through the grid, provision of sanitation services); flood defences (urban and rural projects for mitigating the effects of flooding); and irrigation (facilities and systems of artificial irrigation). Transport includes roads and paths; urban mass transportation; railway transportation (infrastructure and rolling stock); air transport; and fluvial and maritime transportation. Energy includes generation, transmission and distribution of electricity; and transmission and distribution of natural gas.

Source: (Infralatam, 2022[15]).

StatLink https://stat.link/lhrent

A sustainable transport sector is fundamental to boosting structural change

Achieving sustainable transport in LAC is challenged by the current public investment bias towards roads in the transport sector. In 2019, for example, the region's average investment for roads was 42.3% of total investment in infrastructure, while for railways it was only 3.4%. Considering environmental conditions, distances and socio-economic needs, public investment urgently needs to increase in areas of transport other than roads. To make transport inclusive and sustainable, investment in roads must be complemented by investment in sustainable public transport and electrification of the different types of transportation (OECD et al., 2022[17]).

More and better investment in transport connectivity will also prove crucial, as the condition of available transport infrastructure has direct impacts on the ability to attract new investments and on developing potential trade relations among countries in the region. As it also supports extension of commercial connectivity among the local territories of each country, quality transport infrastructure can expand and strengthen the production transformation (CAF, 2021[18]).

Inland waterways and maritime transport received the LAC region's second-largest share (5.4% of total investment) of public investment in transport infrastructure in 2019, with Chile, Panama and Uruguay having the highest investments in this subsector (Infralatam, 2022[15]). In South America, maritime transport accounted for approximately 95% of total foreign trade operations, making it the subregion's dominant mode of transportation. This is being driven by the increased share in total trade of agricultural and mining goods, which demand port infrastructure for handling bulk cargo. In Mexico and Central America, maritime transport is also the primary mode (48%) of transportation for international trade, followed by road transport (42%). Maritime transport can boost production transformation by connecting the LAC region's products with potential markets overseas. Ports, however, represent a particular challenge: Europe has 45% more maritime connectivity than the average of selected LAC countries. Key strategies for improving maritime transport in LAC include: investing in better port infrastructure; ensuring complementarity in port improvements; reducing vessel waiting times; and embracing the digitalisation of logistic procedures (CAF, 2021[18]).

Within the transport sector in LAC, the smallest shares of public investment (on average) have gone to air transport (only 0.04% of GDP) and railways (0.08% of GDP) (Infralatam, 2022[15]). In South America in 2018, air transport and railways together represented less than 1% of total foreign trade operations, well below the 10% directed to railways in North and Central America (ECLAC, 2019[19]). Governments in the region should continue exploring the benefits of promoting these means of transport. Boosting investment in sustainable railway infrastructure could, for example, provide a cheaper and more sustainable means of transport for exporting goods by connecting different stages of strategic value chains. Regarding air transport, closer collaboration with the private commercial airline sector could help to expand export capacity for certain products without causing fleet multiplication and additional impacts on the environment.

To address the rising energy-related greenhouse gas (GHG) emissions in LAC driven by the transport sector, governments must prioritise environmentally responsible investment in transport infrastructure. Future investments represent an opportunity to advance infrastructure that: promotes public and electric transport over private mobility; and is adapted to its environment, respecting local communities and wildlife. Notably, urban passenger and freight transport demand in the LAC region currently outpaces global averages: by 2050, passenger demand is projected to increase by 3.5 times and freight demand by 1.9 times (OECD et al., 2022[17]). Long-term planning is crucial to clarify actions and secure funding for transport decarbonisation, particularly in light of constrained public funding and the potential of private sector involvement and international funding options (Chapter 5) (ITF and IADB, 2022[20]).

Enabling investment in telecommunications

LAC governments should mobilise additional public and private investment in telecommunications to advance a sustainable and inclusive development model. While most LAC countries lag behind the OECD average in broadband access, recent progress in availability, usage and skills has been observed in Costa Rica, Suriname, Brazil and Colombia (OECD and IDB, 2016[21]). Investment in telecommunications that increases the levels of coverage can extend the benefits of the production transformation across territories and jurisdictions. It can also increase well-being dimensions such as access to health and education (OECD et al., 2020[22]; IDB, 2023[23]). Investment in R&D is a key complementary area for fostering innovation and digital transformation (Chapter 3).

The level of public investment in telecommunications in LAC is currently low: in 2019, it stood at less than 1% of GDP in almost every country. To close the digital gap between LAC and OECD countries, mobilising further private investment for telecommunications will be crucial. An estimated USD 68 billion will be needed to enlarge mobile and fixed broadband coverage to the necessary level (IDB, 2022[24]). In 2021, the telecommunications industry's gross sales constituted approximately 2.1% of GDP in several LAC countries, including Argentina (1.8%), Brazil (1.5%), Chile (2%), Colombia (2.1%), Mexico (2%), Paraguay (2.9%) and Uruguay (2.5%) (IDB, 2023[23]).

LAC governments have a crucial responsibility to work more closely with the private sector to maximise the socioeconomic benefits of digital transformation. Constant co-ordination between the public and private sectors, a well-established business framework, administrative simplification, and stronger and credible institutions could ensure that investments in telecommunications infrastructure provide a source of knowledge and technology transfer, thereby delivering benefits to both urban and rural areas throughout the region (Chapter 3) (OECD et al., 2020[22]). Implementing a sustainable and inclusive expansion of broadband internet in LAC could not only create more jobs and improve the productivity and efficiency of the public sector but also strengthen health and educational services, facilitate access to cultural content, and promote the preservation of natural and cultural patrimony (Atlantic Council, 2023[25]; IDB, 2022[24]).

Fifth-generation (5G) mobile networks could help to close the urban-rural gap and advance a sustainable and inclusive development model. Notably, 5G mobile networks provide high connection speeds with faster deployment at lower costs. Their deployment could reduce disparities of access in medium- or low-density areas in both large cities and small towns or villages (ECLAC, 2022[26]). To date, however, 5G deployment has been slow in the region, with a penetration rate of just 12% projected for 2025. The investment in capital goods required to roll out these networks in six countries – Argentina, Brazil, Chile, Colombia, Mexico and Peru – would range from USD 50.8 billion to USD 120.07 billion by 2030, depending on whether deployment takes place only in more highly populated areas or nationwide. This implies that telecommunications service operators would have to increase their annual capital expenditures by 10% to 40% (ECLAC, 2021[27]).

The strategic water sector needs further investment

The water sector, and all of its subsectors, requires further and more strategic investment as it is closely linked with human development. In 2019, the largest share of water investment went to the water and sanitation subsector, but the regional average remains low (11.6% of total investment in infrastructure). While LAC has multiple sources of potentially potable water, a pressing need exists for further investment to ensure equitable access, which is vital for development, reducing inequalities, enhancing global food security and alleviating poverty. Currently, 34% of Latin American households rely on bottled water as their main water source; of those connected to water networks, 41% reported having insufficient potable water (IDB, 2022[28]).

The water sanitation subsector requires comprehensive capacity building that combines physical infrastructure investment with institutional development to address knowledge gaps, staffing issues and obsolete infrastructure. Additionally, to foster well-functioning institutions that support effective investments in water development, it is crucial to create stable and sufficient revenue sources at sub-national levels while considering various financing challenges associated with the different water cycles (services, ecosystems and natural resources) (OECD, 2012[29]). Moreover, improving the quantity and quality of investment in the water and sanitation subsector could help LAC governments move closer to SDG 6.1, which aims to achieve universal access to safe drinking water, with an emphasis on safely managed access.

The situation is similar in the irrigation and flood defences subsector, closely linked to the production transformation. In 2019, only 3.24% of total infrastructure investment in LAC went to irrigation and 4.05% to flood defences (Infralatam, 2022[15]). Both of these subsectors are crucial to limiting the impacts of climate change in strategic sectors, such as the sustainable agro-livestock industry. Better irrigation systems could help fight the consequences of droughts in rural areas, while better flood defences could help avoid the consequences of flooding in areas dedicated to sustainable fish cultivation.

In coastal countries, sustainable investment in maritime infrastructure can bring multiple benefits to the surrounding communities and environment. Construction of sustainable coastlines can directly boost strategic sectors such as sustainable fishery and tourism, while platforms for wind power projects can foster the generation of renewable energy. In 2018, ocean services contributed USD 25 billion to total GDP for LAC as a whole, and USD 7 billion for Caribbean countries alone (OECD et al., 2022[17]).

Boosting investment requires good public governance and transparency

Governments have a central role in creating an environment conducive to investment through good public governance. This requires a mix of co-ordinated policy efforts, as described by the OECD Policy Framework for Investment (Box 2.2) (OECD, 2015[5]).

Box 2.2. The OECD Policy Framework for Investment

The OECD Policy Framework for Investment (PFI) is a comprehensive tool for evaluating and enhancing the investment climate in a country. It covers ten policy areas: investment policy; trade policy; competition policy; taxation; corporate governance; business conduct; human resource development; infrastructure; financing; and public governance.

Under the PFI, key pillars for ensuring good and efficient public governance include quality regulation, transparency, openness and integrity. These dimensions span issues such as improving regulatory frameworks; administrative simplification; regulatory impact assessments; regulatory compliance and enforcement; governance and institutional structure; regulatory coherence across levels of government and jurisdictions; open government; public integrity and public procurement. The PFI also covers conflict-of-interest management, application enforcement and review of anti-corruption laws and regulations as well as international anti-corruption and integrity standards and initiatives. Having effective measures in place for all of these can significantly enhance investor confidence.

Regulatory frameworks and public integrity play a pivotal role in shaping the investment climate. Regulations that are poorly conceived or weakly enforced can obstruct market entry, drain resources that could be better invested elsewhere, limit job growth and generally discourage investment. Investor confidence in regulation is perhaps bolstered most strongly by the assurance of stability and the understanding that the rules are effective in meeting their intended goals. The quality of public services, determined both by internal government regulations and by those imposed on private sector providers, greatly impacts the investment climate. From an investor's perspective, regulatory policy should deliver clear directives and standards for governmental officials, as well as clearly defining what investors can anticipate in terms of government regulation.

Source: OECD Policy Framework for Investment (OECD, 2015[5]).

Governments need to be trustworthy and transparent to attract investments. This is particularly true for infrastructure, as these are usually long-term investments that require a predictable and stable horizon. Political certainty, trustworthiness and an integrity culture help to encourage confidence among investors that the country's policies, regulations and contracts will be honoured and that any changes will be consulted on and implemented fairly and predictably. These elements reduce potential risks for investors and enhance the country's reputation as a secure place to do business (OECD, 2015[5]). Transparency ensures that investors have access to the information they need to make informed decisions. This includes information about the country's laws, regulations, economic indicators and specific investment opportunities. Transparency can also help to ensure that investments are applied efficiently and effectively, rather than misallocated or misused whether due to corruption or negligence.

The adoption of a transparency normative framework, such as "access to information" acts and regular exercises of accountability, can serve as a positive sign for potential investors from the private sector (OECD, 2015[5]). Governments could strengthen trust among stakeholders by encouraging fiscal transparency, access to information on how projects and investments are assigned, and asset disclosure.

Transparent public procurement at national and local levels can also reassure stakeholders from the private sector and civil society. By aiming for efficient, effective, economic and accountable processes of procurement, governments can help to prevent misuse of funds, increase customer satisfaction and promote better services (OECD, 2015[5]). The OECD Recommendation on Public Procurement highlights the importance of ensuring transparency throughout the procurement process, both by providing clear and fair conditions for potential suppliers and by enabling access to updated information for everyone (OECD, 2015[30]).

Policy coherence can ensure that the investment mobilised helps to achieve the SDGs and the objectives of sustainable and inclusive production transformation. Given the long timeframe of infrastructure investment, it is also crucial to align the objectives of public infrastructure with those of national development and investment plans. Moreover, given the number of stakeholders involved in the financing and implementation of infrastructure projects, active co-operation among all relevant jurisdictions will be needed to ensure inclusive and participative policy design (Chapter 4).

Investment regulatory frameworks should aim not only to increase participation of the private sector but also ensure the generation of positive externalities in the surrounding communities and environment. To achieve this, regulations should include a number of strategic elements.

First, the design of the regulatory framework for infrastructure should promote competition among investors, which in turn could generate more innovation and sustainable methods of production. The new regulations should aim to assure clarity and transparency, enabling investors to plan their investments over long-term periods. Similarly, a clear distribution of responsibilities among stakeholders for each investment can help to avoid future conflicts or create additional costs. Finally, efforts to achieve vertically harmonised regulations in line with similar national, regional and international frameworks could avoid duplication of processes and provide more clarity (OECD et al., 2020[22]). Similarly, horizontal harmonisation of regulations across investment, trade and fiscal systems could also prove beneficial to boost production and avoid tax evasion.

Up-to-date and reliable data are also crucial for understanding the needed investment and for mobilising private investment towards strategic sectors. LAC currently suffers a lack of information on issues such as: which private investors will invest or are already investing in which sectors; how much they are investing; and under what conditions. Governments will need to strengthen their collaboration with the private sector and academia to promote easy access to relevant databases and ensure efficient use of the resources already deployed. Good data are essential for sound cost-benefit analyses and successful promotion of investment.

Voluntary government-led initiatives, such as contract guidelines and data partnerships, can enhance access to and sharing of data. The Netherlands' Dare-2-Share Co-operation Agreement is a good example of how collaboration among stakeholders can help define legal standards and references to assist entrepreneurs in establishing trustworthy and transparent agreements during the phase of collaboration in innovation, allowing data exchange between large and small businesses. Similarly, Digital Hub Denmark promotes exchange between the public and private sectors to mutually enrich their data sets. In LAC, a regional effort is the Caribbean Open Institute, which encourages open development approaches to inclusion, participation and innovation, using open data as a catalyst (OECD, 2019[31]). Reliable information about strategic sectors can facilitate the analysis of potential investments, while up-to-date information on current infrastructure can strengthen the policy-making process and attract private investors. Box 2.3 presents an example of a partnership between the public and academic sectors to improve statistical measurement in infrastructure.

Box 2.3. **From Mexico, a guide for strengthening statistical measurement of infrastructure**

Detailed and reliable information is necessary for clear measurement of infrastructure investments. This information should cover every jurisdiction, from national to local infrastructure.

A Mexican initiative offers an example of a partnership between the public and academic sectors that aims to improve data on infrastructure. The country's National Institute of Statistics and Geography (INEGI for its initials in Spanish) and the University Programme of Development Studies at the National Autonomous University of Mexico (UNAM) collaborated to develop a step-by-step guide to strengthening national measurement systems for public infrastructure.

In line with this guide, governments could benefit from efforts to:

- collect, organise and build existing infrastructure databases
- choose and adopt a definition of infrastructure to better delineate the extent and type of information that should be collected
- prioritise the main sectors to be included in the measurement and assign the research to experts who know the particularities of each sector
- decide whether measurement of public infrastructure will be done in physical terms (e.g. number of km) or monetary terms (e.g. as a percentage of GDP)
- choose between the two main methodologies – i.e. the perpetual inventory system and the common inventory method – for evaluating the efficiency of the sums invested
- engage in peer learning exercises to learn from successful cases.

Regarding methodology, the perpetual inventory system has proven to be the most widely used form of valuation as it allows construction of capital stock data taking account of investment flows. The main information to be gathered is capital investment data in constant prices and the economic lifetime of each asset. After estimating the consumption of fixed capital and specifying its depreciation, it is possible to move from a stock of gross capital to a stock of net capital.

Regarding peer learning, an interesting example comes from Canada, where the government developed an Infrastructure Statistical Hub, with statistical information on the amount of investment, type of assets, economic contribution and environmental impact.

Note: Additional considerations for the measurement of the perpetual inventory system are included in the original recommendation.

Source: (INEGI, 2023[32]).

Good governance of the LAC region's infrastructure is crucial to ensuring that investment in infrastructure, both public and private, brings well-being to the citizens without harming the surrounding environment and wildlife. Recommendations from the OECD on the governance of infrastructure provide detailed guidance for countries (Box 2.4).

Box 2.4. OECD recommendations on the governance of infrastructure

The OECD recommendations on the governance of infrastructure cover ten priority areas.

Of special interest for LAC is a recommendation inviting countries to promote a coherent, predictable and efficient regulatory framework. It encourages governments to identify their main policy goals and to complement them, if necessary, with new regulations and additional means to find the best approach to promote their objectives. The recommendation also suggests including relevant stakeholders in the design and implementation of new regulations, from representatives of different levels of government to relevant stakeholders, such as the private sector. The OECD highlights the importance of implementing systematic reviews of existing regulations to ensure their validity and of promoting good governance practices such as transparency and accountability, among others.

Another recommendation of interest for LAC invites countries to promote evidence-informed decision making. It suggests identifying and clearly allocating institutional responsibilities for collecting, processing and disseminating reliable data, and calls for establishing systems that gather relevant information throughout the entire life cycle of an infrastructure project. The recommendation highlights the need to harness digital technologies and data analytics "to reduce administrative burdens, increase transparency, understand performance, inform decision making and take preventive actions" to respond to risks.

The OECD recommendations also call for:

1. adopting a long-term vision
2. guarding fiscal sustainability, affordability and value for money
3. ensuring efficient and effective procurement of infrastructure projects
4. ensuring transparent, systematic and effective stakeholder participation
5. co-ordinating infrastructure policy across levels of government
6. implementing a whole-of-government approach to manage threats to integrity
7. making sure the asset performs throughout its life
8. strengthening critical infrastructure resilience.

The main governance messages in Chapter 4 provide further details on the OECD recommendations.

Source: (OECD, 2020[33]).

Effective PPPs can help boost investment in public infrastructure in LAC

Governments across the LAC region can harness PPPs as a powerful tool to accelerate the development of strategic sectors that are pivotal for a production transformation. The evolution of PPPs for public infrastructure projects in LAC as a percentage of the region's GDP has oscillated in recent years, with the largest share in 2012 (1.3%) and the lowest in 2018 (0.32%) (Figure 2.7). In 2021, LAC's share of PPPs for public infrastructure (0.46% of GDP) was larger than those of Sub-Saharan Africa (0.31%), South Asia (0.26%), East Asia and the Pacific (0.16%), and the Middle East and North Africa (0.05%), and was only slightly surpassed by Europe and Central Asia (0.47%) (World Bank, 2021[34]). Between 2009 and 2022, 94.5% of the active or concluded infrastructure projects in LAC were conducted by private parties having at least a 60% participation in the project contract (World Bank, 2023[35]).

Figure 2.7. **PPPs for public infrastructure projects in LAC as a percentage of GDP, 2010-21**

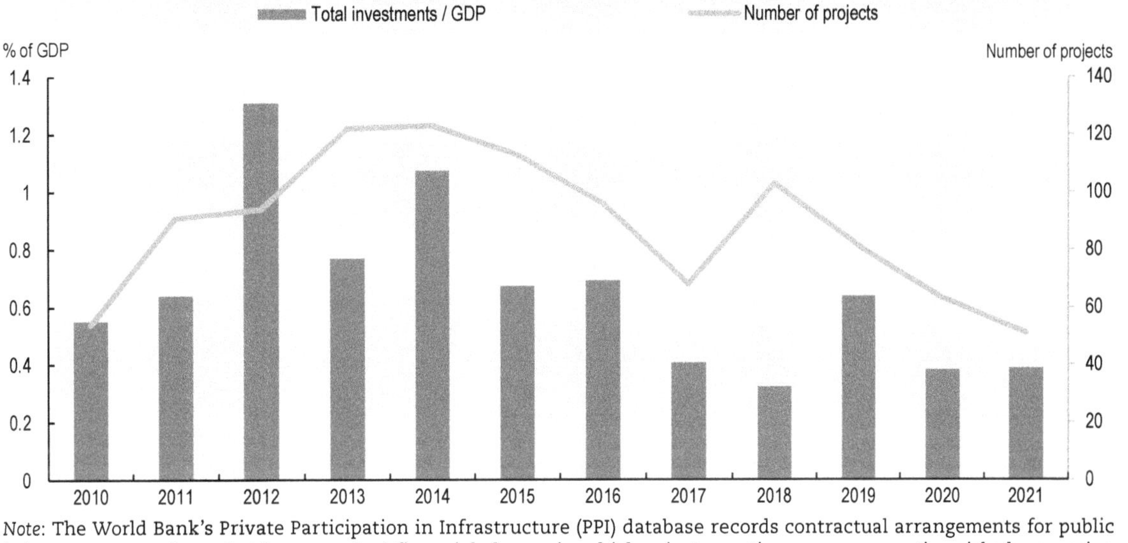

Note: The World Bank's Private Participation in Infrastructure (PPI) database records contractual arrangements for public infrastructure projects that have reached financial closure in which private parties assume operating risks by covering projects with at least a 20% private ownership stake (except for divestitures, which are included with at least a 5% stake) and may include public participation. The World Bank's estimation of the percentage of GDP considers all kinds of projects, including those interrupted and cancelled. "Total Investment" is the sum of investment in physical assets and payments to the government; it is recorded in millions of USD. The World Bank Indicator "GDP at current USD" was used to build the ratio with the total investments variable.

Source: Authors' elaboration based on (World Bank, 2023[35]); (World Bank, 2023[36]).

StatLink https://stat.link/jvo346

The evolution of the total number of infrastructure projects in LAC has followed the trend of PPP as a percentage of GDP (Figure 2.7). This tendency applies as well to the types of projects that normally receive funding, indicating that room exists for diversification. In 2022, the majority of 80 active or concluded infrastructure projects with private participation in LAC took place in Brazil (more than 64%), followed – at much lower shares – by Colombia (11%) and Peru (9%). The fewest such projects took place in Jamaica, El Salvador, Mexico and Paraguay, with only 1 PPP each (1.25%) (World Bank, 2023[35]). Most PPP investment in LAC is directed toward the energy sector (67.5% of total projects), followed by the transport sector (26.25%). The least-funded sectors are water and sewerage (5%) and municipal solid waste (1.25%). To cite the value of one instance, the use of PPPs in water management in Cartagena, Colombia, substantially improved service quality by expanding water supply coverage and providing access to piped water (World Bank, 2016[37]; OECD, 2009[38]).

The increasing adoption of PPPs in LAC over the past decade reflects progress in the region's regulatory, institutional and economic climate. An analysis of the environment for PPPs in 21 LAC countries showed that, by 2019, 14 had established markets for undertaking PPPs, up from just five in 2014. Additionally, it showed that partnerships were established in sectors ranging from conventional areas (such as transport, energy and water) to more innovative areas (e.g. government offices, health care, sports and justice) (EIU, 2019[39]). Progress over the last decade is also evident in that 16 countries set up agencies dedicated to promoting, supervising and providing technical assistance for PPPs (Economist Impact, 2022[40]). Notably, Chile, Colombia, Costa Rica, Mexico and Peru adhered to the OECD Recommendation on Principles for Public Governance of Public-Private Partnerships. However, while political endorsement of private investment in infrastructure development is increasing, areas for improvement remain, including enhanced transparency, accountability and sustainable practices.

Elements that create an enabling environment for PPPs in a country include regulations and institutions; project preparation and sustainability; financing; risk management and contract monitoring; and performance evaluation and impact (Economist Impact, 2022[40]).

Although some LAC countries have shown strong improvements in adherence to PPP regulations and have more robust financial capacities, significant regional disparities exist in project preparation and sustainability. Notably, substantial gaps exist in the management of PPPs, with improvements needed in risk management, project monitoring, and assessment of the economic and social impacts of operational PPPs (Figure 2.8) (Economist Impact, 2022[40]).

Figure 2.8. **Key aspects that determine a country's readiness and capacity to implement PPPs**

Infrascope Index, 2021/22

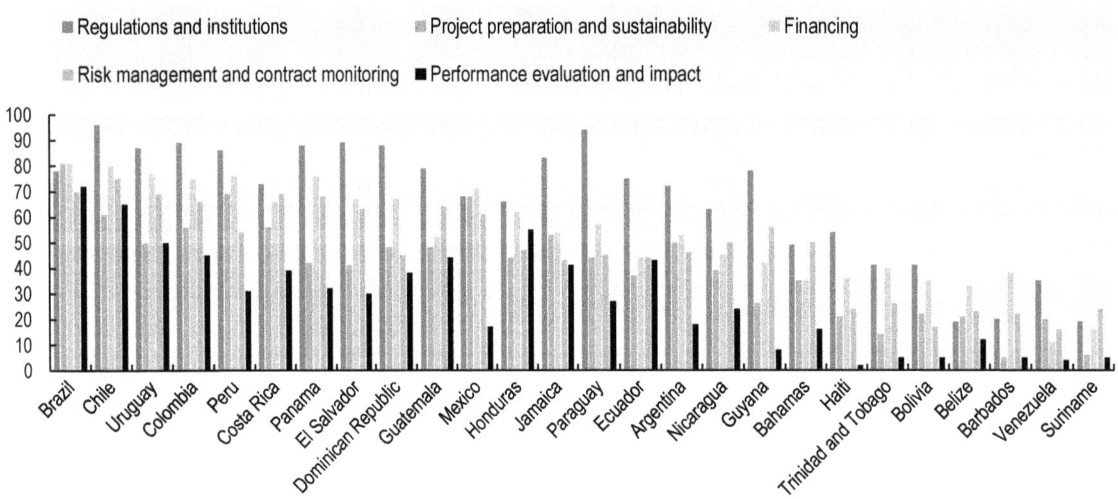

Note: Scores from 0 to 100, where 100 = best. The countries are ordered according to their overall score, from highest to lowest.

Source: (Economist Impact, 2022[40]).

StatLink https://stat.link/kvx4o1

Successful implementation of PPPs depends on underlying regulatory and institutional factors. Institutional inadequacy, uncertainty posed by political instability, endemic corruption and hurdles in long-term financing have presented significant difficulties for the deployment of effective PPPs in some LAC countries. Weak state institutions, unclear legislation and deficient contract design, for example, have allowed for frequent and costly renegotiation of road concessions (Bitrán, Nieto Parra and Robledo, 2013[41]). There is thus a substantial risk of inefficiencies such as poor project selection, cost overruns, delays and misallocated risk distribution. These factors contribute to an investment environment that discourages effective private-sector participation, further undermining the development of PPPs in LAC (CAF, 2018[42]).

Addressing these concerns requires a robust regulatory framework characterised by transparency, capacity building and political stability (Engel, Fischer and Galetovic, 2021[43]). Regulatory clarity and consistency ensure investor confidence, and thus the longevity of PPPs, while integrity and transparent processes mitigate the risk of corruption and enhance value for money. Essential to the success of PPPs is the ability of governments to build technical expertise for the design, implementation and oversight of such projects. Moreover, political stability, marked by the honouring of contracts across political cycles, can bolster an environment conducive to long-term investment in PPPs.

Citizen participation in PPPs fosters transparency, accountability and social inclusion (World Bank, 2019[44]). In turn, it enhances the credibility of the partnership by allowing for the incorporation of diverse perspectives, thereby contributing to more effective and inclusive decision making (Chapter 4). Moreover, public involvement improves the social acceptability of projects, reduces the risk of public backlash and can contribute to identifying local needs, ultimately leading to better targeted and more sustainable solutions. Efforts should be made to enhance citizens' capacity to engage meaningfully in these processes, ensuring that citizen participation leads to tangible impact rather than being a mere formality (ECLAC, 2020[45]).

Given the long-term framework of infrastructure projects, governments can promote PPPs by establishing regular consultations with representatives from the private sector throughout the investment cycle to ensure against interruptions and prevent potential conflicts. To avoid uncertainties and, in the end, further fiscal costs, well-designed regulatory and institutional frameworks are fundamental to reducing the risk of renegotiation costs.

The share of public investment and the availability of blended finance mechanisms – with de-risking elements offered by national governments – could contribute to encouraging private investors to participate in PPPs (Chapter 5). About 27% (on average) of the active or concluded PPPs in Latin America from 2010 to 2017 received some form of direct or indirect government support. Payment guarantees were the most common (14.4%), followed by tax deductions (10.0%), capital subsidies (7.5%) and revenue subsidies (1.6%) (World Bank, 2023[35]).

If well designed and implemented, PPPs could help LAC governments attract private funding into public infrastructure projects with high social impact and promote innovation, thus contributing to a sustainable and inclusive production model. The public sector currently accounts for the largest share of total public infrastructure investment in the region, with around 33.3% provided by the private sector (IDB, 2022[46]). While private investment in public infrastructure is low in LAC compared with OECD countries, it remains higher than in other developing regions. In terms of percentage of regional GDP, LAC had the highest share of private participation in infrastructure in 2022 (0.53%), above South Asia (0.34%), Sub-Saharan Africa (0.25%), and East Asia and Pacific (0.21%) (World Bank, 2022[47]).

It is important to note that PPPs can sometimes be at odds with environmental considerations, due to the inherent tension between infrastructure development and long-term sustainability goals. Incorporating a comprehensive environmental impact assessment in the planning stages of PPPs is essential to mitigate these potential conflicts (OECD, 2008[48]) (Chapter 4). Robust policy frameworks and enforcement mechanisms are also key to ensuring adherence to environmental regulations, along with the promotion of transparency and stakeholder engagement to guarantee environmentally and socially responsible land use. International partnerships can play an important role in mobilising greater public and private investments that yield greater social impact (Chapter 5).

Enhancing quality foreign direct investment

Although global FDI decreased by 24% in 2022, FDI inflows increased by 55% in LAC, reaching almost USD 225 billion.[1] In relative terms, with inflows equivalent to 4% of GDP, LAC was the top destination for FDI in 2022, a position also held in 2018 and 2020. In 2022, the LAC region was followed by East Asia and Pacific (2.2% of GDP), Middle East and North Africa (2%), North America (1.6%), Sub-Saharan Africa (1.5%), South Asia (1.3%) and the EU (0.6%). The rise in FDI inflows in LAC was driven by a marked interest in services, hydrocarbons and manufactures in the countries with the largest capacities (ECLAC, 2023[49]) (Figure 2.9).

FDI represents a substantial influx of capital for LAC countries compared to the Marshall Plan. FDI to the LAC region represented USD 464 billion between 2017 and 2019, and it decreased slightly to USD 445 billion during the post-COVID, from 2020 to 2022 (ECLAC, 2023[49]; ECLAC, 2023[50]). To put these FDI inflows into perspective, for the periods 2017-19 and 2020-22, FDI represented the equivalent to 290% (USD 464 billion) and 278% (USD 445 billion), respectively, of the financial resources provided by the Marshall Plan to promote Europe's recovery after World War II (USD 13 billion in 1948 equivalent to USD 160 billion in 2022). Similarly, while the Marshall Plan amounted to around 2% of the combined national incomes of the recipient countries between 1948 and 1951 (Eichengreen, 2010[60]), FDI in LAC surpassed 3% of GDP in the periods 2017-19 and 2020-22 (and 4% of GDP in 2022).

Figure 2.9. **FDI inflows as a share of GDP, by region, 2010-22**

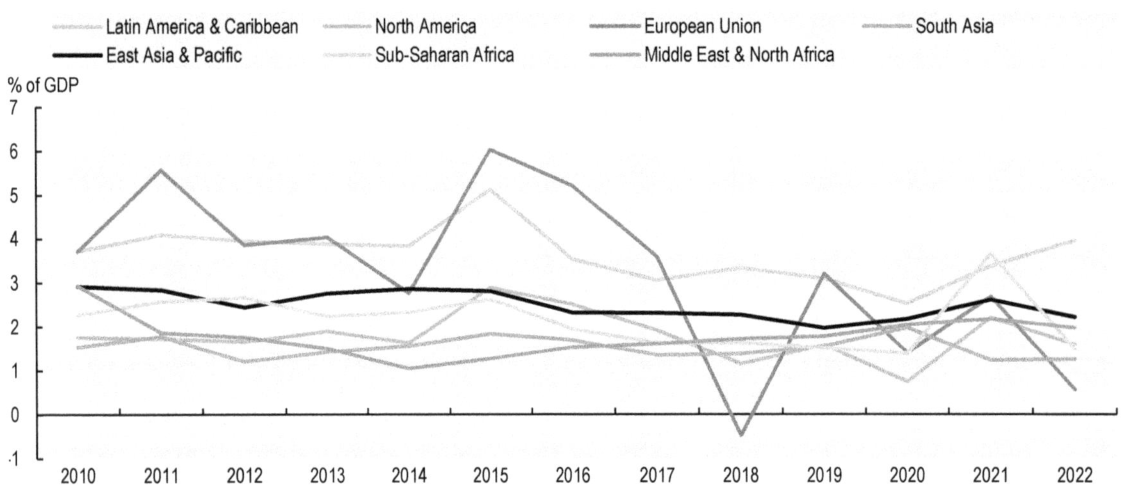

Note: As in (World Bank, 2023[36]), data for each region corresponds to weighted averages. For the LAC region, 37 countries were taken into account with available data for 2022: Antigua and Barbuda, Argentina, Aruba, Bahamas, Barbados, Belize, Bolivia, Brazil, Cayman Islands, Chile, Colombia, Costa Rica, Curacao, Dominica, Dominican Republic, Ecuador, El Salvador, Grenada, Guatemala, Guyana, Haiti, Honduras, Jamaica, Mexico, Nicaragua, Panama, Paraguay, Peru, Saint Kitts and Nevis, Saint Lucia, Saint Vincent and the Grenadines, Saint Maarten, Suriname, Trinidad and Tobago, Turks and Caicos, Uruguay and Venezuela. The latest data available for Aruba, Curacao and Cayman Islands corresponds to 2021, while for Venezuela it corresponds to 2014.

Source: Authors' elaboration based on (World Bank, 2023[36]).

StatLink https://stat.link/6giqkh

More than half of FDI inflows to the LAC region in 2022 went to Brazil and Mexico. In Brazil, the inflow totalled USD 91 billion (41% of LAC FDI) while Mexico received USD 39 billion (17%). For Brazil, the share of FDI exceeded its participation in LAC's GDP

(34%), while for Mexico it was lower (25%). Although FDI inflows received by the region expanded by 55% from 2021 to 2022 – and grew significantly in most subregions, notably in South America (81.8%) – they decreased by 11.9% in Central America (excluding Mexico).[2]

Wide heterogeneity in FDI flows is evident across LAC countries. Uruguay (13.1%), Nicaragua (8.3%), Chile (6.9%) and Costa Rica (5.4%) performed exceptionally well with FDI levels above the LAC average of 4% of GDP. In contrast, the lowest levels of FDI went to Paraguay (1.1%) and Ecuador (0.7%), while Bolivia presented disinvestment, with negative FDI inflows of -0.1% (Figure 2.10).

Figure 2.10. **FDI inflows as a percentage of GDP, selected LAC countries, 2013-22**

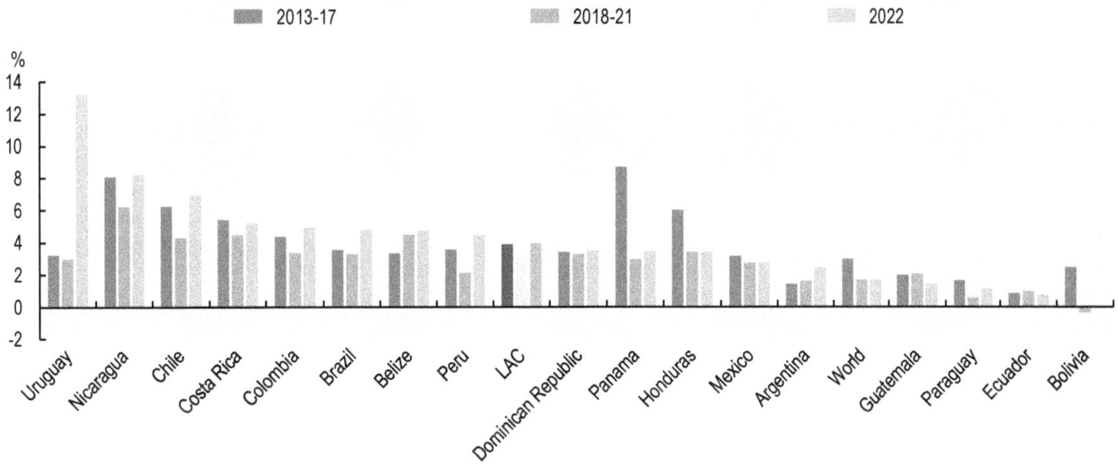

Note: The data for 2013-17 and 2018-21 corresponds to averages over time. As in (World Bank, 2023[36]), the 2022 data for LAC corresponds to a weighted average which includes 33 countries: Antigua and Barbuda, Argentina, Bahamas, Barbados, Belize, Bolivia, Brazil, Chile, Colombia, Costa Rica, Dominica, Dominican Republic, Ecuador, El Salvador, Grenada, Guatemala, Guyana, Haiti, Honduras, Jamaica, Mexico, Nicaragua, Panama, Paraguay, Peru, Saint Kitts and Nevis, Saint Lucia, Saint Vincent and the Grenadines, Sint Maarten, Suriname, Trinidad and Tobago, Turks and Caicos and Uruguay. For Aruba, Curacao and Cayman Islands the latest data available corresponds to 2021, while for Venezuela the latest data available corresponds to 2014.

Source: Authors' elaboration based on (World Bank, 2023[36]).

StatLink https://stat.link/83p2ca

Based on the final destination of investment by FDI project announcements, the EU and the United States of America (USA) are the largest investors in LAC, consistently accounting for more than half of the region's FDIs.[3] In 2022, the top investor was the USA, with 41% of the value of project announcements, followed by the EU (20%). About 8% of FDI in the region originated from LAC countries, followed by the People's Republic of China (hereafter "China") (4%), the United Kingdom (4%) and Canada (2%), while other countries combined accounted for 20%. Although EU investment in LAC decreased in 2022 (by 6 percentage points from 2021), the European Union maintains a strong position as a main FDI partner for LAC over the years (Figure 2.11). Within the European Union, the largest FDI partners from 2013-22 were Spain (9.5%), Germany (5.1%), France (4.3%) and Italy (4.1%).

Figure 2.11. **Origin of FDI project announcements in LAC as a share of total value, 2003-22**

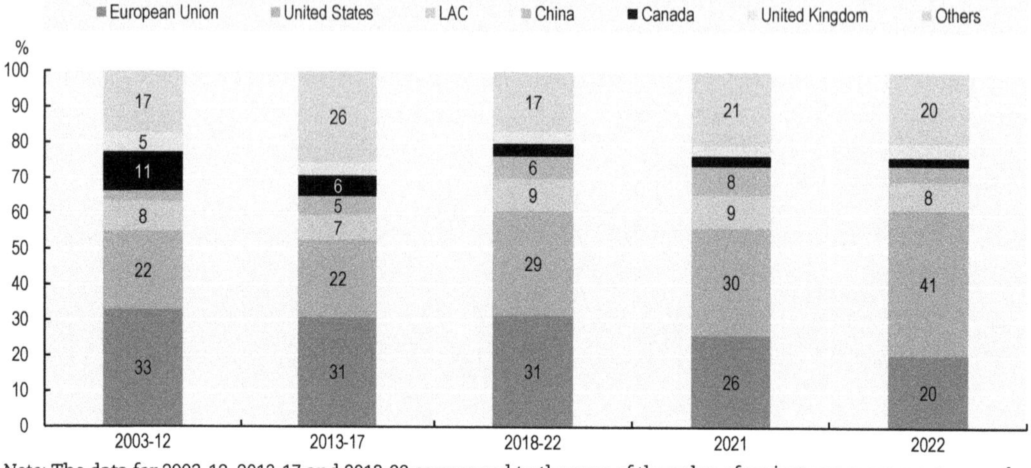

Note: The data for 2003-12, 2013-17 and 2018-22 correspond to the sum of the value of project announcements over the years. The LAC country group includes 27 countries: Antigua and Barbuda, Argentina, Bahamas, Barbados, Belize, Bolivia, Brazil, Chile, Colombia, Costa Rica, Cuba, Dominican Republic, Ecuador, El Salvador, Guatemala, Guyana, Honduras, Jamaica, Mexico, Nicaragua, Panama, Paraguay, Peru, Saint Lucia, Trinidad and Tobago, Uruguay, and Venezuela.
Source: Authors' elaboration based on (fDi Markets, 2023[51]).

StatLink https://stat.link/0pxhco

FDI project announcements in LAC have been concentrated around five key sectors. From January 2003 to May 2023, 47% of the value of FDI projects announced in the region belonged to manufacturing, followed by coal, oil and gas (14%), services (11%), and renewable energy and ICT (10% each) (Figure 2.12, Panel A). In 2022, a slight shift is noticeable with the sectors that received more FDI being manufacturing (45%), coal, oil and gas (23%), renewable energies (11%) and services (8%) (Figure 2.12, Panel B). It is important to note that FDI flows tend to be very volatile. For example, while coal, oil and gas represented only 5% of project announcements in LAC in 2021 (ECLAC, 2022[52]), this sector represented 23% of total announcements in 2022, reflecting two large investment projects in Guyana and Mexico (ECLAC, 2023[49]). For this reason, it is preferable to use a long timeframe for considering project announcements.

Figure 2.12. **Value of FDI project announcements in LAC, distribution by sector**

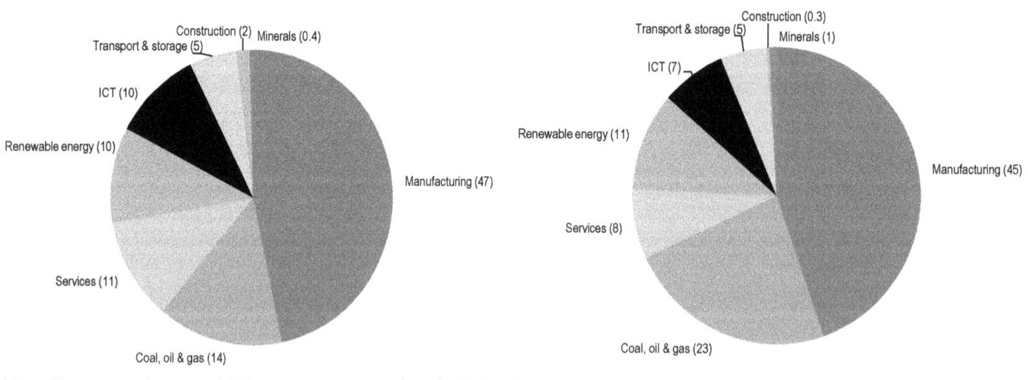

Note: Data cover January 2003 to May 2023. Services includes: business services, financial services, health care, hotels and tourism, and leisure and entertainment. Construction includes: real estate. ICT includes: communications, and software and IT services. The LAC country group includes 27 countries: Antigua and Barbuda, Argentina, Bahamas, Barbados, Belize, Bolivia, Brazil, Chile, Colombia, Costa Rica, Cuba, Dominican Republic, Ecuador, El Salvador, Guatemala, Guyana, Honduras, Jamaica, Mexico, Nicaragua, Panama, Paraguay, Peru, Saint Lucia, Trinidad and Tobago, Uruguay, and Venezuela.
Source: Authors' elaboration based on (fDi Markets, 2023[51]; ECLAC, 2023[49]).

StatLink https://stat.link/tzed9a

Foreign direct investment for better jobs

FDI from the EU and the USA has contributed significantly to formal job creation in the LAC region over the last two decades. In fact, since 2006, investments originating in these two territories have consolidated as the main foreign generators of formal jobs in the region. Investments announced in 2022 coming from the United States are expected to generate almost 108 000 jobs and EU investments 86 000 jobs, followed by Canada (10 000) and China (9 000). FDI originating from LAC countries announced in 2022 is expected to generate around 30 000 jobs (Figure 2.13).

Figure 2.13. **Total formal jobs created by FDI in LAC, by country of origin, 2003-22**

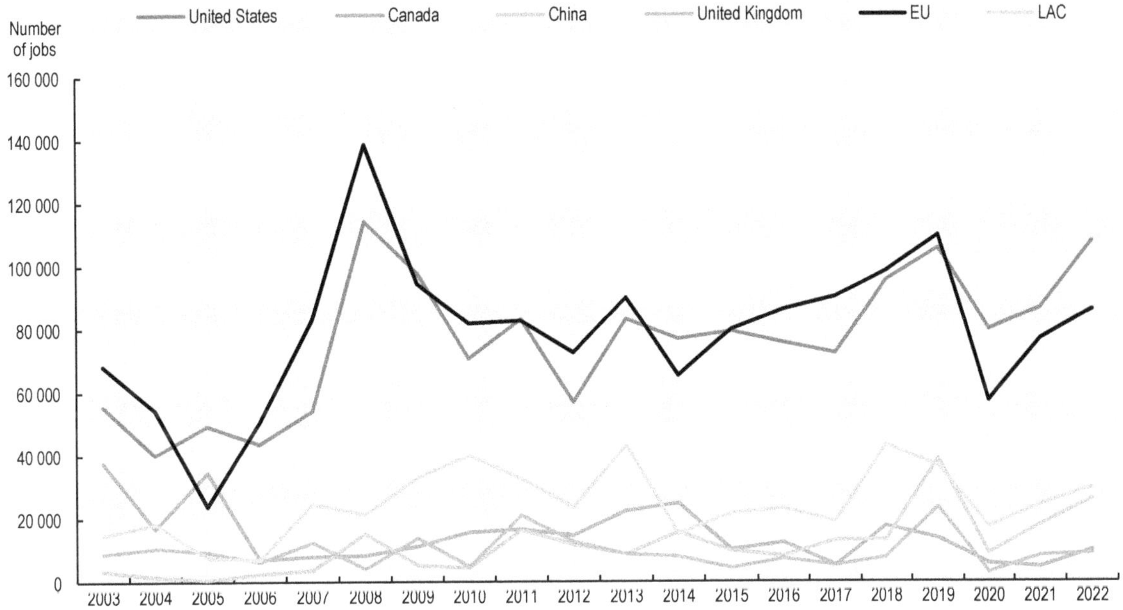

Note: fDi Markets reports how many jobs are expected to be generated from each FDI announcement. The LAC country group includes 27 countries: Antigua and Barbuda, Argentina, Bahamas, Barbados, Belize, Bolivia, Brazil, Chile, Colombia, Costa Rica, Cuba, Dominican Republic, Ecuador, El Salvador, Guatemala, Guyana, Honduras, Jamaica, Mexico, Nicaragua, Panama, Paraguay, Peru, Saint Lucia, Trinidad and Tobago, Uruguay, and Venezuela.

Source: Authors' elaboration based on (fDi Markets, 2023[51]).

StatLink https://stat.link/gkw8m1

At the sectoral level in LAC, the majority of FDI goes to manufacturing and the energy and extraction sectors. Manufacturing has been the top destination sector in the last 20 years, with more than 40% of participation in FDI (Figure 2.14, Panel A). This sector is also first in job generation from FDI in LAC (Figure 2.14, Panel B). For all main partners, the manufacturing sector's participation in jobs generated is higher than its participation in capital invested, showing a high contribution to the economy. The services sector also has a high impact on job generation, especially in the case of investments originating in the European Union and the United States. In contrast, the energy and extraction sector has a small impact on employment, as it has higher participation in capital invested than in jobs generated (for all countries considered). For instance, in the case of the European Union, 31% of the capital is invested in energy and extraction but only 6% of jobs generated are in that sector. In the same vein, 24% of the region's FDI from the United States targeted the energy and extraction sector, but this only created 3% of jobs (Figure 2.14, Panels A and B). Additionally, it's worth noting that FDI in renewable energy results in higher job creation than FDI in fossil fuels. To illustrate, a USD 1 billion investment in fossil fuels generates around 500 new jobs in LAC, while the same investment in renewables creates 800 jobs.

Data can be a powerful tool to broaden the impact of FDI on employment. Knowing precisely what type of operations are run by foreign companies in the LAC region – and the type of skills and capacities they are demanding – could help to guide better labour policies and create new formal jobs.

Figure 2.14. **Capital expenditure and formal jobs created by FDI in LAC, January 2003-May 2023**

By sector and selected countries of origin

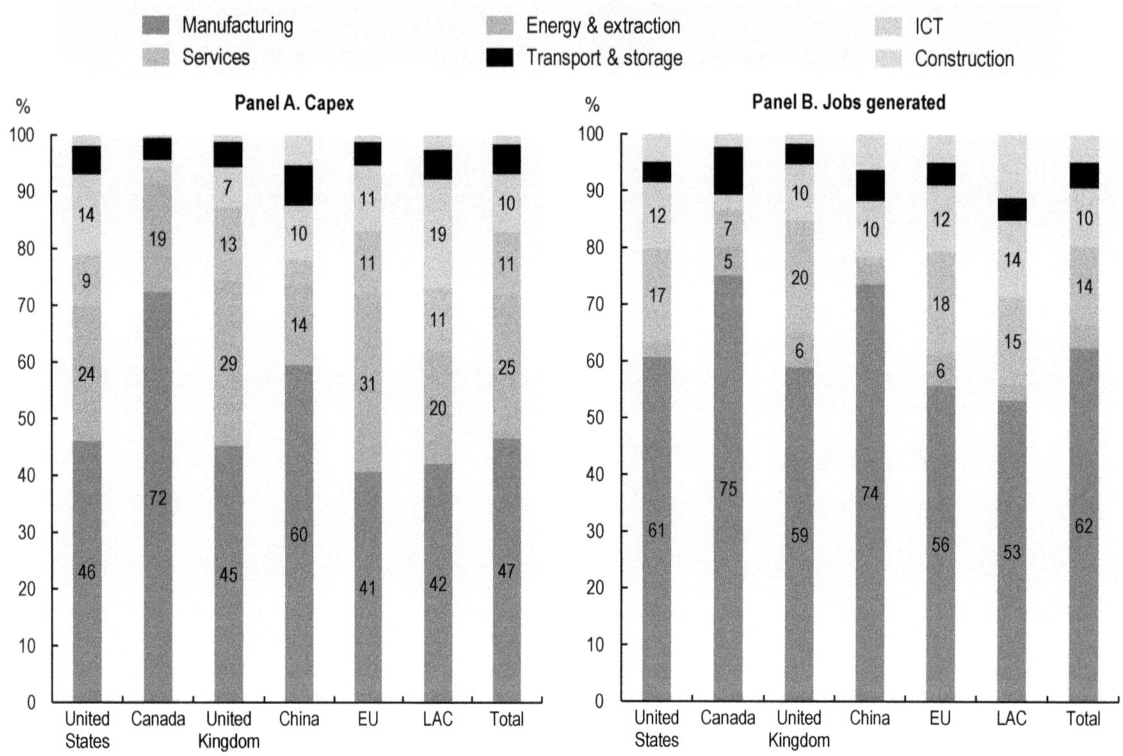

Note: ICT = information and telecommunication technologies. Capex = capital expenditures. Data covers January 2003 to May 2023. Energy and extraction includes: coal, oil and gas; minerals and renewable energy. Services includes: business services, financial services, health care, hotels and tourism, and leisure and entertainment. Construction includes: real estate. ICT includes: communications, and software and IT services. The LAC country group includes 27 countries: Antigua and Barbuda, Argentina, Bahamas, Barbados, Belize, Bolivia, Brazil, Chile, Colombia, Costa Rica, Cuba, Dominican Republic, Ecuador, El Salvador, Guatemala, Guyana, Honduras, Jamaica, Mexico, Nicaragua, Panama, Paraguay, Peru, Saint Lucia, Trinidad and Tobago, Uruguay, and Venezuela.

Source: Authors' elaboration based on (fDi Markets, 2023[51]).

StatLink https://stat.link/i26hkt

FDI could be a source not only of higher employment but also of better quality jobs and the development of human capital (OECD, 2023[53]). The OECD's FDI Qualities Indicators seek to shed light on the extent to which FDI contributes to sustainable development, focusing on productivity and innovation, job quality and skills, gender equality, and the low carbon-transition (OECD, 2019[54]; OECD, 2022[55]).

In the case of the LAC region, the FDI Qualities Indicators show that foreign firms tend to offer higher average wages, suggesting that the enhanced productivity level they enjoy is at least in part transferred to employees (Figure 2.15, Panel A). At the same time, in the majority of Latin American countries considered, foreign firms tend to employ a higher proportion of unskilled workers than domestic firms do and are significantly more likely to offer training opportunities (Figure 2.15, Panels B and C). This suggests that foreign investors are an important source of employment for low-skilled workers in Latin

America and can make a significant contribution to upgrading their skills and increasing their opportunities for future employment. To enhance FDI's contribution to quality job creation, investment promotion efforts in LAC should be aligned with well-defined production development policies that promote economic diversification and with other investment-related policies (OECD et al., 2021[56]; OECD, 2022[1]; OECD, 2022[55]; ECLAC, 2023[49]).

Figure 2.15. **Job-related FDI Qualities Indicators for selected LAC countries, 2019**

Foreign firms perform better than domestic firms if value > 0

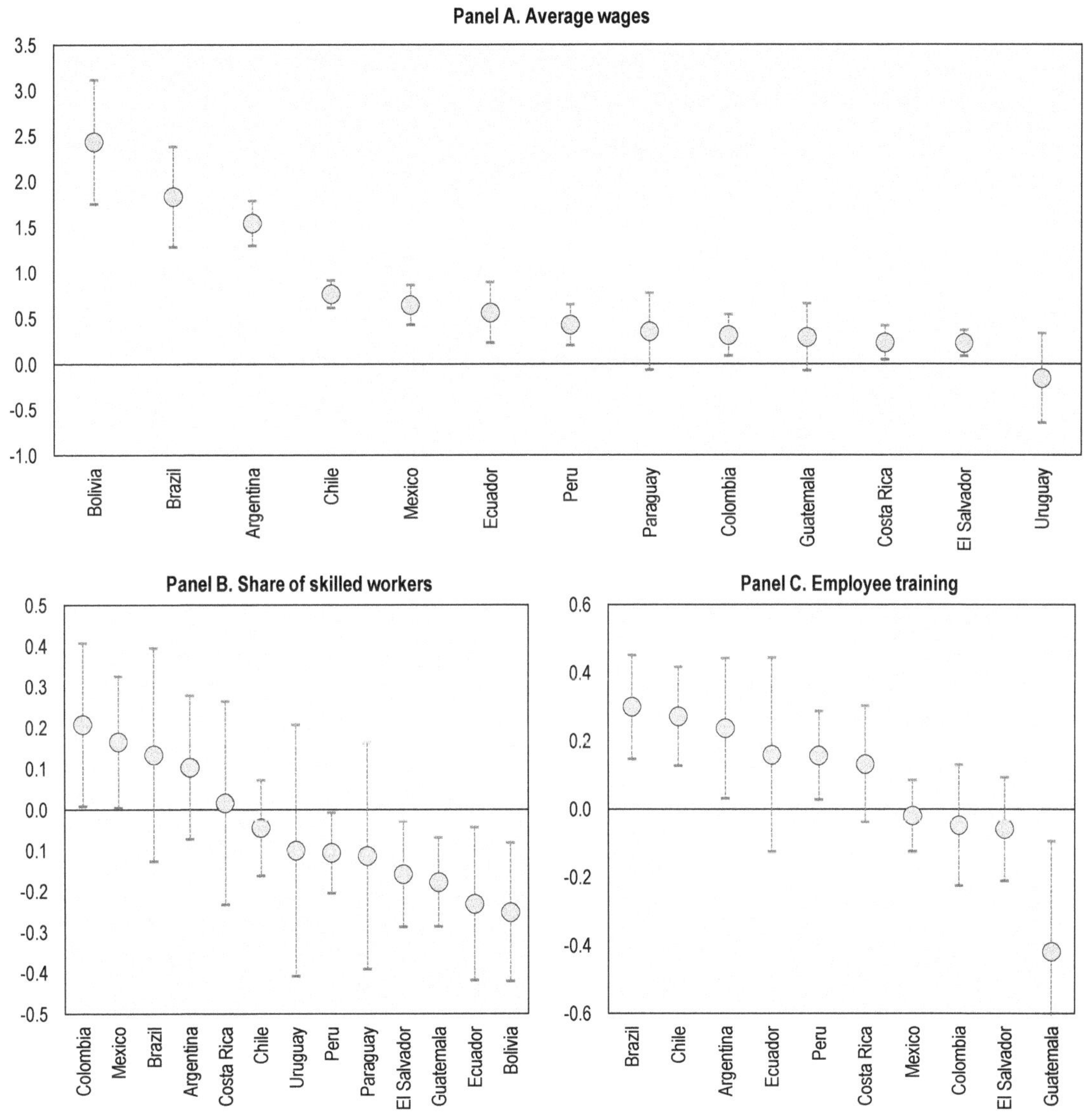

Note: In the figure, the orange dots depict the estimation of the indicator while the dash lines represent the corresponding confidence interval. If the value is >0, foreign firms perform better than domestic firms. Based on 2019 data or the latest.
Source: Based on (OECD et al., 2021[56]; OECD, 2019[54]).

StatLink https://stat.link/290j1c

The impact of FDI on productivity, innovation and environmental sustainability

FDI also has the potential to influence innovation and productivity in the host economies. According to the OECD FDI Qualities Indicators, and across most countries for which data are available, foreign investors are more productive and more likely to introduce product innovation or invest in R&D than domestic firms (Figure 2.16, Panels A-C). This productivity and innovation gap suggests that potential exists for knowledge and technology spillovers from foreign to domestic firms. To maximise the impact of FDI on productivity and innovation, policy objectives must be aligned across government levels and policy areas; this includes co-operation from public institutions at national and subnational levels, and co-ordinating with SMEs to create stronger business linkages and innovation ecosystems (OECD, 2022[1]).

Figure 2.16. **Productivity and innovation: FDI qualities indicators for selected LAC countries, 2019**

Foreign firms perform better than domestic firms if value > 0

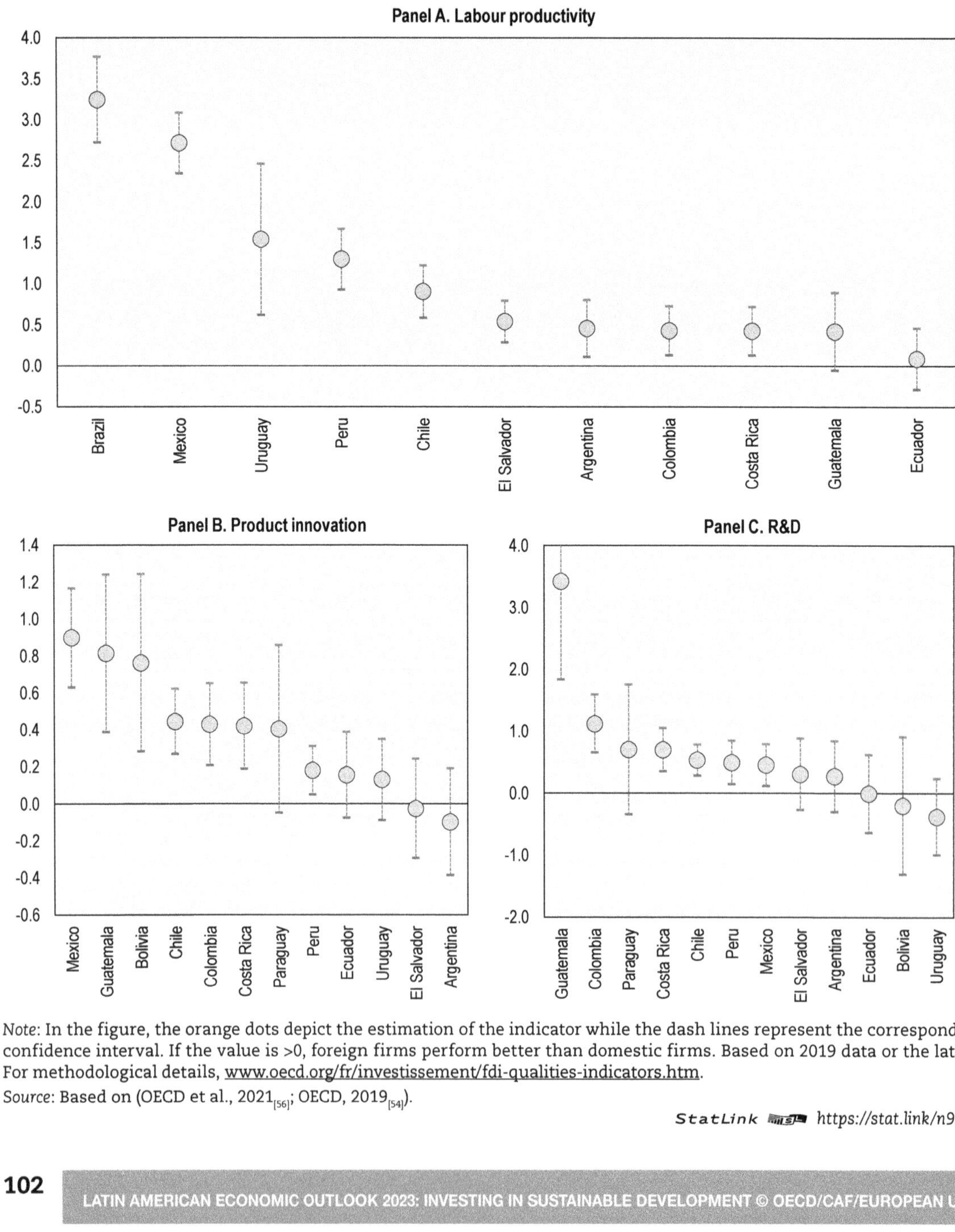

Note: In the figure, the orange dots depict the estimation of the indicator while the dash lines represent the corresponding confidence interval. If the value is >0, foreign firms perform better than domestic firms. Based on 2019 data or the latest. For methodological details, www.oecd.org/fr/investissement/fdi-qualities-indicators.htm.

Source: Based on (OECD et al., 2021[56]; OECD, 2019[54]).

StatLink https://stat.link/n9xfj2

Although FDI shows great potential to contribute to sustainable development, at the aggregate level in most LAC economies, it currently appears more carbon intensive than domestic investment. However, some industries with high emissions per unit of output benefit from the presence of foreign firms with lower carbon intensity.

In terms of the overall economy, foreign firms in LAC economies generate between 4% and 75% more emissions per unit of output than domestic firms (Figure 2.17). Example of places where the differences are greatest – as measured by metric tonnes (Mt) of carbon dioxide (CO_2) emissions per unit of output – include the coke and refined petroleum products industry in Costa Rica, where foreign firms emit about 24 more $MtCO_2$, and electricity and other utilities in Colombia (6 more $MtCO_2$). Foreign companies in the Mexican transport and storage sector and in the Brazilian wood industry also have a higher carbon intensity than domestic competitors, although at a lower level, suggesting that scope remains for improving the carbon performance of FDI in these sectors (OECD, 2023[57]).

Figure 2.17. **Carbon intensity of output by ownership, $MtCO_2$ per million USD**

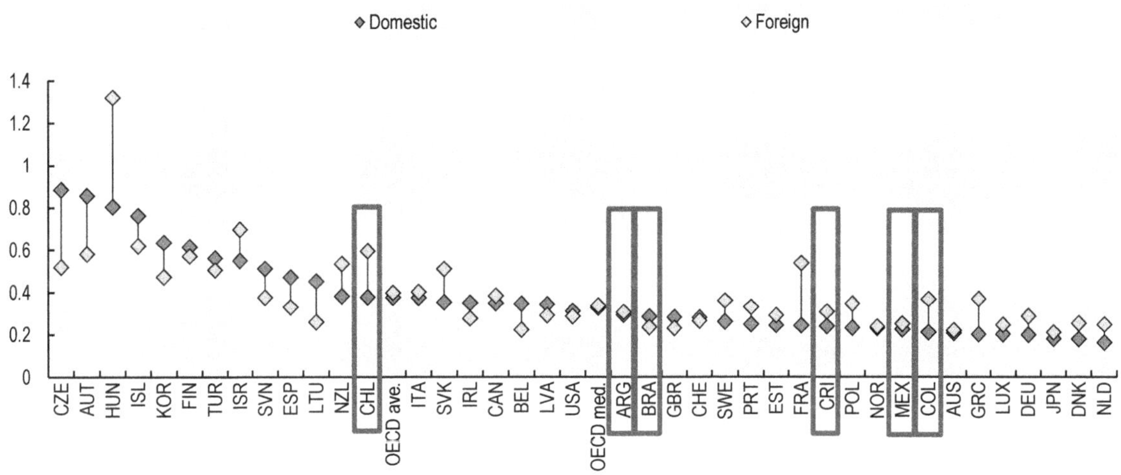

Note: The figure shows carbon intensities – i.e. carbon emissions per unit of output – of foreign and domestic firms at the aggregate country level. To obtain country-level values, values for individual sectors were aggregated using shares of each sector's output in the country's total output as weights.
Source: (OECD, 2023[57]).

StatLink https://stat.link/uvsdx5

Given its natural endowments, such as wind and sun, the LAC region has capacity to attract large investments in renewable energy. New FDI projects in renewable energy (greenfield projects) have been rising over the last two decades, while FDI projects in fossil fuels have slightly decreased (Figure 2.18, Panel A). Since 2011, FDI in renewable energy has surpassed FDI in fossil fuels almost steadily, highlighting FDI's growing contribution to the energy transition. However, the increase in cross-border investment in renewables has been uneven across LAC economies, and FDI in renewable energy has not yet recovered from the COVID-19 crisis (OECD, 2023[57]). Box 2.5 presents a brief compilation of messages on how LAC countries can deepen and expand relations to scale up cross-border investment in renewables.

Box 2.5. LAC countries can further expand investment relations with OECD countries for renewable energy FDI

Given that LAC governments are already facing a tight fiscal space, FDI has a crucial role in securing essential resources for the green transition (Chapter 1). To decarbonise the energy mix by 2050, the LAC region will need to invest USD 1 billion in total (UNEP, 2016[58]).

Even if FDI projects in renewable energy increased more than sixfold over the past two decades in LAC, investment remains highly concentrated. Brazil, Chile and Mexico together received three quarters of all opened and announced renewable energy FDI in the region since 2003 (Chapter 3).

To promote more and better cross-border investment in renewables, other LAC countries could leverage the funds coming from the main investors from OECD countries. Argentina, Colombia, Costa Rica, the Dominican Republic, Ecuador, El Salvador, Guatemala, Honduras, Paraguay, Peru, Uruguay and other countries could further target the main investors in renewable energy. Currently, with 27% of total investment, Spain represents the primary source of greenfield FDI (i.e. new projects in which a company constructs its own new operational facilities), closely followed by the United States and Canada. When considering the combined contributions of these three nations, they collectively account for 44% of the total greenfield FDI in renewable energy.

Nevertheless, LAC countries have a valuable opportunity to further expand investment relations with major countries investing in renewable energy abroad. Countries such as Australia, France, Germany, Italy and Ireland host a significant portion of global FDI projects in renewables, yet their representation within the region remains relatively small in terms of percentage. For example, Germany accounts for 10% of global FDI projects in renewable energy (2003-22) but only represents 5% in LAC.

Source: Authors' elaboration based on (UNEP, 2016[58]; OECD, 2023[57]).

The variation in FDI in energy remains wide across LAC countries. In Argentina, Colombia, Ecuador, El Salvador, Guatemala, Mexico and Peru fossil fuels account for about 10% to 50% of total greenfield FDI accumulated since 2003 and for more than 50% of FDI stocks in the energy sector (Figure 2.18, Panel B). Conversely, in Paraguay, Brazil, Uruguay, Dominican Republic, Honduras and Chile, renewable energy FDI dominates the energy sector and has attracted a sizable share of total greenfield FDI, ranging from 10% in Paraguay to 30% in Chile. Especially in Honduras, almost all open and announced FDI projects in the energy sector are directed to renewable energy (93%). Notably, Honduras has the lowest level of rural electrification among the LAC economies under consideration; it can thus benefit from renewable energy FDI not only to reduce emissions but also to close the gap in access to energy and to promote sustainable development (OECD, 2023[57]). Moreover, quality FDI could contribute to the development in LAC of strategic sectors such as the energy, sustainable mobility, pharmaceuticals and sustainable agribusiness (Chapter 3). These sectors can foster a more dynamic and resilient economy while helping to advance the green transition.

Figure 2.18. **Share of greenfield FDI by energy type for LAC and selected LAC countries, 2003-22**

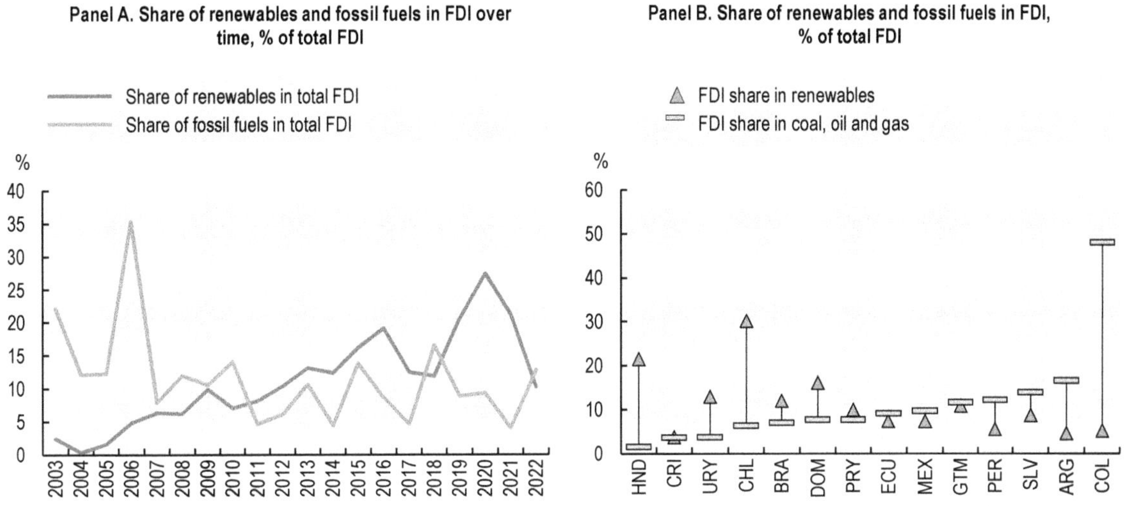

Note: This figure shows the share of all opened and announced greenfield FDI projects in renewables and fossil fuels as a share of total greenfield FDI in LAC over time (Panel A) and by country (Panel B). In Panel A, LAC comprises Argentina, Brazil, Chile, Colombia, Costa Rica, Dominican Republic, Ecuador, El Salvador, Guatemala, Honduras, Mexico, Paraguay, Peru, and Uruguay. Panel B corresponds to the stock for 2003-22.

Source: (OECD, 2023[57]).

StatLink https://stat.link/tcs6id

Key policy messages

The LAC region is experiencing lower levels of investment than any other developing region. Total investment as a percentage of GDP was falling already before the COVID-19 crisis. After a small rebound, it averaged 20.4% of GDP in 2022.

Although heterogeneity is evident across LAC countries, to ensure an inclusive and sustainable structural transformation, total investment will have to increase in all strategic sectors. To achieve this, governments from LAC will have to mobilise more and better private and public investment. Quality public infrastructure in key sectors, including sustainable transport, telecommunications, and water, can boost the well-being of citizens and help LAC countries move towards the SDGs.

Governments from the region can raise investment levels through good governance and a series of financing tools and strategies. Properly designed PPPs, accompanied by elements of de-risking, can motivate the private sector to invest in strategic long-term public projects with high social impact. FDI can also play a strategic role in filling the current investment gap. LAC already attracts larger sums of FDI than other developing regions and could build on this to amplify future investments. By strategically targeting FDI with a larger potential to share know-how, create quality jobs and implement sustainable methods of production, governments could support the objectives of sustainable and inclusive production transformation in LAC. Box 2.6 presents the main policy messages for achieving the objectives described throughout the chapter.

Box 2.6. Key policy messages

Towards more and better investments to drive sustainable and inclusive development

- Advance in creating a better investment climate through a mix of co-ordinated policy efforts, as described by the OECD Policy Framework for Investment. In terms of public governance, four key pillars stand out: quality regulation, transparency, openness and integrity.
- Develop clear and accessible datasets on infrastructure investment. This information should provide tools and evidence for policy makers to properly design public policy for better investments and to better assess potential investment, including by carrying out sound cost-benefit analyses. Such datasets should also allow the rest of the stakeholders to better understand who is developing each sector.
- Strengthen government collaboration with the private sector and academia to further promote reliable and accessible infrastructure databases and to ensure efficient use of the resources already deployed.
- Develop investment regulatory frameworks on infrastructure and enhance co-ordination among jurisdictions to:
  - promote coherent, predictable and efficient regulatory frameworks
  - promote competition among investors
  - provide clarity and transparency (enabling investors to plan their investment for long-term periods)
  - distribute clear responsibilities among stakeholders for each investment, and
  - achieve harmonised regulations in line with similar national, regional and international frameworks (vertical harmonisation) and across investment, trade and fiscal systems to boost production and avoid tax evasion (horizontal harmonisation).
- Ensure the governance of infrastructure brings well-being to citizens by including relevant stakeholders in its design and implementation, basing infrastructure decisions on reliable evidence, and using digital technologies to facilitate easy access to information and transparency.
- Adopt the OECD Recommendations on the Governance of Infrastructure to:
  - maximise the impact of investment in sustainable infrastructure to ensure its resilience over time, including to the effects of increasing extreme weather events.
  - actively include methods of citizen participation to ensure that new infrastructure is truly inclusive and respects local communities and the environment.
- Ensure that investment in transport promotes appropriate modes of transportation, the use of sustainable public transport and shared mobility.
- Work closely with telecommunications enterprises to promote further investment. Key objectives should include: strengthening the weakest territories and agents and helping boost the technological absorption of the economy; facilitating the transformation of business models; and consolidating the integration into more dynamic and innovative production systems.
- Ensure that investment in water infrastructure provides equitable and inclusive access to drinkable water. Expand the water network to ensure the amount and quality of drinkable water are adequate. Adapt future investment in water infrastructure to increase resilience to face future risks such as droughts or sea-level rise.

Box 2.6. **Key policy messages** *(cont.)*

Towards sound PPP frameworks

- Enhance the regulatory framework for PPPs (e.g. comprehensive rules for project selection, risk allocation and contract management) and build technical capacity in their design, implementation and oversight to avoid costly renegotiations and ensure their success.
- Create a predictable and transparent investment environment that bolsters investor confidence and maximises the socioeconomic and environmental impacts of PPPs.
- Enable efficient and effective citizen participation in the decision-making process to foster a sense of ownership and greater accountability, which in turn could help avoid social conflicts throughout the projects.
- Promote sustainable and diversified PPPs to achieve balanced development across sectors and ensure long-term sustainability. Governments should advocate to incorporate comprehensive environmental impact assessments into PPP planning.

Towards the attraction of quality FDI to boost strategic sectors

- Align efforts to promote investment in well-defined production sectors, including renewable energy, to enhance the contribution of FDI to inclusive and sustainable development in LAC.
- Channel FDI to create quality jobs and support skills development. This requires collecting information about the operations of foreign firms as well as skills needs to create skills anticipation systems, training programmes and wide pro-competition policies that increase potential labour-market gains.
- Create successful investment promotion policies by ensuring co-ordination among public institutions at national and subnational levels within the framework of production development policies.
- Involve SMEs in the process, including them in international agreements, providing technical and financial assistance, and promoting intersectoral connections to create business linkages.

Notes

1. This LAC figure includes 30 countries with available data: Antigua and Barbuda, Argentina, Bahamas, Barbados, Belize, Bolivia, Brazil, Chile, Colombia, Costa Rica, Dominica, Dominican Republic, Ecuador, El Salvador, Grenada, Guatemala, Guyana, Honduras, Jamaica, Mexico, Nicaragua, Panama, Paraguay, Peru, Saint Kitts and Nevis, Saint Lucia, Saint Vincent and the Grenadines, Suriname, Trinidad and Tobago, and Uruguay.
2. Mexico is not included. Countries included are Costa Rica, El Salvador, Guatemala, Honduras, Nicaragua and Panama.
3. When identifying the origin of investment in the region, different sources of information exist. Sources such as fDi Markets and Thomson Reuters are transaction based and therefore take into account the final destination of investments. Official figures reported by the United Nations Conference on Trade and Development (UNCTAD), in contrast, do not take the final destination into account. This difference can cause large discrepancies, especially in the LAC region since many Caribbean Islands are considered Offshore Financial Centres (OFCs) (Ding et al., 2021[59]). For example, China does not seem particularly relevant when looking at official sources, as investments are channelled via OFCs. In 2019, official data indicated that Asia's contribution to total FDI in LAC was 4%. However, when incorporating OFCs in the calculation of Asia's FDI stock in LAC, especially from China, this figure surged to 31%. In the same year, a total of USD 4.3 billion – out of USD 6.4 billion in FDI that entered LAC from China – was registered as OFCs, which were not the final destination of the investment (Ding et al., 2021[59]).

References

Atlantic Council (2023), *Unlocking Economic Development in Latin America and the Caribbean: Five Opportunities for Private-Sector Leadership and Partnership*, Atlantic Council, Washington, DC, https://www.atlanticcouncil.org/wp-content/uploads/2023/06/AALAC_IDB_Report_060823_complete.pdf. [25]

Bitrán, E., S. Nieto Parra and J. Robledo (2013), "Opening the black box of contract renegotiations: An analysis of road concessions in Chile, Colombia and Peru", *OECD Development Centre Working Papers*, No. 317, OECD Publishing, Paris, https://doi.org/10.1787/5k46n3wwxxq3-en. [41]

CAF (2021), *Pathways to Integration: Trade Facilitation, Infrastructure and Global Value Chains*, Development Bank of Latin America (CAF), Caracas, https://scioteca.caf.com/handle/123456789/1823. [18]

CAF (2018), *Public-Private Partnership in Latin America. Facing the Challenge of Connecting and Improving Cities*, Development Bank of Latin America (CAF), Bogota, https://scioteca.caf.com/bitstream/handle/123456789/1549/Public-Private_Partnership_in_Latin_America._Facing_the_challenge_of_connecting_and_improving_cities..pdf. [42]

Ding, D. et al. (2021), "Chinese investment in Latin America: Sectoral complementarity and the impact of China's rebalancing", *IMF Working Papers*, No. 160, Washington, DC, https://www.imf.org/en/Publications/WP/Issues/2021/06/07/Chinese-Investment-in-Latin-America-Sectoral-Complementarity-and-the-Impact-of-Chinas-50217. [59]

ECLAC (2023), "CEPALSTAT", *Foreign direct investment (FDI) inflows*, https://agenda2030lac.org/estadisticas/regional-data-bank-statistical-follow-up-sdg-1.html?indicator_id=4231&lang=en (accessed on 5 September 2023). [50]

ECLAC (2023), *Foreign Direct Investment in Latin America and the Caribbean 2023*, United Nations Economic Commission for Latin America and the Caribbean, Santiago, https://www.cepal.org/en/publications/48979-foreign-direct-investment-latin-america-and-caribbean-2023. [49]

ECLAC (2022), *Economic Survey of Latin America and the Caribbean 2022: Trends and Challenges of Investing for a Sustainable and Inclusive Recovery*, United Nations Economic Commission for Latin America and the Caribbean, Santiago, https://repositorio.cepal.org/bitstream/handle/11362/48078/7/S2201057_en.pdf. [11]

ECLAC (2022), *Foreign Direct Investment in Latin America and the Caribbean 2022*, United Nations Economic Commission for Latin America and the Caribbean, Santiago, https://repositorio.cepal.org/bitstream/handle/11362/48521/3/S2200561_en.pdf. [52]

ECLAC (2022), *Redes 5G en América Latina: Desarrollo y potencialidades*, United Nations Economic Commission for Latin America and the Caribbean, Santiago, https://repositorio.cepal.org/handle/11362/48485. [26]

ECLAC (2021), *"Digital technologies for a new future"*, United Nations Economic Commission for Latin America and the Caribbean, Santiago, http://repositorio.cepal.org/handle/11362/46817. [27]

ECLAC (2020), *"Public-private partnerships under the 'people-first' approach"*, United Nations Economic Commission for Latin America and the Caribbean, Santiago, https://repositorio.cepal.org/bitstream/handle/11362/46538/1/S2000676_en.pdf. [45]

ECLAC (2019), *Perspectivas del Comercio Internacional de América Latina y el Caribe 2019: El adverso contexto mundial profundiza el rezago de la región*, United Nations Economic Commission for Latin America and the Caribbean, Santiago, https://www.cepal.org/es/publicaciones/44918-perspectivas-comercio-internacional-america-latina-caribe-2019-adverso-contexto. [19]

ECLAC (2018), *Economic Survey of Latin America and the Caribbean 2018*, United Nations Economic Commission for Latin America and the Caribbean, Santiago, https://www.cepal.org/en/publications/43965-economic-survey-latin-america-and-caribbean-2018-evolution-investment-latin. [13]

ECLAC (2012), *"Public-private partnerships in renewable energy in Latin America and the Caribbean"*, United Nations Economic Commission for Latin America and the Caribbean, Santiago, https://www.cepal.org/es/publicaciones/4016-public-private-partnerships-renewable-energy-latin-america-and-caribbean. [7]

ECLAC (2004), *"La inversión para la provisión de servicios públicos y su financiamiento en América Latina y el Caribe: evolución reciente, situación actual y políticas"*, United Nations Economic Commission for Latin America and the Caribbean, Santiago, https://repositorio.cepal.org/handle/11362/5396. [8]

Economist Impact (2022), *"Evaluating the environment for public-private partnerships in Latin America and the Caribbean: The 2021/22 Infrascope"*, Economist Impact, New York, https://infrascope.wpengine.com/wp-content/uploads/2019/04/EIU_INFRASCOPE_2021_12.pdf. [40]

Eichengreen, B. (2010), *Lessons from the Marshall Plan*, https://documents1.worldbank.org/curated/en/907961468155715855/pdf/620420WP0Lesso0BOX0361475B00PUBLIC0.pdf. [60]

EIU (2019), *"Evaluating the environment for public-private partnerships in Latin America and the Caribbean:*

The 2019 Infrascope", The Economist Intelligence Unit, New York, https://infrascope.eiu.com/wp-content/uploads/2019/04/EIU_2019-IDB-Infrascope-Report_FINAL-1.pdf. [39]

Engel, E., R. Fischer and A. Galetovic (2021), "*When and how to use public-private partnerships in infrastructure: Lessons from the international experience*", National Bureau of Economic Research, Cambridge, MA, https://www.nber.org/papers/w26766. [43]

European Commission et al. (2008), *System of National Accounts 2008*, European Communities, IMF, OECD, UN, WB, New York, https://unstats.un.org/unsd/nationalaccount/docs/sna2008.pdf. [3]

fDi Markets (2023), *fDi Markets*, https://www.fdimarkets.com/. [51]

IDB (2022), *Informe anual del Índice de Desarrollo de la Banda Ancha: Brecha digital en América Latina y el Caribe*, Inter-American Development Bank, Washington, DC, https://doi.org/10.18235/0004379. [24]

IDB (2022), *Sustainable Financing of Economic and Social Infrastructure in Latin America and the Caribbean: Trends, Key Agents and Instruments*, Inter-American Development Bank, Washington, DC, https://publications.iadb.org/publications/english/viewer/Sustainable-Financing-of-Economic-and-Social-Infrastructure-in-Latin-America-and-the-Caribbean-Trends-Key-Agents-and-Instruments.pdf. [46]

IDB (2022), *Water access in Latin America and the Caribbean: Definitions and data*, Inter-American Development Bank, Washington, DC, https://doi.org/10.18235/0004493. [28]

IDB (2021), *The Infrastructure Gap in Latin America and the Caribbean: Investment Needed Through 2030 to Meet the Sustainable Development Goals*, Inter-American Development Bank, Washington, DC, https://publications.iadb.org/en/infrastructure-gap-latin-america-and-caribbean-investment-needed-through-2030-meet-sustainable. [16]

IDB (2023), *Brecha de conectividad y necesidades de inversión en América Latina y el Caribe: una perspectiva económico-financiera*, Inter-American Development Bank, Washington, DC. [23]

IMF (2023), *World Economic Outlook Database*, International Monetary Fund, Washington, DC, https://www.imf.org/en/Publications/WEO/weo-database/2023/April/weo-report (accessed on 5 September 2023). [10]

IMF (2022), *Investment and Capital Stock Dataset*, International Monetary Fund, Washington, DC, https://data.imf.org/?sk=1CE8A55F-CFA7-4BC0-BCE2-256EE65AC0E4&sId=1390030341854 (accessed on 5 September 2023). [12]

INEGI (2023), *Recomendaciones para la Generación de Información sobre Infraestructura en México*, National Institute of Statistics and Geography (INEGI), Aguascalientes, https://www.inegi.org.mx/infraestructura/modelos/. [32]

Infralatam (2022), *Data on Public Investment in Economic Infrastructure in Latin America and the Caribbean (database)*, http://infralatam.info/en/home/ (accessed on 5 September 2023). [15]

ITF and IADB (2022), *Decarbonising Transport in Latin American Cities. A Review of Policies and Key Challenges*, Inter-American Development Bank, Washington, DC, https://publications.iadb.org/publications/english/viewer/Decarbonising-Transport-in-Latin-American-Cities-A-Review-of-Policies-and-Key-Challenges.pdf. [20]

OECD (2023), *"Investment (GFCF)" (indicator)*, https://doi.org/10.1787/b6793677-en (accessed on 24 August 2023). [2]

OECD (2023), *FDI Qualities Review of Chile: Boosting Sustainable Development and Diversification*, OECD Publishing, Paris, https://doi.org/10.1787/98bf1829-en. [53]

OECD (2023), *OECD Foreign direct investment (FDI)*, OECD Publishing, Paris, https://doi.org/10.1787/9a523b18-en. [9]

OECD (2022), "FDI Qualities Indicators: Measuring the sustainable development impacts of investment", OECD, https://www.oecd.org/investment/fdi-qualities-indicators.htm. [55]

OECD (2022), *FDI Qualities Policy Toolkit*, OECD Publishing, Paris, https://www.oecd-ilibrary.org/finance-and-investment/fdi-qualities-policy-toolkit_7ba74100-en. [1]

OECD (2021), *OECD Implementation Handbook for Quality Infrastructure Investment*, OECD Publishing, Paris, https://www.oecd.org/finance/oecd-implementation-handbook-for-quality-infrastructure-investment.htm. [6]

OECD (2020), *"Recommendation of the Council on the Governance of Infrastructure", OECD Legal Instruments*, OECD Publishing, Paris, https://legalinstruments.oecd.org/en/instruments/OECD-LEGAL-0460. [33]

OECD (2020), *OECD Compendium of Policy Good Practices for Quality Infrastructure Investment*, OECD Publishing, Paris, https://www.oecd.org/finance/OECD-compendium-of-policy-good-practices-for-quality-infrastructure-investment.pdf. [14]

OECD (2019), *Effective Public Investment Across Levels of Government: Implementing the OECD Principles*, OECD Publishing, Paris, https://www.oecd.org/effective-public-investment-toolkit/OECD_Public_Investment_Implementation_Brochure_2019.pdf. [4]

OECD (2019), *Enhancing Access to and Sharing of Data: Reconciling Risks and Benefits for Data Re-use across Societies*, OECD Publishing, Paris, https://doi.org/10.1787/276aaca8-en. [31]

OECD (2019), *FDI Qualities Indicators: Measuring the sustainable development impacts of investment*, OECD Publishing, Paris, https://www.oecd.org/investment/FDI-Qualities-Indicators-Measuring-Sustainable-Development-Impacts.pdf. [54]

OECD (2015), *Policy Framework for Investment, 2015 Edition*, OECD Publishing, Paris, https://doi.org/10.1787/9789264208667-en. [5]

OECD (2015), *Recommendation of the Council on Public Procurement*, OECD Publishing, Paris, https://legalinstruments.oecd.org/en/instruments/OECD-LEGAL-0411. [30]

OECD (2009), *Private Sector Participation in Water Infrastructure: OECD Checklist for Public Action*, OECD Publishing, Paris, https://www.oecd.org/env/resources/42350657.pdf. [38]

OECD (2008), *Conducting Sustainability Assessments*, OECD Sustainable Development Studies, OECD Publishing, Paris, https://doi.org/10.1787/9789264047266-en. [48]

OECD (2023), *Harnessing the Potential of Foreign Direct Investment to Advance the Low-Carbon Transition in Latin America and the Caribbean*, OECD, Paris, https://storageprdv2inwink.blob.core.windows.net/fd64104f-b9d5-4759-8902-1297bb45b3fd/477af9b7-c0cd-4b91-8dee-20b657717e27. [57]

OECD and IDB (2016), *Broadband Policies for Latin America and the Caribbean: A Digital Economy*, OECD Publishing, Paris, https://doi.org/10.1787/9789264251823-en. [21]

OECD et al. (2022), *Latin American Economic Outlook 2022: Towards a Green and Just Transition*, OECD Publishing, Paris, https://doi.org/10.1787/3d5554fc-en. [17]

OECD et al. (2021), *Latin American Economic Outlook 2021: Working Together for a Better Recovery*, OECD Publishing, Paris, https://doi.org/10.1787/5fedabe5-en. [56]

OECD et al. (2020), *Latin American Economic Outlook 2020: Digital Transformation for Building Back Better*, OECD Publishing, Paris, https://doi.org/10.1787/e6e864fb-en. [22]

OECD (2012), *Water Governance for Latin America and the Caribbean: A Multi-level approach*, OECD Studies on Water, OECD Publishing, Paris, https://doi.org/10.1787/9789264174542-en. [29]

UNEP (2016), *Carbono cero América Latina: Una Vía para la Descarbonización Neta de la Economía Regional Para Mediados de Este Siglo - Documento de Visión*, https://wedocs.unep.org/20.500.11822/26305. [58]

World Bank (2023), *"World Development Indicators" (database)*, World Bank Group, Washington, DC, https://data.worldbank.org/indicator (accessed on 19 September 2023). [36]

World Bank (2023), *Private participation in infrastructure (database)*, World Bank Group, Washington, DC, https://ppi.worldbank.org/en/customquery (accessed on 5 September 2023). [35]

World Bank (2022), *Private Participation in Infrastructure (PPI): 2022 Annual Report*, World Bank Group, Washington, DC, https://ppi.worldbank.org/content/dam/PPI/documents/PPI-2022-Annual-Report.pdf. [47]

World Bank (2021), *Private Participation in Infrastructure: 2021 Annual Report*, World Bank Group, Washington, DC, https://ppi.worldbank.org/content/dam/PPI/documents/PPI-2021-Annual-Report.pdf. [34]

World Bank (2019), *A Guide to Community Engagement for Public-Private Partnerships: Draft for Discussion*, World Bank Group, Washington, DC, https://ppp.worldbank.org/public-private-partnership/library/guide-community-engagement-public-private-partnerships-june-2019. [44]

World Bank (2016), *Public and private paths to sustainable water supply and sanitation in Colombia*, World Bank Group, Washington, DC, https://ieg.worldbankgroup.org/sites/default/files/Data/reports/ppar_colombia_01132017.pdf. [37]

Annex 2.A. Methodological annex

Figure 2.2. Total investment as a percentage of GDP in selected LAC countries, 2022

Regarding the investment and capital stock dataset (IMF, 2022[12]): Public investment is measured using gross fixed capital formation of the general government (i.e. central plus subnational governments). This approach does not include: i) investment grants, which are transfers from central and/or subnational governments to public and private entities outside the general government to support investment in fixed assets; ii) loan guarantees; iii) tax concessions, such as those for mortgage interest, R&D, and municipal bonds; iv) the operations of public financial institutions, such as development banks, that provide long-term funding at subsidised rates; and v) government-backed saving schemes.

Statistics for the OECD countries are taken from the December 2020 version of the OECD Economic Outlook. Specifically, the series retrieved (in national currency and constant prices) is comprised of general government GFCF and total GFCF.

Figure 2.5. Public investment in infrastructure in LAC, as a percentage of GDP, Panel B

Argentina: The data include investment by the central government, subnational governments and public companies. However, in subnational investments, only investments made with funds transferred from the national government are recorded. Central government data include real direct investment from the national public administration, advances to long-term suppliers (priority investment projects), and capital transfers (excluding capital transfers to companies and provincial and municipal institutions). Data from subnational governments include capital transfers to provincial and municipal institutions. Investment expenditures financed with resources collected by the provinces and municipalities are excluded.

Chile: Investments made by the infrastructure concessions programme are not included.

El Salvador: The water and sanitation data include non-financial public companies and a part of local governments. There are no data on investment in water and sanitation executed by the central government and by non-business decentralised institutions.

Guatemala: Subnational investments are not included; since local governments report total investments without discrimination, it is not possible to identify investments corresponding to infrastructure sectors.

Honduras: As of 2018, "total transportation" includes the "transportation and public works" category. "Total energy" for 2020 and 2021 includes renewable energies, while the data for 2019 may include them. Regarding subnational investments, only investments made by the city government of Tegucigalpa for 2011, 2012 and 2013 are included. Data are unavailable for 2008, 2009 and 2010, and for other subnational governments.

Panama: The investment made by the Panama Canal Authority is included.

Dominican Republic: Data since 2009. The "water and sanitation" statistics from 2009 to 2015 cover only sanitation (residual water management, drainage and sewerage). In transportation data from 2016, the total is greater than the sum of its parts because it contains an additional category called "transportation planning, management, and monitoring".

Uruguay: Data from subnational or departmental governments include only transportation; within this category, only road transportation is included (i.e. urban road infrastructure is not included).

Depending on the sector and the year, statistics were available from different countries. For instance, the calculations corresponding to Figure 2.5, Panel B, for 2021 include:

	Energy	Telecommunications
2021	Belize, Bolivia, Dominican Republic, El Salvador, Guatemala, Guyana, Honduras, Panama, Trinidad and Tobago	Argentina, Belize, Bolivia, Trinidad and Tobago, Uruguay
	Transport	**Water**
2021	Argentina, Belize, Bolivia, Dominican Republic, El Salvador, Guatemala, Guyana, Honduras, Panama, Trinidad and Tobago, Uruguay	Argentina, Belize, Bolivia, Dominican Republic, El Salvador, Guatemala, Guyana, Honduras, Panama, Trinidad and Tobago, Uruguay

Chapter 3

Towards a new structure of production and employment: The role of investment

More and better investments could help transform the production structure of the Latin America and the Caribbean (LAC) region to advance a more sustainable and just development model that creates quality formal jobs. This chapter analyses the current structure of production in the region. It explores the dynamics of the labour market, the importance of advancing a renewed investment agenda to create formal jobs and the role of human talent in the production transformation. Finally, the chapter identifies strategic sectors to drive investment and advance sustainable development. The chapter concludes with key policy messages.

LAC needs more strategic investments to transform its production and employment structures

The region should rethink its production transformation model

Labour productivity gap

LAC labour productivity relative to the USA

49% (1980) → 26% (2022)

Manufacturing gap

In 2021, the share of LAC's manufacturing sector in the total economy fell to **13.2% of GDP**

Innovation gap

R&D investment in LAC has stagnated at around **0.65%** of GDP, representing only 2.3% of the world total

Investment in green and digital can create better jobs and increase dynamism

Green sectors with the highest job creation potentials by 2030 in LAC

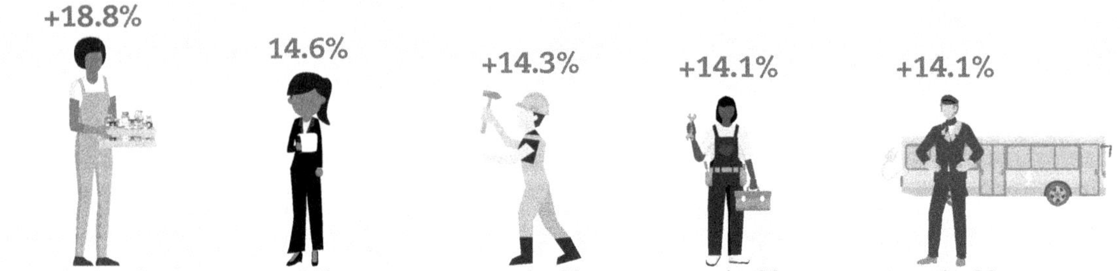

Sustainable food manufacturing	+18.8%
Public administration	14.6%
Sustainable construction	+14.3%
Sustainable commerce	+14.1%
Sustainable transport	+14.1%

Strategic sectors for public and private investments to drive sustainable development

Green transition

- Energy transition
- Circular economy
- Sustainable water management
- Electromobility
- Sustainable tourism

Digital transformation

- Digital economy
- Export of modern services
- Advanced manufacturing

Health and the care economy

- Pharmaceutical and medical devices industry
- Care society

Sustainable agriculture and food systems

- Bioeconomy
- Sustainable food production

Introduction

Countries in Latin America and the Caribbean (LAC) face the challenge of creating a better production structure to increase productivity, generate quality job opportunities and move towards a more sustainable and inclusive development model.

Against this background, the region needs strategic actions to narrow the gaps in human capital, technological and production standards with respect to more advanced economies (ECLAC, 2022[1]). Such actions must aim to upgrade and diversify the economy and involve various factors, including: i) changing the production and service delivery by shifting from low knowledge content activities to those of higher knowledge for transformative change which boosts economic growth (OECD, 2016[2]); ii) creating new sources of dynamism for a better development model with a fairer distribution of income, while minimising environmental impacts and improving quality of life (ECLAC, 1996[3]); and iii) creating better jobs through the collaborative work of governments, firms and individuals (CAF, 2014[4]).

Among these actions, promoting and facilitating investment in physical capital, knowledge and innovation, whether from domestic or foreign sources, can be a fundamental driver of production transformation. Investment can increase dynamism – through productivity growth, technological upgrading, development of suppliers and production linkages, as well as territorial development, human capital and formal job creation – in ways that are more environmentally sustainable. Both the scale and the focus of the investment matter.

In LAC the high degree of informal employment poses challenging conditions for governments to increase investment and redesign their production structure (Chapter 1). In such circumstances, education and technical training are particularly relevant as they can provide workers with the necessary skills to seize the benefits linked to incorporating more advanced technologies across different economic sectors and activities.

Improving the structure of production should be based on a comprehensive set of policies at national and local levels, capable of addressing all the different and interconnected dimensions of productive development. Such policies must aim to enhance, in particular: technology adoption and innovation; supply chain development; diversification of production capabilities; export promotion; incorporation of informal enterprises into the formal sector; and the development of human talent.

The public sector should play an active role in facilitating production transformation – in co-ordination with the private sector, academia and civil society – by identifying and prioritising sectors and strategic areas with greater technological intensity and greater potential for learning, innovation and market expansion, while also prioritising societal challenges. Global transformations are creating new opportunities, hence the need to adapt production transformation efforts to harness the potential of the green and digital transitions, the increasing demands for healthcare, and the need to guarantee a sustainable supply of food (ECLAC, 2022[1]; ECLAC, 2020[5]; OECD et al., 2021[6]; OECD et al., 2022[7]).

This chapter has five sections. The first section analyses the challenges of productivity in LAC countries, as productivity growth is at the heart of production transformation and remains a fundamental driver of quality job creation. The second section delves more deeply into the analysis of the production structure in the region, to identify key challenges and opportunities and to highlight the role of investment for production transformation. The third section examines the dynamics of labour markets in LAC, underscoring the importance of boosting job formalisation and reducing education and skill gaps, which will require further investments. The fourth section identifies strategic sectors with potential for driving sustainable development and that show opportunities for investment in the region. The chapter concludes with key policy messages.

Boosting productivity remains a persistent challenge in LAC

For several decades, LAC countries have experienced low aggregate productivity growth. Potential GDP per-capita growth has been below 1% since 1980, increasing slightly during the commodity boom (between 2003 and 2013). Since then, per-capita potential output growth has stagnated. Potential GDP per-capita growth has remained consistently below the level of advanced economies, hampering the convergence of per-capita income (Chapter 1) (OECD et al., 2022[7]; OECD et al., 2021[6]; OECD et al., 2020[8]).

From a comparative perspective, LAC economies show a widening productivity gap relative to advanced economies. The productivity gap vis-à-vis the United States, for example, has been growing in the last decades (Figure 3.1). This gap cannot be attributed to variations in the use of human capital in the production process, as the average hours that workers dedicate to the production process are, in fact, greater in the LAC region.

Figure 3.1. **Labour productivity in LAC countries relative to the United States, 1951-2022**

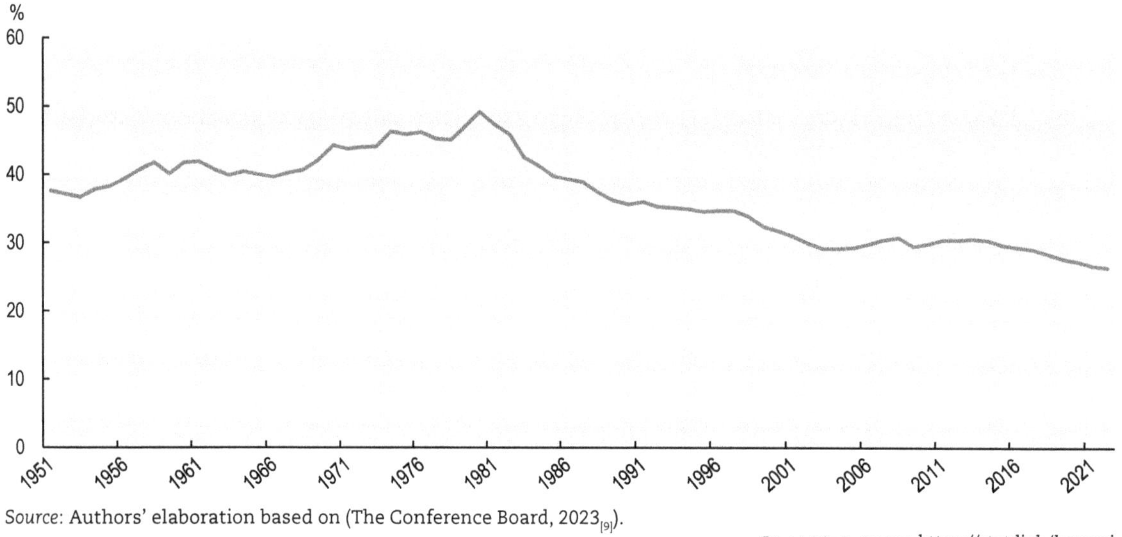

Source: Authors' elaboration based on (The Conference Board, 2023[9]).

StatLink https://stat.link/kmxeni

In LAC countries for which data are comparable, variation in labour productivity at the sectoral level has been evident since the 1990s. Agriculture productivity has increased twofold, while productivity of the industrial sector has followed the same trend as aggregate productivity in LAC economies, increasing by 60% (LA-KLEMS, 2021[10]). Sectors with the lowest gains include mining, financial and business services, and commerce. Although productivity is improving in some sectors, high levels of heterogeneity persist. Even in some sectors in which productivity growth is observed (e.g. agriculture, forestry and fisheries), this growth often starts from low levels of value added per person employed – far below the levels observed in more developed countries (Figure 3.2). The productivity gaps are particularly large in labour-intensive sectors, which explains the difference in average labour productivity between LAC and developed economies.

Figure 3.2. **Labour productivity and employment participation in LAC, by main economic sectors, 2021**

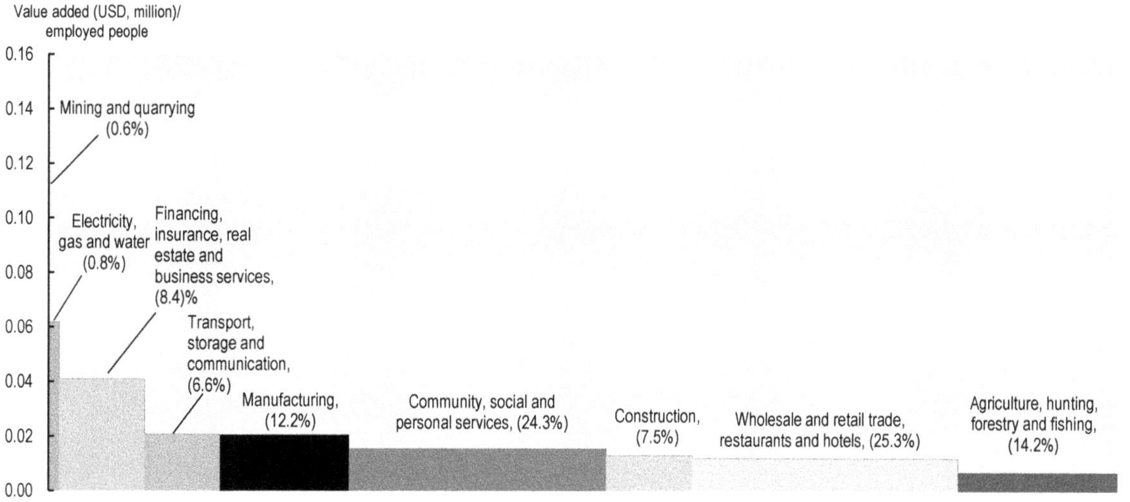

Note: Data on the vertical axis refer to labour productivity per person employed. On the horizontal axis, data refer to the share of employment across main industries, as defined by ISIC Rev. 3 classification. Sectors are ranked according to the respective level of productivity (from highest to lowest). Data shown in the labels refer to the share of employment in each sector.
Source: ECLAC estimates based on data from national statistical offices.

StatLink https://stat.link/xdml2r

Intersectoral improvements have driven productivity growth in LAC, while resource reallocation has not. Shifting resources to higher productivity sectors ("structural change effect") is usually a driver of growth; however, this has not yet been the case in LAC (Figure 3.3). Rather, sectoral productivity increases ("within sectors effect") via increases in physical/human capital, technological changes, closing low-productivity businesses and starting efficient ones have been the main drivers of LAC productivity growth. Ideally, intersectoral improvements and resource reallocation happen together. Stimulating productivity growth based on resource reallocation therefore remains an important opportunity in the region (CAF, 2018[11]; ECLAC and ILO, 2022[12]).

Figure 3.3. **Decomposition of labour productivity growth in LAC countries, 1991-2021**

Unweighted average of 18 LAC countries

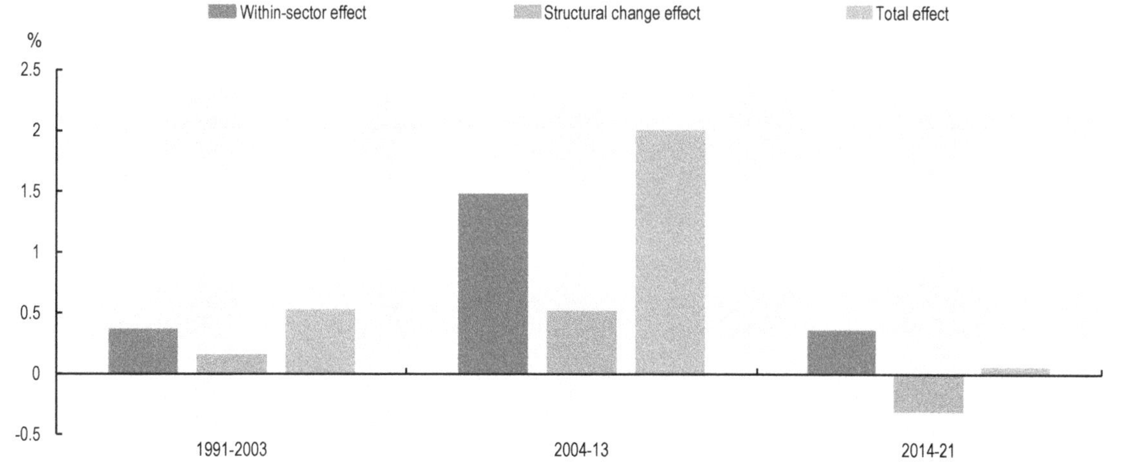

Note: The data refer to an unweighted average of data from the following countries: Argentina, Bolivia, Brazil, Chile, Colombia, Costa Rica, Ecuador, Dominican Republic, El Salvador, Guatemala, Honduras, Mexico, Nicaragua, Panama, Paraguay, Peru, Uruguay and Venezuela (Bolivian Republic of).
Source: (ECLAC and ILO, 2022[12]).

StatLink https://stat.link/mjrlcv

A complex set of policies is needed to support the increase of productivity within and among sectors. The institutions that shape the productive environment of firms (regardless of sectors in which they operate) need to be strengthened (CAF, 2018[11]). In addition, incentives and profitability signals must be aligned to enable the redirection of investments towards sectors that benefit from greater market and technological dynamism and innovation potential (ECLAC, 2020[5]; ECLAC, 2022[1]). To have a positive impact on productivity and economic growth, these policies must be complemented by others aimed at strengthening the local capacities essential for investment.

Examining the structure of production in LAC

The sectors and activities in which a country's production and exports are concentrated are key factors in its development model, determining different growth paths. When technology- and productivity-intensive sectors are more prevalent, greater efficiencies are generated in the form of technological development, learning and positive spillover effects to other sectors (ECLAC, 2022[1]). When sectors are part of an expanding international market, they will also boost demand for skilled labour and better-paid jobs (ECLAC, 2022[1]).

Traditionally, the competitiveness of most LAC countries has been based on natural resources and low-skilled labour. These factors have led to an incomplete industrialisation and are the basis of static comparative advantages. These are known as "spurious competitiveness", as opposed to "authentic competitiveness", based on technology and innovation, which delivers dynamic competitive advantages (Fajnzylber, 1983[13]). The region has made some progress in terms of digitalisation and modernisation of production. By moving towards a model in which the generation and adoption of technology and innovation are at the centre, LAC should achieve high levels of competitiveness and be able to guarantee growth that is compatible with better income distribution and environmental protection.

Structural heterogeneity is another key feature of the LAC region. This can be observed by significant productivity differentials both between and within sectors: very dynamic and high-productivity sectors, that are generally export oriented, coexist with less dynamic sectors and with high rates of informality. Broad heterogeneity in productivity is also evident at the subnational level. The difficulty in achieving greater convergence is due not only to the low technological intensity of production, but also to insufficient linkages among sectors, companies and territories, and the low capacity of diffusion of technical progress of natural resource branches to the whole structure of production (OECD, 2016[2]). Such features condition the fragile insertion of LAC in global value chains, deepen external constraints and increase vulnerability to external shocks (Chapter 1). Nearshoring can help further LAC's integration into global value chains by relocating investments in global production chains to nearby geographical locations. When implemented effectively, it can help bridge productivity differentials, promote linkages among sectors and territories, and foster a more dynamic and interconnected regional economic landscape.

The pattern of production and exports presents important specificities at the subregional level in LAC. In South America, production linked to natural resources and primary activities dominates and it is increasing. Central America and Mexico have a greater focus on manufacturing, contract manufacturing, and service export industries. The Caribbean relies on natural resources in sectors from manufacturing to tourism (ECLAC, 2022[1]).

Cross-cutting aspects will be key to effectively advancing sectoral strategies and to successfully promoting investment in LAC. Sectoral strategies should be aligned with overarching horizontal aspects as well as with cross-sectoral implications such as institutional frameworks, sound analytical tools and co-ordinated policy responses (Chapters 2 and 4) (CAF, 2018[11]).

Manufacturing is losing ground in LAC as services become more dynamic

Manufacturing remains relevant to long-term growth in the LAC region. It can provide rapid productivity increases, generate quality jobs, and be a source of innovation and dissemination of technical knowledge throughout the economy. Its importance also derives from the significant complementarities with the agricultural and services sectors. Measures to strengthen these tie-ins are a crucial step towards generating technological spillovers and backward and forward linkages in the value chains (ECLAC, 2008[14]).

The relative importance of manufacturing in the regional economy, however, has been declining. The share of LAC's manufacturing sector fell to 13.2% of GDP in 2021, its lowest level in the last two decades (Figure 3.4). This has been driven by South American countries in which a gradual decline in the relative weight of the manufacturing industry is associated with increased specialisation in primary activities. At the same time, the services sector has gained relative importance in the composition of GDP in most LAC countries.

Figure 3.4. **Change in the share of the manufacturing sector, LAC subregions, 2000-21**

Index of manufacturing value added as a percentage of GDP, base year 2000 = 1

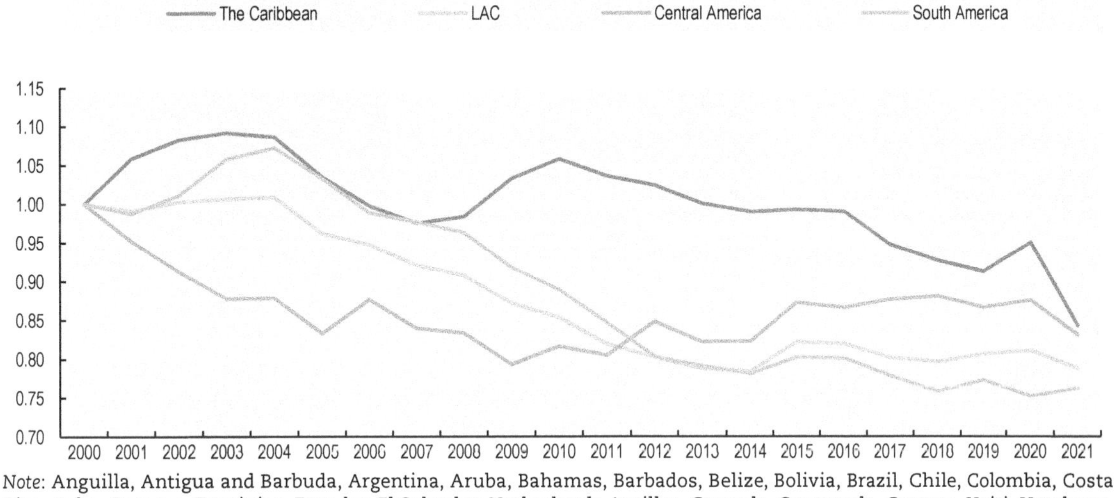

Note: Anguilla, Antigua and Barbuda, Argentina, Aruba, Bahamas, Barbados, Belize, Bolivia, Brazil, Chile, Colombia, Costa Rica, Cuba, Curaçao, Dominica, Ecuador, El Salvador, Netherlands Antilles, Grenada, Guatemala, Guyana, Haiti, Honduras, Cayman Islands, Turks and Caicos Islands, British Virgin Islands, Jamaica, Mexico., Montserrat, Nicaragua, Panama, Paraguay, Peru, Puerto Rico, Dominican Republic, Saint Kitts and Nevis, Sint Maarten (Dutch part), Saint Vincent and the Grenadines, Saint Lucia, Suriname, Trinidad and Tobago, Uruguay, Venezuela (Bolivarian Republic of).

Source: (ECLAC, 2023[15]).

StatLink https://stat.link/2h3luk

Foreign direct investment (FDI) directed towards manufacturing has declined from 40% in the period 2010-19 to 23% in 2021, while FDI inflows to the services sector has increased (ECLAC, 2022[16]). The correlation between foreign capital inflows and the performance of a given sector demonstrates the importance of an integrated vision of processes of structural change and investment attraction and allocation. To promote more technologically sophisticated sectors and activities, as well as industries with expanding global demand, LAC policies for attracting and allocating investments must align with that objective (ECLAC, 2022[16]).

Closing the region's productivity and territorial gaps is key for better development

Micro, small and medium-sized enterprises (MSMEs) play an essential role in LAC economies, accounting for 99% of formal enterprises and 66% of formal employment (Dini and Stumpo, 2020[17]). The difference between the labour productivity of smaller formal enterprises relative to large ones, however, is much more substantial in LAC than in developed regions (Figure 3.5). In 2018, the labour productivity of LAC's medium-sized enterprises was only 65% of that of large enterprises, while much lower levels were reached for small (38%) and micro (17%) enterprises. The differentials are more pronounced when comparing firms' productivity in selected countries: microenterprise productivity in Brazil, for example, represents 4% that of large companies compared with 74% in France (OECD et al., 2020[8]).

Figure 3.5. **Labour productivity relative to large firms, by firm size, LAC and European Union (%)**

LAC = 2008 and 2018; EU = 2016

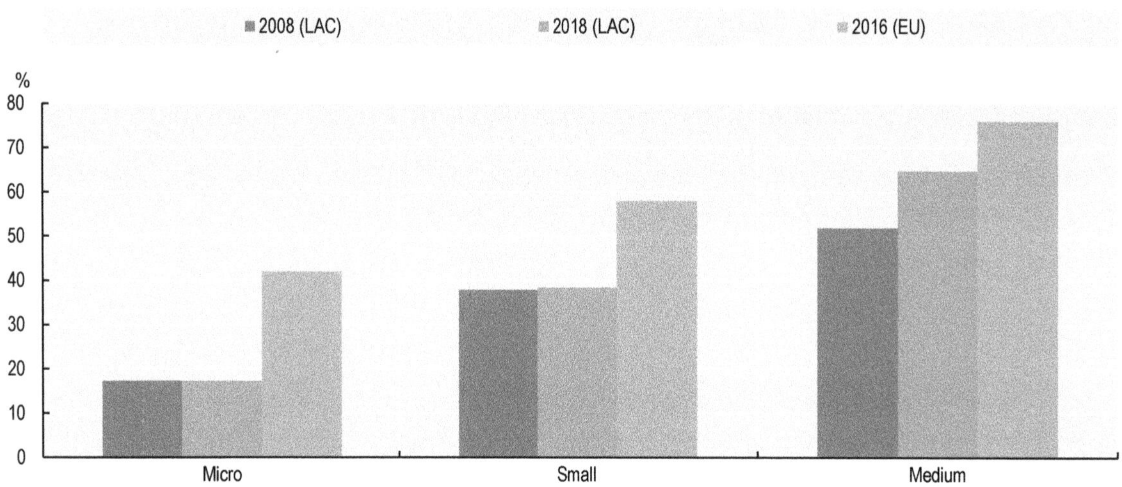

Note: LAC data refer to Argentina, Brazil, Chile and Mexico.
Source: (ECLAC, 2022[1]).

StatLink https://stat.link/z9maqb

These differences stem from the fact that MSMEs in the European Union constitute a key, dynamic and integrated component of the structure of production, conditions that are not replicated in LAC (Dini and Stumpo, 2020[17]). With rare exceptions, MSMEs in the LAC region tend to specialise in low-productivity sectors and their contribution to exports remains very limited. Only occasionally do they manage to establish relationships with large and more dynamic firms. Additionally, they often face difficulties in incorporating technologies and promoting innovation. Moreover, evidence suggests that low productivity in LAC MSMEs is also related to weak management practices, which could be improved through technological extension services (Bloom et al., 2013[18]; McKenzie, 2020[19]; Shapira et al., 2015[20]). Thus, despite progress achieved, policy efforts to support MSMEs in LAC could be strengthened.

Heterogeneity among production units of similar size also stands out in LAC. The region's many informal, low-productivity MSMEs coexist with technology-based and fast-growing start-ups. These start-ups are an important source of innovation, and thus of the creation and transformation of industries and business models. In addition, they carry the potential to contribute to renewing business leadership in the region. Although investments in this domain are high risk and uncertain, if successful they pay off with great potential for contributing to economic growth, job creation and sustainable development (Audretsch et al., 2020[21]). As such, promoting entrepreneurship and innovative start-ups deserves attention and action from policy makers, independent of the need for addressing low productivity and informality.

LAC shows a significant rise in the number of start-ups in the last decade, concentrated particularly in South America. They tend to be digitally based and operate mostly in the software and financial intermediation sectors although some companies focus on commerce, education and health-related services (Box 3.1).

Box 3.1. The start-up landscape in LAC

Start-ups are concentrated in South America and in digital sectors

South America is home to 83% of the LAC region's start-ups, with 58% of companies headquartered in Brazil, 8% in Argentina, 8% in Chile and 5% in Colombia. Another 12% are based in Mexico. According to a new study by the UN Economic Commission for Latin America and the Caribbean (ECLAC), the main sectors for the region's start-ups are software (19%), financial intermediation (19%), commerce (9%), education (8%) and health-related activities (6%). Their business models rely predominantly on the internet and internet-based activities: in fact, 58% of LAC start-ups are digital services providers or offer digital-based solutions.

Financing is challenging for most start-ups in the region

Accessing development funding is challenging for most start-ups in the LAC region. A mere 20 companies raised half of the region's total start-up development funds. Remarkably, nine of those companies each received at least USD 20 million. This contrasts sharply with the funding reality experienced by the remaining companies in the sample, which received USD 714 000 per start-up on average. Given this huge gap, median funding was considerably lower, at USD 171 000 per start-up.

Start-ups operating in the financial services industry received the most individual funding, at USD 420 000 per start-up. This helps to explain why Colombia, which has a significant concentration of start-ups in this sector, stands out with the highest values for individual financing.

Start-ups in LAC also face financial constraints due to the limited availability of funding sources: 57% of companies have only a single investor. Overall, private investors provide 81% of the funding to such companies, which rely on credit for remaining 19%.

Other constraints faced by start-ups in the LAC region include lack of qualified human resources, a high tax burden and stringent labour regulations, as well as (to a lesser extent) factors linked to corruption and political instability (Federico and Ibarra Garcia, 2014[22]).

Public policies can help promote the necessary conditions for start-up growth

In this context, it is important to highlight the role of public policies in promoting the conditions necessary for the growth of start-up ventures, such as incentives for the development of science, technology and innovation, along with education and facilitating access to financing (Mageste et al., forthcoming[23]).

Market-based financing instruments, such as equity and debt, are essential tools in the development of medium-sized companies in emerging economies. However, LAC economies lag behind other emerging economies in the use of these instruments. To reverse this trend, the region needs to improve regulatory and institutional frameworks based on more and better information from SMEs on financing needs (Medina et al., forthcoming[24]).

Note: The information in this box originates from an ECLAC study conducted by (Mageste et al., forthcoming[23]) and elaborated on the basis of Crunchbase and Dataprovider (data for Brazil, Chile, Colombia and Mexico).

Source: (Mageste et al., forthcoming[23]); (Medina et al., forthcoming[24]); (OECD/UN, 2018[25]); (Federico and Ibarra Garcia, 2014[22]).

Although the LAC region has the potential to generate and nurture technology-based companies, the crisis caused by the COVID-19 pandemic affected both demand and funding in this segment. Globally, venture funding attracted by start-ups dropped from USD 21.5 billion in 2021 to USD 7.8 billion in 2022 (CBInsights, 2022[26]). In line with a worldwide trend of decline after the boom in unicorn companies (start-ups valued at more than USD 1 million), the emergence of unicorns also slowed in LAC, falling from 17 in 2021 to 4 in 2022 (Kantis, Caicedo and Ibarra Garcia, 2023[27]). As of April 2023, LAC counted 31 unicorn companies (CBInsights, 2022[26]). Almost half were focused on fintech (45%), followed by e-commerce (23%), logistics and supply chains (13%), and artificial intelligence solutions (nearly 7%).

Promoting entrepreneurship and boosting risk capital should be parts of a broader strategy to promote production transformation and innovation in the LAC region. Given that smaller enterprises and start-ups are highly concentrated in certain areas within countries, significant disparities exist among territories.

The challenges of just and sustainable development models can be categorised into vertical and horizontal inequalities, which are closely interrelated. The vertical aspect – i.e. inequality among individuals or households – is crucial for individual development. Horizontal inequalities – i.e. inequalities among groups and especially territorial inequalities – persist throughout individuals' lives and contribute to reinforcing structural disparities among those residing in different territories (e.g. regions, provinces, urban areas and peripheral areas).

The region's economic dynamism, which is increasingly reliant on agglomeration economies, has resulted in a growing spatial and economic divide between territories that are lagging or declining and more prosperous ones that offer better employment prospects and well-being. As mentioned above, large productivity heterogeneity is evident across LAC countries. Even in countries transitioning to high-income status, pockets of economic stagnation still exist in certain regions (OECD et al., 2019[28]). In other words, many impoverished territories have remained trapped in low-income conditions despite the overall economic growth of their country (Figure 3.6).

Figure 3.6. **GDP per capita and territorial gaps in LAC vs. developed countries, 2020**

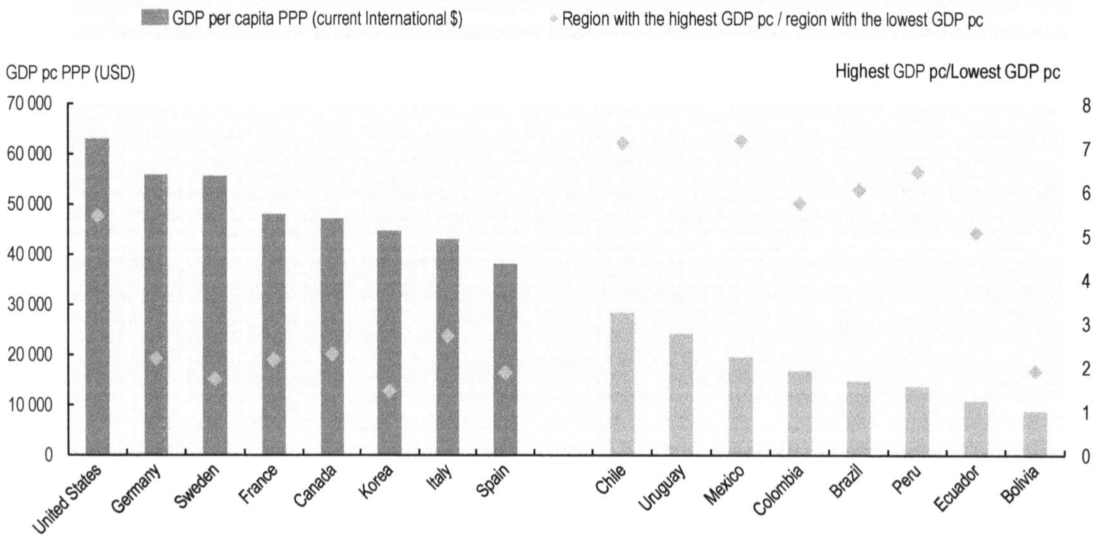

Note: PPP refers to purchasing power parities. Data on the right-hand axis refer to the ratio between the GDP per capita of region with the highest GDP per capita and the GDP per capita of the region withe lowest GDP per capita. Two OECD datasets were used for GDP per capita; i) National Accounts; and ii) Regions and Cities databases. The regions considered in each country are: United States, District of Columbia and Mississippi; Germany, Hamburg and Saxony-Anhalt; Sweden, Stockholm and North Middle Sweden; France, Île de France and Mayotte; Canada, Nunavut and Prince Edward Island; Korea, Seoul and Jeju; Italy, Province of Bolzano and Calabria; Spain, Madrid and Canary Islands; Chile, Antofagasta and Ñuble; Mexico, Campeche and Chiapas; Colombia, Bogota Capital District and Vichada; Brazil, Distrito Federal and Maranhão; Peru, Moquegua and San Martín.
Source: Authors' calculations based on (OECD.Stat, 2020[29]) and ECLAC.

StatLink https://stat.link/grcu7w

Colombia illustrates these disparities. The regions of Bogotá, Antioquia, Cundinamarca, Valle del Cauca and Santander, which account for 48.6% of the population, hold 63.3% of the country's domestic income, while six regions that comprise 13% of the total population have a mere 7% of the national income. In another example, with 8.6% of its population living in extreme poverty, poverty in Chile appears to be relatively low. In reality, extreme poverty ranges from 2.1% in XII Region (Magallanes and Chilean Antarctica) to a staggering 17.2% in IX Region (Araucania). Addressing this local dimension of inequality is crucial for ensuring the long-term stability of economic development. A strong focus on reducing disparities and promoting equitable development is essential at the regional level (OECD/UN/UNIDO, 2019[30]; OECD/UN, 2018[25]).

Territorial inequalities have wide-ranging effects on development progress beyond just GDP per capita. They impact aspects such as access to opportunities, health, education, the labour market and public goods. Disparities are evident not only between urban and rural areas but also within metropolitan areas. Being born or residing in a particular locality has a profound influence on the distribution of people's opportunities (OECD et al., 2019[28]).

Developing a robust production foundation is crucial for expanding opportunities, particularly for individuals whose prospects are heavily influenced by their geographic circumstances. It is through territorial development policies that governments can establish the appropriate conditions to stimulate new investments, improve access to human capital and skills upgrading, accelerate the adoption of new technologies, and enhance resource efficiency. In the LAC context, internationalisation can offer opportunities to develop regions in resilient and sustainable ways, fostering new economic sectors and creating quality formal jobs linked to new investments (OECD, 2023[31]). Given the pronounced territorial needs and opportunities in LAC, relying solely on national sectoral and industrial policies may yield limited results. Instead, policy development needs to be approached with a territorial lens, considering and adapting to the specific assets of each local area. In this regard, it is essential to put in place policies and programmes that boost local and regional development, strengthen community resilience and foster formal job creation (OECD, 2023[31]).

Reducing large productivity heterogeneity among sectors, companies and territories is fundamental to reducing the gaps that LAC presents compared to more developed economies. To this end, cluster-based policy initiatives can be effective for strengthening territorial productive development.

The necessary production and territorial convergence must be stimulated through improved public support of MSMEs – such as nurturing the conditions for their formalisation, better integration and performance – so that they can play a central role as agents of change in the development model.

Investment in R&D and innovation is necessary to transform LAC's production structure

Both the quantity and quality of investments matter in efforts to promote technological sophistication and the upgrading and diversification of production via new industries and production linkages, innovation capabilities, and capacities to use medium and high technologies.

Investments also need to reflect strategic choices, including a focus on sectors with competitive advantages based on technology and growing demand (as noted earlier, these entail Schumpeterian and Keynesian efficiencies). Such strategic choices can stimulate change from a vicious specialisation pattern to a virtuous one, capable of moving workers from low-productivity sectors to those with higher productivity and higher wages (ECLAC, 2022[1]).

Public investment must be rolled out on adequate scales and in sustained manners over time. Public finance can work as a catalyst if it spans the entire innovation chain – including post-research stages, which are high-risk and capital-intensive, where support for companies is often lacking.

Innovation performance depends on a great deal more than investment. It relies on systems comprised of a complex set of interactions among a variety of actors, including firms, research institutions, funding bodies, regulatory bodies, users and others (Lundvall, 2010[32]; Freeman, 1995[33]). The main policy implications are twofold. On the one hand, a systemic approach is needed in each context to deal with the different factors and forces that shape innovation processes. On the other hand, it is important to stimulate and support interactions among actors to foster effective generation and diffusion of knowledge in more systematic ways.

Innovation – and the science and technology that underpin it – is an engine for development, as it is capable of spurring and sustaining long-term growth. New products, new processes, new ways of organising production and business, along with new technological paradigms open new opportunities while shaping different development patterns. In turn, some trajectories have greater potential than others to promote enhanced productive and territorial linkages and higher levels of quality employment.

However, investment in research and development (R&D) has stagnated in LAC in the last two decades. As a percentage of GDP, investment in R&D in LAC countries remained at around 0.65% between 2017 and 2020, representing only 2.3% of the world total (Figure 3.7). This contrasts with the world's leading economies, which have consistently increased R&D investment in recent years, a trend that intensified in the context of measures adopted to recover from the COVID-19 crisis. In LAC, low, fragmented and dispersed investment in R&D is combined with an emphasis on basic research. There is insufficient support for applied R&D, which is key to fostering innovative capacity. Given the backdrop of accelerated digital and green transformations, in which the frontiers of technology and innovation are rapidly shifting, it is all the more important to increase R&D investment in the LAC region. Otherwise, the asymmetries with more developed economies could widen.

Figure 3.7. **Investments in R&D as a share of GDP, LAC vs. selected countries and blocs, 2011-20**

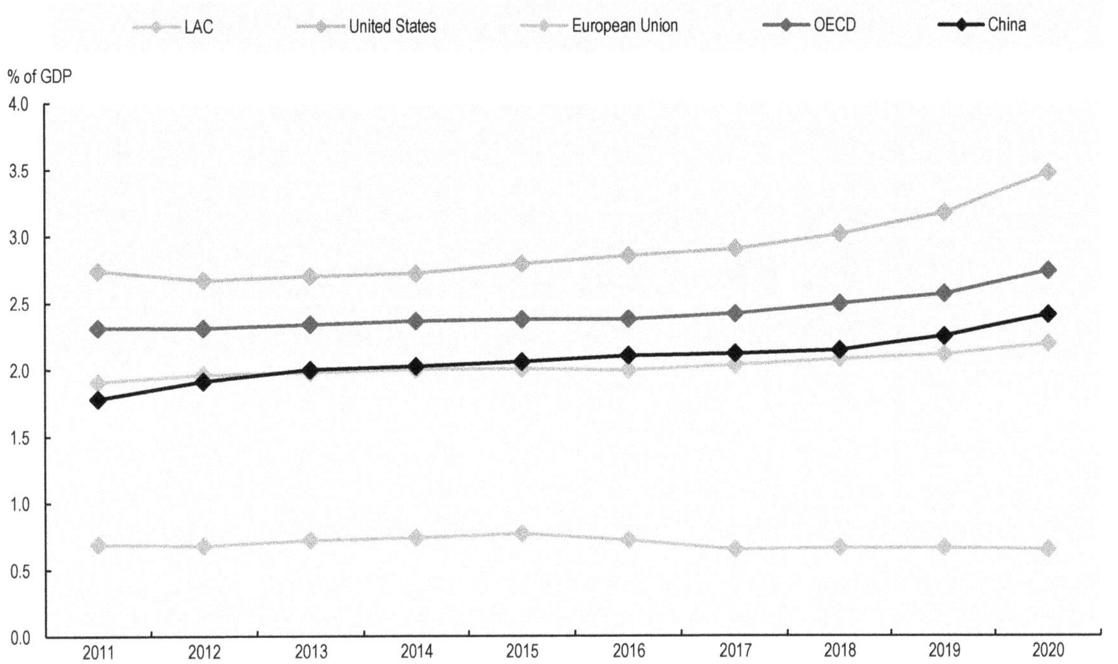

Note: Data for LAC are estimated.

Source: Authors' elaboration on the basis of the Network for Science and Technology Indicators' Ibero-American and Inter-American (RICYT), http://app.ricyt.org/ui/v3/comparative.html?indicator=GASTOxPBI&start_year=2011&end_year=2020, for LAC; the OECD's STI. Scoreboard, https://stip.oecd.org/stats/SB-StatTrends.html?i=G_XGDP&v=3&t=2011,2020&s=EU27_2020,OECD, for the United States, European Union and OECD; and UNESCO, http://data.uis.unesco.org/index.aspx?queryid=181, for China.

StatLink https://stat.link/jwtyh6

Significant heterogeneity is evident across LAC countries in R&D expenditures. In absolute terms, Argentina, Brazil and Mexico accounted for 86% of the region's R&D expenditures in 2020. Brazil, which alone accounted for 65%, invested the highest proportion of its GDP (nearly 1.2% in 2020), followed by Argentina and Cuba (0.52%). In contrast, investment levels in Guatemala and Trinidad and Tobago were close to 0.05% of GDP (RICYT, 2022[34]). As capacities vary tremendously, countries in the region face specific policy challenges in terms of improving their technological sophistication and the innovative potential of their structures of production.

At the sectoral level, most sectors in LAC invest a medium or medium-low percentage of value added in R&D. This contrasts with more developed countries, in which more sectors invest a medium-high or high percentage of value added in R&D (Figure 3.8). Within LAC, Mexico's sectors invest the most in R&D, while sectoral investment in R&D is declining in Peru and Brazil. In developed countries, particularly the United States, Germany and Korea, the range of sectors that invest a high percentage of value added in R&D are increasing.

Figure 3.8. **Distribution of sectors by investment rate in R&D, selected countries, 2015-21**

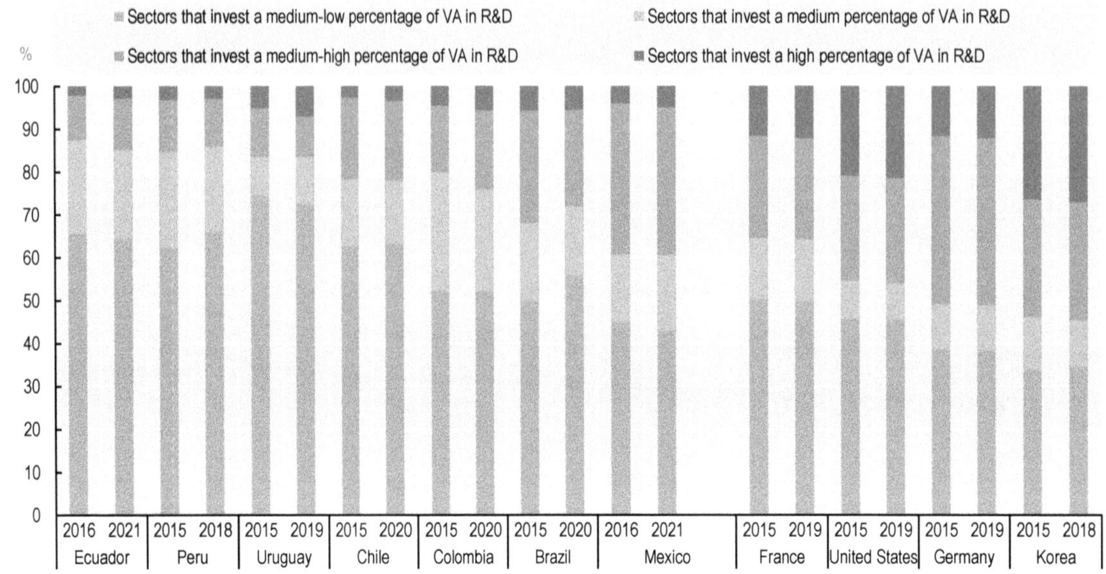

Note: VA = value added.

Source: ECLAC estimates based on data from National Statistical Offices.

StatLink https://stat.link/u6zp3w

Both public and private sources of investment are needed to develop and disseminate innovations and technologies on the scale required to address contemporary challenges and achieve sustainable development in LAC. Deepening the share of private investment in R&D remains difficult in LAC countries, where governments are the main funding source, contributing nearly 60%[1] (Figure 3.9). In more developed economies, the business sector contributes far more to R&D, exceeding 60% in the United States, the European Union and most OECD member countries and reaching nearly 80% in the People's Republic of China (hereafter "China"). Moreover, the share of R&D financed by the business sector has been increasing in those countries over the last decade, possibly driven by new technological opportunities. The very low levels of private R&D investment in LAC deserve attention from policy makers.

Figure 3.9. **Share of R&D investments by funding source in LAC and other territories, 2011-20**

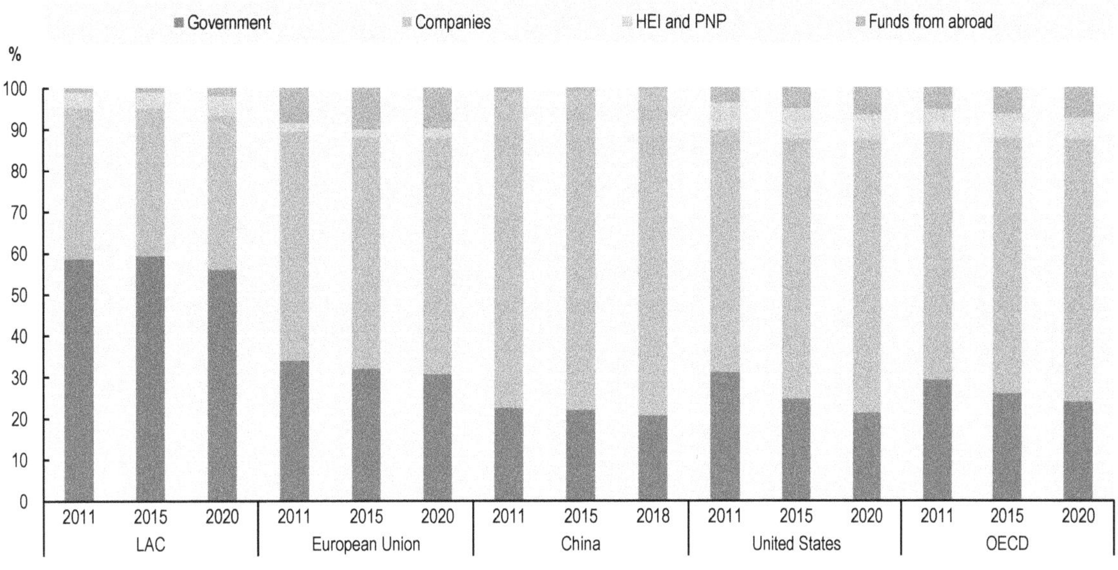

Note: HEI = higher education institutions. PNP = private non-profit organisations.
Source: Authors' elaboration based on (RICYT, 2020[35]) for LAC and OECD's STI Scoreboard for the other territories.
StatLink https://stat.link/4uge8z

A worldwide trend towards an increase in patenting over the last decade is not evident in LAC. The region's patent applications have fluctuated over the years and remain low compared to other regions, both in absolute terms and as a proportion of the population (the latter being a better metric of technological development) (Figure 3.10) (WIPO, 2022[36]).

Figure 3.10. **Patent applications by region, 2012-21**

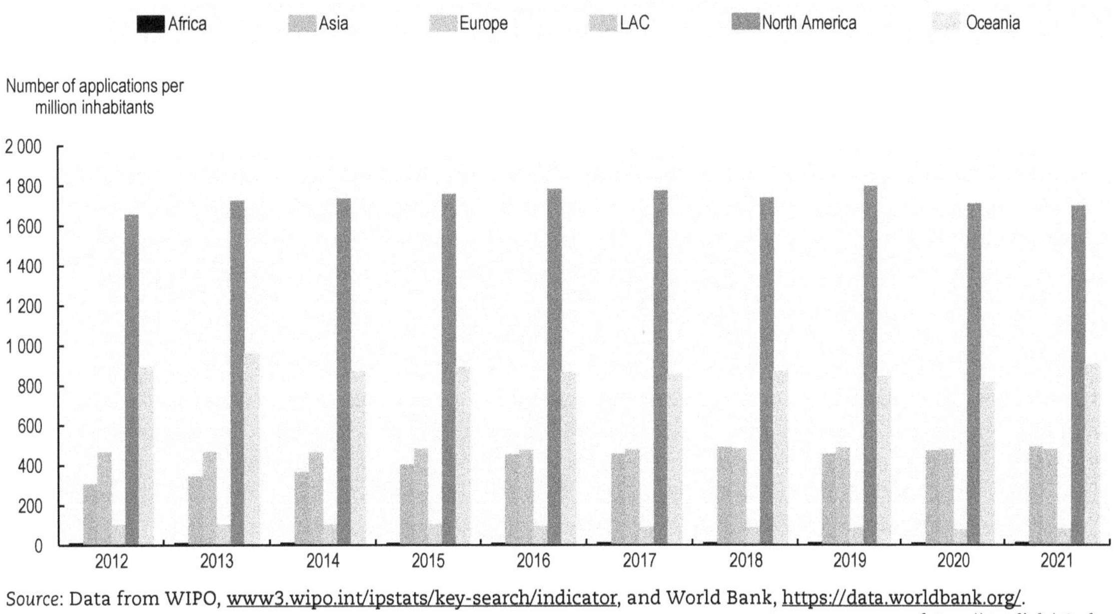

Source: Data from WIPO, www3.wipo.int/ipstats/key-search/indicator, and World Bank, https://data.worldbank.org/.
StatLink https://stat.link/z9wlog

Another particularity of LAC countries is that patent applications have been heavily dominated (87%) by non-resident applicants in recent years. This is in stark contrast to more developed countries, where most patent applications are submitted by residents (Figure 3.11). This indicates who is appropriating the knowledge registered in a country, regardless of where it was generated. Moreover, as of 2020, the number of researchers in LAC represented 4.1% of the global total, well below Asia (43.3%), Europe (30.4%), and the United States and Canada (19.6%), but above Africa (1.4%) and Oceania (1.7%).

Figure 3.11. **Share of resident applicants to national patent offices, selected countries 2019-21**

Percentages (weighted averages)

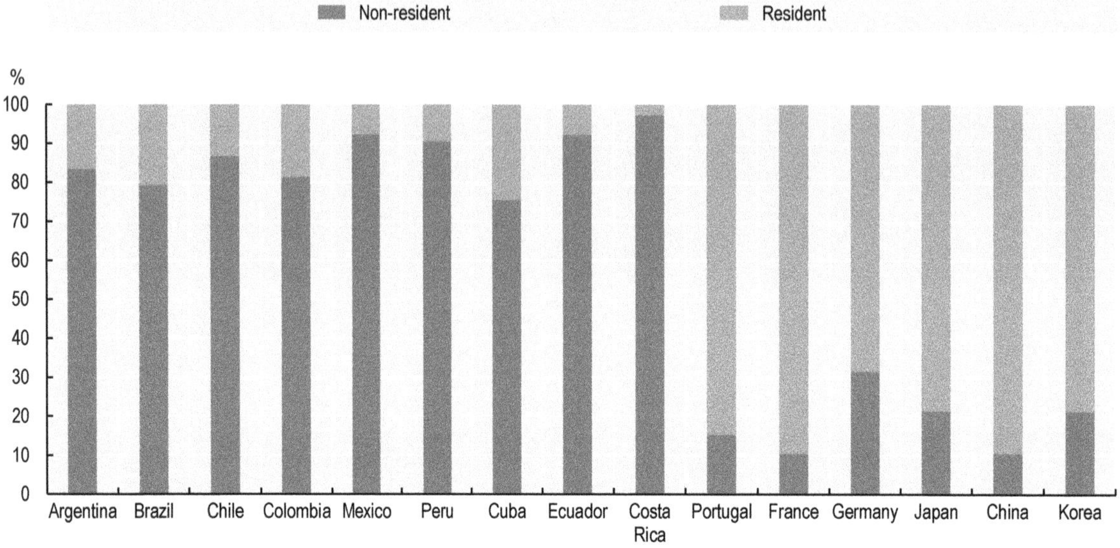

Source: Data from WIPO, www3.wipo.int/ipstats/ips-search/patent.

StatLink https://stat.link/5mwzi3

The development and accumulation of capabilities to generate, absorb and appropriate knowledge and technologies is a lengthy and difficult process that requires the collaboration of multiple actors. These capabilities can be fully developed only in a context of (formal and informal) networks among different types of players. The role of the state, however, goes beyond supporting actors and fostering these networks; it also involves establishing constituting innovation systems of various scopes (national, sectoral or subnational).

Indeed, aligning science, technology and innovation (STI) efforts and their actual contribution to addressing development needs or overcoming bottlenecks is not a natural or automatic process. Mission-oriented and transformative innovation policies are approaches that LAC countries are starting to explore in their endeavour to prioritise and mobilise resources and capacities towards solving national or subnational challenges. The effectiveness of innovation efforts also relies on horizontal factors such as education, institutional frameworks and development of physical, scientific and technological infrastructures – none of which may be disregarded. Equally relevant is ensuring that effective increases in public investment in R&D are properly directed – for example, geared to the digital paradigm and promoting a green and just transition, such that they align with national priorities. More generally, it is critical to align STI efforts with the productive development policies of LAC countries and their territories.

Dynamics of the labour market and human talent gaps: the role of investment

Analysing the labour market, investment dynamics and challenges regarding human talent and innovation capacity can help to clarify why the LAC region has, to date, not been able to increase productivity (OECD et al., 2020[8]; CAF, 2018[11]).

Since 1990, investments have not had the quality and impact desirable to advance towards better development in LAC. Investments have not been sufficiently correlated to productivity and employment growth. This section will show that improving physical and human capital investments in green sectors could be a way to contribute to creating better formal jobs.

In the last decade (as compared with previous trends), lower economic growth in LAC has been accompanied by lower employment growth, lower real hourly wages and lower productivity growth. Total employment in the region grew at a rate of 3.9% in the 1970s, 3.2% in the 1980s, and 2.4% in the 1990s and 2000s, but by just 1.5% in the 2010s (ECLAC, 2021[37]; ECLAC and ILO, 2022[12]). This dynamic is also reflected in real hourly wages, which have stagnated over the last three decades, growing at an annual rate of 2% at the aggregate level.

The shares of employment in market services in LAC countries, with low productivity growth, have been growing (ECLAC and ILO, 2022[12]). The same is true in construction and in social communities and personal services; the share of employment in both manufacturing and agriculture, by contrast, has shrunk over the last two decades (Figure 3.12). The increase in the share of employment in market services with low productivity growth is associated with a lack of structural change to boost productivity and quality job creation in the region.

Figure 3.12. **Employment by sector of economic activity in LAC, 1991-2021**

Unweighted average of 18 LAC countries

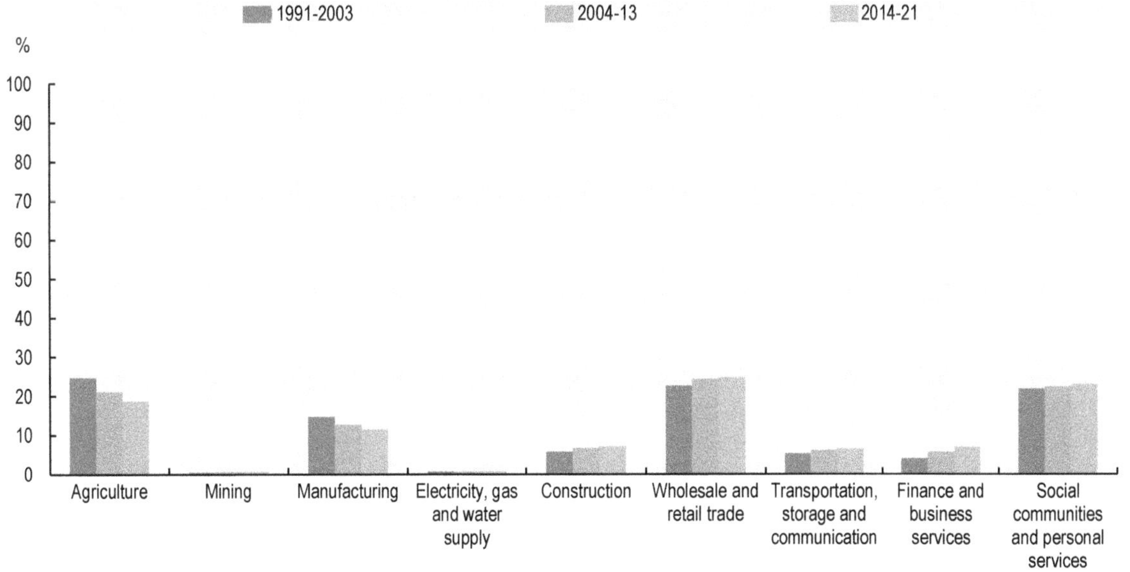

Note: The data refer to an unweighted average for the following countries: Argentina, Bolivia, Brazil, Chile, Colombia, Costa Rica, Ecuador, Dominican Republic, El Salvador, Guatemala, Honduras, Mexico, Nicaragua, Panama, Paraguay, Peru, Uruguay and Venezuela (Bolivarian Republic of).

Source: Data from (ECLAC and ILO, 2022[12]).

StatLink https://stat.link/t93uxc

Boosting formalisation could have a strong impact on improving productivity

Informality is a complex and multifaceted phenomenon, with different connotations and meanings. Some people may choose not to become formal (in terms of employment) when the perceived costs of formalisation outweigh the perceived benefits. Informal employment often acts more as a subsistence strategy in the absence of decent job opportunities. Such subsistence is associated with a low level of worker skills and productivity, as well as a lack of opportunities in the overall economy, which is closely related to a production model's ineffectiveness to absorb formal workers (Maloney, 2004[38]; Fernández and Villar, 2016[39]; Fernández et al., 2017[40]; La Porta and Shleifer, 2014[41]; OECD et al., 2019[28]). In general, informality goes beyond workers' preference for self-employment or informal work based on economic considerations; rather, it is a consequence of limited opportunities to enter the formal labour market. The lack of formal employment opportunities in LAC reflects the absence of dynamism in the formal sector, meaning that formal firms do not grow much, and tend to remain at relatively low levels of productivity. As a result, the distribution of firms by size in the formal sector is skewed toward smaller firms (OECD et al., 2021[6]; ECLAC, 2008[14]).

The high levels of informality in LAC expose workers to significant vulnerabilities in terms of income stability, working conditions, access to labour rights and social protection. These inequalities are compounded by interconnected disparities based on gender, race, ethnicity and geographic location. The limited capacity of higher-productivity sectors to create formal employment leads to a segmented labour market with unequal access to quality jobs and social protection, contributing to significant income inequality within and among households (ECLAC, 2022[1]).

As informality lowers the average productivity of an economy, it has direct impacts on economic growth. Workers in the formal sector are almost twice as productive as those working in the informal sector (CAF, 2013[42]). Given that more than half of salaried workers in LAC are informal, this considerably reduces aggregate labour productivity. If labour and capital were totally reallocated into formal firms, hourly labour productivity and wages could increase by up to 24%, even controlling for the characteristics of workers (CAF, 2013[42]). In the case of large-scale formalisation of firms, aggregate labour productivity would potentially increase by around 30% (CAF, 2018[11]).

The reallocation of factors of production from informal to formal companies within each industry or sector is relevant in LAC. At the micro level in certain LAC countries, considerable disparities exist in the return to factors of production between companies within each industry (Pagés, 2010[43]). Recent evidence from Mexico shows the interplay of the misallocation of labour and capital and low productivity, emphasising the role of the informal sector in shaping labour productivity dynamics (Levy, 2018[44]).

The relationships among productivity, investment, real wages and employment growth

Understanding the relationships among productivity, wages and labour demand in developing and emerging economies is a complex challenge. Yet such understanding is crucial to interpret how the process of innovation may be interlinked with both productivity and wage growth.[2] As heterogeneity is high across the region's countries, the specific characteristics of LAC economies must be considered to understand the role of investment in shaping these relationships. Policy recommendations should be tailored to take account of this complexity and of each country's context.

In recent decades in LAC, empirical evidence has shown a positive correlation between labour productivity and real hourly wage growth at the sectoral level: 0.72 in the short term and 0.87 in the long term between 1990 and 2016 (Figure 3.13, Panel A). However, employment growth was weakly associated with productivity growth (Figure 3.13, Panel B). In the presence of low aggregate and sectoral productivity growth, labour was structurally allocated in sectors with very low growth potential.

In the past, the disconnection between investment and productivity growth within each sector in LAC economies has been striking. From 1990-2016, the correlation between investment growth and productivity growth was not statistically different from zero in the short term and was extremely low in the long term (Figure 3.14, Panel A). Investment was not particularly associated with employment growth (Figure 3.14, Panel B).

Figure 3.13. **Labour productivity growth compared to real wages and employment growth in LAC**

Percentage differences, 1990-2016

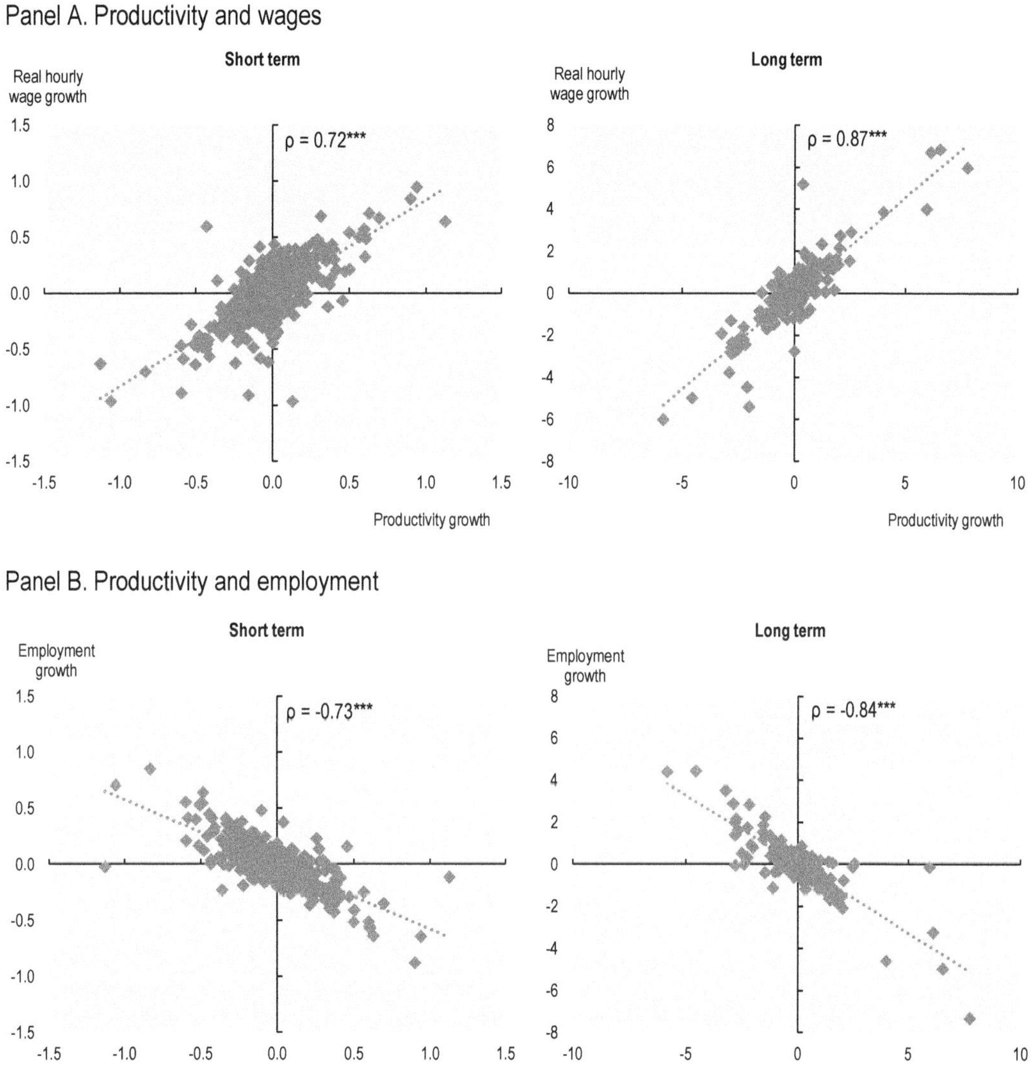

Note: Countries covered by data are: Chile, Colombia, Costa Rica, Dominican Republic, El Salvador, Honduras, Mexico and Peru. The charts show the correlation between productivity growth and hourly real wages growth (1990-2016) within the following sectors: agriculture; mining; manufacturing; electricity, gas and water supply; construction; wholesale and retail trade; transportation, storage and communication; finance and other business services; and communities and personal services (as defined following ISIC Rev. 3.1). Productivity is defined as value added per hour worked, deflated by the deflator of value added, in each industry. Real hourly wages are defined as compensation of employees per hour worked, deflated by the deflator of value-added, in each industry. Employment is defined as the number of people employed in each industry. Growth in the short term refers to year-on-year changes; in the long term refers to five years of cumulative changes. Both correlations are controlled for country-per-sector fixed effects (to show with-industries association) and for time-fixed effects (to control for possible shocks common to all industries across the countries covered). Stars refer to the significance level of each correlation: no star stands for insignificant, * stands for 10%, ** for 5%, *** for 1%.

Source: OECD estimates based on (LA-KLEMS, 2021[10]).

StatLink https://stat.link/k0mw7o

Figure 3.14. **Investment growth compared to labour productivity and employment growth in LAC**

Percentage differences, 1990-2016

Panel A. Investment and productivity

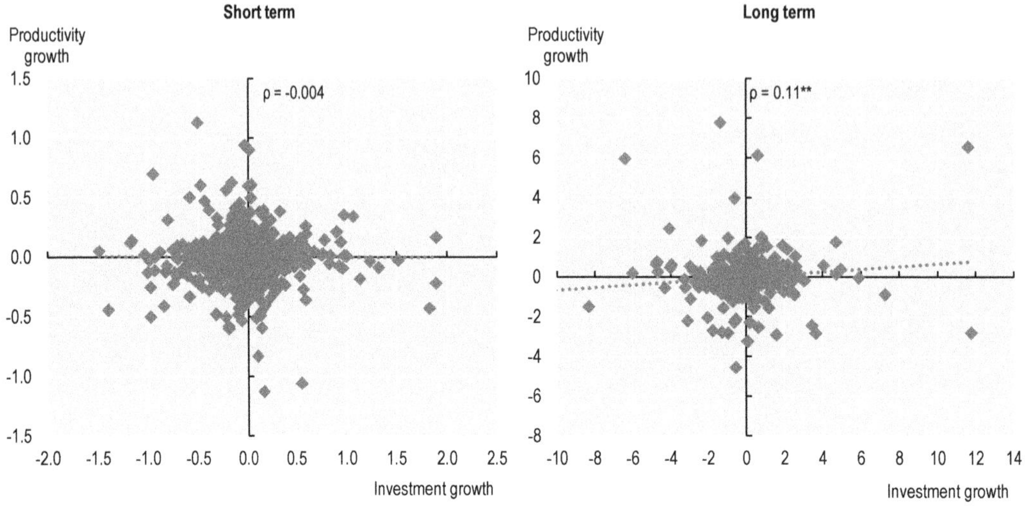

Panel B. Investment and employment

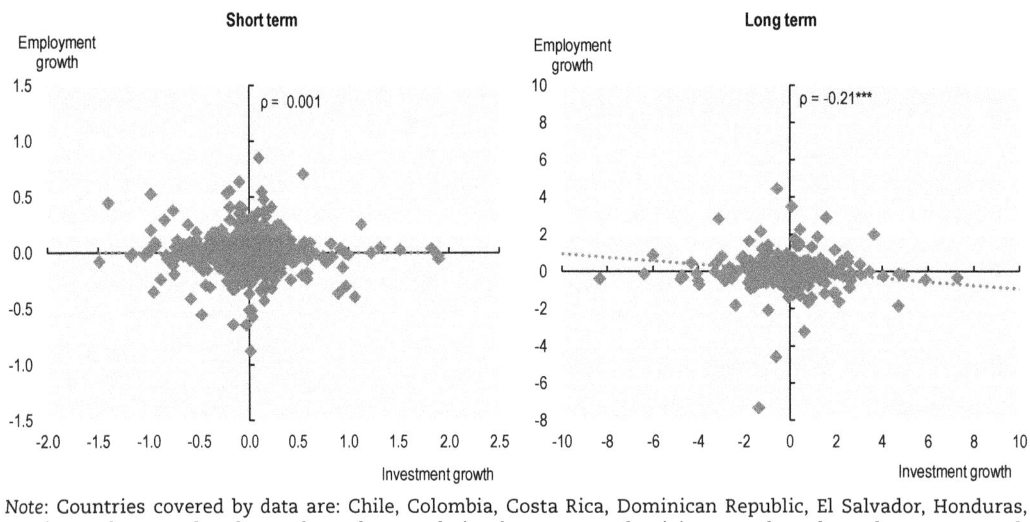

Note: Countries covered by data are: Chile, Colombia, Costa Rica, Dominican Republic, El Salvador, Honduras, Mexico and Peru. The charts show the correlation between productivity growth and employment growth (1990-2016) within the following sectors: agriculture, mining, manufacturing, electricity, gas and water supply, construction, wholesale and retail trade, transportation, storage and communication, finance and other business services, communities, and personal services (as defined following ISIC Rev. 3.1). Productivity is defined as value added per hour worked, deflated by the deflator of value-added, in each industry. Investment is defined as total real gross fixed capital formation. Employment is defined as the number of people employed in each industry. Growth in the short term refers to year-on-year changes; in the long term refers to five years of cumulative changes. Both correlations are controlled for country-per-sector fixed effects (to show with-industries association) and for time-fixed effects (to control for possible shocks common to all industries across the countries covered). Stars refer to the significance level of each correlation: no star stands for insignificant, * stands for 10%, ** for 5%, *** for 1%.

Source: OECD estimates based on (LA-KLEMS, 2021[10]).

StatLink https://stat.link/da49p2

The decoupling between productivity and employment growth in LAC calls for specific policies to restore the right incentives for firms to innovate and invest more in both physical and human capital. The region's production transformation presents a unique opportunity to provide workers with the right incentives to invest more in their skills, education and training, especially given that workers in LAC find themselves trapped in low-productive informal jobs (OECD et al., 2021[6]; OECD et al., 2020[8]).

Notably, high-skilled job creation in LAC was significantly correlated with investment growth in information and communications technology (ICT) between 2000 and 2015 (Figure 3.15). Channelling both public and private investment more effectively is a key policy priority in LAC countries to foster the recoupling of productivity, real wages and high-quality jobs. Increasing the number of interventions based on industrial policy initiatives for ICT investment, such as in broadband or other digital fixed capital investments, is crucial in LAC. For instance, closing the broadband quality gap in LAC compared to OECD countries would generate more than 15 million direct jobs, boost regional GDP by 7.7% and increase productivity by 6.3% (IDB, 2020[45]). Moreover, these policies could help to advance the formalisation of workers, given that employment is highly formal in this industry (ILO, 2022[46]).

Figure 3.15. **Investment in ICT and high-skilled jobs in LAC, 1990-2015**

Correlation coefficients between ICT investment and the growth of high-skilled jobs

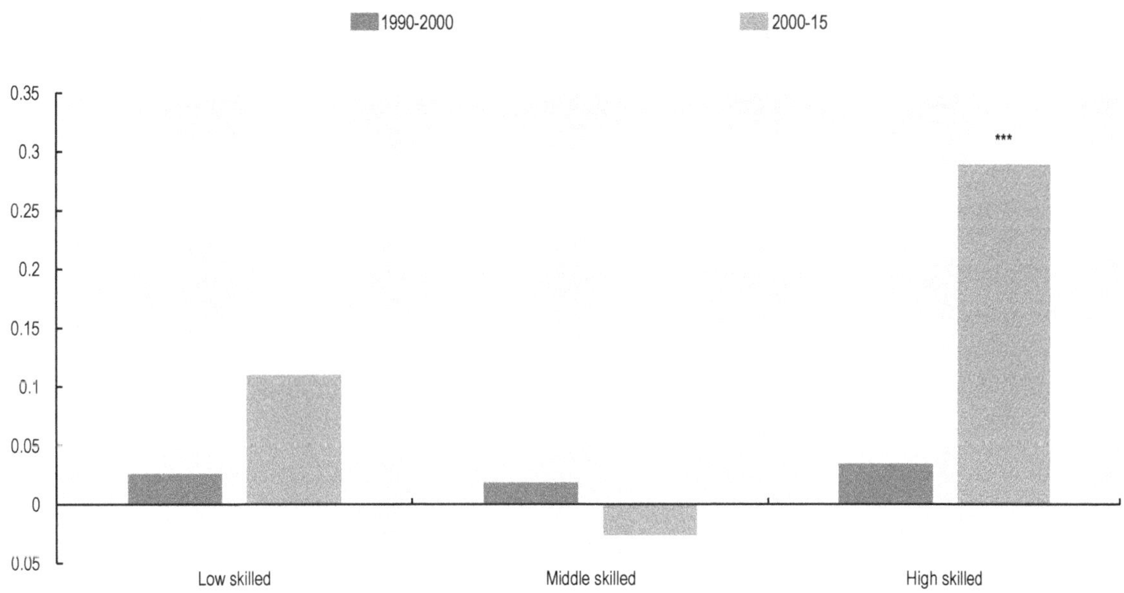

Note: Countries covered by data are: Chile, Colombia, Costa Rica, Dominican Republic, El Salvador, Honduras, Mexico, and Peru. The charts show the correlation between productivity growth and employment growth (1990-2016), within the following sectors: agriculture, mining, manufacturing, electricity, gas and water supply, construction, wholesale and retail trade, transportation, storage and communication, finance and other business services, communities, and personal services (as defined following ISIC Rev. 3.1). Investment in ICT is defined as real gross fixed-capital formation in computer and communication equipment and software. Employment is defined as the number of people employed, in each industry, by level of education, following the ISCED classification. The correlations refer to five years of cumulative changes in ICT investment and employment by educational attainment. Both correlations are controlled for country-per-sector fixed effects, so that they show with-industries association, and for time-fixed effects, to control for possible shocks common to all industries across the countries covered. Stars refer to the significance level of each correlation: no star stands for insignificant, * stands for 10%, ** for 5%, *** for 1%.

Source: OECD estimates based on (LA-KLEMS, 2021[10]).

StatLink https://stat.link/8z23qu

The role of education, skills and evolving job tasks for the production transformation

Increasing productivity levels requires more than implementing initiatives for the production sector and the promotion of innovation, research and technology. It also requires the development of individuals' capabilities in conjunction with social protection and labour policies, while addressing the challenges arising from shifts in the labour landscape.

Labour force participation in LAC is strongly associated with national levels of education. The participation rates of the adult population vary from 68% for those who completed five years or less of education to more than 80% for those who studied for more than ten years. The COVID-19 crisis exacerbated pre-existing inequalities. An entire generation of students experienced up to two full academic years of discontinuity of their studies and/or patchy remote access. This has led to widening gaps in skills development, loss of learning opportunities and the risk of increased school dropout. It could also cause more acute productivity and employability gaps in future (OECD et al., 2021[6]; ECLAC, 2022[47]).

Workers in LAC present lower levels of literacy and numeracy proficiency than workers in OECD countries (OECD, 2019[48]). In Mexico and Chile, 20% of the adult workforce has an exceptionally low level of literacy proficiency, compared to just 5% across OECD countries. In Ecuador and Peru, this share is above 30%. The situation is worse for proficiency in numeracy (Figure 3.16). More than one-third (35.2%) of Latin American adults have little or no computer experience; this negatively affects the level of economic development and ICT penetration in their countries (OECD, 2019[48]; OECD et al., 2020[8]).

Figure 3.16. **Literacy and numeracy proficiency levels, selected LAC countries and OECD, 2019**

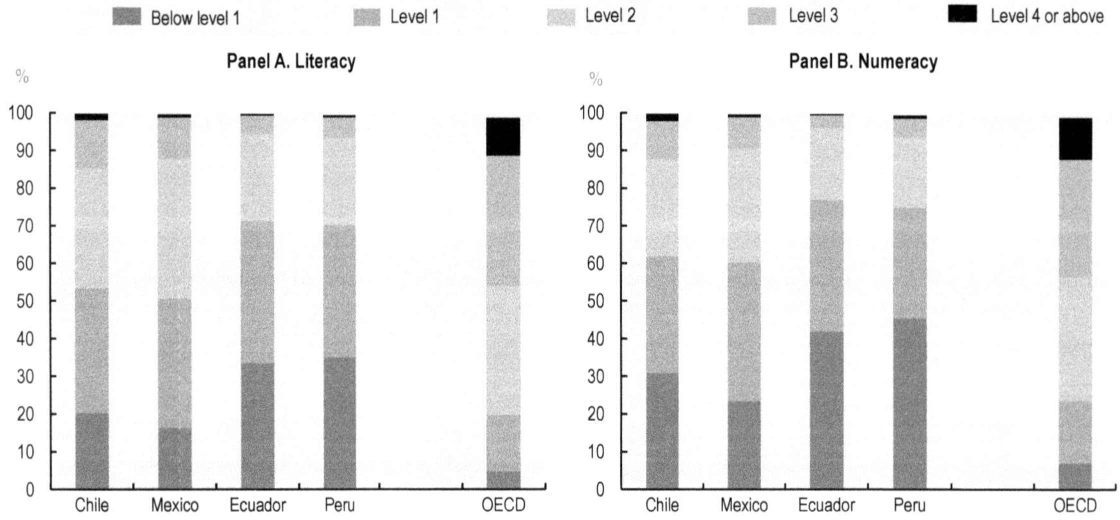

Note: In each of the two domains assessed, proficiency is considered to be a continuum of ability involving the mastery of information-processing tasks of increasing complexity. The results are represented on a scale ranging from 0 to 500. Each proficiency scale is divided into "proficiency levels", defined by score-point ranges, that have a descriptive purpose. They aim to aid in the interpretation and understanding of the reporting scales by describing the attributes of the tasks that adults with particular proficiency scores can successfully complete. It is emphasised that the proficiency levels have no normative element and should not be understood as "standards" or "benchmarks".

Source: Estimates based on (OECD, 2019[48]).

StatLink *https://stat.link/wr2z9d*

LAC labour markets show an important mismatch between proficiency and the skills that are effectively used at work. This mismatch is correlated with low productivity, low innovation and non-functional labour markets, and is highly correlated with the level of informality. The greater the skills gap between what is learned in higher education and what is demanded by the market, the lower the probability of formal employment (Ropero Santiago and Cortés, 2022[49]). Proficiency alone explains a small part of the variation of skills used at work in LAC. It represents only 1% to 6% of skills used at work (OECD et al., 2020[8]). In fact, skills utilisation – the extent to which skills are effectively applied in the workplace to maximise workplace and individual performance – depends on incentives, worker initiative and/or the demand by firms for skills required for a specific job.

There is much to be done in terms of identifying skills mismatches at a more granular level, including which profiles and competencies are needed by the production sector – and in particular those sectors prioritised under the production transformation policies of LAC countries and their territories. This identification should be based not only on information provided by the production sector (through surveys or through their participation in institutional mechanisms), but also through the use of digital technologies (such as artificial intelligence and digital labour platforms). Upon identification of skills mismatches, programmes and initiatives should be put in place to address them. This process should be supported by institutional arrangements that guarantee the participation of the public sector, the private sector and academia.

Another issue is potential job losses driven by technological change and globalisation, a matter that has caused widespread anxiety across OECD countries in recent years (OECD, 2019[50]). In LAC, some 25% of jobs in Chile, Ecuador, Mexico and Peru are at high risk of automation, according to OECD task analysis estimates. An additional 35% of jobs in these countries may undergo substantial changes in the tasks performed and how they are carried out (OECD, 2019[48]; OECD et al., 2020[8]). Similar estimates on a larger set of LAC countries, using occupational analysis, suggest that 16% of jobs are at high risk of automation (Weller, Gontero and Campbell, 2019[51]).

However, new tasks and new jobs are also emerging, which is driving shifts in skills requirements (Amaral et al., 2018[52]). Recent LinkedIn hiring data for some LAC countries (e.g. Argentina, Brazil, Chile and Mexico) show fast-growing demand for advanced digital and tech-related skills. The shift in occupations also appears to be driving an increase in categories linked with the tech industry, such as marketing, advertising, graphic design and digital marketing. As such, the digital transformation presents a unique opportunity to boost production transformation in LAC (OECD et al., 2020[8]).

The green agenda in LAC will also affect labour markets and workers' tasks and skills. As new green tasks appear and green sectors expand, job losses are expected in high carbon-emitting "brown" industries. However, the net effect of the green transition on employment could be positive. The final outcome will depend on adaptation mechanisms to create formal jobs resulting from the implementation of green policies (OECD et al., 2022[7]).

As a result of labour market transformations, most LAC labour markets have experienced losses of middle-skilled occupations, such as clerical jobs (Figure 3.17). In the last two decades, the share of middle-skilled jobs in LAC has decreased relative to the share of workers in both high and low-skilled occupations (Autor, Katz and Kearney, 2006[53]; Goos and Manning, 2007[54]; OECD, 2017[55]).[3]

Figure 3.17. **Changes in urban employment by skills level, selected LAC countries, 2000-21**

Percentage-point change in urban employment share, by skills level of occupations

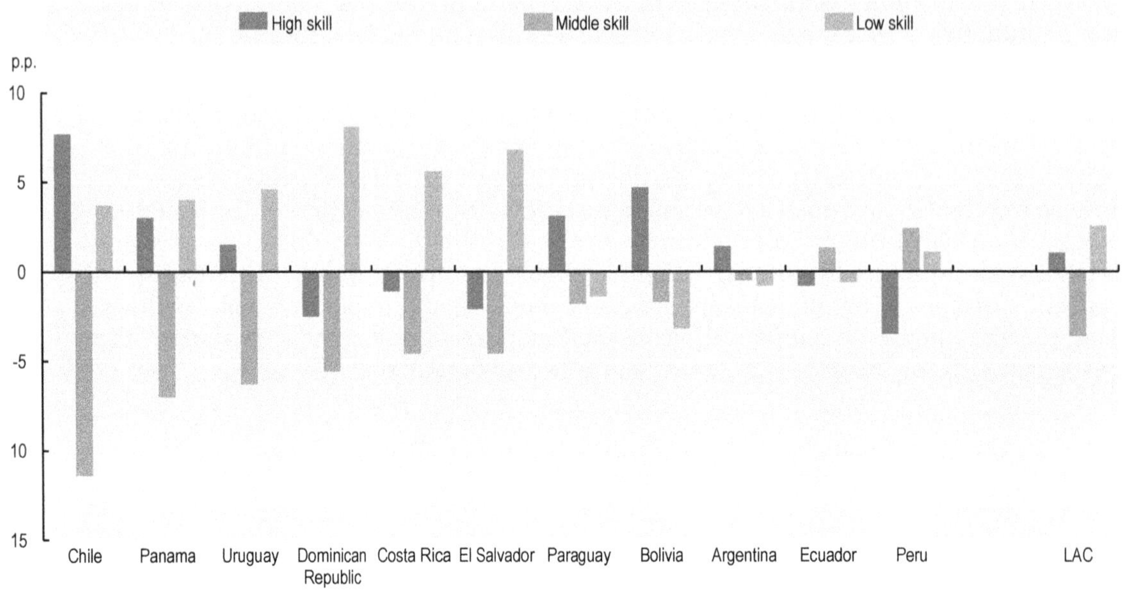

Note: High-skilled occupations include jobs classified under the ISCO-88 major groups 1, 2 and 3: legislators, senior officials and managers (group 1); professionals (group 2); and technicians and associate professionals (group 3). Middle-skilled occupations include jobs classified under the ISCO-88 major groups 4, 6, 7 and 8; clerks (group 4); skilled agriculture workers (group 6), craft, and related trades workers (group 7); and plant and machine operators and assemblers (group 8). Low-skilled occupations include jobs classified under the ISCO-88 major groups 5 and 9: service workers and shop and market sales workers (group 5); and elementary occupations (group 9), including non-skilled agriculture workers. Data refer to employment in urban areas only.

Source: OECD estimates based on ECLAC data, https://statistics.cepal.org/portal/cepalstat/dashboard.html?lang=en.

StatLink https://stat.link/yd67bl

Nine of the eleven LAC countries for which data are available have experienced a decline in the share of middle-skilled occupations. In Argentina, Bolivia, Chile, Panama, Paraguay and Uruguay, this process has been associated with an increase in high-skilled jobs; by contrast, in Costa Rica, the Dominican Republic, El Salvador, Ecuador and Peru, the share of high-skilled workers has also shrunk over the same period. In fact, both trends show the need for policies that support skills improvement for middle-skilled workers in line with future demands of the labour market, such as re-training or vocational education and training (VET) programmes (OECD, 2019[56]). The impact of the COVID-19 pandemic on learning in general, and among more vulnerable segments in particular, threatens to widen long-term disparities in terms of employability and access to formal and/or well-paid jobs. Gaps in access to and quality of education are barriers to the accumulation of skills within the active population. As such skills gaps have consequences for productivity and social and labour market inclusion, they are also a major hindrance to development (ECLAC, 2022[47]).

Investing in strategic sectors for sustainable development

Productive development efforts should prioritise areas or sectors with strong potential for long-term productivity growth (including knowledge-intensive activities) and in which investment could act as a catalyst. These efforts should promote higher productivity, better quality jobs, and the development of sustainable and inclusive value chains (OECD et al., 2022[7]).

Considering the breadth of the sectoral and horizontal challenges faced by LAC countries, it will be fundamental to strengthen capacities related to the policy-making process (e.g. planning, execution and monitoring of public policies) and financing (e.g. mobilising financial resources to support structural reform, including, among others, the financing of productive development agendas). Better understanding of the links and common causalities among different sectoral policy issues and horizontal cross-cutting policy objectives will be critical to developing responses that address their complex interactions while identifying win-win policies that promote synergies and help manage trade-offs (Chapters 2 and 4) (CAF, 2018[11]).

Figure 3.18 presents a set of strategic sectors that have potential to drive sustainable development in the LAC region. The figure uses coloured boxes to identify each sector's potential to contribute to areas of sustainable development, social inclusion and productivity (see colour key above the figure). Investments in these areas could both catalyse the production transformation of LAC countries and also help them to make progress towards the United Nations Sustainable Development Goals (SDGs) of the 2030 Agenda for Sustainable Development (ECLAC, 2023[15]; ECLAC, 2023[57]; ECLAC, 2023[58]).

Figure 3.18. Sectors with high potential to drive sustainable development

Sustainable development components

- Social inclusion
- Economic recovery/employment generation
- Production diversification
- Knowledge/technology intensive
- Productivity increase
- Export opportunity
- Climate change / green transition
- Trends/new development models
- Sovereignty/national security/resilience
- Skilled employment

Green transition:

Energy transition
Combating climate change requires moving towards a clean energy supply matrix, as well as progressing towards sustainable consumption by increasing the incorporation of renewable energies. Electrification and the development of green hydrogen and critical minerals and their value chains can play a key role in achieving decarbonisation goals.

Circular economy
The circular economy could have significant impacts on the economy in terms of increases in GDP and employment, while also delivering reductions in greenhouse gas emissions.

Sustainable water management
Even though LAC hosts the second-largest water resources in the world, 161 million people still do not have access to drinking water. There is a need, and therefore an opportunity, to promote investment to universalise water coverage.

Electromobility
The transition towards low-carbon transportation, particularly based on electricity and through quality public transport service provision, is key to fighting climate change and environmental pollution. It also offers opportunities to generate new economic activities.

Sustainable tourism
After a long period of restrictions on movement due to the COVID-19 pandemic, LAC countries aim to rebuild the tourism sector. In this context, sustainable tourism comes as an interesting option, taking full account of its current and future economic, social and environmental impacts.

Digital transformation:

Digital economy
Digital development has potential to increase the well-being of people, the productivity of companies, the efficiency and effectiveness of the public sector, and environmental sustainability. This could come as the result of synergies among key dimensions including connectivity, adoption of digital technologies and fostering the digital economy.

Export of modern services
Digitally deliverable services (modern services) have been the most dynamic sectoral category of world trade in the last 20 years. Digital technologies have facilitated cross-border trade in a variety of services that until recently were considered untradable, such as business, financial, engineering, design, educational and medical services.

Advanced manufacturing
Advanced manufacturing and Industry 4.0 technologies represent the frontier of industrial production. The arrival of Industry 4.0 implies changes and shocks to the current production structure in LAC, but also offers opportunities to address industrialisation in an innovative and efficient way.

Health and the care economy

Pharmaceutical and medical devices industry
The health-care manufacturing industry, which includes pharmaceuticals and medical devices, could have a strategic role, not only because of its direct impacts on people's health, but also because it generates high-quality jobs, is supported on solid production value chains, and promotes technical progress via high intensity in R&D and important knowledge externalities.

Care society
The care society represents a great opportunity for growth and employment, particularly in a region in which the population is aging and women have been providing care services to children, homes and the elderly under informal conditions. Investing in the care society could reduce the unpaid work carried out mostly by these women and contribute to reducing restrictions on their participation in the labour market, politics and society.

Sustainable agriculture and food systems:

Sustainable food production
Additional demand from a growing world population will require significant increases in food production. The LAC region has 16% of the world's agricultural land and 33% of the unused agricultural area. Investment in technology, infrastructure and training aimed at improving productivity will be a key factor in agricultural development.

Bioeconomy
The bioeconomy encompasses the production, sustainable use, conservation and regeneration of biological resources to provide products, services, processes and information to all economic sectors. It fosters biorefinery and bio-industrialisation processes producing goods and services in rapidly expanding market segments. That is the case of the biotechnology, biofertilisers and biopharmaceuticals markets, all of which are expected to double within the next four to seven years, opening opportunities for investment in LAC.

Source: Authors' elaboration based on (ECLAC, 2023[15]; ECLAC, 2023[57]; ECLAC, 2023[58]; ECLAC, 2022[1]; ECLAC, 2020[5]).

Each sector in Figure 3.18 represents opportunities for investment for both the public and private sectors. Although the list is not exhaustive and could evolve over time, these areas could provide significant opportunities for transforming LAC economies. Each country could focus its productive development policies on economic activities related to these areas, defined according to the country's characteristics, strengths and priorities (ECLAC, 2020[5]).

These sectors can be grouped in four broad areas which are interlinked and where significant transformations are taking place, opening up new opportunities for investment and job creation. These four areas are: i) the green transition; ii) the digital transformation; iii) health and the care economy; and iv) sustainable agriculture and food systems. These areas not only have potential to stimulate production transformation in LAC countries, they can also contribute to the energy transition (green transition); address weaknesses and alleviate dependencies revealed during the COVID-19 crisis (health and the care economy); mitigate some of the consequences of Russia's war of aggression against Ukraine (sustainable agriculture and food systems); and help to build resilience and strengthen national sovereignty, taking advantage of technological progress as an enabler for improving productivity and competitiveness (digital transformation).

The green transition

The green transition offers an unprecedented opportunity for advancing production transformation and improving well-being in LAC (OECD et al., 2022[7]). In recent decades, green sectors in the region have shown more dynamic growth than the rest of the economy. Since 2005, these green sectors have grown by 3.3% every year, compared to 2.8% for the total economy (Figure 3.19).[4]

Figure 3.19. **Growth of value added in green sectors vs. the rest of the economy in LAC, 2005-21**

Average yearly growth rates

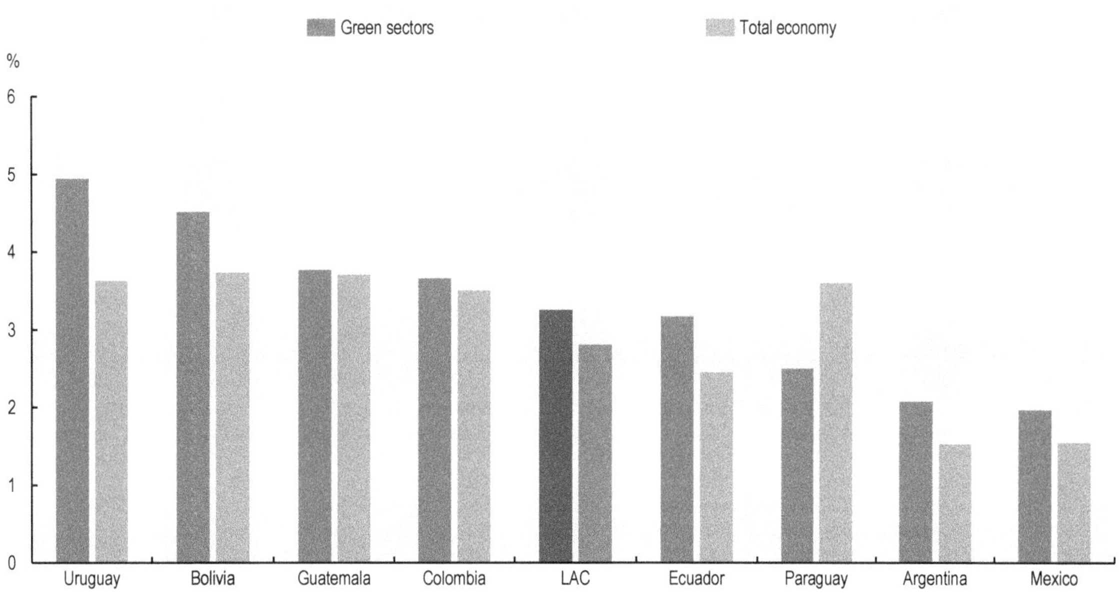

Note: Green sectors are defined in each country by first identifying the number of green tasks that workers perform in their occupations and then by looking at the top ten industries in which those jobs are distributed. Value added is defined at chained-linked constant prices.

Source: Authors' calculations based on (OECD et al., 2022[7]) and countries' national accounts.

StatLink https://stat.link/elq9md

The effects of climate mitigation and adaptation policies on labour markets of LAC countries will involve creating new job opportunities, as well as loss of some jobs due to decarbonisation policies in brown sectors. The net effect on jobs will depend on the industrial structure of each country and the effectiveness of investment packages in boosting green job creation while softening any negative impacts of climate mitigation policies on specific firms and the labour market more broadly (OECD et al., 2022[7]; OECD, 2023[59]). Thanks to a relatively high proportion of green sectors to brown sectors in LAC, the green transition's net effect on employment could be positive, as brown sectors in LAC represent 35% of total employment, compared to 55% for green sectors. The actual outcome will, however, depend on the investment agenda for implementing adaptation mechanisms to create formal jobs in green sectors. Even in a scenario in which investment grows by just one percentage point per year, the effects would be positive compared to the business-as-usual (BAU) scenario. If, for instance, green sectors created jobs according to a low-impact scenario (with investment increasing by one percentage point each year) while jobs in brown sectors were destroyed according to a high-impact scenario (with value-added in each brown sector decreasing by five percentage points per year), this would still translate into 1.8% more total employment in 2030. In the case of medium-impact (investment growing each year by two percentage points) and high-impact policies (annual growth of three percentage points) for green sectors, additional job creation in 2030 would be 6.0% (medium-impact) and 10.5% (high-impact) of total employment in the brown and green sectors (Figure 3.20).

Figure 3.20. **Net employment change by 2030 through investment in green sectors in LAC**

% change in employment compared to 2020 business-as-usual, different scenarios

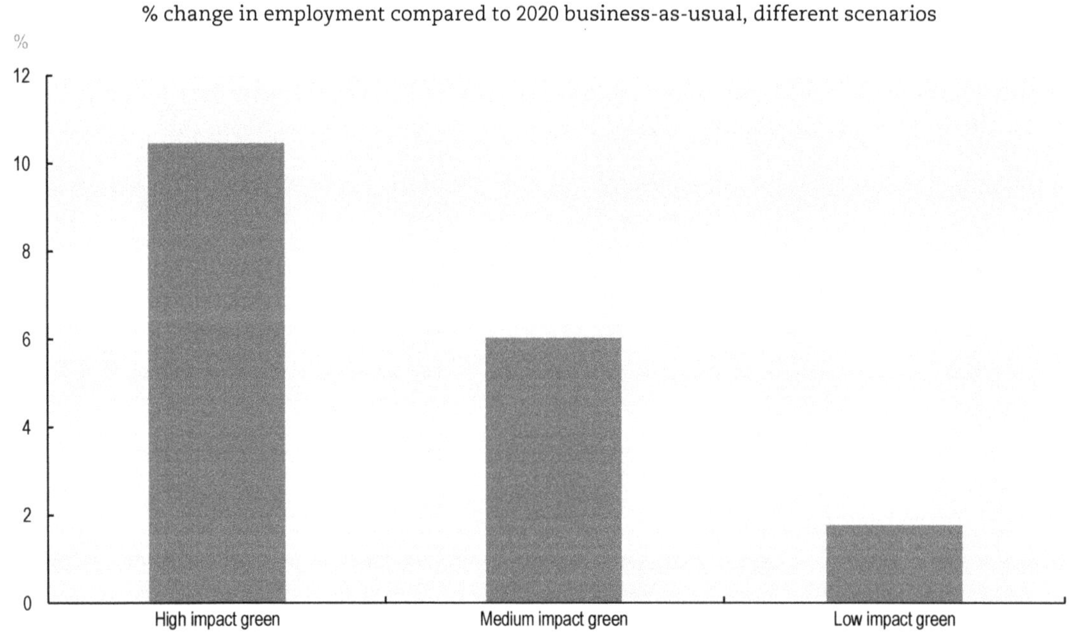

Note: LAC countries included are: Argentina, Bolivia, Brazil, Colombia, Ecuador, Guatemala, Mexico, Paraguay and Uruguay. The data refer to an unweighted average over the countries' forecasts. Green sectors are defined in each country by first identifying the number of green tasks that workers perform in their occupations and then by looking at the top ten industries in which those jobs are distributed. The BAU scenario assumes that, in each green sector, value added and employment will follow the same dynamic as in the past ten years. The counterfactual scenarios are defined according to the impact of green policies that aim to boost investment in fixed and human capital, with a positive impact on value-added growth in each green sector. The high-impact scenario assumes that the value added in each sector will increase by 3 percentage points per year, adjusting to the new equilibrium. The medium-impact scenario assumes that the value added will increase by 2 percentage points, while the low-impact scenario assumes that it will increase by 1 percentage point. Brown sectors are defined according to the CAIT definition (https://datasets.wri.org/dataset/cait-country. The BAU scenario assumes that, in each brown sector, GHG emissions, value added and employment will follow the same dynamic as in the past ten years. The counterfactual scenarios are defined according to the impact of green policies that aim to reduce total GHG net emissions by 50% in 2030 (compared to the 2020 levels) in each brown sector. Figure 3.20 assumes a high-impact scenario in which the value added in each brown sector will decrease by 5 percentage points per year, adjusting to the new equilibrium. In all forecasts, total factory productivity (TFP) will increase by 1 percentage point due to lower climate damages and new technology-induced change. Employment change is forecast using the estimated short-term elasticity to the value added (using a panel dynamic model), defined by each sector and country, in the last ten years.

Source: (OECD et al., 2022[7]).

StatLink https://stat.link/2hknxe

The identification of green sectors depends on the distribution of green tasks across occupations, as well as on the industrial structure of each LAC country. Analysis of nine countries (Argentina, Bolivia, Brazil, Colombia, Ecuador, Guatemala, Mexico, Paraguay and Uruguay) in this regard reveals some important regional insights. In a high-impact scenario where investments in green sectors increase by 3 percentage points annually, several economic sectors are at the centre of green job creation in the region: sustainable food manufacturing (+18.8% green jobs by 2030) is related to more sustainable production models in agriculture, food and beverages, and sustainable intermediate products; public administration (+14.6%) includes activities related to the planning and implementation of sustainable policies (from general administration to sustainable local development or energy market policies). It also comprises supervision and administration of social and economic life such as public activities related to the care economy; construction (+14.3%) is mainly linked to new sustainable building constructions, installations and completions that should improve buildings' energy efficiency thanks to the use of new technologies. It also includes repair, additions and alterations to improve environmentally existing constructions; transport (+14.1%) reflects the need for more sustainable passenger and freight transportation systems, and to support sustainable transport activities, including the ones linked to digital transformation through telecommunications; finally, commerce (14.1%) represents the growing new business models of selling goods and services, and to repair goods that should contribute to developing the circular economy (Figure 3.21). Country-specific analyses are necessary to determine sectors that would benefit the most from the green transition.

Figure 3.21. **Potential employment change in green sectors in LAC by 2030**

% change in employment compared to 2020 BAU, high-impact scenario of investments in fixed and human capital

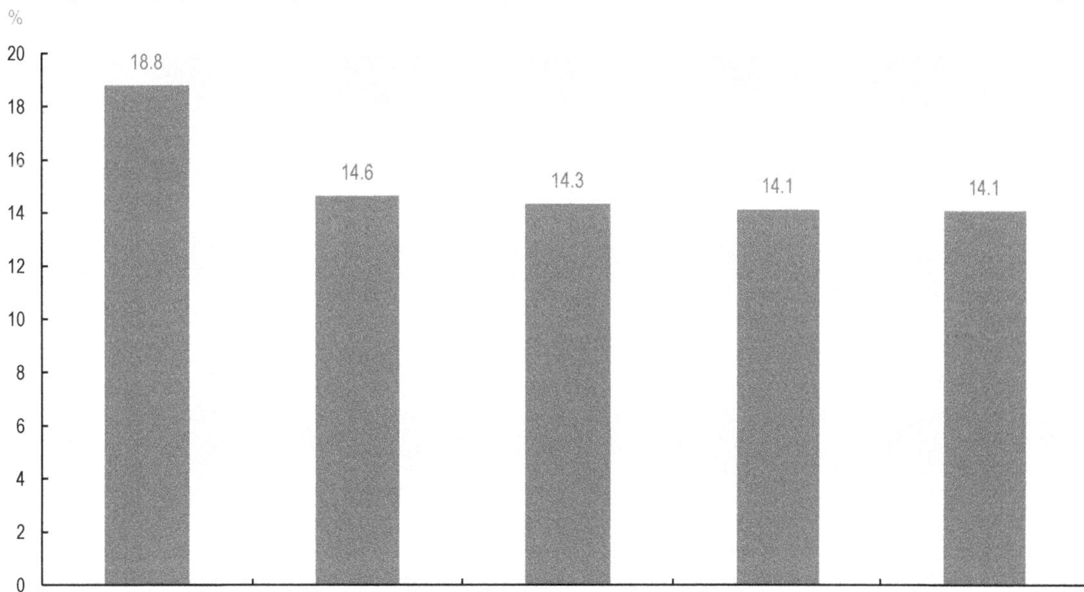

Note: LAC countries included are: Argentina, Bolivia, Brazil, Colombia, Ecuador, Guatemala, Mexico, Paraguay and Uruguay. The data refer to an unweighted average over the countries' forecasts. Green sectors are defined in each country by first identifying the number of green tasks that workers perform in their occupations and then by looking at the top ten industries in which those jobs are distributed. The BAU scenario assumes that, in each green sector, value added and employment will follow the same dynamic as in the past ten years. The counterfactual scenarios are defined according to the impact of green policies that aim to boost investment in fixed and human capital, with a positive impact on value-added growth in each green sector. The high-impact scenario assumes that the value added in each sector will increase by 3 percentage points each year, adjusting to the new equilibrium. In all forecasts, TFP will increase by 1 percentage point due to lower climate damages and new technology-induced change. Employment change is forecast using the estimated short-term elasticity to the value added (using a panel dynamic model), defined by each sector and country, in the last ten years.

Source: Authors' calculations based on (OECD et al., 2022[7]).

StatLink https://stat.link/j20x6a

The green transition also presents a unique opportunity to boost job quality in the LAC region. New green occupations are mostly related to advanced scientific knowledge and skills. Workers with a high intensity of green tasks performed on the job are more likely to be highly educated and formal than the general population of LAC workers (Figure 3.22). However, large gender differences persist in LAC in terms of student disposition towards science-related careers. Although similar shares of boys (34%) and girls (35%) report that they expect to work in a science-related occupation, they appear to select different fields. Girls choose health professions more than boys, while boys choose ICT, science or engineering professions more than girls (OECD et al., 2020[8]). To achieve outcomes that are more balanced just in terms of job quality and formalisation, policies should aim to narrow the gender bias in career selection.

Figure 3.22. **Workers in green jobs are likely to be male, highly educated and formal in LAC**

Odds ratios

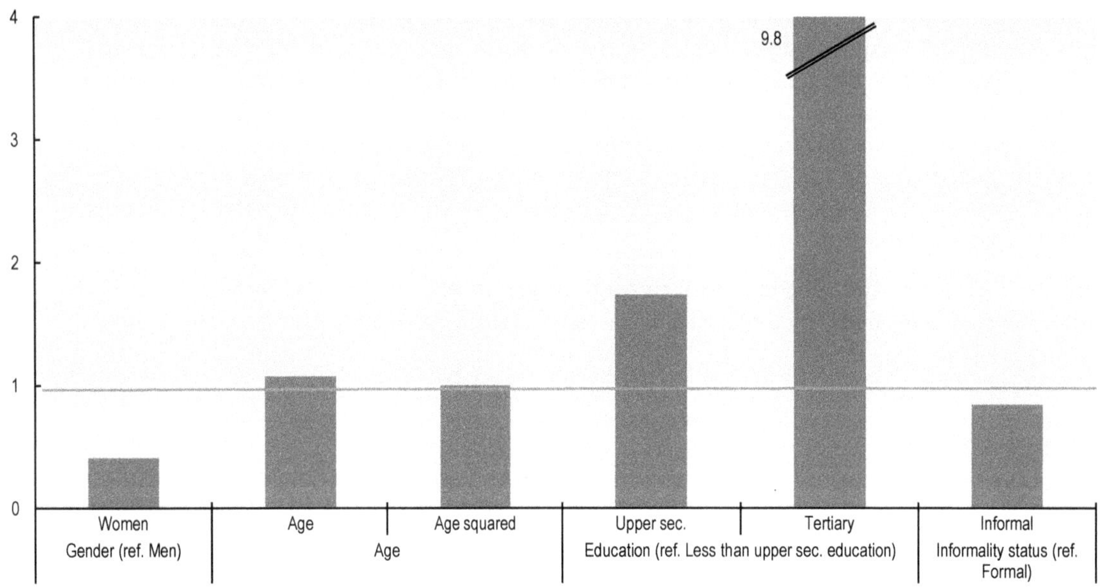

Note: The figure shows the odds ratios of a logistic regression of holding a job with a high intensity of green tasks, with the regressors shown in the chart. The odds ratio is the ratio of the odds of an event occurring in one group to the odds of it occurring in another group. An odds ratio greater than 1 indicates that the condition or event is more likely to occur in the first group. An odds ratio less than 1 indicates that the condition or event is less likely to occur in the first group. For instance, in the chart the odds of holding a green job for women is 0.4 times the odds for men, meaning that women are less likely than men to be employed in a green occupation. The data refer to a pooled sample of workers in Argentina, Bolivia, Brazil, Colombia, Ecuador, Guatemala, Mexico, Paraguay and Uruguay in 2021. Green tasks are identified using the methodology of (Vona et al., 2018[60]).

Source: Authors' calculations based on national labour-force surveys.

StatLink https://stat.link/b80nez

An effective green transition will need substantial public and private investments in physical capital, and proper policies to anticipate the skills demand for the new jobs that will be created. Education and training policies are therefore necessary to move towards a more inclusive and just development model and increase people's welfare. Effective employment services can help workers to move from brown to green sectors. Depending on the sector and region, it should be noted, that workers' displacement may be substantial (OECD et al., 2021[6]; OECD et al., 2022[7]).

The potential of the energy transition to advance the green production transformation in LAC countries is explored below. Other sectors described in Figure 3.18, like electromobility, the circular economy, sustainable tourism and sustainable water management, also play a central role in making the green transition possible and promoting sustainable development the region.

Energy transition

Fighting climate change requires moving towards a low-carbon energy supply matrix and accelerating sustainable consumption habits. Renewables represented 33% of the primary energy supply in LAC in 2020, substantially above the global level of 13%, but fossil fuels still represented 67%. In sectoral terms, transport is the region's largest final consumer of energy (35%), which comes almost exclusively from fossil fuels, followed by industry (30%) and residential use (18%) (OECD et al., 2022[7]).

To meet potential demand for clean energy and electrification in LAC, investments in the electricity sector will have to double before the end of this decade and grow even more to three times current levels by 2050 (IRENA, 2021[61]). To increase investments in renewable energy to the magnitude necessary for achieving the energy transition, LAC countries need to adopt comprehensive policies and adequate instruments to attract private investment (Chapters 2 and 4). Investment policies need to be designed within the broader context of energy transition and productive development policies. Such policies need to consider the drivers of investment, market forces and international technology development to calibrate the toolbox and steer investments towards priority technologies, sectors or stages of the value chain (ECLAC, 2023[62]; OECD, 2023[63]). Renewable energies and electrification, along with green hydrogen and critical minerals, will play key roles in making the energy transition possible in LAC.

Renewable energies and electrification

LAC countries have well-developed energy markets as well as great potential in terms of their endowment of renewable energy resources. Satisfying the region's growing electricity demand requires replacing fossil fuels with renewable energies, concentrating efforts on the management of national power grids, and promoting and strengthening regional electrical integration initiatives. Besides, to secure the resources needed to advance the energy transition, LAC countries will have to implement medium- and long-term strategies that mobilise domestic and international investment in renewable energy development. FDI can play a vital role in this process (ECLAC, 2023[62]; OECD et al., 2022[7]).

Renewable energy installed capacity in LAC increased by 5% between 2019 and 2020, with hydropower production capacity representing more than 70% of total renewables. Solar energy experienced the greatest increase (36%), followed by wind energy (18%), bioenergy (2%) and hydroelectric power (1%) (Figure 3.23, Panel A). Over the last two decades, FDI project announcements for renewables in LAC, both in value and number, have mainly involved Brazil, Chile and Mexico (Figure 3.23, Panel B).

Figure 3.23. **Renewables in LAC: installed capacity and FDI project announcements, 2005-22**

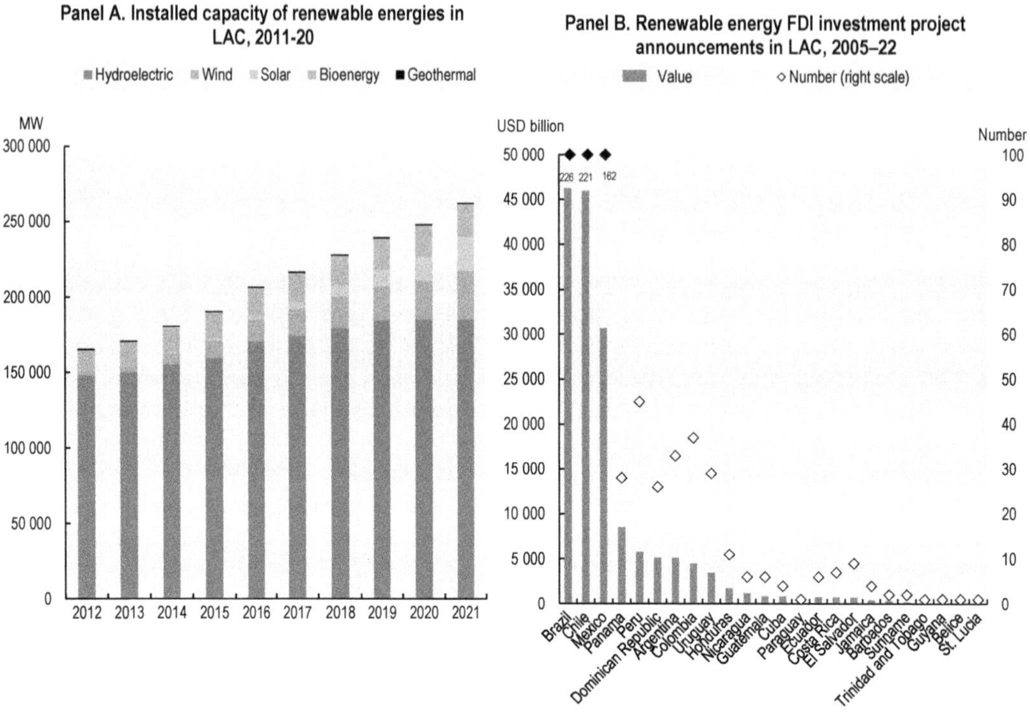

Source: Authors' elaboration based on (IRENA, 2021[61]) and (ECLAC, 2023[62]).

StatLink https://stat.link/flaz8p

Achieving universal access to electricity remains a challenge in LAC. A total of 17 million people in the region still do not have access to electricity – especially in rural areas, where the electrification rate in some countries is around 76% (OECD et al., 2022[7]). For all to have access, 1.3% of regional GDP should be invested annually for ten years, and renewables technologies (mostly solar and wind) should increase in line with the SDG 7 targets on access to affordable and clean energy. These changes could create 7 million new green jobs and reduce greenhouse gas emissions by more than 20% (OECD et al., 2022[7]).

Green hydrogen

Green hydrogen is an energy carrier produced through a process that is powered by renewable energy; as such, it releases no pollution into the atmosphere. Given LAC's abundant and competitive renewable energy resources (hydroelectric, solar and wind power), green hydrogen could thus be a driver of the next phase of the region's clean energy transition, while also contributing to achieving energy security and resilience goals (RICYT, 2022[34]). Hydrogen is also one of the leading options for storing renewable energy (IEA, 2019[64]).

Although there is no commercial-scale production of green hydrogen in the region yet, several LAC countries have official strategies and roadmaps, as well as pilot projects, to develop production that could supply both local and international markets (OECD et al., 2022[7]). Green hydrogen pilot-scale projects are currently being implemented in LAC in transportation (buses, long-distance trucks, shipping) and mining (especially as a replacement for truck diesel). For example, in 2022, Uruguay presented its Green Hydrogen roadmap with the goal of developing a domestic market and first pilot projects by 2025;

scaling up the domestic market and having the first export-scale project, by 2030; and consolidating the domestic market, aiming to produce 20 GW of electricity and 10 GW of electrolysers, by 2040 (MIEM, 2022[65]).

Policies should promote the green hydrogen industry as an engine for sustainable reindustrialisation, supported by industrial clusters distributed throughout the region, which could be strengthened through cluster initiatives under the productive development policies of LAC countries. A key challenge is the lack of appropriate technologies (specifically, electrolysis machines) in the region to produce green hydrogen, making it imperative to develop capacities and train experts to develop this industry (RICYT, 2022[34]).

Critical minerals

LAC is in a strategic position to supply critical minerals (e.g. lithium and copper) that are essential inputs for scaling up renewable energy technologies. Such technologies (and, thus, the minerals) are needed for the green transition in areas such as wind turbines, solar photovoltaic panels, lithium-ion batteries for electromobility and transmission infrastructure. LAC has 61% of global lithium reserves, 39% of global copper and 32% of global reserves of both nickel and silver. At present, it is responsible for 37% of global production of both copper and lithium (OECD, 2022[66]). Demand for critical minerals is expected to grow exponentially by 2040 (compared to 2020 levels): lithium by up to 42 times; graphite by 25 times; cobalt by 21 times; nickel by 19 times; and copper by 2.7 times (IEA, 2021[67]). To meet the growth in global demand and avoid rigidities on the supply side, the extractive and processing capacity of critical minerals in the LAC region will have to be multiplied considering socio-environmental impacts.

Digital transformation

Digital transformation can potentially increase the well-being of people, the productivity of companies, the efficiency and effectiveness of the public sector, and the sustainability of environments. Progress towards digital transformation is advancing as a result of the synergies between key dimensions including connectivity, the adoption of digital technologies and fostering of digital economies (ECLAC, 2021[68]). The ability of LAC countries to provide adequate digital infrastructure for operating digitally enabled international production networks could become a new key determinant in the location decisions of transnational firms.

At present, the availability and use of digital technologies varies widely across LAC. Despite advances in connectivity, significant gaps persist in access and use of digital technologies within and between LAC countries, especially when compared to most advanced economies. In 2021, penetration of household fixed broadband in LAC was 62%, well below North America (close to 100%) and Europe (90%). Gaps in LAC also reflect income inequalities: 66% of rural households and 43% of households in the two lowest income quintiles still need to be connected to the internet, while only 25% of urban households are not yet connected (ECLAC, 2022[69]).

The quality of fixed broadband connections varies among LAC countries (OECD et al., 2020[8]). Brazil, Chile, Colombia, Panama and Uruguay stand out for having high average download speeds (more than 100 megabits per second, or Mbps) and low latency (less than 20 milliseconds). This is above the world average and comparable to the quality of connections in advanced economies such as Japan, the Republic of Korea and the United States. Argentina, Costa Rica, Mexico, Paraguay and Peru are in an intermediate situation, with speeds of more than 50 Mbps (equalling the LAC average), while Bolivia, El Salvador, Guatemala, Haiti and Honduras lag behind (Figure 3.24, Panel A). Mobile broadband connections are the main access modality in the region. Their quality is more homogeneous (than fixed broadband), with speeds of close to 30 Mbps and latency of 35 milliseconds in general, although this lags further behind the quality in more advanced countries (Figure 3.24, Panel B).

Figure 3.24. **Fixed and mobile download speeds in LAC, 2022**

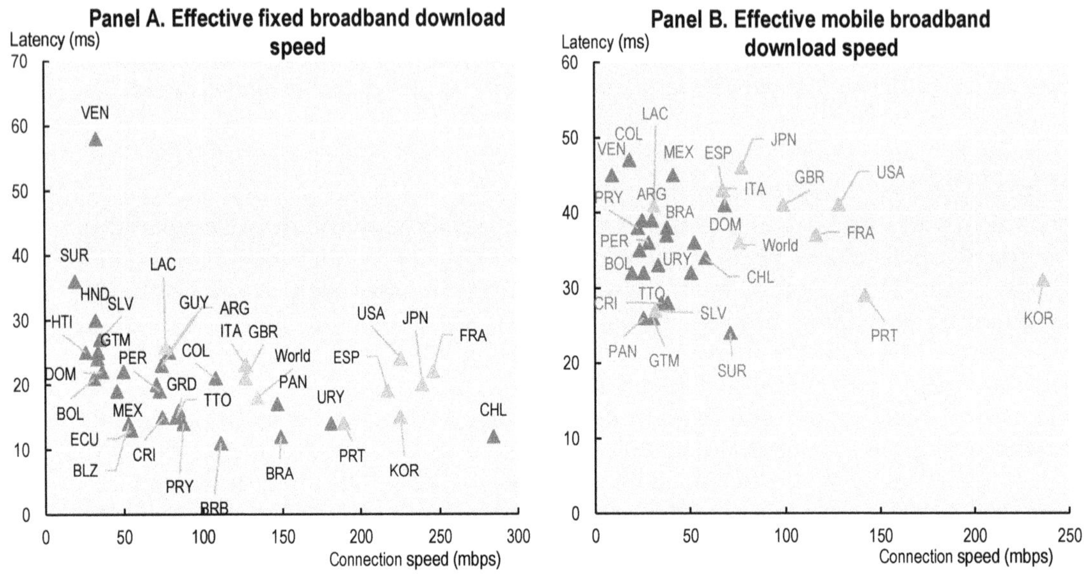

Source: ECLAC, Regional Digital Development Observatory, on the basis of Speedtest Global Index (www.speedtest.net/global-index).

StatLink https://stat.link/6u72fq

Digital infrastructure is necessary for optimal operation of digitally enabled international production networks. If LAC countries can provide adequate digital infrastructure, it could attract transnational firms to the region.

Adoption of advanced technologies is accelerating in the production sectors

While LAC companies have a high level of connectivity, they lag far behind companies in more developed countries in the use of digital technologies in supply, manufacturing and distribution processes. However, LAC companies have dramatically accelerated the adoption of advanced digital technologies since the COVID-19 pandemic (this is particularly true of large companies with more than 200 employees). Cloud computing was the technology most used by companies in Argentina, Brazil, Chile, Colombia and Mexico in 2020 (55%), and also the technology with the highest growth during the pandemic (26%), followed by big data and digital platforms (19% in both cases), the Internet of Things (18%) and artificial intelligence (16%) (Basco and Lavena, 2021[70]). Yet more than 70% of companies in LAC have only a passive presence on the internet through their websites, illustrating the large adoption gaps with regards to both emerging and mature digital technologies. As such, much can be done to help companies, especially MSMEs, to adopt existing digital technologies (Vilgis, Jordán and Patiño, 2023[71]).

FDI in the digital economy is increasing in LAC

New FDI project announcements in the digital economy are increasing in LAC, along with mergers and acquisitions in sector. However, the region received only 7% of global FDI projects in 2021 (compared to 33% in Western Europe, 18% in Asia and the Pacific, and 12% in North America). The number of announced investment projects increased from 118 in 2005 to 396 in 2021, while mergers and acquisitions of companies related to the digital economy increased from 8% of the total number of operations in 2005 to 17% in 2021. The investment amount of announced projects peaked at USD 33 billion in 2021.

Telecommunications project announcements have concentrated the largest FDI investment in the region, with around 70% of the total between 2005 and 2021. In terms of the number of projects, 60% were announced in software and computer services, and 30% in telecommunications.

In recent years, some important venture capital players have turned their attention to sectors related to the digital transition in LAC. In 2022, venture capital investments in the region reached USD 7.8 billion, the highest value on record (LAVCA, 2023[72]).

Health and the care economy

The pharmaceutical industry has a strategic role that goes beyond health. It can also create high-quality jobs. Thanks to the intensity of R&D in the sector, it can also promote technical progress and relevant positive spill-overs on knowledge.

The supply-chain disruption caused by the COVID-19 pandemic revealed weaknesses of this industry in the LAC region. To be better able to cope with future health emergencies, it is urgent to reduce LAC's high degree of dependence on transnational companies. This requires developing more resilient and self-sufficient local industries by strengthening the region's scientific, technological and production capacities. The region took a step in this direction in 2021 by approving a Plan for Self-Sufficiency in Health Matters (ECLAC, 2021[73]).[5]

National and regional investments must play a central role in generating the conditions for the development and strengthening of capacities in those LAC countries that have a health-related manufacturing industry. Foreign investment will also be essential to facilitate technology transfer and the integration of LAC companies into global value chains. However, the region received only 0.55% of global investment in the sector between 2005 and 2021 (ECLAC, 2022[16]).

The pharmaceutical sector presents opportunities for LAC

Many countries in LAC have developed pharmaceutical production capacities, although transnational companies still dominate the market for brand-name medicines. In Argentina, Brazil and Mexico, national laboratories play a fundamental role in the production of medicines, biosimilars and generics. Of 15 sales laboratories, 8 are in Argentina and Brazil, 6 in Mexico and 1 in Colombia (ECLAC, 2021[73]).

However, the region's participation in international trade in pharmaceutical and biopharmaceutical products represented only 0.7% of world exports in 2020. The value of LAC's pharmaceutical exports decreased by 32% between 2012 and 2020, falling to USD 4.9 billion, and the region has a persistent trade deficit in the sector. In 2020, it imported six times more pharmaceutical products than it exported (ECLAC, 2021[73]).

The pharmaceutical sector presents important opportunities for LAC countries. First, the number of micromolecular medicines and brand-name medicines with patents that are expiring will double by 2028. This market segment offers new possibilities for producers in LAC that have already developed capacities in the production of generics. The biosimilars market also represents a safe and low-cost alternative to biological medicines for which patents will expire in the short term.

Clinical trials are the main stage of the sector's R&D process and one of the most promising markets for LAC. Although the region has increased its participation and capacities for developing clinical trials, most clinical studies are submitted by international laboratories or institutions.

Large multinational pharmaceutical companies have a weak presence in LAC

LAC has not been a prominent destination for greenfield projects in the pharmaceutical sector. The region received only 5% of the global total of projects announced between 2005 and 2021. Ten companies (six European, three American and one Canadian) accounted for 50% of the announced investment amount projects in LAC. Brazil received 33.9% of total announcements and Mexico 17.4% (ECLAC, 2023[57]). Moreover, pharmaceutical project announcements in LAC have targeted mainly production-stage activities. There was less emphasis on pre-production investments than the global average, especially R&D activities, and a greater volume of post-production investments, especially in logistics and retail services (Figure 3.25).

Figure 3.25. **FDI projects announced in the pharmaceutical industry in LAC and globally, 2003-21**

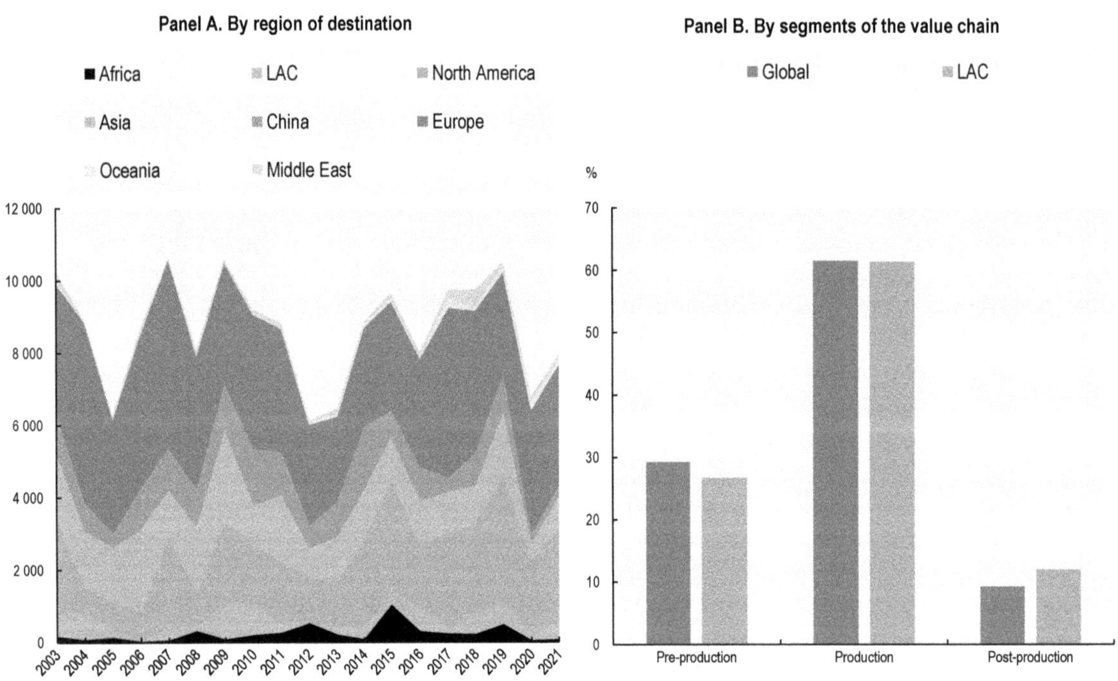

Source: Authors' calculations based on Financial Times, fDi Markets.

StatLink https://stat.link/q6cah9

LAC has the potential to strengthen its pharmaceutical industry and move towards a greater supply of medicines within the regional market. Technological and structural changes in the pharmaceutical industry require an investment effort to improve innovation and production capacities and capabilities and to turn pharmaceuticals into a development engine for the region. To attract FDI, it is necessary to fulfil the basic prerequisites of the sector: skilled labour; basic infrastructure; access to inputs; adequate institutional frameworks; proper health and intellectual property regulation; increasing investment in R&D; and consolidating regional integration in production and distribution chains. This action agenda requires partnerships and collaboration on at least two levels. It implies working on regional initiatives, such as the implementation of the Plan for Self-Sufficiency in Health Matters while also strengthening productive development policies at the national and subnational levels (ECLAC, 2021[73]).

LAC countries are lagging behind in the global market of medical devices

The medical devices market can be a strategic sector for LAC countries. In 2018, the medical device industry was estimated at USD 430 billion and global production is largely located in the United States, Europe and Japan (ECLAC, 2023[57]). In the last twenty years, the relocation of some manufacturing stages of this sector has started, opening potential opportunities for LAC countries to position themselves in the global value chains of these products. Currently, most LAC countries are net importers of medical devices from high-income countries. Just a small fraction of local demand is satisfied with products made by small domestic enterprises with a low or medium level of technological sophistication. Brazil is an exception, as 50% of its demand for medical devices is satisfied with domestic products (Drucaroff, 2021[74]). Costa Rica, the Dominican Republic and Mexico have started hosting multinational companies that export medical devices to the North American market. For example, Mexico's medical devices sector has capitalised on nearshoring practices and geographical proximity in fostering strategic coupling with the US economy. From 2003 to 2020 Mexico's exports of medical devices grew by 8.6% annually, on average, and almost 97% of them were exported to the United States.

Building a care society is key for a new and more just sustainable development model

The care society is a strategic opportunity to build sustainable and equitable growth in LAC. Policies should aim at merging economic and environmental dimensions, as well as at reversing social and gender inequality, to place the care of people and the planet at the heart of a sustainable development model. In 2022, the Buenos Aires Commitment has been adopted. LAC countries agreed to "design, implement and evaluate macroeconomic policies, particularly fiscal policies (income, spending and investment), from a gender equality and human rights perspective to guarantee universal access to affordable and quality care services" (ECLAC, 2023[75]). To achieve this, the right to care needs to be recognised, guaranteeing the right of each person in three basic dimensions – providing care, being cared for and caring for oneself. This is particularly true in the context of ageing LAC societies. Population ageing, higher life expectancies and the COVID-19 crisis have increased the burden of care work, with important changes to the demand for care. In the region, more than 8 million people aged 60 years or older (corresponding to more than 1% of the region's population) need help in carrying out basic life activities (ECLAC, 2022[47]). Care work can be approximately measured by unpaid work in the home. In LAC unpaid work ranges between 15.9% of GDP (Argentina) and 27.6% of GDP (Mexico). On average, women perform 74% of it (ECLAC, 2023[57]).

Large investments are required to move forward the care society agenda, in LAC, but the returns would be sizable, both in terms of new jobs and additional tax revenues. Some studies conducted in Uruguay and Mexico suggest that boosting universal and free childcare systems would require an annual investment of 2.8% of GDP in Uruguay and of 1.2% of GDP in Mexico (De Henau et al., 2019[76]; UN-Women, 2020[77]). If that were the case, women's employment rates would increase by 4.2 percentage points in Uruguay while total employment levels would increase by 3.9% in Mexico. The jobs created would generate additional tax revenues reducing the net financing gap to 1.4% of GDP in Uruguay, while in Mexico, additional revenues could be close to 0.3% of GDP.

Sustainable agriculture and food systems

World food consumption will increase by 1.4% per year in the next decade, mainly due to population growth (OECD/FAO, 2022[78]). Agriculture and agribusiness are key sectors for LAC economies. With 16% of the world's agricultural land and 33% of its unused agricultural area, the region has the world's largest reserve of land with agricultural potential (ECLAC, 2019[79]). The sector is key to ensuring food security in the region, as well as being a source of food for the rest of the world, while also having potential to generate productivity growth and employment. However, the region needs to increase productivity in agribusiness, decarbonise food production and improve access to food for the most vulnerable population.

Productivity challenges are heterogeneous in LAC's agricultural sector

Due to restrictions on the expansion of exploitable lands, most of the increase in agricultural production in LAC should come from productivity increases. Greater investment in technology, infrastructure and training aimed at improving productivity will be a key factor in agricultural development. For example, the yield in cereal production in the United States is double the LAC average (and the world average) and triple the average achieved in the Caribbean and in the LAC group of net food importing countries. In the case of soybeans, the yield in South American countries (especially in Brazil) is practically equal to that of the United States. For livestock, a relevant productivity indicator is the weight per animal. In the United States, this indicator for cattle is 70% higher than the world average and around 2.5 times higher than the average for the Caribbean and net food importing countries. In the case of poultry, the United States and South America (especially Brazil) have similar yields, 30% higher than the world average (ECLAC, 2023[57]).

Private and public investment is required to increase agriculture productivity

LAC should invest around USD 60 billion per year to reach the relative level of investment in agriculture in advanced economies. Agricultural productivity is directly related to the intensity of investment in the sector.[6] The intensity of agricultural investment in the European Union is four times that of South America and about six times that of Central America and the Caribbean. In the United States, agricultural investment is three times more intense than in South America and about five times that of Central America and the Caribbean (ECLAC, 2023[57]).

The agri-food sector is marked by uncertainty and volatility. Two central functions of public investment (beyond generating public goods) are helping to eliminate investment risks through reliable information and analysis, and developing skills and competencies in the institutions and actors that participate in the sector. Although public spending is important to make private investment in agriculture viable, LAC countries tend to allocate relatively few public resources to the sector. As a percentage of the value of agricultural production, the United States allocates between 4 and 13 times more public resources to the sector than do selected countries in the LAC region. To reach the relative level of the United States, the LAC countries shown in Figure 3.26 would have to allocate an additional USD 48 billion annually.

Figure 3.26. **Gross capital formation and public expenditure in agriculture, 2020**

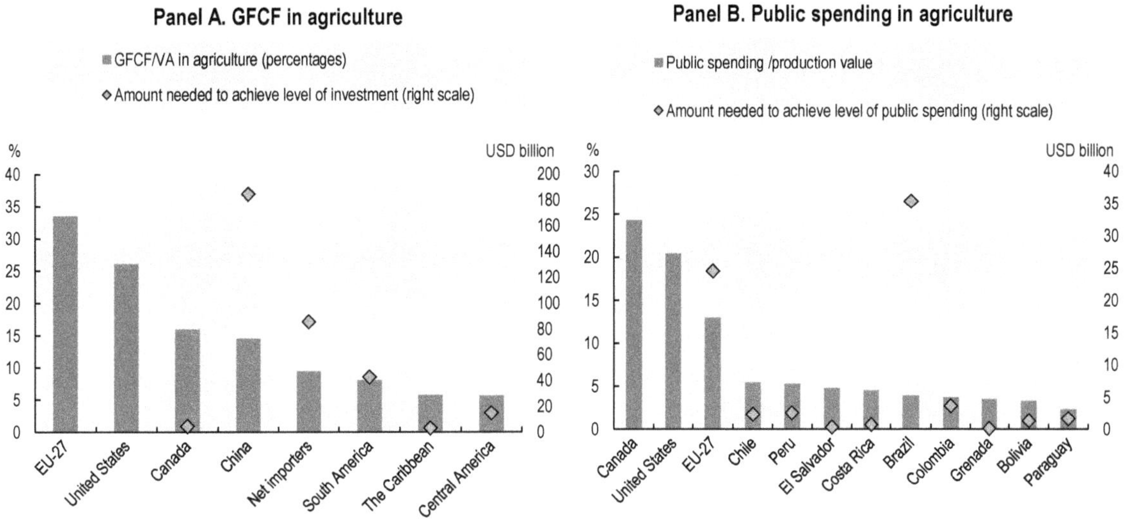

Note: Data in Panel A refer to gross fixed capital formation (GFCF) as a percentage of value added (/VA) in agriculture. In Panel B, they refer to public spending on agriculture as a percentage of the production value in agriculture.
Source: ECLAC, based on the FAOSTAT online database (www.fao.org/faostat/en/#home).
StatLink https://stat.link/13lw4p

Transnational companies are present in LAC's agri-food industry

Transnational companies have a strong presence in the LAC region's main agri-food export chains. Companies from the United States, the European Union and China, as well as Latin American transnationals, are strong players in the production and marketing of soybeans, sugar, coffee, beef, corn, bananas, chicken meat and cereals. European companies have led the announcements of investment projects in the food and beverage industry in the region, with close to USD 9 billion or 38% of the total announced between 2017 and 2021. In addition, accounting for 6% of the value of projects in the period, agri-food ranks seventh among the ten main sectors for investment within the announcements of European firms (ECLAC, 2023[57]).

Key policy messages

Successful public policies to advance production transformation in LAC need to address both horizontal and vertical bottlenecks that hinder the upgrading and diversification of the region's economies. In particular, this includes closing technological and production gaps with more developed economies, and productivity gaps among sectors, firms and territories.

Production development policies should adopt comprehensive, holistic and systemic approaches with a comprehensive set of tools, which are still lacking in LAC countries, both at national and local levels (Chapter 4). Moreover, they should address the different interconnected dimensions of production transformation including: human talent development; formalisation of informal enterprises; technology adoption and innovation; supply chain development; and diversification of production and export capabilities. To achieve a more sustainable and just development model, it is essential to align the prioritisation of strategic sectors – those showing greater technological intensity and greater potential for learning, innovation and market expansion – with the key societal challenges and cross-cutting issues faced by LAC societies.

Important differences remain across LAC countries. A set of key policy messages can nonetheless contribute to guiding each country to implement its own policy mix to advance a production transformation process that catalyses investments, creates formal jobs and increases people's well-being (Box 3.2).

Box 3.2. Key policy messages

Towards improved productivity and job creation

- Include sectoral production development policies that align with horizontal cross-cutting policies as an integral part of development strategies.
- Strengthen and diversify national and local production, technological and innovation capacities for investment to have positive impacts on productivity and quality job creation.
- Develop strategies to achieve higher investments in green sectors, in both fixed and human capital, to produce net positive effects in terms of job creation.

Towards production and territorial economic convergence

- Implement cluster-based policies to strengthen territorial production development. Help to finance and promote innovation among cluster participants and complement or strengthen missing or weaker links in local value chains.
- Provide support and access to finance for start-up companies with high growth potential to allow them to harness their dynamism and consolidate.
- Promote the performance, formalisation and better integration of MSMEs in local and national value chains.

Towards improving investments in R&D and innovation

- Increase public investment in STI. Structure business support to cover all stages of the innovation chain, co-ordinating policy instruments and public institutions for this purpose.
- Enable the institutional conditions and create a business environment to increase private investment in R&D.
- Articulate innovation policies with production development policies in close co-ordination with the private sector.

Towards boosting quality labour and upskilling for all

- Complement production transformation policies by labour market and social policies to better integrate informal workers into the formal economy and to protect the members of households whose income comes entirely or partially from informal work.
- Invest in human capital, talents and new skills to better match the present and future demand for skills and the supply of education and training. Co-ordinate public and private efforts at the national and local levels.
- Introduce policies to enhance STEM careers for women and most vulnerable groups to increase their access to green jobs given that workers holding green jobs are more likely to be highly educated and formal than most workers and that large gender differences persist in green sectors.

Box 3.2. **Key policy messages** *(cont.)*

Towards investment in strategic sectors for sustainable development

- Adopt a strategic sectorial approach, aligned with horizontal cross-cutting policies, to boost production transformation in LAC. This approach will benefit from greater technological and market dynamism and innovation.
- Promote investments in key activities, including the green transition, digital transformation, health and the care economy, and sustainable agriculture and food systems, to stimulate structural change, boost productivity and positively impact social inclusion and sustainability.

Notes

1. This is an underestimation, given that data on business investment includes investments made by state-owned enterprises.
2. Standard models assume that technological change is exogenous in the short and medium term. Technological progress is considered as external and not dependent on current investment in human or physical capital. However, if innovation is assumed to be endogenous, depending on wages as well as capital costs and the investment decisions of firms, employment may well decline, even if productivity and wages grow at the same rate (Hellwig and Irmen, 2001[80]).
3. OECD countries have experienced a similar mega-trend. In almost all OECD countries for which data are available, this process has resulted in a shift of employment towards high-skilled occupations.
4. This is true for all LAC countries for which data are available except Paraguay.
5. In September 2021, at a request from the Community of Latin American and Caribbean States (CELAC), the United Nations Economic Commission for Latin America presented a Plan for Self-Sufficiency in Health Matters. The plan, which was unanimously approved by the country members, is comprised of seven lines of action and defines a clear regional roadmap to enhance productive capacities and resilience. In June 2022, with this plan as a reference and within the framework of the EU Global Gateway strategy, a new initiative was launched: the European Union – Latin America and the Caribbean partnership on local manufacturing of vaccines, medicines and other health technologies, and strengthening health systems resilience. The partnership aims to increase Latin America's manufacturing capacity, foster equitable access to health products, strengthen health resilience and improve capacities to address non-communicable diseases.
6. Gross fixed capital formation in agriculture as a percentage of value added in the sector is used as a proxy for investment intensity.

References

(UN-Women), U. (ed.) (2019), "Investing in free universal childcare in South Africa, Turkey and Uruguay: A comparative analysis of costs, short-term employment effects and fiscal revenue", *Discussion Paper, No. 28*, https://www.unwomen.org/sites/default/files/Headquarters/Attachments/Sections/Library/Publications/2019/Discussion-paper-Investing-in-free-universal-childcare-in-South-Africa-Turkey-and-Uruguay-en.pdf. [76]

Amaral, N. et al. (2018), "How far can your skills take you: Understanding skill demand changes due to occupational shifts and the transferability of workers across occupations", *Technical Note*, No. IDB-TN-01501, Labour Markets and Social Security Division, Inter-American Development Bank, Washington, DC, https://doi.org/10.18235/0001291. [52]

Audretsch, D. et al. (2020), "Innovative start-ups and policy initiatives", *Research Policy*, Vol. 49/10, https://doi.org/10.1016/j.respol.2020.104027. [21]

Autor, D., L. Katz and M. Kearney (2006), "The Polarization of the U.S. Labor Market", *American Economic Review*, Vol. 96/2, pp. 189-194, https://doi.org/10.1257/000282806777212620. [53]

Basco, A. and C. Lavena (2021), *América Latina en movimiento: competencias y habilidades para la cuarta revolución industrial en el contexto de pandemia*, Inter-American Development Bank, Washington, DC, https://publications.iadb.org/es/america-latina-en-movimiento-competencias-y-habilidades-para-la-cuarta-revolucion-industrial-en-el. [70]

Bloom, N. et al. (2013), "Does Management Matter? Evidence From India", *The Quarterly Journal of Economics*, pp. 1-51, https://doi.org/10.1093/qje/qjs044. [18]

CAF (2018), *RED 2018. Instituciones para la productividad: hacia un mejor entorno empresarial*, Development Bank of Latin America (CAF), Bogota, http://scioteca.caf.com/handle/123456789/1343. [11]

CAF (2014), *What is production transformation?*, Development Bank of Latin America (CAF), Caracas, https://www.caf.com/en/currently/news/2014/05/what-is-productive-transformation/#:~:text=Productive%20transformation%20is%20about%20creating,firms%20and%20individuals%20working%20together (accessed on 18 September 2023). [4]

CAF (2013), *RED 2013: Emprendimientos en América Latina. Desde la subsistencia hacia la transformación*, Development Bank of Latin America (CAF), Caracas, https://scioteca.caf.com/bitstream/handle/123456789/168/red_2013.pdf?sequence=1&isAllowed=y. [42]

CBInsights (2022), "*Research Briefs*", https://www.cbinsights.com/research/unicorn-startup-market-map/ (accessed on 18 September 2023). [26]

Dini, M. and G. Stumpo (2020), "Mipymes en América Latina: un frágil desempeño y nuevos desafíos para las políticas de fomento", *Documentos de Proyectos*, No. LC/TS.2018/75/Rev.1, United Nations Economic Commission for Latin America and the Caribbean, Santiago, https://repositorio.cepal.org/server/api/core/bitstreams/2c7fec3c-c404-496b-a0da-e6a14b1cee48/content. [17]

Drucaroff, S. (2021), *Análisis de las fortalezas y debilidades de la industria de equipos e insumos médicos en América Latina y el Caribe*, unpublished, United Nations Economic Commission for Latin America and the Caribbean, Santiago. [74]

ECLAC (2023), *Buenos Aires Commitment*, United Nations Economic Commission for Latin America and the Caribbean, https://conferenciamujer.cepal.org/15/en/documents/buenos-aires-commitment. [75]

ECLAC (2023), *Foreign Direct Investment in Latin America and the Caribbean 2023*, United Nations Economic Commission for Latin America and the Caribbean, Santiago, https://www.cepal.org/en/publications/48979-foreign-direct-investment-latin-america-and-caribbean-2023. [62]

ECLAC (2023), *Halfway to 2030 in Latin America and the Caribbean: Progress and recommendations for acceleration*, United Nations Economic Commission for Latin America and the Caribbean, Santiago, https://repositorio.cepal.org/server/api/core/bitstreams/9481d2a0-70cf-4a5a-a128-5a95123c1ec7/content. [15]

ECLAC (2023), *Iberoamérica: espacio de oportunidades para el crecimiento, la colaboración y el desarrollo sostenible*, United Nations Economic Commission for Latin America and the Caribbean, Santiago, https://www.cepal.org/es/publicaciones/48769-iberoamerica-espacio-oportunidades-crecimiento-la-colaboracion-desarrollo. [58]

ECLAC (2023), *Investment and cooperation opportunities for Latin America and the Caribbean and the European Union*, United Nations Economic Commission for Latin America and the Caribbean, Santiago, https://www.cepal.org/en/publications/48992-investment-and-cooperation-opportunities-latin-america-and-caribbean-and-european. [57]

ECLAC (2022), *A digital path for sustainable development in Latin America and the Caribbean*, United Nations Economic Commission for Latin America and the Caribbean, Santiago, https://repositorio.cepal.org/bitstream/handle/11362/48461/4/S2200897_en.pdf. [69]

ECLAC (2022), *Foreign Direct Investment in Latin America and the Caribbean 2022*, United Nations Economic Commission for Latin America and the Caribbean, Santiago, https://www.cepal.org/en/publications/48521-foreign-direct-investment-latin-america-and-caribbean-2022. [16]

ECLAC (2022), *Social Panorama of Latin America and the Caribbean 2022: Transforming education as a basis for sustainable development*, United Nations Economic Commission for Latin America and the Caribbean, Santiago, https://www.cepal.org/en/publications/48519-social-panorama-latin-america-and-caribbean-2022-transforming-education-basis. [47]

ECLAC (2022), *Towards transformation of the development model in Latin America and the Caribbean: production, inclusion and sustainability*, United Nations Economic Commission for Latin America and the Caribbean, Santiago, https://www.cepal.org/en/publications/48309-towards-transformation-development-model-latin-america-and-caribbean-production. [1]

ECLAC (2021), *Digital technologies for a new future*, United Nations Economic Commission for Latin America and the Caribbean, Santiago, https://www.cepal.org/sites/default/files/publication/files/46817/S2000960_en.pdf. [68]

ECLAC (2021), *Estudio Económico de América Latina y el Caribe*, United Nations Economic Commission for Latin America and the Caribbean, Santiago, https://repositorio.cepal.org/bitstreams/dae0d47c-e8bc-4bf6-b6a4-fd9ab98ba8d6/download. [37]

ECLAC (2021), *Plan for self-sufficiency in health matters in Latin America and the Caribbean: lines of action and proposals*, United Nations Economic Commission for Latin America and the Caribbean, Santiago, https://repositorio.cepal.org/handle/11362/47253. [73]

ECLAC (2020), *Building a New Future: Transformative Recovery with Equality and Sustainability. Summary*, United Nations Economic Commission for Latin America and the Caribbean, Santiago. [5]

ECLAC (2019), *Foreign Direct Investment in Latin America and the Caribbean 2019*, United Nations Economic Commission for Latin America and the Caribbean, Santiago, https://repositorio.cepal.org/server/api/core/bitstreams/715e2868-75ac-4e6c-867f-5a6dddbf0200/content. [79]

ECLAC (2008), *Structural change and productivity growth, 20 years later: old problems, new opportunities*, United Nations Economic Commission for Latin America and the Caribbean, Santiago, https://repositorio.cepal.org/handle/11362/2890. [14]

ECLAC (1996), *Changing production patterns with social equity: the prime task of Latin American and Caribbean development in the 1990s*, United Nations Economic Commission for Latin America and the Caribbean, Santiago, https://repositorio.cepal.org/handle/11362/37869. [3]

ECLAC and ILO (2022), "Dinámica de la productividad laboral en América Latina", *Coyuntura Laboral en América Latina y el Caribe*, No. 27 (LC/TS.2022/213), United Nations Economic Commission for Latin America and the Caribbean, International Labour Organization, https://www.ilo.org/wcmsp5/groups/public/---americas/---ro-lima/---sro-santiago/documents/publication/wcms_863688.pdf. [12]

Fajnzylber, F. (1983), *La industrialización trunca de América Latina*, Editorial Nueva Imagen, S. A., México D.F., https://repositorio.cepal.org/handle/11362/43130. [13]

Federico, J. and S. Ibarra Garcia (2014), "Los obstáculos al desarrollo de las empresas jóvenes: Un análisis comparado", in *¿Emprendimientos dinámicos en América del Sur?: la clave es el (eco) sistema*, Red Mercosur de Investigaciones Económicas, Buenos Aires, https://www.redsudamericana.org/sites/default/files/doc/Emprendimientos.pdf. [22]

Fernández, C. et al. (2017), *Reconciling opposing views towards labour informality. The case of Colombia and South Africa*, Fedesarrollo, Bogota, https://repository.fedesarrollo.org.co/handle/11445/3621?locale-attribute=en (accessed on 27 September 2021). [40]

Fernández, C. and R. Villar (2016), "The Impact of Lowering the Payroll Tax on Informality in Colombia", *Documentos de Trabajo*, No. 72, Fedesarrollo, Bogota, https://www.repository.fedesarrollo.org.co/handle/11445/3300. [39]

Freeman, C. (1995), "The "National System of Innovation" in historical perspective", *Cambridge Journal of Economics*, Vol. 19, pp. 5-24, https://doi.org/10.1093/oxfordjournals.cje.a035309. [33]

Goos, M. and A. Manning (2007), "Lousy and lovely jobs: The rising polarization of work in Britain", *The Review of Economics and Statistics*, Vol. 89/1, pp. 118-133, https://www.jstor.org/stable/40043079. [54]

Hellwig, M. and A. Irmen (2001), *Wage Growth, Productivity Growth, and the Evolution of Employment*, https://cepr.org/publications/dp2927. [80]

IDB (2020), *Informe anual del Índice de Desarrollo de la Banda Ancha. Brecha digital en América Latina y el Caribe*, Inter-American Development Bank, Washington, DC, https://publications.iadb.org/publications/spanish/document/Informe-anual-del-Indice-de-Desarrollo-de-la-Banda-Ancha-IDBA-2020-Brecha-digital-en-America-Latina-y-el-Caribe.pdf. [45]

IEA (2021), *The Role of Critical Minerals in Clean Energy Transitions*, IEA, Paris, License: CC BY 4.0, https://www.iea.org/reports/the-role-of-critical-minerals-in-clean-energy-transitions. [67]

IEA (2019), *The Future of Hydrogen*, IEA, Paris, License: CC BY 4.0, https://www.iea.org/reports/the-future-of-hydrogen. [64]

ILO (2022), *E-formalización en América Latina: acelerando en una región llena de brechas*, International Labour Office, Geneva, https://www.ilo.org/wcmsp5/groups/public/---americas/---ro-lima/documents/publication/wcms_854208.pdf. [46]

IRENA (2021), "International Renewable Energy Agency (IRENA)", *Renewable energy statistics 2021*, https://www.irena.org/publications/2021/Aug/Renewable-energy-statistics-2021 (accessed on 18 September 2023). [61]

Kantis, H., V. Caicedo and S. Ibarra Garcia (2023), *Unicornios y ecosistemas en América Latina: ¿del boom al final de fiesta?*, PRODES, https://prodem.ungs.edu.ar/publicaciones_prodem/unicornios-y-ecosistemas-en-america-latina-del-boom-al-final-de-fiesta/. [27]

La Porta, R. and A. Shleifer (2014), "Informality and Development", *American Economic Association*, Vol. 28/3, pp. 109-126, https://doi.org/10.3386/w20205. [41]

LA-KLEMS (2021), *Crecimiento Económico y Productividad en América Latina - Julio 2021*, http://www.laklems.net/ (accessed on 18 September 2023). [10]

LAVCA (2023), *LAVCA Trends in Tech 2023*, LAVCA, New York, https://lavca.org/industry-data/2023-lavca-trends-in-tech/. [72]

Levy, S. (2018), *Under-rewarded efforts: The elusive quest for prosperity in MexicoUnder-rewarded efforts: The elusive quest for prosperity in Mexico*, Inter-American Development Bank, Washington, DC, https://doi.org/10.18235/0001189. [44]

Lundvall, B. (2010), *National Systems of Innovation: Toward a Theory of Innovation and Interactive Learning*, Anthem Press, London, http://www.jstor.org/stable/j.ctt1gxp7cs. [32]

Mageste, S. et al. (forthcoming), *Startups en América Latina y el Caribe*, United Nations Economic Commission for Latin America and the Caribbean, Santiago. [23]

Maloney (2004), "Informality Revisited", *World Development*, Vol. 32/7, pp. 1159-1178, https://doi.org/10.1016/j.worlddev.2004.01.008. [38]

McKenzie, D. (2020), "Small Business Training to Improve Management Practices in Developing Countries: Reassessing the Evidence for "Training Doesn't Work"", *Policy Research Working Paper*, No. 9408, World Bank Group, Washington, DC, https://documents1.worldbank.org/curated/en/593081600709463800/pdf/Small-Business-Training-to-Improve-Management-Practices-in-Developing-Countries-Reassessing-the-Evidence-for-Training-Doesn-t-Work.pdf. [19]

Medina, A. et al. (forthcoming), *Promoting access to financial markets to SMEs and growth companies in LAC*, OECD Publishing, Paris. [24]

MIEM (2022), *Hoja de Ruta de Hidrógeno Verde en Uruguay.* [65]

OECD (2023), "OECD Initiative on Global Value Chains (GVCs), Production Transformation and Development", OECD, Paris, https://www.oecd.org/dev/Global-value-chaines-Initiative-Production-Transformation-Development-Update-April-2023.pdf. [63]

OECD (2023), *Transición verde y formalización laboral en Colombia*, Making Development Happen, OECD Publishing, Paris, https://www.oecd.org/dev/Transicion-verde-empleo-en-Colombia.pdf. [59]

OECD (2022), *Global Outlook on Financing for Sustainable Development 2023*, OECD Publishing, Paris, https://doi.org/10.1787/fcbe6ce9-en. [66]

OECD (2019), *OECD Employment Outlook 2019: The Future of Work*, OECD Publishing, Paris, https://doi.org/10.1787/9ee00155-en. [50]

OECD (2019), *OECD Skills Strategy 2019: Skills to Shape a Better Future*, OECD Publishing, Paris, https://doi.org/10.1787/9789264313835-en. [56]

OECD (2019), *Skills Matter: Additional Results from the Survey of Adult Skills*, OECD Skills Studies, OECD Publishing, Paris, https://doi.org/10.1787/1f029d8f-en. [48]

OECD (2017), *OECD Employment Outlook 2017*, OECD Publishing, Paris, https://doi.org/10.1787/empl_outlook-2017-en. [55]

OECD (2016), "Production Transformation Policy Reviews (PTPRs): A Policy Assessment and Guidance Tool to Improve the Effectiveness of Production Transformation Strategies", DEV/GB(2016)2, OECD Development Centre, Paris, https://www.oecd.org/dev/Session2_PTPR.pdf. [2]

OECD (2023), *Regional Attractiveness in the New Global Environment: Argentina, Chile and Colombia. Synthesis report*, Making Development Happen, OECD Development Centre, Paris https://www.oecd.org/dev/mdh.htm. [31]

OECD et al. (2022), *Latin American Economic Outlook 2022: Towards a Green and Just Transition*, OECD Publishing, Paris, https://doi.org/10.1787/3d5554fc-en. [7]

OECD et al. (2021), *Latin American Economic Outlook 2021: Working Together for a Better Recovery*, OECD Publishing, Paris, https://doi.org/10.1787/5fedabe5-en. [6]

OECD et al. (2020), *Latin American Economic Outlook 2020: Digital Transformation for Building Back Better*, OECD Publishing, Paris, https://doi.org/10.1787/e6e864fb-en. [8]

OECD et al. (2019), *Latin American Economic Outlook 2019: Development in Transition*, OECD Publishing, Paris, https://doi.org/10.1787/g2g9ff18-en. [28]

OECD.Stat (2020), "Region and Cities", *Regional demography*, https://stats.oecd.org/Index.aspx?DataSetCode=REGION_DEMOGR (accessed on 18 September 2023). [29]

OECD/FAO (2022), *OECD-FAO Agricultural Outlook 2022-2031*, OECD Publishing, Paris, https://doi.org/10.1787/f1b0b29c-en. [78]

OECD/UN (2018), *Production Transformation Policy Review of Chile: Reaping the Benefits of New Frontiers*, OECD Development Pathways, OECD Publishing, Paris, https://doi.org/10.1787/9789264288379-en. [25]

OECD/UN/UNIDO (2019), *Production Transformation Policy Review of Colombia: Unleashing Productivity*, OECD Development Pathways, OECD Publishing, Paris, https://doi.org/10.1787/9789264312289-en. [30]

Pagés, C. (2010), *La era de la productividad : cómo transformar las economías desde sus cimientos*, Inter-American Development Bank, Washington, DC, https://publications.iadb.org/publications/spanish/viewer/La-era-de-la-productividad-C%C3%B3mo-transformar-las-econom%C3%ADas-desde-sus-cimientos.pdf. [43]

RICYT (2022), *El estado de la ciencia: principales indicadores de ciencia y tecnología iberoamericanos / interamericanos 2022*, Altuna Impresores S.R.L., Buenos Aires, https://oei.int/oficinas/argentina/publicaciones/el-estado-de-la-ciencia-principales-indicadores-de-ciencia-y-iberoamericanos-interamericanos-2022. [34]

RICYT (2020), *Network for Science and Technology Indicators –Ibero-American and Inter-American– (RICYT)*, http://www.ricyt.org/en/ (accessed on 18 September 2023). [35]

Ropero Santiago, S. and D. Cortés (2022), *Encontrar trabajo formal en Colombia. ¿Cuestión de habilidades?*, Universidad del Rosario, Bogota, https://dev.focoeconomico.org/2022/09/14/encontrar-trabajo-formal-en-colombia-cuestion-de-habilidades/. [49]

Shapira, P. et al. (2015), *Institutions for Technology Diffusion*, Inter-American Development Bank, Washington, DC, https://publications.iadb.org/en/institutions-technology-diffusion. [20]

The Conference Board (2023), *Total Economy Database*, https://www.conference-board.org/data/economydatabase (accessed on 18 September 2023). [9]

UN-Women (2020), "Costs, returns, and effects of a universal, free, and quality child care system in Mexico", https://mexico.unwomen.org/sites/default/files/Field%20Office%20Mexico/Documentos/Publicaciones/2021/twopager_pobinfantilENG.pdf. [77]

Vilgis, V., V. Jordán and A. Patiño (2023), *Medición de la economía de Internet en América Latina: los casos del Brasil, Chile, Colombia y México*, United Nations Economic Commission for Latin America and the Caribbean, Santiago, https://www.cepal.org/es/publicaciones/48908-medicion-la-economia-internet-america-latina-casos-brasil-chile-colombia-mexico. [71]

Vona, F. et al. (2018), "Environmental Regulation and Green Skills: An Empirical Exploration", *Journal of the Association of Environmental and Resource Economists*, Vol. 5/4, https://www.journals.uchicago.edu/doi/suppl/10.1086/698859/suppl_file/2015197Appendix.pdf. [60]

Weller, J., S. Gontero and S. Campbell (2019), "Cambio tecnológico y empleo: Una perspectiva latinoamericana. Riesgos de la sustitución tecnológica del trabajo humano y desafíos de la generación de nuevos puestos de trabajo", *Macroeconomía del Desarrollo*, No. 201 (LC/TS.2019/37), United Nations Economic Commission for Latin America and the Caribbean, Santiago, https://hdl.handle.net/11362/44637. [51]

WIPO (2022), *World Intellectual Property Organization (WIPO)*, https://www.wipo.int/portal/en/ (accessed on 18 September 2023). [36]

Chapter 4

Unleashing LAC's production potential: The role of public institutions and financing

This chapter examines key elements necessary to mobilise investment and drive a production transformation that brings greater well-being for all citizens in Latin America and the Caribbean (LAC). It emphasises the vital role of public institutions, which are key to creating the conditions conducive to investment and to making the production transformation more connected to the demands of citizens and the broader development strategies of LAC countries. The chapter also explores financing mechanisms that can help to unlock the region's financial markets. Public development finance institutions (DFIs) and innovative debt instruments such as green, social and sustainability-linked (GSSS) bonds can be used to boost private and public investment. The chapter concludes with key policy messages.

Towards better institutions and financing to boost investment

The involvement of citizens and other stakeholders is key to enhancing the impact of investments on well-being and strengthening the social contract

Perception of investments' impact

Positive citizen perceptions of FDI in LAC

71% (2016) → 54% (2020)

Trust in companies

55% of LAC citizens had little to no trust in national and international companies in 2020

Social conflict

Almost **90%** of all social conflicts related to the environment that arose in LAC from 2000-22 were still unresolved by the end of 2022

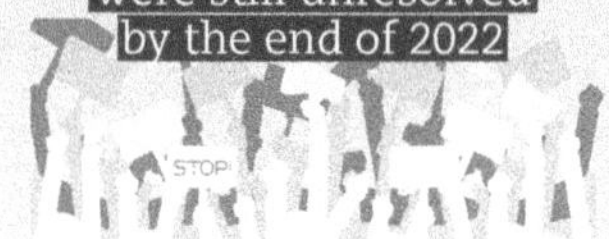

Promoting investment: what are the priorities in LAC countries?

Our analysis of National Development Plans in 14 countries reveals the following strategic sectors:

Energy transition and related industries

Digital transformation

Care economy, pharmaceutical and health industry

Sustainable agribusiness

Sustainable tourism

Circular economy

Development finance institutions (DFIs): a key for smaller firms to invest in strategic sectors

Access finance through different mechanisms: credits, factoring, leasing, guarantees, etc.

National and subnational DFIs can help MSMEs:

Contribute to investments in strategic sectors

Contribute to green, digital and gender goals

Introduction

The role of investment is paramount in driving production transformation, which in turn is essential for achieving greater well-being in Latin America and the Caribbean (LAC). A structural transformation of the economy involves diversifying and upgrading the production apparatus across all LAC countries. This can lead to stronger economic growth and productivity, more quality jobs, and enhanced economic resilience – essential elements for closing inequality gaps and improving living standards (ECLAC, 2022[1]).

Two dimensions are vital to turn investment and production transformation strategies into key drivers of inclusive and sustainable development in the region: public institutions and financing.[1]

First, public institutions can ensure that production transformation strategies are built on inclusive dialogue among all stakeholders, thus enhancing linkages between investment efforts and social priorities, and strengthening the social contract within the region. Public institutions can also improve the investment climate, creating more conducive and predictable conditions by strengthening the rule of law and backing it up with quality regulation, transparency, openness and integrity (OECD, 2015[2]) (Chapter 2). These are fundamental ingredients for building trust, which facilitates investment by boosting compliance and investor confidence. Finally, public institutions can also establish a strategic approach to investment and production transformation, ensuring that these efforts are coherent with broader national development and productive development strategies, and that an integrated and co-ordinated approach is adopted across institutions, levels of government and stakeholders. In this sense, public institutions can take the lead in establishing an approach that is centred on citizen well-being (OECD, 2021[3]), that maintains alignment with the UN Sustainable Development Goals (SDGs), and that commits to contributing to equitable and sustainable development (OECD et al., 2019[4]).

Financing is the second major dimension. Mobilising massive financial resources from public and private sources will be required to finance investment gaps in crucial sectors in LAC, such as quality infrastructure. To stimulate this, the region will need to unlock the potential of its financial markets, with a crucial role for development finance institutions (DFIs) in supporting access to finance and in driving investments in strategic sectors. There is increasing potential in the region for innovative financial tools, such as Green, Social, Sustainability and Sustainability-linked (GSSS) bonds, which can promote public and private investment with the support of more consolidated and harmonised sustainable finance frameworks.

This chapter addresses the question of how to unleash LAC's production potential and make it a catalyst for better development. The chapter begins by analysing how public institutions can help to foster investments and production transformation, and to focus their impact on well-being. The chapter then explores how to improve access to the necessary financing. It emphasises the role of DFIs, the potential of innovative debt instruments such as GSSS bonds and the need to strengthen sustainable finance frameworks. The chapter concludes with key policy messages.

Public institutions are vital to making the production transformation a driver of well-being and central to a new social contract

Production transformation – and the investments needed to make it happen – can have a significant impact on living standards across socio-economic groups in LAC. Engaging strategic stakeholders to agree on the strategies for production transformation and investment will be crucial, both to make the strategies and investments possible and to avoid potential conflict. This involves understanding stakeholders' priorities and incorporating them throughout the policy-making process. Ensuring that efforts to attract and mobilise investment are human-centred will strengthen the social contract.

Such renewed social contract will only endure and bear long-term effects if positions the priorities of main stakeholders around a strategic vision. In other words, investment and production strategies should derive from a whole-of-government approach and be directly linked to national development strategies to guarantee policy coherence, long-term planning and co-ordination across levels of government and key stakeholders. These points will each be addressed below.

Confidence in the impact of investments on well-being remains low in the region

The pursuit of new and more diversified sources of investment and more sustainable forms of production will have multidimensional impacts on citizens' lives in LAC and could thus lay the foundations for a new social contract. A social contract is understood as an intangible but shared acceptance of what society needs and how to achieve these needs through a series of rules and institutions (ECLAC/OECD, 2018[5]).

To ensure the impacts of changes leading to a new social contract meet the expectations and desires of citizens, their opinions must be heard and considered. The only way to guarantee the production transformation is truly sustainable and inclusive is by involving citizens in its design, implementation and evaluation phases. Achieving a broad consensus around the priorities of the production transformation will also prove crucial to efforts to achieve the SDG goals by 2030 and beyond.

Understanding citizens' perceptions about how investments will impact their lives, and on the roles of key stakeholders within the production transformation, will be crucial to building social support, tightening links among stakeholders and, ultimately, strengthening the social contract.

LAC citizens have generally low levels of trust in their national governments and weak levels of satisfaction with their democratic systems. Only around half (48%) of the population surveyed in 2023 preferred democracy over other systems (Latinobarómetro, 2023[6]). Trust in governments stood at just 27% in 2020 (Latinobarómetro, 2020[7]), well below the 41% average in OECD countries (OECD, 2022[8]).

Securing trust in public institutions is essential. A stable institutional environment is crucial for attracting investments and creating for stakeholders a predictable horizon of the production transformation. In fact, low confidence levels may signal that the public sector lacks sufficient capacities to guide a successful production transformation strategy.

Trust in public institutions is particularly relevant in a context of increasing political polarisation observed both in LAC and globally. Low levels of trust may become a significant barrier to investment in LAC, as a heightened political divide often introduces uncertainty into the investment climate (Azzimonti, 2011[9]). This uncertainty arises from the possibility of unexpected policy changes, especially concerning taxation, regulations, foreign trade and the potential nationalisation of industries (Biglaiser and Staats, 2010[10]). Political instability can also lead to social unrest, disrupting business operations and discouraging investment. Additionally, deeply polarised environments sometimes struggle with issues such as governmental gridlock and corruption, which also have negative impacts on investment.

As enterprises are central to production transformation and a main source of investment, citizens' perceptions of their role is crucial. At present, however, LAC citizens have low trust in national and international companies. Asked in 2020 about their views of national and international companies, LAC citizens polled had either no trust at all (20.3% and 24.4%) or little confidence (35% and 34.2%) – adding up to a slight majority overall (Figure 4.1) (Latinobarómetro, 2020[7]). This could be partially explained by a lack of information and low visibility of the roles played by firms. But it also suggests that citizens see strong potential for improving the impacts – social, economic and environmental – of private-sector activities. Governments from the region could promote a more active role for the private sector through a more ambitious adoption of the *OECD Responsible Business Conduct Guidelines* (see below on stakeholder participation), among other efforts.

Figure 4.1. **Most LAC citizens have little trust in national and international companies**

Level of confidence among LAC citizens in national and/or international companies, 2020

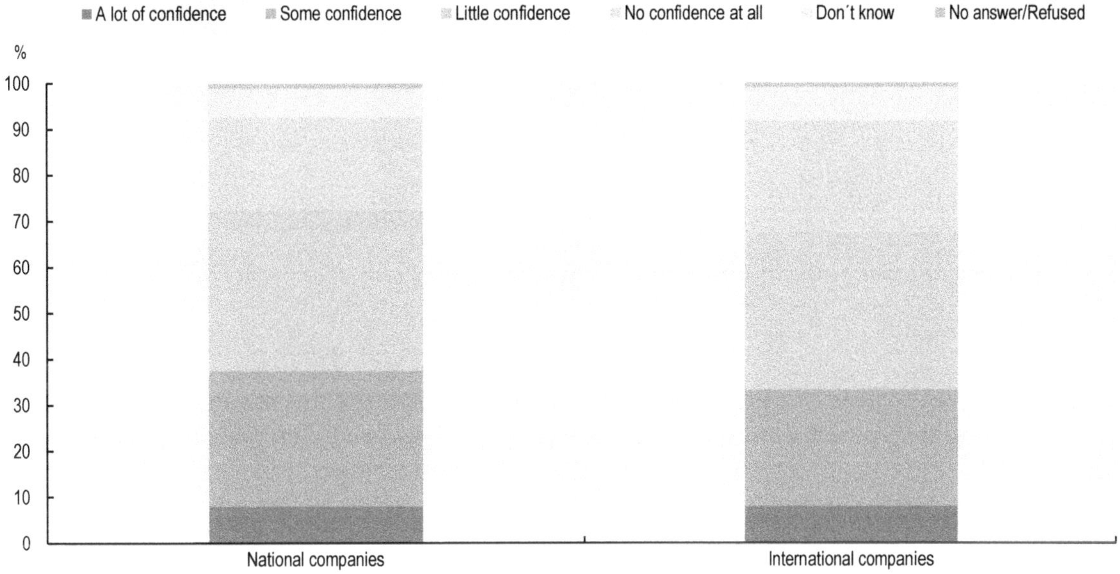

Note: Question: "Please look at this card and tell me how much trust you have in each of the following groups/institutions. Would you say you have a lot, some, a little or no trust in?"

Source: (Latinobarómetro, 2020[11]).

StatLink https://stat.link/ufjq4o

While perceptions that foreign direct investment (FDI) has positive impacts on economic development remain relatively high in LAC, they have been dropped substantially in recent years. FDI was seen as beneficial by 53.6% of the population surveyed in 2020, down from 70.7% in 2016 and the lowest level to date (Figure 4.2). This decline coincides with an increasing lack of awareness about FDI among LAC citizens: in 2020, 28.8% of respondents said they did not know enough to answer whether the effects of FDI were beneficial or detrimental to the economic development of their country (10 percentage points more than in 2017). Citizens' perceptions of FDI vary depending on the type of investment concerned. The purchase of national companies by foreign investors is seen by 40% of citizens as positive for their country, while 72% think the building of factories by foreign companies is a good thing for their country (Pew Research Center, 2020[12]). These trends underscore the importance of raising awareness of the positive impacts that FDI can have (Chapter 2), and of developing mechanisms to make FDI more connected to the development priorities of countries, sub-national regions, and citizens.

Figure 4.2. **Positive perceptions of FDI have declined among LAC citizens**

Share who consider that FDI is beneficial or detrimental for their country's economic development, 1995-2020

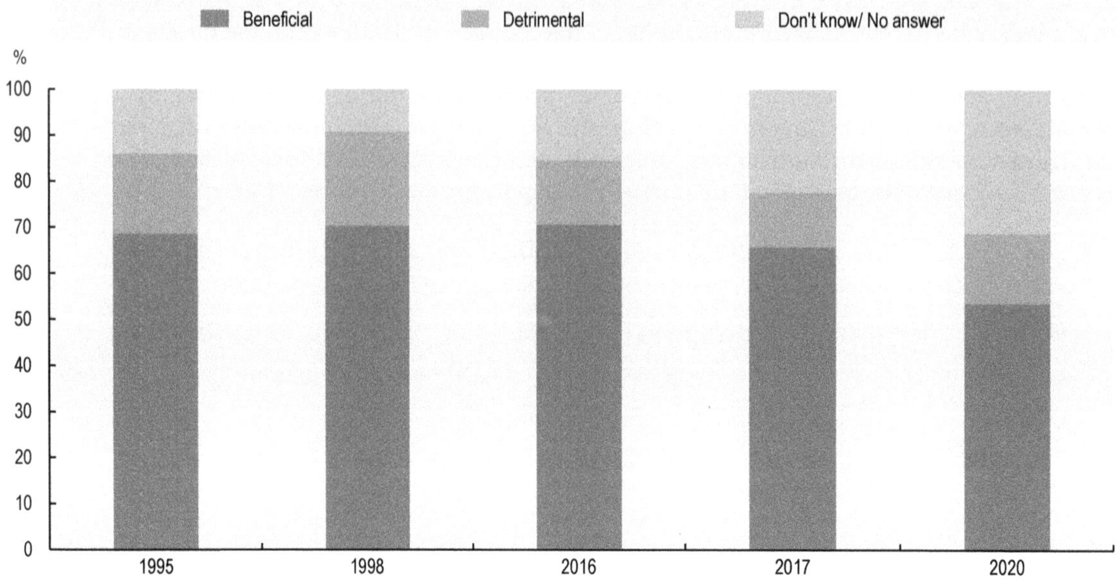

Note: Question: "Is foreign investment beneficial or harmful for the economic development of the country or do you not know enough to say?"

Source: (Latinobarómetro, 2020[11]).

StatLink https://stat.link/5uym6l

In designing policies to mobilise investment and improve the investment climate, understanding the opinions of private-sector representatives can be crucial. The most problematic factors for doing business in the LAC region have been identified by business leaders as inefficient government bureaucracy (12.9%), corruption (11.9%) and high tax rates (9.8%) (Figure 4.3). In the 2020 Doing Business Survey, enterprise owners in the LAC region expressed a significantly higher number of concerns regarding bureaucratic obstacles and the costs associated with formal market operations. The LAC region is ranked 119th out of 190, a position considerably lower than the 56th ranking occupied by the OECD countries. Regarding tax rates, business leaders signalled the pressure of the high contribution rate, particularly during the second year of operation (47.03%), which is well above the averages for the OECD (39.86%), other developing regions such as the Middle East (32.48%), and East Europe and Central Asia (32.10%) (World Bank, 2020[13]). Working more closely with the private sector will help LAC governments better understand the wide range of factors that influence how companies allocate investment.

Figure 4.3. **Business leaders' perceptions of the most problematic factors for doing business in LAC**

Ranking of the most problematic factors for doing business in LAC according to business executives, 2017

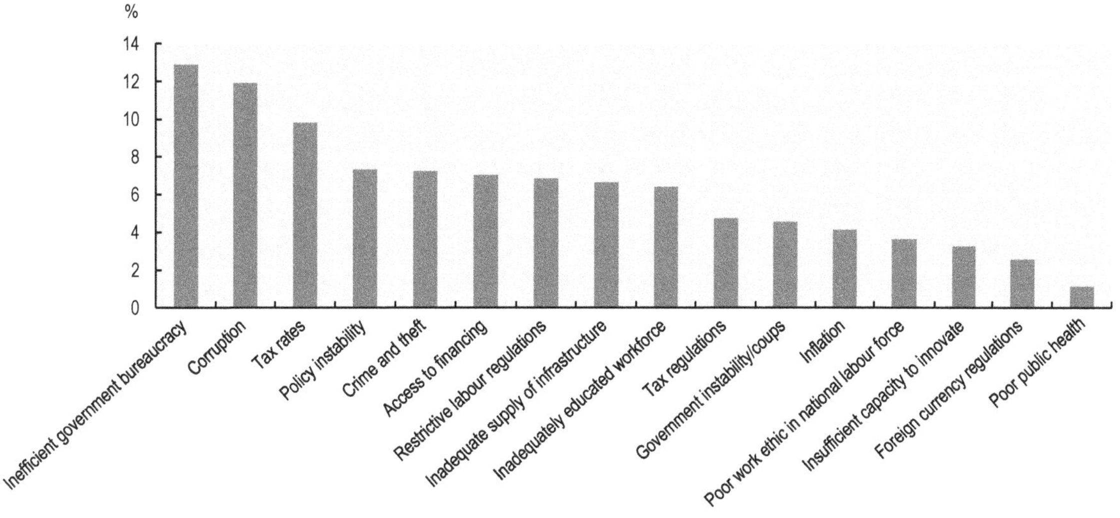

Note: Question: "Select the five most problematic factors for doing business in your country and rank them between 1 (most problematic) and 5." For the LAC region, the simple average of 20 countries was calculated: Argentina, Brazil, Chile, Colombia, Costa Rica, Dominican Republic, Ecuador, El Salvador, Guatemala, Haiti, Honduras, Jamaica, Mexico, Nicaragua, Panama, Paraguay, Peru, Trinidad and Tobago, Uruguay, and Venezuela.

Source: (World Economic Forum, 2018[14]).

StatLink https://stat.link/gi9yxj

Low levels of confidence in the capacity of both public institutions and national and international firms to improve well-being reveal the need to better connect investment and production transformation strategies with development outcomes. To achieve this, it is important that LAC governments reinforce mechanisms for dialogue across stakeholders, so that production transformation is built upon agreement and considers its diverse impacts. Similarly, investment and production transformation efforts should be aligned with broader development strategies and should result from a co-ordinated effort across policies and sectors.

Improving the impact of investments on overall well-being requires that public institutions foster and ensure inclusive dialogues among stakeholders

By creating the conditions for active stakeholder participation, public institutions can play a pivotal role in ensuring that the production transformation is truly inclusive and brings well-being to all. This is crucial to ensure human-centred investments. A diversity of views from the actors involved in investments and production transformation efforts will not only legitimise the process and reduce trade-offs; it can also contribute to the success of such efforts by bringing in new visions and experiences.

Dialogue with society to foster inclusion and manage potential social conflict

Citizen involvement throughout the investment cycle results in projects that are more effective, sustainable and equitable. Input from citizens can help to meet their needs and improve trust in government; it can also prevent the capture of projects by special interest groups (OECD, 2014[15]).

Inclusive dialogue is particularly relevant because of the risk that production transformation can lead to social conflict due to the potential detrimental impacts of some investments on specific groups, territories or communities. These conflicts emerge due to various economic, social and environmental factors. For instance, when undertaken without appropriate consultation or compensation, land acquisition for projects can result in the displacement of local communities, triggering social tensions. Economic disparities resulting from unequal distribution of project benefits can also exacerbate conflicts. Opposition may arise as well over the environmental consequences of large-scale projects that are potentially detrimental to biodiversity and local livelihoods, especially mining projects (Bebbington and Bury, 2013[16]). These considerations are of particular relevance in a context in which the LAC region holds a significant share of critical minerals for advancing the green transition globally, or a need exists for immense investments in various areas that can potentially create tensions across socio-economic groups and territories (OECD et al., 2022[17]).

Many social conflicts around environmental issues have erupted in the LAC region in recent years. Of 742 social conflicts that arose in LAC from 2000 to 2022, 661 were still unresolved by the end of 2022. About one-third of the conflicts still open in 2022 concentrated on mining (33.7%), followed by water management (16.2%), biomass and land conflicts (14.8%), and fossil fuels and climate/energy justice (14.1%) (Figure 4.4) (CALAS, 2019[18]; Environmental Justice Atlas, 2023[19]; Latin American Observatory of Environmental Conflicts, 2023[20]). In mining in particular, the number of conflicts shot up by 236% from 2010 to 2023, affecting more than 300 local communities (OCMAL, 2023[21]).

Figure 4.4. **Number of open social conflicts in LAC linked to environmental issues, by category, 2022**

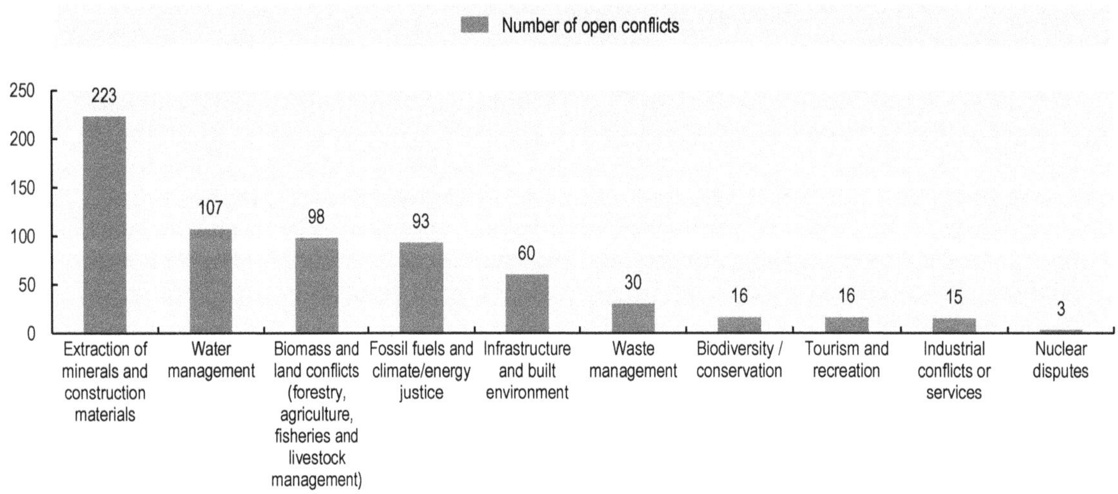

Note: These conflicts are defined as mobilisations by local communities and social movements, which might also include support of national or international networks against particular economic activities, such as infrastructure construction or waste disposal/pollution, whereby environmental impacts are a key element of the grievances. The figure shows unresolved conflicts started in the period 2020-2022.

Source: (Environmental Justice Atlas, 2023[19]).

StatLink https://stat.link/b4sk7r

In order to build support for the production transformation while preventing and/or handling potential social conflicts and corruption, it is vital that governments establish mechanisms to ensure effective citizen participation, rigorous and standard environmental and social impact assessments, and more equitable distribution of the benefits of investment projects (OECD/CAF/ECLAC, 2018[22]).

Regarding citizen participation, several tools can help governments to promote bottom-up collaboration and engage citizens throughout decision making for investment and production transformation policies. The *OECD Guidelines for Citizen Participation* present a ten-step path for planning and implementing a citizen participation process, including:

identifying the problem to solve and the moment for participation; defining the expected results; identifying the relevant group of people; choosing the participation method; choosing the right digital tools; communicating about the process; implementing the participation process; using citizen input; evaluating the process; and fostering a culture of participation (OECD, 2022[23]). These guidelines also present eight different methods that can be effective in involving citizens in decision-making processes, notably: access to information and data; open meetings; public consultations; open innovation; citizen science; civic monitoring; participatory budgeting; and representative deliberative processes.

Several projects in the LAC region have already incorporated citizen participation throughout the development stages. For instance, Chile co-ordinated a participatory process across 15 regions when developing its Energy Route 2018-22: Leading Modernisation with a Citizen Seal, an initiative of the Ministry of Energy aiming to gather citizen input ahead of energy modernisation efforts (Ministerio de Energía, 2017[24]). In Costa Rica, residents were involved throughout the design of the National Development and Public Investment Plan (Reyes and Ríos, 2016[25]; ECLAC, 2021[26]). Examples of civic monitoring include the Marea Digital civic technology platform in Buenaventura in Colombia, which allows citizens to identify and report local issues affecting the community, and the Promise Tracker in Brazil, a collaborative data collection platform that allows citizens to define an issue they would like to tackle and then collect data about it to be shared with decision makers (OECD/WB, 2022[27]). Another good example of multi-actor engagement within a local productive transformation agenda is the Smart Specialisation Strategy of Bogota-Cundinamarca, implemented in Colombia between 2016 and 2020 (Llinás, 2021[28]).

Local governments have a vital role in promoting citizen participation. Given that investment projects often have direct impacts on specific communities and territories, local governments must enable citizen participation from the very beginning of projects. Participatory tools should ensure the widest access for all citizens, and especially for the most vulnerable groups, which in LAC includes women, people with disabilities, Afro-descendants and indigenous peoples. Early citizen participation is crucial in decisions such as the location of facilities or the terms of an environmental impact assessment. Among other useful practices, neighbourhood assemblies and visits to the facilities can allow broad consultations with enterprises and government representatives. Temporary co-ordination committees can prove useful to create smaller opportunities to gather representatives of companies, civil associations, neighbourhood groups and local government representatives to supervise the progress of projects. In turn, collaboration with local universities or non-governmental organisations (NGOs) can be useful for providing technical assistance, especially at key moments such as pre-feasibility studies or environmental or social impact assessments.

Citizen oversight committees, or *veedurías ciudadanas*, are an interesting example of monitoring mechanisms being applied in several LAC countries. These committees empower citizens to monitor public administration activities, including the execution of public contracts and public service management. These watchdog groups ensure transparency, efficiency and legality by vigilantly tracking the performance of public officials and institutions. They report irregularities to the appropriate authorities and play a pivotal role in preventing corruption and mismanagement. In the context of large public infrastructure projects, *veedurías* contribute significantly to ensuring that project implementation goes as planned and that funds are used appropriately, thereby effectively addressing community concerns.

Other examples of good practices in the region include guides from Chile's Environmental Assessment Service on in-person activities and early community participation (SEA, 2013[29]; SEA, 2017[30]), and a guide to citizen participation from the Colombian Foreign Ministry (Ministerio de Relaciones Exteriores de Colombia, 2016[31]).

NGOs also play a critical role in promoting citizen participation in decision making on investment projects. One example in LAC is the Propaz Foundation in Guatemala, which trains and educates citizens on alternative methods of conflict resolution, constructive communication, social leadership, consensus building and do-no-harm methodology. In Argentina, the Democratic Change Foundation provides technical support for indigenous communities, while the Environment and Natural Resources Foundation aims for collective construction of democratic and participatory citizenship in areas linked to environmental sustainability. At the international level, the Extractive Industries Transparency Initiative is an international standard that promotes transparency in payments made by extractive companies to governments and vice versa. This includes dialogue and consultation with civil society and involves civil society organisations (CSOs) in data collection and analysis.

Social and environmental impact assessments are essential tools for measuring and understanding the effects that projects, policies or activities may have on society and the environment. These assessments are fundamental for informed decision making; protection of the environment and communities; transparency and citizen participation; regulatory compliance; and long-term sustainability. Social and environmental impact assessments encourage dialogue among different stakeholders, such as local communities, businesses, government and NGOs. This dialogue facilitates understanding of the concerns and expectations of each stakeholder and seeks consensual solutions to achieve sustainable development.

Several institutions in LAC aim to manage social and environmental impact assessments. In Chile, for instance, Law 20.417 established the Environmental Impact Assessment System (SEIA), which requires public participation as part of the environmental assessment process for large projects. In December 2021, the bodies in charge of the environmental impact assessment systems of Argentina, Chile, Colombia, Costa Rica and Peru signed the statutes of the Latin American Network of Environmental Impact Assessment Systems (REDLASEIA), which was created in October of the same year to strengthen impact assessments in the region and to exchange best practices and lessons learned (MSGP, 2010[32]; SEA, 2021[33]).

Transparent and clear redistributive measures can also help to reduce tensions arising from investment projects. For example, to manage potential conflict emerging from activities with potential environmental impact, it is important to emphasise the development of sustainable alternative activities, such as allocating part of the benefits obtained into human development, education and the health of local communities, and into research, development and innovation (Box 4.1) (IDB, 2021[34]).

Box 4.1. **Costa Rica grants access to natural resources in exchange for benefit sharing**

Costa Rica has implemented a mechanism to ensure that local communities receive a direct benefit from private research and development (R&D) based on their surrounding biodiversity (or access and benefit sharing, ABS).

The National Commission for Biodiversity Management (CONAGEBIO) grants multi-year access contracts for private enterprises to research Costa Rica's biodiversity and genetic resources for commercialisation. This procedure requires prior informed consent and mutually agreed conditions with local producers. Since 2016, Costa Rica has already granted permits to seven enterprises.

Following this initiative, Costa Rica also created the *Distintivo* ABS, the first label in LAC that certifies the compliance of products with the ABS regulations and good practices.

Source: (OECD, 2023[35]).

Engaging with the private sector to improve its beneficial impact on development

Making the production transformation a driver of well-being also involves incentivising enterprises to evolve into purpose-driven organisations (Schoenmaker, 2020[36]). Powerful tools for moving in this direction are the *OECD Guidelines for Multinational Enterprises on Responsible Business Conduct* (RBC) and the associated *OECD Due Diligence Guidance for RBC* (OECD, 2018[37]). As of 2023, eight LAC countries had adhered to these guidelines: Argentina, Brazil, Chile, Costa Rica, Colombia, Mexico, Peru and Uruguay.

National contact points (NCPs) for responsible business conduct can prove useful as alternative mechanisms for mediating and resolving conflicts that may arise between private sector companies, civil society and governments. In 2019, Chile's NCP helped resolve a conflict between trade unions and a private enterprise in the manufacturing industry that had been accused of not respecting workers' human rights. Similarly, Brazil's NCP mediated a conflict between a corporate group accused of not respecting the areas bordering the installation of its mines and a neighbouring association (OECD, 2020[38]). Regardless of the policy mix used to promote a bottom-up approach, it will be essential for governments to seek a balance of stakeholders, views and interests to avoid policy capture – i.e. situations in which public decisions over policies are consistently or repeatedly directed away from the public interest towards a specific interest (OECD, 2017[39]).

A wide array of additional actions exists to further engage the private sector to improve its beneficial impacts on development. Clear regulations to promote the use of public-private partnerships (PPPs) can help the private sector to better identify priority sectors in each country and its territories, and to incentivise investments in strategic projects with social impacts (Chapter 2). Promoting strategic activities based on moderate capital inputs can also help – by avoiding market concentration and democratising market access to small and medium-sized enterprises (SMEs) with higher impact in local communities (Chapter 3). To promote further and better investment, governments could also guarantee fair and depoliticised resource allocation to increase trust within the private sector. For example, for infrastructure projects, governments could implement a transparent system of project selection, based on solid cost-benefit analysis, with co-designed guidelines for prioritising projects and improved environmental, social and governance (ESG) assessments (KPMG, 2021[40]). Finally, the private sector can actively help to address multidimensional inequalities. For example, private enterprises can address the gender gap in certain industries that are key for the production transformation by providing training and skills development. Companies can also address gender-biased inequalities by closing the gender pay gap (Atlantic Council, 2023[41]) or by identifying the additional burden women face at home, such as caregiving or unpaid domestic work, and providing incentives such as flexible hours.

Open government as a crucial dimension of promoting stakeholder engagement

Open government policies are fundamental for building trust, enhancing transparency and promoting stakeholder engagement. Ensuring readily available and comprehensible information on governmental actions, economic performance, business regulations and investment opportunities reduces investment risks and fosters informed decision making. Governments in the LAC region have shown progress in adopting open government principles in recent years. As of 2022, 16 LAC countries were members of the Open Government Partnership. Additionally, at least 67 Plans of Action for Open Government were implemented in LAC between 2011 and 2022.

Centres of government (CoGs) can play a fundamental role in promoting open government. They can have significant impacts by providing more transparency at every stage of the investment process, including: i) clear information about how to register a foreign enterprise; ii) access to amendments and draft bills; iii) consistency of investment regulations and mechanisms to signal incongruencies; iv) interactive platforms showing the prioritisation of projects with private investment and the budget of each project; and v) information about the origin of private funds assigned to projects with direct impacts on citizens' well-being. LAC governments should seize the opportunities provided by the digital transition and make all of these tools available in digital formats, multiplying the range of stakeholders able to access the information. At present, CoGs in LAC countries are involved in fewer stages of the transparency policy process than those of OECD countries. LAC's CoGs tend to focus on the design, communication and monitoring stages, and to leave the implementation, co-ordination and evaluation stages to ministries or agencies in charge of the policy (OECD, 2020[42]).

Envisioning whole-of-government, long-term strategies for production transformation

Production transformation entails gradual and lengthy structural changes that require policy coherence, a whole-of-government approach and long-term policy planning. Co-ordinated public policies, both horizontally (across sectors) and vertically (across government levels), optimise resource utilisation and enhance the impact of investments. Aligning policy objectives across various sectors and government levels steers investments efficiently towards strategic sectors for production transformation, while avoiding potential policy conflicts and addressing trade-offs. Such coherence significantly mitigates uncertainty for investors. Similarly, policy planning makes it possible to identify investment priorities (Chapter 3), align policy objectives, and facilitate coherent and co-ordinated actions beyond political cycles (OECD, 2018[43]).

The absence of political consensus on state policies has been a common challenge in LAC countries, harming both investment levels and production transformation. Uncertainty stemming from inconsistent policies dissuades investment due to higher perceptions of risk, while the fluctuations of policy cycles disrupt long-term investment plans. Since inconsistent policies convey a lack of effective governance, investor confidence diminishes, inhibiting domestic and foreign investments. Furthermore, fragmented policies impede the formulation of coherent industrial strategies, while the absence of long-term planning hinders sustainable development efforts. Production transformation requires the establishment of stable and comprehensive policies that garner wide-ranging political support.

National development plans can be a powerful tool in production transformation efforts

Most LAC countries have a national development plan (NDP), or national development strategy, that serves as the country's main strategic policy roadmap and can act as a first guide to policy efforts linked to investment and production transformation. NDPs establish long-term policy directions. If agreed upon by most key stakeholders, they can contribute to reinforcing the social contract in the region. The process of elaborating an NDP often includes mechanisms to incorporate civic participation and foster the inclusion of a diversity of views. Critically, some NDPs go beyond the policy cycle or include specific protocols to prevent changes in government from affecting the continuity of policy priorities (OECD, 2021[3]). In addition to NDPs, many countries have production development policies that aim to upgrade and diversify the economy as a vehicle for increasing productivity. To achieve this, these policies generally include both horizontal and vertical instruments and programmes that prioritise the strategic sectors on which many production development efforts and resources are focused.

Typically, NDPs outline strategic development guidelines that serve as orientation tools for both public and private investments. National investment plans need to be connected to policy guidelines outlined in NDPs. Similarly, NDPs can significantly influence private investment decisions by offering a strategic roadmap for future growth and stability, a key dimension for investor confidence. NDPs provide predictability, and thus incentivise private capital flows towards certain strategic sectors in which private investors foresee potential growth. By outlining infrastructure development, capacity-building initiatives or possible economic incentives, NDPs outline new market opportunities, enhancing the country's attractiveness to investors.

To ensure effective implementation, NDPs should define the budget allocation for each priority or provide links to specific sources of financing; for instance, dedicated funds or resources from specific sectors, such as the extractive industries. Additional specific measures that can contribute to operationalising priority objectives are: i) including a sectoral and territorial approach to create a national productive map; ii) increasing the availability of land for productive strategic sectors; iii) mapping main stakeholders from the public and private sectors and assigning specific responsibilities over the long term; and iv) specifying concrete tools for horizontal (sectoral) and vertical (subnational) co-ordination. Finally, it will be crucial to specify how, when and with which funds monitoring and evaluation will take place.

NDPs are typically designed to capitalise on a country's strengths, resources and potential areas for growth, such as natural resources, industry strengths, workforce skills and geographical advantages. They provide a roadmap to guide public and private investment towards sectors in which the country has or seeks to develop competitive advantages.

Most NDPs in LAC countries include public policy guidelines associated with strategic sectors with high potential to drive sustainable development. Chapter 3 provides a list of strategic sectors that have potential to enhance productivity, foster social inclusion and promote sustainability in the LAC region. These sectors present appealing prospects for investment, and they include: sustainable agribusiness; the circular economy and sustainable water management; the care economy; sustainable mobility; the pharmaceutical and healthcare industry; digital transformation and digital services; energy transition and related industries; and sustainable tourism (ECLAC, 2023[44]; ECLAC, 2023[45]).

An analysis of the NDPs from 14 LAC countries indicates that among these strategic areas, there are agendas like digital transformation which appear rather prominently in most LAC NDPs, with countries such as Costa Rica, Ecuador, and Peru showing greater relative relevance. The pharmaceutical and healthcare industry receives significant attention in most countries, with Guatemala, Honduras, and Panama addressing this agenda more notably relative to other strategic sectors. Energy transition is also addressed in most NDPs, though not all, and it is dealt with particular emphasis in Argentina and Brazil. Interest surrounding the care economy is also variable among countries, with nations like Chile, Colombia, and the Dominican Republic leading in addressing this agenda. The approach to sustainable tourism is balanced across all countries, with Guatemala giving greater relative importance to this area. Although it receives slightly less relative attention, sustainable agribusiness is addressed in all countries, with some such as Bolivia and Guatemala giving it greater relative importance. The circular economy is addressed in a balanced way in most NDPs, although in most countries is not one of the sectors receiving most attention. Lastly, sustainable mobility appears with low emphasis in all the NDPs. (Figure 4.5).

Figure 4.5. **Prioritisation of strategic economic sectors in LAC national development plans, 2023**

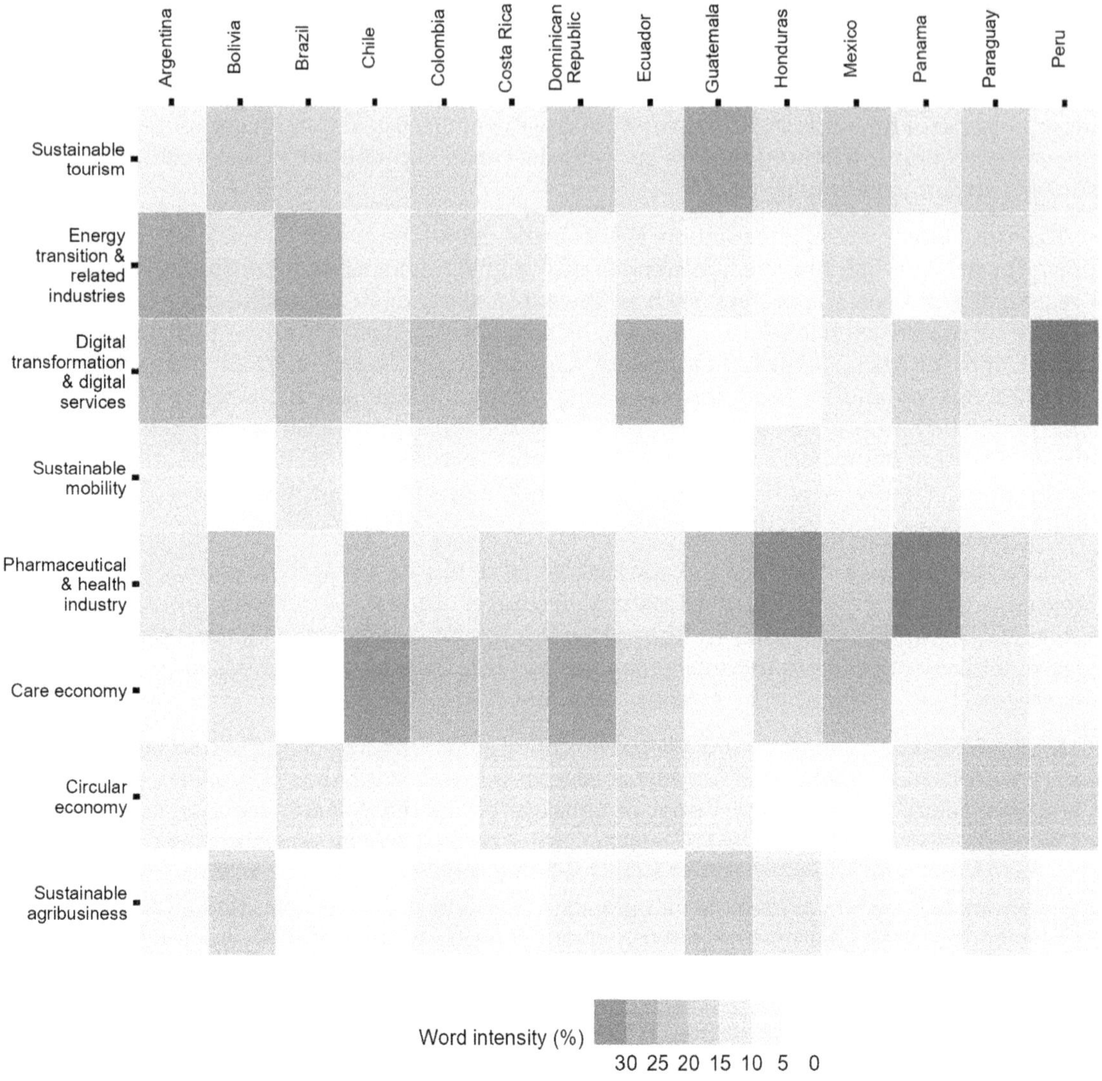

Note: Word intensity refers to the frequency with which a specific set of words associated to a strategic sector appears in each NDP. The idea is that the more frequently a set of words appears, the more "intense" or important they might be in the context of the text being analysed. This intensity, measured by frequency, can be indicative of the prominence or significance of a particular topic within the text. Darker colours indicate higher frequency of references to a given strategic sector within the plan. The sum of the relative frequencies across all economic sectors in a country's NDP is 100. Each country's text data come from the latest development plan (or its equivalent), published by October 2023.

Source: Authors' elaboration using the National Development Plans of 14 LAC countries: Argentina (MECON, 2023[46]); Bolivia (MPDB, 2021[47]); Brazil (MEB, 2020[48]); Chile (Government of Chile, 2022[49]); Colombia (DNP, 2023[50]); Costa Rica (MIDEPLAN, 2022[51]); Dominican Republic (MEPyD, 2012[52]); Ecuador (SNPE, 2021[53]); Guatemala (SPPPG, 2014[54]); Honduras (Government of Honduras, 2022[55]); Mexico (PREUM, 2019[56]); Panama (Government of Panama, 2019[57]); Paraguay (STPP, 2021[58]); and Peru (CEPLAN, 2022[59]).

StatLink https://stat.link/i79mst

It is important to note that the level of coverage and depth of NDPs varies significantly across countries, which can have impacts on the intensity with which specific policy areas appear. Similarly, some countries have specific sectoral strategies for certain sectors that are not particularly prominent in the NDPs. While there may be country-specific explanations as to why some sectors appear more prominently than others, some general conclusions can be drawn. First, some sectors may appear less prominently not because they are less relevant for development in the country, but because other bodies or institutions take a strong role in defining the strategic orientation in that specific sector (e.g. financial issues are usually led by the Ministry of Finance or financial regulatory and supervisory bodies). Second, NDPs sometimes focus on new and emerging areas rather than on policy areas that are well-developed or have a more consolidated policy framework.

Box 4.2. Colombia's strategic roadmap for public investment

In Colombia, the national government formulates a strategic mid-term roadmap for public investment every four years. This is accomplished through a series of processes, bodies, and instances governed by Colombia's National Planning System. After each new administration takes office, the National Planning Department (DNP) prepares a National Development Plan (NDP) based on the elected government's proposals. This initial draft undergoes a review by three separate bodies to ensure various criteria are met: civil society participation (via the National Planning Council [CNP]), technical and economic feasibility (through the National Council of Economic and Social Policy [CONPES]), and legal compliance (assessed by the National Congress).

Each NDP is accompanied by a budgeting component known as the Multi-year Investment Plan approved by Congress. In this plan, the national government estimates its medium-term capacity to achieve its public investment objectives while adhering to the Medium-Term Fiscal Framework set by the Ministry of Finance. The 2022-26 NDP "Colombia, a Global Power of Life" identifies five key areas essential for the implementation of the government's agenda; the Multi-year Investment Plan and their corresponding legislation, Law 2294 of 2023, set a strategic and detailed distribution across these five key policy areas. These are human security and social justice (64.4% of total public investment for the period 2023-26); regional convergence (12%); production transformation, internationalisation, and climate action (9.9%); human right to food (4%); and territorial planning around water and environmental justice (2.5%). The remaining is allocated to macroeconomic stability (7.2%), which is defined as a cross-cutting element in the NDP. Additionally, the National Public Investment Plan outlines a multi-year cross-sectoral investment plan to allocate supplementary budgeting for the Peace Process programmes.

Source: DNP (2023[50]); Congress of Colombia (2023[60]); DNP (2023[61]); Montoya and Nieto-Parra (forthcoming[62]).

National public investment systems help connect investments with specific objectives

National public investment systems (NPISs) play a key role in development strategies. They encompass the set of state institutions that govern a country's public investment process, and employ methodologies, standards and procedures to guide the formulation, execution and evaluation of investment projects. NPISs are key to enhancing the economic and social impact of public investment by improving the quality and efficiency of public spending (ECLAC, 2023[63]). They facilitate strategic decision making on infrastructure and social investments, aligning them with development goals, fostering economic growth and enhancing competitiveness.

NPISs can also serve as catalysts to attract private investment, acting as a guarantee of project continuity and minimising risk for investors. Enhancing the role of NPISs to stimulate private-sector participation could be achieved by improving the credibility, transparency and predictability of public policies. These improvements could attract more FDI and drive a significant transformation of the production base, in turn stimulating innovation, upgrading value chains and creating high-quality jobs.

Several critical elements underpin successful NPISs. First and foremost, strategic alignment with a country's NDP ensures that investment initiatives contribute to wider socio-economic objectives. A robust institutional framework, characterised by clearly defined roles and responsibilities, facilitates efficient co-ordination and decision making. Transparent and efficient procedures are necessary for prioritising, implementing and evaluating impactful projects. Fiscal sustainability is a key consideration in all investment decisions, as is the active participation of stakeholders, which enhances investment quality and public support. A well-structured regulatory framework safeguards the interests of all involved parties, promoting an environment conducive to investment. Lastly, integration of public investments with annual and medium-term budgeting processes assures financial viability (ECLAC, 2023[63]).

Sectoral development plans are strategic roadmaps that provide a framework for promoting growth and development in specific economic sectors. These plans are typically produced by governments, often in consultation with stakeholders from the private sector, academia and civil society. They identify key goals, targets and strategies for developing different sectors, and may also outline specific policies or initiatives to be implemented. For example, Chile has a Green Hydrogen National Strategy (ME, 2020[64]); Costa Rica has a National Energy Plan 2015-30 (MINAE, 2015[65]) and a National Tourism Plan 2022-27 (ICTCR, 2022[66]); Colombia has a National Energy Plan 2020-50 (UPME, 2021[67]) and a Tourism Sector Plan 2022-26 (MCIT, 2022[68]), and is currently putting in place a new Reindustrialisation Policy that prioritises five strategic sectors; Peru has a National Infrastructure Plan for Competitiveness (MEF Peru, 2022[69]); and the Dominican Republic has a National Infrastructure Plan 2020-30 (MEPyD, 2020[70]).

Beyond fostering policy co-ordination and private-sector collaboration, these plans can attract domestic and foreign investment to support transformation efforts. By enhancing sectoral competitiveness, they can stimulate innovation, skills development, infrastructure upgrades and regulatory advancements. For example, Ecuador's National High-Yield Seed Plan was a successful multi-stakeholder plan for boosting the productivity of small farmers, with public and private actors and financing (Box 4.3).

Box 4.3. **A successful initiative in Ecuador to boost the productivity of small farmers**

Ecuador's National High-Yield Seed Plan was initiated in 2013 by the Ministry of Agriculture and Livestock and involved multiple stakeholders. The plan primarily focused on delivering technological packages to small corn producers to enhance their overall productivity. Instrumental to its success was a network involving national government, local governments, private companies and banks.

The Ministry of Agriculture and Livestock led and co-ordinated the project, while local governments played a key role in formalising small farmers. Private companies were vital anchors for corn purchases, while private suppliers facilitated necessary resources for the technological packages. Financial support was made available by private banks and development banks. The Development Bank of Latin America and the Caribbean (CAF) provided funding to improve the capacity of companies to purchase corn produced under the programme. Ecuador's Internal Revenue Service created a simplified tax regime.

Developing such multi-stakeholder strategies for increasing sectoral productivity can boost the impact of investment resources. This initiative more than doubled average corn yields, from 3.8 tonnes to 7.66 tonnes per hectare, while the net profit of the beneficiaries ranged from USD 890 to USD 1 292 per hectare in 2017 – compared to just USD 102 per hectare for non-beneficiary producers.

Source: CAF (2019[71]).

Multi-level governance can foster the potential of investments

The multiplicity of policies and actors involved in investment and production transformation efforts demands a high degree of co-ordination. Effective multi-level governance (MLG) is needed to co-ordinate national policy objectives with institutions and actors at the subnational and local level. The implementation of MLG tools for production transformation can take place vertically or horizontally, involving national, subnational and local governments as well as key stakeholders such as the private sector and neighbourhood associations.

Certain MLG tools can serve as a model, although each country will need to adjust them to its specificities (Allain-Dupré, 2020[72]). Creating a map of the main stakeholders and their channels of communication can help to identify potential gaps and understand the distribution of responsibilities in terms of sectors and functions (OECD, 2017[73]). Contracts, which are widely used tools in OECD countries, allow the responsibilities of all actors to be established in advance: the national government, which decides on the prioritisation and awarding of projects; the investors, which must comply with social and environmental standards; and local governments, which must provide certain goods and services (Charbit, 2020[74]). In other MLG schemes, the strategic priorities are defined at the subnational level. This was the case with the Research and Innovation Smart Specialisation Strategies implemented in the European Union in the last decade (Foray, David and Hall, 2009[75]). Adding co-financing clauses to these contracts can help ensure that all parties comply with their responsibilities. Cross-jurisdictional co-operation involving more than one municipality in the production of a particular good or service can foster local value chains. This type of MLG process could prove particularly useful for co-ordinated investment strategies or rural-urban partnerships, generating positive spillovers, increasing efficiency through economies of scale, and enhancing synergies among the policies of neighbouring municipalities (OECD, 2019[76]).

Local governments have a central role in production transformation efforts – and in connecting investments with the needs and potential of specific territories and communities. For instance, local governments can attract FDI by facilitating information and access to local suppliers for investors and by connecting them with local firms (OECD, 2015[2]). Similarly, local governments have the responsibility to provide goods and services that have direct impacts on development of local communities and their production activities and on attracting investments (OECD, 2015[2]). The OECD has developed a framework with key policy dimensions to improve attractiveness in specific regions of three South American countries: Argentina (Misiones), Chile (Valparaiso and Magallanes), and Colombia (Cordoba and Pacífico) (OECD, 2023[77]).

Spatial planning policies and land-use allocation are intimately related to the type of activities that can be developed at the local level. Currently all 33 LAC countries have a land-use planning law, policy and/or plan; however, only 19 have co-ordination mechanisms between sectoral and territorial planning (ECLAC, 2023[78]). This responsibility of local governments is particularly important as clear information about land tenure can encourage new investments (OECD, 2015[2]). Also, the different uses that municipalities grant for each parcel of land will directly determine what type of investors can locate in the area. The allocation of land for future investments should have a high degree of citizen participation (see above on stakeholder participation). Spatial planning and cadastral management are essential for investment and territorial development, but they also serve to improve fiscal management and support the integration of all legal, property and physical information (OECD, 2023[77]).

Alternative institutional arrangements, such as cluster initiatives, have potential to enhance co-ordination among the private sector, public sector, academia and civil society. These collaborative frameworks aim to address strategic priorities collectively, fostering the development of prioritised sectors in production strategies. Such initiatives offer a conduit for bridging national and local development endeavours, thereby serving as an MLG tool. Use of cluster initiatives has garnered significant traction across the LAC region, with notable experiences in Argentina, Colombia, Costa Rica, Mexico and the Caribbean. Their implementation could be improved, however, particularly regarding the need for increased financial allocation. Comprehensive efforts should be directed towards harmonising the quality and depth of cluster agendas, and a more seamless integration with overarching national strategies and local production development policies must be ensured (Salazar-Xirinachs, 2020[79]; Salazar-Xirinachs, 2020[80]; Llinás, 2021[28]). A better and more widespread use of cluster initiatives in implementing productive development policies in LAC could prove key in upgrading and diversifying the region's economies.

Financing the investments needed for the development agenda

LAC will require a vast mobilisation of public and private resources to finance the investments needed in the region. Two policy areas stand out for their ability to channel investments directly towards strategic development objectives. The first is linked to public development finance institutions (DFIs), the role of which can be strengthened in the region. The second is the development of innovative financing instruments, including green, social, sustainability and sustainability-linked (GSSS) bonds.

DFIs, mostly represented by national and subnational public development banks, play a crucial role in providing innovative financial services, technical and digital support, and expanded access for firms to financial markets.[2] They are well positioned to offer affordable access to financing to the micro-, small- and medium-sized enterprises (MSMEs) that drive employment. Public DFIs can offer unique opportunities to finance all stages of growth, especially for MSMEs, covering most of their working capital and investment needs. They can also facilitate MSMEs' access to capital markets, which is crucial for raising long-term funds, and can align investments to the country's economic priorities. These investments can be used to improve vital infrastructure, key economic sectors, R&D initiatives, and projects that promote gender equality, digital transformation and the green transition. By offering tailored financial and non-financial services to municipalities, local public institutions and national governments, DFIs can also boost public investment in key economic sectors, such as infrastructure and health.

Economic, social and governance (ESG) debt instruments, are key to mobilising and leveraging finance where needs are greatest for both public and private sector issuers. GSSS bonds, as a key asset class within the wider universe of ESG assets, represent a unique opportunity for the LAC region to link its debt requirements to sustainability criteria. To enhance GSSS bond financing, it is necessary to expand and harmonise sustainable finance frameworks, including principles, standards and taxonomies (OECD, 2023[81]). It is also important to consolidate reliable monitoring and verification systems to maintain market transparency and to avoid green/SDG-washing, or efforts by businesses to promote their positive contributions to some SDGs while not mentioning their negative impacts on others.

This section addresses how leveraging the financial and technical services of public DFIs can help MSMEs to make key investments that can drive the production transformation and address cross-cutting challenges. It explains how DFIs support governments, municipalities and public institutions in advancing investment in key sectors. It then focuses on GSSS bonds and how they can promote public and private investments with the support of more consolidated and harmonised sustainable finance frameworks.

DFIs can be crucial facilitators of private and public investments

National and subnational DFIs are uniquely positioned to mobilise essential resources to achieve the SDGs and guide a production transformation in an equitable and sustainable manner (ALIDE, 2023[82]). DFIs have a mandate to promote economic development and employment, and to facilitate investment and projects that align with the country's development objectives. Public DFIs include mostly national development banks (NDBs) and subnational development banks (SDBs). They also include specialised financial institutions and funds at the national and local levels. In the LAC region, the asset average of DFIs corresponds to 9.4% of GDP in Costa Rica, followed by Uruguay (7.9%), Panama (7.9%) and Chile (7.4%) (ALIDE, 2020[83]).

Public DFIs possess unparalleled knowledge of local markets and have long-standing relationships with local private and public sector actors. This advantageous positioning enables them to assess risks, develop project pipelines, generate investment prospects, and facilitate the flow of domestic and international capital between the public and private sectors (Feyertag, Attridge and Kumar, 2022[84]). Public DFIs can also play a catalytic role by using blended finance mechanisms to create more favourable risk-adjusted returns for international private investors (Chapter 5). Given the heterogeneity of capacities and skills among different DFIs, some are better equipped than others to support the LAC region's green, digital and social transitions. Not all DFIs have the same lending capacity or access to the same financing conditions. Constraints affecting some institutions, particularly domestic banks, include poor access to low-cost, long-term capital. Another major associated challenge is lending to entities that do not have a clear guarantee from their government. This issue is especially important when it comes to financing projects for highly indebted municipal entities and local governments.

The potential of DFIs is often underutilised in LAC countries, especially at national and subnational levels (Feyertag, Attridge and Kumar, 2022[84]; Smits and Rodríguez, 2022[85]). With their diverse and innovative financial instruments, DFIs can play a crucial role in addressing the lack of depth in LAC's financial markets by redistributing risks and making markets more inclusive. In turn, DFIs also have potential to bridge financing gaps faced by enterprises and help expand the market. Although substantial heterogeneity exists across LAC countries, financial systems in the region remain underdeveloped relative to the economic level of most countries. In domestic credit to the private sector as a percentage of GDP, at 59.5% the LAC region is far below levels of 171.5% in East Asia and the Pacific, and 160.7% in OECD countries (Figure 4.6, Panel A). As a result, 75% of the financing needs of LAC MSMEs remain unfunded (Figure 4.6, Panel B).

Figure 4.6. **Depth of LAC's financial markets**

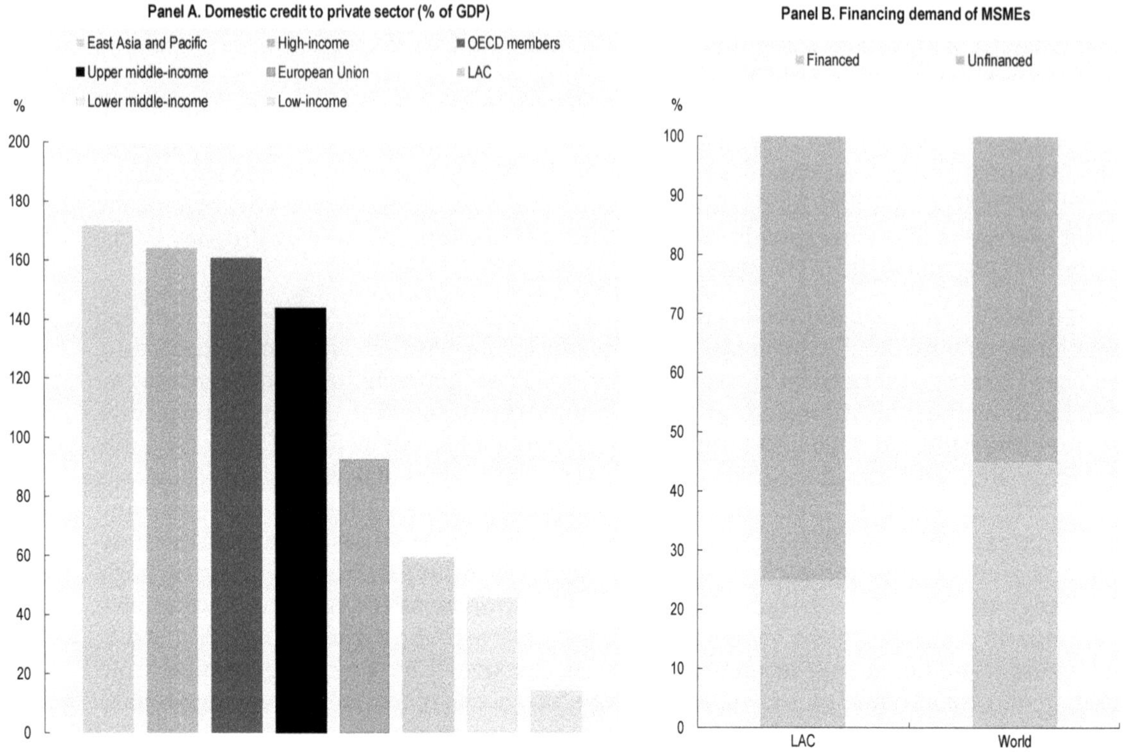

Source: (World Bank, 2023[86]); (SME Finance Forum, 2017[87]).

StatLink https://stat.link/b1ij4f

MSMEs account for 99% of formal enterprises and 66% of formal employment in LAC (Dini and Stumpo, 2020[88]). While MSMEs contribute 20% of GDP in Europe, in LAC they contribute only 3.2%. This difference is due, in part, to the current financing gap, and to limited efforts by MSMEs in LAC to adopt technologies and improvements in production processes (Oliveira de Paiva, 2020[89]) (Chapter 3). Since MSMEs can represent a significant segment for sustained economic recovery and job creation, it is crucial to address one of the main structural barriers they face: the financing gap (López-Calva, 2021[90]).

An analysis in 2023 of financial instruments used by 38 national and subnational public DFIs[3] across 13 LAC countries highlights the crucial role of DFIs in financing MSMEs in the region (Figure 4.7). Of 473 financial instruments mapped, 42% target both MSMEs and large companies, 39% target only MSMEs, 7% target public institutions including national governments and municipalities, and 4% are directed only to large companies.

Figure 4.7. **Targets of financial instruments in selected DFIs in LAC, 2023**

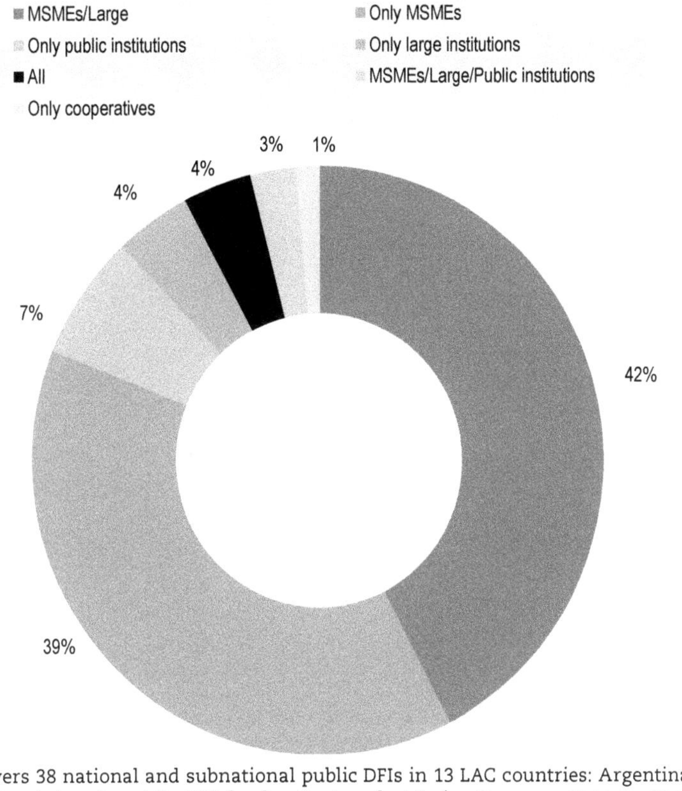

Note: The database covers 38 national and subnational public DFIs in 13 LAC countries: Argentina, Brazil, Chile, Colombia, Costa Rica, Dominican Republic, El Salvador, Guatemala, Mexico, Paraguay, Panama, Peru and Uruguay.
Source: Authors' elaboration based on public data (annual and sustainability reports) accessed in 2023 from 38 public DFIs in 13 LAC countries.

StatLink https://stat.link/evdwly

DFIs offer MSMEs a diverse pool of instruments and services

DFIs offer MSMEs in LAC a variety of tailored financial instruments that cater to financial needs at every stage of development. These instruments can be grouped into five types of financing: i) financing day-to-day operations (working capital, payroll, inventory, rent); ii) financing investment; iii) financing foreign trade; iv) emergency financing; and vi) risk mitigation and security instruments. The main types of financing offered through the 38 DFIs under discussion are financing investment (45%) and financing day-to-day operations (34%). This shows the commitment of DFIs to guaranteeing the working capital, liquidity and long-term investment needs of MSMEs. Other types of financing are less common and are primarily intended to enhance the financial inclusion and competitiveness of MSMEs (Figure 4.8).

Figure 4.8. **Distribution of financing types offered to MSMEs by public DFIs in LAC, 2023**

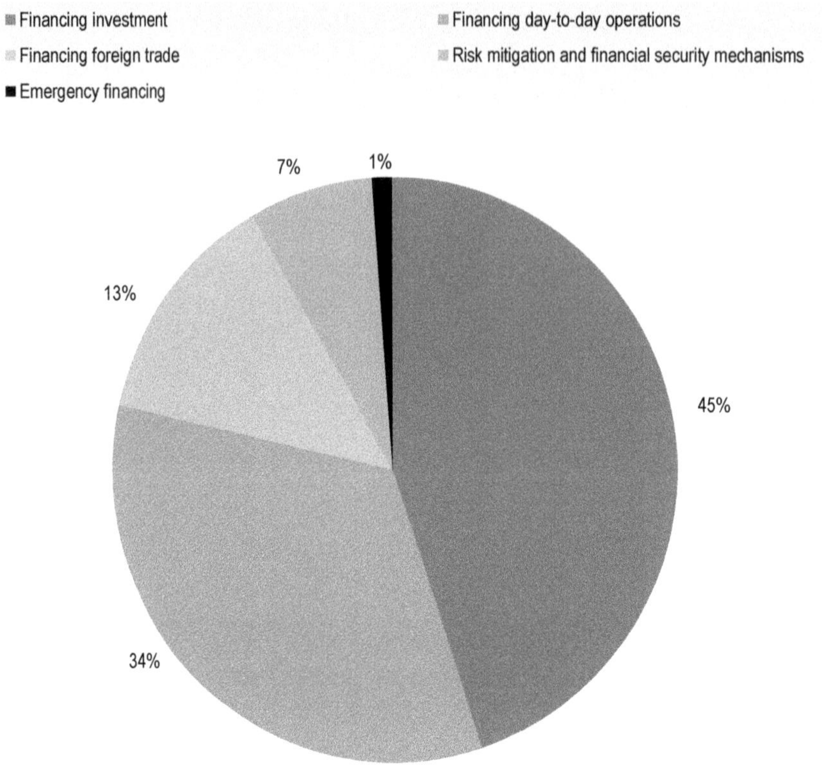

Note: The database covers 38 national and subnational public DFIs in 13 LAC countries: Argentina, Brazil, Chile, Colombia, Costa Rica, Dominican Republic, El Salvador, Guatemala, Mexico, Paraguay, Panama, Peru and Uruguay.
Source: Authors' elaboration based on public data (annual and sustainability reports) accessed in 2023 from 38 public DFIs in 13 LAC countries.

StatLink https://stat.link/ukundc

Multiple tools exist to support MSMEs in financing their investment needs. These investments are essential for MSMEs to undertake renovations or expansions, acquire new capital goods, and launch projects that foster innovation. Credits are the most common instrument offered to finance investment projects (87.6%). Although other types of financing are utilised less, they can also be useful for developing MSMEs. Financing mechanisms offered to grant MSMEs access to capital markets (5.1%) can allow them to participate in crucial investment portfolios. Leasing (4.0%) is offered as an innovative instrument that can allow MSMEs to finance long-term productive investment. This is done through a subsidised rate to foster the acquisition of capital goods aimed at increasing productivity in key sectors of the economy. Guarantees and credit funds are other financial instruments used by DFIs to help boost investment (Figure 4.9).

DFIs can also finance the day-to-day expenses of MSMEs, including working capital, inventory, payroll and rent. Credits are again the most common instrument (69.6%) and have the objective of maintaining and/or generating jobs and the acquisition of machinery. Long-term credits can allow MSMEs to purchase inputs, raw material or fuel so that they can focus on maintaining their production activity and improving their competitiveness. Deferred payment mechanisms (10.1%) are used to help with commercial development, while factoring (9.4%) is offered to MSMEs to boost their competitiveness and increase liquidity for day-to-day operations. Other financial instruments used to help boost liquidity and access to working capital include credit cards, leasing or leaseback, trusts, guarantees credit funds and cancellation of liabilities (Figure 4.9).

Figure 4.9. **Distribution of financial instruments offered to MSMEs by type of financing (%), 2023**

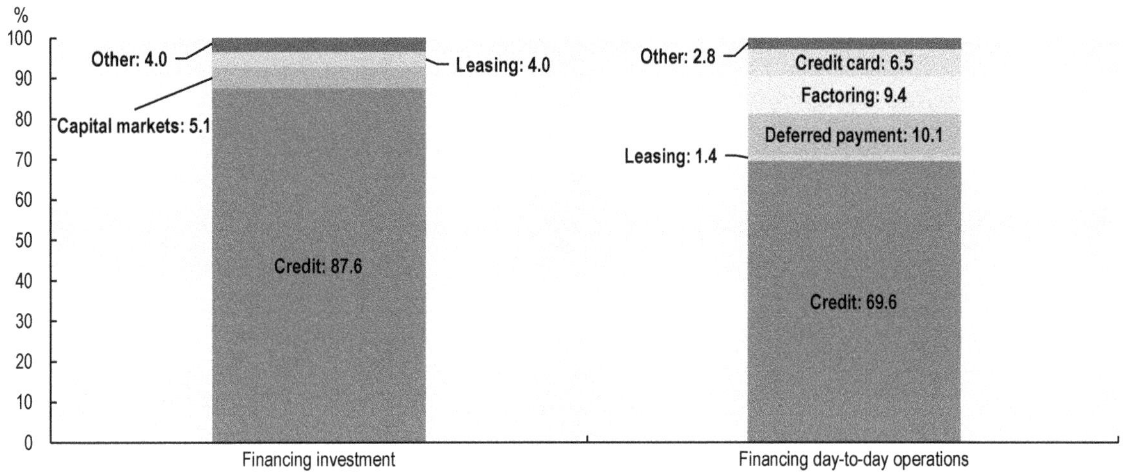

Note: The database covers 38 national and subnational public DFIs in 13 LAC countries: Argentina, Brazil, Chile, Colombia, Costa Rica, Dominican Republic, El Salvador, Guatemala, Mexico, Paraguay, Panama, Peru and Uruguay. The category "Other" includes the following financial instruments: Non-reimbursable financial support; Credit fund; Guarantee; Trusts; and cancellation of liabilities.

Source: Authors' elaboration based on public data (annual and sustainability reports) accessed in 2023 from 38 public DFIs in 13 LAC countries.

StatLink https://stat.link/cul87e

Some DFIs have developed significant expertise in financing the foreign trade needs of MSMEs. This is done through mechanisms that provide guarantees and/or funding for pre-export and post-export financing operations of goods and services. To help MSMEs protect themselves against natural hazards and disasters, public DFIs in the LAC region also offer emergency financing (credit) lines, which can finance the acquisition of new capital goods and/or the construction of facilities.

Trust funds and guarantees are also important risk mitigation and security instruments offered by public DFIs seeking to help MSMEs access project financing in strategic sectors. Trust funds offered to MSMEs mainly support economic and/or social development programmes aligned with national priorities that aim to foster job creation and promote environmental sustainability. Guarantees can also enhance financial inclusion by reducing credit risk and providing security to lenders. This is particularly relevant for MSMEs with limited assets or credit histories. Well-evaluated public DFIs allow MSMEs to acquire financing under better conditions, for example with longer terms, lower entry requirements and lower interest rates. MSMEs in the LAC region mostly use loans and credit lines in climate-related finance, highlighting the need to scale up guarantees that can help reduce risks and attract new investment. Ensuring that credit-guarantee schemes preserve market discipline in credit allocation is a key issue (Blancher et al., 2019[91]).

As key public entities, DFIs have potential to increase the supply and quality of financial instruments. Such instruments can encourage innovative and long-term investment and employment by the private sector, especially MSMEs. Increasing the capacity and accessibility to innovative financial instruments by MSMEs in LAC is fundamental to combatting the current limitations of the region's financial systems (Coalición Regional, 2016[92]). Multilateral Development Banks (MDBs), such as CAF or the Inter-American Development Bank (IDB), can play a key role in providing technical support and transferring strategic know-how to DFIs. MDBs can help build institutional capacity in financial instruments related to capital markets development and the issuance of GSSS bonds. This role can be instrumental in mainstreaming climate- and social-related debt instruments and advancing the sustainable agenda within the region's capital markets (see section on GSSS bonds). It is also necessary to consolidate monitoring and follow-up systems for each financial instrument to better understand their impact and fine-tune them according to companies' needs. The diversity of tools that DFIs offer to key economic sectors, accompanied by the necessary technical and digital support, can help consolidate LAC's production transformation and prepare for and play an active role in shaping a new international financial architecture.

DFIs can boost key production sectors

National and subnational DFIs can play a significant role in promoting investments in key production sectors. They have potential to increase companies' access to finance, thereby boosting development and job creation (ALIDE, 2022[93]). Customised financial instruments can address sector-specific challenges and align sectors with national goals. Of 38 national and subnational DFIs mapped, 87% have one or more financial instruments that target specific sectors. Of 473 financial instruments identified, 41% have a sectoral perspective. One instrument can target several sectors in parallel. Of the total financial instruments with a sectoral perspective, 30% target the agriculture, hunting and forestry sector; 14% the electricity, gas and water supply sector; 13% the manufacturing sector; and 7% the transport, storage and communications sector (Figure 4.10).

Figure 4.10. **Distribution of the sector-targeted financial instruments offered to MSMEs by DFIs, 2023**

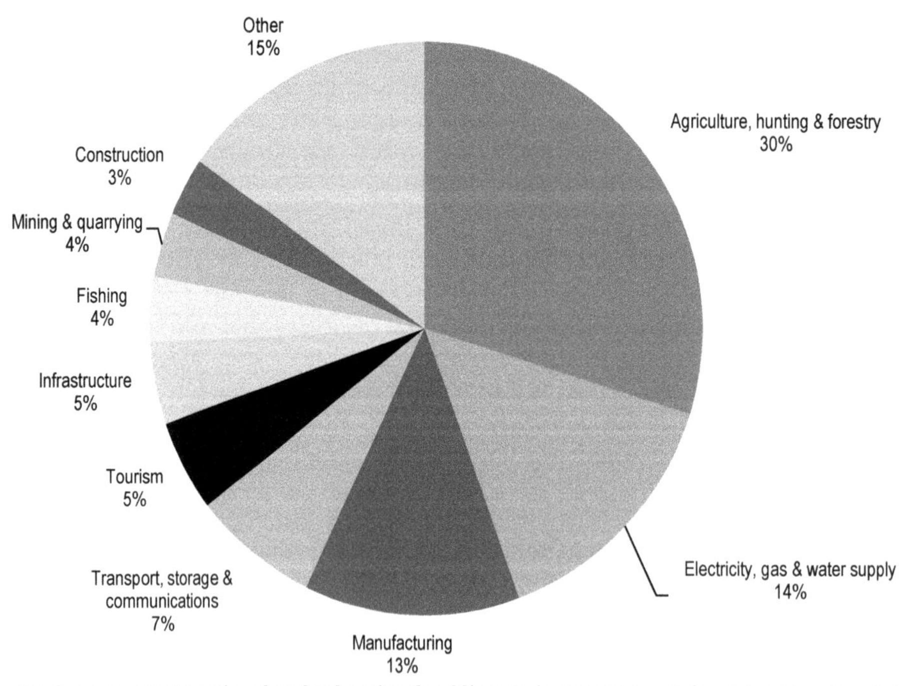

Note: The database covers 38 national and subnational public DFIs in 13 LAC countries: Argentina, Brazil, Chile, Colombia, Costa Rica, Dominican Republic, El Salvador, Guatemala, Mexico, Paraguay, Panama, Peru and Uruguay. The category "Other" includes the following sectors: Wholesale and retail trade; Financial intermediation; Real estate, renting and business activities; Public administration and defence; Education; Health and social work; Other community, social and personal service activities; Information and Communication Technology (ICT); and creative industries.

Source: Authors' elaboration based on public data (annual and sustainability reports) accessed in 2023 from 38 public DFIs in 13 LAC countries.

StatLink https://stat.link/sb8tjv

The agricultural, hunting and forestry sector is the most targeted by all types of financing instruments that are provided by public DFIs in LAC to MSMEs (Figure 4.11). Among these instruments, those financing investment help to support various sectors (such as agri-food or bioeconomy) by providing resources for diverse activities (such as vegetable growing, cattle milk production, poultry farming, beekeeping and meat-processing plants). In this way, they contribute to diversifying a country's production structure. Instruments financing day-to-day operations can also contribute to diversification by helping MSMEs to stabilise and thus become better equipped to focus on long-term planning and on exploring new investment opportunities.

The electricity, gas and water supply sector is targeted through instruments for financing investment, financing day-to-day operations, and supporting risk mitigation and security. Financing investment often includes incentives to improve energy-environmental efficiency and production certification.

The manufacturing sector is often targeted by DFIs, especially through financing of investment and day-to-day operations. Instruments for financing investment for this sector focus on the acquisition of projects with industrial units already built or under construction (Figure 4.11).

Figure 4.11. **Sectoral distribution of financing instruments provided by DFIs to MSMEs in LAC, 2023**

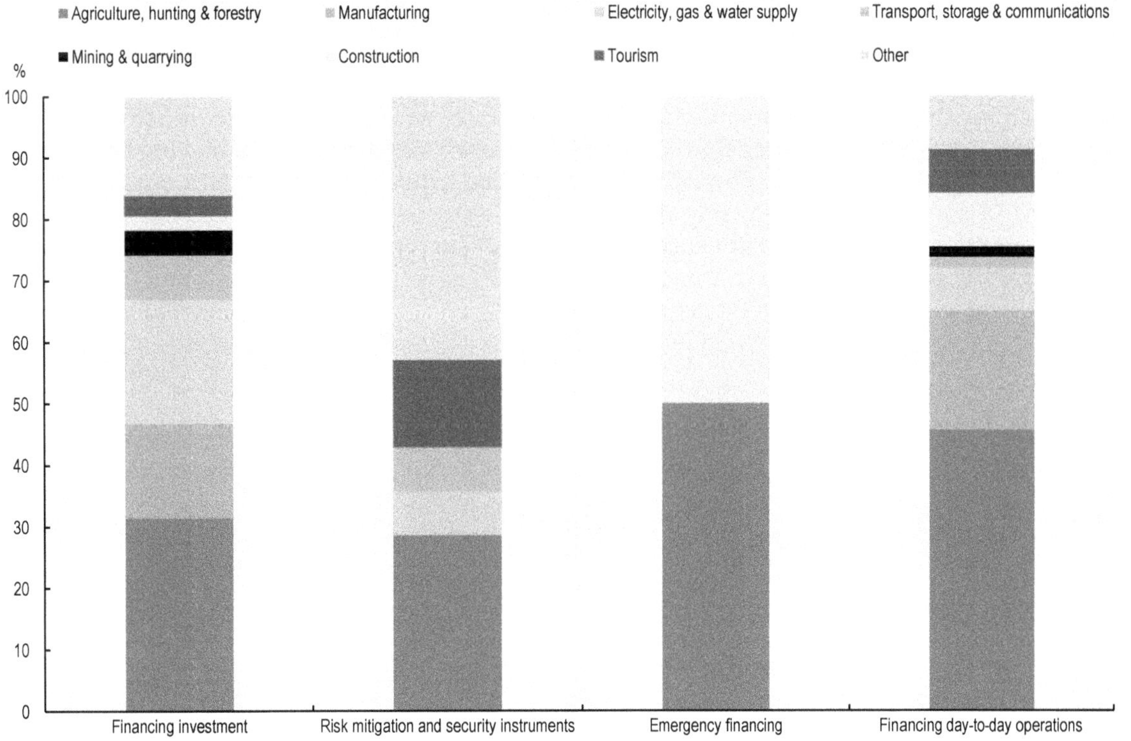

Note: The database covers 38 national and subnational public DFIs in 13 LAC countries: Argentina, Brazil, Chile, Colombia, Costa Rica, Dominican Republic, El Salvador, Guatemala, Mexico, Paraguay, Panama, Peru and Uruguay. The category "Other" includes the following sectors: Fishing; Wholesale and retail trade; Financial intermediation; Real estate, renting and business activities; Public administration and defence; Education; Health and social work; Other community, social and personal service activities; ICT; and creative industries.

Source: Authors' elaboration based on public data (annual and sustainability reports) accessed in 2023 from 38 public DFIs in 13 LAC countries.

StatLink https://stat.link/hl3yun

For DFIs to help effectively drive the LAC region's production transformation, it is important that they function within the framework of well-defined national development strategies. These strategies should allocate DFIs a distinct and strategic mandate, particularly in relation to their role in promoting key production transformation sectors. DFIs must also advance in their efforts to develop instruments that respond to the specific needs and singularities of each production sector. In order to offer the right kind of instruments, DFIs need to develop capabilities and skills within their country's sectoral priorities.

Niche sectors within the larger sector categories are also relevant when developing targeted financial instruments. Green hydrogen, for instance, is a growing niche sector in different LAC countries and requires that DFIs address its emerging needs. This includes financing human capital development in the industry or technologies required, and providing support for products that utilise green hydrogen. Establishing closer contact with companies and getting to know their aspirations and installed capabilities at the sector level can facilitate development of better targeted instruments. Fine tuning these processes requires that DFIs expand their technical knowledge on specific sectors and invest in capacity-building strategies. The Latin American Association of Development Financing Institutions (ALIDE) can become a crucial platform for national and subnational public DFIs to access sectoral information. By bringing together the experience and knowledge of financial experts from across the region, ALIDE could take the lead in improving the design of sector-specific financial services.

DFIs can help MSMEs contribute to green, digital and gender goals

The commitment of national and subnational DFIs to the SDGs could work in favour of developing financial instruments for MSMEs that have sustainable, gender-sensitive and digital objectives. This can help channel private investments towards achieving key development goals. At present, however, of 473 financial instruments for MSMEs offered by public DFIs in the LAC region, only 19% address at least one of the three cross-cutting challenges. Of the financial instruments that address at least one cross-cutting challenge, 51% target the green transition in some dimension, 29% target gender equality, and 20% target digital and innovation challenges (Figure 4.12).

Figure 4.12. **Distribution of financial instruments targeting green, digital and gender dimensions, 2023**

Instruments offered by DFIs to MSMEs in LAC

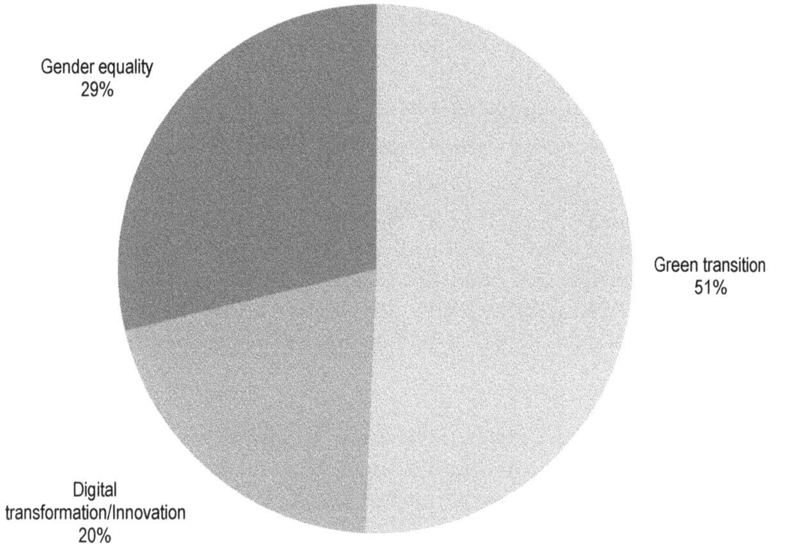

Note: Distribution shows cross-cutting challenges only for those DFIs that had one or more services targeting a green, digital or gender dimension. The following DFIs offered financial instruments targeting at least one cross-cutting challenge: Banco de Inversión y Comercio Exterior S.A. (BICE); Banco de La Pampa, Banco de la Provincia de Buenos Aires (BAPRO); Banco de la Nación Argentina; Banco de Desenvolvimento de Minas Gerais S.A. (BDMG); Banco do Nordeste do Brasil S.A. (BNB); Banco Nacional de Desenvolvimento Econômico e Social (BNDES); Banco Regional de Desenvolvimento do Extremo Sul (BRDE); Desenvolve SP – Agência de Fomento do Estado de São Paulo S.A.; Fondo para el Financiamiento del Sector Agropecuario (FINAGRO); Banco Nacional de Costa Rica; Banco Popular y de Desarrollo Comunal; Instituto Nacional de Desarrollo Agropecuario (INDAP); Banco Nacional de las Exportaciones (BANDEX); Corporación Nacional de Finanzas Populares y Solidarias (CONAFIPS); Banco de Desarrollo Rural S.A. (BANRURAL); Banco de Desarrollo de El Salvador (BANDESAL); Nacional Financiera S.N.C. (NAFIN); Banco Nacional de Comercio Exterior S.N.C. (BANCOMEXT); Fideicomisos Instituidos en Relación con la Agricultura (FIRA); Banco de México; Banco Nacional de Fomento (BNF); Agencia Financiera de Desarrollo; Corporación Financiera de Desarrollo S.A. (COFIDE).
Source: Authors' elaboration based on public data (annual and sustainability reports) accessed in 2023 from 38 public DFIs in 13 LAC countries.

StatLink https://stat.link/1bgom8

To increase green investments, DFIs in LAC offer financial services to MSMEs to support projects related to renewable energy (energy generation and efficiency), and to mitigate crises related to natural disasters. To accelerate the green transition, it is essential for DFIs to provide financing mechanisms that target the most critical sectors. This will support countries in achieving their climate-change mitigation and adaptation objectives. Among the financial services targeting the green transition with a sectoral perspective, 33% focus on the electricity, gas and water supply sector; 17% on the agriculture, forestry and fishing sector; and 10% on the transport, storage and communications sector. Other less-targeted sectors include mining and quarrying, as well as manufacturing, with each accounting for 6.8%. Despite being less targeted, these sectors play crucial roles in achieving countries' mitigation and adaptation goals (UNEP, 2023[94]). Therefore, it is necessary for public DFIs to expand their financial services and offer more targeted support to these sectors with high greenhouse gas (GHG) emissions.

DFIs have also developed financial frameworks to facilitate women-led investments. Financial support for women includes, for example, investment loans for MSMEs that are 51% owned by women or those with women ownership of at least 25% that have at least one woman on their board of directors or in their senior management. However, much room for improvement still exists. The proportion of disbursements to women-led MSMEs is still very small compared to the total. More opportunities should be generated, not only to increase the supply of financial services to women but also to stimulate demand, for instance through gender-focused financial education programmes.

DFIs can also help to increase digital, research, innovation and technology-oriented investments. DFIs offer trusts to stimulate the information and communications technology sector, loans to foster innovation and financial support for developing new products, processes or services. Public DFIs are also innovating in the financial technology (fintech) sector by offering MSMEs financing platforms to promote financial inclusion. In parallel, public DFIs are increasing focus on their own digital transformation, including by integrating applications and automating operations through digital channels.

To boost investment in these dimensions, DFIs can establish specific programmes for: i) project preparation; and ii) technical support during project implementation. It is important for DFIs to engage actively in policy dialogues concerning the green transition, digital transformation and gender equality (Smits and Rodríguez, 2022[85]). This should include offering insights into the constraints and catalysts they have identified. Lastly, DFIs need to develop the capacity to articulate and measure the impact of their financial instruments on work towards the SDGs and climate-related objectives.

DFIs can support investments by local governments in targeted sectors

National and subnational DFIs in LAC have an important role in financing public investments, for example by providing national or local governments with permanent financing lines such as credits, capital market access mechanisms, guarantees, leasing, deferred payment and trusts (Figure 4.13). Credits often target improvements in infrastructure and public services at the local level. Some investment credits focus on municipal projects that target SDGs in areas including energy efficiency, smart cities, renewable and clean energy, water supply and sewage treatment, among others. To finance investment, DFIs also support public institutions in accessing capital markets. Leasing is emerging as a novel instrument enabling government institutions to access new equipment and technologies for investments. It allows regular equipment renewal at low credit costs, improving the investment capacity of local governments and enhancing public services for the population (Jouglard, 2019[95]).

Figure 4.13. **Distribution of financial instruments offered to the public sector by public DFIs in LAC, 2023**

By type of instrument and objective

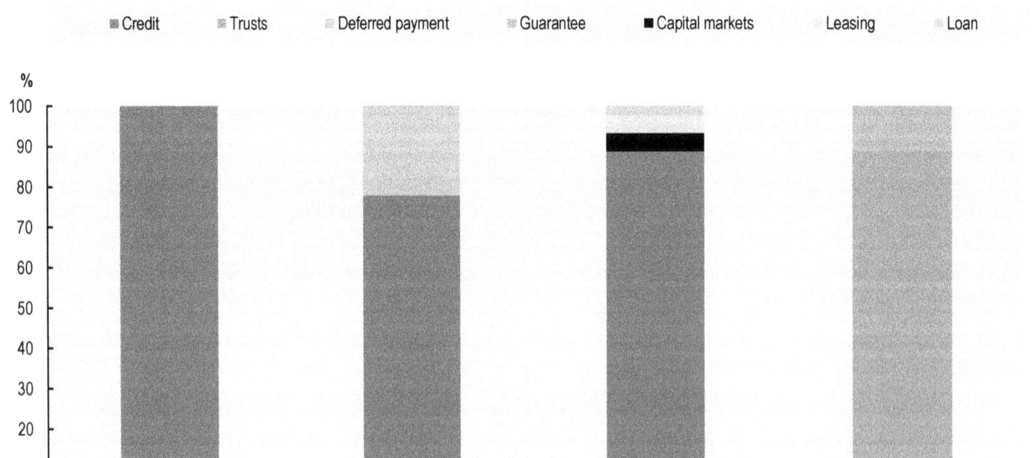

Note: The database covers 38 national and subnational public DFIs in 13 LAC countries: Argentina, Brazil, Chile, Colombia, Costa Rica, Dominican Republic, El Salvador, Guatemala, Mexico, Paraguay, Panama, Peru and Uruguay.
Source: Authors' elaboration based on public data (annual and sustainability reports) accessed in 2023 from 38 public DFIs in 13 LAC countries.

StatLink https://stat.link/uckoeh

DFIs in LAC also offer targeted financial instruments to public institutions to facilitate mobilising resources to key sectors. Of the total instruments offered, 24% target the infrastructure sector; 20% the electricity, gas and water supply sector; 15% the transport, storage and communications sector; and 11% the agriculture, hunting and forestry sector (Figure 4.14). Most of the credits offered to public institutions focus on developing urban infrastructure and public services. These credits allow the financing of roads and bridges, as well as infrastructure projects in the energy, tourism, culture and sports sectors.

Figure 4.14. **Sectoral distribution of financial instruments offered to the public sector by public DFIs, 2023**

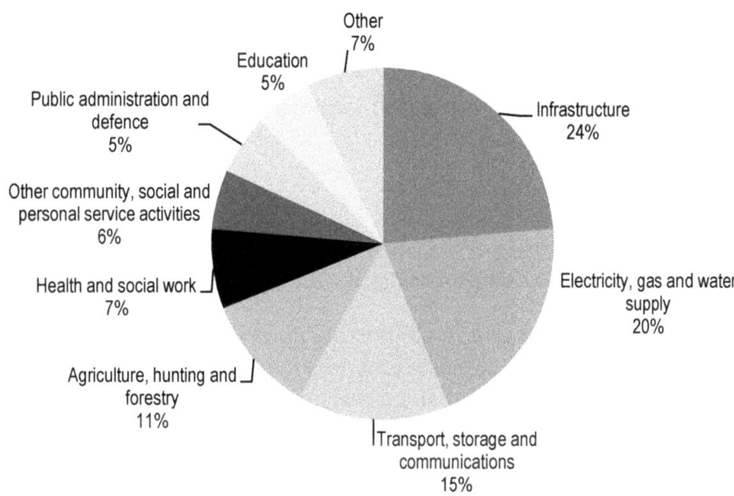

Note: The database covers 38 national and subnational public DFIs in 13 LAC countries: Argentina, Brazil, Chile, Colombia, Costa Rica, Dominican Republic, El Salvador, Guatemala, Mexico, Paraguay, Panama, Peru and Uruguay. The category "Other" includes the following sectors: Fishing; Mining and quarrying; Wholesale and retail trade; Repair of motor vehicles, motorcycles and personal and household goods; and ICT.

Source: Authors' elaboration based on public data (annual and sustainability reports) accessed in 2023 from 38 public DFIs in 13 LAC countries.

StatLink https://stat.link/ws25e6

DFIs can also provide technical and digital support to public entities. They can offer the public sector specialised and advisory services as well as technical assistance by creating partnerships with state secretariats, ministries and municipalities. In May 2023, the state of Pernambuco in Brazil sought technical assistance from the Brazilian Development Bank (BNDES) to expand its sanitation infrastructure. BNDES will oversee specialised consultants conducting preliminary studies, including a sector diagnosis, investment estimates, an assessment of financing options and economic viability studies (BNDES, 2023[96]). Some DFIs also offer training on digital platforms for efficient credit access and assist in disseminating information on available credit lines.

DFIs in LAC still have a long way to go in providing and expanding some of these instruments to the public sector. Access to these instruments and services must be increasingly improved through digital innovations that streamline the application and procurement processes for the different lines of financing. Some misunderstanding still exists, especially in small public entities, of how these new types of financial products and services work. It is thus necessary that public DFIs increase technical and digital services to support municipalities and also help to "professionalise" the public sphere by progressively aligning its practices with those of the private sector (Jouglard, 2019[95]).

Innovative financial tools, such as GSSS bonds, can help to finance investments

Capital markets serve as a vital component of the LAC region's financial system, and their potential can be strengthened. Capital markets can help to mobilise financing for strategic sectors such as infrastructure and housing, facilitate funding for SMEs, and foster innovation (World Bank, 2022[97]). By functioning as a hub for investors and issuers, capital markets in LAC facilitate economic growth and enable companies and governments to access necessary funds for expansion and development.

In addition to traditional instruments (such as equities, fixed-income assets and derivatives in the foreign-exchange market) in LAC capital markets, new instruments have been developed. Equity instruments such as venture capital funds are gaining importance and showing growth in the region. These funds aim to increase financing for early-stage and high-growth companies (Box 4.4). There has also been significant growth in the issuance of GSSS bonds, reflecting rising investor interest in ESG-themed products (ECLAC, 2022[98]).

Box 4.4. Unleashing the potential of venture capital funds to finance start-ups in the LAC region

Venture capital plays a crucial role in supporting start-ups and companies at different stages of growth, from initial development to expansion and acquisition activities (OECD, 2015[99]). Venture capital funds can be classified into three main types: early-stage financing, expansion financing and acquisition/buyout financing. Early-stage financing encompasses seed financing, start-up financing and first stage financing, providing capital for start-ups to qualify for loans, complete product development and initiate full-scale business activities. Expansion financing supports growing companies and includes second-stage financing, bridge financing and third-stage financing. This type of financing enables companies to pursue growth opportunities and utilise initial public offerings (IPOs) as a strategic business approach. In IPOS, shares of a private company are offered to the public for the first time, raising additional funds and providing access to public markets. Acquisition financing involves financing to purchase other companies or parts of them, while leveraged buyout financing facilitates the acquisition of specific products (Nayak, 2018[100]).

Many medium-sized companies face challenges when seeking conventional financing due to the inherent risks involved in their ventures (Rudolph, Faruk and Gonzalez-Uribe, 2023[101]). Venture capitalists bridge this funding gap by offering capital, expertise and networks. Their involvement supports the growth of promising start-ups and contributes to developing entrepreneurial ecosystems in the region. Through their support, they facilitate connections for start-ups with mentors, industry experts and potential collaborators, fostering knowledge sharing.

The venture capital landscape in LAC has experienced remarkable growth in recent years, with venture capital investments surging from around USD 1 million in 2015 to nearly USD 20 billion in 2021 (Rudolph, Faruk and Gonzalez-Uribe, 2023[101]). This surge surpassed corporate debt financing and approached the levels of equity financing raised through IPOs in the region's primary markets. It can be attributed to the entrance of deep-pocketed venture capital investors actively pursuing both early-stage and late-stage deals. These opportunities, predominantly facilitated by non-domestic investors in the LAC venture capital market, have played a significant and instrumental role in driving overall investment value and participation in deals, further fuelling growth and development of the LAC venture capital ecosystem.

Box 4.4. **Unleashing the potential of venture capital funds to finance start-ups in the LAC region** *(cont.)*

In 2021, LAC's venture capital investment as a percentage of GDP reached a rate of 0.38%, surpassing Southeast Asia's rate of 0.27% but below the global average of 0.57% (Endeavor Intelligence & Glisco Partners, 2022[102]). Notably, Colombia and Brazil have emerged as frontrunners with investment rates of 0.52% of GDP within the same year, showcasing their strength in attracting venture capital. Despite facing a decline in FDI, in 2021 Mexico achieved a record level of venture capital investment with USD 3.7 billion (0.29% of GDP). These figures demonstrate the increasing prominence and attractiveness of venture capital opportunities in the region, and indicate the potential for further expansion and innovation in the coming years.

Sustainable debt market instruments are key to addressing development challenges

Developing sustainable debt market instruments can help mobilise resources where needs are greatest. Increasing demand for ESG-linked assets, and especially for GSSS bonds, has contributed to raising public and private funds for crucial projects.

For sovereigns in the LAC region, raising funds through these assets has become an attractive option to increase the return on liquid global capital, diversify the investor base, mobilise direct capital into sustainable activities, and acquire financial support for creating sustainable capital markets. In the aftermath of the COVID-19 pandemic, impact investing through bonds has become increasingly important, especially since European funds are willing to take a longer-term view of risk (Gavin, 2022[103]). For sovereigns in LAC, bond proceeds can fund sustainable public expenditure and infrastructure, as well as sustainable policies and national commitments, such as the Nationally Determined Contributions (NDC) set under the Paris Agreement on climate change (Frisari, Carlino and Palacios, 2022[104]).

For corporates in LAC, issuing debt in international markets is attractive as it often offers lower interest rates and greater potential for capital gains. Bond proceeds can also benefit sectoral investments in LAC, such as the agricultural sector (agribusiness, food and beverages, forestry), the financial sector (commercial banks, financial services companies, finance development banks/multilateral agencies), and the energy sector (utilities, oil, gas, power) (ECLAC, 2023[105]).

There are two types of structures in the sustainability debt market: green, social and sustainable (GSS) bonds which are "use-of-proceeds" bonds designed to finance sustainable projects, and sustainability-linked bonds which are "target-linked" bonds tied to specific sustainability targets (Figure 4.15). As defined by the International Capital Market Association (ICMA), use-of-proceeds bonds (also called GSS bonds) are fixed-income instruments, the proceeds of which are exclusively applied to finance or refinance green, social and sustainable projects, either entirely or partially. With target-linked bonds (also called sustainability-linked bonds [SLBs]), the proceeds are used for general purposes. The issuers choose the associated targets they want to achieve through the issuance of the bond; ultimately, they accrue additional payments to bondholders if the predetermined targets are not met. These bonds are generally tracked by assessing key performance indicators (KPI) and sustainability performance targets (SPTs) (OECD et al., 2022[17]; Núñez, Velloso and Da Silva, 2022[106]).

Figure 4.15. **Types of structure in the sustainability debt market**

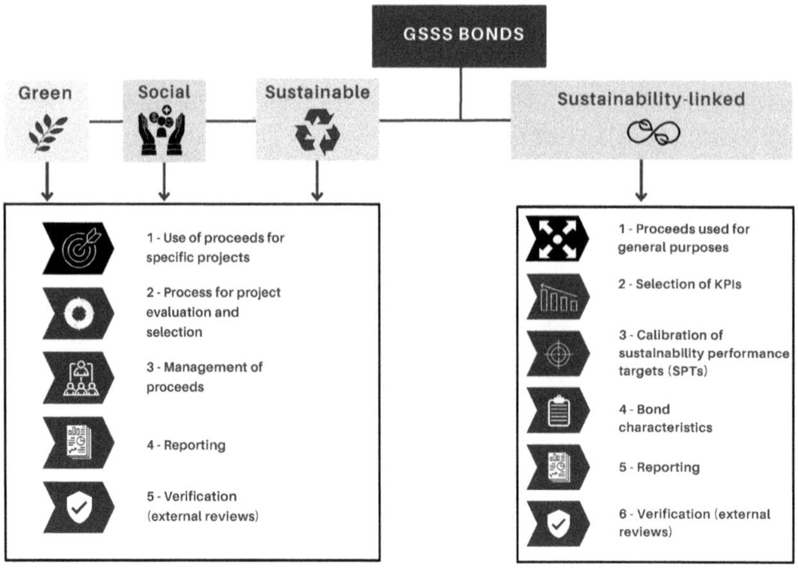

Source: Authors' elaboration based on ICMA Principles.

To date, the GSSS bond market represents only a small fraction of the global bond market. It is still considered a niche sector, representing only 1% of total assets outstanding and around 2% of new issuances globally (OECD, 2022[107]). In the LAC region, however, even with tight financial markets, GSSS bonds continue to be an attractive financing mechanism, representing 32% of total international LAC bond issuance. The region issued USD 20.1 billion of international GSSS bonds in 2022, down 56% from 2021 but still the second-highest year recorded. Between 2014 and 2022, the GSSS international bond market reached a cumulative value of close to USD 100 billion, of which green bond issuance alone accounted for USD 33.4 billion, followed by bonds linked to sustainability criteria (USD 24.4 billion) (Figure 4.16).

Figure 4.16. **International bond issuance in LAC: GSSS by type and as percentage of total, 2014-22**

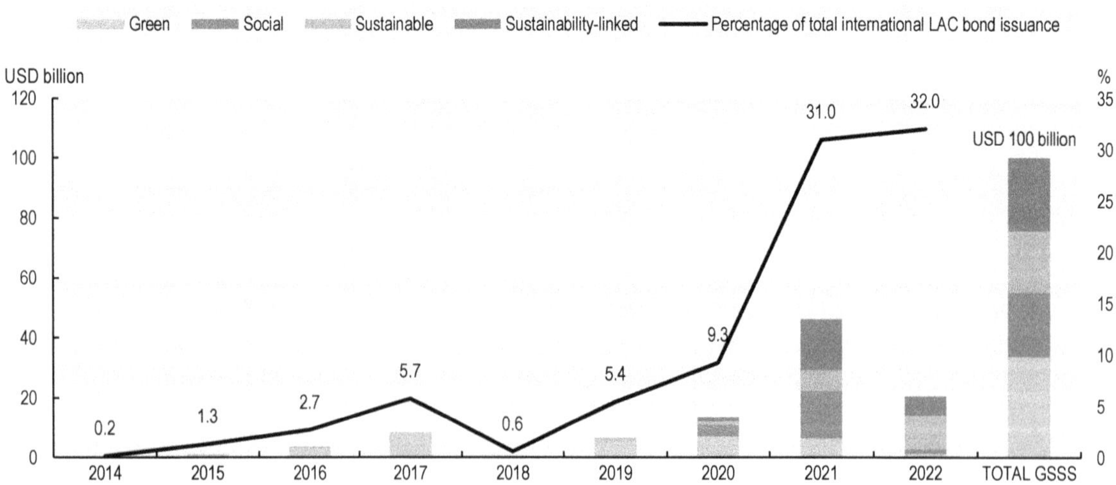

Note: GSSS refers to green, social, sustainability and sustainability-linked bonds. Total sustainable bonds for 2022 include two blue bonds issued by the Bahamas.

Source: (Núñez, Velloso and Da Silva, 2022[106]; ECLAC, 2023[105]).

StatLink https://stat.link/0xsh8z

Sovereign GSSS issuance has been growing as a share of total GSSS bond issuance in LAC. In 2022, sovereign GSSS bond issuance in international markets in the region accounted for 35.7% of the total sovereign issuance of all types of bonds in international markets. During the first six months of 2023 this figure increased to 43.5%. Until June 2019, all LAC GSSS bond issuances originated in the corporate sector, and corporates continued to lead total GSSS bond volumes in 2019 with a 44% share of the total, while sovereign issuances represented 37%, and supranational issuers 19%. Sovereign issuances have since been rising. In 2022, sovereigns led with a 57% share of total GSSS bond issuance in LAC, followed by corporates (23%) and supranational and quasi-sovereign issuers (20%) (ECLAC, 2023[105]) (Figure 4.17, Panel A). In June 2019, Chile issued the region's first green sovereign bond in international markets. By 2022, seven countries had followed (Ecuador, Guatemala, Mexico, Peru, Bahamas and Uruguay [in order of appearance]) by issuing green (or blue), social, sustainability and sustainability-linked bonds in international markets (Figure 4.17, Panel B) (ECLAC, 2023[105]). Regarding sovereign issuances in the domestic market, in 2021 Colombia became the first emerging economy worldwide to issue a sovereign green bond in local currency (TES Verdes) (OECD et al., 2022[17]).

Figure 4.17. **GSSS sovereign bond issuance in international markets**

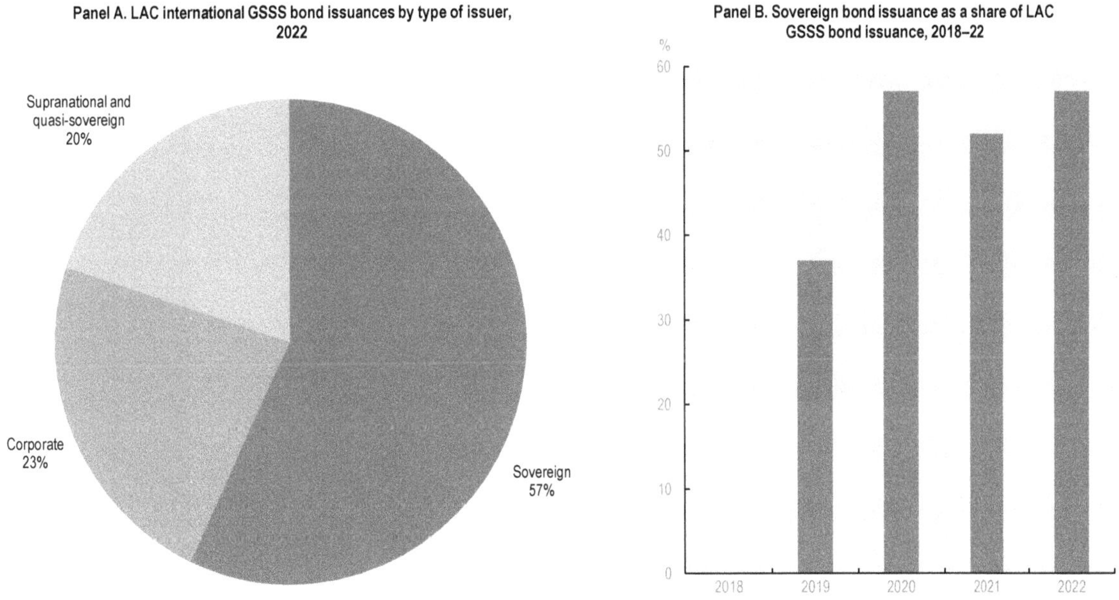

Note: Quasi-sovereign issuers are defined as companies with full or partial government ownership or control. Supranational issuers are defined as entities formed by two or more central governments to promote economic development for the member countries.

Source: (ECLAC, 2023[105]).

StatLink https://stat.link/vbd30z

The share of SLBs in total GSSS bond issuance fell to 31% in 2022, from 37% in 2021. These bonds can be prone to greenwashing. Since issuers self-impose KPIs and SPTs that can be very difficult to verify externally, increased market scrutiny and fear of greenwashing may slow the growth of this type of bond in the short term. Nonetheless, SLBs offer issuers the opportunity to redirect capital flows to achieve multiple sustainable objectives at the same time. Two LAC countries, Chile and Uruguay, became pioneers in 2022 as the world's first nations to issue sovereign sustainability-linked bonds; as of mid-2023, they remained the sole issuers in the LAC region (OECD, 2023[81]). In March 2022, Chile issued a USD 2 billion sovereign bond tied to two key performance indicators: reducing GHG emissions and boosting energy production. With the issuance, Chile became the first government to link its official NDC commitment on climate change to a bond issuance. In November 2022, Uruguay issued its first bond indexed to indicators of climate change (BIICC).

GSSS bonds have emerged as attractive instruments for specific sectors to raise capital and address the LAC region's pressing sectoral challenges. Between 2014 and April 2022, the main sectors that issued GSSS bonds, after sovereign (39%), were finance (14%), the chemical industry (10%) and energy (9%) (Figure 4.18). Diversification across sectors in the GSSS market in LAC has increased since 2019 (Núñez, Velloso and Da Silva, 2022[106]). Until 2018, the only sectors issuing GSSS bonds were pulp and paper, food and beverage, and energy. Since 2019, new sectors have accessed the sustainable market, including auto and related activities, technology, chemicals, telecommunications, consumer products, real estate, transportation, and sugar and ethanol (Núñez, Velloso and Da Silva, 2022[106]). Sectoral distribution indicates that these bonds have potential to increase finance investment in projects in key sectors with sustainability impacts.

Figure 4.18. **GSSS bond issuance in international markets, sectoral distribution, LAC**

December 2014 to April 2022

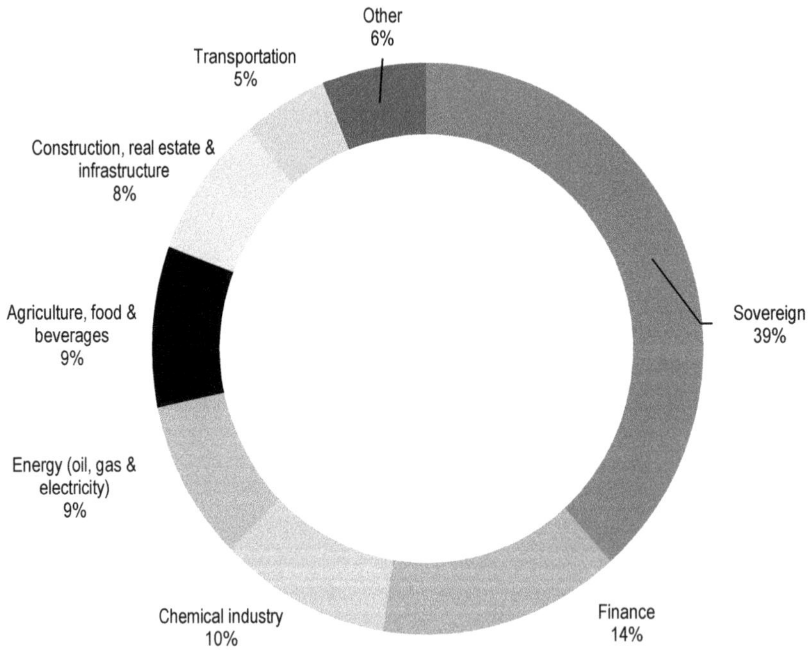

Note: The category "Other" includes the following sectors: Telecommunications; Forestry & paper; and retail & consumer products.

Source: (OECD et al., 2022[17]; Núñez, Velloso and Da Silva, 2022[106]).

StatLink https://stat.link/l68n0x

GSSS bonds can unlock key investments to address gender equality and digital inclusion

The LAC region has become a leader in gender bond issuance, with a total of ten issuances between 2016 and 2022 from sovereign, corporate and supranational issuers (Sacristán, 2022[108]). Gender bonds are a type of social, sustainable or sustainability-linked bond that aims to raise capital earmarked for new or existing projects that support the advancement, empowerment and equality of women. For instance, Ecuador's Banco Pichincha issued two gender bonds in 2022. The first funded loans to women-led small businesses. Half of the bond sale was subscribed to IDB Invest and the other half to the

International Finance Corporation (IFC).The second gender bond was a private placement, backed by diversified payment rights (DPR) to fund loans for MSMEs owned by women (ECLAC, 2022[109]; OECD et al., 2022[17]).

Regarding digital inclusion, GSSS bonds are being used globally to address the digital divide. By issuing GSSS bonds with a digital inclusion component, companies, governments and multilateral organisations in LAC can raise funds to support the region's digital transformation efforts (Norton and Horton, 2021[110]). Digital inclusion bond financing enables commitments to digital inclusion projects and KPIs that may relate to investing in broadband infrastructure, digital skills training, financial inclusion, and access to quality health care and education, among other priorities (Norton and Horton, 2021[110]). In LAC, in 2022 IDB Invest issued its first silver economy social bond to support seniors' financial inclusion, including through digital solutions. The proceeds will be directed to fund social projects with a focus on alleviating poverty and reducing inequalities that affect senior citizens and retirees in LAC (IDB Invest, 2022[111]).

GSSS bonds in LAC would benefit from harmonised regulation and monitoring

Countries in LAC are focusing on expanding, improving and harmonising sustainable finance frameworks, which are essential to regulating, monitoring and verifying the issuance of GSSS bonds and other instruments. Frameworks that are more consolidated have potential to reduce transaction costs for investors, making capital markets in the region more attractive (Salazar-Xirinachs, 2023[112]). Such frameworks may include principles, standards and/or taxonomies that serve two main purposes: i) reducing and managing the ESG risks of financial activities; and ii) encouraging the flow of capital to assets, projects, sectors and companies that have environmental, climate and social benefits.

Sustainable finance frameworks guide the issuance of GSSS bonds at international, regional and national levels. The ICMA principles and the Helsinki Principles[4] are often used as overarching guiding frameworks for the issuance of GSSS bonds at the regional and national levels (Figure 4.19). The ICMA principles, for instance, provide a set of specific procedural guidelines for each type of bond issuance. This benefits investors, as it allows them to make better-informed decisions on their investments. ICMA's suite of instruments – i.e. Green Bond Principles (GBP), Social Bond Principles (SBP), Sustainability Bond Guidelines (SBG) and Sustainability-Linked Bond Principles (SLBP) – have become increasingly important in international markets. Several countries and corporates around the world now use them as reference to develop their own frameworks for the issuance of GSSS bonds (Núñez, Velloso and Da Silva, 2022[106]) (ICMA, 2023[113]).

The framework for GSS bonds is different from that of SLBs. For use-of-proceeds or GSS bonds, standards and taxonomies have been developed to guide issuance, certification and verification (Figure 4.19, Panel A). For target-linked bonds or SLBs, standards have also been developed to guide issuance, certification and verification, except the final step involves evaluating issuer level "self-imposed" KPIs and SPTs (Figure 4.19, Panel B).

Figure 4.19. **Overview of sustainable finance frameworks for GSSS bonds**

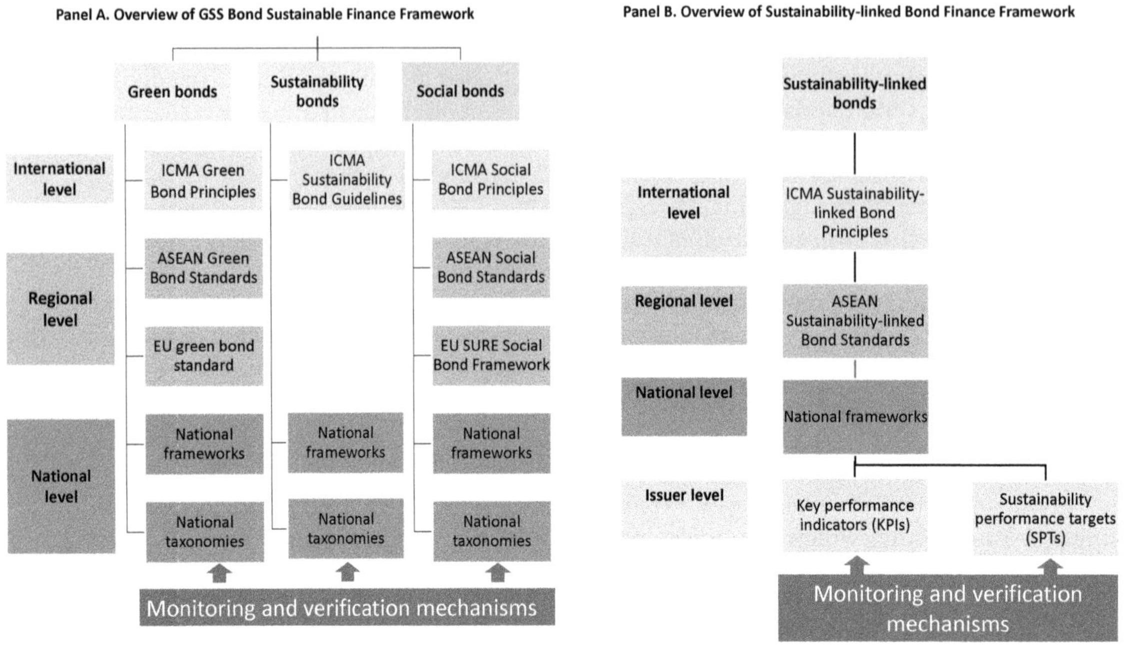

Source: Authors' elaboration.

In both cases, overarching principles and guidelines serve only to advise issuers under a general framework. It is therefore important that issuers at the regional and national levels develop clearer and more binding standards and taxonomies, rather than relying solely on the market to self-regulate through principles. Chile presents a good example of how standards have been gradually developed for all types of GSSS bond issuances. In 2019, Chile's Ministry of Finance published a Sovereign Green Bond Framework in collaboration with the Ministry of Environment. In 2020, it published a Sustainable Bond Framework that set standards for the issuance of not only green bonds, but also social and sustainable bonds. In 2022, the Ministry of Finance developed a Sustainability-Linked Bond Framework prior to issuing (March 2022) its first sovereign sustainability-linked bond (OECD et al., 2022[17]).

Green and sustainable taxonomies have been developed in the LAC region. As of mid-2023, they have been implemented in Mexico and Colombia, and are under development in countries such as Brazil, Chile, Dominican Republic, and Peru and in sub-regions such as Central America (UNEP, 2023[94]). These are tools to manage financial risks related to environmental and social issues and to avoid greenwashing. Taxonomies can also be used as industrial policy tools. Creating technical assessment criteria for defining a green activity allows financial and environmental authorities, along with industry stakeholders, to engage in comprehensive sustainability discussions. Such dialogue is essential for a well-informed green transition in the region. In April 2022, the Colombian government published the region's first green taxonomy, which seeks to help identify projects with environmental objectives, develop capital markets, and promote effective mobilisation of private and public resources (OECD et al., 2022[17]). In June 2023, the UN system in LAC also launched the first Common Framework of Sustainable Finance Taxonomies through the Working Group on Taxonomies of Sustainable Finance in Latin America and the Caribbean.[5] This regional framework is intended as a voluntary guidance document for actors in the region that are in the process of developing or intend to develop taxonomies.

The framework also provides guidance for interoperability of taxonomies within LAC and globally (UNEP, 2023[94]). Harmonising the methodologies behind the different taxonomies will increase trust among investors and reduce transaction costs.

To maintain market transparency and avoid greenwashing/SDG-washing, it is crucial to consolidate reliable monitoring and verification systems. LAC's GSSS bond market has made progress from self-labelling to becoming an externally reviewed market, yet still has a long way to go (EU-LAC Foundation, 2020[114]; Núñez, Velloso and Da Silva, 2022[106]). External reviews, i.e. pre-issuance reviews and/or post-issuance reviews, must be installed and enhanced (Table 4.1). To date, the absence of internationally recognised credit ratings attached to emerging market green bonds has limited investment opportunities. The challenge pertains to assessing the creditworthiness of bond issuers in the region. However, since 2021, a growing proportion of issuers from emerging economies have secured credit ratings from at least one major credit rating agency. In 2021, of all the green bonds issued by emerging economies worldwide, 14% received an investment-grade rating, while another 9% were rated as non-investment grade. The remaining bonds were not rated at all, and a minor percentage were withdrawn. The lower percentage of internationally rated bonds in 2021 compared with 2020 is a result of the overall higher issuance in the People's Republic of China (hereafter "China"), where many issuers have relied on local credit ratings (Amundi and IFC, 2021[115]).

With green, social and sustainable projects, issuers should develop an initial methodological framework that establishes clear and measurable objectives for external verification and monitoring. In the case of SLBs, KPIs and SPTs should be public, clear and measurable from the beginning and include signals for improved performance. The benefit of developing and strengthening these mechanisms is twofold. First, greater transparency avoids green-/SDG-washing. Greenwashing can occur, for instance, when the definition of a green bond implies that resources are somehow linked to an investment in sustainability projects (water, electricity, solar panels, etc.) but the yield on the bond is not linked to indicators that effectively measure improvements in the issuer's environmental impacts. Second, reinforcement of verification and monitoring promotes the harmonisation of taxonomies and impact reporting practices.

Table 4.1. **External reviews for GSSS bond issuance**

	Mechanism
Pre-issuance reviews	Second-party opinion (SOP): An institution with environmental, social, or sustainability expertise that is independent of the issuer and provides an opinion about the framework.
	Verification: An issuer can obtain independent verification against a designated set of criteria.
	Certification: An issuer can have its GSSS framework certified against a recognised external GSSS standard or label.
	GSSS scoring/rating: An issuer can have its GSSS bond framework evaluated or assessed by third parties, such as specialised research providers of rating agencies, according to an established scoring/rating methodology (ICMA, 2021[116]).
Post-issuance reviews	Second- or third-party assurance report: This provides assurance of the allocation of proceeds to eligible GSSS projects.
	Impact reporting: This seeks to quantify numerically the environmental, social or sustainable impacts of a project/asset. With GSS bonds, the impact report can detail whether the proceeds are being used effectively to meet the GSS objectives set out at the start of the project. With SLBs, the report can measure performance against KPIs and STIs set at the time of issuance.

Source: Authors' elaboration based on (CBI, 2023[117]).

Key policy messages

Public institutions play a fundamental role in enhancing the impacts of investments on the well-being of LAC citizens. This involves creating attractive and predictable conditions for investments to flow (Chapter 2). It also involves developing investment and production transformation strategies that reflect broad agreement among stakeholders, are connected to the broader development strategy of each country, and are ultimately an essential part of a renewed social contract in the region.

The investments required for the region's development agenda will need to come from both public and private sources. In addition to improvements in fiscal frameworks (Chapter 1), two areas are particularly promising. First, strengthening national and subnational DFIs can support access to finance, particularly for MSMEs, and drive investments in key sectors. Second, the development of capital markets in the region is essential. Potential is increasing for innovative financial tools such as GSSS bonds, which can promote public and private investment with the support of more consolidated and harmonised sustainable finance frameworks. Box 4.5 presents the key policy messages for achieving the objectives described throughout this chapter.

Box 4.5. **Key policy messages**

Towards inclusive dialogue to build consensus around investment and production transformation strategies

- Promote spaces for citizen participation, following the OECD Guidelines for Citizen Participation Processes. Public consultations, participatory budgeting and representative deliberative processes are relevant methods to foster citizen participation.
- Strengthen the social and environmental impact assessments of investment projects with relevant citizen participation.
- Develop transparent and clear redistributive measures to support socio-economic groups, territories and communities that may be negatively affected by investment projects.
- Support the adoption of the OECD Responsible Business Conduct Guidelines, strengthening the role of National Contact Points as relevant instances to mediate and resolve conflicts that may arise among private-sector companies, civil society and governments.
- Empower local governments to boost inclusive citizen participation in investment and production decisions, involving vulnerable groups, collaborating with local institutions and using tools to foster innovation, prevent conflicts and ensure sustainable investments.
- Enhance open government policies and strengthen the role of Centres of Government to provide transparency at every stage of the investment process, including transparency tools (e.g. clear registration information; access to amendments; consistent regulations; interactive project platforms; and disclosure of the origins of private funds).

Towards whole-of-government investment and production transformation efforts

- Ensure effective implementation of national development plans (NDPs), deepening the focus on long-term strategic planning and ensuring policy continuity beyond political cycles. Sector-specific strategies should be well connected to broader development strategies.
- Define the budget allocation for each priority in NDPs to ensure effective implementation.

Box 4.5. **Key policy messages** *(cont.)*

- Strengthen national public investment systems via greater aligment with NDPs; mechanisms for efficient co-ordination and decision making across stakeholders; transparent procedures for prioritisation, implementation and evaluation of impactful projects; and clear linkages with annual and medium-term budgeting processes to ensure financial viability.
- Enhance policy co-ordination and multi-level governance and create a map of main stakeholders in the investment arena and their channels of communication to help identify potential gaps and improve the distribution of responsibilities.

Towards financing the production transformation and mobilising investments for strategic sectors

- To increase private investment, especially by MSMEs, public DFIs in the region can:
  - Expand and evaluate further the supply of financial instruments that incentivise innovative and long-term investment by the private sector. These instruments are aimed at financing key aspects including working capital, sustainable investment, foreign trade, and climate emergencies.
  - Advance efforts to develop instruments that answer the specific needs and singularities of key production sectors within the framework of a well-defined national development strategy.
  - Invest in capacity building in niche sectors to provide improved sector-specific financial, digital and technical services, enabling MSMEs to meet their financial requirements.
- To address the finance gap faced by MSMEs by scaling up financial instruments that have sustainable, gender-sensitive and digital objectives, DFIs can establish specific programmes for project preparation and for technical support during project implementation.
- To boost public investment, DFIs can increase their offer in technical and digital services by creating partnerships with state secretariats, ministries and municipalities, and improve capacity-building for these entities.
- To promote capital market instruments that support investments in key development areas, countries in the region can:
  - Support the expansion and attractiveness of venture capital funds to finance start-ups. Continue efforts to create a more favourable business growth environment (e.g. by crafting legal frameworks that enhance investment in technology-based businesses).
  - Support the expansion and adjustment of SLBs, redirecting capital flows towards projects that promote climate-change mitigation and adaptation while strengthening the social and sustainable dimensions.
  - Enhance sustainable financing frameworks for GSSS bonds and foster co-ordination and harmonisation across countries. It is crucial to consolidate reliable monitoring and verification systems to maintain market transparency and avoid green-/SDG-washing. Pre- and post-issuance external reviews must be established and enhanced.

Notes

1. The word "institutions" in this chapter refers to government agencies or public agencies.
2. "DFIs" in this document will always refer only to national and subnational public development finance institutions.
3. The 38 national and subnational DFIs are the following. From Argentina: Banco de Inversión y Comercio Exterior S.A. (BICE); Banco de La Pampa; Banco de la Provincia de Buenos Aires

(BAPRO); Banco de la Nación Argentina; Fondo de Garantías Buenos Aires – FOGABA. From Brazil: Banco de Desenvolvimento de Minas Gerais S.A. (BDMG); Banco do Nordeste do Brasil S.A. (BNB); Banco Nacional de Desenvolvimento Econômico e Social (BNDES); Banco Regional de Desenvolvimento do Extremo Sul (BRDE); Agência de Fomento do Estado de São Paulo S.A. (Desenvolve SP). From Chile: Instituto Nacional de Desarrollo Agropecuario (INDAP); Corporación de Fomento de la Producción (CORFO). From Colombia: Fondo para el Financiamiento del Sector Agropecuario (FINAGRO); Banco de Comercio Exterior de Colombia (Bancoldex); Instituto Financiero para el Desarrollo del Valle del Cauca (Infivalle); Instituto para el Desarrollo de Antioquía (IDEA). From Costa Rica: Banco Nacional de Costa Rica; Banco Popular y de Desarrollo Comunal. From the Dominican Republic: Banco Nacional de las Exportaciones (BANDEX); Banco de Reservas de la República Dominicana (BR). From Ecuador: Banco de Desarrollo del Ecuador B.P. (BdE); BanEcuador B.P.; Corporación Financiera Nacional B.P. (CFN); Corporación Nacional de Finanzas Populares y Solidarias (CONAFIPS). From El Salvador: Banco de Desarrollo de El Salvador (BANDESAL); Federación de Cajas de Crédito y de Bancos de los Trabajadores (FEDECRÉDITO); Banco de Fomento Agropecuario (BFA). From Guatemala: Banco de Desarrollo Rural S.A. (BANRURAL). From Mexico: Banco del Bienestar; Banco Nacional de Obras y Servicios Públicos S.N.C. (BANOBRAS); Sociedad Hipotecaria Federal S.N.C. (SHF); Fideicomisos Instituidos en Relación con la Agricultura (FIRA) – Banco de México; Nacional Financiera S.N.C. (NAFIN); Banco Nacional de Comercio Exterior S.N.C. (BANCOMEXT). From Panama: Caja de Ahorros. From Paraguay: Agencia Financiera de Desarrollo; Banco Nacional de Fomento (BNF); Crédito Agrícola de Habilitación (CAH). From Peru: Corporación Financiera de Desarrollo S.A. (COFIDE); Banco de la Nación, Banco Agropecuario – Agrobanco. From Uruguay: Banco de la República Oriental del Uruguay (BROU).

4. The Helsinki Principles (agreed upon in 2019) are the shared principles of the Coalition of Finance Ministers for Climate Action, which is comprised of members from more than 80 governments and is supported by 25 institutional partners. These principles are aspirational and serve to give a common purpose to member countries, which are committed to taking collective and domestic action on climate change and achieving the Paris Agreement's objectives.

5. The Working Group on Sustainable Finance Taxonomies in Latin America and the Caribbean is comprised of the United Nations Environment Programme (UNEP), the World Bank Group, the United Nations Development Programme (UNDP), the Economic Commission for Latin America and the Caribbean (ECLAC), the Inter-American Development Bank (IDB), the Development Bank of Latin America (CAF), and the Food and Agriculture Organization of the United Nations (FAO).

References

ALIDE (2023), *Potential an opportunities for Latin America and the Caribbean in the current scenario and the support of development banking*, General Secretariat of ALIDE, Lima, http://www.alidedatabank.org/1001/plantilla/documentoPublicacionAlide/Basic%20Document%20Asemmbly%202023.pdf. [82]

ALIDE (2022), *Repensando la matriz productiva de América Latina y el Caribe para el mundo que viene*, ALIDE, Buenos Aires, http://www.alidedatabank.org/1001/plantilla/documentoPublicacionAlide/REUNI%C3%93N-DE-ECONOMISTAS-JEFES-2022.pdf. [93]

ALIDE (2020), *Activos*, ALIDE, Lima, http://hubdebanca.alide.org/community-practice/portal-de-datos/alide/. [83]

Allain-Dupré, D. (2020), "The multi-level governance imperative", *The British Journal of Politics and International Relations*, Vol. 22/4, pp. 800-808, https://doi.org/10.1177/1369148120937984. [72]

Amundi and IFC (2021), *Emerging Market Green Bonds Report*, Amundi Asset Management and International Finance Corporation, Washington, DC, http://www.ifc.org/content/dam/ifc/doc/mgrt/202206-emerging-market-green-bonds-report-2021-vf-2.pdf. [115]

Atlantic Council (2023), *Unlocking economic development in Latin America and the Caribbean: Five opportunities for private-sector leadership and partnership*, Atlantic Council, Washington, DC, http://www.atlanticcouncil.org/wp-content/uploads/2023/06/AALAC_IDB_Report_060823_complete.pdf. [41]

Azzimonti, M. (2011), "Barriers to Investment in Polarized Societies", *American Economic Review*, Vol. 101/5, pp. 2182-2204, http://www.aeaweb.org/articles?id=10.1257/aer.101.5.2182. [9]

Bebbington, A. and J. Bury (eds.) (2013), *Subterranean Struggles. New Dynamics of Mining, Oil, and Gas in Latin America*, University of Texas press, https://www.crolar.org/index.php/crolar/article/view/169. [16]

Biglaiser, G. and J. Staats (2010), "Do Political Institutions Affect Foreign Direct Investment? A Survey of U.S. Corporations in Latin America", *Political Research Quarterly*, Vol. 63/3, pp. 508–522, http://www.jstor.org/stable/25747955. [10]

Blancher, M. et al. (2019), *Financial inclusion of small and medium-sized enterprises in the Middle East and Central Asia*, International Monetary Fund, Washington, DC, http://www.imf.org/en/Publications/Departmental-Papers-Policy-Papers/Issues/2019/02/11/Financial-Inclusion-of-Small-and-Medium-Sized-Enterprises-in-the-Middle-East-and-Central-Asia-46335. [91]

BNDES (2023), *Agência BNDES de notícias*, BNDES, Rio de Janeiro, http://api.mziq.com/mzfilemanager/v2/d/0a296115-dd7d-454b-ba26-369893ae3f0c/9b522068-6622-15cc-aae1-5b43cd781bfa?origin=2. [96]

CAF (2019), *Institutions for productivity: towards a better business environment*, Corporación Andina de Fomento, Buenos Aires, https://scioteca.caf.com/bitstream/handle/123456789/1410/Institutions%20for%20productivity.pdf?sequence=1&isAllowed=y. [71]

CALAS (2019), *Las fronteras del neoextrativismo en América Latina*, http://calas.lat/sites/default/files/svampa_neoextractivismo.pdf. [18]

CBI (2023), *External Review*, Climate Bonds Initiative, London, https://www.climatebonds.net/market/second-opinion. [117]

CEPLAN (2022), *Plan Estratégico de Desarrollo Nacional al 2050*, Centro Nacional de Planeamiento Estratégico del Perú (CEPLAN), Lima. [59]

Charbit, C. (2020), "From 'de jure' to 'de facto' decentralised public policies: The multi-level governance approach", *The British Journal of Politics and International Relations*, Vol. 22/4, pp. 809–819, https://doi.org/10.1177/1369148120937624. [74]

Coalición Regional (2016), *Papel de los Bancos Nacionales de Desarrollo en la estructura del financiamiento regional en América Latina*, Centro de Estudios para el Desarrollo Laboral y Agrario (CEDLA), Bogota, https://cedla.org/publicaciones/cedla/papel-de-los-bancos-nacionales-de-desarrollo-en-la-estructura-del-financiamiento-regional-en-america-latina/#. [92]

Congress of Colombia (2023), *Law 2294 of 2023: 2022-26 National Development Plan "Colombia World Power for Life"*, Congress of the Republic of Colombia, Bogota. [60]

Dini, M. and G. Stumpo (2020), *Mipymes en América Latina: un frágil desempeño y nuevos desafíos para las políticas de fomento*, United Nations Economic Comission for Latin America and the Caribbean, Santiago,https://repositorio.cepal.org/server/api/core/bitstreams/2c7fec3c-c404-496b-a0da-e6a14b1cee48/content. [88]

DNP (2023), *Bases del Plan Nacional de Desarrollo 2022-2026. Colombia, Potencia Mundial de la Vida*, National Planning Department (DNP) of Colombia, Bogota. [50]

DNP (2023), *Multi-year Investment Plan*, National Planning Department (DNP) of Colombia, Bogota. [61]

ECLAC (2023), *Capital flows to Latin America and the Caribbean: 2022 year-in-review and early 2023 developments*, United Nations Economic Commission for Latin America and the Caribbean, Santiago, http://www.cepal.org/sites/default/files/news/files/kflows2023final_web.pdf. [105]

ECLAC (2023), *CEPAL insta a los países a revitalizar los compromisos y acelerar el paso hacia el cumplimiento de los Objetivos de Desarrollo Sostenible*, United Nations Economic Commission for Latin America and the Caribbean, Santiago, http://www.cepal.org/es/noticias/cepal-insta-paises-revitalizar-compromisos-acelerar-paso-cumplimiento-objetivos-desarrollo. [45]

ECLAC (2023), *Iberoamérica: espacio de oportunidades para el crecimiento, la colaboración y el desarrollo sostenible*, XXVIII Cumbre Iberoamericana de Jefes y Jefas de Estado y de Gobierno. Santo Domingo 24 y 25 de marzo de 2023, http://repositorio.cepal.org/bitstream/handle/11362/48769/4/S2300098_es.pdf. [44]

ECLAC (2023), *Observatorio Regional de Planificación para el Desarrollo de América Latina y el Caribe*, United Nations Economic Commission for Latin America and the Caribbean, Santiago, http://observatorioplanificacion.cepal.org/. [63]

ECLAC (2023), *Ordenamiento Territorial*, Observatorio Regional de Planificación para el Desarrollo de América Latina y el Caribe, United Nations Economic Commission for Latin America and the Caribbean, https://observatorioplanificacion.cepal.org/es/territorial-planning. [78]

ECLAC (2022), *Capital Flows to Latin America and the Caribbean: 2021 year-in-review and the first four months of 2022*, United Nations Economic Commission for Latin America and the Caribbean, Santiago, http://www.cepal.org/en/notes/capital-flows-latin-america-and-caribbean-2021-year-review-and-first-four-months-2022. [98]

ECLAC (2022), *Capital Flows to Latin America and the Caribbean: the first eight months of 2022*, United Nations Economic Commission for Latin America and the Caribbean, Santiago, http://www.cepal.org/es/node/57377. [109]

ECLAC (2022), *Hacia la transformación del modelo de desarrollo en América Latina y el Caribe: producción, inclusión y sostenibilidad*, United Nations Economic Commission for Latin America and the Caribbean, Santiago, http://repositorio.cepal.org/bitstream/handle/11362/48308/3/S2200584_es.pdf. [1]

ECLAC (2021), *Los planes nacionales de inversión pública en América Latina y el Caribe*, Observatorio Regional de Planificacion para el Desarrollo de América Latina y el Caribe, United Nations Economic Commission for Latin America and the Caribbean, https://observatorioplanificacion.cepal.org/es/nota/los-planes-nacionales-de-inversion-publica-en-america-latina-y-el-caribe. [26]

ECLAC/OECD (2018), *Emerging challenges and shifting paradigms: New approaches on international co-operation for development*, United Nations Economic Commission for Latin America and the Caribbean, Santiago, http://repositorio.cepal.org/bitstream/handle/11362/44002/1/S1800619_en.pdf. [5]

Endeavor Intelligence & Glisco Partners (2022), *Venture Capital and Growth Equity Ecosystem in Latin America*, Endeavor Intelligence, https://gliscopartners.com/wp-content/uploads/2022/10/Venture-Capital-LATAM-ENG.pdf. [102]

Environmental Justice Atlas (2023), *Environmental Justice World Map*, https://ejatlas.org/. [19]

EU-LAC Foundation (2020), *The Potential of the Green Bond Markets in Latin America and the Caribbean*, EU-LAC Foundation, Hamburg, https://eulacfoundation.org/en/potential-green-bond-markets-latin-america-and-caribbean-0. [114]

Feyertag, J., S. Attridge and N. Kumar (2022), *GFANZ: a watershed moment or a drop in the ocean of the Global South's climate finance needs?*, The Overseas Development Institute (ODI), Wales., https://odi.org/en/insights/gfanz-a-watershed-moment-or-a-drop-in-the-ocean-of-the-global-souths-climate-finance-needs/. [84]

Foray, D., P. David and B. Hall (2009), "Smart specialisation – The concept", *Knowledge economists policy brief*, Vol. 9/85, p. 100. [75]

Frisari, G., M. Carlino and A. Palacios (2022), "Sovereign Sustainable Bonds as Core Financing Instruments for Sustainable Development", *IDB Blogs*, Inter-American Development Bank, Washington, DC, http://blogs.iadb.org/sostenibilidad/en/sovereign-sustainable-bonds-as-core-financing-instruments-for-sustainable-development/. [104]

Gavin, E. (2022), *Latin America leads the way in sovereign thematic bonds*, Verisk Maplecroft, London, http://www.maplecroft.com/esg-weekly/latin-america-leads-the-way-in-sovereign-thematic-bonds/. [103]

Government of Chile (2022), *Programa de Gobierno 2022-2026. Apruebo Dignidad*, Government of Chile, Santiago, http://observatorioplanificacion.cepal.org/sites/default/files/plan/files/Plan%2Bde%2Bgobierno%2BAD%2B2022-2026%2B%282%29.pdf. [49]

Government of Honduras (2022), *Plan de Gobierno para Refundar Honduras 2022-2026*, Government of Honduras, Tegucigalpa, http://observatorioplanificacion.cepal.org/sites/default/files/plan/files/PLAN-DE-GOBIERNO-XIOMARA-CASTRO_0.pdf. [55]

Government of Panama (2019), *Plan Estratégico 2020-2024*, Government of Panama, Panama City. [57]

ICMA (2023), *External Reviews*, International Capital Market Association, Paris, https://www.icmagroup.org/sustainable-finance/external-reviews/. [113]

ICMA (2021), *Guidelines for Green, Social, Sustainability and Sustainability-Linked Bonds External Reviews*, International Capital Market Association, Paris, https://www.icmagroup.org/assets/documents/Sustainable-finance/Guidelines-for-GreenSocialSustainability-and-Sustainability-Linked-Bonds-External-Reviews-February-2021-170221.pdf. [116]

ICTCR (2022), *Plan nacional de turismo de Costa Rica 2022-2027*, Instituto Costarricense de Turismo de Costa Rica (ICTCR), San José, https://www.ict.go.cr/pdf/Plan%20nacional%20de%20turismo%202022-2027.pdf. [66]

IDB (2021), *Documento de Marco Sectorial de Industrias Extractivas*, Inter-American Development Bank, Washington, DC, http://www.iadb.org/es/acerca-del-bid/documentos-de-marco-sectorial. [34]

IDB Invest (2022), *IDB Invest Launches Its First Silver Economy Social Bond to Support Financial Inclusion of Seniors in Latin America and the Caribbean*, Inter-American Development Bank, Washington, DC, https://www.idbinvest.org/en/news-media/idb-invest-launches-its-first-silver-economy-social-bond-support-financial-inclusion. [111]

Jouglard, P. (2019), "Leasing: an opportunity for the public sector", *Blog*, BNP Paribas, https://leasingsolutions.bnpparibas.com/en/leasing-an-opportunity-for-the-public-sector/. [95]

KPMG (2021), *Los cambios en infraestructura en América Latina. Perspectivas del sector publico*, KPMG, http://assets.kpmg.com/content/dam/kpmg/pe/pdf/kpmg_cambios_infraestructura_AmericaLatina.pdf. [40]

Latin American Observatory of Environmental Conflicts (2023), *Latin American Observatory of Environmental Conflicts*. [20]

Latinobarómetro (2023), *Informe Latinobarómetro 2023: La recesión democrática de América Latina*, Latinobarómetro, Santiago, http://www.latinobarometro.org/lat.jsp?Idioma=724. [6]

Latinobarómetro (2020), *Latinobarómetro (database)*, Latinobarómetro, Santiago, http://www.latinobarometro.org/lat.jsp?Idioma=724, accessed 18 September 2023. [11]

Latinobarómetro (2020), *Latinobarómetro 2021: Adios a Macondo*, Latinobarómetro, Santiago, http://www.latinobarometro.org/latContents.jsp. [7]

Llinás, M. (2021), *Iniciativas cluster: una forma concreta y efectiva de "mover la aguja" de la productividad*, Editorial Puntoaparte, Bogota. [28]

López-Calva, L. (2021), *Supporting productive SMEs as an engine of recovery in LAC*, UN Development Program, New York, https://www.undp.org/latin-america/blog/graph-for-thought/small-businesses-big-impacts-supporting-productive-smes-engine-recovery-lac. [90]

MCIT (2022), *Plan Sectorial de Turismo 2022- 2026: Turismo en armonía con la vida*, Ministerio de Comercio, Industria y Turismo (MCIT), Bogota, http://www.mincit.gov.co/participa/consulta-ciudadana/20-12-2022-plan-sectorial-de-turismo-vfpp.aspx. [68]

ME (2020), *Estrategia Nacional Hidrógeno Verde: Chile, fuente energética para un planeta cero emisiones*, Ministerio de Energía, Santiago, https://energia.gob.cl/sites/default/files/estrategia_nacional_de_hidrogeno_verde_-_chile.pdf. [64]

MEB (2020), *Estratégia Federal de Desenvolvimento Para O Brasil 2020-2031*, Ministério da Economia do Brasil, Brasilia, http://observatorioplanificacion.cepal.org/sites/default/files/plan/files/efd-2020-2031_v2_1.pdf. [48]

MECON (2023), *Argentina Productiva 2030. Plan para el Desarrollo Productivo, Industrial y Tecnológico*, Ministerio de Economía de Argentina (MEA), Buenos Aires, http://www.argentina.gob.ar/sites/default/files/documento_resumen_de_misiones_1.pdf. [46]

MEF Peru (2022), *Plan Nacional de Infraestructura para la Competitividad 2022-2025*, Ministerio de Economía y Finanzas (MEF Peru), Lima, https://www.mef.gob.pe/index.php?option=com_content&view=article&id=6082&Itemid=100674&lang=es&language=es-ES. [69]

MEPyD (2020), *Plan nacional de infraestructura 2020-2030*, Ministerio de Economía, Planificación y Desarrollo (MEPyD) de la República Dominicana, Santo Domingo, https://mepyd.gob.do/publicaciones/Plan-nacional-de-infraestructura-2020-2030. [70]

MEPyD (2012), *Ley 1-12. Estrategia Nacional de Desarrollo 2030*, Ministerio de Economía, Planificación y Desarrollo de la República Dominicana (MEPyD), Santo Domingo, http://mepyd.gob.do/wp-content/uploads/drive/UAAES/END/Informes%20Anuales%20END/end_2030.pdf. [52]

MIDEPLAN (2022), *Plan Nacional de Desarrollo e Inversión Pública 2023-2026*, Ministerio de Planificación Nacional y Política Económica de Costa Rica (MIDEPLAN), San José. [51]

MINAE (2015), *Plan Nacional de Energía 2015-2030*, Ministerio de Ambiente y Energia (MINAE) de Costa Rica, San José, https://cambioclimatico.go.cr/wp-content/uploads/2018/08/VII_Plan_Nacional_de_Energia_2015-2030.pdf. [65]

Ministerio de Energía (2017), "Primera piedra del Parque Eólico Punta Sierra", Ministerio de Energía, Gobierno de Chile, https://energia.gob.cl/noticias/coquimbo/primera-piedra-del-parque-eolico-punta-sierra. [24]

Ministerio de Relaciones Exteriores de Colombia (2016), *Guía de Participación Ciudadana 2016*, https://www.cancilleria.gov.co/sites/default/files/Fotos2017/guia_de_participacion_ciudadana_2016.pdf. [31]

Montoya, N. and S. Nieto-Parra (forthcoming), *Policymaking beyond GDP in Latin America: Case studies and lessons*, OECD Publishing, Paris. [62]

MPDB (2021), *Plan de Desarrollo Económico y Social 2021-2025. Reconstruyendo la Economía para Vivir Bien, Hacia la Industrialización con Sustitución de Importaciones*, Ministerio de Planificación del Desarrollo de Bolivia (MPDB), La Paz, http://observatorioplanificacion.cepal.org/sites/default/files/plan/files/PDES_2021-2025a_compressed_0.pdf. [47]

MSGP (2010), *Ley 20.417. Crea el ministerio, el servicio de evaluación ambiental y la superintendencia del medio ambiente*, Ministerio Secretaría General de la Presidencia (MSGP) de Chile, Santiago, https://www.bcn.cl/leychile/navegar?idNorma=1010459. [32]

Nayak, T. (2018), "A Study on the Growth of Venture Capital Financing in India", *Journal of Advances and Scholarly Researches in Allied Education*, Vol. 15/1, pp. 1455-1461, http://ignited.in/I/a/304322. [100]

Norton, B. and B. Horton (2021), *Innovative debt financing could close the digital access gap. Here's how*, World Economic Forum, New York, http://www.weforum.org/agenda/2021/09/debt-financing-close-digital-access-gap/. [110]

Núñez, G., H. Velloso and F. Da Silva (2022), *Corporate governance in Latin America and the Caribbean: Using ESG debt instruments to finance sustainable investment projects*, United Nations Economic Commission for Latin America and the Caribbean, Santiago, http://repositorio.cepal.org/server/api/core/bitstreams/0db29a24-a0b0-4421-a4ca-a47fca752e2d/content. [106]

OCMAL (2023), *Map of Mining Conflicts in Latin America (database)*, Observatory of Mining Conflicts (OCMAL), Santiago, http://www.ocmal.org/. [21]

OECD (2023), *OECD Sovereign Borrowing Outlook 2023*, OECD Publishing, Paris, https://doi.org/10.1787/09b4cfba-en. [81]

OECD (2022), *Building Trust to Reinforce Democracy: Main Findings from the 2021 OECD Survey on Drivers of Trust in Public Institutions*, Building Trust in Public Institutions, OECD Publishing, Paris, https://doi.org/10.1787/b407f99c-en. [8]

OECD (2022), *Green, social, sustainability and sustainability-linked bonds in developing countries: How can donors support public sector issuances?*, OECD Publishing, Paris, http://www.oecd.org/dac/green-social-sustainability-and-sustainability-linked-bonds.pdf. [107]

OECD (2022), *OECD Guidelines for Citizen Participation Processes*, OECD Public Governance Reviews, OECD Publishing, Paris, https://doi.org/10.1787/f765caf6-en. [23]

OECD (2021), *How's Life in Latin America? Measuring Well-being for Policy Making*, OECD Publishing, Paris, https://doi.org/10.1787/2965f4fe-en. [3]

OECD (2020), *Government at a Glance: Latin America and the Caribbean 2020*, OECD Publishing, Paris, https://doi.org/10.1787/13130fbb-en. [42]

OECD (2020), *National Contact Points for Responsible Business Conduct: Providing access to remedy, 20 years and the road ahead*, OECD Publishing, Paris, http://mneguidelines.oecd.org/NCPs-for-RBC-providing-access-to-remedy-20-years-and-the-road-ahead.pdf. [38]

OECD (2019), *Making Decentralisation Work: A Handbook for Policy-Makers*, OECD Multi-level Governance Studies, OECD Publishing, Paris, https://doi.org/10.1787/g2g9faa7-en. [76]

OECD (2018), *OECD Due diligence guidance for responsible business conduct*, OECD Publishing, Paris, http://mneguidelines.oecd.org/OECD-Due-Diligence-Guidance-for-Responsible-Business-Conduct.pdf. [37]

OECD (2018), *Policy Coherence for Sustainable Development 2018: Towards Sustainable and Resilient Societies*, OECD Publishing, Paris, https://doi.org/10.1787/9789264301061-en. [43]

OECD (2017), *Making Decentralisation Work in Chile. Towards Stronger Municipalities*, OECD Publishing, Paris, https://doi.org/10.1787/9789264279049. [73]

OECD (2017), *Preventing Policy Capture: Integrity in Public Decision Making*, OECD Public Governance Reviews, OECD Publishing, Paris, https://doi.org/10.1787/9789264065239-en. [39]

OECD (2015), *New Approaches to SME and Entrepreneurship Financing: Broadening the Range of Instruments*, OECD Publishing, Paris, https://doi.org/10.1787/9789264240957-en. [99]

OECD (2015), *Policy Framework for Investment, 2015 Edition*, OECD Publishing, Paris, https://doi.org/10.1787/9789264208667-en. [2]

OECD (2014), *Inversión Pública Efectiva en todos los niveles de Gobierno. Principios de Acción*, OECD Publishing, Paris, http://www.oecd.org/effective-public-investment-toolkit/Recomendaci%C3%B3n-sobre-Inversi%C3%B3n-Publica-Efectiva.pdf. [15]

OECD (2023), *OECD Environmental Performance Reviews: Costa Rica 2023*, OECD Environmental Performance Reviews, OECD Publishing, Paris, https://doi.org/10.1787/ec94fd4e-en. [35]

OECD (2023), *Regional Attractiveness in the New Global Environment: Argentina, Chile and Colombia. Synthesis report*, Making Development Happen, OECD Development Centre, Paris https://www.oecd.org/dev/mdh.htm. [77]

OECD et al. (2022), *Latin American Economic Outlook 2022: Towards a Green and Just Transition*, OECD Publishing, Paris, http://www.oecd-ilibrary.org/deliver/3d5554fc-en.pdf?itemId=%2Fcontent%2Fpublication%2F3d5554fc-en&mimeType=pdf. [17]

OECD et al. (2019), *Latin American Economic Outlook 2019: Development in Transition*, OECD Publishing, Paris, https://doi.org/10.1787/g2g9ff18-en. [4]

OECD/CAF/ECLAC (2018), *Latin American Economic Outlook 2018: Rethinking Institutions for Development*, OECD Publishing, Paris, https://doi.org/10.1787/leo-2018-en. [22]

OECD/WB (2022), *Indicators of Product Market Regulation*, Organisation for Economic Co-operation and Development, Paris/World Bank Group, Washington, DC, http://www.oecd.org/economy/reform/indicators-of-product-market-regulation/. [27]

Oliveira de Paiva, T. (2020), *The SME leap in Latin America*, International Finance Corporation, Washington, DC, http://www.ifc.org/content/dam/ifc/doc/mgrt/2020-12-call-for-insights-e-publication.pdf. [89]

Pew Research Center (2020), *Pew Research*, https://www.pewresearch.org/short-reads/2020/08/10/globally-views-of-foreign-direct-investment-vary-depending-on-type-of-investment/. [12]

PREUM (2019), *Plan Nacional de Desarrollo 2019-2024*, Presidencia de la República de los Estados Unidos Mexicanos, Mexico City, http://observatorioplanificacion.cepal.org/sites/default/files/plan/files/Plan%20Nacional%20de%20Desarrollo%20de%20M%C3%A9xico.pdf. [56]

Reyes, F. and E. Ríos (2016), *Participación ciudadana en proyectos de inversión: Lecciones desde la experiencia internacional*, https://www.espaciopublico.cl/wp-content/uploads/2021/05/73.pdf. [25]

Rudolph, H., M. Faruk and J. Gonzalez-Uribe (2023), *Venture Capital in Latin America and the Caribbean*, World Bank Group, Washington, DC, https://documents1.worldbank.org/curated/en/099060223062519487/pdf/P17865500ba5cc0e9081f30b5948199b92f.pdf. [101]

Sacristán, G. (2022), *Latin America, World Leader in Gender Bonds*, IDB Invest, Inter-American Development Bank, Washington, DC, http://idbinvest.org/en/blog/gender/latin-america-world-leader-gender-bonds. [108]

Salazar-Xirinachs, J. (2023), *Common Framework of Sustainable FInance Taxonomies in LAC*, United Nations Environment Programme, Geneva., http://www.unepfi.org/wordpress/wp-content/uploads/2023/07/Common-Framework-of-Sustainable-Finance-Taxonomies-LAC.pdf. [112]

Salazar-Xirinachs, J. (2020), *Cluster-Based Policies: What Have We Learned?*, Oxford University Press, http://global.oup.com/academic/product/the-oxford-handbook-of-indust. [79]

Salazar-Xirinachs, J. (2020), *Estado de las políticas de desarrollo de clústeres para la exportación en América Latina y el Caribe con énfasis en su institucionalidad y gobernanza*, Inter-American Development Bank, Washington, DC, https://redclustercolombia.gov.co/storage/resources/documents/informe-estado-de-las-politicas-de-desarrollo-de-clusteres-para-la-exportacion-bidpdf. [80]

Schoenmaker, D. (2020), "The impact economy: balancing profit and impact", *Working Paper 2020/04*, Bruegel, https://www.bruegel.org/sites/default/files/wp_attachments/WP-2020-04-Impact-Economy-D.-Schoenmaker.pdf. [36]

SEA (2021), *Entidades ambientales de Latinoamérica firman los estatutos de la REDLASEIA y eligen a su presidente pro tempore*, Servicio de Evaluación Ambiental (SEA) de Chile, Santiago, http://sea.gob.cl/noticias/entidades-ambientales-de-latinoamerica-firman-los-estatutos-de-la-redlaseia-y-eligen-su. [33]

SEA (2017), *Guía metodológica de actividades presenciales del Servicio de Evaluación Ambiental con la ciudadanía*, Servicio de Evaluación Ambiental (SEA) de Chile, Santiago, http://sea.gob.cl/sites/default/files/imce/archivos/2017/07/27/web_guia_metodologica_de_actividades_presenciales_del_sea.pdf. [30]

SEA (2013), *Guía para la participación anticipada de la comunidad en proyectos que se presentan al SEIA*, Servicio de Evaluación Ambiental (SEA) de Chile, Santiago, http://sea.gob.cl/sites/default/files/migration_files/guias/GuiaPAC_anticipada_FINAL_20130711.pdf. [29]

SME Finance Forum (2017), *MSME Finance Gap*, International Finance Corporation, Washington, DC, http://www.smefinanceforum.org/data-sites/msme-finance-gap. [87]

Smits, S. and M. Rodríguez (2022), *Public development banks in the water sector: Case studies from Latin America*, AFD éditions, Paris, https://www.afd.fr/en/rt65_water_case_studies_latin_america_crespi_reghizzi. [85]

SNPE (2021), *Plan de Creación de Oportunidades 2021-2025*, Secretaría Nacional de Planificación del Ecuador, Quito, https://www.planificacion.gob.ec/wp-content/uploads/2021/09/Plan-de-Creacio%CC%81n-de-Oportunidades-2021-2025-Aprobado.pdf. [53]

SPPPG (2014), *Plan Nacional de Desarrollo K'atun: nuestra Guatemala 2032*, Secretaría de Planificación y Programación de la Presidencia de Guatemala (SPPPG), Guatemala, http://pnd.gt/Documentos/undp_gt_PND_Katun2032.pdf. [54]

STPP (2021), *Plan Nacional de Desarrollo Paraguay 2030*, Secretaría Técnica de Planificación del Desarrollo Económico y Social del Paraguay (STPP), Asunción, http://www.stp.gov.py/pnd/. [58]

UNEP (2023), *Common Framework of Sustainable FInance Taxonomies in Latin America and the Caribbean*, United Nations Environment Programme, Geneva, http://www.unepfi.org/wordpress/wp-content/uploads/2023/07/Common-Framework-of-Sustainable-Finance-Taxonomies-LAC.pdf. [94]

UPME (2021), *Plan energético nacional 2020 – 2050: Transformación energética para el desarrollo sostenible*, Unidad de Planeación Minero Energética (UPME) de Colombia, Bogota, https://www1.upme.gov.co/DemandayEficiencia/Paginas/PEN.aspx. [67]

World Bank (2023), *World Development Indicators*, World Bank, Washington, DC, https://databank.worldbank.org/source/world-development-indicators. [86]

World Bank (2022), *Capital Markets*, World Bank Group, Washington, DC, http://www.worldbank.org/en/topic/financialsector/brief/capital-markets. [97]

World Bank (2020), *Doing Business*, World Bank Group, Washington, DC, http://archive.doingbusiness.org/en/doingbusiness. [13]

World Economic Forum (2018), *The Global Competitiveness Report 2017–2018*, https://www3.weforum.org/docs/GCR2017-2018/05FullReport/TheGlobalCompetitivenessReport2017%E2%80%932018.pdf. [14]

Chapter 5

International partnerships for more and better investments

Countries in Latin America and the Caribbean (LAC) must forge stronger, modernised and strategic alliances to attract investments that drive the region's production transformation. New tools in development co-operation, such as blended finance, present an opportunity for LAC to mobilise greater investments through private-sector engagement. To attract investments with the potential to transform the region's economic and productive structures, it is key to maximise the potential of international investment treaties, foster an environment for sustainable finance, provide capacity building and technology transfer, establish co-ordination platforms, and promote linkages to support local and national development. Strengthening international partnerships that stimulate co-operation, investment promotion and policy dialogue will boost LAC's production transformation goals and have positive social impacts. Regional integration is an important step for reaching sustainable production transformation through more and more strategic investment. Finally, maximising the EU-LAC Global Gateway Investment Agenda can promote investments that drive the transformation of LAC's development model.

International partnerships: Keys to mobilising more and better investments

International partnerships can make investments yield greater socio-economic impacts

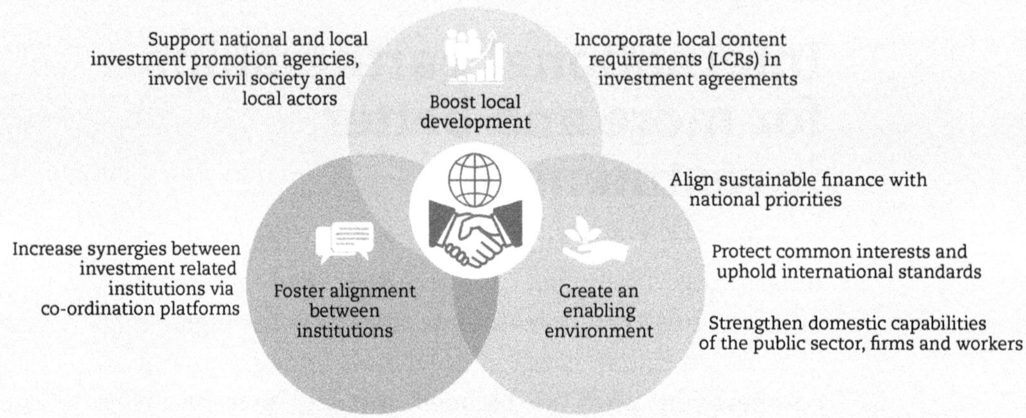

Further regional integration can accelerate the shift to more sustainable production

Shares of intra-regional exports in total goods exports, 1995-2021

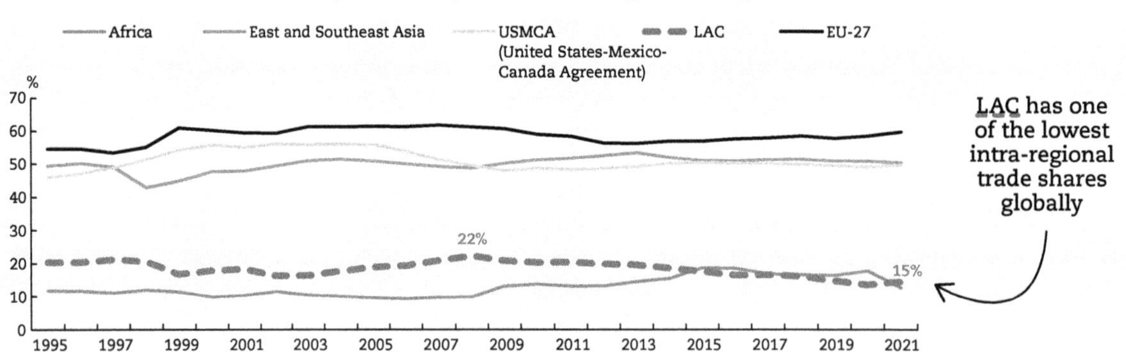

A new EU-LAC agenda for production transformation

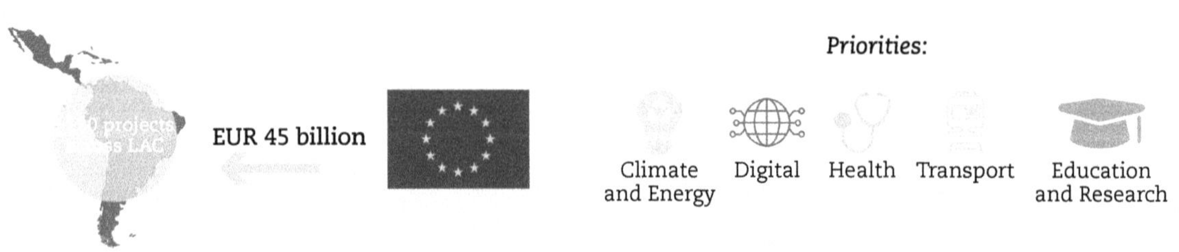

Introduction

The nature of international partnerships and co-operation is being reshaped by evolving global dynamics and trends. Today's geopolitical landscape is characterised by a confluence of interconnected challenges, from the lingering effects of the COVID-19 pandemic and the Russian invasion of Ukraine to the worsening impacts of climate change. In fact, the world is moving further away from reaching the UN Sustainable Development Goals (SDGs): a preliminary assessment reveals that only about 15% of the targets are currently on track (United Nations, 2023[1]).

This new geopolitical landscape has expedited the imperative for countries of any income level to make progress in their interconnected "triple transition" – green, digital and social. These agendas represent new models of socio-economic development, encompassing the essential framework required to facilitate sustainable production transformation (Chapter 3). For instance, the European Green Deal and the NextGenerationEU programme propose mechanisms to accelerate the EU's triple transition, which includes the climate goals set forth in the Paris Agreement (Sanahuja, 2022[2]).

These new agendas navigate the complexities of an adverse international landscape and its impact on the way international co-operation and partnerships are evolving. Back in 2015, the Addis Ababa Action Agenda was already calling for a more prominent role for the private sector in advancing the SDGs. These calls have grown stronger in recent years, with increasing reliance on concessional funds to attract private-sector engagement.

In this light, countries in Latin America and the Caribbean (LAC) need to advance stronger, modernised and strategic partnerships to attract more and better investments that drive capacity building, create quality jobs, generate production linkages, and facilitate the transfer of skills, innovation and technologies. Governments, international organisations and development agencies, while recognising the importance – but also the limitations – of public resources, are turning towards new approaches to attract private capital to development projects. LAC countries need to ensure that this new model attracts and retains investments that contribute to transforming the region's development models, breaking the vicious circle of low productivity and lack of diversification.

This chapter first explores opportunities to mobilise greater investments in LAC by engaging the private sector in development co-operation. It provides an overview of blended finance as a possible effective tool. Second, the chapter highlights the need to think beyond the amounts mobilised and ensure that investments can promote sustainable production transformation. It examines how international partnerships can promote better investments by supporting an enabling environment, upholding international standards, harnessing the full potential of international investment treaties (IITs), promoting capabilities and skills, creating co-ordination platforms, and boosting local development. Third, the chapter focuses on the potential for regional and subregional integration, and on how trade within LAC can boost partnership efforts for production transformation. Fourth, it explores how strengthening partnerships and co-operation with the European Union has the potential to help LAC countries advance along their paths towards reindustrialisation and sustainable production transformation. Finally, the chapter provides key policy messages.

Opportunities in a changing co-operation landscape: Role of the private sector

A noticeable shift has taken place in international co-operation and development finance towards recognising the potential of the private sector in advancing the SDGs. This shift is captured in the Addis Ababa Action Agenda on Financing Development of 2015, which recognised the importance of private investments to meet the SDGs.

Following the COVID-19 pandemic, the SDG financing gap in developing countries is estimated at USD 3.9 trillion, a 56% increase from pre-COVID estimates (OECD, 2022[3]). With official development assistance (ODA) amounting to USD 185.9 billion in 2021, this gap significantly exceeds the development co-operation budget worldwide (OECD, 2023[4]). While ODA continues to play an important role in supporting development initiatives, recognition of the limitations of public funding has prompted a strategic re-evaluation of financing models. In response, the development co-operation community is scaling up its engagement with the private sector to mobilise additional finance, create and strengthen partnerships, and help build inclusive markets and values chains across key sectors (GPEDC, 2019[5]).

Global co-operation is shifting, with a focus on scaling investments

International partnerships based on a model of mobilising investments for production transformation first came about via developing countries and South-South co-operation actors – with trade and investment playing greater roles in mutual interest partnerships, a more holistic approach to development initiatives emerged (Chaturvedi, 2016[6]).This shift is captured by China's Belt and Road Initiative (BRI), an investment plan launched in 2013 that seeks to connect China with the rest of the world via land and maritime networks (EBRD, 2023[7]). The BRI represents a new approach to global collaboration, albeit with several nuances, placing a strong emphasis on trade and investment as drivers of development co-operation. China has used its global trade networks to engage actively with countries and regions around the world, offering investment opportunities to contribute to their structural transformation (Vadell, Brutto and Leite, 2020[8]). The BRI highlights a departure from the traditional aid-based model of international co-operation, as China actively seeks foreign investments and partnerships to fund and implement ambitious infrastructure projects across Asia, Europe, Africa and the Americas (Freymann and García-Herrero, 2022[9]; Ministry of Foreign Affairs of the People's Republic of China, 2016[10]). Since its inception, the BRI has faced some opposition. Worsened by the COVID-19 pandemic and the war in Ukraine, a growing number of borrowing countries have accumulated unsustainable levels of debt to China, surpassing 20% of GDP in some countries (McBride, Berman and Chatzky, 2023[11]).

Other development partners are also taking a lead in this shifting focus of development co-operation. The European Union (EU) has been a significant leader in mobilising private finance. The European Fund for Sustainable Development (EFSD), established in 2017 and expanded as EFSD+ in 2021, is an example. These funds aim to encourage investment in developing countries and the European neighbourhood through blending mechanisms, guarantees and other financial operations, combining EU grants with loans or equity from public and private investors to generate higher investment volumes (Box 5.1) (European Commission, 2022[12]). More recently, the European Union has launched the Global Gateway, aiming to significantly expand its efforts. With a commitment to mobilise EUR 45 billion in LAC by 2027, the EU-LAC Global Gateway Investment Agenda (GGIA) aims to enhance smart, clean and secure links in the digital, climate, energy and transport sectors while also strengthening health, education and research systems in partner countries (European Commission, 2023[13]).

The United States has also made a significant step in this direction by approving the BUILD Act of 2018, which established the International Development Finance Corporation (DFC). This legislation was a response to the increasing importance of private finance in development and an attempt to make development finance tools more efficient (CSIS, 2018[14]). The DFC can make equity investments and provide technical assistance; notably, it has a higher spending cap than its predecessor and can facilitate broader engagement with the private sector for development financing. Another initiative is the Americas

Partnership for Economic Prosperity (APEP), which groups the United States, Canada and several LAC countries. The APEP acts as a framework for regional co-operation to foster regional competitiveness, resilience, shared prosperity, and inclusive and sustainable investment (SICE, 2023[15]).

Box 5.1. **EFSD+ in Latin America and the Caribbean**

EFSD+ is part of the EU's investment framework for external action. As such, it serves as the main financial tool for mobilising investments under Global Gateway, the EU strategy for narrowing the global investment gap (European Commission, 2022[12]). To promote sustainable development, the EFSD+ aims to raise financial resources to support investment in partner countries for decent job creation, strengthening public and private infrastructure, fostering renewable energy and sustainable agriculture, and supporting the digital transition, among other goals. Through EFSD+, the European Union will provide stronger leadership for shared investment priorities, respecting the need for financial institutions to diversify their risks (geographically and across sectors).

When projects have a public added value and the de-risking cannot be addressed by guarantees, the European Union can use the EFSD+ blending facilities. These facilities use grants to de-risk investment projects in EU partner countries and subsequently leverage loans from development finance institutions (public investment) that will enhance the investment's sustainability, climate proofing and development impact.

Blending has proven to be a successful and transformative tool in the LAC region. Since 2010, the Latin America Investment Facility (LAIF) and the Caribbean Investment Facility (CIF) have contributed more than EUR 597 million to support 67 projects (LAIF, 2023[16]; LAIF, 2023[17]). The global scope of the Neighbourhood, Development, and International Co-operation Instrument (NDICI) has allowed for the merging of both facilities into one: Latin America and Caribbean Investment Facility (LAIF).

The guarantees are used for de-risking activities and leveraging private investment, working together with the European Investment Bank (EIB) and other European financial institutions. The EFSD+ budgetary guarantees investment programmes are implemented via two main paths. First, in partnership with the EIB, the European Union plans to provide a global-level guarantee of up to EUR 26.7 billion. This funding is intended to bolster investments in areas such as clean energy, environmentally friendly infrastructure, and healthcare (European Commission, 2022[18]). The guarantees focus on facilitating Global Gateway investments in partner countries where issues related to sovereign and public sector risks still pose significant obstacles. Second, through the EFSD+ open architecture, the European Union will extend financial guarantees of up to EUR 13 billion worldwide by 2027 (European Commision, 2022[19]). These guarantees will be administered by a variety of implementing partners, including international financial institutions and European development finance institutions. The overarching aim is to stimulate private investments that contribute to achieving the SDGs in EU partner countries.

The first call of the EFSD+ open architecture, launched mid-2022, was structured around six investment windows: i) micro, small and medium enterprises (MSMEs) finance for inclusive and green growth; ii) sustainable cities; iii) sustainable agriculture (including biodiversity, forests, and water); iv) connectivity (including energy, transport and digital); v) sustainable finance; and vi) human development.

In December 2022, the EFSD+ Operational Board approved EUR 6.05 billion to support 40 new guarantee programmes in Sub-Saharan Africa, LAC, and Asia and the Pacific (European Commision, 2022[19]), with 18 to be implemented in LAC.

Beyond bilateral investment agendas, the urgent need of scaling development finance has called for the reform of multilateral development banks (MDBs). MDB reform encompasses a series of initiatives aimed at improving the operations and impact of the international financial system to provide financial and technical assistance to developing countries. A key area of focus is to align MDB strategies with the SDGs and expand the overall volume of development finance (Peter Lankes and Prizzon, 2023[20]). These include efforts to enhance project implementation by ensuring transparency, accountability, and efficiency. In response to the MDB reform agenda for instance, the IDB is undertaking multiple efforts in balance sheet optimisation, allowing the IBD to increase its risk-absorbing capacity and lending headroom over the next ten years. For example, the Bank is seeking to: i) receive credit substitution guarantees from high-rated countries which would unlock capital for the Bank, ii) receive committed lines of credit from high-rated countries to replace debt funding liquidity, and iii) issue hybrid capital that is purchased by donor countries to increase the amount of equity in the Bank. These reforms would allow the IDB to be more effective to the evolving development needs of LAC, while aligning their activities with broader development and sustainability objectives.

LAC can boost production transformation by tapping into international flows

The shift in international co-operation towards attracting private investments offers considerable potential for LAC. The region is characterised by a mix of lower middle-, upper middle- and high-income countries, many of which are experiencing important levels of economic growth. However, they also confront ongoing development challenges, including issues such as inequality, low levels of productivity and infrastructure gaps (OECD et al., 2019[21]). Despite these challenges, LAC has positioned itself as an important recipient of foreign direct investment (FDI). Regarding cross-border capital inflows into the region, FDI remained the largest and least volatile source of capital in 2021 (ECLAC, 2023[22]). In addition, LAC's heterogeneous economies and rich environmental resources present a promising landscape for impact investment, offering opportunities to improve the production structure and create positive effects connected to productivity, social, environmental and institutional development traps (Dallmann, 2021[23]). The global impact investing market is estimated at USD 1.164 trillion in 2022, with experts pointing to climate change and increased demand for transparent reporting standards as the main drivers of overall investment activity (Almaguer and Davidson, 2023[24]). While the economic fallout of the COVID-19 pandemic reduced interest from venture investors, overall investment activity in LAC has steadily increased over the last couple of years, with more than USD 25 billion in impact-investing assets focused on the region (Schwartz and Arévalo-Carpenter, 2021[25]).

LAC is mostly comprised of upper-middle-income countries, defined under the World Bank's country classification system as those with gross national income (GNI) per capita of between USD 4 466 and USD 13 854 (Hamadeh, Van Rompaey and Metreau, 2023[26]). As such, the region shows little and decreasing reliance on concessional sources of financing such as ODA, when measured as a share of GNI (Figure 5.1). While the share of ODA as a percentage of GNI remains relatively low on average, ODA represents an important source of finance for the least developed countries (LDCs) in LAC, including small island states in the Caribbean. For instance, ODA accounts for 14.3% of GNI in Saint Vincent and the Grenadines, 6.4% in Granada, and 5.8% in Saint Lucia. In this context, while FDI is a key indicator for LAC economies, ODA continues to provide key support to certain LAC economies, and its importance should not be overlooked.

Figure 5.1. **ODA as a percentage of GNI and FDI as a percentage of GDP, 2021**

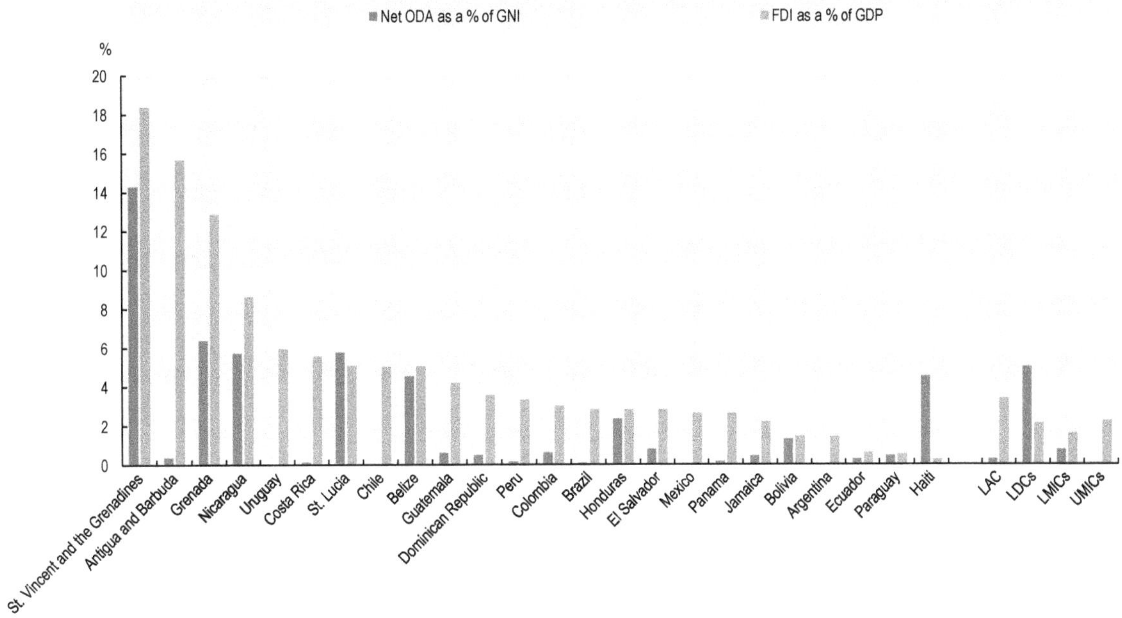

Note: As in (World Bank, 2023[27]), the 2022 data for LAC corresponds to a weighted average which includes 33 countries: Antigua and Barbuda, Argentina, Bahamas, Barbados, Belize, Bolivia, Brazil, Chile, Colombia, Costa Rica, Dominica, Dominican Republic, Ecuador, El Salvador, Grenada, Guatemala, Guyana, Haiti, Honduras, Jamaica, Mexico, Nicaragua, Panama, Paraguay, Peru, Saint Kitts and Nevis, Saint Lucia, Saint Vincent and the Grenadines, Sint Maarten, Suriname, Trinidad and Tobago, Turks and Caicos and Uruguay. For Aruba, Curacao and Cayman Islands the latest data available corresponds to 2021, while for Venezuela the latest data available corresponds to 2014. As per UN classification: LDCs = least-developed countries; LMICs = lower-middle-income. countries; UMICs = upper-middle-income countries.

Source: Authors' elaboration based on (World Bank, 2023[27]); (OECD, 2023[28]).

StatLink https://stat.link/b4gdsi

Development co-operation is essential for LAC to tap into international financial flows. While LAC remains an attractive destination for FDI, countries in the region sometimes face challenges in attracting these investments. This can be partially explained by actual or perceived risks that make it more difficult for the private sector to invest (OECD/UNCDF, 2020[29]). Other challenges include political and administrative transitions, as well as policy and regulatory upheavals across many LAC countries, which can increase uncertainty (Chapter 2). By offering access to de-risking instruments, such as blended finance or guarantees offered at concessional or competitive terms to unlock private finance, development co-operation can help to lower investment barriers such as perceived risks (OECD, 2022[30]). Development partners also play an important role in supporting governments in efforts to enhance the attractiveness of the region as an investment destination.

Blended finance can unlock private-sector investments

Increased pressure, particularly since 2015, to narrow the SDG financing gap has placed mobilisation of private-sector finance at the centre of development co-operation (OECD, 2022[30]). Donors have developed various tools to increase private participation in development goals, including the use of blended finance, defined as the strategic use of development finance to mobilise additional finance towards sustainable development projects (OECD, 2023[31]). By leveraging a mix of public and private funds, as well as philanthropic funds, blended finance mobilises new sources of private capital towards the SDGs, especially to address specific targets such as decent work, economic growth and climate action (Convergence, 2022[32]). It achieves this through de-risking instruments such as guarantees, reducing perceived risks and making investments more financially attractive to private investors. Blended finance also includes provisions for capacity building, strengthening the capabilities of local stakeholders and creating an enabling environment for sustainable investments.

Development finance institutions (DFIs) and multilateral development banks (MDBs) have mobilised significant private finance in LAC (Convergence, 2022[32]; OECD. Stat, 2023[35]). Blended finance flows in the LAC region remained constant, even amid the COVID-19 pandemic, exceeding an aggregate of USD 22 billion in 2021 and 2022 and reaching a total of 154 transactions by 2022 (Convergence, 2023[33])[1] (Figure 5.2). However, compared to domestic resource mobilisation or public debt (Chapter 1), blended finance resources have remained low in the past decade.

Figure 5.2. **Market size and growth of blended finance in LAC, 2012-22**

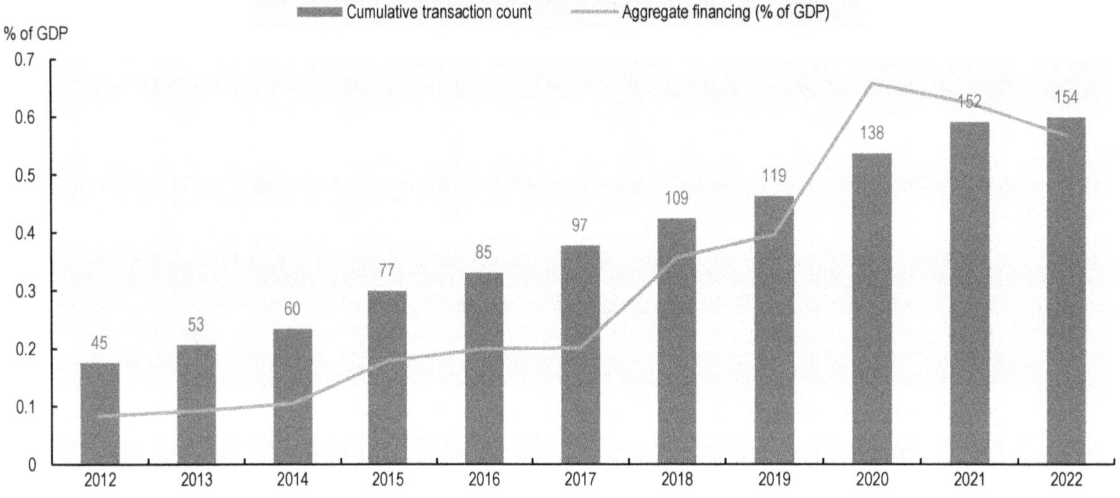

Note: The year 2012 includes accumulated transactions since 1990.
Source: Authors' elaboration based on (Convergence, 2023[33]).

StatLink https://stat.link/0x8l4j

From 2018-20, LAC accounted for approximately 15% of the global total amount mobilised from the private sector by official development interventions (OECD, 2023[4]).[2] During the last decade, LAC has experienced an increase in the share of mobilised private finance as a percentage of GDP, from 0.06% (USD 3 billion) in 2016 to 0.18% (USD 9 billion) in 2021 (Figure 5.3). Top LAC countries include Mexico, Peru, Ecuador and Colombia, in that order (Faty Dembele, 2022[34]).

Figure 5.3. **Amounts mobilised from the private sector by official development finance interventions, 2012-21**

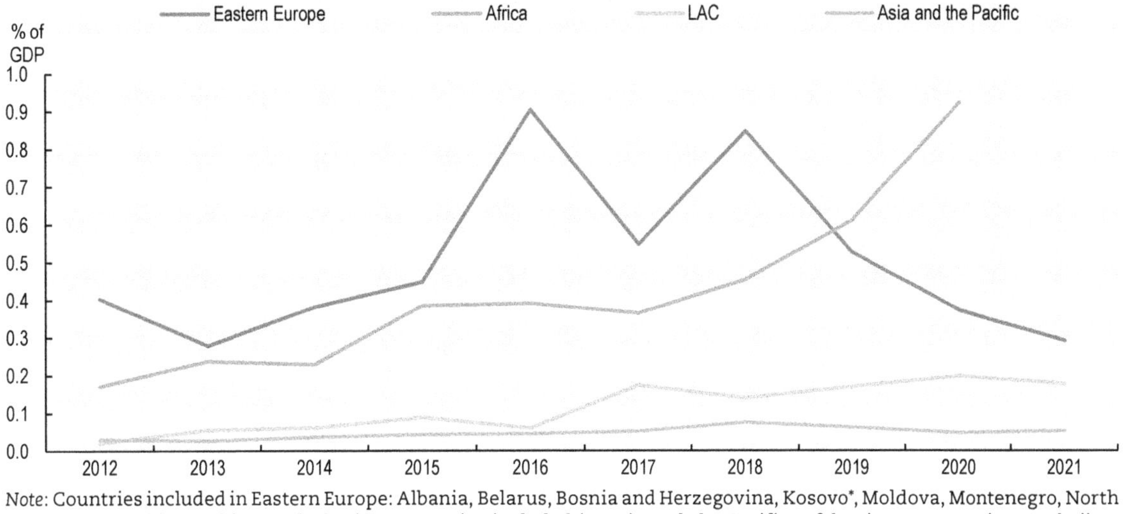

Note: Countries included in Eastern Europe: Albania, Belarus, Bosnia and Herzegovina, Kosovo*, Moldova, Montenegro, North Macedonia, Serbia, Türkiye, and Ukraine. Countries included in Asia and the Pacific: Afghanistan, Armenia, Azerbaijan, Bangladesh, Bhutan, Cambodia, China, Fiji, Georgia, India, Indonesia, Iran, Iraq, Jordan, Kazakhstan, Kiribati, Kyrgyzstan, Lao PDR, Lebanon, Malaysia, Maldives, Micronesia, Mongolia, Myanmar, Nepal, Niue, Palau, Pakistan, Papua New Guinea, Philippines, Samoa, Solomon Islands, Sri Lanka, Syrian Arab Republic, Tajikistan, Thailand, Timor-Leste, Tonga, Turkmenistan, Tuvalu, Uzbekistan, Vanuatu, Viet Nam, West Bank and Gaza Strip, and Yemen. Countries included in LAC: Antigua and Barbuda, Argentina, Belize, Bolivia, Brazil, Chile, Colombia, Costa Rica, Cuba, Dominica, Dominican Republic, Ecuador, El Salvador, Grenada, Guatemala, Guyana, Haiti, Honduras, Jamaica, Mexico, Nicaragua, Panama, Paraguay, Peru, Saint Lucia, Saint Vincent and the Grenadines, Suriname, Uruguay, Venezuela. Africa includes all African countries. Data for 2021 are being reviewed.

* This designation is without prejudice to positions on status, and is in line with United Nations Security Council Resolution 1244/99 and the Advisory Opinion of the International Court of Justice on Kosovo's declaration of independence.

Source: Authors' calculations based on (OECD.Stat, 2023[35]) and (IMF, 2023[110]).

StatLink https://stat.link/xco6es

Almost three-quarters (72%) of private finance mobilised in LAC in 2018-20 was directed towards sectors that fall under economic infrastructure and services. This includes banking and financial services, energy, and transport and storage (Figure 5.4). Most of the financing for banking and financial services came from guarantees, credit lines and syndicated loans, instruments that are generally used for supporting the development of small and medium-sized enterprises (SMEs) and financial inclusion (OECD, 2023[4]).

Figure 5.4. **Share of mobilised private finance by sector (%), LAC 2018-20 average**

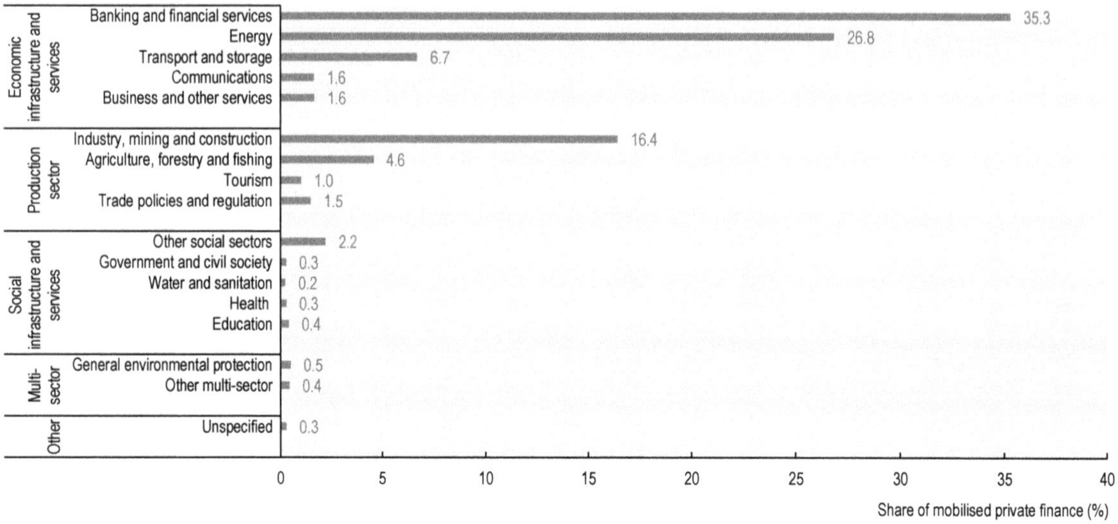

Note: Data for 2021 were not included since a large share of mobilised private finance went to the health sector due to the COVID-19 pandemic. Listed sectors are based on the Development Assistance Committee (DAC) sector classification.
Source: (OECD.Stat, 2023[35]).

StatLink https://stat.link/sak0h9

Energy sector transactions are essential in the region, with ten countries in LAC committing to generate 70% (above the current target of 40%) of their total energy consumption from renewable energy by 2030 as part of the Renewable Energy for Latin America and the Caribbean (RELAC) initiative. The main financial instruments used to mobilise private finance in the energy sector were guarantees (47.6%), and direct investment in companies (DIC) and project finance special purpose vehicles (SPVs), with 41.4% going to DIC/SPVs. Blended finance can help bridge the financing gap for critical sectors such as renewable energy, sustainable agriculture and infrastructure by unlocking resources for projects that have both financial viability and positive social and environmental impacts. For example, Uruguay is using a blended finance approach to accelerate its second energy transition (Box 5.2).

Box 5.2. **Uruguay's Renewable Energy Innovation Fund (REIF)**

Uruguay is supporting its second energy transition through its Renewable Energy Innovation Fund (REIF), a blended finance approach that combines private capital and UN funds to promote energy transition projects in the country. The fund mobilises private and public investments to stimulate innovative private projects in the renewable energies sector, which presents a certain level of risk and therefore requires an initial blended finance contribution to attract financing and de-risk private sector investments (REIF, 2023[36]). The REIF programme was due to receive a grant of USD 10 million from the UN's Joint SDG Fund and to leverage co-financing of more than USD 77 million from regional development banks and private commercial banks (UNIDO, 2022[37]). Four major banks in Uruguay have signed a co-operation agreement with the programme: BBVA, Heritage, Santander and Itau.

Box 5.2. **Uruguay's Renewable Energy Innovation Fund (REIF)** *(cont.)*

REIF works in collaboration with several government agencies: the Ministry of Industry, Energy and Mining; the Ministry of Environment; the Office of Planning and Budget; and the National Administration of Power Plants and Electrical Transmissions (the country's government-owned power company, better known as UTE). The programme seeks to accelerate Uruguay's compliance with the UN's 2030 Agenda for Sustainable Development. REIF's main impact areas include: enhanced private-sector competitiveness; environmental sustainability; social and gender inclusiveness; and enhanced financial sector capabilities for SDG investment.

Note: Other partners include United Nations Industrial Development Organization (UNIDO), United Nations Development Programme (UNDP) and UN Women.

Source: (REIF, 2023[36]); (UNIDO, 2022[37]).

Only 3% (USD 282 million) of total private finance mobilised in LAC in 2018-20 was directed towards the social infrastructure and services sectors. However, private investments in social sectors have been gaining traction in recent years to address social and development challenges in the region. Most notably, and in response to the pandemic, investments in the health sector increased dramatically between 2020 and 2021, from USD 47.9 million to USD 334.5 million, a rise of 598.3% (OECD.Stat, 2023[35]). While private investments in social infrastructure and services may have positive impacts, important factors must be considered. Since private investments tend to be driven by profit motives, blended finance projects need to be carefully monitored and their development impacts measured (Attridge and Engen, 2019[38]). Ensuring a robust monitoring and evaluation mechanism is essential to maximise the positive impact of private investments, particularly in the social infrastructure and services sector.

In 2018-20, the main private mobilisation leveraging mechanisms in LAC were guarantees (38%) and DICs/SPVs (30%) (Figure 5.5). Guarantees, which have the advantage of not requiring upfront funding as loans do, accounted for one-third of the private capital mobilised between 2012 and 2020 (Alvarez Pagliuca et al., 2022[39]). Syndicated loans, which usually arise when a project requires too large of loan for a single lender, represented 17% of the total. Although amounts mobilised through credit lines (8%), simple co-financing (4%) and shares in collective investment vehicles (CIVs) (3%) were relatively low, these leveraging tools can still be effective in certain mobilisation contexts, such as access to SME financing and projects with limited bankability potential (OECD, 2023[4]).

Figure 5.5. **Private mobilisation by leveraging mechanism, LAC, 2018-20 average**

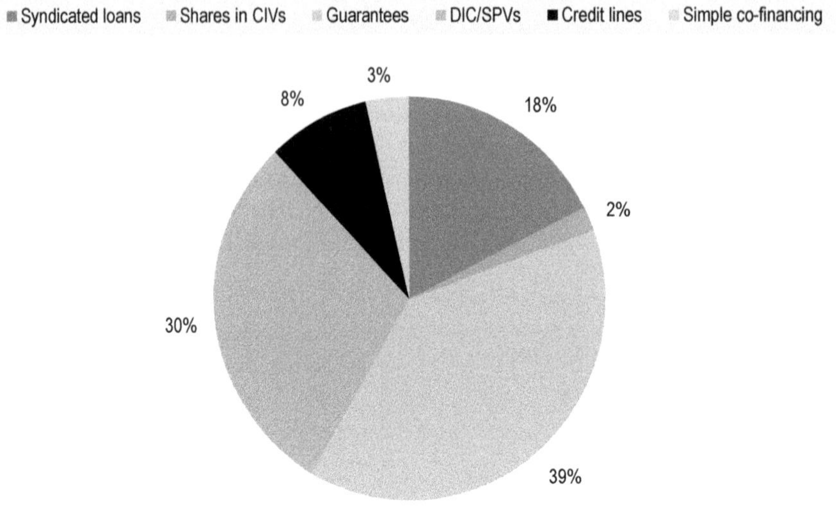

Note: CIVs = collective investment vehicles; DIC/SPVs = direct investment in companies and project finance special purpose vehicles.
Source: (OECD.Stat, 2023[35]).

StatLink https://stat.link/m9gylu

Blended finance operations targeting SMEs in several key sectors of LAC economies are also essential for filling private investment gaps and fostering the region's economic transformation. As climate change adds to the challenge of protecting and sustainably managing this natural wealth, blended finance initiatives play a crucial role though the support of domestic SMEs. For instance, in 2022, the Central America Small Enterprise Investment Fund IV (CASEIF IV) committed USD 75 million of growth capital to SMEs operating in Central and South America and the Caribbean, with a particular focus on the agro-industry, food and beverage, manufacturing, and telecommunications sectors (SIFEM, 2023[40]). Moreover, the European Union LACIF has contributed EUR 16.4 million to support the Eco.business Fund, a collaborative effort channelling funds to local financial institutions to promote the sustainable use of natural resources and to mitigate the impacts of climate change (LACIF, 2023[41]; Eco.business Fund, 2023[42]). Since the fund's inception in December 2014, it has supported more than 816 000 jobs related to sustainable resource management, sustainably managed 1 093 700 hectares of farmland, kept 144 000 litres of herbicides out of the environment, and saved 5.3 million cubic metres of irrigation water in both LAC and Sub-Saharan Africa (Eco.business Fund, 2023[43]). The EU's financial support has enabled technical assistance for 62 projects in 14 countries in the region, guiding investments towards more sustainable outcomes.

MDBs have assumed an increasingly important role in global efforts to address the climate crisis and its far-reaching consequences. Since 2016, the emergence of new climate-focused multilateral providers, such as the Global Environment Facility and the Green Climate Fund, has significantly increased the mobilisation of private finance for climate-related investments. In recent years, a notable rise has been evident in the proportion of private funds allocated towards climate-related initiatives by MDBs, with a peak in 2017 (Figure 5.6). Of USD 7.8 billion mobilised in 2017 by development funds, nearly half (USD 3.84 billion) targeted climate-related projects. In 2022, the Inter-American Development Bank (IDB) alone mobilised USD 2.82 billion to support the region's development, engaging in 111 transactions with over 61 partners (IDB, 2023[44]). The bank prioritised key areas of focus, including climate action and addressing the social issues impeding the region's recovery.

Figure 5.6. **Total mobilised private finance by MDBs, 2012-21**

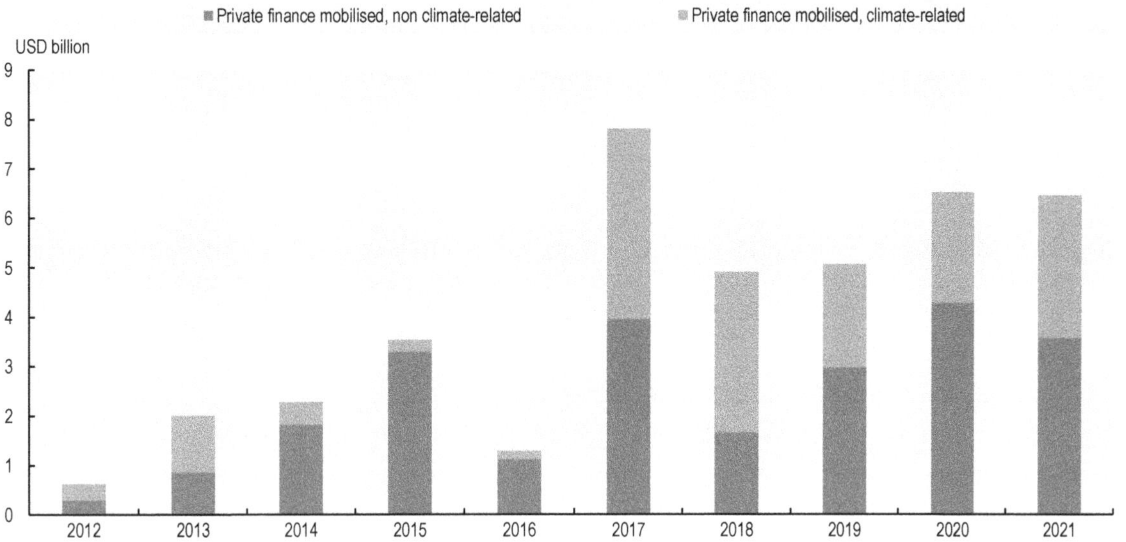

Note: Multilateral providers in LAC include the Caribbean Development Bank, Development Bank of Latin America, EU Institutions, International Fund for Agricultural Development (IFAD), IDB Group, World Bank Group, Nordic Development Fund, Private Infrastructure Development Group, Global Environment Facility, Green Climate Fund, North American Development Bank, and OPEC Fund for International Development.

Source: (OECD.Stat, 2023[35]).

StatLink https://stat.link/i8w7am

MDBs also facilitate private sector financing for development through innovative mechanisms that de-risk investments and target sustainability goals. For instance, the IDB and The Nature Conservancy agreed on a debt-for-nature swap with Barbados that provided the country with USD 10 million to support its blue economy and partnered with the U.S. Development Finance Corporation to implement another debt-for-nature swap worth USD 450 million to protect the Galápagos Islands in Ecuador (IDB, 2022[45]) (Reuters, 2023[46]). In addition, the IDB has become the first multilateral development bank to offer a financing tool – the Biodiversity and Climate-Linked Mechanism for Ambition (IDB CLIMA) – that rewards countries for achieving nature and climate objectives. This will provide the borrower with a discount when nature and climate objectives of selected loan projects are met (IDB, 2023[47]).

Beyond these opportunities from blended finance, the shift in development co-operation towards mobilising private finance must be taken with caution. Setting up de-risking initiatives to attract private capital to development projects still raises some concerns. For instance, the very definition of blended finance is still under debate. Institutions take different approaches regarding the actors involved in blended finance, the underlying presumptions regarding beneficiaries and how best to measure its impact. The lack of an official definition can present problems in data collection and comparability (OECD/UNCDF, 2020[29]). Furthermore, MDBs and DFIs also compile data on blending, giving importance as well to combining concessional finance from donors or third parties alongside the normal own-account finance and/or commercial finance from other investors (IFC, 2023[48]).

Another crucial concern with the blended finance approach is the risk of diverting public funds away from the poorest countries, which are less attractive to private investors due to higher perceived risks and lower return potential (Attridge and Engen, 2019[38]). This could exacerbate inequalities between and within countries. There is also a concern about transparency and accountability in blended finance operations

(Hausmann, 2023[49]). As public and private actors have different accountability structures and reporting standards, this could complicate the process of tracking how funds are used and guaranteeing that they contribute to sustainable development (Oxfam/Eurodad, 2017[50]). In terms of transparency and public access to information, it is crucial as well to ensure the participation of civil society and local actors in monitoring and accountability (Chapters 2 and 4). Blending also presents the challenge of ensuring that the private sector's needs and motivations do not overshadow development objectives and outcomes (Attridge and Engen, 2019[38]). Blended finance must be based on careful and measured consideration of the impact of partnerships, while also ensuring that assumptions made regarding the actors involved are borne out by evidence (Oxfam, 2019[51]). Therefore, blended finance projects should be evaluated across both the short and long term, while also ensuring their transparency through public accessibility.

International partnerships to ensure better investments in LAC

International partnerships are important in LAC not only for mobilising greater resources from the private sector, but also to ensure that investments yield greater socio-economic impacts. A key challenge for LAC countries is to achieve a sustainable production transformation via a fair, green and digital transition. This is important given the region's structural and systemic economic growth problems, which have been exacerbated by the COVID-19 pandemic, inflation and disruptions in global value chains (Chapter 1).

The challenges faced by LAC in attracting quality FDI can be attributed (in large part) to three main factors: lack of adequate infrastructure; gaps in skills and education compared to other regions; and lags in research and development (R&D) and technological innovation. Together, these can limit the region's attractiveness to knowledge-intensive sectors (Chapter 3). Due to the drop in FDI relative to GDP, LAC may have missed out on 0.08-0.64 percentage point of GDP growth per capita every year from 2013 to 2020 (Chapter 2) (Maloney et al., 2023[52]).

Leveraging LAC's comparative advantages – in sustainable energy production, the commodities necessary for emerging green industries and its unique natural capital – offers a new potential source of growth. But this will require policies to facilitate access to global markets, capital and technology. The effectiveness of foreign investment in these sectors that hold potential may depend on various factors. For example, better absorption capacities are related to higher FDI productivity, enhanced human capital, deeper financial systems, improved institutional quality, and the stability of regulatory and political systems (Maloney et al., 2023[52]).

International partnerships can play a significant role in attracting quality FDI to the region. By pooling expertise, knowledge and resources, LAC countries can address critical regional needs, such as stimulating a production transformation across all economies or creating forward linkages in value chains in a more comprehensive manner. FDI quality is typically seen as investment that goes beyond mere financial contributions, leading to sustainable economic, social and environmental outcomes. FDI quality is measured in terms of its contribution to promoting productivity and innovation, employment, job quality, skills and gender equality while also reducing the carbon footprint (OECD, 2019[53]) (Chapter 2).

Foreign investment in LAC countries has already had positive impacts in terms of productivity, innovation, R&D investment and real wages (Chapter 2). However, further efforts to attract quality FDI are needed in order to promote an inclusive and sustainable transformation model. Development partners have a key role to play. The OECD's FDI

Qualities Guide for Development Co-operation provides a framework for reinforcing the role of the development co-operation community in mobilising FDI and enhancing its impact in developing countries (OECD, 2022[30]).

Focusing on three main objectives can help international partnerships to ensure that they mobilise more and better investments. First, these partnerships can strive to create an enabling environment that attracts and facilitates investments conducive to the region's production transformation. Second, they can foster alignment and collaboration among institutions, such as MDBs and DFIs, to enhance co-ordination and effectiveness. Third, they can boost local development by implementing measures such as local content requirements that strengthen local economies and value chains, and by aligning support with national development strategies (Table 5.1).

Table 5.1. **International mechanisms to ensure better investments**

Objective	Existing or potential instrument	Description
Create an enabling environment	International standards and frameworks	Creates an environment and common understanding of due diligence for investors and private capital mobilisation.
	International investment treaties	Commits contracting parties to afford specific standards of treatment to foreign investors.
	Capacity building and technology transfer	Supports governments in: i) design of coherent strategies on investment attraction and production transformation through training in strategic sectors; ii) assessing and monitoring the impact of investments in job creation; and iii) improving transparency and standards.
		Ensures commitment from the private sector to invest in education and training.
		Ensures the transfer of technology within investment in specific sectors, building upper value chains in key strategic sectors.
Foster alignment between institutions	Co-ordination platforms among institutions	Articulates development and non-development instruments and institutions by increasing synergies between the public actors of development policies and public actors supporting commercial endeavours (e.g. IPAs, trade and export credit agencies).
		Articulates efforts of MDBs and DFIs operating in LAC, avoiding overlap and creating synergies within strategic sectors and countries.
		Promotes business-to-government dialogue, enabling feedback about policies and investment barriers.
Boost local development	Platforms for aligning investments with national priorities	Supports national and local IPAs and local financial institutions to align sustainable finance with national priorities.
		Provides support to strategic sectors in co-ordination with national development strategies, aligning all relevant actors.
		Ensures the participation of civil society and local actors in monitoring projects to promote transparency and accountability.
	Local content requirements	Strengthens the development of local supply chains and increases labour productivity.

Source: Authors' elaboration.

Creating an enabling environment to attract more and better investments

Establishing favourable conditions and frameworks can encourage both domestic and foreign investors to allocate their resources in a particular country or region. This includes adopting policies and regulations that promote transparency, predictability and legal protection for investors. It also entails adhering to international standards and best practices in areas such as governance, environmental protection and labour rights. Furthermore, it involves adhering to international investment treaties to provide additional safeguards and incentives for investors.

Aligning domestic frameworks with international standards can support sustainable investments in LAC. By joining major international instruments, such as the Paris Agreement, core conventions of the United Nations (UN) and the International Labour Organization (ILO), and international instruments on responsible business conduct (RBC), governments can protect the public interest from potential negative impacts of business activities (OECD, 2015[54]). Ensuring RBC can attract responsible investors, mitigating the risks of potential adverse impacts of investments, and can promote broader sustainable development (OECD, 2018[55]).

To date, 50 countries, including Argentina, Brazil, Costa Rica, Colombia, Mexico, Peru and Uruguay, have adhered to the OECD Due Diligence Guidance for RBC (OECD, 2022[56]). These guidelines provide non-binding recommendations designed to assist businesses in managing risk and promoting positive impacts on matters related to environmental protection, human rights, labour rights, bribery and corruption, and other issues related to sustainable development. They also seek to promote a common understanding among governments and other stakeholders on due diligence for RBC (Table 5.2) (OECD, 2018[55]). Recently, momentum has been growing around mandatory due diligence legislation on RBC and mandatory human rights due diligence (mHRDD) to ensure companies undertake environmental and human rights due diligence (OECD, 2022[57]; OHCHR, 2023[58]). Examples include the French Duty of Vigilance Law and the proposal in 2022 for an EU-wide law (Business & Human Rights Resource Centre, 2023[59]). These steps towards mandatory due diligence legislation can establish new requirements for companies to adhere to, thereby protecting the public from the negative impacts of business activities.

Table 5.2. **Key elements of OECD Due Diligence Guidance**

Topics	Recommendations
Human rights	Provides recommendations on how businesses can respect human rights, including issues such as child labour, forced labour and freedom of association; draws on and is aligned with the UN Protect, Respect and Remedy Framework and Guiding Principles on Business and Human Rights.
Employment and industrial relations	Focuses on the role of due diligence in promoting observance among multinational enterprises of international labour standards developed by the ILO.
Environmental responsibility	Urges businesses to identify and manage environmental risks, actively mitigate pollution and address climate change impacts within their operations and supply chains.
Combating bribery, bribe solicitation and extortion	Encourages businesses to level the international playing field by fighting to eliminate bribery.
Disclosure	Encourages businesses to report on their due diligence efforts and to communicate with stakeholders about their responsible business conduct.

Source: Authors' elaboration based on (OECD, 2018[55]).

Consideration of environmental, social and governance (ESG) standards in financial decision making is a crucial aspect that is advancing in LAC (Chapter 4). Financing from banks, private equity, multilateral financial institutions and institutional investors is increasingly linked to ESG criteria (Beeber, Li and Schulz, 2022[60]). ESG taxonomies, i.e. criteria for evaluating which investments are considered environmentally or socially sustainable, are a key example (UNCTAD, 2022[61]). They provide guidelines for classifying investments based on their ESG characteristics. Taxonomies now exist at the global and regional levels to support the development of investment markets. Many are the result of partnerships between countries within a given region and other institutions. Colombia's national green taxonomy, for example, was developed with the support of the World Bank and the International Finance Corporation (World Bank, 2022[62] ; Chapter 4).

Common standards will be imperative for protecting the Amazon, an ecosystem shared by eight countries in LAC. By establishing standards for projects, countries can ensure responsible business activity to minimise environmental and social impacts. In 2023, the IDB launched Amazonia Forever, an umbrella programme that brings together relevant stakeholders to strengthen the planning and execution of projects in the Amazon region (IDB, 2023[63]). Through this platform, partners can share knowledge, evidence-based innovations and leverage expertise to support policy development, enhancing regional collaboration and co-ordination. Within Amazonia Forever, the IDB and the Brazilian Development Bank (BNDES) launched the Green Coalition to carry out collaborative, sustainable development initiatives among development banks from the Amazon basin countries (IDB, 2023[64]). This has increased the scale and impact of projects in the Amazon region, while respecting local and regional characteristics. By establishing these platforms for shared practices and common standards, countries can mitigate conflicts over land use, resource extraction, and infrastructure development, as well as protect the Amazon's ecosystem, biodiversity and local communities.

International frameworks that specifically target infrastructure also contribute to creating an enabling environment for investments in strategic sectors related to production transformation. Such frameworks can enable LAC countries to guarantee the quality of infrastructure investments. The region has experienced a persistent decline in infrastructure investments since the 1990s, leading to a widening infrastructure gap. As a result, countries are now looking into measures that can ensure FDI quality. The G20 Principles for Quality Infrastructure Investment (QII) provide a set of voluntary, non-binding principles for countries to maximise the positive impacts of infrastructure in order to achieve sustainable growth and development (OECD, 2023[65]). These principles provide a framework to bridge the infrastructure gap while ensuring quality infrastructure investments that promote strong, sustainable and balanced growth. Chile has proved to be a success story in terms of strong institutions, processes and regulatory frameworks for quality infrastructure investments, often in line with international good practices and standards (OECD, 2021[66]).

Policy dialogue and exchange also play important roles in fostering investments by creating a conducive environment for investors through the development of transparent, stable and investor-friendly policies. These processes build trust among investors and policy makers, ultimately attracting capital that can drive economic growth and development. The OECD-LAC regional networks provide a mechanism for member countries to engage in constructive policy discussions by facilitating dialogue among policy makers, experts, and stakeholders to exchange ideas, experiences, and best practices (Box 5.3).

Box 5.3. **Regional policy networks: contributing to the enabling environment for investments**

The OECD Latin America and the Caribbean (OECD-LAC) regional policy networks play a crucial role in enhancing a conducive environment for investments across the region. These networks act as knowledge-sharing platforms that bring together policy makers, experts and stakeholders from diverse sectors to collaborate on shaping policies that promote investment, integrity, regulation, competition and effective corporate governance. By fostering cross-border co-operation and dialogue, these networks facilitate the exchange of best practices, experiences and data-driven insights, which are essential for creating robust frameworks that attract and sustain investments in the LAC region.

In terms of investment, these networks enable member countries to pool their collective expertise and devise strategies to attract both domestic and foreign investments. Through shared experiences, participating countries can design targeted policies that address investment challenges, reduce barriers, and provide transparent and predictable rules for investors. For instance, a focus on integrity ensures that anti-corruption measures are in place, enhancing the trust of investors and safeguarding their interests. By collaborating on regulatory frameworks, the networks assist member countries in developing efficient and streamlined processes that encourage business growth while

Box 5.3. Regional policy networks: contributing to the enabling environment for investments *(cont.)*

upholding necessary standards. The emphasis on fair competition drives economic dynamism, innovation and efficiency, thereby fostering an environment that appeals to investors seeking vibrant markets. In addition, the networks' guidance on corporate governance practices nurtures responsible business conduct, which not only attracts investors but also strengthens the overall business ecosystem in the LAC region. Lastly, the fiscal policy network facilitates discussions on fiscal responsibility, transparency and effective resource allocation. This network helps member countries design fiscal policies that create the necessary fiscal space for public investments while maintaining macroeconomic stability.

Source: (OECD, 2023[67]).

LAC countries have also made use of IITs (also known as international investment agreements) as a mechanism for reducing investor uncertainty. Such treaties commit contracting parties to afford specific standards of treatment to foreign investors (OECD, 2015[54]). The general purpose of IITs is to promote investments by granting certain protections and benefits to foreign investors, including recourse to investor-State dispute settlement (ISDS) to resolve disputes with host states. In general, IITs aim to provide a level of certainty and security for investors, reducing the risks they perceive and encouraging investment. However, in the last decade more IITs have been terminated than new ones created. In 2021, for example, 86 IITs were terminated but only 13 were created, bringing the total number of agreements to 3 288 (UNCTAD, 2022[61]). As of June 2023, LAC countries had signed a total of 706 treaties related to international investment (Figure 5.7).

The design and negotiation of IITs is a complex, evolving process, and such treaties have both critics and proponents (Dixon and Haslam, 2016[68]). Many of these treaties were designed decades ago, within a different global economy and with different concerns in mind. Proponents argue that they provide necessary protections for investors to encourage capital flows; critics argue that IITs can constrain the policy space of host countries and erode their ability to regulate in the public interest. Despite these opposing views, IITs continue to be signed in LAC. Therefore, it is essential to ensure that new IITs pursue a development policy agenda favourable to all parties and to production transformation in the region. This requires transparent regulatory frameworks for investment flows.

Today's challenges – such as climate change, achieving the SDGs and pandemic recovery – are global in nature with local impacts. As such, they can be met only through international co-operation. Investment treaties establish frameworks through which countries can address complex transnational issues collectively. Well-designed IITs that protect common interests and uphold international norms and standards can help countries face these global challenges (Gaukrodger, 2021[69]). For example, recent revisions to EU agreements with Chile and Mexico introduce provisions on e-commerce, environmental sustainability, labour standards, gender equality and support for small businesses. These agreements also establish a contemporary framework for foreign investment and dispute resolution, encouraging investment in vital sectors for sustainable and inclusive growth. Over time, a common foundation of similar agreements with the European Union could facilitate the alignment of diverse economic integration efforts within the LAC region (ECLAC, 2023[70]).

Investment treaties are being reconsidered in this new context to ensure that they address new social and environmental standards. Issues being revisited are related to climate change, pandemic recovery and digital transformation, as well as how to deal with disputes over existing agreements. New approaches have emerged that would lead to better outcomes on matters related to the efficient allocation of capital, regulation in the public interest and the promotion of sustainable development. These include recommendations to: i) ensure that treaties contribute to sustainable development and do not hamper legitimate regulation in the public interest; ii) provide a framework to support market openness, facilitate investment and promote responsible business conduct; iii) consider a more flexible range of procedures and remedies when treaties are implemented; and iv) examine which issues may be best addressed in treaties, and which may be better suited for regulation through domestic law, international guidance or other tools (Gaukrodger, 2021[69]). Other notable developments in recent years include the conclusion of new-generation, megaregional economic agreements, the termination of bilateral investment treaties, and multilateral discussions on reforming investor-state dispute settlement mechanisms (UNCTAD, 2022[61]). Within the World Trade Organisation (WTO), plurilateral negotiations towards a new agreement on investment facilitation for development were successfully concluded in July 2023. More than 110 WTO members participated in the talks, including a large number of LAC countries.

Figure 5.7. **Number of IITs signed and terminated in LAC and worldwide, 1960-2023**

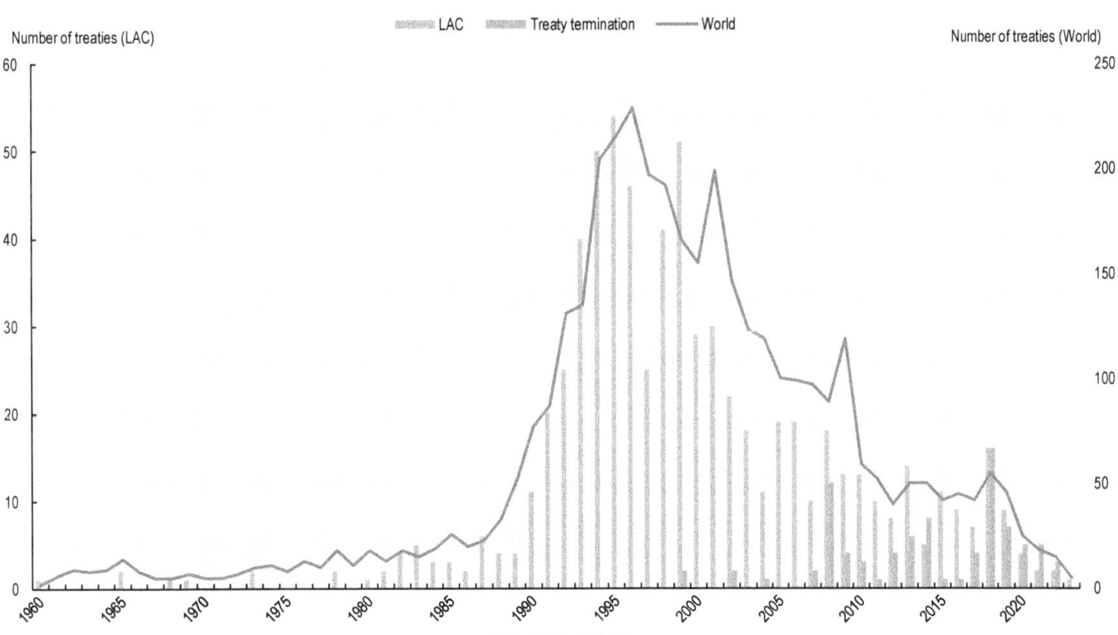

Note: Type of agreements include bilateral investment treaties (BITs) and treaties with investment provisions (TIPs). Date of signature includes treaties that are in negotiation, signed, in force and terminated.
Source: (UNCTAD, 2023[71]).

StatLink https://stat.link/q68r5y

Domestic conditions are also a key enabler for investments. Development partners can help build the domestic capabilities of firms and workers by supporting local capacity building, thereby driving the LAC region's production transformation and fostering sustainable economic development. Capacity building initiatives focused on enhancing human capital development, including training programmes and re-skilling in sectors in transition, will help to attract FDI and foster positive impacts in LAC (OECD, 2022[30]).

This involves identifying strategic sectors with high potential for job creation and growth that align investment with production transformation goals. In turn, these strategic sectors should be aligned with those prioritised by LAC countries and their territories under their productive development policies. By investing in vocational training centres and R&D institutions, LAC can equip workers with the skills and knowledge necessary to participate in high value chains and foster decarbonisation, productivity and innovation, as well as job quality and gender equality (OECD, 2022[30]). For instance, to support the region's research in genomics databases, the European Bioinformatics Institute (EMBL-EBI) collaborated with nine research institutes in Latin America in 2017 to launch the CABANA project (Stroe, 2017[72]). Funded by the Global Challenges Research Fund, CABANA aims to accelerate data-driven biology in the LAC region through capacity-building programmes that will train Latin America's diverse biological and biomedical sciences communities (CABANA, 2023[73]).

Fostering alignment among investment-related actors will enhance their effectiveness

The finances and policies of MDBs and other international actors are regaining centre stage in debates on financing for development. Securing resources to progress toward the SDGs remains a major challenge, with developing countries facing a growing finance gap estimated at USD 4.2 trillion per year in key sustainable development sectors (Joint SDG Fund, 2023[74]). Multilateral and public development banks are crucial in this context given they jointly manage USD 23 trillion in assets and provide over USD 2.7 trillion in development financing each year (FICS, 2022[75]). MDBs have the potential to boost their contribution to financing sustainable development by expanding their lending capacity and increasing their effectiveness when addressing global challenges, including by adopting common standards and co-ordinating better as a system, including with other financial institutions such as DFIs (Bilal, 2021[76]).

The problem of co-ordination among MDBs and DFIs primarily stems from their overlapping roles and responsibilities, as well as the diverse nature of their operations. While both aim to promote economic development and poverty reduction in developing countries, their approaches, mandates and financing mechanisms often differ, leading to co-ordination challenges. MDBs primarily provide loans, grants and policy advice to governments, whereas DFIs focus on financing private-sector projects through equity investments, loans, guarantees or technical assistance. The differing financing mechanisms can result in differences in project selection, risk tolerance and evaluation criteria. Co-ordinating these diverse financing approaches can be challenging, especially when joint projects or co-financing arrangements are pursued. Effective co-ordination requires timely sharing of information, experiences and best practices. However, MDBs and DFIs may have different reporting mechanisms, data requirements and evaluation frameworks, making it challenging to exchange relevant information. Insufficient knowledge sharing can result in missed opportunities for collaboration and hinder the efficient use of resources.

By signing co-financing agreements, MDBs and DFIs can mitigate co-ordination challenges and expand the volume of co-financing. These agreements are key mechanisms for leveraging resources for development projects as they help reduce transaction costs and processing times. For example, the IDB holds co-financing agreements with the French Development Agency (AFD), the European Commission, the EIB, and the Spanish Agency for International Development Cooperation (AECID) to streamline co-financing procedures and pre-define terms and conditions for co-financing projects. As such, co-financing agreements can help mobilise greater investments and enhance the impact of development initiatives.

Another important dimension is to better articulate and operationalise the synergies among international development actors such as MDBs, international financial institutions (IFIs) and public actors supporting commercial endeavours, including export credit agencies (ECAs), trade entities and investment promotion agencies (IPAs). IPAs promote the country's advantages, business opportunities and incentives via marketing efforts and collaboration with relevant government departments, fostering an investor-friendly environment. Between 2002 and 2018, the number of national and subnational IPAs grew from 112 to 170 worldwide (Steenbergen, 2023[77]). IPAs not only support the creation of an attractive economy for investments, but also help to ensure that FDI generates positive spillovers for developing poorer areas, fostering skills transfer and job creation, and enhancing the overall competitiveness of the respective region (OECD, 2020[78]). Development actors have an important role in ensuring co-ordination across various actors, thereby fostering the scalability of the support and further alignment with national priorities.

Existing collaboration platforms could be put at the service of scaling co-ordination for production transformation. CooperaNet, an online co-operation exchange hub run by the Organization of American States (OAS), facilitates regional co-operation and technical assistance through horizontal and South-South co-operation among OAS member states and with the private sector, sectoral experts, civil society, foundations, international organisations and others (OAS, 2023[79]). CooperaNet currently has 214 co-operation offers from 7 OAS member states, 20 co-operation offers from OAS development partners, and 10 needs from 8 countries in the areas of technological innovation, sustainable agriculture, food security, environmental conservation, sustainable communities, risk management, renewable energy, micro-, small- and medium-sized enterprises (MSMEs), education and gender equality. Another co-ordination mechanism is the European Financial Architecture for Development (EFAD), a network of institutions that includes EU member states, DFIs, public development banks, implementing agencies, MDBs and private actors. Through co-ordination of development and commercially-focused public actors, private entities have the potential to participate more effectively and at a greater scale (Bilal and Karaki, 2023[80]).

FDI, when aligned with national strategies, can boost sustainable local development

Beyond supplying capital, FDI can be a source of valuable technology and know-how for local firms, and thus contribute to production transformation.

A relevant approach for development partners is to align FDI with national priorities to the greatest extent possible, as defined under countries' productive development policies, for example. Supporting and strengthening national and local IPAs and financial institutions can enable co-ordination with the country's sustainable development objectives. With enhanced capacity and outreach, these institutions can play a pivotal role in attracting foreign investments that align with national development strategies, focusing on strategic sectors with high growth potential.

Another way of promoting local development and the social impact of foreign investment is through local content requirements (LCRs). Incorporating LCRs in investment agreements can enhance the social and economic transformation impact of FDI. These requirements incentivise foreign companies to engage with and invest in local firms, fostering valuable technology transfer, knowledge exchange and skills development. This can significantly contribute to jumpstarting the local economy and creating long-term sustainable benefits for the nation.

The incentives provided by LCRs can be key to strengthening the development of local supply chains and catalysing labour productivity, for instance in green industries. An example is the successful expansion of the solar and wind energy sectors in Uruguay and Brazil. In 2009, Uruguay opened an auction call to expand small wind farms, requiring 20% local content and 80% local contracting, and that the control centre be based in Uruguay. This initiative not only provided quality employment to expand the renewable energy sector, but also leveraged local content requirements to benefit local manufacturing. Similarly, in 2002, Brazil launched the Alternative Electricity Sources Incentive Programme, with a 60% local content requirement. This catalysed the national supply chain and has given rise to more than 300 companies; in 2014, the Brazilian wind energy manufacturing sector used 89% national content (IDB/ILO, 2020[81]).

The success of LCRs depend, however, on balancing rising local production costs with appropriate public policy instruments. LCRs do not offer guaranteed results, and the evidence on how best to apply them is mixed (Hansen et al., 2019[82]). Literature suggests that countries with better local content outcomes, both in LAC and Africa, use sound local content frameworks that are well structured and positioned within the country's legislation, and that include clear implementation and monitoring mechanisms (Mushemeza et al., 2017[83]).

Examples indicate that LCRs are best applied in countries where the level of skills and human capital is sufficient for the adoption of new technologies to improve productivity locally, thereby increasing efficiency while supporting national growth. This illustrates the need to, at the same time, invest more in training and skills development, and to expand the capabilities of existing industries (Da Costa and Caicedo, 2023[84]).

It is important to consider that policies aimed at attracting FDI must be accompanied by measures to enhance the local capacity to absorb investment to ensure that FDI becomes effective as a mechanism to transfer knowledge and technology. These measures include investing in education, strengthening institutional frameworks, and developing physical, scientific and technological infrastructure. It is thus crucial to establish a comprehensive framework that combines efforts to attract FDI with production development policies. Development partners can support efforts to upgrade productive development policies via international partnerships and co-operation. A good example of how international co-operation is helping local production transformation is Mexico's *Sembrando Vida* programme in El Salvador and Honduras (Box 5.4).

Box 5.4. **International co-operation for production transformation: Mexico's *Sembrando Vida***

Across the LAC region, bold international development policies are needed to help the most disadvantaged communities. One such innovative initiative is the Mexican government's *Sembrando Vida* ("Sowing Life") project, which seeks to contribute to food security in low-income rural localities of Honduras and El Salvador through agro-forestry systems that encourage self-consumption and the sale of surpluses. The programme is currently helping 10 000 small producers in each country with monthly economic support, as well as support in kind and technical assistance for contributing to food security.

The design of *Sembrando Vida* incorporates monitoring and follow-up mechanisms. A total of 40 biofactories have been built in El Salvador and 232 in Honduras; in El Salvador, 300 irrigation systems were also built. In terms of results, the planting of vegetables and fruit and/or timber trees has increased by more than 150%, with more than 90% of the beneficiaries reporting increases in their production. Positive spillovers are also evident.

Box 5.4. International co-operation for production transformation: Mexico's *Sembrando Vida* (cont.)

For example, *Sembrando Vida* also generated additional jobs, as the beneficiaries hired day labourers. More than 20 000 additional jobs were created in each country. In turn, the intention to migrate was reduced by 90% among the beneficiaries.

With this work, Mexico seeks to contribute to changing development models, as well as being a leader of innovation and an agent of transformation.

Source: (UNDP, 2022[85]).

The role of regional integration in production transformation and employment

Regional integration in LAC plays a vital role in promoting productive diversification, employment and industrialisation. Regional and subregional trade blocs can create larger markets and increase participation in regional value chains. By creating a favourable environment for economic integration, scalability of projects, and co-operation among member countries and development partners, they can also promote investments in LAC that are conducive to production transformation.

Intra-regional trade and production integration can drive sustainable development

It is important to consider that the organisation of productive activity spans national borders, and many forces exist by which internationalisation can drive production transformation. Regional integration opens opportunities to generate more sophisticated, resilient and secure value chains. For LAC countries to leverage these opportunities, public policies geared toward productive development and trade, and international dialogue and co-operation are essential.

One key achievement of LAC economic integration lies in its significant reduction of tariff barriers, making entry to the regional market more attractive for FDI. As of 2019, the average tariff imposed on trade within the region was a mere 2% (ECLAC, 2021[86]). Establishing a normative framework of rules for trade and FDI is another valuable asset.

Subregional trade blocs can also help to harmonise regulations and standards across member countries. Aligning regulations related to customs, taxation, investment procedures and business practices helps to reduce barriers for investors. It can also enhance transparency and predictability, making it easier for businesses to operate and invest across borders. Various subregional blocs in LAC have made noteworthy progress in formulating regulations pertaining to service trade, trade facilitation, public procurement, foreign investment treatment and electronic commerce, among other relevant subjects. As the literature suggests that regional integration has a positive effect on extra-region inward FDI, an indeterminate effect on intra-region FDI and a positive overall effect on FDI attraction, these assumptions should be analysed case by case (Sánchez-Martín, de Arce and Escribano, 2014[87]).

LAC countries have established several regional integration mechanisms (Figure 5.8), although not all share the same characteristics and depth in terms of liberalisation policies. The Common Market of the South (Mercosur), the Andean Community of Nations (CAN), the Central American Common Market (CACM), and the Caribbean Community (Caricom) were formally founded as customs unions. In these bodies, in addition to the internal liberalisation of tariffs and non-tariff barriers (NTBs), a common external tariff (CET) was to be established. In practice, implementation of a CET varies widely among these blocs. In contrast, the Pacific Alliance (PA) and the United States-Mexico-Canada Agreement (USMCA) are free trade agreements, in which the signatory countries have reduced tariffs and NTBs to internal trade and co-ordinated a series of other policies (e.g. government procurement, services) but maintain their independence in terms of external tariffs (CAF, 2021[88]). The Pacific Alliance aimed to facilitate trade and investment flows with the Asia-Pacific region. The integration of the Andean Community, Mercosur and the Central American Common Market, should be revitalised to open paths for productive transformation. Improving co-ordination among subregional integration mechanisms would help overcome the current fragmentation of the regional market and consolidate partnerships at the international level to further attract investments in the LAC region.

Figure 5.8. **LAC subregional integration mechanisms**

Note: The USMCA entered into force in July 2020 and substituted the North America Free Trade Agreement (NAFTA).
Source: Authors' elaboration based on (CAF, 2021[88]).

Regional trade agreements, however, are not sufficient for fostering productive and commercial integration. Despite some progress, LAC countries show limited levels of such integration among themselves, with only a few exceptions. This trend has become more pronounced since the 2010s. In 2008, intra-regional trade accounted for a maximum of 22% of LAC total goods; this figure has since declined steadily. It fell to 15% in 2021, one of the lowest intra-regional trade shares globally (Figure 5.9). In 2017, the share of imported goods from the region in total exports of major LAC economies averaged only 3% (Figure 5.10).

Figure 5.9. **Participation of intra-group exports in total goods exports, 1995-2021**

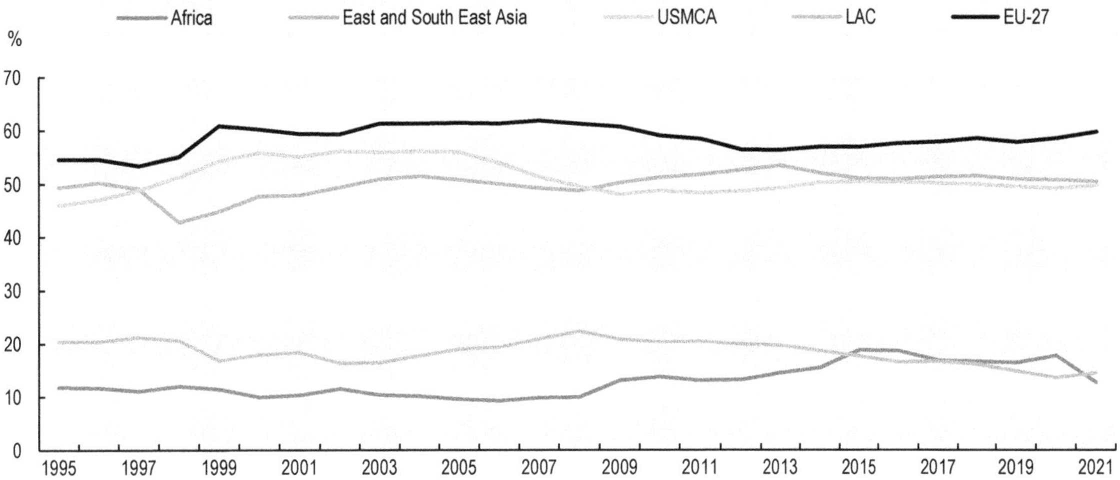

Note: USMCA = United States-Mexico-Canada Agreement.

Source: Authors' elaboration based on (UNCTADStat, 2023[89]).

StatLink https://stat.link/b4p8ig

Figure 5.10. **Structure of the imported content of exports, 2017**

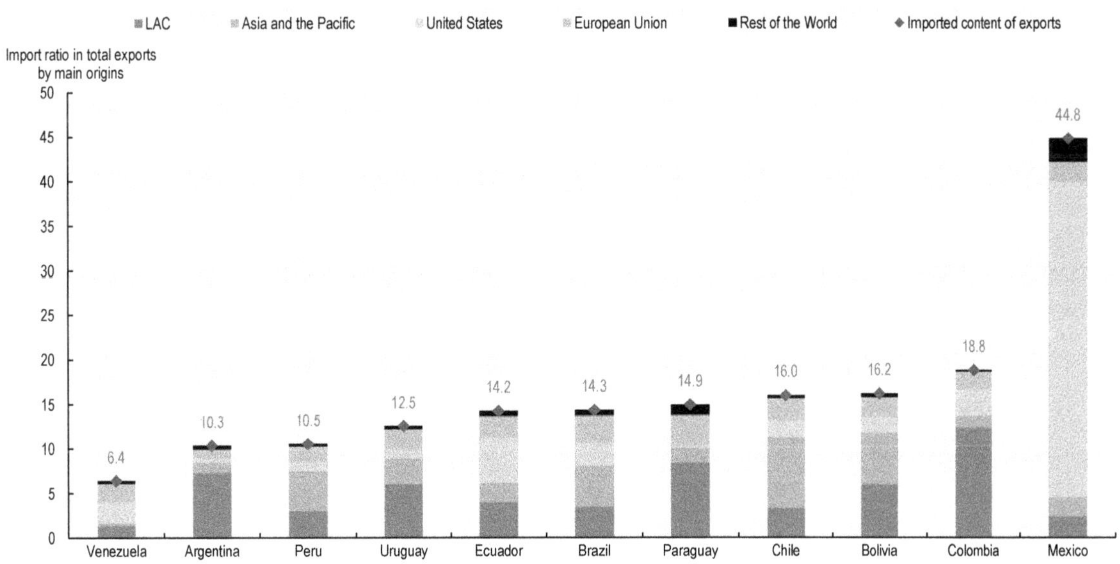

Source: Authors' elaboration based on the 2017 global input-output matrix on (ECLAC, 2020[90]).

StatLink https://stat.link/hjr9am

The decline in economic integration observed in the LAC region since the mid-2010s is concerning, especially considering the emerging global trends moving in the opposite direction. In response to vulnerabilities exposed by the COVID-19 pandemic and geopolitical disruptions in global value chains, several major players in the world economy are actively promoting greater regionalisation of their trade and production networks. Their aim is to attain greater strategic autonomy in sourcing key products and inputs. Given these global developments, revitalising regional integration in LAC is of utmost importance. Not only will it foster productive and export diversification, it will also enhance resilience in the face of future external shocks.

Several factors contribute to the low levels of intra-regional trade in LAC. First, limited economic complementarity arises from the similarity of the productive structures across many of the countries. This is particularly notable among the South American nations, which share an abundance of natural resources. Additionally, Mexico's deep integration into North American value chains has resulted in reduced trade with LAC. In 2021, LAC received only 4.4% of Mexico's total exports and account for 3.5% of its imports.

Compounding these challenges is the significant deficit in transport and logistics infrastructure across the region (Chapter 2). This hampers the formation of productive networks and exacerbates the difficulties arising from LAC's vast territorial expanse and complex topography (Pérez and Sánchez, 2019[91]; CAF, 2021[88]). Furthermore, substantial disparities persist in the rules and regulations applicable within each subregional bloc, such as technical standards and labelling requirements. This heterogeneity adds to trade costs among different blocs, particularly impacting SMEs.

Other factors contribute significantly to the low levels of intra-regional trade. For example, although the average applied tariff on intra-regional trade is low, at around 2%, there is still limited tariff liberalisation (or a partial absence thereof) in commercial relations among some key economies in the LAC region. Notably, this is evident in the relationships between Mexico and countries such as Argentina and Brazil; Central America and various South American nations; and between Caricom and the rest of the region. Another noteworthy aspect is the negotiation of numerous free trade agreements with partners outside the region, which has intensified competition for Latin American manufacturers. This competition has been further intensified by the influx of Chinese manufactured goods over the past two decades, resulting in a significant shift in regional production across multiple sectors (Durán Lima and Pellandra, 2017[92]).

Despite these challenges, intra-regional trade shows a clear positive potential for production transformation as it accounts for a large proportion of the manufacturing exports of LAC. While the regional market accounted for 15% of exports of manufactured goods from LAC in 2021, it was higher in all countries for which data are available, except Mexico (Figure 5.11). Additionally, intra-regional trade encompasses the broadest range of exported products (Annex 5.A) and involves the highest participation of companies, particularly SMEs (ECLAC, 2021[86]). It thus plays a vital role in terms of promoting productive diversification, employment and industrialisation.

Figure 5.11. **LAC's participation in total manufacturing exports, 2021**

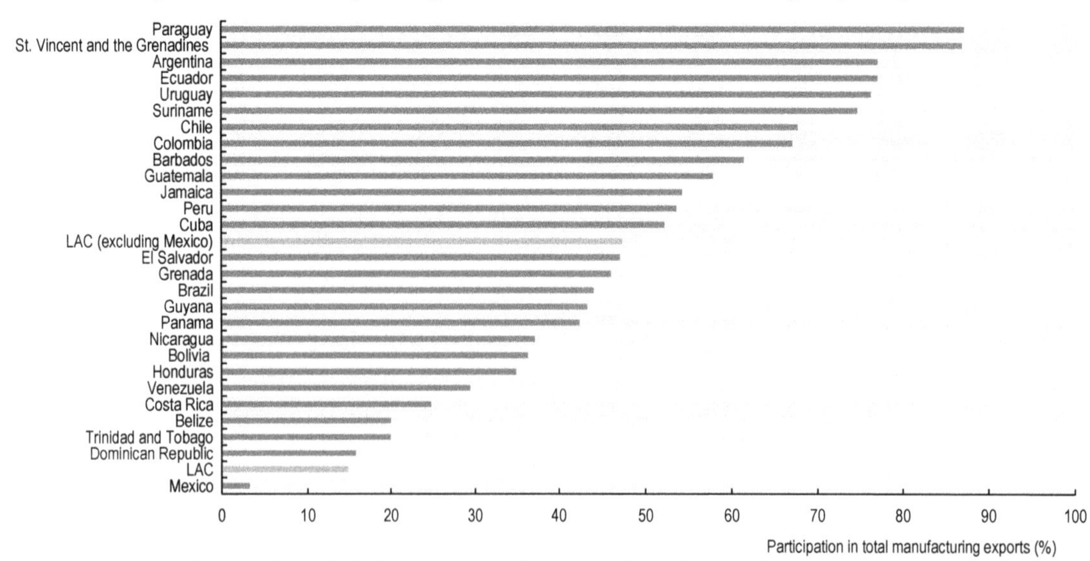

Note: Latin America and the Caribbean includes 27 countries. Figures for Cuba and Venezuela were calculated from mirror statistics.
Source: (UN Comtrade, 2023[93]).

StatLink https://stat.link/v0qdxe

Intra-regional trade is characterised by a lower proportion of raw materials than exports outside the region and generally involves shorter distances, which enhances its environmental sustainability and strategic role for industrialisation. In turn, the greater presence of MSMEs in intra-regional than in extra-regional exports helps to distribute the benefits more equitably. Summing up, the lack of dynamism shown by intra-regional trade in LAC over the last decade poses challenges for achieving a transformative recovery.

The LAC region as a whole could take advantage of strengthened subregional integration blocs, following the successful model demonstrated by Central America (Box 5.5), which has some of the highest levels of intra-regional trade (typically above 25%). This is followed by Mercosur, which actually shows a significant decrease in internal trade flows – from 20% in the mid-1990s to 12% in 2015-18 (CAF, 2021[88]).

Box 5.5. Central America as an example of regional integration

Central America serves as a remarkable example of regional integration due to its concerted efforts to foster regional co-operation and economic development. The establishment of institutions such as the Central American Integration System (SICA) and the Central American Parliament has facilitated dialogue, co-ordination and decision-making processes across the region. In addition, Central American countries have implemented initiatives such as the Central American Common Market (CACM) that promote the free movement of goods, services and people, thereby encouraging trade and investment.

On energy, Central America has taken a significant step forward by forming a regional electricity market and the completing physical interconnections among the six countries involved. The Central American Electrical Interconnection System, completed in 2014, is the greatest achievement in this area. The region has made progress as well in incorporating non-conventional renewable energies (NCREs) into electricity systems, increasing generating capacity. The countries involved have expanded this capacity over the last decade, with NCREs now accounting for slightly more than 20% of total electricity generation (CAF, 2021[88]).

The International Renewable Energy Agency (IRENA) is supporting development of the Clean Energy Corridor of Central America (CECCA), a regional initiative calling for accelerated development and cross-border trade of renewable power in Central America. Implementation of the CECCA initiative and its set of activities within the regional context aims to support the integration of larger amounts of renewables into the Regional Transmission Network. This potential is seen as attractive by partner countries looking to mobilise investments, such as the European Union (EUCA Trade, 2021[94]).

Towards a new agenda for production integration in LAC

To establish economically viable regional production chains, it is crucial to establish a stable market that combines efficient scale with minimising transaction costs associated with cross-border integration. Achieving this requires integration initiatives that surpass existing agreements and foster convergence among various subregional groupings. Several alternatives exist for making progress in this direction, differing in terms of their instruments, time frames, technical complexities and political considerations, among other factors.

Currently, negotiating a large-scale LAC trade agreement seems to be of low priority for most LAC governments. Other regional and subregional integration initiatives are instead gaining relevance, such as strategic use of national public procurement systems, regulatory harmonisation and regional trade facilitation agreements (ECLAC, 2022[95]). One aspect of the convergence agenda that could greatly enhance intra-regional production networks is the gradual harmonisation or mutual recognition of technical, sanitary and phytosanitary standards. Such progress would be particularly advantageous for SME exporters, which often face challenges in dealing with diverse regulatory requirements in different regional markets. Harmonising technical standards becomes pivotal in promoting productive integration, especially in areas critical to the energy transition, such as electromobility.

Trade facilitation, which involves streamlining and simplifying cross-border procedures, plays a crucial role in promoting participation in both regional and global value chains, and in facilitating the internationalisation of SMEs. The positive impacts of trade facilitation measures are amplified when they extend beyond national boundaries and become regional initiatives. Similar to other emerging regions, LAC has made progress since 2019 in simplifying and harmonising documents, automating and streamlining procedures, and improving domestic border agency co-operation (Sorescu and Bollig, 2022[96]). An exemplary case is the Authorised Economic Operator (AEO) regional recognition agreement, signed in May 2022 by the customs services of 11 LAC countries. When fully implemented, this agreement will enable exporting companies certified as an AEO in one member country to enjoy similar benefits in other member countries, simplifying customs procedures and enhancing the security of the logistics chain. Other trade facilitation initiatives in which significant progress is being made at the regional or subregional level include the interoperability of national single windows for foreign trade and the digital certification of origin.

The WTO's Trade Facilitation Agreement (TFA) sets a baseline of disciplines that LAC countries can build upon to pursue more ambitious commitments, particularly regarding the digitisation of procedures. Within this framework, negotiating a regional agreement on trade facilitation would send a robust political signal of commitment to integration and contribute to enhancing the efficiency of intra-regional trade and productive networks. Such an agreement would demonstrate a collective commitment to streamlining processes and reducing barriers, ultimately fostering smoother regional trade flows. In addition to the convergence initiatives discussed earlier, addressing the regional infrastructure deficit is crucial.

The institutional fragility of integration agreements constitutes a crucial barrier in LAC. National stances on integration are frequently subject to shifts due to changing political cycles in different countries. The regional integration project should be seen – independently of the political parties in government – as a regional development strategy to shift LAC's peripheral role in the global market towards a more value-added and central place in regional and global value chains. In turn, this would provide greater sovereignty and room to manoeuvre for the region within the global arena.

LAC can draw valuable lessons on regional integration from Europe, particularly from the experience of the European Coal and Steel Community (ECSC). Established in 1951, the ECSC laid the foundation for the European Union and played a pivotal role in fostering economic integration and political co-operation among European countries. It created a common market for coal and steel by eliminating trade barriers, encouraging competition and ensuring a stable supply of these products. This integration boosted industrial production and facilitated technological advancements. LAC can learn from this success story in prioritising a common market and focusing on strategic sectors that would boost a transformation of production and labour markets. By establishing similar mechanisms tailored to their own context, LAC countries can enhance intra-regional trade, harmonise regulations, and develop common policies on crucial issues such as energy, transportation and environmental protection. The region could also benefit from including regional trade integration as part of the productive development policies of LAC countries and their territories. For example, integration opportunities could be explored through the implementation of cluster initiatives in countries that share common or complementary value chains.

Regional integration blocs in LAC can serve not only to increase FDI for production transformation through better and more regional trade, but also as the basis for a regional platform for co-ordinated investment projects. Recent reports show a promising trend, with an increase of more than 80% in FDI outflows from LAC countries in 2023 (ECLAC, 2023[22]). The amount invested abroad by Latin American transnational companies (known as trans-Latins) reached the historic level of USD 74.677 billion in 2022 (ECLAC, 2023[22]). This trend could be boosted by strengthening regional investment platforms such as Mercosur's Structural Convergence Fund (FOCEM in Spanish), which was established with the aim of reducing asymmetries within the regional bloc. FOCEM comprises larger contributions from its bigger partners (Argentina and Brazil) while its allocations progressively benefit its smaller partners (Paraguay and Uruguay) with a focus on infrastructure projects, business competitiveness and social development. Another example is the Priority Integration Projects Agenda of the Union of South American Nations (UNASUR). This agenda consists of 31 structured projects with an estimated investment amount of USD 20.1 billion (UNASUR, 2023[97]).

The region's vast experience in South-South co-operation provides it with another tool to support coalitions for production transformation. When regional integration blocs become too rigid to provide concrete solutions, countries can resort to more flexible bilateral and subregional alliances that push forward production transformation agendas. For instance, consider the South-South co-operation project between Uruguay and Mexico, which focuses on fostering ecosystem dynamics in research, development, and innovation, while also emphasising value addition in local productive chains, with a particular focus on environmental issues, circular economy, and sustainable development. The project focuses on the exchange of experiences between public and private sectors from both countries, including start-ups from strategic sectors. Experiences such as this one can be replicated or scaled by gradually adding new partners.

A new EU-LAC agenda for production transformation

The European Union is not only one of the top investors in LAC, it is also the region's third-largest trading partner and the leading contributor of development co-operation. More recently, it has also become a significant investment partner in LAC, particularly in countries that receive a considerable share of the region's FDI inflows from the EU, including Brazil (31%) and Mexico (26%), followed by Chile (10%), Argentina (8%) and Colombia (5%) (fDi Markets, 2023[98]) (Chapter 1). This investment has played a crucial role in job creation, particularly in sectors such as services and manufacturing, which are key for LAC's production transformation (Chapter 2). European companies have established production facilities and acquired manufacturing entities, generating employment opportunities in LAC across diverse value chains.

Trade and investment ties between the European Union and LAC have been strengthened through bilateral and regional trade agreements that have facilitated market access and economic integration, leading to a significant increase in two-way trade

(European Commission, 2023[13]). The European Union has signed association agreements with individual countries and regional blocs within LAC, promoting co-operation, political partnership and closer economic relations. Such agreements exist with the Caribbean Forum (Cariforum); Central America; the Andean countries (Colombia, Ecuador and Peru); Chile; and Mexico. Negotiations are ongoing with Mercosur.

The EU's recent shift towards a new development co-operation paradigm based on international partnerships is also changing its approaches towards the LAC region. This shift recognises partner countries in LAC as active participants in shaping their own development agendas, moving away from a recipient-centric approach (ECLAC/OECD, 2018[99]; OECD et al., 2019[21]). It involves engaging in policy dialogue, co-designing policies, and jointly implementing projects that address common challenges (such as the green and digital transitions) while prioritising social inclusion. It promotes joint work across the two regions to harness their collective strengths and defend common interests. This approach also integrates tools such as trade, investments and co-operation in a multidimensional and "whole of government" approach (European Commission, 2023[13]).

The EU's Global Gateway strategy, which aims to mobilise investment, trade and development co-operation, is a turning point towards this new strategic alliance with the LAC region. This new approach places transparency and high standards at the core of EU-LAC relations, offering LAC countries projects that promote wealth creation through partnerships between the public and private sectors. It seeks to generate business investments that contribute to the prosperity of societies in both regions (European Commission, 2023[100]). The new EU-LAC GGIA is a collaborative effort to identify investment opportunities in LAC that will benefit the region's production transformation in sectors such as climate and energy, critical raw materials, infrastructure, SME development, electromobility, and sustainable tourism, among others (Figure 5.12). For example, the EU has worked closely with the IDB Group to identify investment opportunities in LAC. Over the past three years, the IDB has partnered on 58 initiatives alongside 14 European partners in 17 LAC countries, aligned with all key sectors of the GGIA. For each dollar financed by European partners, the IDB Group contributes twice as much, reaching more than USD 10 billion in co-financing and almost USD 200 million in grants.

Within the framework of the Global Gateway strategy, an association between the European Union and LAC for local manufacture of vaccines, medicines and other health technologies was launched in June 2022 (European Commission, 2022[101]). This initiative, which also aims to strengthen the resilience of health care systems, is fully aligned with the plan for self-sufficiency in health matters of the Economic Commission for Latin America and the Caribbean (ECLAC), which was unanimously approved by the heads of state and government in September 2021 (ECLAC, 2021[102]). The ECLAC plan stands out as a framework for co-operation and action across three areas. First, it defines a multilateral approach to enhancing investment in the health sector and promoting regional productive capacities. Second, it sets a vision for integrating health and productive development. Third, it identifies and prioritises high-impact projects that are feasible to implement in the short term.

Figure 5.12. **Global Gateway Investment Agenda: Number of projects by country and sector**

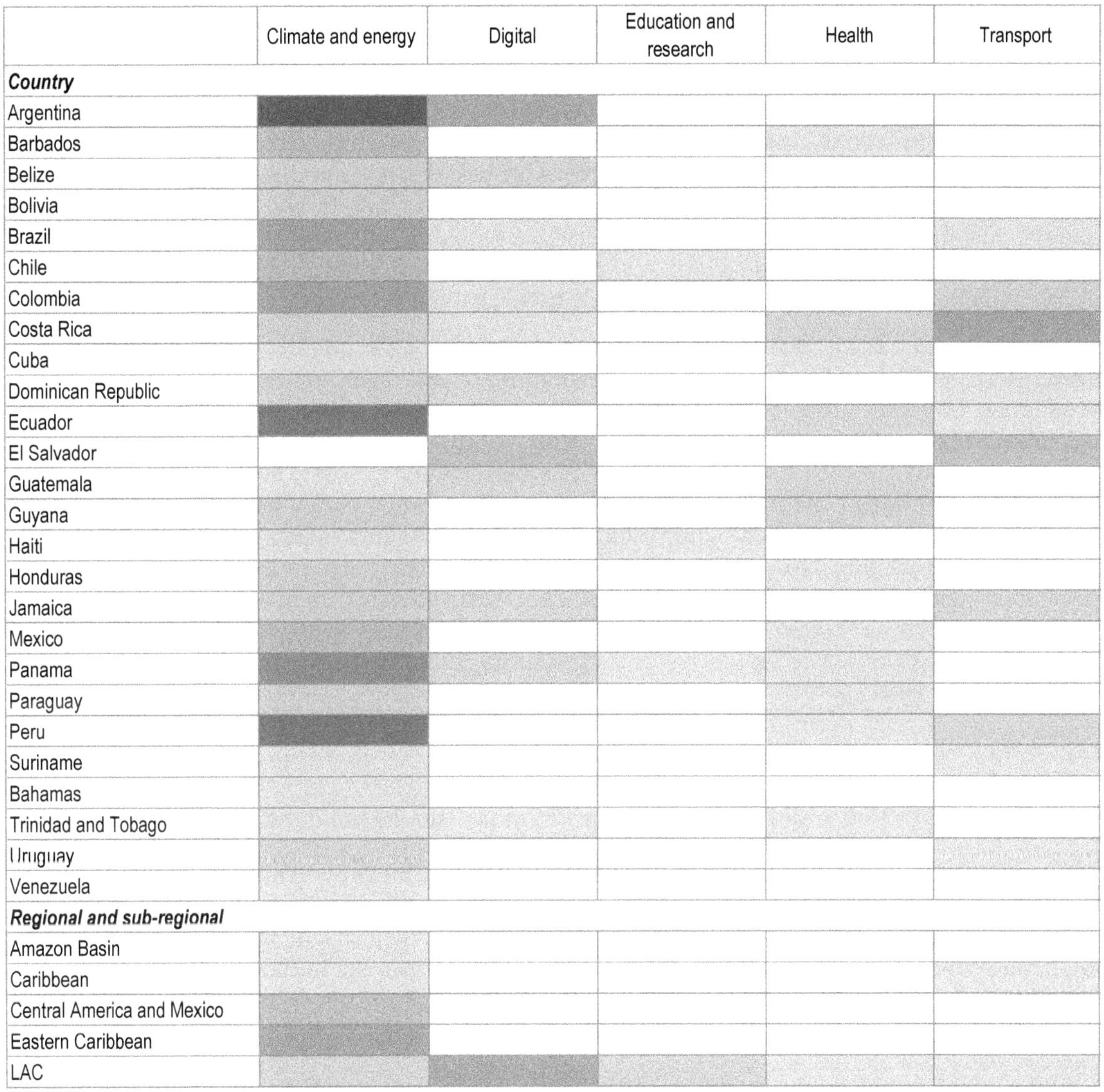

Note: The figure shows the total number of projects by country published by the European Commission. Darker blue shows a higher number of projects (lightest blue = 1 project; darkest blue =7 projects). In addition to the number of projects shown at country level, the number of projects at the regional and subregional level is also included in the Amazon Basin, Caribbean, Central America and Mexico, Eastern Caribbean and LAC regions.

Source: (European Commission, 2023[103]).

StatLink https://stat.link/5op6t9

The transformation of the EU's economic and social model – based on just green and digital transitions – presents an opportunity for exchange with LAC countries in support of their own transformation. The Global Gateway is an important tool in this sense. It needs to be accompanied with political (and policy) dialogue, as well as the necessary adaptation to the region's specific structural conditions and mitigation of potential costs. The July 2023 EU-CELAC Summit marked a turning point in this alliance, showing renewed commitment at the highest political level to pursue joint endeavours across the regions. During the meeting, the IDB, CAF and the European Commission co-hosted an

EU-LAC Business Roundtable, a key step in involving the private sector in the bi-regional partnership towards a production transformation.

Greater policy exchange and dialogue would foster stronger ties, paving the way for the production transformation that LAC countries aspire to achieve. An agenda in which trade, investment and co-operation generate mutual benefits should be based on stronger dialogue, broader and innovative sources of finance, and evidence-based policy recommendations, as well as co-ordination between national and regional levels. Renewed mechanisms of co-ordination and alignment with national development strategies are crucial for ensuring that investments flows follow shared criteria on quality, sustainability and inclusiveness. These mechanisms will need to bring together the investment, trade, and development communities, and ensure that the process accompanying LAC's reindustrialisation aligns with national priorities.

Technical exchanges on smart specialisation strategies – e.g. economic transformation agendas or productive development polices – can be of strategic importance for LAC's production transformation. Such exchanges can contribute to sustainable development by promoting competitiveness and innovation in different regions and reducing territorial inequalities (Di Cataldo, Monastiriotis and Rodríguez-Pose, 2022[104]; Halleux, 2016[105]). The European Union has implemented this innovative policy approach, which could be usefully applied in LAC countries with high subregional economic disparities (UTEC, 2021[106]). Within LAC, Chile's Production Development Corporation (CORFO) has developed such policies. The European Union is currently advising its member countries on how to adapt their strategies to the needs of industrial policies to align with the green and digital transitions. The EU bloc recently joined forces with the LAC region in a new digital alliance (Box 5.6).

Box 5.6. EU-LAC Digital Alliance: A joint effort to close the digital divide in LAC

The European Union-Latin America and the Caribbean (EU-LAC) Digital Alliance (launched in March 2023) seeks to boost digital co-operation between the two regions through concrete actions that promote the development of digital infrastructure and the convergence of policies and regulations that guarantee the protection of human rights online. The initiative is part of Europe's Global Gateway strategy for trusted links with partner countries to contribute to the development of LAC economies and societies. It will rely for co-ordination on Europe's Digital Development Hub (D4D) and ECLAC.

Projects to be developed in the framework of the EU-LAC Digital Alliance are: i) extend the BELLA fibre optic cable connecting Europe and Latin America to create secure digital backbone connectivity and bring researchers from both regions closer together; ii) enhance the Copernicus regional strategy, with regional Copernicus data centres in Panama and Chile; iii) create an EU-LAC Digital Accelerator to boost competitiveness and innovation in the digital field; and iv) strengthen and consolidate a permanent dialogue space between the two regions on issues of meaningful connectivity, regulatory frameworks, governance, cybersecurity and digital transformation.

The EU-LAC Digital Alliance aims to strengthen the institutional capacities of LAC countries and support the production transformation based on digitisation and innovation in the region. It is expected to help LAC countries to close digital gaps and divides, promote social cohesion, boost gender and racial equality, improve youth empowerment, and establish an inclusive digital society and economy that leaves no one behind.

Source: (ECLAC, 2023[107]); (European Commission, 2023[108]).

Policy exchanges on the green transition and international green standards can also benefit both regions. With the EU Green Deal entering into force, the European Union will have regulations on imports of agricultural and agro-industrial goods. The EU's regulatory framework on pesticides and fertilisers, as well as the deforestation-free standards entering into force, will have important effects on the EU-LAC trade balance. Partner countries will need to invest important resources to comply with these regulations and will need to update current processes to new international standards. LAC countries are already advancing in updating their regulations and establishing traceability processes. For instance, a bill is moving forward in Colombia's national congress that seeks to combat deforestation by making beef traceability mandatory, i.e. to monitor livestock to ensure that it is not sourced from illegally deforested areas (Tarazona, 2022[109]). The potential adoption of such a law would put Colombia at the forefront of green regulations and would allow agri-food products to comply with EU requirements in future. Within the framework of a strengthened partnership, it will be crucial for the European Union to provide technical and financial assistance to LAC countries so they can meet the new, more stringent requirements to access the EU market.

The sharing of strategic priorities by LAC and EU countries is an opportunity to build a mutually beneficial alliance around priority areas such as the three transitions: green, digital and social. While distinct, the goals of each transition are complementary, and their paths to realisation intersect.

Key policy messages

International co-operation and partnerships have become crucial in LAC for fostering more and better investments for the production transformation. At a time when a series of mutually reinforcing crises – including climate change, the COVID-19 pandemic, the disruption of global value chains and the war in Ukraine – have fragmented the multilateral system, a co-ordinated response is imperative. The triple transition – green, digital and social – brings an opportunity for LAC to strengthen international partnerships and to build new models of sustainable growth and development to ensure that the region does not fall behind in this new industrialisation agenda. Key policy messages (Box 5.7) highlight how international partnerships can help to:

- overcome the development financial gap by mobilising private-sector capital;
- ensure that investments yield greater social impacts; and
- promote and support regional integration.

These policy messages provide overarching considerations to help LAC countries implement their own policy mix for attracting FDI – and other investment – that drives the production transformation in a sustainable and just way.

Box 5.7. **Key policy messages**

Promote further co-ordination and alignment to mobilise greater and better resources for investment

- Enhance co-ordination among governments, the private sector, international co-operation agencies, MDBs and DFIs through platforms for dialogue and information exchange. This can help to mobilise further private investments that align with national and subnational priorities under the development of strategy agendas, and contribute to improving the region's enabling environment for investment.

Box 5.7. **Key policy messages** *(cont.)*

- Make greater use of mobilisation instruments such as blended finance, which can be used to reduce perceived risk for institutional investors for investment projects in LAC.
- Align national policy frameworks to international standards including taxonomies, international policy instruments or multilateral agreements to create a common understanding and due diligence for private capital mobilisation.
- Assess the potential benefits of introducing new or alternative approaches to investment treaties to ensure that they respect environmental standards, labour rights and social welfare.
- Promote support for capacity building and technology transfer linked to investments in key strategic sectors. This includes further support for national and local IPAs and local financial institutions to align sustainable finance with national priorities.
- Promote the creation of spaces for discussion among national and local IPAs, in support of strategic sectors for investments, involving civil society and local actors, to align investment with national priorities.
- Incorporate local content requirements in international investment agreements to create linkages with domestic SMEs and foster the needed value chains in context-specific investments. This can enhance the social and economic impact of investments, strengthening the development of local supply chains and labour productivity.

Towards revitalised regional integration

- Strengthen intra-regional integration, in particular production integration, to create a large and stable market that enables economies of scale, with reduced transaction costs along with regional infrastructure. This can be accomplished via strategic public procurement, regulatory harmonisation, trade facilitation measures and production development policies that directly target regional integration.
- Give due attention to the regionalisation of trade and production networks, and orient international partnerships towards supporting this effort. This is vital in the quest for greater strategic autonomy in the sourcing of key products and inputs.
- Increase co-operation and policy dialogue with the European Union and other strategic partners, to foster regional integration in LAC that is adapted to the current context of increasing demand for critical raw materials and the need to upgrade value chains in the region.

Towards a new strategic alliance with the European Union

- Strengthen policy exchange and dialogue between LAC and the European Union through the EU Global Gateway Investment Agenda to promote trade and quality investments across the two regions. Such co-operation includes the EU-LAC association for the local manufacture of vaccines, medicines and other health technologies; technical exchanges on smart specialisation strategies; the EU-LAC Digital Alliance; and the green transition.

Notes

1. Two databases, Convergence and OECD, provide insights into the state of blended finance globally. Convergence (Convergence, 2023[111]) data is collected from i) credible public sources like press releases, ii) data sharing agreements, and iii) validation exercises with Convergence members. To be included in Convergence's database, a deal must meet three main criteria:

1. The transaction attracts financial participation from one or more commercial investors that would otherwise not have invested in the opportunity.
2. The transaction uses catalytic capital in one of the following ways: a) Public/philanthropic investors are concessional within the capital structure; b) Public/philanthropic investor provided guarantees or risk insurance priced below market rate; c) Transaction design or preparation is grant funded; d) Transaction is associated with a Technical Assistance facility.
3. The transaction intends to create development impact related to the SDGs in developing countries, or directly impacts beneficiaries in developing countries.

See note 2 for information on the OECD database.

2. The OECD has developed an international standard for measuring and collecting data on the amounts mobilised from the private sector by official development interventions (OECD.Stat, 2023[35]). Referred to as the "Mobilisation database", it describes the causal link between private finance made available for a specific project and an official intervention. Data are collected following instrument-specific methodologies, covering all leveraging mechanisms used by DFIs and MDBs: guarantees, syndicated loans, project finance schemes, shares in collective investment vehicles, direct investment in companies, credit lines and simple co-financing.

References

Almaguer, F. and A. Davidson (2023), *Impact Investing in Latin America: Trends 2020-2021*, Aspen Network of Development Entrepreneurs, Washington, DC, https://andeglobal.org/wp-content/uploads/2023/06/latam-report-2023-v8.pdf. [24]

Alvarez Pagliuca, C. et al. (2022), *Sustainable financing of economic and social infrastructure in Latin America and the Caribbean: trends, key agents, and instruments*, Inter-American Development Bank, Washington, DC, https://doi.org/10.18235/0004497. [39]

Attridge, S. and L. Engen (2019), *Blended finance in the poorest countries: The need for a better approach*, Overseas Development Institute, London, https://cdn.odi.org/media/documents/12666.pdf. [38]

Beeber, M., J. Li and J. Schulz (2022), *The Growth of Impact Investing in Latin America: Insights From Latibex Forum 2022*, Sustainlytics, https://www.sustainalytics.com/esg-research/resource/corporate-esg-blog/impact-investing-in-latin-america-insights-from-latibex-forum-2022. [60]

Bilal, S. (2021), *The rise of public development banks in the European financial architecture for development*, Elcano Royal Institute, Madrid, https://media.realinstitutoelcano.org/wp-content/uploads/2021/12/wp12-2021-bilal-rise-of-public-development-banks-in-european-financial-architecture-for-development.pdf. [76]

Bilal, S. and K. Karaki (2023), "Strengthening the European financial architecture for development through better coordination", *Discussion Paper*, No. 351, The centre for Africa-Europe relations (ECDPM), Maastricht, https://ecdpm.org/application/files/6416/8837/0523/Strengthening-European-Financial-Architecture-Development-Better-Coordination-ECDPM-Discussion-Paper-351-2023.pdf. [80]

Business & Human Rights Resource Centre (2023), *Mandatory Due Diligence*, Business & Human Rights Resource Centre, London, https://www.business-humanrights.org/en/big-issues/mandatory-due-diligence/ (accessed on 31 August 2023). [59]

CABANA (2023), "About the CABANA Network", Capacity Building for Bioinformatics in Latin America, Global Challenges Research Fund, https://cabana.network/about (accessed on 12 July 2023). [73]

CAF (2021), *Pathways to integration: trade facilitation, infrastructure, and global value chains: Executive Summary*, Development Bank of Latin America, Caracas, https://scioteca.caf.com/bitstream/handle/123456789/1823/RED%202021-Executive%20Summary.pdf?sequence=5&isAllowed=y. [88]

Chaturvedi, S. (2016), "The Development Compact: A Theoretical Construct for South-South Cooperation", *RIS Discussion Papers*, No. 203, Research and Information System for Developing Countries, New Delhi, https://www.apccolombia.gov.co/sites/default/files/2022-06/Chaturvedi%20%282016%29%20Development%20Compact.pdf. [6]

Convergence (2023), *Data Methodology (website)*, https://www.convergence.finance/about/data-methodology (accessed on 18 November 2023). [111]

Convergence (2023), *Historical Deals [database]*, https://www.convergence.finance/historical/deal/summary-analysis?sort=eyJjb2x1bW4iOiJhcHByb3ZlZF9hdCIsImRpcmVjdGlvbiI6ImRlc2MifQ%3D%3D&filters=eyJrZXl3b3JkIjpudWxsLCJkZWFsVHlwZXMiOltdLCJibGVuZGluZ0FwcHJvYWNoZXMiOltdLCJ0YWdzIjpbXSwic2VjdG9yc0FuZFN1YlNlY3Rv (accessed on 30 June 2023). [33]

Convergence (2022), *Blended Finance in Latin America & the Caribbean*, Convergence, Toronto, https://www.convergence.finance/resource/blended-finance-in-latin-america-and-the-caribbean/view. [32]

CSIS (2018), *The BUILD Act Has Passed: What's Next?*, Center for Strategic & International Studies, Washington, DC, https://www.csis.org/analysis/build-act-has-passed-whats-next (accessed on 5 May 2023). [14]

Da Costa, R. and A. Caicedo (2023), "Expandir el potencial de la alianza UE-LAC: enfoques integrados para la transición verde justa en América Latina y el Caribe", *Documentos de trabajo*, n°83 (2ª época), Fundación Carolina, Madrid, https://doi.org/10.33960/issn-e.1885-9119.DT83. [84]

Dallmann, J. (2021), *Latin America Is The New Frontier For Impact Investing*, Forbes, https://www.forbes.com/sites/jpdallmann/2021/07/18/latin-america-is-the-new-frontier-for-impact-investing/?sh=4c72d33768bb. [23]

Di Cataldo, M., V. Monastiriotis and A. Rodríguez-Pose (2022), *How 'smart' are smart specialization strategies?*, Industrial Analytics Platform, UNIDO, Vienna, https://iap.unido.org/articles/how-smart-are-smart-specialization-strategies. [104]

Dixon, J. and P. Haslam (2016), "Does the Quality of Investment Protection Affect FDI Flows to Developing Countries? Evidence from Latin America", *The World Economy*, Vol. 39/8, pp. 1080-1108, https://doi.org/10.1111/twec.12299. [68]

Durán Lima, J. and A. Pellandra (2017), "La irrupción de China y su impacto sobre la estructura productiva y comercial en América Latina y el Caribe", *Serie Comercio Internacional n°131*, https://www.cepal.org/es/publicaciones/41021-la-irrupcion-china-su-impacto-la-estructura-productiva-comercial-america-latina. [92]

EBRD (2023), "Belt and Road Initiative (BRI)", *European Bank for Reconstruction and Development*, https://www.ebrd.com/what-we-do/belt-and-road/overview.html (accessed on 30 August 2023). [7]

ECLAC (2023), *América Latina y el Caribe y la Unión Europea refuerzan sus lazos de colaboración con el lanzamiento de la Alianza Digital EU-LAC*, United Nations Economic Commission for Latin America and the Caribbean, Santiago, https://www.cepal.org/en/node/58644 (accessed on 30 August 2023). [107]

ECLAC (2023), *Foreign Direct Investment in Latin America and the Caribbean 2023*, United Nations Economic Commission for Latin America and the Caribbean, Santiago, https://repositorio.cepal.org/server/api/core/bitstreams/fd2ce029-2846-4900-a0e6-14818f6191b3/content. [22]

ECLAC (2023), *Investment and cooperation opportunities for Latin America and the Caribbean and the European Union*, United Nations Economic Commission for Latin America and the Caribbean, Santiago, https://repositorio.cepal.org/bitstream/handle/11362/48992/1/S2300117_en.pdf. [70]

ECLAC (2022), *Towards transformation of the development model in Latin America and the Caribbean: production, inclusion and sustainability*, United Nations Economic Commission for Latin America and the Caribbean, Santiago, https://www.cepal.org/en/publications/48309-towards-transformation-development-model-latin-america-and-caribbean-production. [95]

ECLAC (2021), *International Trade Outlook for Latin America and the Caribbean 2020: Regional integration is key to recovery after the crisis*, United Nations Economic Commission for Latin America and the Caribbean, Santiago, https://www.cepal.org/en/publications/46614-international-trade-outlook-latin-america-and-caribbean-2020-regional-integration. [86]

ECLAC (2021), *Plan for self-sufficiency in health matters in Latin America and the Caribbean: Lines of action and proposals*, United Nations Economic Commission for Latin America and the Caribbean, Santiago, https://repositorio.cepal.org/bitstream/handle/11362/47253/S2100556_en.pdf?sequence=1&isAllowed=y. [102]

ECLAC (2020), *Global Input-Output Tables: Tools for the analysis of the integration of Latin America with the world*, United Nations Economic Commission for Latin America and the Caribbean, Santiago, https://www.cepal.org/en/events/global-input-output-tables-tools-analysis-integration-latin-america-world (accessed on 7 July 2023). [90]

ECLAC/OECD (2018), *Emerging challenges and shifting paradigms: New approaches on international co-operation for development*, United Nations Economic Commission for Latin America and the Caribbean, Santiago, https://www.cepal.org/en/publications/44002-emerging-challenges-and-shifting-paradigms-new-perspectives-international. [99]

Eco.business Fund (2023), *Impact*, Eco.business Fund, Bertrange, https://www.ecobusiness.fund/en/impact (accessed on 1 August 2023). [43]

Eco.business Fund (2023), *The Fund*, Eco.business Fund, Bertrange, https://www.ecobusiness.fund/en/the-fund (accessed on 1 August 2023). [42]

EUCA Trade (2021), *Study on 6 priority sectors for EU Trade and Investment in Central America*, EU-Central America Association Agreement, https://trade.ec.europa.eu/access-to-markets/en/country-assets/euca_01_Study%20on%206%20priority%20sectors%20for%20EU%20trade%20and%20investment%20in%20Central%20America.pdf. [94]

European Commision (2022), "Global Gateway: EU greenlights 40 new guarantee programmes under the European Fund for Sustainable Development plus", *Press release*, European Commission, Brussels, https://ec.europa.eu/commission/presscorner/detail/en/ip_22_7799 (accessed on 29 August 2023). [19]

European Commission (2023), *EU-LAC Global Gateway Investments Agenda - Infographics*, European Commission, Brussels, https://international-partnerships.ec.europa.eu/publications/eu-lac-global-gateway-investment-agenda-infographics_en (accessed on 21 July 2023). [103]

European Commission (2023), "Global Gateway in Latin America and the Caribbean", European Commission, Brussels, https://international-partnerships.ec.europa.eu/policies/global-gateway/initiatives-region/initiatives-latin-america-and-caribbean_en (accessed on 29 August 2023). [100]

European Commission (2023), "Global Gateway: EU, Latin America and Caribbean partners launch in Colombia the EU-LAC Digital Alliance", European Commission, Brussels, https://ec.europa.eu/commission/presscorner/detail/en/ip_23_1598 (accessed on 28 August 2023). [108]

European Commission (2023), "Joint Communication To The European Parliament And The Council: A New Agenda for Relations between the EU and Latin America and the Caribbean", European Commission, Brussels, https://www.eeas.europa.eu/sites/default/files/documents/2023/JOIN_2023_17_1_EN_ACT_part1_v7.pdf. [13]

European Commission (2022), "EU-Latin America and Caribbean Partnership: manufacturing vaccines, medicines and health technologies and strengthening health systems", *Press release*, European Commission, Brussels, https://international-partnerships.ec.europa.eu/news-and-events/news/eu-latin-america-and-caribbean-partnership-manufacturing-vaccines-medicines-and-health-technologies-2022-06-22_en (accessed on 28 August 2023). [101]

European Commission (2022), "European Commission and EIB sign an Agreement to enable further investments worldwide", *Press release*, European Commission, Brussels, https://ec.europa.eu/commission/presscorner/detail/en/IP_22_2870 (accessed on 1 August 2023). [18]

European Commission (2022), "European Fund for Sustainable Development Plus (EFSD+)", European Commission, Brussels, https://international-partnerships.ec.europa.eu/funding-and-technical-assistance/funding-instruments/european-fund-sustainable-development-plus-efsd_en (accessed on 12 July 2023). [12]

Faty Dembele, T. (2022), "Blended finance funds and facilities: 2020 survey results", *OECD Development Co-operation Working Papers*, No. 107, OECD Publishing, Paris, https://doi.org/10.1787/fb282f7e-en. [34]

fDi Markets (2023), *fDi Markets: the in-depth crossborder investment monitor from the Financial Times*, https://www.fdimarkets.com/ (accessed on 11 July 2023). [98]

FICS (2022), *Finance in Common Progress Report to the G20*, Finance in Common, https://financeincommon.org/sites/default/files/2022-10/FICS%20Progress%20Report%20to%20the%20G20%2C%20July%202022_0.pdf (accessed on 29 September 2023). [75]

Freymann, E. and A. García-Herrero (2022), "A new kind of Belt and Road Initiative after the pandemic", *Bruegel Blog*, https://www.bruegel.org/blog-post/new-kind-belt-and-road-initiative-after-pandemic. [9]

Gaukrodger, D. (2021), "The future of investment treaties - possible directions", *OECD Working Papers on International Investment*, No. 2021/03, OECD Publishing, Paris, https://doi.org/10.1787/946c3970-en. [69]

GPEDC (2019), *Kampala Principles on Effective Private Sector Engagement in Development Co-operation*, Global Partnership for Effective Development Co-operation, https://effectivecooperation.org/system/files/2019_07/Kampala%20Principles%20-%20final.pdf. [5]

Halleux, V. (2016), *Smart specialisation: The concept and its application to EU cohesion policy*, European Parliament, Strasbourg, https://www.europarl.europa.eu/RegData/etudes/BRIE/2016/589813/EPRS_BRI(2016)589813_EN.pdf. [105]

Hamadeh, N., C. Van Rompaey and E. Metreau (2023), "World Bank Group country classifications by income level", *World Bank Blogs*, World Bank, Washington, DC, https://blogs.worldbank.org/opendata/new-world-bank-group-country-classifications-income-level-fy24. [26]

Hansen, U. et al. (2019), "The effects of local content requirements in auction schemes for renewable energy in developing countries: A literature review", *Renewable and Sustainable Energy Reviews*, Vol. 127, https://doi.org/10.1016/j.rser.2020.109843. [82]

Hausmann, R. (2023), "Dodgy Climate Finance", *Project Syndicate*, 30 March, https://www.project-syndicate.org/commentary/just-energy-transition-program-announcements-are-misleading-by-ricardo-hausmann-2023-03. [49]

IDB (2023), *2022 Partnership Report: Envisioning a New Future Together*, Inter-American Development Bank, Washington, DC, https://doi.org/10.18235/0004821. [44]

IDB (2023), *Amazonia Forever (website)*, Inter-American Development Bank, Washington, DC, https://www.iadb.org/en/who-we-are/topics/Amazonia (accessed on 5 October 2023). [63]

IDB (2023), *IDB's Innovative Financing Tool Rewards Results on Nature and Climate*, Inter-American Development Bank, Washington, DC, https://www.iadb.org/en/news/idbs-innovative-financing-tool-rewards-results-nature-and-climate (accessed on 27 September 2023). [47]

IDB (2023), "Mobilized by IDB and BNDES, Development Banks Launch Green Coalition for the Amazon", Inter-American Development Bank, Washington, DC, https://www.iadb.org/en/news/mobilized-idb-and-bndes-development-banks-launch-green-coalition-amazon (accessed on 7 October 2023). [64]

IDB (2022), "Barbados Places Climate Financing Firmly on Agenda with IDB, Nature Conservancy Support", Inter-American Development Bank, Washington, DC, https://www.iadb.org/en/news/barbados-places-climate-financing-firmly-agenda-idb-nature-conservancy-support. [45]

IDB/ILO (2020), *Jobs in a Net-Zero Emissions Future in Latin America and the Caribbean*, Inter-American Development Bank and International Labor Organization, Washington, DC/Geneva, Switzerland, https://www.ilo.org/wcmsp5/groups/public/---americas/---ro-lima/documents/publication/wcms_752069.pdf. [81]

IFC (2023), *DFI Working Group on Blended Concessional Finance for Private Sector Projects*, International Finance Corporation, Washington, DC, https://www.ifc.org/content/dam/ifc/doc/mgrt/2023-03-dfi-bcf-joint-report.pdf. [48]

IMF (2023), *World Economic Outlook, October 2023 database*, International Monetary Fund, Washington, DC, https://www.imf.org/en/Publications/WEO/weo-database/2023/October (accessed on 8 November 2023). [110]

Joint SDG Fund (2023), *Finance for the Sustainable Development Goals (website)*, https://www.jointsdgfund.org/sdg-financing (accessed on 28 September 2023). [74]

LACIF (2023), *Facts & figures CIF*, Latin America and Caribbean Investment Facility, Brussels, https://www.eulaif.eu/en/facts-figures-CIF (accessed on 1 August 2023). [17]

LACIF (2023), *Facts & figures LAIF*, Latin America and Caribbean Investment Facility, Brussels, https://www.eulaif.eu/en/facts-figures (accessed on 1 August 2023). [16]

LACIF (2023), *Success Story: eco.business fund for the development of sustainability in Latin America*, Latin America and Caribbean Investment Facility, Brussels, https://www.eulaif.eu/en/success-story-eco-business-fund-development-sustainability-latin-america (accessed on 30 August 2023). [41]

Maloney, W. et al. (2023), *The Promise of Integration: Opportunities in a Changing Global Economy*, Latin America and the Caribbean Economic Review, http://hdl.handle.net/10986/39612. [52]

McBride, J., N. Berman and A. Chatzky (2023), *China's Massive Belt and Road Initiative*, Council on Foreign Relations, New York, https://www.cfr.org/backgrounder/chinas-massive-belt-and-road-initiative (accessed on 31 August 2023). [11]

Ministry of Foreign Affairs of the People's Republic of China (2016), *Build a New Type of International Relations Featuring Win-Win Cooperation*, https://www.fmprc.gov.cn/mfa_eng/wjb_663304/wjbz_663308/2461_663310/201607/t20160701_468628.html (accessed on 21 July 2023). [10]

Mushemeza, E. et al. (2017), "What Matters When it Comes to Adopting Local Content? A comparative analysis of success factors in Africa and Latin America", *ACODE Policy Research Series*, No. 79, Kampala, https://www.acode-u.org/uploadedFiles/PRS79.pdf. [83]

OAS (2023), *CooperaNet*, Organization of American States, Washington, DC, https://www.oas.org/ext/en/development/cooperanet/Cooperation-Exchange (accessed on 16 August 2023). [79]

OECD (2023), *Blended Finance (website)*, OECD, Paris, https://www.oecd.org/development/financing-sustainable-development/blended-finance-principles/ (accessed on 29 August 2023). [31]

OECD (2023), *Improving the Landscape for Sustainable Infrastructure Financing*, OECD Publishing, Paris, https://doi.org/10.1787/bc2757cd-en. [65]

OECD (2023), *OECD-LAC Regional Policy Networks (website)*, OECD, Paris, https://www.oecd.org/latin-america/regional-programme/regional-policy-networks/ (accessed on 29 August 2023). [67]

OECD (2023), *Private finance mobilised by official development finance interventions*, OECD Publishing, Paris, https://www.oecd.org/dac/2023-private-finance-odfi.pdf. [4]

OECD (2023), *Table 25: ODA Receipts and Selected Indicators for Developing Countries and Territories [database]*, OECD, https://webfs.oecd.org/oda/ReadymadeTables/EN/Table25_EN.xlsx (accessed on 13 September 2023). [28]

OECD (2022), *FDI Qualities Guide for Development Co-operation: Strengthening the Role of Development Co-operation for Sustainable Investment*, OECD Development Policy Tools, OECD Publishing, Paris, https://doi.org/10.1787/7f251bac-en. [30]

OECD (2022), *Global Outlook on Financing for Sustainable Development 2023: No Sustainability Without Equity*, OECD Publishing, Paris, https://doi.org/10.1787/fcbe6ce9-en. [3]

OECD (2022), *Responsible Business Conduct in the Financial Sector in Latin America and the Caribbean*, OECD Publishing, Paris, https://mneguidelines.oecd.org/responsible-business-conduct-in-the-financial-sector-in-latin-america-and-the-caribbean.pdf. [56]

OECD (2022), *The role of sustainability initiatives in mandatory due diligence*, Background note on Regulatory Developments concerning Due Diligence for Responsible Business Conduct, http://mneguidelines.oecd.org/the-role-of-sustainability-initiatives-in-mandatory-due-diligence-note-for-policy-makers.pdf. [57]

OECD (2021), *OECD Implementation Handbook for Quality Infrastructure Investment: Supporting a Sustainable Recovery from the COVID-19 Crisis*, https://www.oecd.org/finance/OECD-Implementation-Handbook-for-Quality-Infrastructure-Investment.htm. [66]

OECD (2020), *OECD Investment Policy Reviews: Egypt 2020*, OECD Investment Policy Reviews, OECD Publishing, Paris, https://doi.org/10.1787/9f9c589a-en. [78]

OECD (2019), "FDI Qualities Indicators: Measuring the sustainable development impacts of investment", OECD, Paris, https://www.oecd.org/investment/FDI-Qualities-Indicators-Measuring-Sustainable-Development-Impacts.pdf. [53]

OECD (2018), "OECD Due Diligence Guidance for Responsible Business Conduct", OECD, Paris, https://mneguidelines.oecd.org/OECD-Due-Diligence-Guidance-for-Responsible-Business-Conduct.pdf. [55]

OECD (2015), *Policy Framework for Investment, 2015 Edition*, OECD Publishing, Paris, https://doi.org/10.1787/9789264208667-en. [54]

OECD.Stat (2023), *Mobilisation [database]*, OECD.Stat, https://stats.oecd.org/Index.aspx?DataSetCode=DV_DCD_MOBILISATION (accessed on 23 May 2023). [35]

OECD et al. (2019), *Latin American Economic Outlook 2019: Development in Transition*, OECD Publishing, Paris, https://doi.org/10.1787/g2g9ff18-en. [21]

OECD/UNCDF (2020), *Blended Finance in the Least Developed Countries 2020: Supporting a Resilient COVID-19 Recovery*, OECD Publishing, Paris, https://doi.org/10.1787/57620d04-en. [29]

OHCHR (2023), *Mandatory Human Rights Due Diligence (mHRDD)*, Office of the United Nations High Commissioner for Human Rights, Geneva, https://www.ohchr.org/en/business-and-human-rights/mandatory-human-rights-due-diligence-mhrdd (accessed on 30 August 2023). [58]

Oxfam (2019), "Faith is Not Enough: Ensuring that aid donor-private sector partnerships contribute to sustainable development", *Briefing Paper*, Oxfam, https://policy-practice.oxfam.org/resources/faith-is-not-enough-ensuring-that-aid-donor-private-sector-partnerships-contrib-620839/. [51]

Oxfam/Eurodad (2017), "Blended Finance: What it is, how it works and how it is use", *Research Report*, Oxfam and European Network on Debt and Development, https://www.eurodad.org/blended_finance_what_it_is_how_it_works_and_how_it_is_used. [50]

Pérez, G. and R. Sánchez (2019), *Logistics for production, distribution and trade*, Economic Commission for Latin America and the Caribbean, Santiago, https://www.cepal.org/en/publications/44899-logistics-production-distribution-and-trade. [91]

Peter Lankes, H. and A. Prizzon (2023), *Multilateral development bank reform can – and must – benefit both low- and middle-income countries*, Overseas Development Institute, London, https://odi.org/en/insights/multilateral-development-bank-reform-can-and-must-benefit-both-low-and-middle-income-countries/. [20]

REIF (2023), *Fondo de Innovación en Energías Renovables (website)*, https://reifuruguay.org.uy/ (accessed on 30 August 2023). [36]

Reuters (2023), "Natural evolution: Record Galapagos deal sparks clamour for eco-friendly debt swaps", 11 June, Reuters, https://www.reuters.com/business/environment/natural-evolution-record-galapagos-deal-sparks-clamour-eco-friendly-debt-swaps-2023-06-09/. [46]

Sanahuja, J. (2022), "El Pacto Verde, NextGenerationEU y la nueva Europa geopolítica", *Documentos de Trabajo*, No. 63 (2ª época), Fundación Carolina, Madrid, https://doi.org/10.33960/issn-e.1885-9119.DT63. [2]

Sánchez-Martín, M., R. de Arce and G. Escribano (2014), "Do changes in the rules of the game affect FDI flows in Latin America? A look at the macroeconomic, institutional and regional integration determinants of FDI", *European Journal of Political Economy*, Vol. 34, pp. 279-299, https://doi.org/10.1016/j.ejpoleco.2014.02.001. [87]

Schwartz, J. and M. Arévalo-Carpenter (2021), *Impact investing in Latin America and addressing the 'missing middle'*, World Economic Forum, Cologny, Switzerland, https://www.weforum.org/agenda/2021/03/impact-investing-for-latin-america-s-great-reset-addressing-the-missing-middle. [25]

SICE (2023), *Americas Partnership for Economic Prosperity*, Organization of American States, Washington, DC, http://www.sice.oas.org/TPD/Americas_Partnership/Americas_Partnership_e.asp (accessed on 30 August 2023). [15]

SIFEM (2023), *Central America Small Enterprise Investment Fund IV*, Swiss Investment Fund for Emerging Markets, Geneva, https://sifem.ch/investments/portfolio/detail/central-american-small-enterprise-investment-fund-iv (accessed on 12 July 2023). [40]

Sorescu, S. and C. Bollig (2022), "Trade facilitation reforms worldwide: State of play in 2022", *OECD Trade Policy Papers*, No. 263, OECD Publishing, Paris, https://doi.org/10.1787/ce7af2ce-en. [96]

Steenbergen, V. (2023), "What Makes an Investment Promotion? Findings from a Structural Gravity Model", *Policy Research Working Paper*, N° 10276, World Bank Group, https://doi.org/10.1596/1813-9450-10276. [77]

Stroe, O. (2017), "Bioinformatics in Latin America", in *Bioinformatics in Latin America*, European Molecular Biology Laboratory, https://www.embl.org/news/lab-matters/bioinformatics-latin-america/. [72]

Tarazona, D. (2022), *Colombia: avanza proyecto de ley para combatir la deforestación al regular procedencia de la carne*, Mongabay, Menlo Park, CA, https://es.mongabay.com/2022/12/avanza-proyecto-para-combatir-deforestacion-al-regular-procedencia-de-carne-en-colombia/. [109]

UN Comtrade (2023), *International Trade Statistics Database*, https://comtrade.un.org/ (accessed on 30 August 2023). [93]

UNASUR (2023), *Integration Priority Project Agenda (API)*, Union of South American Nations, Buenos Aires, https://iirsa.org/en/Page/Detail?menuItemId=95 (accessed on 30 August 2023). [97]

UNCTAD (2023), *International Investment Agreements Navigator (database)*, United Nations Conference on Trade and Development, Geneva, https://investmentpolicy.unctad.org/international-investment-agreements/advanced-search (accessed on 23 June 2023). [71]

UNCTAD (2022), *World Investment Report 2022: International Tax Reforms and Sustainable Investment*, United Nations Conference on Trade and Development, United Nations Publications, Geneva, https://unctad.org/system/files/official-document/wir2022_en.pdf. [61]

UNCTADStat (2023), *UNCTADStat database*, United Nations Conference on Trade and Development, Geneva, https://unctadstat.unctad.org/wds/ReportFolders/reportFolders.aspx?sCS_ChosenLang=en (accessed on 30 August 2023). [89]

UNDP (2022), *Our Voices from Below: Diagnosis of the Results of the "Sembrando Vida (Sowing Life) and Jóvenes Construyendo el Futuro (Young People Building the Future)" projects in their Beneficiaries in El Salvador and Honduras*, United Nations Environment Program, Nairobi, https://www.undp.org/sites/g/files/zskgke326/files/2023-01/Diagnostico_SV_CF_2022.en_.pdf. [85]

UNIDO (2022), "Through the Renewable Energy Innovation Fund (REIF), UNIDO and its partners will support Uruguay´s 2nd energy transition by decarbonizing the transportation and industry sectors", United Nations Industrial Development Organization, Vienna, https://www.unido.org/news/through-renewable-energy-innovation-fund-reif-unido-and-its-partners-will-support-uruguays-2nd-energy-transition-decarbonizing-transportation-and-industry-sectors. [37]

United Nations (2023), *The Sustainable Development Goals Report 2023*, Department of Economic and Social Affairs (DESA), United Nations, New York, https://unstats.un.org/sdgs/report/2023/The-Sustainable-Development-Goals-Report-2023.pdf (accessed on 29 August 2023). [1]

UTEC (2021), "Qué es la Estrategia de Especialización Inteligente (EEI) (website)", Universidad Tecnológica, https://utec.edu.uy/es/noticia/que-es-la-estrategia-de-especializacion-inteligente-eei/. [106]

Vadell, J., G. Brutto and A. Leite (2020), "The Chinese South-South development cooperation: an assessment of its structural transformation", *Revista Brasileira De Politica Internacional*, Vol. 63, https://www.scielo.br/j/rbpi/a/7bGWCPphHqQZT7wKDg3SLgw/?lang=en. [8]

World Bank (2023), *World Development Indicators (database)*, World Bank Group, Washington, DC, https://databank.worldbank.org/source/world-development-indicators (accessed on 19 September 2023). [27]

World Bank (2022), *Colombia: Leading the Path to Sustainability in Latin America*, The World Bank, Washington, DC, https://www.worldbank.org/en/news/feature/2022/08/31/colombia-leading-the-path-to-sustainability-in-latin-america. [62]

Annex 5.A.

Table 5.A.1. Number of types of products exported to selected destinations, 2021

	LAC	United States	EU-27	China
Argentina	3 352	1 388	1 479	409
Barbados	671	433	98	13
Belize	85	76	25	1
Bolivia	569	240	225	64
Brazil	4 358	3 311	3 730	1 968
Chile	3 260	1 311	1 391	364
Colombia	3 292	2 022	1 380	234
Costa Rica	2 869	2 015	950	182
Cuba	268	3	373	46
Ecuador	2 267	1 344	789	161
El Salvador	2 412	1 076	567	69
Guatemala	3 536	1 449	741	130
Guyana	769	525	175	40
Honduras	1 823	1 083	364	39
Jamaica	382	348	82	20
Mexico	1 448	2 858	503	361
Nicaragua	1 852	974	255	52
Panama	271	144	64	30
Paraguay	1 388	431	397	106
Peru	3 294	1 867	1 555	266
Dominican Rep.	2 362	2 278	1 288	135
Trinidad and Tobago	1 769	295	508	27
Uruguay	1 490	567	519	140
Venezuela	958	266	613	63
LAC total	**44 745**	**26 304**	**18 071**	**4 920**

Note: Products are defined at the 6-digit level of the Harmonised Commodity Description and Coding System. Data for Cuba, Trinidad and Tobago and Venezuela (Bol. Rep. of) were calculated from mirror statistics. Data for Argentina correspond to 2017. Boxes shaded in light blue correspond to the destination to which the largest quantity of products was exported.

Source: UN Comtrade, International Trade Statistics Database, https://comtrade.un.org/.

Country notes

- Argentina
- Brazil
- Chile
- Colombia
- Costa Rica
- Dominican Republic
- Ecuador
- El Salvador
- Guatemala
- Mexico
- Panama
- Paraguay
- Peru
- Uruguay

READER'S GUIDE

The statistical tables follow key areas identified in the *Latin American Economic Outlook (LEO)*: 1) socio-economic dimension; 2) productivity and innovation; 3) investment and production transformation; 4) citizens' perceptions and institutions; and 5) fiscal position.

Latin America and the Caribbean (LAC) average is a simple average of the largest set of LAC countries for which data are available.

Organisation for Economic Co-operation and Development (OECD) average is a simple average of the largest set of all OECD member countries for which data were available as of July 2023.

To ensure comparability between years, countries for which data are not available for both years of comparison have been excluded from the averages. Exceptions to this are mentioned in the notes.

Applying the same criteria as in previous LEO editions, data selection prioritises comparability across LAC countries and shows the latest comparable data available at the report's publication date.

Social dimension

Extreme poverty:[1] refers to the share (%) of the population whose average per-capita income is below the extreme poverty line, as specified by the United Nations Economic Commission for Latin America and the Caribbean. Method of computation: "n" is defined as the total number of persons and "i" is the number of people whose per-capita income is below the extreme poverty line; the percentage of people living in extreme poverty is expressed as I=(i/n)x100 (known as "headcount index"). The average per-capita income (yPC) is calculated by dividing the total income of each household by the number of people forming it. Data from ECLAC (2023[1]), *Social Panorama of Latin America and the Caribbean*, https://repositorio.cepal.org/server/api/core/bitstreams/a4d96610-6048-4044-bf89-2eb3c31fc369/content.

Poverty:[1] refers to the share (%) of the population whose average per-capita income is below the poverty line, as specified by the United Nations Economic Commission for Latin America and the Caribbean. Method of computation: "n" is the total number of people and "p" is the number of people whose per-capita income is below the poverty line; the percentage of people living in poverty is expressed as P=(p/n)x100. This indicator includes people under the extreme poverty line, by definition. The average per-capita income (yPC) is calculated by dividing the total income of each household by the number of people forming it. Data from ECLAC (2023[1]), *Social Panorama of Latin America and the Caribbean*, https://repositorio.cepal.org/server/api/core/bitstreams/a4d96610-6048-4044-bf89-2eb3c31fc369/content.

Gini index:[2] measures the extent to which the distribution of income (or, in some cases, consumption expenditure) among individuals or households within an economy deviates from a perfectly equal distribution. A Gini index of zero represents perfect equality; an index of 100 represents perfect inequality. Data from (World Bank, 2023[2]), *World Bank Open Data*, https://data.worldbank.org/indicator/SI.POV.GINI.

Share of internet users: measures people with access to the internet from any location in the last three months as a percentage of the total population. It includes access via a computer, mobile phone, personal digital assistant, games machine, digital TV, etc. Data from (International Telecommunication Union, 2023[3]), *Global ICT Statistics*, www.itu.int/en/ITU-D/Statistics/Pages/stat/default.aspx.

Share of total population in informal households overall and by quintile:[3] provides the distribution of the total population living in informal households overall and by quintile. An informal household has all its workers in informal work. Quintiles are based on monthly total household consumption or income. Data from (OECD, 2023[4]), *Key Indicators of Informality based on Individuals and their Households (KIIbIH) database*, www.oecd.org/dev/key-indicators-informality-individuals-household-kiibih.htm.

SIGI index: measures discrimination against women in social institutions (e.g. formal and informal laws, social norms, and practices). Lower values indicate lower levels of discrimination in social institutions: the SIGI ranges from 0% for no discrimination to 100% for very high discrimination. Data from (OECD, 2023[5]), *Social Institutions and Gender Index (SIGI)*, https://stats.oecd.org/Index.aspx?DataSetCode=SIGI2019.

PISA score in science:[4] indicates the mean score in science performance as measured by the Programme for International Student Assessment (PISA) for each country. Scientific performance measures the scientific literacy of a 15-year-old in the use of scientific knowledge to identify questions, acquire new knowledge, explain scientific phenomena and draw evidence-based conclusions about science-related issues. Data from (OECD, 2023[6]), *Science performance (PISA) indicator*, https://data.oecd.org/pisa/science-performance-pisa.htm#indicator-chart.

Productivity and innovation

Labour productivity: estimation that measures output per employed person as a percentage of United States output per employed person (in 2022 international USD, converted using purchasing power parities). Data from (The Conference Board, 2023[7]), *Total Economy Database*, www.conference-board.org/data/economydatabase/totaleconomy-database-productivity.

High-technology exports:[5] measures exports of products with high research and development (R&D) intensity as a percentage of total manufactured exports. Data from (World Bank, 2023[2]), *World Bank Open Data*, https://data.worldbank.org/indicator/TX.VAL.TECH.MF.ZS.

Research and development expenditure:[6] measures capital and current expenditures as a percentage of GDP in four main sectors: business enterprise, government, higher education and private non-profit. R&D covers basic research, applied research and experimental development. Data from (World Bank, 2023[2]), *World Bank Open Data*, https://data.worldbank.org/indicator/GB.XPD.RSDV.GD.ZS

Investment and production transformation

Total investment:[7] measures the gross fixed capital formation (GFCF) as a percentage of GDP. GFCF includes land improvements (fences, ditches, drains, etc.); plant, machinery, and equipment purchases; and the construction of roads, railways, and the like (including schools, offices, hospitals, private residential dwellings, and commercial and industrial buildings). According to the 1993 SNA, net acquisitions of valuables are also considered capital formation. Data from (World Bank, 2023[2]), *World Bank Open Data*, https://data.worldbank.org/indicator/NE.GDI.FTOT.ZS.

Foreign direct investment (FDI):[8] measures the net inflows of investment to acquire a lasting management interest (10% or more of voting stock) in an enterprise operating in an economy other than that of the investor as a percentage of GDP. It is the sum of equity capital, reinvestment of earnings, other long-term capital, and short-term capital as shown in the balance of payments. This series shows net inflows (new investment inflows less disinvestment) in the reporting economy from foreign investors and is divided by GDP. Data from (World Bank, 2023[2]), *World Bank Open Data*, https://data.worldbank.org/indicator/BX.KLT.DINV.WD.GD.ZS.

Private investment: measures private GFCF as a percentage of GDP. Private GFCF was derived as the residual of total GFCF and general government GFCF. Data from (International Monetary Fund, 2023[8]), *IMF Data*, https://data.imf.org/?sk=388dfa60-1d26-4ade-b505-a05a558d9a42.

Public investment in economic infrastructure:[9] measures resources for investment in economic infrastructure: water and sanitation, flood defences, energy, irrigation, telecommunications, and transport. It considers investment by the public sector, including both non-financial public enterprises and general government, the latter of which may comprise three or more levels of government (central; state, provincial or regional; and local). Data from (Infralatam, 2023[9]), *Data on Public Investment in Economic Infrastructure in LAC*, http://infralatam.info/.

Citizens' perceptions and institutions

Share (%) of population who perceive FDI as beneficial: percentage of respondents answering that "foreign investment is beneficial" to the question: Do you consider foreign investment to be beneficial or detrimental to the economic development of the country or do you not know enough to give an opinion? Data from (Latinobarómetro, 2023[10]), *Opinión Pública Latinoamericana*, www.latinobarometro.org/latOnline.jsp.

Share (%) of population who consider that, in general, domestic products are of lower quality than imported ones: percentage of respondents who agree or strongly agree with the following statement: In general, domestic products are of lower quality than imported products. Data from (Latinobarómetro, 2023[10]), *Opinión Pública Latinoamericana*, www.latinobarometro.org/latOnline.jsp.

Corruption Perception Index: measures citizens' perceptions of the levels of local corruption in their country, where 0 is completely corrupt and 100 is totally clean. Data from (Transparency International, 2023[11]), *Corruption Perception Index*, www.transparency.org/en/cpi/2022.

Security Risks Indicator: considers the security threats to a state, such as bombings, attacks and battle-related deaths, rebel movements, mutinies, coups, or terrorism. The Security Risks Index also considers serious criminal factors, such as organised crime and homicides, and the perceived trust of citizens in domestic security. 0 means low security risks and 10 means high security risks. Data from (The Fund for Peace, 2023[12]), *Fragile States Index*, https://fragilestatesindex.org/global-data/.

Science and technology: average reaction to the statement "Because of science and technology, there will be more opportunities for the next generations," where 1 is completely disagree and 10 is completely agree. Data from (World Values Survey, 2023[13]), *Online Data Analysis*, www.worldvaluessurvey.org/WVSOnline.jsp.

Education: share (%) of population who worry (very much or a great deal) about not being able to provide a good education for their children. Data from (World Values Survey, 2023[13]), *Online Data Analysis*, www.worldvaluessurvey.org/WVSOnline.jsp.

Fiscal position

Total tax revenues:[10] measures total tax revenues as a percentage of GDP. Data from (OECD, 2022[14]), *Revenue Statistics in Latin America and the Caribbean 2022*, https://stats.oecd.org/Index.aspx?DataSetCode=RS_GBL.

Environmentally related tax revenue:[11] measures the revenues from environmentally related taxes as a percentage of GDP. It includes taxes on greenhouse gas (GHG) emissions, fuel taxes, taxes on road use, forestry taxes and revenue from auctioned permits of emission trading systems for GHGs. Data from (OECD, 2023[15]), *Environmentally related tax revenue*, https://stats.oecd.org/Index.aspx?DataSetCode=ERTR.

Share of VAT (value added tax):[10] measures VAT as a percentage of GDP. Data from (OECD, 2022[14]), *Revenue Statistics in Latin America and the Caribbean 2022*, https://stats.oecd.org/Index.aspx?DataSetCode=RS_GBL.

Share of PIT (personal income tax):[10] measures taxes on the income, profits and capital gains of individuals as a percentage of GDP. Data from (OECD, 2022[14]), *Revenue Statistics in Latin America and the Caribbean 2022*, https://stats.oecd.org/Index.aspx?DataSetCode=RS_GBL.

Share of CIT (corporate income tax):[10] measures taxes on the income, profits and capital gains of corporations as a percentage of GDP. Data from (OECD, 2022[14]), *Revenue Statistics in Latin America and the Caribbean 2022*, https://stats.oecd.org/Index.aspx?DataSetCode=RS_GBL.

Perception of tax evasion: measures the share of the population, as a percentage of the adult population, that claims to have heard of people who paid less taxes than they should have. Data from (Latinobarómetro, 2023[10]), *Opinión Pública Latinoamericana*, www.latinobarometro.org/latOnline.jsp.

Social expenditure:[12] measures public social spending as a percentage of GDP. The main social policy areas are: old age, survivors, incapacity-related benefits, health, family, active labour market programmes, unemployment, housing, and other social policy areas. For OECD countries, data refer to *Social expenditure* from (OECD, 2022[14]), *Revenue Statistics in Latin America and the Caribbean 2022* OECD Data Explorer • Social expenditure aggregates. For LAC countries, data refer to *Social public expenditure* from (ECLAC, 2023[1]), CEPALSTAT, https://statistics.cepal.org/portal/cepalstat/dashboard.

Debt service: measures debt service as a percentage of tax revenue. Debt service is calculated as general government primary lending/borrowing minus general government net lending/borrowing. Authors' calculations are based on data from (International Monetary Fund, 2023[16]), *World Economic Outlook Database*, www.imf.org/en/Publications/WEO/weo-database/2023/April and (OECD, 2022[14]), *Revenue Statistics in Latin America and the Caribbean 2022*, https://stats.oecd.org/Index.aspx?DataSetCode=RS_GBL.

Notes

1. Poverty and extreme poverty: All data are national-level data, except for Argentina for which only urban-level data are available (as such, Argentina is excluded from the LAC averages). Brazil does not have an official poverty estimation. The data correspond to estimates from the Brazilian Institute of Geography and Statistics (IBGE) indicated in the source based on the lines used by the World Bank for low- and lower middle-income countries. The data for Colombia in 2021 and 2022 correspond to new series, based on the framework of the 2018 National Census of Population and Housing, and are not comparable with data from previous years. For Ecuador, the measurement by ECLAC considers the annual accumulated sample from 2021. Official data for Ecuador is based on the sample from December of each year. Weighted LAC averages for poverty and extreme poverty can be consulted in Chapter 1.
2. Gini index: For the OECD and LAC averages in 2016, data for Chile is from 2015. For the LAC average in 2021, data for Chile and Mexico are from 2020, and for Honduras are from 2019. For the OECD average in 2020: data for Iceland are from 2017; data for Australia, Canada, Israel and Switzerland are from 2018; and data for Germany, Norway, Poland and Türkiye are from 2019.
3. Informality indicators: For the averages of informality by quintiles and overall: in 2009, data for Argentina, Costa Rica, Colombia, Mexico and Peru are from 2010; data for El Salvador and Honduras

are from 2014; and data for Uruguay is from 2008. For the averages in 2021, data for Chile is from 2017; data for Argentina, Bolivia, Dominican Republic, Paraguay and Uruguay are from 2018; data for Brazil, Honduras and Peru are from 2019; and data for Costa Rica and Mexico are from 2020. Countries for which data are not available for both years of comparison have not been excluded from the averages for the indicators on the share of total population in informal households overall and by quintile.

4. PISA score in science: average for LAC and OECD countries is simple and not weighted following the scheme of replicated weights as in www.oecd.org/pisa/sitedocument/PISA-2015-Technical-Report-Chapter-8-Survey-Weighting.pdf.
5. High-technology exports: For the LAC average in 2016, data for Belize are from 2017. For the LAC average in 2021, data for St. Kitts and Nevis are from 2017; data for Antigua and Barbuda and Bahamas are from 2018; data for Honduras and St. Lucia are from 2019; and data for Costa Rica, Jamaica, Peru and Uruguay are from 2020. For the OECD average in 2021, data for Costa Rica, Ireland and Korea are from 2020.
6. Research and development expenditure: For the OECD average in 2016, data for Australia, Switzerland and New Zealand are from 2017. For the OECD and LAC averages in 2019, data for Costa Rica are from 2018.
7. Total investment: For the LAC average in 2022, data for Panama are from 2017 and data for Bolivia are from 2021. For the OECD average, data for Japan, New Zealand and the United States are from 2021.
8. Foreign direct investment: For the LAC average in 2022, data are from 2021 for Antigua and Barbuda, Barbados, Bermuda, Grenada, Guatemala, Guyana, Haiti, Panama, St. Kitts and Nevis, St. Lucia, St. Vincent and the Grenadines, and Trinidad and Tobago. For the OECD average in 2022, data for Austria, Luxembourg and Portugal are from 2021.
9. Public investment in economic infrastructure: For the LAC average in 2021, data for Brazil, Colombia, Nicaragua and Peru are from 2019; and data for Chile, Costa Rica and Mexico are from 2020.
10. Tax revenues: For the OECD average of total tax revenues in 2021, data for Australia and Japan are from 2020. For the OECD averages of the shares of VAT/PIT/CIT in 2021, data for Australia, Greece and Japan are from 2019.
11. Environmental tax revenue: For the LAC average, data for Colombia are from 2020. For the OECD average, data for Colombia, Greece and Switzerland are from 2020.
12. Social expenditure: For the LAC average in 2021, data for Bolivia, Cuba and Panama are from 2020. For the OECD average in 2021, data for Australia, Mexico and Türkiye are from 2019, and data for Canada, Costa Rica and Japan are from 2020.

References

ECLAC (2023), *Social Panorama of Latin America and the Caribbean 2023: Labour inclusion as a key axis of inclusive social development*, United Nations Economic Commission for Latin America and the Caribbean, Santiago, https://repositorio.cepal.org/server/api/core/bitstreams/a4d96610-6048-4044-bf89-2eb3c31fc369/content. [1]

Infralatam (2023), *Data on Public Investment in Economic Infrastructure in Latin America and the Caribbean*, http://infralatam.info/. [9]

International Monetary Fund (2023), *IMF Data: Access to Macroeconomic & Financial data*, https://data.imf.org/?sk=388dfa60-1d26-4ade-b505-a05a558d9a42. [8]

International Monetary Fund (2023), *World Economic Outlook Database*, https://www.imf.org/en/Publications/WEO/weo-database/2023/April. [16]

International Telecommunication Union (2023), *Statistics, International Telecommunication Union, Geneva*, https://www.itu.int/en/ITU-D/Statistics/Pages/stat/default.aspx. [3]

Latinobarómetro (2023), *Latinobarómetro: Opinión Pública Latinoamericana*, https://www.latinobarometro.org/latOnline.jsp. [10]

OECD (2023), *Key Indicators of Informality based on Individuals and their Household (KIIbIH)*, https://www.oecd.org/dev/key-indicators-informality-individuals-household-kiibih.htm. [4]

OECD (2023), *OECD.Stat*, https://stats.oecd.org/Index.aspx?DataSetCode=ERTR. [15]

OECD (2023), *Science performance (PISA)*, https://doi.org/10.1787/91952204-en (accessed on 8 September 2023). [6]

OECD (2023), *Social Institutions and Gender Index*, https://stats.oecd.org/Index.aspx?DataSetCode=SIGI2023. [5]

OECD (2022), *OECD.Stat: Revenue Statistics in Latin America and the Caribbean 2022*, https://stats.oecd.org/Index.aspx?DataSetCode=RS_GBL. [14]

The Conference Board (2023), *The Conference Board Total Economy Database™, April 2023*, http://www.conference-board.org/data/economydatabase/total-economy-database-productivity. [7]

The Fund for Peace (2023), *Fragile States Index*, https://fragilestatesindex.org/global-data/. [12]

Transparency International (2023), *Corruption Perception Index*, http://www.transparency.org/en/cpi/2022. [11]

World Bank (2023), *World Bank Open Data*, https://data.worldbank.org/. [2]

World Values Survey (2023), *World Values Survey: Online Data Analysis*, http://www.worldvaluessurvey.org/WVSOnline.jsp. [13]

ARGENTINA

1. Recent trends

Poverty in Argentina increased from 21.5% in 2016 to 30.1% in 2022, above the Latin America and the Caribbean (LAC) average of 24.1%. Extreme poverty also increased, from 2.9% in 2016 to 3.9% in 2022, yet remained below the LAC average (8.3%). The Gini index remained unchanged at 42.0 between 2016 and 2021, also below the LAC average (44.8). Regarding investment and production transformation indicators, total investment in Argentina increased from 14.3% of GDP in 2016 to 17.3% in 2022 but remained below the LAC average, which increased from 20.8% to 21.3% over the same period. Private investment, however, decreased slightly, from 8.0% of GDP to 7.7%, well below the LAC average (15.8% in 2019). Argentina's labour productivity, measured against output per employed person in the United States, decreased from 40.7% in 2016 to 34.9% in 2023, remaining above the LAC average of 27.1% in 2023. The share of exports of high-tech products in total exported manufactured goods declined in the country from 9.0% in 2016 to 4.4% in 2021, below the LAC average (7.2%). Positive perceptions of foreign direct investment (FDI), which declined across the LAC region, also fell in Argentina, from 59.3% in 2016 to 44.3% in 2020. The country's tax revenue decreased slightly from 30.7% of GDP in 2016 to 29.1% in 2021, still significantly above the regional average of 21.5%. Environment-related tax revenues decreased from 2.1% of GDP in 2016 to 1.1% in 2021.

2. Long-term policies to promote investment and production transformation

Argentina has made significant efforts **to attract and mobilise high-quality investment**, focusing mainly on facilitating access to finance for companies carrying out investment projects. It established CreAR, a credit programme for micro, small, medium and large enterprises that carry out investment projects and show potential to change the production structure by promoting development of strategic value chains, boosting exports and efficiently replacing imports. Since 2009, Argentina has also implemented a Competitiveness Support Programme for micro, small and medium enterprises (MSMEs) that co-finances, through Non-Refundable Contributions, technical assistance to companies to develop business capacities and improve their competitiveness. In line with these efforts, since 2016, Argentina has implemented the National Supplier Development Programme, which aims to develop national supplier companies in strategic sectors, boost industry, diversify the national production matrix, and promote competitiveness and production transformation.

To advance an inclusive and sustainable production model, Argentina has focused its national programme for developing industrial parks on four fundamental axes: territorial planning, promotion of local productive planning, employment generation, and encouragement of corporate and associative schemes. In 2022, the Dynamic Entrepreneurship Programme was established to facilitate the start-up of underfunded projects through granting of non-refundable contributions.

In terms of **regional and international partnerships** to support the attraction of quality investments, Argentina has established collaborative initiatives with partners both within and beyond LAC. **Within** the region, the Ministry of Science, Technology and Innovation of Argentina, together with the Ministry of Science, Technology and Innovations of Brazil, and the Ministry of Education and Culture of Uruguay, created the Latin American Biotechnology Centre. The Centre comprises a network of biotechnology research groups and promotes the implementation of joint research and development (R&D) projects and the training of high-level human resources. **Beyond** LAC, Argentina and the European Union (EU) formalised (in 2023) a memorandum of understanding focused on integrating sustainable raw materials value chains, as part of the EU's Global Gateway Initiative. Additional key goals are: develop sustainable raw materials value chains, advance R&D activities; align environment, sustainability and governance (ESG) criteria; infrastructure development; capacity building; and create quality employment to support economic growth and the clean energy transition. Argentina also participates in a co-operation agreement with Spain's Centre for the Development of Industrial Technology. This agreement finances the business projects, on a pilot and/or prototype scale, of companies involved in collaborative initiatives to develop innovative technologies with market prospects.

Key indicators – Argentina

	Argentina		LAC		OECD	
Social						
	2016	**2022**	**2016**	**2022**	**2016**	**2022**
Extreme poverty	2.9	3.9	8.1	8.3	N/A	N/A
Poverty	21.5	30.1	25.9	24.1	N/A	N/A
	2016	**2021**	**2016**	**2021**	**2016**	**2021**
Share of internet users (% of population)	71.0	87.2	54.5	74.2	81.8	89.6
	2016	**2021**	**2016**	**2021**	**2016**	**2020**
Gini index	42.0	42.0	46.3	44.8	34.1	33.6
	2010	**2018**	**2009**	**2021**	**2009**	**2021**
Share of total population in informal households (%)	34.5	36.8	44.2	46.8	N/A	N/A
Share of total population in informal households, upper-income quintile (%)	12.2	14.1	23.9	21.8	N/A	N/A
Share of total population in informal households, lower-income quintile (%)	72.8	35.0	77.6	78.5	N/A	N/A
	2019	**2023**	**2019**	**2023**	**2019**	**2023**
SIGI index	N/A	17.7	25.4	21.6	17.5	15.3
	2015	**2018**	**2015**	**2018**	**2015**	**2018**
PISA score in science	432	404	411	407	489	487
Productivity and innovation						
	2016	**2023**	**2016**	**2023**	**2016**	**2023**
Labour productivity (% of the United States)	40.7	34.9	29.3	27.1	70.0	68.5
	2016	**2021**	**2016**	**2021**	**2016**	**2021**
High-tech exports (% of manufactured exports)	9.0	4.4	8.4	7.2	16.5	16.0
	2016	**2019**	**2016**	**2019**	**2016**	**2019**
R&D expenditures (% of GDP)	0.6	0.5	0.3	0.4	1.8	2.0
Investment and production transformation						
	2016	**2022**	**2016**	**2022**	**2016**	**2022**
Total investment, gross fixed capital formation (% of GDP)	14.3	17.3	20.8	21.3	21.9	22.8
Foreign direct Investment (FDI), net capital inflow (% of GDP)	0.6	2.4	4.4	4.6	6.8	3.5
	2016	**2019**	**2016**	**2019**	**2016**	**2019**
Private investment (% of GDP)	8.0	7.7	16.1	15.8	18.2	18.8
	2016	**2021**	**2016**	**2021**	**2016**	**2021**
Public investment in economic infrastructure (% of GDP)	1.1	1.0	2.3	1.6	N/A	N/A
Citizens' perceptions and institutions						
	2016	**2020**	**2016**	**2020**	**2016**	**2020**
Share of population who perceive FDI as beneficial (%)	59.3	44.3	70.9	53.9	N/A	N/A
	2018	**2020**	**2018**	**2020**	**2018**	**2020**
Share of population who consider that, in general, domestic products are of lower quality than imported ones (%) (agreeing or strongly agreeing)	34.6	34.0	44.6	42.7	N/A	N/A
	2016	**2022**	**2016**	**2022**	**2016**	**2022**
Corruption Perception Index (score on a scale of 0 [highly corrupt] to 100 [totally clean])	36.0	38.0	41.2	40.6	67.3	66.3
Security risks indicator (score from 0 [low security risks] to 10 [high security risks])	4.0	4.6	5.9	5.6	2.8	2.6
	2010-14	**2017-22**	**2010-14**	**2017-22**	**2010-14**	**2017-22**
Belief that science and technology will create more opportunities for the next generation (score on a scale from 1 [strongly disagree] to 10 [strongly agree])	7.5	7.6	7.3	7.2	7.6	7.2
Share of population who worry (very much or a great deal) about not being able to provide a good education for their children (%)	48.0	48.0	75.4	74.0	49.8	41.4
Fiscal position						
	2016	**2021**	**2016**	**2021**	**2016**	**2021**
Total tax revenues (% of GDP)	30.7	29.1	22.0	21.5	33.6	34.1
Environmentally related tax revenue (% of GDP)	2.1	1.1	1.1	0.9	2.4	2.0
Share of VAT (% GDP)	7.1	7.0	5.9	6.1	6.6	7.0
Share of PIT (% GDP)	2.1	2.2	2.0	2.0	7.8	8.3
Share of CIT (% of GDP)	2.9	2.5	3.2	3.4	2.9	3.1
Debt service (% of total tax revenue)	6.2	6.2	11.3	12.3	5.4	5.3
Social expenditure (% of GDP)	14.2	14.6	11.3	13.3	20.1	22.0
	2016	**2020**	**2016**	**2020**	**2016**	**2019**
Perception of tax evasion (%)	N/A	34.7	N/A	27.3	N/A	N/A

Note: See the Reader's Guide for definitions and sources.

StatLink https://stat.link/1uc0ni

BRAZIL

1. Recent trends

Poverty in Brazil decreased from 20.9% in 2016 to 19.5% in 2022, below the Latin America and the Caribbean (LAC) average of 24.1%. Extreme poverty was at 5.3% in 2022, below the LAC average (8.3%). The Gini index decreased from 53.3 in 2016 to 52.9 in 2021, remaining above the LAC average (44.8). Regarding investment and production transformation indicators, total investment in Brazil increased from 15.5% of GDP in 2016 to 18.8% in 2022, following the LAC average trend, which increased from 20.8% to 21.3% over the same period. Private investment represented 14.2% of GDP, somewhat below the LAC average (15.8% in 2019). Brazil's labour productivity, measured against output per employed person in the United States, was 24.7% in 2023, below the LAC average of 27.1%. The share of exports of high-tech products in total exported manufactured goods declined from 16.0% in 2016 to 9.0% in 2021 while remaining above the LAC average (7.2%). Positive perceptions of foreign direct investment (FDI), which declined across the LAC region, also fell slightly in Brazil, from 63.4% in 2016 to 60.0% in 2020. The country's tax revenue increased from 31.6% of GDP in 2016 to 33.5% in 2021, in contrast to regional trends. Environment-related tax revenues remained almost unchanged at 0.7% in 2021.

2. Long-term policies to promote investment and production transformation

Brazil has made significant efforts **to attract and mobilise high-quality investment**, focusing mainly on stimulating the production, acquisition, and export of capital goods and technological innovation. In 2009, it established the Investment Support Programme, which operates through BNDES on-lendings. Starting in 2011, the Investment Support Programme was also operated by Finep, to support innovative projects that seek to develop new or significantly improved products and processes which involve technological risk but have market opportunities. The federal government, along with its agencies, also seeks to promote innovative businesses and start-ups through public programmes and regulations. In 2021, Brazil approved the Legal Framework for Start-ups, aiming to reduce bureaucracy for small innovative businesses. Public programmes to foster the development of start-ups include: *Inovativa Hub*, a free start-up acceleration programme; *Centelha*, to foster the creation of innovative businesses; *Garagem*, funded by BNDES, to support early and mid-stage start-ups; *Innovation Diplomacy*, from the Ministry of Foreign Affairs, to internationalise Brazilian innovation ecosystems; *Startup Outreach*, a multistakeholder programme to bring mid-to-late-stage start-ups to promising international innovation ecosystems; and *Sebrae Start-ups*, a training and acceleration programme targeted to start-ups. Regarding boosting private investment in research and development (R&D), since 2013 *EMBRAPII (Empresa Brasileira de Pesquisa e Inovação Industrial)*, a funding agency focused on building bridges between research centres and private companies, invested around USD 648 million in financing R&D projects in Brazil.

To advance an inclusive and sustainable production model, Brazil has focused its 2030 Sustainable Development Plan of the Brazilian Development Association on five missions with transformative potential: digital, smart, and inclusive future; innovation ecosystem in the bioeconomy and for the Amazon; committed agribusiness; sustainable infrastructure and cities; and health as a driver of development. In addition, the Brazilian government is actively involved in infrastructure development managed by the Special Secretariat for the Investment Partnerships Programme (SEPPI). Since 2016, over 321 projects have been completed in various sectors that align with national priorities, such as transportation, energy, 5G and healthcare. Additionally, the new *Programa de Aceleração do Crescimento* (PAC), a federal programme in partnership with various stakeholders, plans to invest BRL 1.7 trillion over four years to stimulate economic growth and reduce inequalities, focusing mainly on nine axes: inclusive social infrastructure; efficient and sustainable transportation; digital inclusion and connectivity; water for all; energy transition and security; innovation for the defence industry; education, science and technology; sustainable and resilient cities; and health.

In terms of **regional and international partnerships** to support the attraction of quality investments, Brazil has established collaborative initiatives with partners both within and beyond LAC. **Within** the region, Brazil established a training programme open to LAC countries to advance competition advocacy. The programme aims to develop and strengthen the position of the Brazilian system as a reference for competition authorities and to promote the dissemination of a competition culture in the region. Brazil and Uruguay, supported by the Development Bank of Latin America and the Caribbean (CAF), are exploring the creation of a shared waterway (*Lagoa Mirim* and *Canal de São Gonçalo/rs*), aiming to create positive economic and environmental impacts. **Beyond** the region, Brazil developed a support programme for urban development in Mozambique. The programme aims to: help elaborate housing policy; transfer non-conventional construction methodologies and technologies to create business incubators; formulate a methodology for implementing a monitoring system for construction costs and indices; and develop a project to expand the *Namialo* Technological Centre. **Beyond** the region, Brazil holds a co-operation agenda with the European Union. In the framework of the EU Global Gateway Initiative, the EU committed to invest EUR 2 billion to support Brazil's production of green hydrogen and to promote energy efficiency in the industrial sector. The EU will continue to support ongoing co-operation projects such as the *EllaLink* fibre-optic cable, co-funded by Brazil, and research and investment in biofuels and information technology.

Key indicators – Brazil

	Brazil		LAC		OECD	
Social						
	2016	**2022**	**2016**	**2022**	**2016**	**2022**
Extreme poverty	5.3	5.3	8.1	8.3	N/A	N/A
Poverty	20.9	19.5	25.9	24.1	N/A	N/A
	2016	**2021**	**2016**	**2021**	**2016**	**2021**
Share of internet users (% of population)	60.9	80.7	54.5	74.2	81.8	89.6
	2016	**2021**	**2016**	**2021**	**2016**	**2020**
Gini index	53.3	52.9	46.3	44.8	34.1	33.6
	2009	**2019**	**2009**	**2021**	**2009**	**2021**
Share of total population in informal households (%)	37.7	29.8	44.2	46.8	N/A	N/A
Share of total population in informal households, upper-income quintile (%)	20.2	7.9	23.9	21.8	N/A	N/A
Share of total population in informal households, lower-income quintile (%)	72.7	75.5	20.2	7.9	N/A	N/A
	2019	**2023**	**2019**	**2023**	**2019**	**2023**
SIGI index	21.2	21.6	25.4	21.6	17.5	15.3
	2015	**2018**	**2015**	**2018**	**2015**	**2018**
PISA score in science	401	404	411	407	489	487
Productivity and innovation						
	2016	**2023**	**2016**	**2023**	**2016**	**2023**
Labour productivity (% of the United States)	26.6	24.7	29.3	27.1	70.0	68.5
	2016	**2021**	**2016**	**2021**	**2016**	**2021**
High-tech exports (% of manufactured exports)	16.0	9.0	8.4	7.2	16.5	16.0
	2016	**2019**	**2016**	**2019**	**2016**	**2019**
R&D expenditures (% of GDP)	1.3	1.2	0.3	0.4	1.8	2.0
Investment and production transformation						
	2016	**2022**	**2016**	**2022**	**2016**	**2022**
Total investment, gross fixed capital formation (% of GDP)	15.5	18.8	20.8	21.3	21.9	22.8
Foreign direct investment (FDI), net capital inflow (% of GDP)	4.1	4.8	4.4	4.6	6.8	3.5
	2016	**2019**	**2016**	**2019**	**2016**	**2019**
Private investment (% of GDP)	13.5	14.2	16.1	15.8	18.2	18.8
	2016	**2019**	**2016**	**2021**	**2016**	**2021**
Public investment in economic infrastructure (% of GDP)	0.5	0.4	2.3	1.6	N/A	N/A
Citizens' perceptions and institutions						
	2016	**2020**	**2016**	**2020**	**2016**	**2020**
Share of population who perceives FDI as beneficial (%)	63.4	60.0	70.9	53.9	N/A	N/A
	2018	**2020**	**2018**	**2020**	**2018**	**2020**
Share of population who consider that, in general, domestic products are of lower quality than imported ones (%) (agreeing or strongly agreeing)	47.1	48.0	44.6	42.7	N/A	N/A
	2016	**2022**	**2016**	**2022**	**2016**	**2022**
Corruption Perception Index (score on a scale of 0 [highly corrupt] to 100 [totally clean])	40.0	38.0	41.2	40.6	67.3	66.3
Security risks indicator (score from 0 [low security risks] to 10 [high security risks])	6.4	6.5	5.9	5.6	2.8	2.6
	2010-14	**2017-22**	**2010-14**	**2017-22**	**2010-14**	**2017-22**
Belief that science and technology will create more opportunities for the next generation (score on a scale from 1 [strongly disagree] to 10 [strongly agree])	7.6	7.1	7.3	7.2	7.6	7.2
Share of population who worry (very much or a great deal) about not being able to provide a good education for their children (%)	82.0	75.0	75.4	74.0	49.8	41.4
Fiscal position						
	2016	**2021**	**2016**	**2021**	**2016**	**2021**
Total tax revenues (% of GDP)	31.6	33.5	22.0	21.5	33.6	34.1
Environmentally related tax revenue (% of GDP)	0.9	0.7	1.1	0.9	2.4	2.0
Share of VAT (% GDP)	6.6	7.6	5.9	6.1	6.6	7.0
Share of PIT (% GDP)	2.6	3.0	2.0	2.0	7.8	8.3
Share of CIT (% of GDP)	3.2	3.7	3.2	3.4	2.9	3.1
Debt service (% of total tax revenue)	20.5	15.0	11.3	12.3	5.4	5.3
Social expenditure (% of GDP)	17.3	17.3	11.3	13.3	20.1	22.0
	2016	**2020**	**2016**	**2020**	**2016**	**2019**
Perception of tax evasion (%)	N/A	24.5	N/A	27.3	N/A	N/A

Note: See the Reader's Guide for definitions and sources.

StatLink https://stat.link/ft5cna

CHILE

1. Recent trends

Poverty in Chile was at 8.1% in 2022, remaining below the Latin America and the Caribbean (LAC) average of 24.1%. Extreme poverty was at 2.1% in 2022, below the LAC average (8.3%). The Gini index was 44.9 in 2020, almost on par with the LAC average (44.8). Regarding investment and production transformation indicators, total investment in Chile increased from 24.1% of GDP in 2016 to 24.8% in 2022, remaining above the LAC average, which increased from 20.8% to 21.3% over the same period. Private investment slightly rose in Chile, from 20.9% of GDP in 2016 to 21.1% in 2019, above the LAC average (15.8% in 2019). Chile's labour productivity, measured against output per employed person in the United States, remained almost unchanged, increasing from 41.3% in 2016 to 41.4% in 2023, substantially above the LAC average of 27.1% in 2023. The share of exports of high-tech products in total exported manufactured goods increased from 8.4% in 2016 to 12.4% in 2021, above the LAC average (7.2%). Positive perceptions of foreign direct investment (FDI), which declined across the LAC region, dropped significantly in Chile as well, from 68.1% in 2016 to 45.7% in 2020. Contrary to a declining trend in the region, Chile's fiscal revenues increased from 20.2% of GDP in 2016 to 22.2% in 2021. Similar to the LAC average, environment-related tax revenues remained almost unchanged at 1.0% of GDP in 2021.

2. Long-term policies to promote investment and production transformation

Chile has made significant efforts **to attract and mobilise high-quality investment**, focusing mainly on simplifying, facilitating and optimising investment processes. It established the *Invirtamos en Chile* plan to: establish tax incentives for private investment; improve access to finance; generate proposals to improve public investment; promote foreign investment; improve the efficiency of regulatory and permit procedures; and promote public-private partnerships for investment. Since 2016, Chile has had an FDI promotion agency called *InvestChile*, created by Law 20.848. *InvestChile* leads the active search for specific foreign companies to attract to the country. In turn, it supports them in their prospecting and installation process. The agency also promotes reinvestment of companies already established in Chile to develop new projects and deepen their ties with local producers, particularly with small firms and companies located at the sub-national level. Since 2023, *InvestChile* has been implementing its Strategy for the Promotion and Encouragement of Foreign Direct Investment, which seeks to actively contribute, through a proactive policy of attracting FDI projects, to the economic recovery and sustainable development.

To advance an inclusive and sustainable production model, Chile has focused its 2030 Agenda for Sustainable Development on strategic lines of action: people; planet; prosperity; peace, justice and institutions; and partnerships. The main objective of this agenda is to provide a roadmap for sustainable and inclusive development in a context of peace, justice and partnership. It is flexible and adaptable to the specific needs of each region and locality, as it intends to generate the enabling conditions for elaborating sub-national strategies for sustainable development, based on a national roadmap and a sub-national organisation that facilitates representation of diverse local actors. Since 2020, Chile has a National Green Hydrogen Strategy, which has three main stages: the first (2020-25) seeks to activate the domestic industry and develop exports; the second (2025-30) aims to leverage local experience to enter strongly into international markets; and the third (2030 onwards) will exploit synergies and economies of scale to advance as a global supplier of clean energy.

In terms of **regional and international partnerships** to support the attraction of quality investments, Chile has established collaborative initiatives with partners both within and beyond LAC. **Within** the region, Chile has several co-operation projects with Argentina, such as the initiative "Transfer of experiences and good practices in the area of foreign trade, opportunities and barriers for the free flow of goods and services between the Province of Neuquén and the Region of La Araucanía," which aims to strengthen trade between these two regions. **Beyond** LAC, Chile and the European Union (EU), as part of the EU's Global Gateway Initiative, are co-operating to create local value chains for critical raw materials that support the clean energy and digital transitions (e.g. lithium), develop green hydrogen and produce carbon-neutral fuels using wind energy. The European Investment Bank (EIB) will finance climate action projects in Chile for more than EUR 300 million. Under the Ecovivienda programme, its first green mortgage loan outside Europe, the EIB will finance mortgages for new homes with improved energy efficiency standards. The EIB while also support Chile's renewable hydrogen industry, which will contribute to reaching the country's goal of 100% clean energy by 2050.

	Key indicators – Chile					
	Chile		LAC		OECD	
Social						
	2015	**2022**	**2016**	**2022**	**2016**	**2022**
Extreme poverty	1.8	2.1	8.1	8.3	N/A	N/A
Poverty	13.7	8.1	25.9	24.1	N/A	N/A
	2016	**2021**	**2016**	**2021**	**2016**	**2021**
Share of internet users (% of population)	83.6	90.2	54.5	74.2	81.8	89.6
	2015	**2020**	**2016**	**2021**	**2016**	**2020**
Gini index	44.4	44.9	46.3	44.8	34.1	33.6
	2009	**2017**	**2009**	**2021**	**2009**	**2021**
Share of total population in informal households (%)	24.5	20.2	44.2	46.8	N/A	N/A
Share of total population in informal households, upper-income quintile (%)	17.3	7.0	23.9	21.8	N/A	N/A
Share of total population in informal households, lower-income quintile (%)	39.4	46.0	20.2	7.9	N/A	N/A
	2019	**2023**	**2019**	**2023**	**2019**	**2023**
SIGI index	36.1	27.2	25.4	21.6	17.5	15.3
	2015	**2018**	**2015**	**2018**	**2015**	**2018**
PISA score in science	447	444	411	407	489	487
Productivity and innovation						
	2016	**2023**	**2016**	**2023**	**2016**	**2023**
Labour productivity (% of the United States)	41.3	41.4	29.3	27.1	70.0	68.5
	2016	**2021**	**2016**	**2021**	**2016**	**2021**
High-tech exports (% of manufactured exports)	8.4	12.4	8.4	7.2	16.5	16.0
	2016	**2019**	**2016**	**2019**	**2016**	**2019**
R&D expenditures (% of GDP)	0.4	0.3	0.3	0.4	1.8	2.0
Investment and production transformation						
	2016	**2022**	**2016**	**2022**	**2016**	**2022**
Total investment, gross fixed capital formation (% of GDP)	24.1	24.8	20.8	21.3	21.9	22.8
Foreign direct investment (FDI), net capital inflow (% of GDP)	4.6	6.9	4.4	4.6	6.8	3.5
	2016	**2019**	**2016**	**2019**	**2016**	**2019**
Private investment (% of GDP)	20.9	21.1	16.1	15.8	18.2	18.8
	2016	**2020**	**2016**	**2021**	**2016**	**2021**
Public investment in economic infrastructure (% of GDP)	2.6	2.3	2.3	1.6	N/A	N/A
Citizens' perceptions and institutions						
	2016	**2020**	**2016**	**2020**	**2016**	**2020**
Share of population who perceive FDI as beneficial (%)	68.1	45.7	70.9	53.9	N/A	N/A
	2018	**2020**	**2018**	**2020**	**2018**	**2020**
Share of population who consider that, in general, domestic products are of lower quality than imported ones (%) (agreeing or strongly agreeing)	37.7	58.2	44.6	42.7	N/A	N/A
	2016	**2022**	**2016**	**2022**	**2016**	**2022**
Corruption Perception Index (score on a scale of 0 [highly corrupt] to 100 [totally clean])	66.0	67.0	41.2	40.6	67.3	66.3
Security risks indicator (score from 0 [low security risks] to 10 [high security risks])	2.9	3.9	5.9	5.6	2.8	2.6
	2010-14	**2017-22**	**2010-14**	**2017-22**	**2010-14**	**2017-22**
Belief that science and technology will create more opportunities for the next generation (score on a scale from 1 [strongly disagree] to 10 [strongly agree])	7.5	6.8	7.3	7.2	7.6	7.2
Share of population who worry (very much or a great deal) about not being able to provide a good education for their children (%)	65.0	66.0	75.4	74.0	49.8	41.4
Fiscal position						
	2016	**2021**	**2016**	**2021**	**2016**	**2021**
Total tax revenues (% of GDP)	20.2	22.2	22.0	21.5	33.6	34.1
Environmentally related tax revenue (% of GDP)	1.2	1.0	1.1	0.9	2.4	2.0
Share of VAT (% GDP)	8.3	9.5	5.9	6.1	6.6	7.0
Share of PIT (% GDP)	1.8	2.4	2.0	2.0	7.8	8.3
Share of CIT (% of GDP)	4.2	3.8	3.2	3.4	2.9	3.1
Debt service (% of total tax revenue)	1.4	2.8	11.3	12.3	5.4	5.3
Social expenditure (% of GDP)	16.2	24.9	11.3	13.3	20.1	22.0
	2016	**2020**	**2016**	**2020**	**2016**	**2020**
Perception of tax evasion (%)	N/A	14.1	N/A	27.3	N/A	N/A

Note: See the Reader's Guide for definitions and sources.

StatLink https://stat.link/iw3y86

COLOMBIA

1. Recent trends

Poverty in Colombia increased from 30.9% in 2016 to 34.5% in 2022, remaining above the Latin America and the Caribbean (LAC) average of 24.1%. Extreme poverty also increased, from 12.0% in 2016 to 16.9% in 2022, standing above the LAC average (8.3%). The Gini index increased from 50.6 in 2016 to 51.5 in 2021, remaining above the LAC average (44.8). Regarding investment and production transformation indicators, total investment in Colombia is at 19.0% in 2022 compared to 21.3% for the LAC average over the same period. Colombia's labour productivity, measured against output per employed person in the United States, increased from 25.9% in 2016 to 28.1% in 2023, above the LAC average of 27.1%. The share of exports of high-tech products in total exported manufactured goods decreased from 10.2% in 2016 to 8.2% in 2021 but remained above the LAC average (7.2%). Positive perception of foreign direct investment (FDI), which declined across the region, dropped markedly in Colombia, from 55.9% in 2016 to 37.2% in 2020. The country's tax revenue slightly increased from 19.1% of GDP in 2016 to 19.5% in 2021, avoiding the regional downward trend. Environment-related tax revenues decreased slightly from 0.8% of GDP in 2016 to 0.6% in 2020.

2. Long-term policies to promote investment and production transformation

Colombia has made significant efforts **to attract and mobilise high-quality investment**, focusing mainly on promoting higher levels of business formality in the economy. In 2019, Colombia introduced the Business Formalisation Policy (CONPES document No. 3956), which streamlines the formalisation processes of businesses, enhances regulatory enforcement, gathers better business data, and shares evidence on policy impacts. To make this possible, the formalisation policy lowered commercial registration fees, resulting in entrepreneurs collectively saving around COP 85 393 million by 2022. The policy also expanded the "one-stop business window" to 57 locations nationwide, facilitating the creation of 177 599 companies from June 2018 to December 2022. In 2020, Colombia formalised the Articulation for Competitiveness Methodology (ArCo), based on five main objectives: promote articulation from and towards users; improve the efficiency of public spending; orient the budget towards results; define a regionalised offer; and strengthen transparency of and access to information. In the same year, the national government launched the *Innovamos* platform to consolidate all public calls and programmes related to competitiveness and innovation in science, technology, and innovation (STI). This platform has simplified the application process for citizens and firms seeking to avail themselves of national policy instruments, efficiently providing relevant information.

To advance **an inclusive and sustainable production model**, Colombia developed the 2022-2026 National Development Plan (NDP), titled Colombia, a Global Power of Life. This plan is structured around five essential transformations: i) territorial planning around water and environmental justice; ii) preserving natural wealth, human security, and social justice; iii) human right to food; iv) production transformation, internationalisation, and climate action; and v) regional convergence. In terms of inclusive growth, Colombia's NDP established the Council of Popular Economy, which aims to strongly incentivise grassroots economies by bolstering small and medium-sized productive units. In 2022, Colombia also updated, approved and started implementing the first phase of the action plan of the National Climate Finance Strategy: Closing the Gap. Its objective is to efficiently mobilise resources to finance mitigation and adaptation initiatives throughout the entire policy cycle, aiming to achieve national climate change goals with equity and justice.

In terms of **regional and international partnerships** to support the attraction of quality investments, Colombia has established collaborative initiatives with partners both within and beyond LAC. **Within** the region, Colombia offers and receives South-South and triangular co-operation related to productive transformation, employment and competitiveness, with Chile, the Dominican Republic, Ecuador, Guatemala, Honduras, Uruguay, and the Inter-American Development Bank (IDB), among others. **Beyond** LAC, the European Union supports initiatives to mitigate, adapt and reduce vulnerability to climate change and funds projects that seek to build sustainable development models and promote peace-building initiatives. In addition, together with the United Kingdom and Germany, Colombia participates in the Climate Finance Corridor. Finally, the EU-LAC Digital Alliance should promote the use of digital technologies for the peace agenda, the green transition, the conservation of natural resources, and for closing both social and geographic gaps in Colombia.

	Key indicators – Colombia					
	Colombia		LAC		OECD	
Social						
	2016	**2022**	**2016**	**2022**	**2016**	**2022**
Extreme poverty	12.0	16.9	8.1	8.3	N/A	N/A
Poverty	30.9	34.5	25.9	24.1	N/A	N/A
	2016	**2021**	**2016**	**2021**	**2016**	**2021**
Share of internet users (% of population)	58.1	73.0	54.5	74.2	81.8	89.6
	2016	**2021**	**2016**	**2021**	**2016**	**2020**
Gini index	50.6	51.5	46.3	44.8	34.1	33.6
	2010	**2021**	**2009**	**2021**	**2009**	**2021**
Share of total population in informal households (%)	62.6	54.1	44.2	46.8	N/A	N/A
Share of total population in informal households, upper-income quintile (%)	44.3	17.9	23.9	21.8	N/A	N/A
Share of total population in informal households, lower-income quintile (%)	69.6	90.2	44.3	17.9	N/A	N/A
	2019	**2023**	**2019**	**2023**	**2019**	**2023**
SIGI index	15.0	23.5	25.4	21.6	17.5	15.3
	2015	**2018**	**2015**	**2018**	**2015**	**2018**
PISA score in science	416	413	411	407	489	487
Productivity and innovation						
	2016	**2023**	**2016**	**2023**	**2016**	**2023**
Labour productivity (% of the United States)	25.9	28.1	29.3	27.1	70.0	68.5
	2016	**2021**	**2016**	**2021**	**2016**	**2021**
High-tech exports (% of manufactured exports)	10.2	8.2	8.4	7.2	16.5	16.0
	2016	**2019**	**2016**	**2019**	**2016**	**2019**
R&D expenditures (% of GDP)	0.3	0.3	0.3	0.4	1.8	2.0
Investment and production transformation						
	2016	**2022**	**2016**	**2022**	**2016**	**2022**
Total investment, gross fixed capital formation (% of GDP)	22.1	19.0	20.8	21.3	21.9	22.8
Foreign direct investment (FDI), net capital inflow (% of GDP)	4.9	4.9	4.4	4.6	6.8	3.5
	2016	**2019**	**2016**	**2019**	**2016**	**2019**
Private investment (% of GDP)	18.2	18.2	16.1	15.8	18.2	18.8
	2016	**2019**	**2016**	**2021**	**2016**	**2021**
Public investment in economic infrastructure (% of GDP)	1.7	1.4	2.3	1.6	N/A	N/A
Citizens' perceptions and institutions						
	2016	**2020**	**2016**	**2020**	**2016**	**2020**
Share of population who perceive FDI as beneficial (%)	55.9	37.2	70.9	53.9	N/A	N/A
	2018	**2020**	**2018**	**2020**	**2018**	**2020**
Share of population who consider that, in general, domestic products are of lower quality than imported ones (%) (agreeing or strongly agreeing)	38.2	29.6	44.6	42.7	N/A	N/A
	2016	**2022**	**2016**	**2022**	**2016**	**2022**
Corruption Perception Index (score on a scale of 0 [highly corrupt] to 100 [totally clean])	37.0	39.0	41.2	40.6	67.3	66.3
Security risks indicator (score from 0 [low security risks] to 10 [high security risks])	7.0	6.6	5.9	5.6	2.8	2.6
	2010-14	**2017-22**	**2010-14**	**2017-22**	**2010-14**	**2017-22**
Belief that science and technology will create more opportunities for the next generation (score on a scale from 1 [strongly disagree] to 10 [strongly agree])	7.0	7.2	7.3	7.2	7.6	7.2
Share of population who worry (very much or a great deal) about not being able to provide a good education for their children (%)	91.0	69.0	75.4	74.0	49.8	41.4
Fiscal position						
	2016	**2021**	**2016**	**2021**	**2016**	**2021**
Total tax revenues (% of GDP)	19.1	19.5	22.0	21.5	33.6	34.1
	2016	**2020**	**2016**	**2021**	**2016**	**2021**
Environmentally related tax revenue (% of GDP)	0.8	0.6	1.1	0.9	2.4	2.0
	2016	**2021**	**2016**	**2021**	**2016**	**2021**
Share of VAT (% GDP)	4.8	5.9	5.9	6.1	6.6	7.0
Share of PIT (% GDP)	1.1	1.3	2.0	2.0	7.8	8.3
Share of CIT (% of GDP)	4.9	4.6	3.2	3.4	2.9	3.1
Debt service (% of total tax revenue)	10.1	14.7	11.3	12.3	5.4	5.3
Social expenditure (% of GDP)	12.5	15.0	11.3	13.3	20.1	22.0
	2016	**2020**	**2016**	**2020**	**2016**	**2019**
Perception of tax evasion (%)	N/A	25.5	N/A	27.3	N/A	N/A

Note: See the Reader's Guide for definitions and sources.

StatLink https://stat.link/wjhexr

COSTA RICA

1. Recent trends

Poverty in Costa Rica was at 16.6% in 2022, substantially below the Latin America and the Caribbean (LAC) average of 24.1%. Extreme poverty decreased from 4.2% in 2016 to 3.3% in 2022, also well below the LAC average (8.3%). The Gini index remained unchanged at 48.7 from 2016 to 2021, above the LAC average (44.8). Regarding investment and production transformation indicators, total investment in Costa Rica remained almost unchanged in the past years at close to 18% of GDP in 2022 (vs. 21.3% for the LAC average in the same year). Private investment decreased from 13.3% of GDP to 11.1%, below the LAC average (15.8% in 2019). Costa Rica's labour productivity, measured against output per employed person in the United States, increased from 38.8% in 2016 to 39.1% in 2023, above the LAC average of 27.1% in 2023. The share of exports of high-tech products in total exported manufactured goods represented 15.7% in 2020, more than double the LAC average (7.2%). Positive perceptions of foreign direct investment (FDI), which declined across the region, also dropped in Costa Rica, from 70.8% in 2016 to 62.1% in 2020. In contrast to a regional declining trend, the country's tax revenue increased from 23.5% of GDP in 2016 to 24.2% in 2021. Environment-related tax revenues remained almost unchanged over that period at 2.1% in 2021, more than double the LAC average (0.9% of GDP in 2021).

2. Long-term policies to promote investment and production transformation

Costa Rica has made significant efforts **to attract and mobilise high-quality investment**, focusing mainly on simplifying, facilitating and optimising investment processes. It established a one-stop investment window, which corresponds to an inter-institutional effort to facilitate processes to encourage investment, eliminate unnecessary requirements, reduce time and costs, and promote traceability, transparency, and legal certainty. Since 2023, Costa Rica also upgraded its Foreign Direct Investment Strategy to attract and retain FDI that contributes to three key areas: export diversification, job creation, and sustainable and inclusive development across all regions, with a special focus on the Greater Metropolitan Area.

To advance **an inclusive and sustainable production model**, the National Development and Public Investment Plan for 2023-26 focuses the investment agenda on seven fundamental sectors: education; culture; public finance; agriculture and livestock; health; public security and justice; and public works and transport. Achieving the plan's objectives will require an estimated total investment of more than USD 13.8 billion. In 2022, Costa Rica published its National Strategic Plan 2050, which aims to transition from a historically centralised development model to one based on a *3D economic and social development model*: decentralised, digitalised and decarbonised. With the commitment to become a modern, green and emission-free economy, Costa Rica defined a National Decarbonisation Plan 2018-50, which focuses on the sectors of transport and mobility, energy, environment, agriculture, industry, construction and land-use planning.

In terms of **regional and international partnerships** to support the attraction of quality investments, Costa Rica has established collaborative initiatives with partners both within and beyond LAC. **Within** the region, Costa Rica signed an agreement on co-operation for cross-border development with Panama, which aims to deepen co-operative relations thanks to socio-economic, environmental and political improvements in the border region, as well as to boost integration between both countries. Within the framework of this agreement, the Atlantic Road Corridor was built in the Sixaola/Guabito border, promoting road integration of both countries through an efficient, economic and safe transport system. This will foster economic and social development of the Atlantic region while reducing vehicle operating costs. **Beyond** the LAC region, Costa Rica participates in several co-operation actions with the European Union (EU). These include: strengthening the Administrative Associations of Water and Sewage Systems (ASADAS) of the Greater Metropolitan Area and peripheral cities to improve system management and boost resilience to climate change; capacity building for disaster risk reduction due to floods and drought; institutional capacity building to promote and develop organic agricultural production; and development of the National Action Strategy for Climate Empowerment.

Key indicators – Costa Rica	Costa Rica		LAC		OECD	
Social						
	2016	**2022**	**2016**	**2022**	**2016**	**2022**
Extreme poverty	4.2	3.3	8.1	8.3	N/A	N/A
Poverty	16.5	16.6	25.9	24.1	N/A	N/A
	2016	**2021**	**2016**	**2021**	**2016**	**2021**
Share of internet users (% of population)	65.9	82.8	54.5	74.2	81.8	89.6
	2016	**2021**	**2016**	**2021**	**2016**	**2020**
Gini index	48.7	48.7	46.3	44.8	34.1	33.6
	2010	**2020**	**2009**	**2021**	**2009**	**2021**
Share of total population in informal households (%)	26.9	26.8	44.2	46.8	N/A	N/A
Share of total population in informal households, upper-income quintile (%)	5.9	2.8	23.9	21.8	N/A	N/A
Share of total population in informal households, lower-income quintile (%)	69.3	81.4	77.6	78.5	N/A	N/A
	2019	**2023**	**2019**	**2023**	**2019**	**2023**
SIGI index	27.9	10.9	25.4	21.6	17.5	15.3
	2015	**2018**	**2015**	**2018**	**2015**	**2018**
PISA score in science	420	416	411	407	489	487
Productivity and innovation						
	2016	**2023**	**2016**	**2023**	**2016**	**2023**
Labour productivity (% of the United States)	38.8	39.1	29.3	27.1	70.0	68.5
	2016	**2020**	**2016**	**2021**	**2016**	**2021**
High-tech exports (% of manufactured exports)	18.4	15.7	8.4	7.2	16.5	16.0
	2016	**2018**	**2016**	**2019**	**2016**	**2019**
R&D expenditures (% of GDP)	0.4	0.4	0.3	0.4	1.8	2.0
Investment and production transformation						
	2016	**2022**	**2016**	**2022**	**2016**	**2022**
Total investment, gross fixed capital formation (% of GDP)	18.8	17.9	20.8	21.3	21.9	22.8
Foreign direct investment (FDI), net capital inflow (% of GDP)	4.5	5.2	4.4	4.6	6.8	3.5
	2016	**2019**	**2016**	**2019**	**2016**	**2019**
Private investment (% of GDP)	13.3	11.1	16.1	15.8	18.2	18.8
	2016	**2020**	**2016**	**2021**	**2016**	**2021**
Public investment in economic infrastructure (% of GDP)	2.5	1.7	2.3	1.6	N/A	N/A
Citizens' perceptions and institutions						
	2016	**2020**	**2016**	**2020**	**2016**	**2020**
Share of population who perceive FDI as beneficial (%)	70.8	62.1	70.9	53.9	N/A	N/A
	2018	**2020**	**2018**	**2020**	**2018**	**2020**
Share of population who consider that, in general, domestic products are of lower quality than imported ones (%) (agreeing or strongly agreeing)	34.9	30.5	44.6	42.7	N/A	N/A
	2016	**2022**	**2016**	**2022**	**2016**	**2022**
Corruption Perception Index (score on a scale of 0 [highly corrupt] to 100 [totally clean])	58.0	54.0	41.2	40.6	67.3	66.3
Security risks indicator (score from 0 [low security risks] to 10 [high security risks])	3.3	3.2	5.9	5.6	2.8	2.6
	2010-14	**2017-22**	**2010-14**	**2017-22**	**2010-14**	**2017-22**
Belief that science and technology will create more opportunities for the next generation (score on a scale from 1 [strongly disagree] to 10 [strongly agree])	N/A	N/A	7.3	7.2	7.6	7.2
Share of population who worry (very much or a great deal) about not being able to provide a good education for their children (%)	N/A	N/A	75.4	74.0	49.8	41.4
Fiscal position						
	2016	**2021**	**2016**	**2021**	**2016**	**2021**
Total tax revenues (% of GDP)	23.5	24.2	22.0	21.5	33.6	34.1
Environmentally related tax revenue (% of GDP)	2.3	2.1	1.1	0.9	2.4	2.0
Share of VAT (% GDP)	4.4	5.1	5.9	6.1	6.6	7.0
Share of PIT (% GDP)	1.3	1.6	2.0	2.0	7.8	8.3
Share of CIT (% of GDP)	2.3	2.4	3.2	3.4	2.9	3.1
Debt service (% of total tax revenue)	11.8	20.0	11.3	12.3	5.4	5.3
Social expenditure (% of GDP)	11.9	11.7	11.3	13.3	20.1	22.0
	2016	**2020**	**2016**	**2020**	**2016**	**2019**
Perception of tax evasion (%)	N/A	33.8	N/A	27.3	N/A	N/A

Note: See the Reader's Guide for definitions and sources.

StatLink https://stat.link/p253lm

DOMINICAN REPUBLIC

1. Recent trends

Poverty in the Dominican Republic decreased in recent years, from 26.7% in 2016 to 20.4% in 2022, and is now below the Latin America and the Caribbean (LAC) average of 24.1%. Extreme poverty also decreased, from 7.0% in 2016 to 5.1% in 2022, also below the LAC average (8.3%). The Gini index sharply decreased from 45.7 in 2016 to 38.5 in 2021, and again is now below the LAC average (44.8). Regarding investment and production transformation indicators, total investment in the Dominican Republic increased substantially from 22.9% of GDP in 2016 to 33.2% in 2022, far surpassing the trend for the LAC average, which increased from 20.8% to 21.3% over the same period. Private investment also rose in the Dominican Republic, from 20.5% of GDP to 21.7%, exceeding the LAC average (15.8% in 2019). Labour productivity, measured against output per employed person in the United States, increased from 29.6% in 2016 to 33.5% in 2023, above the LAC average of 27.1% in 2023. The share of exports of high-tech products in total exported manufactured goods almost doubled, from 4.4% in 2016 to 8.5% in 2021, above the LAC average (7.2%). Positive perceptions of foreign direct investment (FDI), which declined across the LAC region, dropped sharply in the Dominican Republic, from 85.1% in 2016 to 65.3% in 2020. The country's tax revenue increased from 13.0% of GDP in 2016 to 14.5% in 2021, but remains far below the regional average of 21.5%. Environment-related tax revenues remained almost unchanged, declining from 1.8% of GDP in 2016 to 1.7% in 2021, which is almost double the regional average of 0.9%.

2. Long-term policies to promote investment and production transformation

The Dominican Republic has made significant efforts **to attract and mobilise high-quality investment**, focusing mainly on a broad system of incentives that aim to develop and dynamise important sectors of the national economy. It established Law No. 16-95 on Foreign Investment and its Implementing Regulations No. 214-04 of 11 March 2004 to achieve two main aims: i) favour foreign investors, guaranteeing them the same legal protection afforded to domestic investors; and ii) liberalise dividends and repatriation of capital. In 2020, the Dominican Republic enacted Law No. 47-20, which regulates public-private partnerships (PPPs) and established the General Directorate of Public-Private Partnerships (DGAPP). This directorate played a vital role in ensuring a legal framework that fosters investment, attracting both local and foreign capital to stimulate socio-economic growth and infrastructure development. In 2021, the Dominican Republic has implemented Law No. 12-21, which creates the Special Zone for Integrated Border Development as well as an incentive regime that covers the provinces of Pedernales, Independencia, Elías Piña, Dajabón, Montecristi, Santiago Rodríguez and Bahoruco. Since 2021, the Dominican Republic has been implementing the Zero Bureaucracy Programme: Towards an Efficient Government, the objectives of which are to: increase productivity; reduce the social cost of regulations; facilitate access to services; streamline and minimise requirements and formalities; strengthen economic growth and social welfare; and reduce response times in public services.

To advance an inclusive and sustainable production model, the Dominican Republic has focused its National Development Strategy for 2010-30 on four fundamental axes: a State with efficient and transparent institutions, at the service of a responsible and participatory citizenry; a cohesive society, with equal opportunities and low levels of poverty and inequality; an articulated, innovative and sustainable economy, with a productive structure that generates high and sustained growth with decent employment; and a sustainable management of the environment and adequate adaptation to climate change. In 2007, the government established Law No. 57-07 on Incentives for the Development of Renewable Energy Sources and their Special Regimes, which provides for: exemption of all types of import taxes on equipment and accessories necessary to produce energy from renewable sources; reduction of taxes on financing paid abroad; and a tax incentive for energy self-producers.

In terms of **regional and international partnerships** to support the attraction of quality investments, the Dominican Republic has established collaborative initiatives with partners both within and beyond LAC. **Within** the region, the Dominican Republic is part of the Regional Framework Policy for Mobility and Logistics in Central America. The main objective is to provide and dynamise a regional framework for articulating national mobility and logistics policies that are strengthened in complementarity, comprehensiveness, and sustainability. This also contributes to orienting national policies towards common and strategic regional objectives. **Beyond** LAC, the Dominican Republic and the European Union (EU) are co-operating in the framework of the Multiannual Indicative Programme (MIP) for 2021-2024. The main priority areas are: strategies to foster employability and entrepreneurship, particularly among women and youth; the protection and sustainable use of ecosystems and biodiversity; and the efficient provision of public services while strengthening public planning. The Dominican Republic is a member of the Green MSMEs II Initiative, together with Germany, the Central American Bank for Economic Integration, and other member countries of the Central American Integration System (SICA). This programme aims to promote the financing of environmental investments to boost the infrastructure needed for energy conversion, transport and storage.

	Key indicators – Dominican Republic					
	Dominican Republic		**LAC**		**OECD**	
Social						
	2016	**2022**	**2016**	**2022**	**2016**	**2022**
Extreme poverty	7.0	5.1	8.1	8.3	N/A	N/A
Poverty	26.7	20.4	25.9	24.1	N/A	N/A
	2016	**2021**	**2016**	**2021**	**2016**	**2021**
Share of internet users (% of population)	63.9	85.2	54.5	74.2	81.8	89.6
	2016	**2021**	**2016**	**2021**	**2016**	**2020**
Gini index	45.7	38.5	46.3	44.8	34.1	33.6
	2009	**2018**	**2009**	**2021**	**2009**	**2021**
Share of total population in informal households (%)	N/A	42.3	44.2	46.8	N/A	N/A
Share of total population in informal households, upper-income quintile (%)	N/A	15.7	23.9	21.3	N/A	N/A
Share of total population in informal households, lower-income quintile (%)	N/A	74.9	77.6	78.2	N/A	N/A
	2019	**2023**	**2019**	**2023**	**2019**	**2023**
SIGI index	18.2	14.8	25.4	21.6	17.5	15.3
	2015	**2018**	**2015**	**2018**	**2015**	**2018**
PISA score in science	332	336	411	407	489	487
Productivity and innovation						
	2016	**2023**	**2016**	**2023**	**2016**	**2023**
Labour productivity (% of the United States)	29.6	33.5	29.3	27.1	70.0	68.5
	2016	**2021**	**2016**	**2021**	**2016**	**2021**
High-tech exports (% of manufactured exports)	4.4	8.5	8.4	7.2	16.5	16.0
	2016	**2019**	**2016**	**2019**	**2016**	**2019**
R&D expenditures (% of GDP)	N/A	N/A	0.3	0.4	1.8	2.0
Investment and production transformation						
	2016	**2022**	**2016**	**2022**	**2016**	**2022**
Total investment, gross fixed capital formation (% of GDP)	22.9	33.2	20.8	21.3	21.9	22.8
Foreign direct investment (FDI), net capital inflow (% of GDP)	3.3	3.5	4.4	4.6	6.8	3.5
	2016	**2019**	**2016**	**2019**	**2016**	**2019**
Private investment (% of GDP)	20.5	21.7	16.1	15.8	18.2	18.8
	2016	**2021**	**2016**	**2021**	**2016**	**2021**
Public investment in economic infrastructure (% of GDP)	1.4	0.6	2.3	1.6	N/A	N/A
Citizens' perceptions and institutions						
	2016	**2020**	**2016**	**2020**	**2016**	**2020**
Share of population who perceive FDI as beneficial (%)	85.1	65.3	70.9	53.9	N/A	N/A
	2018	**2020**	**2018**	**2020**	**2018**	**2020**
Share of population who consider that, in general, domestic products are of lower quality than imported ones (%) (agreeing or strongly agreeing)	55.7	51.1	44.6	42.7	N/A	N/A
	2016	**2022**	**2016**	**2022**	**2016**	**2022**
Corruption Perception Index (score on a scale of 0 [highly corrupt] to 100 [totally clean]).	31.0	32.0	41.2	40.6	67.3	66.3
Security risks indicator (score from 0 [low security risks] to 10 [high security risks])	5.5	5.8	5.9	5.6	2.8	2.6
	2010-14	**2017-22**	**2010-14**	**2017-22**	**2010-14**	**2017-22**
Belief that science and technology will create more opportunities for the next generation (score on a scale from 1 [strongly disagree] to 10 [strongly agree])	N/A	N/A	7.3	7.2	7.6	7.2
Share of population who worry (very much or a great deal) about not being able to provide a good education for their children (%)	N/A	N/A	75.4	74.0	49.8	41.4
Fiscal position						
	2016	**2021**	**2016**	**2021**	**2016**	**2021**
Total tax revenues (% of GDP)	13.0	14.5	22.0	21.5	33.6	34.1
Environmentally related tax revenue (% of GDP)	1.8	1.7	1.1	0.9	2.4	2.0
Share of VAT (% GDP)	4.6	4.8	5.9	6.1	6.6	7.0
Share of PIT (% GDP)	1.2	1.3	2.0	2.0	7.8	8.3
Share of CIT (% of GDP)	2.0	2.8	3.2	3.4	2.9	3.1
Debt service (% of total tax revenue)	19.5	21.5	11.3	12.3	5.4	5.3
Social expenditure (% of GDP)	7.7	8.9	11.3	13.3	20.1	22.0
	2016	**2020**	**2016**	**2020**	**2016**	**2019**
Perception of tax evasion (%)	N/A	27.9	N/A	27.3	N/A	N/A

Note: See the Reader's Guide for definitions and sources.

StatLink https://stat.link/xwv0m5

ECUADOR

1. Recent trends

Poverty in Ecuador was 25.7% in 2022, above the Latin America and the Caribbean (LAC) average of 24.1%. Extreme poverty fell from 7.5% in 2016 to 6.9% in 2022, below the LAC average (8.3%). The Gini index was 45.8 in 2021, remaining above the LAC average (44.8). Regarding investment and production transformation indicators, total investment in Ecuador decreased from 25.1% of GDP in 2016 to 21.3% in 2022. In the same period, total regional investment increased on average from 20.8% to 21.3%. Notably, in parallel, private investment rose sharply, from 13.1% of GDP to 17.8%, rising above the LAC average (15.8% in 2019). Ecuador's labour productivity, compared to output per employed person in the United States, decreased from 20.5% in 2016 to 18.2% in 2023, falling further below the LAC average of 27.1% in 2023. The share of exports of high-tech products in total exported manufactured goods was 4.8% in 2021, well below the LAC average (7.2%). Positive perceptions of foreign direct investment (FDI), which declined across the LAC region, dropped sharply in Ecuador, from 83.9% in 2016 to 48.3% in 2020. The country's tax revenue decreased slightly, from 19.9% of GDP in 2016 to 19.4% in 2021 (below 21.5% as the LAC average). Environment-related tax revenues remained low and almost unchanged, at 0.4% of GDP in 2016 and 0.3% in 2021.

2. Long-term policies to promote investment and production transformation

Ecuador has made significant efforts **to attract and mobilise high-quality investment**, focusing mainly on simplifying, facilitating and optimising investment processes. It established a National System for Investment Attraction and Facilitation aiming to: reduce the time, costs and procedures for private investment; improve the effectiveness of actions to attract and promote investment; and better manage and evaluate the implementation of investment projects. Since 2021, Ecuador has also implemented a One-Stop Investment Window that offers investors a single channel to manage the necessary permits and authorisations to start operations quickly and transparently. In line with these efforts, Executive Decree No. 68 of 2021 declares as priority public policies the efforts to facilitate trade and production, and to simplify procedures and the country's Competitiveness Agenda.

To advance an inclusive and sustainable production model, Ecuador has focused its Opportunity Creation Plan for 2021-25 on five fundamental axes: economic, social, comprehensive security, environmental and institutional. The plan has an estimated total investment of more than USD 14 billion. In 2021, the Technical Secretariat for Public-Private Partnerships and Delegated Management was established, along with regulation for public-private partnerships (PPPs). This entity co-ordinates and articulates inter-institutional actions to attract, facilitate, materialise and maintain private investments, focused on the generation of infrastructure and provision of public services through various modalities of delegated management. To **strengthen the energy sector**, Ecuador designed an Electricity Master Plan 2020-31. As of 2022, six hydroelectric, one wind and one photovoltaic projects were under implementation, while nine additional projects are due to be operational by 2024. In terms of climate change mitigation, in June 2023, Ecuador issued the Technical regulation establishing the greenhouse gas emissions compensation scheme in Ecuador, which aims to reduce emissions and increase the removal of greenhouse gases.

In terms of **regional and international partnerships** to support the attraction of quality investments, Ecuador has established collaborative initiatives with partners both within and beyond LAC. **Within** the region, Ecuador's Public-Private Investment Secretariat signed an Inter-Institutional Co-operation Framework Agreement for the period 2023-25 with Peru's Private Investment Promotion Agency (Proinversión). The agreement aims to promote co-operation, exchange of experiences and mutual assistance between the institutions, with a special focus on the transfer of knowledge related to PPPs. **Beyond** LAC, Ecuador is a member of Euroclima, the European Union's flagship programme to promote green action in LAC countries. The EU-LAC Global Gateway Investment Agenda can further strengthen efforts to promote sustainable development and both local and international investments. Some specific ongoing projects on climate and energy are: "A green deal for Ecuador" promoting actions and institutional frameworks to implement low-carbon and climate mitigation projects at the subnational level; supporting the development of a green bond market; strengthening regional energy integration in the Andean region, particularly electricity transmission infrastructure between Ecuador and Peru; and the *Ukumari* EU-Ecuador Forest Partnership to promote sustainable use of forest biodiversity, agroforestry and forest recovery, including the protection of the *Galápagos* reserve.

	Key indicators – Ecuador					
	Ecuador		LAC		OECD	
Social						
	2016	**2022**	**2016**	**2022**	**2016**	**2022**
Extreme poverty	7.5	6.9	8.1	8.3	N/A	N/A
Poverty	24.3	25.7	25.9	24.1	N/A	N/A
	2016	**2021**	**2016**	**2021**	**2016**	**2021**
Share of internet users (% of population)	54.1	76.2	54.5	74.2	81.8	89.6
	2016	**2021**	**2016**	**2021**	**2016**	**2020**
Gini index	45.0	45.8	46.3	44.8	34.1	33.6
	2009	**2021**	**2009**	**2021**	**2009**	**2021**
Share of total population in informal households (%)	N/A	N/A	44.2	46.8	N/A	N/A
Share of total population in informal households, upper-income quintile (%)	N/A	N/A	23.9	21.3	N/A	N/A
Share of total population in informal households, lower-income quintile (%)	N/A	N/A	77.6	78.2	N/A	N/A
	2019	**2023**	**2019**	**2023**	**2019**	**2023**
SIGI index	28.9	17.0	25.4	21.6	17.5	15.3
	2015	**2018**	**2015**	**2018**	**2015**	**2018**
PISA score in science	N/A	N/A	411	407	489	487
Productivity and innovation						
	2016	**2023**	**2016**	**2023**	**2016**	**2023**
Labour productivity (% of the United States)	20.5	18.2	29.3	27.1	70.0	68.5
	2016	**2021**	**2016**	**2021**	**2016**	**2021**
High-tech exports (% of manufactured exports)	9.2	4.8	8.4	7.2	16.5	16.0
	2016	**2019**	**2016**	**2019**	**2016**	**2019**
R&D expenditures (% of GDP)	N/A	N/A	0.3	0.4	1.8	2.0
Investment and production transformation						
	2016	**2022**	**2016**	**2022**	**2016**	**2022**
Total investment, gross fixed capital formation (% of GDP)	25.1	21.3	20.8	21.3	21.9	22.8
Foreign direct investment (FDI), net capital inflow (% of GDP)	0.8	0.7	4.4	4.6	6.8	3.5
	2016	**2019**	**2016**	**2019**	**2016**	**2019**
Private investment (% of GDP)	13.1	17.8	16.1	15.8	18.2	18.8
	2016	**2021**	**2016**	**2021**	**2016**	**2021**
Public investment in economic infrastructure (% of GDP)	2.9	0.3	2.3	1.6	N/A	N/A
Citizens' perceptions and institutions						
	2016	**2020**	**2016**	**2020**	**2016**	**2020**
Share of population who perceive FDI as beneficial (%)	83.9	48.3	70.9	53.9	N/A	N/A
	2018	**2020**	**2018**	**2020**	**2018**	**2020**
Share of population who consider that, in general, domestic products are of lower quality than imported ones (%) (agreeing or strongly agreeing)	51.4	45.8	44.6	42.7	N/A	N/A
	2016	**2022**	**2016**	**2022**	**2016**	**2022**
Corruption Perception Index (score on a scale of 0 [highly corrupt] to 100 [totally clean])	31.0	36.0	41.2	40.6	67.3	66.3
Security risks indicator (score from 0 [low security risks] to 10 [high security risks])	6.5	5.6	5.9	5.6	2.8	2.6
	2010-14	**2017-22**	**2010-14**	**2017-22**	**2010-14**	**2017-22**
Belief that science and technology will create more opportunities for the next generation (score on a scale from 1 [strongly disagree] to 10 [strongly agree])	7.3	7.0	7.3	7.2	7.6	7.2
Share of population who worry (very much or a great deal) about not being able to provide a good education for their children (%)	78.0	80.0	75.4	74.0	49.8	41.4
Fiscal position						
	2016	**2021**	**2016**	**2021**	**2016**	**2021**
Total tax revenues (% of GDP)	19.9	19.4	22.0	21.5	33.6	34.1
Environmentally related tax revenue (% of GDP)	0.4	0.3	1.1	0.9	2.4	2.0
Share of VAT (% GDP)	6.0	6.2	5.9	6.1	6.6	7.0
Share of PIT (% GDP)	N/A	N/A	2.0	2.0	7.8	8.3
Share of CIT (% of GDP)	N/A	N/A	3.2	3.4	2.9	3.1
Debt service (% of total tax revenue)	7.7	6.7	11.3	12.3	5.4	5.3
Social expenditure (% of GDP)	8.8	11.0	11.3	13.3	20.1	22.0
	2016	**2020**	**2016**	**2020**	**2016**	**2019**
Perception of tax evasion (%)	N/A	27.9	N/A	27.3	N/A	N/A

Note: See the Reader's Guide for definitions and sources.

StatLink https://stat.link/h4ukiw

EL SALVADOR

1. Recent trends

Poverty in El Salvador decreased markedly in recent years, from 40.4% in 2016 to 29.8% in 2022, but remains above the Latin America and the Caribbean (LAC) average of 24.1%. Extreme poverty also decreased, from 10.7% in 2016 to 8.7% in 2022, slightly above the LAC average (8.3%). The Gini index decreased from 40.0 in 2016 to 39.0 in 2021, remaining below the LAC average (44.8). Regarding investment and production transformation indicators, total investment in El Salvador increased from 15.5% of GDP in 2016 to 20.0% in 2022, showing a stronger growth rate than the LAC average trend, which increased from 20.8% to 21.3% over the same period. Private investment also rose in El Salvador, from 13.6% of GDP to 15.8%, equalling the LAC average (15.8% in 2019). The share of exports of high-tech products in total exported manufactured goods increased from 5.4% in 2016 to 7.4% in 2021, placing it slightly above the LAC average (7.2%). Positive perceptions of foreign direct investment (FDI), which declined across the LAC region, showed a slight increase in El Salvador, from 71.3% in 2016 to 72.0% in 2020. The country's tax revenue increased from 20.5% of GDP in 2016 to 23.3% in 2021, contrary to a regional declining trend. Environment-related tax revenues remained unchanged at 0.6% of GDP from 2016 to 2021, below the LAC average of 0.9%.

2. Long-term policies to promote investment and production transformation

El Salvador has made significant efforts **to attract and mobilise high-quality investment**, focusing mainly on creating new institutions to help promote investment. It created a new Investment and Export Promotion Agency of El Salvador (INVEST) to enhance the attraction of quality investment in selected priority sectors: agro-industry; energy; tourism; pharmaceutical chemicals; manufacturing; textile and apparel; bitcoin; digital technologies; and services. From 2023 to 2027, El Salvador will implement the Strategy for the Streamlining and Modernisation of Foreign Trade Services through the Centre for Import and Export Procedures, which seeks to facilitate, modernise and promote foreign trade in El Salvador, as well as to improve the provision of public services and inter-institutional collaboration, by simplifying and centralising procedures.

To advance **an inclusive and sustainable production model**, El Salvador has focused its Trade and Investment Policy 2020-2050 on three main macro-objectives: increasing the importance of exports in GDP; eliminating the balance of payments deficit; and increasing the stock of FDI. El Salvador's National Trade Facilitation Strategy 2023-2027 focuses on six main axes: streamlining and digitising procedures for a competitive climate; modernising logistics infrastructure for a new way of doing business; promoting co-ordinated and unified border management; modernising the legal framework for foreign trade; fostering transparency and availability of foreign trade information; and human talent management.

In terms of **regional and international partnerships** to support the attraction of quality investments, El Salvador has established collaborative initiatives with partners both within and beyond LAC. **Within** the region, El Salvador participates (alongside Honduras and Guatemala) in a programme that aims to integrate the Northern Triangle countries into regional value chains. This programme also aims to boost higher education completion by equipping workers with essential English language skills and IT certifications. A total of 191 people finalised the English training, with 131 being hired as a result. A pilot training programme in French is planned. **Beyond** the region, El Salvador and the European Union (EU), through the EU Global Gateway Initiative, co-operate in an investment agenda comprising several infrastructure projects including: first, linking the ports of Acajutla and San Salvador through 108 km of train rails; second, developing an electric passenger transportation system in the metropolitan area of San Salvador; and third, providing broadband connectivity to public schools and health centres in non-served areas, among others. El Salvador participates in the USAID Economic Competitiveness Project, a five-year initiative that seeks to strengthen the capacities of micro, small and medium-sized enterprises to increase the country's competitiveness by expanding competition in domestic and export markets. The digital platform MiEmpresa.gob.sv has been created as a one-stop shop to facilitate and digitise the formalisation process of entrepreneurs and companies starting operations. The project was technically supported by the UN Conference on Trade and Development (UNCTAD) and funded by Luxemburg and the United States.

	Key indicators – El Salvador					
	El Salvador		LAC		OECD	
Social						
	2016	**2022**	**2016**	**2022**	**2016**	**2022**
Extreme poverty	10.7	8.7	8.1	8.3	N/A	N/A
Poverty	40.4	29.8	25.9	24.1	N/A	N/A
	2016	**2021**	**2016**	**2021**	**2016**	**2021**
Share of internet users (% of population)	29.0	62.9	54.5	74.2	81.8	89.6
	2016	**2021**	**2016**	**2021**	**2016**	**2020**
Gini index	40.0	39.0	46.3	44.8	34.1	33.6
	2015	**2021**	**2009**	**2021**	**2009**	**2021**
Share of total population in informal households (%)	52.4	54.4	44.2	46.8	N/A	N/A
	2014	**2021**	**2009**	**2021**	**2009**	**2021**
Share of total population in informal households, upper-income quintile (%)	20.5	20.7	23.9	21.3	N/A	N/A
Share of total population in informal households, lower-income quintile (%)	90.4	95.0	77.6	78.2	N/A	N/A
	2019	**2023**	**2019**	**2023**	**2019**	**2023**
SIGI index	22.9	19.6	25.4	21.6	17.5	15.3
	2015	**2018**	**2015**	**2018**	**2015**	**2018**
PISA score in science	N/A	N/A	411	407	489	487
Productivity and innovation						
	2016	**2023**	**2016**	**2023**	**2016**	**2023**
Labour productivity (% of the United States)	N/A	N/A	29.3	27.1	70.0	68.5
	2016	**2021**	**2016**	**2021**	**2016**	**2021**
High-tech exports (% of manufactured exports)	5.4	7.4	8.4	7.2	16.5	16.0
	2016	**2019**	**2016**	**2019**	**2016**	**2019**
R&D expenditures (% of GDP)	0.1	0.2	0.3	0.4	1.8	2.0
Investment and production transformation						
	2016	**2022**	**2016**	**2022**	**2016**	**2022**
Total investment, gross fixed capital formation (% of GDP)	15.5	20.0	20.8	21.3	21.9	22.8
Foreign direct investment (FDI), net capital inflow (% of GDP)	2.0	0.0	4.4	4.6	6.8	3.5
	2016	**2019**	**2016**	**2019**	**2016**	**2019**
Private investment (% of GDP)	13.6	15.8	16.1	15.8	18.2	18.8
	2016	**2021**	**2016**	**2021**	**2016**	**2021**
Public investment in economic infrastructure (% of GDP)	1.2	1.7	2.3	1.6	N/A	N/A
Citizens' perceptions and institutions						
	2016	**2020**	**2016**	**2020**	**2016**	**2020**
Share of population who perceive FDI as beneficial (%)	71.3	72.0	70.9	53.9	N/A	N/A
	2018	**2020**	**2018**	**2020**	**2018**	**2020**
Share of population who consider that, in general, domestic products are of lower quality than imported ones (%) (agreeing or strongly agreeing)	51.1	50.9	44.6	42.7	N/A	N/A
	2016	**2022**	**2016**	**2022**	**2016**	**2022**
Corruption Perception Index (score on a scale of 0 [highly corrupt] to 100 [totally clean])	36.0	33.0	41.2	40.6	67.3	66.3
Security risks indicator (score from 0 [low security risks] to 10 [high security risks])	7.0	6.3	5.9	5.6	2.8	2.6
	2010-14	**2017-22**	**2010-14**	**2017-22**	**2010-14**	**2017-22**
Belief that science and technology will create more opportunities for the next generation (score on a scale from 1 [strongly disagree] to 10 [strongly agree])	N/A	N/A	7.3	7.2	7.6	7.2
Share of population who worry (very much or a great deal) about not being able to provide a good education for their children (%).	N/A	N/A	75.4	74.0	49.8	41.4
Fiscal position						
	2016	**2021**	**2016**	**2021**	**2016**	**2021**
Total tax revenues (% of GDP)	20.5	23.3	22.0	21.5	33.6	34.1
Environmentally related tax revenue (% of GDP)	0.6	0.6	1.1	0.9	2.4	2.0
Share of VAT (% GDP)	7.5	9.6	5.9	6.1	6.6	7.0
Share of PIT (% GDP)	3.0	3.2	2.0	2.0	7.8	8.3
Share of CIT (% of GDP)	3.2	3.8	3.2	3.4	2.9	3.1
Debt service (% of total tax revenue)	14.2	19.5	11.3	12.3	5.4	5.3
Social expenditure (% of GDP)	7.8	12.6	11.3	13.3	20.1	22.0
	2016	**2020**	**2016**	**2020**	**2016**	**2019**
Perception of tax evasion (%)	N/A	27.0	N/A	27.3	N/A	N/A

Note: See the Reader's Guide for definitions and sources.

StatLink https://stat.link/kt8z64

GUATEMALA

1. Recent trends

Regarding investment and production transformation indicators, total investment in Guatemala increased from 13.9% of GDP in 2016 to 16.8% in 2022, following the average trend for the Latin American and Caribbean (LAC) region, which increased from 20.8% to 21.3% over the same period. Private investment rose slightly in Guatemala, from 12.6% of GDP to 12.8%, but remains below the LAC average (15.8% in 2019). Guatemala's labour productivity, measured against output per employed person in the United States, remained largely unchanged at 15.7% in 2016 and 15.8% in 2023, below the LAC average of 27.1% in 2023. The share of exports of high-tech products in total exported manufactured goods declined from 5.8% in 2016 to 5.2% in 2021, below the LAC average (7.2%). Positive perceptions of foreign direct investment (FDI), which declined across the LAC region, fell in Guatemala from 55.1% in 2016 to 45.5% in 2020. The country's tax revenue increased from 13.2% of GDP in 2016 to 14.2% in 2021, remaining below the regional average of 21.5%. Environment-related tax revenues remained almost unchanged, declining from 0.9% of GDP in 2016 to 0.8% in 2021.

2. Long-term policies to promote investment and production transformation

Guatemala has made significant efforts **to attract and mobilise high-quality investment**, focusing mainly on creating new and good-quality jobs. It established the *Guatemala No se detiene* plan, which aims to strengthen sectors in which Guatemala already performs efficiently to increase exports by USD 5 billion by 2030 and attract new investments by leveraging the competitive advantages of its proximity to important markets worldwide. The main sectors identified were pharmaceuticals, medical devices, electronic devices, and the provision of outsourcing services for business process and information technology (IT). This plan supports the attraction of more FDI to the country by addressing five main axes: prioritisation of sectors, human capital, infrastructure, legal certainty and tourism.

To advance **an inclusive and sustainable production model**, Guatemala has focused its National Competitiveness Policy for 2018-32 on three strategic guidelines, called 11-11-9: 11 clusters with the greatest potential for employment generation; 11 priorities that Guatemala must address in terms of competitiveness; and 9 territories suitable for consolidation as intermediate cities. In 2015, the National Entrepreneurship Policy *Guatemala Emprende* was formulated, which influences most of the country's economic sectors. The policy's main objective is to foster an entrepreneurial culture that promotes new ways of thinking and acting, which contribute to the human, economic, social and environmental development of the country. This can be achieved by facilitating the creation, establishment and strengthening of sustainable enterprises, generating wealth, establishing a good business climate for attracting investment, and creating quality jobs for Guatemalans.

In terms of **regional and international partnerships** to support the attraction of quality investments, Guatemala has established collaborative initiatives with partners both within and beyond LAC. Guatemala has formalised frameworks of co-operation with the United Nations system, the European Union (EU), and the Governments of Spain, Colombia, the United States, and Chile to promote sustainable development. Initiatives of South-South co-operation have focused on employment and investment, priorities of the country's National Development Plan. National institutions involved in these initiatives were (among others) the Ministry of Labour and Social Welfare (MINTRAB), the Ministry of Agriculture, Livestock, and Food (MAGA), and the Superintendency of Tax Administration (SAT). Key projects in this context included Labor Inclusion and Youth Entrepreneurship Networks for Job Generation. Guatemala is also a member of Euroclima, the EU's flagship programme to promote green action in LAC countries. Euroclima's Multi-Year Indicative Programme 2021-24 for Guatemala focuses on three priority areas: i) a Green Deal supports the development of inclusive, sustainable and resilient small-scale agriculture; ii) sustainable and inclusive growth promotes an open, inclusive and competitive economic structure and fosters a sound investment climate; and iii) good governance and human development promotes strong, accountable and transparent national, regional and local administrations.

Key indicators – Guatemala

	Guatemala		LAC		OECD	
Social						
	2016	**2022**	**2016**	**2022**	**2016**	**2022**
Extreme poverty	N/A	N/A	8.1	8.3	N/A	N/A
Poverty	N/A	N/A	25.9	24.1	N/A	N/A
	2016	**2021**	**2016**	**2021**	**2016**	**2021**
Share of internet users (% of population)	34.5	50.8	54.5	74.2	81.8	89.6
	2016	**2021**	**2016**	**2021**	**2016**	**2020**
Gini index	N/A	N/A	46.3	44.8	34.1	33.6
	2009	**2021**	**2009**	**2021**	**2009**	**2021**
Share of total population in informal households (%)	N/A	N/A	44.2	46.8	N/A	N/A
Share of total population in informal households, upper-income quintile (%)	N/A	N/A	23.9	21.3	N/A	N/A
Share of total population in informal households, lower-income quintile (%)	N/A	N/A	77.6	78.2	N/A	N/A
	2019	**2023**	**2019**	**2023**	**2019**	**2023**
SIGI index	28.6	25.7	25.4	21.6	17.5	15.3
	2015	**2018**	**2015**	**2018**	**2015**	**2018**
PISA score in science	N/A	N/A	411	407	489	487
Productivity and innovation						
	2016	**2023**	**2016**	**2023**	**2016**	**2023**
Labour productivity (% of the United States)	15.7	15.8	29.3	27.1	70.0	68.5
	2016	**2021**	**2016**	**2021**	**2016**	**2021**
High-tech exports (% of manufactured exports)	5.8	5.2	8.4	7.2	16.5	16.0
	2016	**2019**	**2016**	**2019**	**2016**	**2019**
R&D expenditures (% of GDP)	0.0	0.0	0.3	0.4	1.8	2.0
Investment and production transformation						
	2016	**2022**	**2016**	**2022**	**2016**	**2022**
Total investment, gross fixed capital formation (% of GDP)	13.9	16.8	20.8	21.3	21.9	22.8
	2016	**2022**	**2016**	**2022**	**2016**	**2022**
Foreign direct investment (FDI), net capital inflow (% of GDP)	1.3	1.4	4.4	4.6	6.8	3.5
	2016	**2019**	**2016**	**2019**	**2016**	**2019**
Private investment (% of GDP)	12.6	12.8	16.1	15.8	18.2	18.8
	2016	**2021**	**2016**	**2021**	**2016**	**2021**
Public investment in economic infrastructure (% of GDP)	0.5	0.8	2.3	1.6	N/A	N/A
Citizens' perceptions and institutions						
	2016	**2020**	**2016**	**2020**	**2016**	**2020**
Share of population who perceives FDI as beneficial (%)	55.1	45.5	70.9	53.9	N/A	N/A
	2018	**2020**	**2018**	**2020**	**2018**	**2020**
Share of population who consider that, in general, domestic products are of lower quality than imported ones (%) (agreeing or strongly agreeing)	46.6	41.4	44.6	42.7	N/A	N/A
	2016	**2022**	**2016**	**2022**	**2016**	**2022**
Corruption Perception Index (score on a scale of 0 [highly corrupt] to 100 [totally clean])	28.0	24.0	41.2	40.6	67.3	66.3
Security risks indicator (score from 0 [low security risks] to 10 [high security risks])	7.3	6.5	5.9	5.6	2.8	2.6
	2010-14	**2017-22**	**2010-14**	**2017-22**	**2010-14**	**2017-22**
Belief that science and technology will create more opportunities for the next generation (score on a scale from 1 [strongly disagree] to 10 [strongly agree])	N/A	7.1	7.3	7.2	7.6	7.2
Share of population who worry (very much or a great deal) about not being able to provide a good education for their children (%)	N/A	76.0	75.4	74.0	49.8	41.4
Fiscal position						
	2016	**2021**	**2016**	**2021**	**2016**	**2021**
Total tax revenues (% of GDP)	13.2	14.2	22.0	21.5	33.6	34.1
Environmentally related tax revenue (% of GDP)	0.9	0.8	1.1	0.9	2.4	2.0
Share of VAT (% GDP)	4.8	5.6	5.9	6.1	6.6	7.0
Share of PIT (% GDP)	0.4	0.7	2.0	2.0	7.8	8.3
Share of CIT (% of GDP)	2.9	2.8	3.2	3.4	2.9	3.1
Debt service (% of total tax revenue)	11.6	12.1	11.3	12.3	5.4	5.3
Social expenditure (% of GDP)	7.2	7.6	11.3	13.3	20.1	22.0
	2016	**2020**	**2016**	**2020**	**2016**	**2019**
Perception of tax evasion (%)	N/A	22.3	N/A	27.3	N/A	N/A

Note: See the Reader's Guide for definitions and sources.

StatLink https://stat.link/0d3p2v

MEXICO

1. Recent trends

Poverty in Mexico decreased from 37.6% in 2016 to 28.6% in 2022, remaining above the Latin America and the Caribbean (LAC) average of 24.1%. Similarly, extreme poverty fell from 8.4% in 2016 to 6.2% in 2022, below the LAC average (8.3%). The Gini index decreased from 47.7 in 2016 to 45.4 in 2020, above the LAC average (44.8). Regarding investment and production transformation indicators, total investment in Mexico was at 21.2% in 2022, similar to the LAC average of 21.3% over the same period. Private investment represented 15.0% of GDP in 2019, slightly below the LAC average (15.8% of GDP). Mexico's labour productivity, measured against output per employed person in the United States, decreased from 38.2% in 2016 to 32.7% in 2023 yet remains above the LAC average of 27.1% in 2023. The share of exports of high-tech products in total exported manufactured goods represented close to 20% in 2021, substantially above the LAC average (7.2%). Positive perceptions of foreign direct investment (FDI), which declined across the LAC region, fell from 59.3% in 2016 to 54.3% in 2020. In contrast to a decline in the LAC average, tax revenue in Mexico increased slightly from 16.6% to 16.7% of GDP. Environment-related tax revenues decreased from 1.6% of GDP in 2016 to 1.0% in 2021 but are still slightly above the LAC average (0.9% of GDP in 2021).

2. Long-term policies to promote investment and production transformation

Mexico has made significant efforts **to attract and mobilise high-quality investment**, focusing mainly on attracting investment in industrial activities. In 2023, Mexico approved a decree to promote investment by taxpayers who carry out productive economic activities at the Isthmus of Tehuantepec within the Development Poles for Well-being (*Polos de Desarrollo para el Bienestar*). Mexico also implemented, in 2019, the Mobilising Sustainable Finance Strategy (*Estrategia de Movilización de Financiamiento Sostenible*), with the overall objective to mobilise, redirect and improve access to public and private sources of finance to develop activities and projects compatible with national sustainable development, climate change and biodiversity conservation goals.

To advance **an inclusive and sustainable production model**, Mexico published a Sustainable Taxonomy in 2023. This corresponds to a public financial policy instrument for sustainability that sets out technical parameters and criteria to identify activities, assets or investment projects with positive environmental and social impacts. The Taxonomy provides a catalogue of 124 activities, distributed across six strategic sectors of the economy: agriculture and forestry; energy and water; manufacturing; transport; construction; and waste management. In August 2020, the Infrastructure for Quality Law (LIC) came into effect in Mexico, which aims to promote technological innovation in goods, services and processes to: improve quality of life; facilitate creation of greater physical and digital infrastructure (through standardisation, accreditation, conformity assessment and metrology activities); and foster economic development and quality in the production of goods and services (by expanding productive capacity and ensuring better insertion in value chains).

In terms of **regional and international partnerships** to support the attraction of quality investments, Mexico has established collaborative initiatives with partners both within and beyond LAC. **Within** the region, Mexico promoted the *Sembrando Vida* programme with investments in El Salvador (USD 15.5 million) and Honduras (USD 20 million). This innovative project seeks to contribute to food security in low-income rural areas through agroforestry systems that encourage self-consumption and the commercialisation of surpluses. **Beyond** the LAC region, Mexico is a member of Euroclima, the flagship programme of the European Union (EU) to promote green action in LAC countries. This active participation will contribute significantly to the implementation of the EU Global Gateway Investment Agenda in the region, further strengthening efforts to promote sustainable development and attractiveness for both local and international investments.

Key indicators – Mexico

	Mexico		LAC		OECD	
Social						
	2016	**2022**	**2016**	**2022**	**2016**	**2022**
Extreme poverty	8.4	6.2	8.1	8.3	N/A	N/A
Poverty	37.6	28.6	25.9	24.1	N/A	N/A
	2016	**2021**	**2016**	**2021**	**2016**	**2021**
Share of internet users (% of population)	59.5	75.6	54.5	74.2	81.8	89.6
	2016	**2020**	**2016**	**2021**	**2016**	**2020**
Gini index	47.7	45.4	46.3	44.8	34.1	33.6
	2010	**2020**	**2009**	**2021**	**2009**	**2021**
Share of total population in informal households (%)	41.6	36.8	44.2	46.8	N/A	N/A
Share of total population in informal households, upper-income quintile (%)	13.4	14.4	23.9	21.3	N/A	N/A
Share of total population in informal households, lower-income quintile (%)	80.7	72.5	77.6	78.2	N/A	N/A
	2019	**2023**	**2019**	**2023**	**2019**	**2023**
SIGI index	29.0	21.9	25.4	21.6	17.5	15.3
	2015	**2018**	**2015**	**2018**	**2015**	**2018**
PISA score in science	416	419	411	407	489	487
Productivity and innovation						
	2016	**2023**	**2016**	**2023**	**2016**	**2023**
Labour productivity (% of the United States)	38.2	32.7	29.3	27.1	70.0	68.5
	2016	**2021**	**2016**	**2021**	**2016**	**2021**
High-tech exports (% of manufactured exports)	20.6	19.8	8.4	7.2	16.5	16.0
	2016	**2019**	**2016**	**2019**	**2016**	**2019**
R&D expenditures (% of GDP)	0.4	0.3	0.3	0.4	1.8	2.0
Investment and production transformation						
	2016	**2022**	**2016**	**2022**	**2016**	**2022**
Total investment, gross fixed capital formation (% of GDP)	22.8	21.2	20.8	21.3	21.9	22.8
Foreign direct investment (FDI), net capital inflow (% of GDP)	3.6	2.8	4.4	4.6	6.8	3.5
	2016	**2019**	**2016**	**2019**	**2016**	**2019**
Private investment (% of GDP)	16.0	15.0	16.1	15.8	18.2	18.8
	2016	**2020**	**2016**	**2021**	**2016**	**2021**
Public Investment in Economic Infrastructure (% of GDP)	1.8	0.5	2.3	1.6	N/A	N/A
Citizens' perceptions and institutions						
	2016	**2020**	**2016**	**2020**	**2016**	**2020**
Share of population who perceive FDI as beneficial (%)	59.3	54.3	70.9	53.9	N/A	N/A
	2018	**2020**	**2018**	**2020**	**2018**	**2020**
Share of population who consider that, in general, domestic products are of lower quality than imported ones (%) (agreeing or strongly agreeing)	37.7	41.0	44.6	42.7	N/A	N/A
	2016	**2022**	**2016**	**2022**	**2016**	**2022**
Corruption Perception Index (score on a scale of 0 [highly corrupt] to 100 [totally clean])	30.0	31.0	41.2	40.6	67.3	66.3
Security risks indicator (score from 0 [low security risks] to 10 [high security risks])	8.0	8.6	5.9	5.6	2.8	2.6
	2010-14	**2017-22**	**2010-14**	**2017-22**	**2010-14**	**2017-22**
Belief that science and technology will create more opportunities for the next generation (score on a scale from 1 [strongly disagree] to 10 [strongly agree])	7.8	7.5	7.3	7.2	7.6	7.2
Share of population who worry (very much or a great deal) about not being able to provide a good education for their children (%)	92.0	90.0	75.4	74.0	49.8	41.4
Fiscal position						
	2016	**2021**	**2016**	**2021**	**2016**	**2021**
Total tax revenues (% of GDP)	16.6	16.7	22.0	21.5	33.6	34.1
Environmentally related tax revenue (% of GDP)	1.6	1.0	1.1	0.9	2.4	2.0
Share of VAT (% GDP)	3.9	4.3	5.9	6.1	6.6	7.0
Share of PIT (% GDP)	3.4	3.6	2.0	2.0	7.8	8.3
Share of CIT (% of GDP)	3.5	3.4	3.2	3.4	2.9	3.1
Debt service (% of total tax revenue)	18.8	23.1	11.3	12.3	5.4	5.3
Social expenditure (% of GDP)	9.9	9.9	11.3	13.3	20.1	22.0
	2016	**2020**	**2016**	**2020**	**2016**	**2019**
Perception of tax evasion (%)	N/A	24.3	N/A	27.3	N/A	N/A

Note: See the Reader's Guide for definitions and sources.

StatLink https://stat.link/v2udn5

PANAMA

1. Recent trends

Poverty in Panama decreased from 16.7% in 2016 to 14.3% in 2022, well below the Latin America and the Caribbean (LAC) average of 24.1%. Extreme poverty also decreased from 7.4% in 2016 to 6.5% in 2022, below the LAC average (8.3%). The Gini index increased slightly from 50.4 in 2016 to 50.9 in 2021, remaining above the LAC average (44.8). Regarding investment and production transformation indicators, total investment in Panama increased from 38.4% of GDP in 2016 to 39.3% in 2017, remaining well above the LAC average which increased from 20.8% to 21.3% over the same period. Private investment slightly decreased in Panama, from 25.0% of GDP to 24.6% between 2016 and 2019, yet remaining well above the LAC average (15.8% in 2019). The share of exports of high-tech products in total exported manufactured goods declined from 1.2% in 2016 to 0.3% in 2021, below the LAC average (7.2%). Positive perceptions of foreign direct investment (FDI), which declined across the LAC region, dropped in Panama, from 67.8% in 2016 to 50.0% in 2020. The country's tax revenue decreased from 15.5% of GDP in 2016 to 12.7% in 2021, in line with a regional declining trend, and remains well below the LAC average (21.5% in 2021). Environment-related tax revenues declined from 0.7% of GDP in 2016 to 0.4% in 2021, below the average of 0.9% in LAC.

2. Long-term policies to promote investment and production transformation

Panama has made significant efforts **to attract and mobilise high-quality investment**, focusing mainly on boosting participation in the international economy, attracting investments and promoting exports. The country established PROPANAMA to: design and implement the Investment Strategy; design and implement the Integrated Trade Promotion and Export Market Opening Programme; accompany development of the Panama Country Brand; support development of inter-institutional actions; and strengthen its institutional capacity. In 2023, Panama presented its Investment Map for the UN Sustainable Development Goals (SDGs), promoted by the Ministry of Commerce and Industries with the support of the United Nations Development Programme (UNDP). This initiative identifies investment opportunities and business models that have significant potential to promote the SDGs and generate attractive financial returns for investors.

To advance **an inclusive and sustainable production model**, Panama has focused its Strategic Governance Plan for 2021-24 on five fundamental axes: good governance; rule of law; competitive economy to create jobs; poverty and inequality reduction; and education, science, technology, and culture. At the beginning of 2016, the government announced a dialogue to adopt Panama 2030, a National Strategic Plan with a State Vision, aiming to enable achievement of the SDGs. The Plan sets out five goals that form the basis for the country's development: good life for all; growing more and better; environmental sustainability; democracy, institutions and governance; and strategic alliances for development. To move towards circularity, resilience and progressive emission reductions, Panama designed the National Climate Action Plan (PNAC). This key instrument promotes a long-term national and sectoral agenda on climate change, aiming to facilitate and ensure Panama implements its first update of the Nationally Determined Contribution of Panama and fulfils its commitments.

In terms of **regional and international partnerships** to support the attraction of quality investments, Panama has established collaborative initiatives with partners both within and beyond LAC. **Within** the region, Panama signed a ground-breaking agreement in 2015 with Costa Rica to protect the labour rights of migrants, including indigenous populations. This agreement aims to improve collaboration between the two governments in managing dignified, orderly, humane, and safe labour migration, as well as monitoring labour conditions and ensuring access to services such as health, education, and social security. **Beyond** the region, Panama and the European Union have defined diverse co-operation priorities for 2023: on climate and energy (including production of green hydrogen and universal access to energy); health (creation of a regional vaccine development centre and manufacturing plant); and digital education and research (e.g. creation of the Copernicus data centre).

Key indicators – Panama

	Panama		LAC		OECD	
Social						
	2016	**2022**	**2016**	**2022**	**2016**	**2022**
Extreme poverty	7.4	6.5	8.1	8.3	N/A	N/A
Poverty	16.7	14.3	25.9	24.1	N/A	N/A
	2016	**2021**	**2016**	**2021**	**2016**	**2021**
Share of internet users (% of population)	54.0	67.5	54.5	74.2	81.8	89.6
	2016	**2021**	**2016**	**2021**	**2016**	**2020**
Gini index	50.4	50.9	46.3	44.8	34.1	33.6
	2009	**2021**	**2009**	**2021**	**2009**	**2021**
Share of total population in informal households (%)	N/A	N/A	44.2	46.8	N/A	N/A
Share of total population in informal households, upper-income quintile (%)	N/A	N/A	23.9	21.3	N/A	N/A
Share of total population in informal households, lower-income quintile (%)	N/A	N/A	77.6	78.2	N/A	N/A
	2019	**2023**	**2019**	**2023**	**2019**	**2023**
SIGI index	N/A	15.2	25.4	21.6	17.5	15.3
	2015	**2018**	**2015**	**2018**	**2015**	**2018**
PISA score in science	N/A	365	411	407	489	487
Productivity and innovation						
	2016	**2023**	**2016**	**2023**	**2016**	**2023**
Labour productivity (% of the United States)	N/A	N/A	29.3	27.1	70.0	68.5
	2016	**2021**	**2016**	**2021**	**2016**	**2021**
High-tech exports (% of manufactured exports)	1.2	0.3	8.4	7.2	16.5	16.0
	2016	**2019**	**2016**	**2019**	**2016**	**2019**
R&D expenditures (% of GDP)	0.1	N/A	0.3	0.4	1.8	2.0
Investment and production transformation						
	2016	**2017**	**2016**	**2022**	**2016**	**2022**
Total investment, gross fixed capital formation (% of GDP)	38.4	39.3	20.8	21.3	21.9	22.8
	2016	**2021**	**2016**	**2022**	**2016**	**2022**
Foreign direct investment (FDI), net capital inflow (% of GDP)	9.1	3.5	4.4	4.6	6.8	3.5
	2016	**2019**	**2016**	**2019**	**2016**	**2019**
Private investment (% of GDP)	25.0	24.6	16.1	15.8	18.2	18.8
	2016	**2021**	**2016**	**2021**	**2016**	**2021**
Public investment in economic infrastructure (% of GDP)	3.0	1.1	2.3	1.6	N/A	N/A
Citizens' perceptions and institutions						
	2016	**2020**	**2016**	**2020**	**2016**	**2020**
Share of population who perceive FDI as beneficial (%)	67.8	50.0	70.9	53.9	N/A	N/A
	2018	**2020**	**2018**	**2020**	**2018**	**2020**
Share of population who consider that, in general, domestic products are of lower quality than imported ones (%) (agreeing or strongly agreeing)	41.8	39.5	44.6	42.7	N/A	N/A
	2016	**2022**	**2016**	**2022**	**2016**	**2022**
Corruption Perception Index (score on a scale of 0 [highly corrupt] to 100 [totally clean])	38.0	36.0	41.2	40.6	67.3	66.3
Security risks indicator (score from 0 [low security risks] to 10 [high security risks])	5.4	4.9	5.9	5.6	2.8	2.6
	2010-14	**2017-22**	**2010-14**	**2017-22**	**2010-14**	**2017-22**
Belief that science and technology will create more opportunities for the next generation (score on a scale from 1 [strongly disagree] to 10 [strongly agree])	N/A	N/A	7.3	7.2	7.6	7.2
Share of population who worry (very much or a great deal) about not being able to provide a good education for their children (%)	N/A	N/A	75.4	74.0	49.8	41.4
Fiscal position						
	2016	**2021**	**2016**	**2021**	**2016**	**2021**
Total tax revenues (% of GDP)	15.5	12.7	22.0	21.5	33.6	34.1
Environmentally related tax revenue (% of GDP)	0.7	0.4	1.1	0.9	2.4	2.0
Share of VAT (% GDP)	2.6	1.8	5.9	6.1	6.6	7.0
Share of PIT (% GDP)	1.5	1.7	2.0	2.0	7.8	8.3
Share of CIT (% of GDP)	1.8	0.9	3.2	3.4	2.9	3.1
Debt service (% of total tax revenue)	10.5	16.1	11.3	12.3	5.4	5.3
	2016	**2020**	**2016**	**2021**	**2016**	**2021**
Social expenditure (% of GDP)	8.5	11.4	11.3	13.3	20.1	22.0
	2016	**2020**	**2016**	**2020**	**2016**	**2019**
Perception of tax evasion (%)	N/A	29.8	N/A	27.3	N/A	N/A

Note: See the Reader's Guide for definitions and sources.

StatLink https://stat.link/kr6hyl

PARAGUAY

1. Recent trends

Poverty in Paraguay decreased from 24.0% in 2016 to 21.1% in 2022, below the Latin America and the Caribbean (LAC) average of 24.1%. Extreme poverty has remained stable at 7.9% between 2016 and 2022, but remains below the LAC average (8.3%). The Gini index decreased from 47.9 in 2016 to 42.9 in 2021 and is now below the LAC average (44.8). Regarding investment and production transformation indicators, total investment in Paraguay increased from 19.1% of GDP in 2016 to 21.8% in 2022, placing the country slightly above the LAC average of 21.3% over the same period. Private investment, however, slightly decreased, from 11.1% of GDP to 10.7%, remaining below the LAC average (15.8% in 2019). Paraguay's labour productivity, measured against output per employed person in the United States, decreased from 22.9% in 2016 to 22.0% in 2023, below the LAC average of 27.1% in 2023. The share of exports of high-tech products in total exported manufactured goods declined marginally, from 7.6% in 2016 to 7.4% in 2021 but remains above the LAC average in 2021 (7.2%). Positive perceptions of foreign direct investment (FDI), which declined across the region, dropped in Paraguay, from 84.6% in 2016 to 55.4% in 2020. The country's tax revenue increased from 13.4% of GDP in 2016 to 14.0% in 2021 but remains below the LAC average (21.5% of GDP). Environment-related tax revenues remained almost unchanged, declining from 1.0% of GDP in 2016 to 0.9% in 2021, positioning Panama on par with the LAC average.

2. Long-term policies to promote investment and production transformation

Paraguay has made significant efforts **to attract and mobilise high-quality investment**, focusing mainly on incentives that: encourage the adoption of sustainable technologies and practices; boost the digital transformation of businesses; and promote job creation and social inclusion. It established a tax incentive under Law 60/90 Regime of Tax Incentives for the Investment of National and Foreign Capital, to: promote and increase capital investments; increase production of goods and services; create employment; promote exports and import substitution; and incorporate technologies to increase productive efficiency. In the past three decades, Paraguay has been implementing the Law on Free Trade Zones Regime, which fosters economic development and promotes investment in a given region or in the country generally. In line with these efforts, the Law on the Maquiladora Export Industry offers tax incentives to promote industrial development, job creation and increased exports.

To advance **an inclusive and sustainable production model**, Paraguay has focused its 2030 National Development Plan on three fundamental axes: poverty reduction and social development; inclusive economic growth; and Paraguay's insertion into the world. Achieving the plan's objectives will require an estimated total investment of USD 500 million. In 2020, the government introduced structural and cross-cutting guidelines through Law N° 6.490/20 Public Investment Law and its regulation, as a basis for elaborating Paraguay's National Investment Plan. Since the Plan entered into force, only those public investment projects that were included in it can be evaluated and subsequently implemented. The new government's top priorities are job creation and boosting productivity, with the implementation of significant market-friendly reforms. These reforms include: supporting the private sector to stimulate employment and long-term economic growth; requiring co-ordinated efforts across institutions and regions; and collaboration with the production sector.

In terms of **regional and international partnerships** to support the attraction of quality investments, Paraguay has established collaborative initiatives with partners both within and beyond LAC. **Within** the region, Paraguay is part of the intra-Mercosur co-operation and investment facilitation protocol, together with Argentina, Brazil and Uruguay. This protocol seeks to promote co-operation among the member States to facilitate direct investment for sustainable development. Paraguay also adheres to the protocol for reciprocal promotion and protection of investments from non-Mercosur states, such as France, Germany, Great Britain, South Africa, Spain and the United States, among others. This protocol establishes that each state will ensure fair and equitable treatment of investments from third states and will grant full protection to such investments. Paraguay and the European Union (EU) have formed, within the framework of the EU-LAC Global Gateway Investment Agenda, a partnership that includes concrete infrastructure projects in the key fields of: climate (e.g. a green-field pulp mill and forestry plantation project); energy (e.g. renewal of the electricity transmission network); and health (e.g. a water and sanitation project in Asuncion).

	Key indicators – Paraguay					
	Paraguay		LAC		OECD	
Social						
	2016	**2022**	**2016**	**2022**	**2016**	**2022**
Extreme poverty	7.9	7.9	8.1	8.3	N/A	N/A
Poverty	24.0	21.1	25.9	24.1	N/A	N/A
	2016	**2021**	**2016**	**2021**	**2016**	**2021**
Share of internet users (% of population)	53.4	77.0	54.5	74.2	81.8	89.6
	2016	**2021**	**2016**	**2021**	**2016**	**2020**
Gini index	47.9	42.9	46.3	44.8	34.1	33.6
	2009	**2018**	**2009**	**2021**	**2009**	**2021**
Share of total population in informal households (%)	66.3	57.4	44.2	46.8	N/A	N/A
Share of total population in informal households, upper-income quintile (%)	28.8	16.6	23.9	21.3	N/A	N/A
Share of total population in informal households, lower-income quintile (%)	98.0	96.5	77.6	78.2	N/A	N/A
	2019	**2023**	**2019**	**2023**	**2019**	**2023**
SIGI index	32.8	20.6	25.4	21.6	17.5	15.3
	2015	**2018**	**2015**	**2018**	**2015**	**2018**
PISA score in science	N/A	N/A	411	407	489	487
Productivity and innovation						
	2016	**2023**	**2016**	**2023**	**2016**	**2023**
Labour productivity (% of the United States)	22.9	22.0	29.3	27.1	70.0	68.5
	2016	**2021**	**2016**	**2021**	**2016**	**2021**
High-tech exports (% of manufactured exports)	7.6	7.4	8.4	7.2	16.5	16.0
	2016	**2019**	**2016**	**2019**	**2016**	**2019**
R&D expenditures (% of GDP)	0.1	0.1	0.3	0.4	1.8	2.0
Investment and production transformation						
	2016	**2022**	**2016**	**2022**	**2016**	**2022**
Total investment, gross fixed capital formation (% of GDP)	19.1	21.8	20.8	21.3	21.9	22.8
Foreign direct investment (FDI), net capital inflow (% of GDP)	2.1	1.1	4.4	4.6	6.8	3.5
	2016	**2019**	**2016**	**2019**	**2016**	**2019**
Private investment (% of GDP)	11.1	10.7	16.1	15.8	18.2	18.8
	2016	**2021**	**2016**	**2021**	**2016**	**2021**
Public investment in economic infrastructure (% of GDP)	1.8	4.0	2.3	1.6	N/A	N/A
Citizens' perceptions and institutions						
	2016	**2020**	**2016**	**2020**	**2016**	**2020**
Share of population who perceive of FDI as beneficial (%)	84.6	55.4	70.9	53.9	N/A	N/A
	2018	**2020**	**2018**	**2020**	**2018**	**2020**
Share of population who consider that, in general, domestic products are of lower quality than imported ones (%) (agreeing or strongly agreeing)	58.1	41.9	44.6	42.7	N/A	N/A
	2016	**2022**	**2016**	**2022**	**2016**	**2022**
Corruption Perception Index (score on a scale of 0 [highly corrupt] to 100 [totally clean])	30.0	28.0	41.2	40.6	67.3	66.3
Security risks indicator (score from 0 [low security risks] to 10 [high security risks])	6.8	6.0	5.9	5.6	2.8	2.6
	2010-14	**2017-22**	**2010-14**	**2017-22**	**2010-14**	**2017-22**
Belief that science and technology will create more opportunities for the next generation (score on a scale from 1 [strongly disagree] to 10 [strongly agree])	N/A	N/A	7.3	7.2	7.6	7.2
Share of population who worry (very much or a great deal) about not being able to provide a good education for their children (%)	N/A	N/A	75.4	74.0	49.8	41.4
Fiscal position						
	2016	**2021**	**2016**	**2021**	**2016**	**2021**
Total tax revenues (% of GDP)	13.4	14.0	22.0	21.5	33.6	34.1
Environmentally related tax revenue (% of GDP)	1.0	0.9	1.1	0.9	2.4	2.0
Share of VAT (% GDP)	5.1	5.1	5.9	6.1	6.6	7.0
Share of PIT (% GDP)	0.2	0.1	2.0	2.0	7.8	8.3
Share of CIT (% of GDP)	2.0	2.5	3.2	3.4	2.9	3.1
Debt service (% of total tax revenue)	6.6	11.4	11.3	12.3	5.4	5.3
Social expenditure (% of GDP)	8.5	10.3	11.3	13.3	20.1	22.0
	2016	**2020**	**2016**	**2020**	**2016**	**2019**
Perception of tax evasion (%)	N/A	27.0	N/A	27.3	N/A	N/A

Note: See the Reader's Guide for definitions and sources.

StatLink https://stat.link/grxcnh

PERU

1. Recent trends

Poverty in Peru decreased from 19.1% in 2016 to 17.2% in 2022, remaining below the Latin America and the Caribbean (LAC) average of 24.1%. Similarly, extreme poverty decreased from 5.2% in 2016 to 3.3% in 2022, standing below the LAC average (8.3%). The Gini index decreased from 43.6 in 2016 to 40.2 in 2021, remaining below the LAC average (44.8). Regarding investment and production transformation indicators, total investment in Peru increased from 21.4% of GDP in 2016 to 23.6% in 2022, in line with the region's average trend, which increased from 20.8% to 21.3% over the same period. Private investment increased slightly from 15.7% to 15.9%. Peru's labour productivity, measured against output per employed person in the United States, decreased from 19.0% in 2016 to 18.6% in 2023, remaining below the LAC average of 27.1% in 2023. The share of exports of high-tech products in total exported manufactured goods remained unchanged at 4.8% from 2016 to 2020, well below the LAC average (7.2%). Positive perceptions of foreign direct investment (FDI), which declined across the region also dropped in Peru, from 67.8% in 2016 to 41.3% in 2020. The country's tax revenue increased from 16.1% of GDP in 2016 to 17.9% in 2021, remaining below the regional average of 21.5%. Environment-related tax revenues remained the same at 0.5% of GDP between 2016 and 2021, about half of the LAC average of 0.9% in 2021.

2. Long-term policies to promote investment and production transformation

Peru has made significant efforts **to attract and mobilise high-quality investment**, focusing mainly on providing the country with quality economic and social infrastructure. In 2018, it established the National Policy on Competitiveness and Productivity to achieve sustainability and proper operation of economic, social, and environmental infrastructure. This approach centres on territorial growth and the ability to withstand natural disasters. In July 2019, Peru published its first-ever National Infrastructure Plan for Competitiveness (PNIC) for 2019-22, which prioritised implementing 52 projects throughout the country, with an investment worth nearly USD 30 billion. In October 2022, Peru released the National Sustainable Infrastructure Plan for Competitiveness for 2022-25, which builds upon and extends the PNIC 2019-22, adding social aspects and a focus on sustainability.

To advance **an inclusive and sustainable production model**, the General Directorate of Multi-annual Investment Programming of Peru developed its Multiannual State Investment Programme 2021-2023 (*Programa Multianual de Inversiones del Estado [PMIE]*) to allocate public resources towards the construction of public infrastructure that contributes to the country's development. The programme focuses on six key areas for public investment: education; healthcare; transportation and communication; housing and sanitation; agriculture; and energy and mining.

In terms of **regional and international partnerships** to support the attraction of quality investments, Peru has established collaborative initiatives with partners within and beyond LAC. **Within** the region, Peru participates in defining sustainable infrastructure through the Pacific Alliance, together with Chile, Colombia and Mexico. The Pacific Alliance, through the Working Group on Infrastructure Investment, seeks to standardise the concept of sustainable infrastructure among member countries, in line with the conceptual framework of the Inter-American Development Bank (IDB). This framework covers four sustainability dimensions: economic and financial, social, environmental, and institutional. **Beyond** LAC, Peru is also a member of Euroclima, the flagship programme of the European Union (EU) to promote green action in LAC countries. This membership will contribute to implementing the EU Global Gateway Investment Agenda in the region, further strengthening efforts to promote sustainable development and attractiveness for local and international investments.

	Key indicators – Peru					
	Peru		LAC		OECD	
Social						
	2016	**2022**	**2016**	**2022**	**2016**	**2022**
Extreme poverty	5.2	3.3	8.1	8.3	N/A	N/A
Poverty	19.1	17.2	25.9	24.1	N/A	N/A
	2016	**2021**	**2016**	**2021**	**2016**	**2021**
Share of internet users (% of population)	45.5	71.1	54.5	74.2	81.8	89.6
	2016	**2021**	**2016**	**2021**	**2016**	**2020**
Gini index	43.6	40.2	46.3	44.8	34.1	33.6
	2010	**2018**	**2009**	**2021**	**2009**	**2021**
Share of total population in informal households (%)	67.2	60.6	44.2	46.8	N/A	N/A
	2010	**2019**	**2009**	**2021**	**2009**	**2021**
Share of total population in informal households, upper-income quintile (%)	27.6	21.4	23.9	21.3	N/A	N/A
Share of total population in informal households, lower-income quintile (%)	93.5	95.5	77.6	78.2	N/A	N/A
	2019	**2023**	**2019**	**2023**	**2019**	**2023**
SIGI index	24.5	18.6	25.4	21.6	17.5	15.3
	2015	**2018**	**2015**	**2018**	**2015**	**2018**
PISA score in science	397	404	411	407	489	487
Productivity and innovation						
	2016	**2023**	**2016**	**2023**	**2016**	**2023**
Labour productivity (% of the United States)	19.0	18.6	29.3	27.1	70.0	68.5
	2016	**2020**	**2016**	**2021**	**2016**	**2021**
High-tech exports (% of manufactured exports)	4.8	4.8	8.4	7.2	16.5	16.0
	2016	**2019**	**2016**	**2019**	**2016**	**2019**
R&D expenditures (% of GDP)	0.1	0.2	0.3	0.4	1.8	2.0
Investment and production transformation						
	2016	**2022**	**2016**	**2022**	**2016**	**2022**
Total investment, gross fixed capital formation (% of GDP)	21.4	23.6	20.8	21.3	21.9	22.8
Foreign direct investment (FDI), net capital inflow (% of GDP)	3.5	4.5	4.4	4.6	6.8	3.5
	2016	**2019**	**2016**	**2019**	**2016**	**2019**
Private investment (% of GDP)	15.7	15.9	16.1	15.8	18.2	18.8
	2016	**2019**	**2016**	**2021**	**2016**	**2021**
Public investment in economic infrastructure (% of GDP)	2.6	2.1	2.3	1.6	N/A	N/A
Citizens' perceptions and institutions						
	2016	**2020**	**2016**	**2020**	**2016**	**2020**
Share of population who perceive FDI as beneficial (%)	67.8	41.3	70.9	53.9	N/A	N/A
	2018	**2020**	**2018**	**2020**	**2018**	**2020**
Share of population who consider that, in general, domestic products are of lower quality than imported ones (%) (agreeing or strongly agreeing)	33.4	33.7	44.6	42.7	N/A	N/A
	2016	**2022**	**2016**	**2022**	**2016**	**2022**
Corruption Perception Index (score on a scale of 0 [highly corrupt] to 100 [totally clean])	35.0	36.0	41.2	40.6	67.3	66.3
Security risks indicator (score from 0 [low security risks] to 10 [high security risks])	7.3	5.8	5.9	5.6	2.8	2.6
	2010-14	**2017-22**	**2010-14**	**2017-22**	**2010-14**	**2017-22**
Belief that science and technology will create more opportunities for the next generation (score on a scale from 1 [strongly disagree] to 10 [strongly agree])	7.3	6.9	7.3	7.2	7.6	7.2
Share of population who worry (very much or a great deal) about not being able to provide a good education for their children (%)	83.0	81.0	75.4	74.0	49.8	41.4
Fiscal position						
	2016	**2021**	**2016**	**2021**	**2016**	**2021**
Total tax revenues (% of GDP)	16.1	17.9	22.0	21.5	33.6	34.1
Environmentally related tax revenue (% of GDP)	0.5	0.5	1.1	0.9	2.4	2.0
Share of VAT (% GDP)	6.0	7.2	5.9	6.1	6.6	7.0
Share of PIT (% GDP)	1.8	1.9	2.0	2.0	7.8	8.3
Share of CIT (% of GDP)	3.8	4.5	3.2	3.4	2.9	3.1
Debt service (% of total tax revenue)	5.8	7.3	11.3	12.3	5.4	5.3
Social expenditure (% of GDP)	N/A	N/A	11.3	13.3	20.1	22.0
	2016	**2020**	**2016**	**2020**	**2016**	**2019**
Perception of tax evasion (%)	N/A	34.8	N/A	27.3	N/A	N/A

Note: See the Reader's Guide for definitions and sources.

StatLink https://stat.link/d4a6w9

URUGUAY

1. Recent trends

Poverty in Uruguay increased from 3.6% in 2016 to 4.3% in 2022 but remains significantly below the Latin America and the Caribbean (LAC) average of 24.1%. Extreme poverty increased slightly from 0.2% in 2016 to 0.3% in 2022 but is well below the LAC average (8.3%). The Gini index increased from 39.7 in 2016 to 40.8 in 2021, remaining below the LAC average (44.8). Regarding investment and production transformation indicators, total investment in Uruguay increased from 16.9% of GDP in 2016 to 18.5% in 2022, following the LAC average trend, which increased from 20.8% to 21.3% over the same period. Private investment, however, decreased in Uruguay, from 15.0% of GDP to 12.0%, dropping further below the LAC average (15.8% in 2019). Uruguay's labour productivity, measured against output per employed person in the United States, decreased from 39.0% in 2016 to 38.0% in 2023, while remaining well above the LAC average of 27.1% in 2023. The share of exports of high-tech products in total exported manufactured goods declined from 10.6% in 2016 to 9.8% in 2020 but continues to be above the LAC average (7.2%). Positive perceptions of foreign direct investment (FDI), which declined across the region, dropped in Uruguay, from 74.3% in 2016 to 65.0% in 2020. The country's tax revenue increased from 25.6% of GDP in 2016 to 26.5% in 2021, above the regional average of 21.5%. Environment-related tax revenues remained almost unchanged, rising from 1.7% of GDP in 2016 to 1.8% in 2021, above the regional average of 0.9%.

2. Long-term policies to promote investment and production transformation

Uruguay has made significant efforts **to attract and mobilise high-quality investment**, focusing mainly on promoting science, technology, and innovation projects. It established the Uruguay Innovation Hub to attract high-value-added investment, promote venture acceleration, and develop open labs and an innovation campus. This platform aims to create a public-private financing fund to invest in high-potential startups. Since 1998, Uruguay has fostered investments through the Investment promotion law 16.906, with a total of 708 projects promoted by 2022, for about USD 1.2 billion. This law focuses mainly on mobilising investments in the industrial, trade and services, agriculture, and tourism sectors.

To advance **an inclusive and sustainable production model**, Uruguay is developing a National Circular Economy Strategy (ENEC) with three fundamental goals: define the vision of the ENEC; establish the strategic priorities of the ENEC and relevant indicators; and determine short- and medium-term action plans. Since 2011, Uruguay has implemented the public-private participation programme, created by Law 18786 and Decree 49/022. This programme seeks to improve the country's physical infrastructure to increase the factor productivity and consolidate social equity progress. As an example of multi-stakeholder partnerships for development, Uruguay is participating in the UN Global Compact, which gathers private sector institutions worldwide. The country created (in 2021) its national network to promote private sector involvement in policy making and promoting the UN Sustainable Development Goals (SDGs).

Uruguay is embarking on its second energy transition, after achieving its first energy transition, with over 95% of its electricity production coming from renewable sources such as hydro, wind, biomass, and solar. With a focus on decarbonising the transport and industrial sectors, the second transition is built upon three main pillars: continued integration of new renewable energy generation; promotion of electric mobility; and development of green hydrogen and its derivatives. In 2022, Uruguay established a roadmap for Green Hydrogen and its Derivatives, outlining short-, medium- and long-term goals. These goals include generating heavy-duty transport solutions for the domestic market; creating e-fuels; using methanol as a raw material; and producing green fertilisers for export markets. To guide the development of this roadmap, Uruguay established the H2U Programme.

In terms of **regional and international partnerships** to support the attraction of quality investments, Uruguay has established collaborative initiatives with partners both within and beyond LAC. **Within** the region, Uruguay is part of the investment promotion and border development programme with Paraguay, which promotes targeted investment attraction, evaluation and monitoring mechanisms while also identifying good practices for better-integrated border management (among other initiatives). Uruguay and Mexico are collaborating to increase research and development (R&D) investment and value added in local production chains, with an emphasis on sustainable development. With Ecuador, Uruguay is collaborating to establish territorial strategies to support micro, small and medium enterprises (MSMEs) and their entrepreneurship capacities. **Beyond** the region, Uruguay has collaborated with the United Nations Development Programme (UNDP) to support the implementation of the National Preinvestment Fund (FONADEP) and to improve the management, monitoring and evaluation of the Interior Development Fund within the Directorate of Decentralisation and Public Investment. In the field of renewable energy and the energy transition, Uruguay has also collaborated with the UN International Development Organization (UNIDO) through the Renewable Energy Innovation Fund (REIF). The project Strengthening the Energy Transition is an example of triangular co-operation with Germany and Bolivia. Uruguay has also developed multiple partnerships to strengthen the green and circular economy, such as: AL-INVEST green and CoopsUYxDS with the European Union; and the Knowledge Sharing Programme (KSP) with Korea.

	Key indicators – Uruguay					
	Uruguay		LAC		OECD	
Social						
	2016	**2022**	**2016**	**2022**	**2016**	**2022**
Extreme poverty	0.2	0.3	8.1	8.3	N/A	N/A
Poverty	3.6	4.3	25.9	24.1	N/A	N/A
	2016	**2021**	**2016**	**2021**	**2016**	**2021**
Share of internet users (% of population)	66.4	90.1	54.5	74.2	81.8	89.6
	2016	**2021**	**2016**	**2021**	**2016**	**2020**
Gini index	39.7	40.8	46.3	44.8	34.1	33.6
	2008	**2018**	**2009**	**2021**	**2009**	**2021**
Share of total population in informal households (%)	28.5	16.3	44.2	46.8	N/A	N/A
Share of total population in informal households, upper-income quintile (%)	12.9	1.2	23.9	21.3	N/A	N/A
Share of total population in informal households, lower-income quintile (%)	68.7	56.1	77.6	78.2	N/A	N/A
	2019	**2023**	**2019**	**2023**	**2019**	**2023**
SIGI index	22.2	19.4	25.4	21.6	17.5	15.3
	2015	**2018**	**2015**	**2018**	**2015**	**2018**
PISA score in science	435	426	411	407	489	487
Productivity and innovation						
	2016	**2023**	**2016**	**2023**	**2016**	**2023**
Labour productivity (% of the United States)	39.0	38.0	29.3	27.1	70.0	68.5
	2016	**2020**	**2016**	**2021**	**2016**	**2021**
High-tech exports (% of manufactured exports)	10.6	9.8	8.4	7.2	16.5	16.0
	2016	**2019**	**2016**	**2019**	**2016**	**2019**
R&D expenditures (% of GDP)	0.4	0.5	0.3	0.4	1.8	2.0
Investment and production transformation						
	2016	**2022**	**2016**	**2022**	**2016**	**2022**
Total investment, gross fixed capital formation (% of GDP)	16.9	18.5	20.8	21.3	21.9	22.8
Foreign direct investment (FDI), net capital inflow (% of GDP)	-0.9	13.2	4.4	4.6	6.8	3.5
	2016	**2019**	**2016**	**2019**	**2016**	**2019**
Private investment (% of GDP)	15.0	12.0	16.1	15.8	18.2	18.8
	2016	**2021**	**2016**	**2021**	**2016**	**2021**
Public investment in economic infrastructure (% of GDP)	1.9	1.3	2.3	1.6	N/A	N/A
Citizens' perceptions and institutions						
	2016	**2020**	**2016**	**2020**	**2016**	**2020**
Share of population who perceive FDI as beneficial (%)	74.3	65.0	70.9	53.9	N/A	N/A
	2018	**2020**	**2018**	**2020**	**2018**	**2020**
Share of population who consider that, in general, domestic products are of lower quality than imported ones (%) (agreeing or strongly agreeing)	27.4	26.5	44.6	42.7	N/A	N/A
	2016	**2022**	**2016**	**2022**	**2016**	**2022**
Corruption Perception Index (score on a scale of 0 [highly corrupt] to 100 [totally clean])	71.0	74.0	41.2	40.6	67.3	66.3
Security risks indicator (score from 0 [low security risks] to 10 [high security risks])	3.5	3.9	5.9	5.6	2.8	2.6
	2010-14	**2017-22**	**2010-14**	**2017-22**	**2010-14**	**2017-22**
Belief that science and technology will create more opportunities for the next generation (score on a scale from 1 [strongly disagree] to 10 [strongly agree])	7.6	7.4	7.3	7.2	7.6	7.2
Share of population who worry (very much or a great deal) about not being able to provide a good education for their children (%)	64.0	75.0	75.4	74.0	49.8	41.4
Fiscal position						
	2016	**2021**	**2016**	**2021**	**2016**	**2021**
Total tax revenues (% of GDP)	25.6	26.5	22.0	21.5	33.6	34.1
Environmentally related tax revenue (% of GDP)	1.7	1.8	1.1	0.9	2.4	2.0
Share of VAT (% GDP)	7.1	7.2	5.9	6.1	6.6	7.0
Share of PIT (% GDP)	3.0	3.8	2.0	2.0	7.8	8.3
Share of CIT (% of GDP)	2.6	2.8	3.2	3.4	2.9	3.1
Debt service (% of total tax revenue)	9.5	7.7	11.3	12.3	5.4	5.3
Social expenditure (% of GDP)	14.7	15.6	11.3	13.3	20.1	22.0
	2016	**2020**	**2016**	**2020**	**2016**	**2019**
Perception of tax evasion (%)	N/A	32.6	N/A	27.3	N/A	N/A

Note: See the Reader's Guide for definitions and sources.

StatLink https://stat.link/trlb4s

www.ingramcontent.com/pod-product-compliance
Ingram Content Group UK Ltd.
Pitfield, Milton Keynes, MK11 3LW, UK
UKHW051459290926
15471UKWH00008B/1288

9 789264 561366